The Institute of Chartered Accountants in England and Wales

BUSINESS STRATEGY AND TECHNOLOGY

For exams in 2018

Question Bank

www.icaew.com

Business Strategy and Technology
The Institute of Chartered Accountants in England and Wales

ISBN: 978-1-78363-771-3
Previous ISBN: 978-1-78363-468-2

First edition 2008
Eleventh edition 2017

All rights reserved. No part of this publication may be reproduced, stored
in a retrieval system or transmitted in any form or by any means,
graphic, electronic or mechanical including photocopying, recording,
scanning or otherwise, without the prior written permission of the
publisher.

The content of this publication is intended to prepare students for the
ICAEW examinations, and should not be used as professional advice.

British Library Cataloguing-in-Publication Data
A catalogue record for this book is available from the British Library

Originally printed in the United Kingdom on paper obtained from
traceable, sustainable sources.

© ICAEW 2017

Contents

The Study Manual reference column highlights where the questions in this Question Bank have been explicitly referred to in the Study Manual. The references in the Study Manual highlight how key business strategy and technology concepts and theories have been examined in past exam questions. This should be used as a guide to help you with your studies and is not intended to provide any insight into those syllabus areas which may be examined in future sittings. The Sample Paper can also be found at the back of the Study Manual.

Please refer to questions 1, 2 and 3 and the 2017 March, June and September exams to see how technology may be assessed in 2018.

Exam

Your exam will consist of:

3 questions	100 marks
Pass mark	55
Exam length	2.5 hours

The ACA student area of our website includes the latest information, guidance and exclusive resources to help you progress through the ACA. Find everything you need, from exam webinars, past papers, marks plans, errata sheets and the syllabus to advice from the examiners at icaew.com/exams.

Question Bank

ICAEW

1 DA plc (amended)

DA plc (DA) is an information solutions company, listed on the London Stock Exchange.

Company background

DA began trading a number of years ago, providing credit reference services for business customers. Although this remains its primary activity, it has grown organically and now provides financial and statistical information to a variety of UK businesses to help them manage the risk of commercial and financial decisions.

The company is split into three divisions:

- Credit reference services – provides factual information to clients, via credit searches of an individual's financial history, to assist them to lend profitably or offer trade credit.

- Decision software – assists clients in improving the consistency and quality of business decisions in areas such as credit risk, fraud prevention and customer account management.

- Vehicle history – provides financial and statistical information to the automotive industry to help clients understand the risks associated with the purchase or sale of a particular second-hand vehicle.

A breakdown of key data, by division, for 20X7 is as follows:

	Credit reference services	Decision software	Vehicle history	Total
Sales (£m)	166	115	64	345
Operating profit (£m)	41	34	13	88
Growth in sales from 20X6	3%	15%	0%	6%
Number of employees	686	490	300	1,476

Credit reference services

Clients for credit reference services can be split into two groups:

(1) Banks, credit card companies and other financial services organisations which need help assessing the risk associated with lending decisions; and

(2) Commercial companies seeking credit references before supplying goods on credit to other businesses and private customers.

When an individual or business makes an application for credit, the lender or supplier usually asks a credit reference agency (CRA) for a credit search to check the applicant's identity and credit worthiness. The database system operated by a CRA enables different lenders, such as banks, to share information about their customers' credit accounts and repayment histories. Applicants have to give permission for their credit report information to be shared when they apply for credit.

Although a number of companies are currently licensed as CRAs in the UK, DA is the largest, with a 58% market share. DA has built its market position by compiling and managing the most comprehensive credit database in the UK. Communication and information technology are a core part of DA's business. Online systems allow lenders to update data directly, resulting in more accurate information and efficiency gains for DA.

DA's main competitor, CC Inc (CC) is an American-based business with an acknowledged expertise in credit scoring (a statistical technique that combines several financial characteristics to form a single score to represent a customer's creditworthiness). CC has recently announced that, as part of its global expansion strategy, it plans to increase its share of the UK credit market, which is currently 32%. CC intends to use low cost web-based systems to deliver online consumer credit scores directly to lenders and companies extending trade credit. In this way, it hopes to reduce DA's market dominance in the UK.

DA's strategic development

Decision software

Having created a reputation for holding the most comprehensive credit database in the UK, DA has embraced the increasing use of data analytics software and has developed its own in-house analytical software to enable clients to process credit applications and manage customer credit accounts more efficiently.

The software takes data from DA's own credit management database and a range of other sources, such as the client's own customer account information, and uses analytical tools and scoring systems to provide decision support. Typical users of this product are banks, credit card companies, mortgage providers and other organisations that grant personal or trade credit. DA's software has helped to revolutionise the service offered to clients by enabling them to quickly and accurately assess in 'real time' whether to accept a new customer or extend credit arrangements for existing customers. The software can also define the processes the businesses should adopt in managing an account that has fallen into arrears. In recent months a number of large financial institutions have contacted DA with a view to making a use of the service.

Vehicle history

Recognising that it had a core skill in the management of large databases for the financial services industry, DA also decided to provide similar services to the automotive industry. It compiles and manages data on the histories of 30 million vehicles and 25 million car insurance policies in the UK.

This data is used to provide vehicle history information to car dealers, finance providers and insurers. Fraudulent representation of used vehicles is a significant risk for private consumers and a potential financial liability for the businesses involved in the sale or purchase. The vehicle history can assist in establishing the market value of a vehicle; and whether a vehicle is registered as stolen or has outstanding finance.

Proposed diversification

Recently, DA has decided to target a new market, the individual consumer market, with a new online service: 'Checksta'.

Under current UK legislation, individuals have a legal right to see the information about them held by a CRA. In return for a statutory fee of £2, the CRA is legally obliged to provide a written copy of the information held on the individual's credit report. Instead of making a written application for a statutory credit report, individual consumers will be able to pay to subscribe to Checksta.

The Checksta service will allow individuals to check online that their credit report is accurate and up-to-date, as many times as they want. Checksta will send a text or email alert every time there is a significant change to the information held on an individual's credit report. This alert service assists in identifying identity fraud (where somebody applies for credit in another person's name). Individuals will also be able to order a credit score, based on their DA credit report, which will give them an idea of how a lender would view the information, if they were to apply for credit.

The introduction of Checksta is partly in response to the aggressive marketing stance currently being adopted by CC and also as a reaction to the following changes in the external environment:

- **Changing attitudes to money and credit**

  An increase in spending has led to an increase in demand for credit and it is very easy to apply now, both by telephone and online. This means that individuals are more likely to shop around for credit and lenders have to carry out more credit checks.

- **Changes in legislation**

  DA has to conform to the UK laws that govern the way it does business. Government concerns that debt levels are too high have caused a tightening of the legislation to give consumers better access to information held on them, more rights regarding disputes with lenders and more protection from rogue lenders. As a result, CRAs have had to implement a consumer education programme, working closely with consumer organisations to help consumers understand how credit referencing works.

- **The growth of e-commerce (products bought online)**

  This has necessitated more frequent and rapid credit checks and a subsequent upgrading of DA's information technology systems.

- **An increase in identity fraud**

    Identity criminals steal people's personal information and use these details to commit crimes, usually obtaining credit illegally.

Marketing

To date, DA has worked mainly with business clients, attracting business customers through personal selling and retaining them by developing strong client relationships. The sales director is aware that to succeed in the consumer market, DA will need to use a different marketing strategy for Checksta.

DA intends to use its knowledge of consumers who have applied for their statutory credit reports in the past, to build up a profile of the consumers it wants to target with its online service. Preliminary market research suggests that those most likely to be interested are people who are internet users, credit users and those keen to manage their financial affairs effectively. Such people are likely to read the financial pages in newspapers or visit personal finance websites.

Requirements

1.1 Explain the factors that are likely to have contributed to DA's competitive advantage.　　**(6 marks)**

1.2 Using relevant strategic models, analyse the ways in which DA has chosen to expand its business since it began trading, including its plans for Checksta.　　**(10 marks)**

1.3 Prepare a PESTEL analysis on the credit reference industry, clearly explaining the implications for DA's plans to implement the Checksta product.　　**(8 marks)**

1.4 Advise DA on an appropriate marketing strategy for Checksta.　　**(8 marks)**

1.5 Identify the strategic and cyber security risks arising from DA's use of Information Technology and Information Systems and outline the measures that can be implemented to deal with such risks.　　**(8 marks)**

Total: 40 marks

2　e-Parts Ltd (amended)

e-Parts Ltd (EP) is an online retailer which sells spare parts and accessories for a variety of domestic appliances. EP was established two years ago by Kamal Sheikh, who identified a gap in the market after he struggled to find a reasonably priced replacement part for his oven. EP has two types of customer:

- Small specialists who repair and service domestic appliances for individuals and need to access parts quickly at low cost; and

- Individuals who need either parts such as door hinges and seals to carry out their own simple, non-electrical repairs, or accessories such as fridge shelves or dishwasher cutlery baskets.

EP has grown as people try to save money and seek to extend the life of their existing domestic appliances by servicing them rather than replacing them. It now has a database of over two million customers. 90% of orders are placed and paid for online, with the remaining 10% handled by a call centre, which also offers after-sales service and support for online customers. In its warehouse, EP stocks 100,000 different products covering the appliances of 250 different manufacturers. EP's inventory control system allows it to despatch most items on the day that the order is placed.

Competition

Domestic appliance manufacturers charge premium prices for spare parts and accessories, primarily to encourage customers to buy new appliances, but also because they do not find it cost-effective to supply parts and accessories directly to customers. Domestic appliance retailers only stock items for the most popular appliances. EP prices are significantly lower than those charged by the appliance manufacturers. As a result, its only real competition is from other similar online businesses.

Brand and marketing

Kamal has positioned EP as 'a service business which helps customers to repair and enhance appliances'. Via the EP website's advice page, customers can access articles and videos to guide them through the most common repair processes. EP also takes advertising revenue from repair businesses in exchange for listing their services on the website. EP relies heavily on customer feedback. As well as a 'product and service review' facility on the website, Kamal has recently created a social networking page where customers can take advantage of special promotions, exchange information and access free advice from experts.

Risk management and business continuity

At a recent management meeting, Kamal made the following comments:

"Keeping our website operational is key for our business. If the site is down we don't make any money. If new customers visit our site and the online shop is not functioning effectively, they don't come back again. The other key issue for us is our inventory control system which allows us to identify quickly whether an item is in stock and where it is located. So far we have handled everything ourselves, but as a result of our rapid growth I am thinking of outsourcing all our operational systems to a specialist information technology (IT) provider. I have also been told that we should have a formal risk management policy, including a business continuity plan, for the business as a whole, so that if a major incident occurs we can continue to function."

Requirements

2.1 Explain the relevance of risk management to the business as a whole and identify the main factors that would be covered in EP's business continuity plan. **(6 marks)**

2.2 Identify the key IT risks including cyber risks arising for EP as a result of its reliance on IT (other than those relating to business continuity) and recommend how they can be managed. **(8 marks)**

2.3 Explain the factors to be considered by EP in deciding whether to use outsourcing as a method of implementing its IT strategy. **(7 marks)**

Total: 21 marks

3 Marcham plc (amended)

Marcham plc (Marcham) is a major supermarket chain with a loyal customer base and a 30% share of the UK supermarket sector.

MarchamBank

Marcham is proposing to take advantage of recent turmoil in the banking sector and public mistrust of some retail banks by launching its own banking services, under the name of MarchamBank. This will reduce the pressure felt by Marcham's traditional, mature retail business as a result of lower consumer spending, and will take advantage of rising margins for financial products. MarchamBank will operate from 30 branches within the largest existing Marcham stores and will also provide online banking facilities. The strategy is to offer Marcham customers simplified financial products and the marketing literature will emphasise "face-to-face, relationship-driven banking from a name that our customers can trust". Initially MarchamBank will offer simple savings products, short term loans, and a credit card. Once these have all been launched successfully, it will offer current accounts and a mortgage broker service to source mortgages for customers. It does not intend to offer mortgages itself.

Unlike other competitors which have moved into selected personal finance products via joint ventures with major UK banks, Marcham is planning to control its own banking operations. It will hire its own financial services specialists to run its branches and staff its customer service call centre. In view of the collapse of several banks during the financial crisis a number of years ago, the UK government is keen to increase competition in the banking sector and Marcham has already been granted a banking licence. Establishment of the customer service call centre in Scotland (rather than Asia where most competitors base their support services) will allow Marcham to receive a £5 million grant from the UK government.

Customer loyalty card scheme and integrated information system

Marcham has over 20 million customers in the UK and manages its relationship with them via a customer loyalty card. The loyalty card allows customers to earn points in return for cash spent in Marcham stores. Points can be converted into vouchers that can be used to reduce the cost of future purchases. The loyalty card forms part of an integrated data analytics and knowledge management information system which allows Marcham to track the shopping habits of its customers.

The other key element of the integrated system is a sophisticated electronic point of sale (EPOS) and inventory control system. As soon as a sales transaction is recorded, this system updates inventory records, provides valuable sales information regarding product demand and profitability, and facilitates automated purchasing from suppliers. This has enabled Marcham to reduce costs by increasing the frequency and accuracy of ordering, leading to lower levels of inventory and wastage.

The data collected from the various elements of the integrated system are logged in a centralised database with an advanced search engine. The data analytics feature of the system allows Marcham to build a profile of each customer with a loyalty card. This profile can then be used for a variety of purposes including pricing, decisions as to which product ranges to stock, research, marketing and customer service. One of the key benefits is improved customer segmentation, enabling Marcham to promote low price or high quality items as appropriate. The information is also sold to a number of the company's suppliers which use it to refine and develop their products.

Whilst most other supermarkets operate similar customer loyalty schemes, none is as far-reaching as Marcham's, which was the first of its kind. Marcham's research suggests that one in four UK adults belongs to its customer loyalty scheme. A key advantage for Marcham is that the scheme enables it to extend its share of customer spend by identifying other products that the customer is likely to be interested in, based on their profile and spending patterns.

Marcham plans for the loyalty card scheme to be a key driver of competitive advantage for its expansion into banking services, especially as none of the existing retail banks operates a loyalty card scheme. It will provide an immediate customer list for direct marketing purposes and the data may help to assess a customer's credit-worthiness.

Marcham intends to offer its customers a MarchamBank credit card to stand alongside the standard loyalty card scheme. This will further enhance its database by giving it access to information about non-Marcham purchases made by its customers.

Marcham criticised

The following is an extract from an article that appeared recently in a national newspaper:

"Supermarket giant Marcham has been criticised recently. Its customer loyalty card scheme has been labelled as a sophisticated spy system by some critics, allowing it to exploit customers by capturing information that they are not in a position to withhold and then using it to sell them things they don't need. As well, there is a risk that this private shopping information could fall into the wrong hands and might one day be used against people.

Marcham has also been accused of further tightening supplier payment terms to improve its own cash flow, despite continuing to make huge profits – indeed this may be where the money for its proposed expansion into banking services is coming from. Suppliers are, of course, prevented from complaining about low margins and onerous terms and conditions because of fears that they will lose Marcham's business."

Requirements

3.1 In preparation for a meeting of Marcham's senior executives, the operations director has asked you to prepare a report which:

  (a) Explains the potential benefits of an effective data analytics and information system for a supermarket and discuss how Marcham has used its information systems to create competitive advantage in the supermarket industry. **(8 marks)**

  (b) Assesses the suitability, feasibility and acceptability of Marcham's proposed expansion into the banking sector. **(12 marks)**

  (c) Discusses the relative merits of Marcham's intention to expand into banking via organic growth rather than having an established bank as a joint venture partner. **(8 marks)**

3.2 Discuss the ethical issues raised by the newspaper article in respect of Marcham's customer loyalty card and its treatment of suppliers. **(8 marks)**

Total: 36 marks

4 Bigville Council

Bigville Council (the Council) is the local government body responsible for providing community services to residents of Bigville, a large city in the UK. The Council is financed by central government, together with local taxes paid by residents and businesses in the area. Bigville is relatively strong economically. It has a respected university and is well-known as both a business and tourist destination. Around 500,000 people live and/or work in Bigville.

Demand for a community stadium

Bigville's professional rugby club leases its current sports stadium from the Council. As a result of recent success, the club is attracting large crowds to matches played at its stadium (home matches) and this stadium is at full capacity. Aware that Bigville's professional football club is also in need of a new stadium, the rugby club has asked the Council to consider the creation of a council-owned community stadium on a new site, with a shared pitch suitable for both rugby and football. It would also incorporate additional sports facilities which would be available for use by schools, colleges, clubs and other community groups throughout the year. On days when there are no home matches for either rugby or football teams the stadium could be used for a range of other commercial and social events (concerts, weddings, etc).

In the UK, football clubs compete in a series of hierarchical leagues, with the top clubs being promoted to the league above at the end of the playing season and the bottom clubs being relegated to the league below. The same system applies to rugby.

The attendance (number of people attending home matches at the club's stadium) and financial performance of any club is heavily dependent on its team's performance in the league. Bigville's two clubs currently play home matches on different days (football on Saturdays and rugby on Sundays) and their seasons overlap. The football season runs from August through to April, and the rugby season runs from February to September. Both clubs have a strong support base but have lower attendance than their respective league competitors due to restricted capacity. Neither stadium has the scope to be extended.

A new stadium would benefit the two clubs by allowing for increased attendance, which generates revenue from ticket sales, refreshments and merchandising. The improvement in facilities would increase the scope to raise some ticket prices by offering premium seating. For this reason, if the shared stadium goes ahead, the rugby and football clubs have pledged to make initial contributions of £1 million and £2 million respectively towards the capital cost.

Council's strategic priorities

The Council has recently stated publicly that its strategic priorities are as follows:

- To maintain and develop Bigville's successful economy and provide suitable employment opportunities for residents

- To ensure accessible opportunities for all to engage in culture, leisure and recreational activity

- To promote and provide support for local people to make healthy lifestyle choices

- To create, enhance and maintain cleaner, safer and more sustainable environments

The Council believes that a new community stadium would potentially assist in meeting some of these aims. It is therefore making a preliminary assessment of the business case for the community stadium. If this indicates viability, a more detailed feasibility study and financial analysis will be undertaken. The vision is to create a stadium with 6,000 seats, which both the football and rugby clubs will use for home matches and training.

The new stadium will incorporate a community sports centre with an athletics track and all-weather sports pitches. There is an option to enhance the stadium by adding a second level, which could be used commercially as a conference and events centre.

The Council has identified three criteria which it will use to assess the business case:

(1) Ability to raise finance for the initial capital investment
(2) Whether it is a commercially sustainable venture
(3) Alignment with the Council's overall strategic priorities

Council-owned land has already been identified as a suitable site for the stadium. This land is expected to meet the necessary planning criteria. The stadium would be partly sunk into the ground to limit noise problems, reduce the impact on the landscape and maximise environmental efficiency.

Capital costs and financial projections

The new stadium would be partly funded by the sale of the council-owned land on which the rugby club's current stadium stands. If sold to a developer for the construction of a retail site, this land would be expected to realise in the region of £6 million. Initial research suggests that some additional public sector funding would be available in the form of central government grants, provided certain criteria are fulfilled by the new stadium. These criteria include whether it can be demonstrated that the stadium actively increases community participation in sports, creates additional employment or contributes to the sustainability of the local environment. A sponsorship deal would be sought with a large credit card company, Finanex plc, whose headquarters are in Bigville and which is Bigville's largest private sector employer. The company has indicated that it would be prepared to pay an initial £1 million for the stadium to be named 'The Finanex Stadium', and then it would also contribute an amount annually for the right to display its company logos on the exterior and interior of the stadium.

The stadium is likely to cost a total of £10 million to construct. This comprises £6.75 million for the basic stadium and £3.25 million for the community sports facilities. An enhanced stadium, with an additional second level for conference and events facilities, would cost a further £1.1 million. Any shortfall in funding would need to come from the Council's cash reserves and/or debt finance. The Council's strategy department has researched similar community stadia funded by other councils and has produced some initial forecasts for the potential costs and revenue streams associated with the new stadium. These are set out in **Exhibits 1 and 2**.

Management and operation

If the new stadium goes ahead as planned, it will be owned by the Council and operated by a stadium management company (SMC) created as a joint venture between the Council and the two sports clubs. The Council will lease the stadium to SMC, which will then retain any profits or losses made from its operation. The Council, the football club and the rugby club will each have two directors on the board of SMC, although the Council will have a casting vote on certain specified issues. The Council is keen to ensure that it minimises its level of risk and, in particular, the financial liability to which it is exposed. It also wants to retain the ability to control the governance of SMC and the pricing, events scheduling and promotion of the stadium.

Exhibit 1: Forecast annual match revenues and costs for new stadium

	Number of home matches	Expected attendance per match	Total annual attendance	Total annual revenue	Total annual contribution	Traceable annual fixed operating costs	Forecast annual profit/ (loss)
	Note 1	Notes 2 and 3		Note 4			
Football	25	3,200	80,000	£800,000	£640,000	(£644,000)	(£4,000)
Rugby	15	3,000	45,000	£450,000	£270,000	(£214,000)	£56,000

Notes

1   Based on the average number of home matches played last season in each club's existing stadium. This can increase if a club is successful in various additional competitions which are run during the season.

---

2. Initial estimate of expected future attendance provided to the Council by each club, on the basis that it increases its capacity by moving to the new stadium and remains playing within its existing competitive league.

3. The average home match attendance at each club's current stadium is: football: 2,863; rugby: 2,234. Comparable data for similar clubs are as follows:

	Average attendance per match for typical club in:		
	League below	Existing league	League above
Football	1,800	3,050	5,000
Rugby	1,900	2,840	4,000

4. Based on expected average total spend per visitor on tickets, refreshments and merchandising.

Exhibit 2: Forecast annual non-match revenues and costs for new stadium

	Basic stadium £	Enhanced stadium with conference facilities £
Revenues		
Net income from community use of facilities	50,000	50,000
Stadium advertising/sponsorship from Finanex plc	200,000	250,000
Revenue from non-match day activities	187,000	537,000
Costs		
Stadium running costs, not directly traceable to rugby or football matches	(375,000)	(525,000)

Requirements

4.1 Discuss how the objectives of the key stakeholders (the Council, the rugby club and the football club) may conflict in relation to the shared stadium. You should ignore SMC as a separate entity for the purposes of this requirement. **(7 marks)**

4.2 (a) Using the quantitative data in Exhibit 1 relating to the new stadium, estimate the break-even attendance figures for each rugby and football match. **(4 marks)**

(b) Explain the implications of your calculations in (a) for the forecast match profits and discuss the potential variability in the annual attendance for each club, including the impact this is likely to have on the forecast in Exhibit 1. Show any supporting calculations. **(9 marks)**

4.3 Using the quantitative data in Exhibits 1 and 2 and the other qualitative information provided, prepare a report for the Council which evaluates the business case for the new stadium against the Council's three stated criteria, clearly identifying any further information required. **(14 marks)**

4.4 Assess the key risks for the Council in relation to the construction of the stadium and its operation by SMC. **(8 marks)**

Total: 42 marks

5   Beauty Soap Ltd

Beauty Soap Ltd (BS) is a large UK-based company which manufactures and sells personal care products (eg, hand soap, deodorant, shampoo, face cream, toothpaste and other personal hygiene products) throughout Europe.

Company history

BS was established over one hundred years ago as a producer of soap. BS quickly established itself as a major player in the market because of the range of different product sizes and fragrances offered. Initially BS grew organically by investing in research and development to create a wider range of personal care products including shampoo and face cream. As the UK market became increasingly competitive, consolidation took place and the number of competitors reduced. BS however continued to expand through the acquisition of a UK company specialising in dental care products. It also acquired several manufacturers of personal care products in mainland Europe.

Strategic options

BS wants to reduce its dependence on the European market, as the market is mature and market prices are under pressure (see **Exhibit**).

Exhibit: European market for personal care products		
	Revenue	
	20Y0 €m	20Y1 €m
Total European market	11,690	10,989
Market leader	1,489	1,297
BS	444	417

A number of competitors have targeted other international markets. BS is keen to expand into Latin America, as forecasts suggest there is considerable growth potential in some areas of the personal care products market, particularly in Brazil. The population of Brazil is culturally diverse. There are a number of affluent cities, but approximately one third of people live in rural areas, and there is significant poverty. BS is currently considering two alternative methods of development for expansion into Brazil:

(1) Acquire Gomera, a personal care products business based in Brazil. Gomera has an existing product range tailored to the needs of the local market and established supply chain and distribution networks. BS could either rebrand Gomera's products under the existing BS brand or keep Gomera's local brands and gradually introduce other brands from the BS range.

(2) Expand organically. Preliminary research has suggested that the market in Brazil would prefer smaller product sizes and lower prices than BS's traditional European product model, which the market perceives to be priced at a premium compared to local companies. BS plans to introduce new versions of products such as soap, shampoo and toothpaste in small packets containing enough product for a single use. BS already produces a range of similar single-use products for a major European hotel chain but does not currently sell these to individual consumers. The Brazilian government wants foreign-owned companies to demonstrate that they are creating value for the Brazilian economy. BS would therefore use a direct selling model with a workforce of local people, working from home and paid on a commission basis.

Competition

In Brazil the main competition in the personal care product market consists of:

- Two large multinational companies which have entered the market with their own global personal care brands

- Three domestic companies, one of which is Gomera, which produce a range of personal care products

The three domestic companies have established a strong presence in a variety of product segments and have the following advantages:

- An existing wide distribution network which extends to remote rural regions
- Low cost local manufacturing
- An established local supply chain network

They produce good quality products at competitive prices and make reasonable margins, although they lack the advertising budget and product innovation capacity of the multinational firms.

Educational marketing campaign

BS has recently announced plans to launch an education campaign, in conjunction with the governments in the countries in which it operates, to promote the regular washing of hands with BS soap to reduce infection and disease. The campaign will involve posters within schools and hospitals. If undertaken in Brazil there will be an advertising campaign featuring a well-known Brazilian footballer. BS's education campaign has been criticised by some as unethical marketing.

Requirements

5.1 (a) Using relevant strategic models, explain both the ways in which BS has previously chosen to expand its business and its future plans for Brazil. **(7 marks)**

   (b) Using the data in the Exhibit and the other information provided, evaluate the appropriateness of BS's plans to target markets outside Europe, given its current position. For the purposes of this requirement you should ignore the specific methods of expansion being considered. **(8 marks)**

5.2 Explain the choice that companies such as BS face between standardisation and adaptation of products in the context of the global market for personal care products. **(5 marks)**

5.3 Advise BS on the relative merits of the two options being considered for expansion into Brazil. **(8 marks)**

5.4 Discuss the ethical marketing issues raised by BS's proposed education campaign. **(5 marks)**

Total: 33 marks

6 Maureen's Motors

Maureen's Motors (MM), named after its female founder Maureen Docherty, sells motor insurance policies to car owners.

In the UK it is a legal requirement for drivers to have a minimum level of motor insurance cover. This provides compensation in respect of injury or damage to other people or their property resulting from an accident caused by the driver. The main driver of the car is usually the policy-holder, but the policy may also cover additional named drivers. Policy-holders can reduce their premium (the annual price of the policy) by agreeing to an excess (a fixed amount which, in the event of a claim under the policy, will not be paid out by the insurer).

Company background

A gap in the motor insurance market was identified by MM when industry research revealed that although there are many women drivers, a significant number were just covered as a named driver on their partner's car insurance policy rather than being the policy-holder.

MM therefore focuses on motor insurance for female policy-holders, by offering product and service benefits specifically tailored to women, which are not offered by standard car insurers.

MM provides additional cover for handbags and contents, pushchairs and child car seats; 24-hour accident and breakdown recovery (including a guarantee to be there within an hour of any call); a network of female-friendly car repairers; a helpline giving policy-holders advice on all vehicle-related matters; and, if a car is involved in an accident, MM provides a replacement child car seat even if the existing seat has not been damaged.

MM wanted to remove the image of 'insurance as a necessary evil' and to create a reassuring brand for 'real women with real lives'. Three famous actresses from a well-known TV comedy played the role of the '3 Maureens' in a long-running TV advertising campaign. Following this, MM was featured heavily in women's magazines. MM then ran a competition for existing and potential customers to star in a TV and poster advertising campaign. This campaign has significantly increased brand recognition, and using customers rather than celebrities has had the additional benefit of reducing marketing costs.

Pricing

The pricing of motor insurance premiums involves a risk assessment by the insurer of the likely risk of a claim being made and the amount that the insurer may have to pay out. The final price incorporates a number of factors, including:

- the insurance benefits offered
- the policy excess
- the type of vehicle, the expected annual mileage, and the location where the vehicle is normally kept
- the age and claims history of the policy-holder and any named drivers

The larger the pool of insured drivers, the more the risk is spread out for the insurer and the lower the premiums can be. MM offers discounts for customer loyalty and for referring a friend, to help retain customers and market share.

An EU Directive prohibits motor insurers from price discrimination between equivalent men and women. MM therefore offers its car insurance policies to male drivers at the same price as an equivalent female driver and men can also be named as drivers on a female partner's policy. However because of its brand image and the nature of its product offering, MM's current customer base of policy-holders is 90% female.

Insurance industry statistics show that women typically drive fewer miles than men, are responsible for fewer driving convictions and make significantly fewer claims. Where women do make claims, these are usually for less serious accidents and therefore smaller amounts. Statistically women are also less likely to switch insurer and this, coupled with their reduced risk profile, allows MM to make higher margins.

MM has recently attracted some adverse publicity in the national newspapers. It has been criticised for focussing too much attention on marketing to attract new customers rather than on delivering efficient claims handling and customer service to its existing ones.

Requirements

6.1 With reference to relevant models, discuss MM's generic strategy and market positioning.

(7 marks)

6.2 Explain the key elements of the service marketing mix adopted by MM. **(12 marks)**

6.3 In light of the criticism received by MM, recommend, with reasons, three KPIs that MM can implement to help improve its claims handling and customer service. **(6 marks)**

Total: 25 marks

7 Grassgrind Garden Mowers plc

"I really do not believe that accepting this bid is in the best interests of our shareholders. The board needs to convince shareholders that they should reject the bid and support our strategy for growth." The chief executive of Grassgrind Garden Mowers plc (GGM), Sundeep Shiller, was speaking at a board meeting last week.

GGM is a UK company that manufactures two types of upmarket, petrol-powered mower for use by UK households in cutting grass in their gardens. The meeting was held to discuss a take-over bid for GGM by Boston Batteries Inc (BB), a large US company.

You are a senior working for a firm of chartered accountants and business advisers, Puller and Platt LLP (PP). Following the board meeting, Sundeep asked a partner in your firm, Jeff Nelson, to come to see him. You accompany Jeff.

The meeting

It was Sundeep who opened the meeting:

"In making the offer to GGM shareholders, BB has been critical of our strategy and our performance. The GGM board however believes that it has produced a reasonable performance recently and has a better strategy for future growth than BB.

The board needs PP to provide a report to shareholders which evaluates GGM's performance and compares the board's proposed strategy for growth with that of BB.

PP has not carried out any business advisory work for GGM in the past, so I have provided you with:

- Some background notes about GGM (**Exhibit 1**)
- A trade newspaper cutting about the mower industry (**Exhibit 2**)
- Details of the growth strategies proposed by both GGM and BB (**Exhibit 3**)
- Some financial, operating and market data about GGM (**Exhibit 4**)

"In looking at the data in **Exhibit 4**, I am concerned that we allocate fixed operating costs between our two types of mower on the basis of volumes sold. Is this distorting our assessment of profitability? I am wondering whether we should, instead, allocate such costs on the basis of the sales revenues generated by each type of mower, as this would provide a better measure of performance of each product line."

An ethical issue

GGM recently received an email from Hetty Inc (Hetty), a company located in Eurasia, which is a developing nation. The following is an extract from that email:

"We would like to become your first export customer by placing a major order with GGM. However, in order to keep the price low, we would require a modification to your mowers, which is the removal of the safety guard. Unlike the UK, it is not a legal requirement in Eurasia, so it is not necessary for us to have this feature."

Requirements

7.1 Using the quantitative data and other information provided, draft the report requested by Sundeep. In the report you should:

(a) Analyse the performance of GGM, and of each of its two products, in the financial years 20Y1 and 20Y2. **(15 marks)**

(b) Determine the current UK market share of GGM, highlighting any problems that arise in defining market share in order to produce a useful figure. **(5 marks)**

(c) Explain the competitive positioning of GGM in the UK mower market, and assess how this has changed between 20Y1 and 20Y2. **(7 marks)**

(d) Compare the growth strategy of the GGM board with that of BB. Make relevant calculations and refer to appropriate strategic models. **(12 marks)**

7.2 Explain the ethical issues that arise for GGM from Hetty's request to modify its mowers, and outline how GGM should respond.

(6 marks)

Total: 45 marks

Exhibit 1: GGM company background

GGM was established a number of years ago and has always produced upmarket, petrol-powered mowers. Two types of mower are produced by GGM: (1) large mowers with a seat and a steering wheel for the user ('tractor mowers'); and (2) conventional mowers which the user steers by hand while walking. Tractor mowers are sold to high income households as they are only suitable for very large gardens. All tractor mowers are powered by petrol engines, while conventional mowers are powered in a variety of ways.

A feature of both types of GGM product is their high-quality steel cutting blades, which outperform most rivals. All of GGM's sales are in the UK.

GGM's customers are large do-it-yourself (DIY) stores, garden centres and other large retailers. As is normal in the industry, these retailers sell on to households at the price charged by GGM plus 25%.

While most companies in the mower industry also manufacture other types of powered garden tools and equipment, GGM has, to date, only produced mowers.

Exhibit 2: Extract from article in Mower Chronicle, 4th December 20Y2

Mowers – battery power is cutting into the market

Sales of mowers to consumers in the UK amounted to £396 million in 20Y1 at retail prices, making up 45% of the overall gardening tools and equipment market.

The mower industry can be divided into sub-sectors in a variety of ways. These include by style of blade, by type (tractor or conventional) or according to how they are powered (petrol, electric, battery or hand-propelled).

Petrol-powered mowers have the largest market share by value as they are more expensive than electric mowers but, in terms of volumes, electric and hand-propelled mowers have a larger market share.

Conventional petrol-powered mowers have maintained approximately the same market share by value at about 35% of the UK mower market in the last five years, while tractor mowers make up about 9% of the UK mower market.

A recent development in the mower industry has been cordless mowers powered by batteries. Their market share by value reached 10% in 20Y1, from 5% in 20X7.

Exhibit 3: Proposed strategies for growth

GGM strategic plan

The GGM board proposes a new strategy, to diversify into a range of petrol-powered garden tools and equipment, including hedge trimmers, strimmers and chainsaws. The new range would use a smaller version of the petrol engine developed for the GGM mower. Customers (ie, retailers) for the new products would be the same as for the mowers and the same GGM brand name would be used.

Budgets have been produced for the new range of petrol-powered garden tools and equipment, based on market research. The most realistic estimate indicates that 25,000 units will be sold each year, at an average price of £150 and with a 40% contribution margin on selling price. Additional annual fixed operating costs are expected to be £1.4 million. The market researchers have indicated that their estimate of sales volume could be up to 20% higher or 20% lower than their most realistic estimate, depending on market conditions.

BB strategic plan

BB is a US manufacturer of high performance lithium-ion batteries and has diversified in recent years by acquiring companies in industries producing industrial and domestic equipment which uses its batteries.

BB does not manufacture mowers, nor do any of its subsidiaries. As a result, its strategic plan is to acquire GGM and allow it to continue to produce petrol-powered mowers, and to commence producing mowers powered by lithium-ion batteries, using the same cutting blades as currently used by GGM. BB plans to encourage GGM to export battery-powered mowers to the US in future. BB has no plans for GGM to diversify away from mowers into other garden tools and equipment.

In the UK, battery-powered mowers would be sold to the same customers (ie, retailers) as the existing products. The petrol-powered mowers would continue to be branded as GGM, but the battery-powered mowers would be branded under the BB name.

Budgets have been produced by BB that indicate 20,000 battery-powered mowers would be sold worldwide each year at an average price of £500 and with a 30% contribution margin on selling price. Additional annual fixed operating costs are expected to be £2 million, but could be as high as £3 million, or as low as £1 million.

Exhibit 4: GGM financial, operating and market data for years to 31 December

Profit per unit data	20Y1		Estimated 20Y2	
	Conventional mowers £	Tractor mowers £	Conventional mowers £	Tractor mowers £
Price	400.0	2,000.0	400.0	1,800.0
Variable operating costs	240.0	1,000.0	240.0	1,000.0
Fixed operating costs *	112.5	112.5	120.0	120.0
Operating profit per unit sold	47.5	887.5	40.0	680.0

* Fixed operating costs are currently allocated to each mower based on GGM's total sales volume (see Sundeep's comments).

Operating and market data	20Y1		Estimated 20Y2	
	Conventional mowers	Tractor mowers	Conventional mowers	Tractor mowers
Volume sold by GGM (units)	8,100	2,700	7,380	2,820
UK market – volume sold (units)	1.5m	30,000	1.5m	30,600
UK market – sales value (at retail prices)	£360m	£36m	£368m	£36m

---

8 Care 4U Ltd

Care 4U Ltd (C4U) is a large private company which owns a chain of retail pharmacy outlets in the UK. These outlets supply consumers with prescription items (drugs and other products prescribed by health professionals for individual patients), general medicines and a range of other health and personal care products.

Industry background

Products and services

Retail pharmacies have two main sources of revenue:

(1) About 80% from the provision of prescription items to patients by an appropriately qualified pharmacist

(2) About 20% from retail sales by non-qualified staff of over-the-counter (OTC) general medicines and other products

In the UK, the key role of pharmacies is to provide patients with drugs and other items under prescriptions from their doctor or other health professional. Many prescriptions are wholly government-funded and provided free-of-charge to patients. Where the patient is required to pay a charge for a prescription item, this is a fixed amount which is the same irrespective of the purchase cost of the item. Most of a pharmacy's revenue therefore comes directly from the government which pays an amount for each prescription item supplied and makes an additional payment for the service the pharmacy provides to patients.

Many drugs can be obtained only on prescription from qualified pharmacists. However, many types of OTC general medicines, plus other health and personal care products, can be bought at their market price from non-qualified staff at pharmacies and other general retailers.

The retail pharmacy market

Total revenue for pharmacies has the potential to grow, as the volume of demand for prescription items is expected to increase. This is due to an ageing population and constant improvements in healthcare. However, reductions in government expenditure create doubt over the amount of future government funding that will be available for prescription items.

Despite increases in industry revenues, the number of retail pharmacy outlets has declined in recent years. This has been partly due to increased competition in the industry created by deregulation which has permitted price competition on OTC general medicines since 20X1. Since that time, supermarkets have introduced low-price, in-store pharmacies that are open, in some cases, 24 hours a day.

C4U company background

C4U was established over forty years ago. Since that time, commercial success through good centralised management has enabled expansion of the number of pharmacy outlets to 150 and significant growth in revenue per pharmacy.

All purchases are undertaken centrally at head office where key decisions are made. C4U's information technology system helps monitor and manage the performance of individual pharmacies. Typically, an average size C4U pharmacy, once established, would generate annual revenues of about £600,000 and an operating profit of 20% of sales revenue (this is before any central management charges, but after product purchases, salaries and overheads).

C4U has a reputation as a community pharmacy that offers services which are free to customers, including basic health tests (eg, blood tests and health screening) and medical advice. The C4U brand has high and favourable consumer recognition throughout the UK.

At each C4U pharmacy there is a senior qualified pharmacist who, in addition to preparing prescription items, also runs the pharmacy's business activities, including being responsible for: ordering prescription drugs, OTC medicines and other products from head office; administration; hiring staff; and financial arrangements. Depending on the size of the pharmacy, there may be one or more other qualified pharmacists in addition to a senior qualified pharmacist.

A problem has arisen of high staff turnover among qualified pharmacists. Generous salaries are paid which have been successful in recruiting qualified pharmacists to C4U, but there have been problems in motivating and retaining them. In particular, many of C4U's pharmacists carry out the technical functions required of them, but have failed to manage professionally the business activities of the pharmacy by winning new customers, expanding sales and controlling costs. Other C4U pharmacists, having accumulated enough savings, have resigned from C4U to set up their own pharmacies on a self-employed basis.

C4U has borrowing facilities to obtain funding for its desired objective of further expansion, but the C4U board wants to ensure that available funds are used to best effect by opening as many new pharmacy outlets as possible.

C4U proposed expansion

The board has proposed two alternative strategies for expansion. Both strategies are designed to attract independent-minded, qualified pharmacists who wish to operate their own pharmacy, but who do not have enough funds to be self-employed by buying one outright. The two strategies are franchising and shared ownership:

Strategy 1 – franchising

Under this proposal the number of C4U pharmacy outlets would be increased across the UK by offering qualified pharmacists franchise arrangements with the right to use the C4U brand name. Franchisees (ie, the qualified pharmacists) could choose to benefit from some limited support and advice with respect to purchasing and administration, but could choose to reject this help.

C4U would purchase the property and basic fittings for each pharmacy outlet at an average cost of £200,000. The property would be acquired specifically for the purpose of opening a new pharmacy outlet. No existing pharmacy outlets would be franchised.

Each franchise agreement would last for five years and then would either be terminated (ie, C4U would take full ownership of the property and control of the business) or, if both parties agreed, renegotiated on new terms. C4U would charge the franchisee an initial fixed fee of £25,000 and also an annual franchise fee of 5% of total annual revenue. Each franchisee would manage their own performance and would be entitled to all residual profit after franchise fees had been paid.

Franchisees would have strict responsibilities to abide by the terms of the franchise arrangement so C4U can protect its reputation. There would be no constraints on prices charged for non-prescription items, which can be determined by the franchisee.

Strategy 2 – shared ownership

Under this proposal each new pharmacy outlet would be owned by a limited company, with ownership of the company shared equally between C4U and a qualified pharmacist. C4U would lend money to each new company to finance the remaining initial cash requirement of the pharmacy outlet. Typical funding for an average-sized pharmacy outlet would be as follows:

Share capital contributed by C4U	20%
Share capital contributed by pharmacist	20%
Loan from C4U to the company	60%

The average cost of opening a pharmacy outlet would be £200,000, so each qualified pharmacist would need to contribute £40,000 on average to acquire their share capital.

Each pharmacist would be paid a market salary by their company. C4U would receive a management fee from each company for providing intensive support, advice, administration and IT facilities at a market rate averaging £20,000 per annum. This support and monitoring would be a compulsory part of the agreement, so C4U can manage the performance of its investment. If the pharmacist wanted to sell his/her shares to C4U (or conversely to buy C4U's shares) at any stage in the future, this would be possible at a fair value, to be independently determined.

Requirements

8.1 Prepare a SWOT analysis for C4U. Each point should be clearly explained. Conclude by identifying the key issues and justify why they are significant. Ignore the strategies for expansion. **(12 marks)**

8.2 Explain and compare the two strategies for C4U's expansion under each of the following headings:

   (a) Operating profit **for C4U** in respect of one outlet for one year (you should provide supporting calculations)

   (b) Control and management

   (c) Incentives for franchisees compared to shared owners **(19 marks)**

   Total: 31 marks

9 The Mealfest Corporation

The Mealfest Corporation (MC) owns a chain of over 100 mid-market restaurants, located in four countries across Europe: France, Germany, Switzerland and the UK. France and Germany have the euro as their currency.

Company structure and pricing

Until January 20Y2, each restaurant manager was responsible for performance and reported directly to the company's head office in Germany. Menu prices were fixed centrally in euro at 1 January each year and were uniform across all restaurants. The prices in euro were translated into Swiss francs (CHF) and sterling (£) using exchange rates prevailing at that date.

Head office specialists took responsibility for recruiting permanent staff for each restaurant. The same wage, which was reset and retranslated annually, was paid to all staff within each staff grade throughout the company.

On 1 January 20Y2 the company was restructured by having a separate division for each country. Each division has a divisional head. Restaurant managers now report their performance to their divisional heads, who then report total divisional performance to the company's head office. As with the previous structure, performance is evaluated by three measures: revenue, profit and return on assets.

From 1 January 20Y2 a new pricing policy was implemented. Menu prices are now set by divisional heads for their division each year, and can therefore vary between countries, but prices are required to be consistent within each country. Similarly, staff recruitment and remuneration are now decided at divisional level.

In both the pre and post-20Y2 structures, all meal ingredients are purchased centrally by MC from a French wholesaler. They are recharged to restaurants in euro at cost. Similarly, decisions on investment in new restaurants have always been centralised.

Monitoring the new structure and strategy

The MC board is having problems monitoring the success of the new structure and the new pricing strategy. It wishes to evaluate whether the method of assessing performance has improved following the restructuring.

The finance director summarised just one of the issues: 'It is very difficult to compare performance between countries due to exchange rate movements. Under the old pricing policy this meant that we set menu prices centrally in euro, then for the UK and Swiss operations we translated these to sterling and Swiss francs each year. Fluctuations over the year in exchange rates meant restaurant prices in the UK and Switzerland sometimes changed significantly when they were reset the following year. Under the new pricing system there is more pricing flexibility at national level, but we still need to make performance comparisons in euro as a common currency.

"I am not interested in hedging or in financial reporting issues, but I am concerned about the commercial impact of exchange rates on restaurants and customers, and their effect on measuring divisional financial performance."

The chief executive responded: "That is all very well in terms of financial performance, but I am interested in measuring all aspects of performance and in whether we now have the right structure and pricing strategy."

Requirements

9.1 Compare MC's pre-20Y2 and post-20Y2:

  (a) Organisational structure and performance measurement; and
  (b) Pricing strategies. **(14 marks)**

9.2 Explain how benchmarking may be used by MC to evaluate the performance of divisions and individual restaurants. **(10 marks)**

Total: 24 marks

10   Mayhews Ltd (amended)

Mayhews Ltd (Mayhews) is a family-owned business which runs three garages from freehold sites in prime locations in central England. Each garage operates a filling station, which sells fuel (petrol and diesel), and has a facility offering maintenance and repairs for motor vehicles.

Fuel retailing in the UK

Fuel retailing in the UK is a high volume, low margin business, characterised by strong competition. In the industry there are three types of filling station:

- Branded filling stations are either owned and managed by one of the major fuel wholesalers or operated on their behalf by licensees.

- Independent retailers, like Mayhews, are free to obtain fuel supplies from any wholesaler. Over 50% of all filling stations in the UK are independently owned.

- The big supermarket chains operate filling stations alongside their major stores. In recent years, whilst the number of branded filling stations and independent retailers has declined, the number of supermarket-owned sites has increased. This has coincided with the expansion of large out-of-town supermarkets with more people driving to do their shopping and buying fuel at the same time. As a result of their supply chain efficiencies and the large volumes of fuel that they sell, the supermarkets incur lower overheads per litre of fuel sold and are able to charge lower prices. In addition, many offer discounts on fuel based on the amount customers spend on goods in the main store. The average retail price charged by supermarkets in 20Y2 was 130.9 pence per litre compared to an overall UK average of 133.8 pence per litre.

Supply of fuel and pricing in the UK industry

The wholesale supply of fuel to retailers is dominated by a few large companies which produce and refine crude oil into a range of products including fuel. These wholesalers supply fuel to their own branded filling stations and to the supermarkets and independent retailers. 60% of the UK retail fuel price per litre consists of fuel tax and sales tax. On average 35% is paid to the wholesaler and the retailer earns 5% towards overheads and profit. Wholesale fuel prices in the last three years have been very volatile as the price of crude oil has varied significantly. Price volatility is a major problem for independent retailers. When market prices fall, independent retailers are often left with fuel supplies previously bought from the wholesaler at a high price. If they reduce the retail price then they may make a loss. If they keep retail prices high this is likely to have a negative effect on sales volumes. Conversely, when wholesale prices rise, the independent retailer may struggle to afford the increased cost of replenishing fuel supplies.

Demand for fuel in the UK market

Despite increased numbers of cars on the road, sales volumes of fuel are under pressure because of the improved efficiency of vehicle engines, increased fuel prices and the difficult economic climate. Government figures suggest congestion on motorways and major roads has been falling, indicating that people are undertaking fewer journeys by car.

Fierce competition between fuel retailers has led to a significant decline in the number of filling stations. There are now fewer than half the 18,000 filling stations that existed twenty years ago (**Exhibit 1**).

A fuel station's viability depends on two key factors: the gross margin per litre and the volume of fuel sold. Independent filling stations and those in less well-populated rural areas are at the greatest risk of losses due to declining sales volumes and below average margins. They also struggle to justify the additional capital expenditure required to comply with increasingly strict environmental and safety regulations. Many have tried to reduce their reliance on fuel revenue by creating alternative revenue streams such as on-site shops selling snacks, groceries and vehicle accessories. Mayhews does not currently operate a shop at any of its garages.

420 filling stations closed in the UK in 20Y2, of which two-thirds were independent. Some of these filling stations have been bought by property developers, although because of environmental regulations, sites have to be closed and the fuel tanks filled with concrete before being capable of alternative use.

Mayhews' business

The first Mayhews garage was set up a number of years ago by John Mayhew. The boom at this time in vehicle ownership and the later development of the UK motorway network led to a significant increase in demand for fuel and maintenance/repairs and Mayhews soon opened a further two garages. The business is now owned and managed by John's son Barry (aged 60), who is a well-known businessman in the region. After many successful years, Mayhews has been finding the filling stations market increasingly difficult and this is reflected in the company's recent results (**Exhibit 2**).

Although Mayhews has been experiencing a decline in fuel sales, the revenue and profit from maintenance and repairs have been increasing. This part of the business undertakes MOT testing (a compulsory annual test of safety for vehicles over three years old); replacement of parts due to wear and tear (brakes, tyres, wiper blades, lights etc); annual maintenance; and repairs.

Due to the economic climate, people have been slow to replace their old vehicles with new ones. Time pressure, lack of skills and the complexity of vehicles mean people no longer maintain their own vehicles, but they are reluctant to pay the high prices charged by the vehicle retailers for maintenance. Because of its longstanding presence in the region, and also as a result of Barry's contacts, each Mayhews garage has a loyal base of local customers. Mayhews also has contracts with a number of local companies for the maintenance of their corporate vehicles.

There are 32 million vehicles on the UK's roads and the maintenance and repairs market is fragmented. There are around 24,000 garage outlets in the UK offering motor vehicle repairs and maintenance. They are operated by retailers of vehicles, national and regional repairs and maintenance chains, fast-fit centres (specialising in tyres, exhausts and brakes) and many independents.

Strategic dilemma

Your firm acts as business advisers to Mayhews. At a recent meeting, Barry commented:

"We seem to be selling so little fuel these days I can't believe we are making much money from this side of the business. What do you think about us closing one or more of the filling stations and focussing on maintenance and repairs? This is a service-based market with many different providers where trust is really important to the customer. We already have a reputation for being honest and reliable and our brand is well-known locally.

We also have much lower overheads and labour costs than the main vehicle retailers. We can use this to differentiate ourselves by offering vehicle retailer quality service at affordable local garage prices.

Unfortunately, we simply don't have the appropriate technology to deal with the engine management systems in the more modern vehicles so currently we have to refer them to the vehicle retailer. We would need to invest in information technology by purchasing the relevant engine diagnostic equipment and a new computer system.

The new IT system would improve parts management and have marketing benefits. By maintaining their vehicles in good working condition our customers can improve fuel efficiency and drive safely. A key way we can help customers is to anticipate their needs for MOTs and maintenance and contact them in advance based on the age and mileage of their vehicle. The new system would provide us with an advanced data management system incorporating data analytics functionality. This should enable us to offer customers online booking for repairs and maintenance."

Requirements

10.1 Prepare a Porter's Five Forces analysis of the UK fuel retailing industry which might be used to inform further discussions regarding the viability of Mayhews' filling station operations. **(9 marks)**

10.2 Using the quantitative data in the Exhibits, your answer to requirement (10.1), and the other information provided, evaluate the performance of Mayhews' overall business and compare the performance of the individual garages. Make and justify a preliminary conclusion as to whether Mayhews should consider closing one or more of its filling stations to focus on maintenance and repairs. **(16 marks)**

10.3 Discuss the advantages and disadvantages of making the investment in information technology referred to by Barry. You should refer to the use of data analytics in your answer. **(7 marks)**

10.4 Explain how the use of critical success factors (CSFs) may assist Mayhews in establishing a strategic control system. Justify three CSFs for Mayhews' maintenance and repairs business and suggest one appropriate key performance indicator for each CSF identified. **(9 marks)**

Total: 41 marks

Exhibit 1: UK filling stations – market data 20Y2

	Branded filling stations	Independents	Supermarkets	Total
Number of sites	2,605	4,425	1,470	8,500
Millions of litres sold	10,520	7,425	14,950	32,895

Exhibit 2: Mayhews Ltd recent financial performance

	Breakdown of 20Y2			Total company	
	Garage A 20Y2 £'000	Garage B 20Y2 £'000	Garage C 20Y2 £'000	Mayhews Ltd 20Y2 £'000	Mayhews Ltd 20Y1 £'000
Sales:					
Fuel (Note 1)	878	738	776	2,392	2,686
Maintenance and repairs	688	454	755	1,897	1,604
Total sales	1,566	1,192	1,531	4,289	4,290
Gross profit:					
Fuel	103	76	91	270	304
Maintenance and repairs (Note 2)	355	218	415	988	836
Total gross profit	458	294	506	1,258	1,140
Operating costs (Note 3)	269	184	219	672	679
Profit	189	110	287	586	461
Litres of fuel sold (millions)	1.63	1.34	1.43	4.40	5.21

Notes

1   Fuel revenue is stated net of tax, ie, at 40% of the retail fuel price.

2   The gross profit on maintenance and repairs is based on the sales value of work done less the cost of parts and materials.

3   Operating costs include the wages and salaries of all garage staff. The operating costs for garage A also include £45,000 for Barry's salary.

---

11   Cabezada Ltd

Cabezada Ltd (Cabezada) is a relatively new company which uses steel shipping containers to create short-term living accommodation. The standard-sized containers can be transported anywhere by road, rail or sea, modified and then stacked to create the desired number of rooms.

The business is owned and managed by two directors: Sam Lowe, previously chief executive of a hotel group, and Anka Bien, formerly operations director of a large construction company.

Cabezada has two markets:

(1)   Events clients, which require short-term accommodation for employees, media representatives, visitors and participants at a variety of sporting and leisure events.

(2)   Contract clients, including the construction industry, the military and government, which typically require longer-term accommodation. Recent projects include key-worker accommodation and a temporary hospital.

Since starting the company, a number of projects have been completed very successfully for both markets. Cabezada's directors believe the business has significant global appeal and have started to draft a business plan which will be used to attract appropriate local partners to develop a worldwide business. The directors have already written some of the plan, which is included in the **Exhibit**, and have asked your firm of business advisers for help in developing it further.

Requirements

11.1 As a senior in the firm of business advisers, write the sections of the draft business plan indicated in the Exhibit, to cover the following:

    (a)   Strengths and realistic market opportunities (section 2.2.1)
    (b)   Weaknesses and threats (section 2.2.2)
    (c)   Benefits of partnership for both Cabezada and its local partners (section 3)

    You should present your answer in an appropriate style and format, written in such a way as to help Cabezada to attract potential partners. **(16 marks)**

11.2 Recommend any further information that you believe should be included in the plan to enable potential partners to adequately assess Cabezada's partnership proposition. **(8 marks)**

11.3 Cabezada currently segments its market between events and contract clients. Explain the purpose and benefits of market segmentation and discuss other approaches to segmentation which Cabezada could adopt. **(8 marks)**

Total: 32 marks

Exhibit: Draft Business Plan provided by Cabezada's directors

DRAFT: Cabezada Local Partnership Programme 20Y3

1. **Cabezada Local Partnership model**

Cabezada uses steel shipping containers to create temporary living accommodation. Cabezada is regarded as a pioneer in the container accommodation industry and our brand name is well-recognised and trusted. The demand for cheap, flexible, temporary accommodation provided under a sustainable model is a global one. However we believe global business is best done using a local model and we are seeking the right local partners to help us target a wide range of potential markets.

Each local partner will set up a new company in their country or region called 'Cabezada (country/region name)'. Cabezada will have partial ownership of the company with a stake of 20%. The new company will pay a one-off franchise fee for exclusive rights to operate under the Cabezada brand in its defined area. There will be a monthly management charge for the use of all Cabezada information and infrastructure and a royalty fee on all container accommodation sold in the local market.

2. **The Business**

    2.1. **Our product concept**

    Shipping containers are highly durable and provide an ideal building module suitable for all climates and locations. Most new shipping containers are manufactured in China to international-standard sizes at a cost of approximately £4,000 each. Many countries import manufactured goods from Asia in shipping containers. Rather than pay to have these containers shipped back empty, it is often cheaper for Asian suppliers to buy new containers in Asia. As a result there is a plentiful supply of used shipping containers available globally, costing on average £1,000 per container.

    Since the containers are designed to be easily transported by ship, road or rail, distribution costs are low, so accommodation can be provided in whatever location the client requires. Once adapted to make them suitable for living accommodation, the shipping containers can be quickly and easily combined in several storeys without requiring additional structural support.

The modular system offers flexibility of design and the standard of accommodation can range from very basic to luxurious. Depending on the client and location there is scope to create a building façade of brick, timber or marble. Cabezada's design system includes any necessary foundations, communal access arrangements, ventilation and connections to utilities.

For buildings up to five storeys high, container accommodation is significantly cheaper than the cost of erecting a brick-built structure, which takes much longer and requires larger, expensive foundations. Cabezada's whole product concept is more environmentally friendly, ideal for temporary use and consistent with the need for sustainability. Once a project is over, the containers can be refurbished and re-used. There is also a ready market for the sale of containers after use if Cabezada no longer requires them.

2.2. Cabezada position analysis

2.2.1 Strengths and realistic market opportunities (to be completed)
2.2.2 Weaknesses and threats (to be completed)

3. Benefits of partnership for both Cabezada and its local partners (to be completed)

12 Chiba

Chiba is a Japanese company which manufactures a range of liquid foods including rice vinegar and soy sauce.

Different countries make vinegars from their indigenous crops, for example rice vinegar in Japan, oat vinegar in Korea, cider vinegar in the US, wine vinegar in Europe and malt vinegar in the UK. Rice vinegar has no fat or cholesterol and is very low in calories. It is also known for its anti-bacterial properties.

UK expansion strategy

Malegar, a division of a large UK listed food business, makes the UK's leading brand of malt vinegar. The division is currently for sale because Malegar's parent company (VM plc) has incurred significant borrowings and is now moving to a strategy of focusing on a few key profitable food brands.

Chiba wants to increase its market share in the UK and is considering setting up a subsidiary company, Chiba UK, to acquire Malegar, because of Malegar's strong UK heritage and identity. As well as targeting Malegar's traditional food market, Chiba is also keen to promote vinegar as a health product and as a cleaning product. However, Chiba's marketing director is concerned that VM plc would not be selling Malegar if it were a profitable business.

Contamination issue

The directors of Malegar are aware of a recent complaint from a major wholesaler concerning a contaminated batch of malt vinegar. The cause has not yet been confirmed and they are unsure whether the contamination arose in the glass bottles, which are purchased from an external supplier, or within the Malegar factory. Malegar takes health and safety and quality control very seriously, so the directors believe the fault is most likely to lie with the supplier. As Malegar was probably not responsible for the incident, the directors are planning to keep this issue confidential from all parties, including Chiba.

Human resource management

If Chiba's acquisition of Malegar goes ahead, all Malegar employees will transfer their contracts to Chiba UK following an appropriate consultation process. This may take up to twelve months.

Chiba's approach to human resource management is very different from Malegar's. Malegar has a hierarchical structure with a focus on short-term results, and with individual functional managers held accountable for the performance of their function. Employees within Malegar's factory have little involvement in the decision-making process and there is high staff turnover. In contrast, Chiba's approach emphasises job security for core employees, co-operation and mutual trust between employees and managers, collective responsibility and shared decision making. Chiba's directors are concerned about the change management issues that will arise from the integration of the Malegar employees into the Chiba culture.

Requirements

12.1 Explain the ethical issues that arise for Malegar's directors in relation to concealing the possible contamination.

(5 marks)

12.2 In light of the comments by Chiba's marketing director, discuss the possible reasons for the divestment of Malegar by VM plc and the benefits to Chiba of growing by acquisition in the UK.

(8 marks)

12.3 (a) Contrast Chiba's and Malegar's differing approaches to human resource management.

(5 marks)

(b) Explain the change management issues that Chiba is likely to face when integrating the Malegar employees. Refer to relevant models where appropriate.

(9 marks)

Total: 27 marks

13 Hire Value Ltd

Hire Value Ltd (HV) operates in the car hire industry throughout the UK.

The UK car hire industry has two sectors: renting cars to users for the short term, typically between one day and two weeks (the car rental sector); and leasing cars to users for the longer term (the leasing sector). These sectors are of approximately equal size in terms of revenue.

The UK car rental sector

There are about 100 companies operating in the car rental sector in the UK. In 20Y2, these companies generated total revenue of £5,000 million. A few large companies dominate the sector. These larger companies tend to be international, with some companies being subsidiaries of car manufacturers. The car rental sector is also characterised by many medium-sized companies. Some of these have a regional focus, but most operate throughout the UK from airports, where there are clusters of car rental companies providing wide consumer choice.

The larger companies tend to maintain a modern fleet of cars, usually owning each vehicle for an average of only 13 months.

The car rental sector can be segmented in two main ways: by customer (business or leisure) or by location of outlets (airport or non-airport). A high proportion of rentals are dependent on the airline industry. Business customers tend to be companies which negotiate flexible contracts for renting many vehicles for short periods so that, for instance, visiting overseas executives can drive to meetings straight from the airport. An account is set up for each business customer and preferential prices are offered, compared with those for individual customers hiring cars for leisure purposes.

The car rental business tends to be seasonal, with spring and summer (the peak periods for leisure customers) each generating about 30% of annual revenues.

Strategic partnerships are common in the sector. The main examples are partnerships between car rental companies and airlines, which allow the customer to book car rentals on-line with a partner company at the same time as booking flights.

UK car rental market leader

Kerr Karrs plc (KK) is the UK market leader in the car rental sector, which is the only sector in which it operates. KK offers a high level of standard service by renting out modern, relatively good quality cars, charging a price premium compared with the industry average. In addition to its standard range of vehicles, it has a premium range of luxury cars for affluent individuals and senior business executives.

KK operates throughout the UK. It has many large, listed companies as its business customers and has partnerships with many airlines including special arrangements for their first class and business class customers. It tends not to have partnerships with budget airlines.

Hire Value Ltd – company history

HV was established a number of years ago by the current members of its board. HV's business model is to operate in the car rental sector throughout the UK. Its particular focus is to locate its outlets at airports in order to attract business and leisure travellers. The airport outlets also serve customers living or working in the cities closest to these airports. Each outlet consists of a customer service desk in the airport terminal, plus a vehicle collection site in the parking area. Both are distinctively branded to attract travellers and promote brand image. Staff are well trained in customer service.

HV's accounting information system provides an analysis of revenues from business customers and leisure customers separately. However, there is no separate analysis of costs or profit for each of these customer groups, as individual cars are used interchangeably between them.

HV aims to operate mid-market in terms of the service it provides. However, in order to control costs, HV buys cars which are about two years old and then operates them for a further three years. HV has adopted this policy as it believes that customers are more sensitive to price and the type of car they hire than its age.

All customer bookings are made on-line. Car rental charges are payable by credit card or debit card at the time of booking by leisure customers. Business accounts are on credit terms.

Expansion and the business plan

In March 20Y2, the HV directors obtained new equity finance from a venture capital company, TopFin, to expand the business. The business plan included the acquisition of more vehicles and the development of more locations to provide greater economies of scale and more efficient operations. A forecast of rapid growth was therefore a key element in obtaining the new finance from TopFin. The original board members continue to hold 60% of the ordinary share capital of HV; the remaining 40% is owned by TopFin.

A formal agreement was made between the director-shareholders and TopFin that there would be an independent review after a year to monitor the success of HV's growth strategy. In April 20Y3 accountants and business advisers, Gatter LLP, therefore reviewed how the business plan was being implemented and monitored. They reported that, for the year ended 31 March 20Y3, revenues had grown, but the projections in the business plan had not been achieved (see **Exhibit**). TopFin has now asked for a detailed analysis of the data to explain why actual performance has varied from the business plan.

Ethical issues

The review by Gatter LLP also reported that executive directors used some HV assets for personal use, raising a number of ethical issues:

(1) HV cars are sometimes loaned overnight to various executive directors when not rented out to customers. This is done on a casual basis without records. It appears to be accepted by employees as part of HV's corporate culture but, as no records are kept, TopFin has, to date, been unaware of this practice.

(2) One director, Mike Knight, provided an HV car to his friend for a few hours without charge. He told one of the other directors about this, prior to lending the car.

(3) Another director, Sandra Bevan, rented out an HV car for cash under a private arrangement. Initially, she held the cash received in her personal bank account but, after a month, paid it over to HV. This was just prior to the start of the Gatter investigation.

Requirements

13.1 For the year ended 31 March 20Y3 compare the actual performance and competitive position of HV with that of the market leader, KK. Use the data in the Exhibit and the other information provided.
(10 marks)

13.2 Using the quantitative data in the Exhibit and the other information provided, analyse and explain the shortfall between HV's actual performance for the year ended 31 March 20Y3 and its forecast performance in the business plan for the same period. In addition, you should indicate **three** significant matters which require further investigation in order to provide a more complete analysis.
(16 marks)

13.3 Prepare a risk register for what you consider to be the **four** most significant risks of HV. Use a table with three columns which, for each risk, explains:

   (a) The nature of the risk
   (b) The possible impact of the risk and likelihood of it occurring
   (c) Possible risk management procedures
(9 marks)

13.4 Prepare notes for a presentation to the HV board which explain the ethical issues, and the implications that arise from these, for the HV directors (both individually and collectively) as a result of the review by Gatter LLP of HV asset use.
(10 marks)

Total: 45 marks

Exhibit: Financial and operating data for HV and KK

Year ended 31 March 20Y3	HV forecast in Business Plan	HV actual	KK actual
Revenue:			
Business customers (£'m)	13.00	7.00	620.00
Leisure customers (£'m)	17.00	20.00	580.00
Operating profit (£'m)	1.20	1.00	56.00
Number of cars owned (average in year)	3,000	2,800	68,000
Total days of hiring ('000 days)	870	820	21,100
Market values of assets:			
Cars (£'m)	20.25	16.80	816.00
Other assets (£'m)	10.00	10.00	664.00

14   Up 'n' Over plc

Up 'n' Over plc (UnO) manufactures garage doors for domestic properties. It sells entirely to retailers on a business-to-business basis.

Company history

UnO was established over twenty years ago and obtained a listing in 20X5. The directors own 20% of the ordinary share capital, with the other 80% being held by financial institutions.

From incorporation, UnO produced reasonable quality, basic garage doors at relatively low cost. It did not aim to be the cheapest, but it did aim to offer best value to customers, selling garage doors at prices towards the lower end of the market. UnO established a good reputation with end-consumers, who demand a reliable product at reasonable prices.

UnO sells to retailers located throughout the UK. They range from small shops, which buy from UnO only when they receive an order from a customer, up to very large retail chains, which have three-year purchase contracts with UnO. Large chains carry high inventories of UnO doors for immediate delivery to consumers.

A cost reduction policy

In December 20Y1 a new chief executive, Helen Earth, was appointed by UnO to increase profitability. After briefly reviewing the operations of the business, she decided on a cost reduction exercise, commencing in January 20Y2. This involved: reducing the quality of the materials used to make the garage doors; reducing staffing levels; replacing some staff at a lower skill level; freezing any unnecessary capital investment in machinery; and reducing maintenance. Strict performance management procedures were introduced to ensure that output volume was maintained, despite the changes.

The changes had a favourable effect on reported profit in the year ended 31 December 20Y2 (see **Exhibit 1**) but by June 20Y3 some problems were being reported. A board meeting was arranged.

Board meeting

Helen, the **chief executive**, explained the reasoning for her cost reduction plan. "We have not yet developed a long-term strategy, but the cost reductions were immediately necessary just to make a profit.

"We've had some quality problems lately, but the cost of correcting these faults is small in comparison with the cost savings we have made. I realise that the durability of the current products is questionable. Problems will increase after about 18 months of usage of the garage doors, and there may be serious problems after three years of usage. I have made sure, however, that this is not going to be too costly to UnO, by reducing the guarantee period to customers from five years to two years. This means that by the time most doors start to develop serious faults after usage, they are out of guarantee and we have no obligation to repair them.

"As a result, I have prepared a schedule (see **Exhibit 1**) which shows that we expect to make a profit in the year to 31 December 20Y3, whereas we made a loss in 20Y1, and the share price is higher now than then. This demonstrates that the strategy is working. This is a competitive market and we need to compete on low prices, so we must keep our costs low."

The **marketing director** disagreed: "This business model is not sustainable. The number of complaints from our customers is growing and our reputation is declining. One of the large retailers has given us a final warning about quality standards and is threatening to stop buying our products when its long-term agreement period with UnO is completed. This cost reduction policy is just to improve short-term profits and share price. We should try to keep our customers happy in the longer term, so we must return to our previous policy of best value."

The **chairman** joined the discussion: "We need to balance the cost of rectifying faults with operating cost savings, but it's an increasingly competitive market. Personally, I doubt we can sustain our position as a manufacturer. One possibility is to close down our manufacturing facility and import garage doors from Thailand at a cost (including transport) that is just below our expected operating cost per door for 20Y3. In effect, we would become an importer and wholesaler of garage doors. To do this cost-effectively, we would need to order in large batches so we can fill a whole shipping container with each order, as there is a high fixed cost for transporting each container. I would like your views on whether we should consider this possibility further."

Exhibit 1

Years to 31 December	20Y1	20Y2	20Y3 (expected)
Revenue	£32m	£32m	£30m
Selling price to retailer per door	£400	£400	£400
Fixed operating costs	£15m	£14m	£14m
Operating profit/(loss)	£(1m)	£3m	£2m
Number of doors repaired under guarantee	8	24	96
Price per share	£2.10 at 31 Dec 20Y1	£4.50 at 31 Dec 20Y2	£3.20 at 31 May 20Y3

Requirements

14.1 On the basis of the information in the Exhibit, determine:

   (a)   The expected variable cost per garage door for 20Y3; and

   (b)   The break-even level of sales by volume for UnO in each of the years ended 31 December 20Y1 and 31 December 20Y2.

   Briefly comment on the implications for operating risk of these calculations.   **(9 marks)**

14.2 As a business adviser, prepare a report that evaluates the benefits and problems of each of the three strategies for UnO that were discussed at the board meeting:

   (a)   Return to the original strategy of producing in the UK at low cost and selling at best value, as suggested by the marketing director;

   (b)   Continue with the cost reduction programme introduced by the chief executive; or

   (c)   Cease manufacturing and import garage doors from Thailand, as suggested by the chairman.

   In each case, include a brief assessment of the sustainability of each strategy. Provide a reasoned recommendation, justifying your preferred strategy.   **(21 marks)**

                                                                                          Total: 30 marks

15 Moogle plc

The date is June 20X9.

You have recently joined Moogle plc (Moogle), one of the largest supermarket chains in the UK. You are the senior executive manager responsible for all Moogle's pet product sales in all its UK stores.

Initial briefing – chief operating officer

At an initial briefing, Moogle's chief operating officer, Fred Trueblood, outlined what he expected from you in your role:

"Moogle's pet products have underperformed compared with those of our rivals in recent years. I want you to make a difference. You will be responsible for procurement, pricing and profits in respect of all our pet product sales in the UK. This includes pet food and other pet-related accessories (eg, toys, bowls, bedding).

I need you to think strategically and get ahead of market trends. Don't just copy what our competitors have already done, as your predecessor did. He also got too involved in what was happening at individual stores and did not see the bigger picture.

I have outlined a few details for you about the UK pet products retail industry (see **Exhibit 1**) and about Moogle (see **Exhibit 2**), as initial guidance.

I have also arranged for you to meet our head of IT, Walter Weasil. I want you to agree an information strategy, so you have the information that is necessary to guide the strategic and operational decisions you will need to take."

Meeting with the head of IT

Walter Weasil opened the conversation:

"I need to know what key pieces of information you will need to guide your decision making and to help you monitor and control your area of responsibility. Your predecessor wanted every possible piece of information and just could not cope with it all. Try to be more selective and ask only for information that is appropriate to your function and level of management. Include any information you need to monitor any new strategies you may wish to adopt.

We can review matters later but, as a start, set out your regular monthly information needs by identifying three internal and three external pieces of information. In accordance with company policy, you must justify why you need each piece of information."

Requirements

15.1 Prepare a PESTEL analysis for the UK pet products retail industry. **(11 marks)**

15.2 Respond to the head of IT's request by identifying **three** pieces of internal information and **three** pieces of external information that you will require each month in your role. Explain why you will need each piece of information. **(14 marks)**

Total: 25 marks

Exhibit 1: An overview of the UK pet products retail industry

The UK pet products retail industry grew steadily by around 3% per year until 20X4 when it reached total retail sales of £2,500 million. Since 20X4, UK pet products sales have grown more slowly at 1% per year due to an economic downturn.

Pet food makes up about 75% of pet products sales. The remainder comprises: pet accessories (eg, toys, bedding); veterinary services; and pet insurance. Pet insurance sales are growing rapidly, but insurance is highly regulated. Expenditure on products for dogs and cats makes up 93% of UK pet products sales. The highest growth in the pet food sector has been premium quality moist food, which has the highest price, largest margins and lowest consumer price resistance.

Animal welfare has become a key issue with new laws being passed requiring minimum standards of pet living accommodation, diet and medical care.

Pet owners now use social media network sites to share experiences and ideas and to recommend pet products to each other.

There has been a growing trend to tag dogs and cats electronically with microchips, so they can be recovered if they are lost.

Online sales of pet products are increasingly common. There is also significant competition from pet superstores.

Exhibit 2: Moogle company background

Moogle is one of the largest supermarket chains in the UK, with stores throughout the world. Overall, Moogle positions itself as mid-market, but it has many low cost ranges and many premium product ranges.

Stores vary from large out-of-town superstores, to small in-town stores. All Moogle stores carry pet products. However, the proportion of total sales made up by pet product sales at each store varies significantly.

Moogle has a narrow product range for pets, focussing mainly on dogs and cats with a wide range of foods, plus a moderate range of accessories.

16   The Contract Cleaning Corporation Ltd

The Contract Cleaning Corporation Ltd (CCC) is a medium-sized company providing contract cleaning services to businesses in London.

The contract cleaning industry

The market for the contract cleaning industry arises from the outsourcing of cleaning activities by organisations which occupy offices, shops and factories. Contract cleaning market revenues in the UK amounted to £8,500 million in 20Y2.

Contract cleaners tend to be either small or medium-sized specialist cleaning companies or larger facilities management companies. The latter provide a wide range of services including, for example, contract cleaning, catering, building maintenance and security. A large facilities management company will often provide all these services to a client under a single contract.

Cleaning contracts tend to be awarded by clients for between one year and five years, with a break clause half way through in order to allow either party to terminate the agreement under specified conditions. At the end of the contract term there is usually a tender process, which may lead to a change in supplier. Alternatively, there may be a formal renegotiation between the current service provider and the client, resulting in a new price. The tendering process in the industry has become increasingly competitive, not just in terms of price, but also in terms of the quality and scope of the services provided.

The levels of staffing and the management of staff are key issues for cost control and operating efficiency. Small and medium-sized firms pay the statutory minimum wage, or just above this amount, to cleaners. Larger firms tend to pay more, as some of their cleaning processes require specialised skills. To check on the quality and security of work performed, there is a supervisor for each job, who is paid more than cleaners. Staff turnover is high for all companies in the industry.

The Contract Cleaning Corporation

CCC was established as a specialist cleaning company a number of years ago by two sisters, Gaynor and Lisa Harrison. Each owns 50% of the ordinary shares in CCC and they are also directors. Gaynor is primarily responsible for customer-facing activities. Lisa is responsible for internal activities, including staffing and day-to-day operations.

The business operates from leased office premises. There are few business assets, which comprise only vehicles, disposable cleaning equipment and office equipment. Operating staff (cleaners and supervisors) work 28 hours a week.

In April 20Y1, CCC's largest customer, Jarren plc (Jarren), announced that it would not be using CCC for its cleaning requirements after the current contract expired on 30 June 20Y2. In the year ended 30 September 20Y2, Jarren represented 10% of CCC's total annual revenue and 12% of its total annual operating profit.

Partly in response to the loss of Jarren as a customer, CCC engaged in a strategic review and decided to set up a new division to provide building maintenance services. This activity requires mainly part-time operating staff and they are managed separately from the Cleaning Division staff. The target market for the new Maintenance Division is existing contract cleaning clients who wish to widen the scope of services acquired from CCC, as part of a single facilities management contract. The new division commenced operations on 1 October 20Y2.

In November 20Y3, CCC prepared its management accounts for the year ended 30 September 20Y3 and this prompted concerns about performance. Gaynor and Lisa therefore appointed Sam Griffin, a newly-qualified ICAEW Chartered Accountant, as CCC's finance director and asked him to attend a board meeting to discuss performance.

The meeting

Lisa opened the meeting: "Since we lost the Jarren contract I believe the business as a whole has gone into decline. We launched the Maintenance Division in October 20Y2, but it is taking time to become established. I would like Sam to review the performance of CCC and comment on our existing performance management system, which is a balanced scorecard that was introduced in 20Y1 by a university student on an internship with us. Frankly, we do not fully understand the balanced scorecard and we are unsure whether the key performance indicators (KPIs) we have adopted are appropriate. We have provided an outline of our current balanced scorecard and some operating and financial data (**Exhibits 1 and 2**)."

Gaynor joined the discussion: "We have a potential new business opportunity. The CEO of a large facilities management company, Roizer plc (Roizer), approached me recently about a contract which might be mutually beneficial, even though they are a rival company. I have provided details (**Exhibit 3**)."

An ethical issue

As a consequence of decreasing revenues, Gaynor placed an advert in a London newspaper on 2 December 20Y3 which included the following:

The Contract Cleaning Corporation

The CCC is the leading medium-sized cleaning company in London.

- All of our staff receive regular training
- We use environmentally-friendly cleaning materials
- Customer service is our main priority
- We also now offer maintenance services as a major part of our business

Sam discovers that:

- After initial induction training, staff training only takes place every three years
- CCC uses an equal mix of environmentally-friendly and standard chemical cleaning materials

Requirements

16.1 The directors have asked you, Sam Griffin, to complete the following tasks:

(a) Critically appraise the appropriateness of the KPIs in the balanced scorecard (Exhibit 1) that CCC has used in its performance management system. Explain how the performance management system can be improved, including suggestions for more suitable KPIs. You do not need to quantify the suggested KPIs. **(10 marks)**

(b) With reference to Exhibit 2 and the other information supplied, evaluate and explain the performance of CCC for the year ended 30 September 20Y3, compared with the year ended 30 September 20Y2. **(18 marks)**

(c) Using the quantitative data in Exhibit 3 and the other information provided, assess the benefits and risks which may arise from accepting the contract with Roizer. Provide supporting calculations, using the assumption that the Roizer contract would have the same contribution margin (ie, contribution per £1 of sales) that the Cleaning Division had in the year ended 30 September 20Y3. **(9 marks)**

16.2 Discuss the ethical issues arising from the newspaper advert. **(5 marks)**

Total: 42 marks

Exhibit 1: CCC Balanced Scorecard KPIs

Key performance indicators currently used

Financial

   Revenue growth %

   Return on capital employed (ROCE)

Customer

   Total number of customers

   Number of customer complaints to the directors

Internal business

   Cost of cleaning products used

   Number of staff

Innovation and learning

   Hours of staff training carried out

   % of revenue from new clients

Exhibit 2: CCC operating and financial data

Income statements for the years ended 30 September

	Notes	20Y3 Cleaning Division £'000	20Y3 Maintenance Division £'000	20Y3 CCC Total £'000	20Y2 CCC Total £'000
Revenue		7,200	500	7,700	7,800
Direct labour costs		(4,048)	(324)	(4,372)	(4,128)
Other variable costs	1	(2,024)	(162)	(2,186)	(2,477)
Fixed operating costs	2	(950)	(50)	(1,000)	(1,000)
Operating profit/(loss)		178	(36)	142	195

Notes

1   Other variable costs comprise: transport (including vehicle depreciation), cleaning materials, disposable cleaning equipment.

2   Fixed operating costs comprise: administration salaries and other costs, training costs, directors' remuneration, office rent and other office costs including depreciation, insurance, accounting services.

Operating data – year ended 30 September

	20Y3 Cleaning Division	20Y3 Maintenance Division	20Y3 CCC Total	20Y2 CCC Total
Total number of clients during the year	80	5	85	77
Average number of operating staff (treated as direct labour)	440	30	470	430

Exhibit 3: Information for potential contract with Roizer – prepared by Gaynor

Roizer has recently won a facilities management contract with a large pharmaceutical company, GFP plc (GFP), for their London offices. The contract between Roizer and GFP is for four years from 31 January 20Y4, with a break clause after two years.

Roizer provides some cleaning services to existing customers, but cleaning is not a major aspect of their business and they will have trouble staffing this part of the contract at such short notice.

Roizer has therefore offered to sub-contract the GFP cleaning work to CCC on the following terms:

- CCC staff will perform all the cleaning tasks required under Roizer's contract with GFP in accordance with Roizer's service level agreement with GFP

- CCC will invoice Roizer for 60,000 chargeable employee hours per year, at £12 per hour

- CCC will provide all cleaning materials, disposable cleaning equipment, and transport, as for any other client

- The contract between Roizer and CCC would be annual, but renewable each year with the agreement of both parties.

17   The Foto Phrame Company

The date is December 20Y3.

The Foto Phrame Company (FPC) is a listed company manufacturing mid-market cameras from a single factory in Germany.

The camera industry

The first camera was produced over a hundred years ago and, since that time, new technology has enabled improved products to be launched with increasing frequency. Nearly all cameras now produced are digital cameras, which first appeared thirty years ago. However, technology advances quickly in the camera industry and each model of digital camera has a limited life cycle of five to eight years, before being replaced with an updated model. Within this life cycle, minor changes in technology mean that small variations in design, to improve a given model, are implemented each year.

Currently, there are broadly three types of camera: the compact camera (at the lower end of the market); the mirrorless camera (mid-market); the digital SLR (single lens reflex) camera (at the upper end of the market). Smart-phones are a major competitor for compact cameras, but are less of a threat to mirrorless and digital SLR cameras.

Research and development (R&D) is a key feature of product improvement and replacement. The industry is very competitive and owning intellectual property for the latest technology can be important in gaining competitive advantage. However, as technology changes rapidly, any such competitive advantage can be quickly eroded. Industry employees tend to be highly skilled.

The Foto Phrame Company

FPC products

FPC manufactures only mirrorless cameras. It has a highly skilled workforce and it spends a significant amount on R&D. FPC's markets are global. 40% of sales revenues are from European countries and 30% from the United States.

The lens is one of the highest cost components in a camera. FPC currently purchases all of its camera lenses from a German company, Zeegle, which has a factory located 40 kilometres from FPC's factory. Zeegle is in daily communication with FPC procurement staff regarding delivery quantities. However, there have been occasional delays in supply, so FPC holds the equivalent of 15 days of average usage of lenses in inventory. FPC believes that Zeegle's prices are higher than they should be. The Zeegle board has refused to lower the prices, but it has constantly sought to improve product quality and service delivery for FPC.

In June 20Y4 FPC intends to launch a replacement model for its best selling MirrorMinus3 (MM3) camera. This is the MirrorMinus4 (MM4), which has been redesigned to be smaller and lighter, with industry-leading technology. FPC undertakes a strategic review at the end of each model's life cycle. It is currently reviewing its procurement strategy and supply chain management policy as part of the strategic implementation of the new MM4.

Procurement and supply chain management

Two issues have arisen in terms of procurement and supply chain management:

Issue 1:   FPC is unsure whether to procure its lenses for the MM4 from: (1) one supplier, Zeegle; or (2) a range of five suppliers, producing a single type of lens, but competing on price, product quality and service. One of the suppliers would be Zeegle, two other suppliers would be French, and two would be Japanese.

Issue 2:   The MM4 has over 60 other separate components and FPC wishes to reduce costs. It wants to assess the benefits of undertaking a procurement review of all its direct suppliers ('tier 1' suppliers) in order to identify efficiencies. It is also considering managing further up the supply chain to ensure its suppliers' suppliers (ie, 'tier 2' suppliers) are reliable and cost efficient. FPC is unsure whether to conduct its own review of operating procedures in tier 2 suppliers or to ask its tier 1 suppliers to carry out this task on its behalf.

Distribution

A further concern for the FPC board relates to distribution, particularly in the US which is a major and growing market for FPC. US sales have increased from 15% to 30% of FPC's total sales revenue in the last 10 years. Up to now, distribution for this market has occurred from Germany either to US wholesalers or directly to large US retail clients (eg, large chains of specialist camera shops). No inventory is currently held by FPC in the US. However, demand in the US is variable and there have been an increasing number of complaints from US customers that lead times are too long and too uncertain.

The problems have been magnified by the fact that the version of the MM3 sold in the US differs in design from the MM3 sold to other global customers, due to the particular demands of US consumers. As a consequence, production runs for US design cameras at the factory in Germany only take place in the first week of each month. The company expects that variations in design for the US product will also be required for the new MM4.

FPC is considering developing its distribution facilities in the US by one of the following:

Distribution strategy 1:   Open a distribution centre in central US to hold significant inventory for distribution throughout the US using a third party courier.

Distribution strategy 2:   Set up a joint venture with a Japanese camera manufacturer to operate a distribution function in the US. The joint venture would acquire a distribution centre and vans to deliver the cameras of both companies to clients throughout the US.

Under both strategies, distribution would be both to wholesalers and directly to large retailers. However, a greater proportion of deliveries could be made directly to retailers, rather than through wholesalers, compared with existing distribution from Germany. Neither distribution strategy would involve FPC carrying out any further modification of cameras in the US.

Requirements

17.1 Explain the concept of the product life cycle and describe the factors which may affect the length of the product life cycle for FPC's cameras such as the MM3 and the MM4.   **(8 marks)**

17.2 Prepare a report for the board which explains the factors that FPC should consider in evaluating:

(a)   The two procurement and supply chain management issues identified by FPC, providing reasoned advice; and   **(13 marks)**

(b)   Each of the two US distribution strategies identified by FPC, providing reasoned advice.   **(14 marks)**

Total: 35 marks

18   FeedAfrica

FeedAfrica is a UK registered charity. It raises funds throughout the UK so it can support African communities faced with adverse conditions.

A summary of the issues

FeedAfrica has recently appointed Tom Reesing as its new chief executive because the trustees were unhappy with the charity's previous performance. The chair of the trustees summarised the situation in a conversation with Tom:

"We have been carrying out some really effective work in Africa, but we could do so much more. We are rejecting more and more requests for help, because we just do not have the financial or human resources to meet all the demands.

"The problems stem from a lack of public awareness of FeedAfrica's activities and a decline in funds raised in the UK. We need to market ourselves more intelligently to raise public awareness and increase our income. I have provided some background information and financial data (**Exhibit**) but, for me, FeedAfrica is about helping communities in Africa feed themselves sustainably. The charity can do this in three ways: by providing education on farming techniques; by supplying modern agricultural equipment; and by initiating projects to give long-term access to clean water. However, I do not believe we have got this message across to enough individual donors in the UK."

The chief executive's initial review

Based on an initial review, Tom believes that, in order to increase donations from UK individuals, FeedAfrica needs to improve its market research and use this to target its promotional activities. Tom is very concerned that marketing expenditure has been wasted in the past, and that the costs incurred in raising funds have been too high in proportion to the funds generated.

Tom also believes that he could attract more donations from UK companies if he could better demonstrate that the charity's work in Africa is contributing to sustainable development there. However, to do this, FeedAfrica needs to provide appropriate evidence by measuring and monitoring its achievements.

Requirements

18.1 Explain the types of market research that FeedAfrica could carry out to help target its advertising and other promotional activities aimed at individual donors. **(8 marks)**

18.2 Explain how market segmentation may be implemented by FeedAfrica to improve the effectiveness of its promotional activities towards individual donors. **(7 marks)**

18.3 Explain how FeedAfrica can measure and monitor the impact it is having on sustainable development in Africa. **(8 marks)**

Total: 23 marks

Exhibit: FeedAfrica – background information and financial data

FeedAfrica was established thirty years ago in response to a long-term drought in central Africa which caused the failure of crops and led to the starvation of many people. Television coverage meant this hardship was well publicised and significant donations were received at this time by FeedAfrica from both individuals and companies in the UK.

An economic downturn in the UK, and the absence of television coverage in recent years, have together meant that FeedAfrica's income has fallen. Draft financial statements for the year ended 30 November 20Y3 showed the following deficit:

	£'000
Donations from individuals:	
Cash and cheques	1,025
Planned giving (regular amounts by standing order)	1,345
Legacies and bequests	550
Donations from companies	840
Other income	260
Total funds generated	4,020
Costs of generating funds	(760)
Funds spent on charitable activities in Africa	(3,030)
Overheads	(540)
Deficit	(310)

- Drilling wells and accessing other water sources to enable irrigation of crops

- Educating farmers regarding fertilisation and crop rotation to improve crop yields

- Building roads for inward transportation of materials and workers to villages and for outward distribution of harvests to wider communities

- Encouraging the wealth generated by improved agriculture to be used in developing local communities

---

19 Emelius Ltd

Emelius Ltd (Emelius) offers document storage and management services in England. Its clients are organisations which typically process large volumes of paper and need to retain documents for a certain amount of time, for commercial or regulatory purposes. Clients include banks, professional services firms, local government organisations, utility companies and medical practices which find that managing their own documents requires significant amounts of time and storage space.

Document management companies benefit from economies of scale and can provide fast, cost-effective access to business-critical information. They use sophisticated systems to index information, protect documents from loss and alteration, and allow authorised access. Companies in the industry range from large global businesses, which offer comprehensive document storage and electronic data management, to smaller local or regional providers of paper-based storage facilities.

Company information

Emelius' current focus is the physical storage of paper documents. Documents requiring storage are collected from the client and taken to the nearest Emelius facility where they are bar-coded. This allows the documents to be catalogued and computer-indexed. Where relevant, a document is assigned an end-of-life destruction date, selected by the client, before being placed in long-term storage. When the agreed destruction date arrives, the document is shredded and the waste is recycled wherever possible.

Emelius' long-term storage system is suited to paper documents which clients are unlikely to need to access regularly. If access is required, the relevant documents can be retrieved from the storage facility and delivered to the client. Each Emelius storage facility is fitted with advanced fire detection systems and has comprehensive security with 24-hour off-site monitoring of the premises via surveillance cameras.

The document storage and management industry is quite capital intensive. In addition to premises and equipment, significant investment in IT systems is required. To reduce the amount of capital required, Emelius operates its business on a franchise model, with each franchisee granted an exclusive right to run the Emelius business in an agreed region of England. Strict franchise agreements allow Emelius to have tight control over the operations and quality of service provided, and to ensure Emelius' business model is applied consistently. Confidentiality of information and customer satisfaction are important and Emelius takes a strict approach to breaches of security and customer complaints.

Emelius has recently developed a new service, which franchisees will have the option to offer as an alternative to their customers. The new service is the digital data capture of paper documents that clients might need to access regularly. These are taken to the company's single central scanning house, where they are converted and saved in digital form. The original paper document is destroyed and the digital version is made available for clients to access using a web-enabled platform. A value chain analysis for Emelius' new digital data capture service is included in **Exhibit 1**.

Emelius Northern franchise

The Emelius Northern franchise (EN) was set up in 20Y2 by Lee Gryphon. The maximum storage capacity of its existing paper-based facility is 100 million sheets of paper. The business has been experiencing rapid growth (see **Exhibit 2**) and capacity could be increased to 150 million sheets by incurring additional fixed costs of £750,000 pa. EN does not currently offer the new digital data capture service.

Lee is in discussions with a large firm of solicitors, Swinburne LLP (Swinburne), about a potential new contract. Swinburne has five offices in the north of England and its paper document archive consists of 12 million sheets of paper. It wishes to outsource paper-based storage of all these documents to EN.

Swinburne has expressed an interest in using Emelius' new digital data capture service but Lee is unsure whether EN should start offering this service. Swinburne estimates that, once stored, 40% of its archive will need to be accessed regularly. The remainder needs storing for regulatory purposes but is unlikely to be accessed before end-of-life.

Requirements

19.1 Prepare a risk register setting out one significant risk facing Emelius' current paper-based document storage business, in each of the following four risk categories: strategic, operational, hazard and financial.

Use a table with four rows and three columns which explains, for each risk category:

- The nature of the one significant risk you have identified;
- The possible impact of the risk and the likelihood of it occurring; and
- Appropriate risk management procedures. **(12 marks)**

19.2 Explain four key drivers in the value chain for Emelius' new digital data capture service (Exhibit 1).

(12 marks)

19.3 Using the quantitative data in Exhibit 2 and the other information provided in relation to the Emelius Northern (EN) franchise:

- Calculate the expected operating profit for 20Y4, without the Swinburne contract. Analyse the reasons for the improvement in performance of the EN franchise over the period 1 January 20Y2 to 31 December 20Y4.

- Quantify the impact on EN's 20Y4 expected operating profit of accepting the contract to manage Swinburne's document archive in paper format only.

- Explain your results and their implications for EN's decision about whether to introduce the digital data capture service. State any assumptions you have made. **(14 marks)**

19.4 Draft a letter on behalf of Lee Gryphon, the EN franchisee, to Swinburne, which covers the following:

- The benefits that digital data capture might offer Swinburne

- A justification of three performance measures that should be incorporated in the service level agreement for the contract between EN and Swinburne **(10 marks)**

Total: 48 marks

Exhibit 1: Value chain analysis for Emelius' new digital data capture service

FI	10 regional franchises in England; head office provides support services (accounting, marketing, training) and centralised purchasing of all equipment and IT requirements; single centralised scanning house				
TD	Automatic checks on quality/legibility of scanning and exception reporting of scanning errors	Documents stored in standard image and text format to ensure maximum system compatibility	Powerful indexing system with multiple search function allows rapid document retrieval of main and any linked supporting documents		Multiple secure access controls to prevent and detect unauthorised creation, access, alteration or deletion of records
HRM	Relatively unskilled employees at scanning house, minimum wage, strict document processing targets			Existing franchisee responsible for deciding whether to offer new service in their region	Existing head office customer service team responsible for all customer support in relation to digital data service
P	Use of 24-hour national couriers to deliver paper documents from clients to central scanning house	Sole supplier agreement for all IT needs	Maintenance of online platform for document access is outsourced to specialist provider		
PA	High-speed scanners at single central facility, able to cope with multiple document formats and batch-process large volumes Once scanned, paper documents are destroyed	Key data captured and used to index documents Validation of accuracy of indexes Copies of digital documents stored across multiple servers	Web-enabled system allows multiple users to access the same files at the same time Paper copies of documents can be requested by authorised individuals	Distinctive Emelius branding on vans, staff uniforms, correspondence, website and social media	Certificate of destruction issued to client at end-of-life in accordance with regulatory requirements
	Inbound Logistics = Converting paper documents to electronic files by scanning	**Operations =** Indexing and storage of digital documents	**Outbound Logistics =** Providing clients with access to digital documents	**Marketing and Sales =** Informing customers and persuading them to buy	**Service =** Ongoing service support

Margin (on right-hand side)

KEY: FI = firm infrastructure; **TD** = technology development; **HRM** = human resource management; **P** = procurement; **PA** = primary activities

Exhibit 2: Emelius Northern (EN) franchise – operating performance summary

Year ended 31 December	Volume (sheets of paper)	Revenue £'000	Variable costs £'000	Fixed costs £'000	Operating (loss)/profit £'000
20Y2 actual	50 million	1,800	675.0	1,500	(375.0)
20Y3 actual	75 million	2,700	937.5	1,650	112.5

20Y4 working assumptions (without Swinburne contract):

Maximum storage capacity = 100 million sheets of paper.
Anticipated volume = 90 million sheets of paper.
There will be no change in 20Y3 prices to customers.
Variable cost will be 1.15 pence per sheet.
Expected fixed cost = £1,755,000.

20 Boom plc

Boom plc (Boom) is a large, profitable mining company. It is engaged in extracting natural shale gas from underground rock formations at various sites around the world.

The hydraulic fracturing industry

Shale gas is projected to be one of the fastest-growing components of world energy consumption, with production expected to more than double between 2000 and 2020. A plentiful supply of shale gas is contained worldwide in underground rocks. It is much more abundant than conventional gas but cannot be reached by traditional vertical drilling. Instead a mixture of water, sand and chemicals is injected at high pressure, deep underground, to break up rocks and release the gas they hold. This process is known as hydraulic fracturing (fracking). The benefits claimed for shale gas include: reduced reliance on traditional fossil fuels, increased security of energy supply, reduced carbon emissions, and socio-economic development through jobs and tax revenues.

Project SA

Boom has recently discovered a new site in a remote but populated area of South America (Project SA). The local government is willing to grant Boom a lease to proceed with the fracking and the central government anticipates that there will be significant economic benefits from the production of shale gas, in terms of job creation, gross domestic product and tax revenues. Also, an abundant domestic supply of natural shale gas could be used to produce cleaner, cheaper electricity and fuel for the region.

However, there is opposition from environmental groups which claim that the local population has not been sufficiently informed about the long-term environmental issues associated with fracking. They claim that the development would place large demands on already restricted water resources and that Boom would compete with local farmers and residents for water. They also claim that fracking risks contaminating drinking water supplies. Industry experts disagree, pointing out that it is possible to make some use of saline (non-drinking) water and recycle the waste water from the fracking process.

Boom's mission

Boom's mission statement is 'to maximise the return on investment for our shareholders whilst striving to recognise our corporate responsibility to wider society.'

At a recent board meeting to discuss Project SA, Boom's finance director commented: 'Our responsibility as directors is to look after our shareholders. If we have to spend money keeping these environmentalists happy, at best we will reduce profits and at worst some of our projects will not be viable. I think the two parts of our mission statement contradict each other.'

One non-executive director (NED) took a different view. 'I recently attended a conference looking at the NED's role. They said that, as directors, we have a legal duty to promote the success of the company for the benefit of its members as a whole. This means having regard to the long-term consequences of any decision and the impact of the company's operations on the community and the environment as well as its employees, suppliers and customers. This leads to a sustainable business. Surely therefore we need to consider these environmentalists, if only from a risk management point of view.'

Requirements

20.1 Discuss the views of the two directors in relation to Boom's mission statement. In doing so, you should explain the directors' duties in respect of corporate governance and corporate responsibility.

(12 marks)

20.2 Discuss the commercial and ethical issues for Boom which are involved in the decision to extract shale gas in South America.

(10 marks)

Total: 22 marks

21 Tai Ltd and Jelk plc

Tai Ltd (Tai) is a Chinese company and Jelk plc (Jelk) is a UK company. They are currently considering a merger.

Tai Ltd – company information

Tai is well-established in China which is currently its only market. It manufactures and sells high-quality travelators (moving staircases and walkways) for use in shopping malls, offices, hotels, airports and railway stations.

Tai uses high quality materials and prides itself on its research and development team, which has created a range of technologically innovative products with outstanding energy efficiency. An integrated power control system means that Tai's travelators can run at full speed during peak times and automatically slow down or stop when there are no passengers. Safety is critical and the control system helps to minimise the risk of accidents as well as automatically shutting down power in the event of an emergency.

Tai has recently been asked to tender for the supply of 350 travelators for a railway expansion project in China. The contract will be awarded by the Chinese Ministry of Railways which requires the contractor to demonstrate its ability to cope with the scale and complexity of the project and to meet tight deadlines. Post-installation service and maintenance will also be key factors in awarding the contract.

Jelk plc – company information

Jelk is a UK listed company. It began as a manufacturer of elevators (mechanical platforms which move people or goods vertically between different levels of buildings). Jelk currently has contracts to supply and maintain elevators for a variety of major European clients in office and housing developments, hotels, railway stations and airports. Its products range from basic, cost-effective elevators for low-rise residential buildings to sophisticated multi-elevator systems for high-rise office buildings. Jelk has a reputation with its clients for excellent customer service and post-installation maintenance. Jelk makes extensive use of technology, including a state-of-the-art transport management and communication system which optimises travel within multi-elevator buildings, reducing energy use. This gives Jelk a competitive advantage. However the company recently lost a tender for a new project in Poland because the client wanted to install both travelators and elevators and decided to use a single supplier which, unlike Jelk, offered both services.

Jelk also designs, manufactures and installs stairlifts (motorised seats for transporting elderly or disabled people up and down stairs). Due to the decline in the European construction industry, Jelk has become increasingly reliant on its stairlift business. Each year, it sells thousands of stairlifts to individuals, of which 40% are exported from the UK, predominantly to Eurozone countries. Jelk is the acknowledged market leader in product safety, quality of service and innovative product design.

Jelk's headquarters, manufacturing and distribution operations are all based in the UK. It has an extensive network of installation and maintenance engineers located throughout Europe. Jelk does not currently operate in China.

Product life cycles

Travelators, elevators and stairlifts all go through similar stages in their life cycle:

- Installation of new equipment
- Modernisation and maintenance
- Replacement

However the useful lives differ: on average each travelator and elevator lasts 30 years, while each stairlift lasts only 15 years. The energy required to operate a travelator or elevator accounts for up to 80% of its environmental impact over its entire life cycle, so the primary objective when developing new models is to improve their energy efficiency.

Industry and market information: travelators and elevators

Collectively, the top four global manufacturers account for 65% of industry revenue. Demand for travelators and elevators is heavily linked to the construction sector, where macroeconomic conditions remain highly uncertain and market growth rates differ significantly between continents. The depressed construction sector in Europe has led to weak demand, increased competition and an increasingly price-sensitive market. Europe accounts for 48% of all travelators/elevators in operation, but only 23% of new installations.

In contrast, the construction sector continues to expand rapidly in South America and Asia. Due to high urbanisation rates, China represents the fastest growing travelator and elevator market, accounting for 30% of new installations. There is a developing awareness in China of the importance of quality and reliability, and increased demand for post-installation maintenance. There is also a need for basic, cost-effective elevators in the affordable-housing segment, since the Chinese government has announced plans to build 36 million mid-rise housing blocks for low-income families over the next five years.

Industry and market information: stairlifts

Apart from Jelk, the global stairlift industry largely comprises independent manufacturers which focus solely on stairlifts. Jelk is the global market leader, closely followed by two large competitors, both of which also originated in the UK. One of these competitors has recently been acquired by a major global company that provides a range of mobility products for the elderly and disabled.

Key drivers of industry demand are the age and health of the population, type of housing, disposable income and availability of government funding. Over 35% of worldwide sales currently take place in the UK, as government assists in paying for mobility aids for the elderly and disabled whereas, in most other countries, stairlifts are bought privately. Demand in China is growing rapidly because it has an ageing population with increasing levels of disposable income.

Proposed merger

"Despite our cultural differences, the proposed merger with Tai will bring tremendous benefits to both parties," said Jelk's CEO. "With Jelk's strong market share in the stairlift business, as well as Tai's well-established presence in China, the companies complement each other in achieving remarkable geographical market coverage and in offering a comprehensive product portfolio (see **Exhibits 1 and 2**). We are confident we can successfully manage the integration of the two entities."

Requirements

Discuss whether the proposed merger should proceed, referring to relevant models where appropriate.

Use the following headings:

21.1 Product portfolio benefits	(10 marks)
21.2 Other key benefits	(7 marks)
21.3 Key strategic disadvantages and management issues	(9 marks)
21.4 Preliminary conclusions	(4 marks)

Total: 30 marks

Exhibit 1: Market data UK and China

UK market (figures stated in £ millions)

	Jelk sales	Largest competitor	UK market Annual growth rate
Elevators	£54m	£260m	–2%
Travelators	n/a	£182m	Nil
Stairlifts	£96m	£80m	8%

Chinese market (figures stated in US$ millions)

	Tai sales	Largest competitor	Chinese market Annual growth rate
Elevators	n/a	$4,550m	19%
Travelators	$19.6m	$342m	15%
Stairlifts	n/a	$12m	30%

Note: Assume an exchange rate of US$1 = £0.65

Exhibit 2: Analysis of sales revenue mix

	Jelk	Tai
Modernisation and maintenance	66%	12%
New installations	34%	88%

22 Albatross Golf Equipment plc

The date is June 20Y4.

Albatross Golf Equipment plc (AGE) is an unlisted company which manufactures golf clubs.

Market background

Golf clubs are used to play the sport of golf and are sold individually or in sets of clubs. They make up about 70% of the wider golf equipment market which also comprises golf clothing, bags, balls and other items related to playing golf.

Golf equipment is the largest single sector of the sports equipment market in the UK, mainly due to its high price compared to equipment for other sports. The UK golf equipment market amounted to £350 million in 20Y3, using manufacturers' selling prices. This represented a decrease of 16% since 20X8.

Distribution channels for manufacturers comprise general sports retailers and specialist golfing shops.

Company history

A number of years ago Ben Fogan opened AGE's factory in the UK to manufacture a range of high quality golf clubs. All raw materials have always been sourced locally in the UK. AGE has never made any other types of golf equipment.

When he started the business, Ben was a successful amateur golfer and a professional engineer. He made innovative adjustments to the standard design of golf clubs available at that time and patented his idea, under the LazySwing brand name. As a result, many golfers purchased the LazySwing branded clubs and reported improved scores when they played golf with them. Four years after opening the factory AGE's sales experienced a major boost when the winner of the Open Golf Championship, a globally recognised golf competition, used LazySwing golf clubs and this had a favourable reputational impact for the LazySwing brand.

AGE has, to date, sold only to specialist golfing shops, both in the UK and the rest of Europe. These shops are owned by a variety of companies and individuals, and Ben visited them personally on a regular basis to make sure that AGE products were being displayed and promoted, alongside rival brands, in an appropriate manner.

Ben continued to innovate with golf club design, but over time he could not match the rapid changes in technology achieved by larger competitors with significant research and development budgets. As a result, the LazySwing brand declined in reputation, with a decreasing customer base. Ben died in 20X4, by which time sales had fallen significantly from their peak in the early days. In October 20Y3, AGE was acquired by a private equity company, Fuller Finance plc (FF).

Lee Trebino was appointed by FF as the new chief executive of AGE. He immediately undertook a strategic review of AGE in order to explore opportunities for developing the company and returning it to growth. He asked Putt and Pitch LLP (PP), the firm of business advisers for which you work, to attend a meeting to plan the next steps following his review.

Possible strategies

Lee opened the meeting: "When I took over as chief executive of AGE it was clear we needed to make changes to turn the company around. It was in decline and lacked a clear strategic direction. AGE has performed poorly in recent years (**Exhibit**).

"I would like PP to analyse why this is the case and to compare the performance of AGE with that of Galdo plc, the UK market leader in manufacturing golf clubs.

"The LazySwing brand still has a reasonably good reputation. However, it has now become a mid-range brand trying to compete in the high-end sector of the market. I believe it can no longer expect the required price premium or generate the required volume of sales in the high-end sector. I therefore propose a repositioning strategy for the existing LazySwing golf clubs, which is to move the LazySwing brand downmarket into the mid-range sector. We would continue to sell the existing clubs through specialist golfing shops, but at a reduced average selling price of £55 per golf club, to reflect the new mid-range market positioning.

"In addition to repositioning the existing clubs, I believe we can achieve real growth by importing some basic quality golf clubs from JiangGolf, a manufacturer in China. We expect these imported golf clubs to appeal to a wider market than our current range of clubs. We would need to guarantee to purchase a minimum of 100,000 clubs per year under a two-year agreement with JiangGolf. In return, JiangGolf has agreed it would supply AGE at an average price of £15 per golf club which, for the level of quality, is a lower price than any European supplier. I have two alternative strategies for the imported clubs:

Strategy 1: Sell the imported golf clubs under the LazySwing brand through the same specialist golfing shops as our existing LazySwing clubs, but price the imported clubs, on average, at £30 per club. They would therefore typically be the cheapest clubs available in these shops.

Strategy 2: Sell the imported golf clubs under a newly created brand name, 'Eagle', and distribute them through general sports retailers priced, on average, at £25 per club."

Ethical issue

For the last few years, AGE has used a professional golfer, Gary Paler, to promote the LazySwing brand name. Gary signed a new four-year contract with AGE in 20Y2 to promote the LazySwing brand. He was chosen due to his success in golf competitions, but also because of his public image as a player with integrity. At a celebrity party in March 20Y4, Lee was told in confidence, by a professional golfer, that Gary regularly took performance-enhancing drugs. The possession and use of such drugs are banned in many countries.

Lee is aware that, if this information became public, it would significantly damage the LazySwing brand and severely harm Gary's career. Lee said nothing for a few months, but is now very concerned about the ethical implications of the following two options open to him: breach the confidence and disclose the information, which would damage all concerned, or stay quiet until the end of Gary's contract.

Requirements

22.1 Using the quantitative data in the Exhibit and the other information provided, analyse the performance of AGE:

(a) Over the period 20Y1-20Y3; and
(b) In comparison with the performance of Galdo, the UK market leader.

Indicate briefly any further information that would be required to make a more complete analysis.

(18 marks)

22.2 As a business adviser working for PP, write a memorandum to the AGE board which evaluates the chief executive's strategies to: (1) reposition the existing clubs; and (2) import clubs. Use the following headings:

- Supply chain management
- Market positioning and branding **(14 marks)**

22.3 Explain the ethical issues arising for Lee, and for AGE, in relation to Gary Paler. Set out and justify the actions that Lee should now take. **(8 marks)**

Total: 40 marks

Exhibit: Financial, operating and market data

Financial data

	AGE			Galdo		
	20Y1 £'000	20Y2 £'000	20Y3 £'000	20Y1 £'000	20Y2 £'000	20Y3 £'000
Revenue						
UK sales	17,600	16,400	15,455	40,000	38,400	36,800
Export sales	4,400	3,600	2,945	60,000	57,600	55,200
Total	22,000	20,000	18,400	100,000	96,000	92,000
Manufacturing cost	17,600	16,400	15,456	70,000	67,200	64,400
Gross profit	4,400	3,600	2,944	30,000	28,800	27,600
Fixed operating cost	2,900	2,900	2,900	10,000	10,000	10,000
Operating profit	1,500	700	44	20,000	18,800	17,600

Operating data

	AGE			Galdo		
	20Y1	20Y2	20Y3	20Y1	20Y2	20Y3
Number of golf clubs sold (000s)	250	240	234	556	519	484

UK market data – golf equipment

	20Y1 £'000	20Y2 £'000	20Y3 £'000
UK market sales (at manufacturers' selling prices)	380,000	365,000	350,000

23 Best Fresh Bakeries Ltd

Assume the date is 20Y4.

Best Fresh Bakeries Ltd (BFB) is a family-run company with five shops, each of which bakes and sells high quality, fresh produce including breads, pies, cakes and pastries.

Company background

BFB was founded by Henry Hardcastle thirty years ago when he opened one shop in a small town.

Over the following 15 years, Henry opened four further shops in the local area. All the food has always been freshly baked on the premises of each shop and BFB is well-known locally, with a loyal customer base. One of Henry's slogans is 'Baked and sold on the premises, on the same day.'

BFB is a key customer for some of its smaller local suppliers.

There has been no expansion in the number of shops since 20X1. However, in 20X4 Henry's two sons, Ralph and Nigel, joined the business. Henry gave each of them 10% of the ordinary share capital and retained the remaining 80%, with Henry taking the position of chief executive. Ralph and Nigel are the other two directors. Each director has one vote at board meetings. Brief biographies of the three directors are provided (**Exhibit**).

The net assets of BFB recognised in its financial statements are £3 million. Last year the board rejected an offer of £5 million from a large confectionery company for the entire ordinary share capital of BFB.

Henry intends to retire in 20Y9 and it is the intention that his two sons will then buy all his shares at their market value. Henry does not want to expand the business before then, but his sons are keen to grow the business as soon as possible. This caused conflict at a recent board meeting.

Board meeting – expansion strategy

Ralph opened the meeting: 'I think we should expand by centralising baking production at a single new centralised baking facility. We could then distribute the products each morning to our shops. This would give us greater capacity and enable us both to sell internally to our own shops and to make new sales to third parties. The new bakery would be set up as a separate division so we could monitor its performance after implementation. The five shops would together form the other division. I estimate my strategy would require initial capital of £2 million.'

Nigel joined the conversation: 'I agree with Ralph. We can expand the business this way, as larger scale production will deliver greater economies of scale, for instance by bulk buying raw materials and having larger production runs.'

Henry was not pleased with his sons: 'I will retire in five years at which time you can buy me out and do what you want with the business but, until then, I really do not want to invest more capital and incur the risk and effort involved in a major expansion. You both want to expand the business, but you have no money of your own to invest.'

Nigel rejoined the conversation: 'We believe the company can borrow £2 million to finance the new development, so we are not asking for any more personal investment from you. Ralph and I are serious about this; if necessary, we will vote together for the expansion plan at the next board meeting, where we will have a two to one voting majority.'

A governance issue

The day after the meeting Henry was still angry and discussed what had happened with a couple of good friends, Jon and Gemma, who are unconnected to BFB. Henry said: 'Ralph's suggestion might be the best strategy to expand the business, but I just do not want the extra strain from a personal point of view. It's my business and I don't want my sons to take control away from me at board meetings before I retire.'

Jon supported Henry: 'You're the chief executive and major shareholder, so why don't you appoint Gemma and me as non-executive directors? We will vote with you to make sure that you have a majority at board meetings.'

Requirements

23.1 Explain the risks that should be considered in evaluating the expansion strategy from the perspective of: (a) BFB; and (b) each of the three existing shareholder-directors. **(12 marks)**

23.2 Assuming the expansion strategy is implemented, briefly explain the factors that should be considered in determining transfer prices from the new centralised baking production facility to the five individual BFB shops, and recommend how the transfer prices should be set. **(9 marks)**

23.3 In light of Nigel's and Ralph's voting intentions, and Jon's suggestions, explain the governance issues for BFB. **(7 marks)**

Total: 28 marks

Exhibit: Biographies of the directors

Henry – aged 60: Henry owns his own house and has savings of about £200,000, but the proceeds from the sale of his shareholding in BFB will be his main source of retirement funding. Henry intends that his sons should buy all his shares at market value when he retires in about five years' time, even if they have to borrow from their banks to do so. Henry is risk averse.

Ralph – aged 35: Ralph is single, has no savings and rents, rather than owns, his house. He has an extravagant lifestyle, spending nearly all his income, but he has no debts. He believes in taking reasonably high risks.

Nigel – aged 30: Nigel is married with a family. He owns his house, but has a large mortgage. He has some limited savings. He is risk neutral, but ambitious.

---

24 ElectroInfo Ltd

ElectroInfo Ltd (EIL) operates in the electrical and IT services industry. The EIL board is currently reconsidering the company's pricing policy to customers.

Operations

EIL offers electrical and IT services to customers for their homes. These two types of service are offered independently and are provided by different EIL employees. The electrical services provided by EIL include traditional home electrical services, such as wiring and fuse box installation, and also broadband installation and maintenance. The IT services offer solutions to basic software problems experienced by customers on their home PCs, laptops and tablets.

EIL operates from 30 depots located on business parks in towns throughout the UK. The depots are located about 50 kilometres away from each other in places where there is less competition than in large cities and where local reputation can be established more easily. EIL employs qualified electricians and IT specialists. Typically there are three electricians and three IT specialists operating from each depot. Customers all live within 25 kilometres of a depot. The company aims to offer good quality customer service.

EIL has a centralised structure so prices and wages, plus most other aspects of operations, are determined centrally. Each depot head reports directly to EIL's board of directors.

Competition

EIL aims to have a market position between large service companies and small sole proprietor businesses which operate from proprietors' homes. The large service companies tend to carry out both commercial and consumer work, but charge higher prices at £38 per labour hour upwards. Sole proprietor businesses offer lower prices, charging £28 per labour hour or less, but they often lack the most up-to-date training.

Pricing

EIL charges all its services, to all its customers, at a single rate of £32 per chargeable hour. The average variable cost to the company for both IT and electrical services is £20 per chargeable hour.

To increase profits, some directors suggested raising EIL's price to all customers for both types of service, but the **finance director**, Denise Jones, was concerned about this. 'Some customers are willing to pay more, but many are on low incomes. They are resistant to price increases and many would move to lower priced competitors if we raised our price. Instead, I believe we should consider charging a different price for each of our two different services, IT and electrical, to all customers, even though it costs us the same to provide these services in terms of both wages and other costs.'

The **marketing director**, Amy Ashad, disagreed: 'We should be charging different prices to different customers, but pricing each of the two types of service the same.'

Market research

The board agreed to obtain more information about customers' attitudes to price through market research based on questionnaires and examination of actual behaviour in response to previous price changes. This research revealed the following information about the sensitivity of demand (chargeable hours per year) to selling price (£ per chargeable hour):

Selling price per chargeable hour	£30	£32	£34	£36
Demand (chargeable hours per year)	250,000	230,000	200,000	160,000

Further market analysis was completed, using two different approaches to segmenting the customer market for electrical and IT services, firstly by customer income, and secondly by service type.

Segmented by customer income

Selling price per chargeable hour	£30	£32	£34	£36
Demand (chargeable hours per year)				
Low income customers (Note)	85,000	70,000	45,000	20,000
Other customers	165,000	160,000	155,000	140,000

Note: Classified using the estimated value of the customer's house as a rough measure to indicate the level of the customer's income.

Segmented by service type

Selling price per chargeable hour	£30	£32	£34	£36
Demand (chargeable hours per year)				
IT services	125,000	120,000	110,000	100,000
Electrical services	125,000	110,000	90,000	60,000

The **chief executive** has now made a further suggestion: prices should be set locally by each depot head, rather than centrally for all the depots by the directors.

Requirements

24.1 Assume that the same price is charged for both electrical and IT services and that prices are set centrally:

(a) From the four choices of price identified in the tables above, calculate the price per chargeable hour that EIL should charge in order to maximise total contribution under each of the following alternative assumptions:

- A single uniform price is charged to all customers (as per the current policy).

- One uniform price is charged to low income customers and a different uniform price is charged to all other customers.

(b) Discuss the feasibility and benefits of Amy Ashad's suggestion of charging different prices to different customers based on income. Refer to your calculations in (a) above. **(12 marks)**

24.2 Evaluate Denise Jones' suggestion that a different price should be charged for the two different service types, IT and electrical. Provide supporting calculations. Assume the same single uniform price continues to be charged to both low income and all other customers, and that prices are set centrally. **(9 marks)**

24.3 Evaluate the chief executive's suggestion of depot heads setting prices locally and explain the issues which are likely to arise in implementing this policy. **(11 marks)**

Total: 32 marks

25 Forsi Ltd

Forsi Ltd (Forsi) provides forensic science services to private clients and UK public sector organisations, such as the police and HMRC.

Industry information

Forensic scientists examine materials and provide scientific evidence to assist in an investigation or court proceedings. As well as criminal cases, forensic science is used in private disputes concerning accidents, medical negligence, insurance claims and product liability.

Until 20X9, the government-owned Forensic Science Service (FSS) accounted for 60% of the total forensic science market in the UK and handled the majority of the public sector work. However, in 20Y0 a decision was taken to reduce the activities of FSS, leading to its complete closure in 20Y3. As a result there have been several new entrants to the market, which is now very competitive.

Forsi was founded in 20Y0 by four scientists who previously worked for FSS. Forsi and one other key competitor now dominate the UK market. Both offer a wide range of forensic science services to all types of client. A number of smaller providers have also emerged which typically specialise in one particular scientific field eg, fire investigation, toxicology or genetics. Various UK police forces also have their own in-house forensic science laboratories but there is no national police policy, so many police forces outsource work to businesses such as Forsi.

Company information

From the outset, Forsi has operated with an informal structure, to minimise bureaucracy and focus on technical expertise and scientific analysis. The original founders spend little time on administration and management tasks, and instead concentrate on attracting clients and undertaking analytical work. Many support functions (including payroll, accounting and human resources) are outsourced.

As a result of the founders' reputations and technical expertise, and the range of forensic science services provided, Forsi has experienced steady growth. It now employs 40 scientists and five administrators. Work is organised on a project basis, with an appropriate project team created for each specific client request. On smaller projects, scientists may work alone. When they are not working on projects, Forsi's scientists are expected to undertake research to develop new scientific techniques or more efficient processes.

Although Forsi does undertake one-off projects for clients, most of its business is on a repeat basis, eg, a succession of accident investigations for an insurance company. Obtaining such clients is key to revenue growth. Once Forsi has been confirmed as a client's approved supplier, client retention becomes important. Depending on the client and the nature of the work, some projects are negotiated at a fixed price and some are priced on a cost-plus basis. Increasingly clients prefer fixed-price projects so that they can avoid unexpected increases in costs. All dealings and discussions with clients are handled by the four founders.

As a result of the increased competition, Forsi's informal structure has started to present some difficulties and threatens to inhibit its growth. There has been a lack of collaboration between staff, with scientists preferring to work independently on each project, and Forsi has not maximised opportunities for shared learning.

Often, requirements change during the course of a project and delays have arisen whilst one of the founders renegotiates with the client, leading to client complaints. There are few in-house financial controls and although a budgeted cost is established for each project before work starts, this is often exceeded. As a result of these issues, Forsi's profits have fallen (**Exhibits 1 and 2**). It has started to lose some potential projects to competitors and has also had to accept lower margins on repeat business in order to retain clients.

A possible new owner

Recently, Forsi has been approached by an Australian multi-national, Aussi Ltd (Aussi), which undertakes work for global private and public sector clients. Aussi consists of several divisions, each offering a different scientific service (eg, pharmaceutical research, forensic science, aerospace). All support services are provided by a centralised head office function.

Aussi's forensic science division is the market leader in Australia and Asia. In 20Y3 it spent £4.4 million on research and development and £9 million on marketing, and it generated sales revenue of £220.3 million (all figures translated from Australian dollars into £ sterling).

Aussi wants to acquire Forsi to further its expansion in Europe. However, it does not want to destroy Forsi's research-centred culture as it acknowledges that Forsi's success to date has been driven by the founders' knowledge and contacts, and by the skill of the scientists it employs. If the founders agree to sell their shares, Aussi will either allow Forsi to operate autonomously as a separate subsidiary company or integrate it within Aussi's forensic science division.

Whichever structure is chosen, Forsi will be required by Aussi to achieve a target return on capital employed (ROCE) of 15%. It will also have to comply with Aussi's formal project screening process whereby:

- All new projects are required to meet an expected minimum 20% gross margin
- The final agreed project price has to be signed off by Aussi's central finance department

In 20Y3, Aussi's forensic science division generated a gross margin of 25% and ROCE of 18% on net assets of £183.5 million. **Exhibit 2** sets out additional operating data for Aussi.

Requirements

25.1 Using the quantitative data in the Exhibits and the other information provided, analyse the performance of Forsi, contrasting it with Aussi's where appropriate. Suggest other non-financial information that may be useful in ascertaining the causes of the deterioration in Forsi's performance. **(16 marks)**

25.2 Discuss the appropriateness of Forsi's existing structure, referring to relevant models. **(7 marks)**

25.3 Assuming Forsi's founders do **not** agree to be taken over by Aussi, explain why knowledge management is important to Forsi and recommend the steps that Forsi could take to implement a knowledge management strategy. **(8 marks)**

25.4 Assuming Forsi's founders **do** agree to be taken over by Aussi:

(a) Discuss whether Forsi should be operated as a subsidiary of Aussi or as part of Aussi's forensic science division; and

(b) Recommend how Aussi should manage the change when the takeover is announced. **(14 marks)**

Total: 45 marks

Exhibit 1: Financial data for Forsi for the years ended 31 December		
	20Y2	**20Y3**
	£'000	£'000
Sales revenue	5,400	5,088
Direct costs	(4,175)	(4,165)
Gross profit	1,225	923
Research & development	(254)	(260)
Marketing	(108)	(90)
Other operating expenses	(268)	(270)
Operating profit	595	303
Net asset value	4,020	3,910

Exhibit 2: Operating data for Forsi and Aussi

	Forsi 20Y2	Forsi 20Y3	Aussi forensic science division 20Y3
Number of employees	45	45	2,000
Number of projects undertaken in year	108	106	2,448
% of projects completed on time	83%	76%	89%
% of projects completed within budgeted cost	72%	65%	92%
Sales value of projects awarded, but not yet undertaken, at year end	£1,350,000	£855,000	£65,080,000

26 ToyL Ltd

ToyL Ltd (ToyL) is a start-up business. It intends to provide educational toys for children, which will be sold to individual customers and educational establishments.

ToyL has been founded by a husband and wife team, Pavel and Rosemary Bochev. They have prepared the first draft of a business plan to attract additional funding from private investors (**Exhibit**).

You are a consultant in a firm of business advisers that is assisting ToyL. Your manager has undertaken an initial review of the draft business plan and has some concerns about its structure and content. Rosemary and Pavel have never prepared a business plan before and lack financial expertise. Your manager is also concerned that they may have been over-enthusiastic in their desire to present the business in the best possible light to attract potential investors.

Requirements

26.1 Write a report for Pavel and Rosemary which critically assesses the content of the draft business plan and makes recommendations as to how the document may be improved. As part of your appraisal indicate the nature of any missing information and any additional sections of the plan that would be relevant to a prospective investor. **(15 marks)**

26.2 Explain the benefits of outsourcing as a production model for ToyL. **(6 marks)**

26.3 Assume that ToyL successfully raises the necessary finance. Explain how the information requirements of Pavel and Rosemary as managers will be different from the information requirements of the additional private investors, once the business is operational. **(9 marks)**

Total: 30 marks

Exhibit

DRAFT BUSINESS PLAN: ToyL Ltd

Contents

1 Executive summary
2 Introduction and management team
3 Products
4 Marketing
5 Competition
6 Strategy and operations

---

1 Executive summary

Will be completed after the remainder of the business plan is finalised.

2 Introduction and management team

ToyL Ltd (ToyL) will sell educational toys for young children. It is owned and managed by Pavel, an information technology (IT) specialist and his wife, Rosemary, an educational consultant.

Pavel will be in charge of operations, including the one-off manufacture of product prototypes. He has a computer engineering degree. Pavel started his career in the product development department of a large IT company, before moving to a consumer electronics company, where he was responsible for developing hand-held games.

Rosemary will be responsible for marketing and sales. She studied for a Master of Education degree and then spent several years developing educational tools for teachers of pre-school children.

Together Rosemary and Pavel's backgrounds have helped them design products that combine opportunities for learning with the fun aspects of a game.

3   Products

ToyL has developed three distinct educational toys for young children, aged three to five years. These toys use interactive technology to teach numeracy and literacy.

- NumberToy: emits lights and sounds when the child touches a stylus on the appropriate number. In addition to teaching number skills, it also helps with hand-eye co-ordination.

- AlphabetToy: similar to NumberToy, but it teaches the child the alphabet and appears to improve their attention span.

- PhonicToy: an interactive toy that looks similar to a miniature laptop. It contains speech recognition software which allows the child to have a spoken conversation with a cartoon character. The character teaches word pronunciation and reads stories aloud. This is the most expensive product and is designed to help the child read and develop a vocabulary.

Although the toys are currently prototypes, they are functionally complete and ready for manufacture. The prototypes have been tested widely and were well received. Part of the testing has included Rosemary and Pavel observing a variety of children as they interact with the toys.

All products will be designed and initially manufactured in-house. However once a toy design has been tested and approved for sale, its on-going production will be outsourced to suppliers either in the UK or Eastern Europe. ToyL's product range is expected to grow over time as ideas for new toys are generated.

4   Marketing

ToyL has identified two target market segments:

- Individuals, such as parents or grandparents, who will purchase the product for a particular child. We think this market segment currently has about 3.3 million prospective customers and is growing at around 8% pa. Typically these customers are well-educated and have higher disposable incomes. They are keen for the children to develop and believe they are getting value-for-money if the toys have educational as well as entertainment value.

- Educational organisations, such as pre-schools, day care centres and nurseries, which will buy products to use within their institutional environment. Typically they care for children in groups of between 7 and 25 in number. We believe that this market segment contains about 0.7 million prospective customers and is growing annually at around 10%.

ToyL has decided to sell direct to both groups. Its key marketing tool will be its website. Its marketing strategy will recognise the fact that there are two distinct groups that must be attracted.

5   Competition

The UK toy industry is a fragmented market, with many different toy manufacturers. Within the toy industry there is a niche of educational toy manufacturers which is dominated by two global market leaders (Knowall and Brightkidz). These companies sell toys under a range of different brand names to cover several price points. There are also several smaller, regional manufacturers of educational toys.

In addition, educational toy providers compete with the wide range of electronic products produced by the large game manufacturers.

We believe ToyL's competitive advantage comes from products that are superior to those already available in the marketplace. This quality will allow ToyL to achieve market penetration. ToyL will use its educational and engineering expertise to produce toys that are fun to use and which at the same time teach important skills for children. By recognising and exploiting its core competencies, ToyL will quickly gain market share as well as develop a reputation for making effective educational toys.

6   **Strategy and operations**

The company is in its first year. It has incurred set-up costs of around £24,000 but has not yet produced a finished product or made any sales. ToyL hopes to generate sufficient revenues to break-even by the end of year one and then expects strong sales growth for several years. Rosemary and Pavel anticipate sales of £367,000 in year two and £475,000 in year three.

Pavel and Rosemary have invested capital of £60,000 in the business (through personal borrowing) but to develop more products ToyL is seeking additional equity capital of £40,000 from one, or more, private investors.

ToyL has identified three critical success factors (CSFs) that will be instrumental in the sustainability of its business:

- The ability to develop creative, educational, engaging toys

- The need to listen to customers and create a feedback mechanism for new product development and existing product improvement

- The implementation of strict financial controls

27   Water On Tap

'Water On Tap' (Ontap) is a small social enterprise operating in central London. A social enterprise is a business which meets social and environmental aims by trading in a profitable and sustainable way.

Ontap's specific aim is 'to provide a cheaper and more sustainable alternative to bottled water.' Its founder, Nala Delmar, a keen athlete, founded Ontap because she was frustrated by the large amount of money she was spending on bottled drinking water.

Ontap's operations need to be financially viable because it relies on its business activities, not donations, for funding. 70% of Ontap's profits are donated to fund clean water projects in India. Remaining funds are reinvested in the business or used to raise awareness of the damaging effects of bottled water on the environment.

Bottled water industry in the UK

The retail market for bottled water in the UK is worth approximately £1.6 billion, by annual sales revenue. Industry statistics show that the average consumer drinks 33 litres of purchased bottled water per annum.

Despite legislation that requires any establishment serving alcohol to have free tap water available, it has become the social norm to purchase bottled water in such establishments. This has reduced the acceptability of asking for free tap water in restaurants, cafes and bars. It has also created a huge increase in plastic bottle waste. An estimated 18 billion plastic bottles are consumed annually in the UK, of which 75% are not recycled and therefore end up in landfill. The packaging and transportation involved means that bottled water also has a much higher carbon footprint per litre than tap water.

In 20Y2 several UK supermarkets were criticised for selling a product that should have been free, when it became apparent that some of their own-brand bottled water was simply filtered, purified tap water. Some multi-national bottled water companies have also attracted adverse publicity for spending huge sums on advertising in an attempt to make their brand fashionable and appear to offer variety for what is essentially an homogenous product.

About Ontap

The Ontap concept involves a re-fillable water bottle made from recycled aluminium foil, which carries the Ontap logo. Once purchased from Ontap, at a cost of £8, the bottle can be taken to a range of participating cafes and shops (currently only in central London) and re-filled with tap water. These businesses provide their re-filling services for Ontap's customers free of charge, in the hope they will purchase additional products. The Ontap website and free mobile app provide a list of refill sites, all of which prominently display the Ontap logo.

Plans for expansion

In London, Ontap has been a success and proved popular with athletes, commuters and students plus the participating cafes and shops. Ontap has received lots of social media coverage and the brand is currently very fashionable. Nala is keen to expand her original concept.

She is considering two possible options for expansion:

(1) A corporate sales scheme. Nala would like to persuade companies to buy water bottles to replace the plastic cups typically found beside water coolers in most offices. She has read a recent survey reporting that, on average in such offices, each employee throws away four plastic cups a day. Instead, the company would bulk purchase Ontap bottles for their employees, which would then be co-branded with the company's own name.

(2) Geographical expansion. This would necessitate finding cafes and shops outside the central London area which would be willing to be Ontap partners.

Requirements

27.1 Discuss the extent to which Ontap is a sustainable enterprise. **(7 marks)**

27.2 Compare and contrast the ethics of the marketing activities of Ontap with its competitors in the bottled water industry. **(8 marks)**

27.3 Discuss the problems Ontap will face in any expansion of the business and evaluate the two proposed options. **(10 marks)**

Total: 25 marks

28 Confo plc

Confo plc (Confo) is a listed company, operating in the packaged confectionery products (boxes of sweets) industry.

Confo was established a number of years ago, manufacturing boxes of sweets in its factory and selling them in its own shops throughout the UK. Since this time , some of the 240 shops have been operated under exclusive franchise arrangements, while the remainder are still owned by Confo. All products sold at Confo shops (both owned and franchised) are produced in Confo's factory. The company was structured as two separate divisions, Manufacturing and Retail, until 30 September 20Y3 (**Exhibit 1**).

Recovery plan

After a difficult period of trading, a new board was appointed in December 20Y2 and, following a detailed review, it implemented a radical three-year recovery plan from 1 October 20Y3. The recovery plan included: the closure of 70 owned shops; the opening of 30 franchised shops; and the creation of two new sales channels, commercial sales (to UK supermarkets) and export sales (to overseas retailers). As a result, Confo now has two additional divisions, Commercial and Export, and a revised system for pricing transfers (**Exhibit 2**).

Following preparation of the management accounts and operating data for the year ended 30 September 20Y4 (**Exhibit 3**), a board meeting was called to review progress in implementing the three-year recovery plan, and to consider whether any changes to the plan are needed.

Board meeting

The chief executive complained: 'This year's results are disastrous. This was supposed to be a recovery plan, but performance seems to have got worse, not better. Profit has fallen compared with last year.'

The marketing director disagreed: 'I believe that we have great potential for future growth from the commercial and export sales that we started this year. However, we need to give them time to get established and show their potential. You cannot judge performance on one year's figures.'

An ethical issue

From 1 October 20Y3, the sales manager of Confo's Commercial Division, Kirsty Keller, met regularly with John Drake, the procurement manager of a large customer, Lenton Supermarket (Lenton). In November 20Y3, John asked if he could have two small boxes of sweets for his family for Christmas. This type of small gift to customers' staff is common in the sweets industry. In December 20Y3, Kirsty delivered some Confo sweets, with a total value of £10, to John's home as a gift to promote good relations between Confo and Lenton. She informed Confo's commercial director about what she had done and he was happy with this action.

From January 20Y4, John made further requests for gifts of sweets, gradually increasing in both value and frequency. In order to keep a good business relationship with John, Kirsty continued to provide these gifts, but she stopped disclosing them to the commercial director in March 20Y4 when the value of the gifts reached £30 per week. In July 20Y4, when John started asking for gifts valued at £100 per week, Kirsty refused.

In September 20Y4, Lenton stopped purchasing from Confo. Kirsty never made any personal gain from the gifts and there is no documentary evidence relating to them.

Requirements

28.1 Compare and evaluate Confo's pricing of transfers before and after the changes made by implementing the recovery plan on 1 October 20Y3. Suggest and justify alternative methods of pricing transfers that Confo could have adopted on 1 October 20Y3. **(9 marks)**

28.2 Analyse and evaluate the performance of the Manufacturing Division and the Retail Division in the year ended 30 September 20Y4 compared with the year ended 30 September 20Y3. Highlight any problems in comparing the data and set out any additional information that would assist your analysis. **(15 marks)**

28.3 As part of the appraisal of the first year of the recovery plan, write a report which:

  (a) Reviews the strategies adopted by the Export Division and the Commercial Division, and evaluates their performance. Include any relevant strategic models in your appraisal.

  (b) Evaluates the success of the recovery plan for Confo to date.

(15 marks)

28.4 Explain the ethical issues for Kirsty, and for Confo, arising from the matters occurring with Lenton and John Drake. Set out, and justify, the actions that Kirsty and Confo should now take.

(7 marks)

Total: 46 marks

Exhibit 1: Company structure and pricing of transfers – pre 30 September 20Y3

Up to 30 September 20Y3, both Confo divisions, Manufacturing and Retail, were profit centres. The factory's output was transferred by the Manufacturing Division to all Confo shops (owned and franchised) at the same price, full cost plus 20%. In addition to the Retail Division's profits from the owned shops, Confo also earned a total of £1.2 million annually from the fixed fees it charged to franchisees for use of the Confo brand name and for operational and management support.

Consumers are charged the same list prices at all Confo shops. Franchisees are also required to charge these list prices in order not to undercut the prices charged by owned shops, and to avoid cheapening the Confo brand.

The setting of the same prices for transfers from the factory to both owned and franchised shops caused some internal debate. The Retail Division management claimed that prices for transfers to owned shops were too high and should be lower than the prices charged to franchisees. They also believed that the annual fixed fees paid to Confo by franchisees were too low. Confo products are unique and valid comparison with the prices charged by rival manufacturers and retailers cannot be made easily.

Exhibit 2: Company structure and pricing of transfers – post 1 October 20Y3

Since the commencement of the recovery plan on 1 October 20Y3, Confo has operated with four divisions: Manufacturing, Retail, Commercial and Export.

Changes in the Manufacturing Division

From 1 October 20Y3, the Manufacturing Division became a cost centre. It transfers all its output at full cost to the Retail Division, to franchisees, and to the new Commercial and Export Divisions. The reduction in the price of transfers was, in part, intended to increase the volume of sweets purchased by existing franchisees and to encourage more franchises to be taken up. To offset the lost revenue, Confo increased the fixed fee charged to each franchisee. These fixed fees now total £2.5 million.

Changes in the Retail Division

Confo continues to make UK retail sales via owned and franchised shops. The Retail Division still comprises owned shops and remains a profit centre. The review by the new board identified that many owned shops in the retail network were under-performing. On 1 October 20Y3, as part of the recovery plan, 70 poorly performing owned shops were closed. Of these closed shops, 30 were immediately reopened under the management of new franchisees.

The new Commercial and Export Divisions

The Commercial and Export Divisions were opened on 1 October 20Y3 as separate profit centres.

The Commercial Division makes sales to UK supermarkets. The products are all made in Confo's factory, but are packaged by Confo in the client's brand and wrapping (ie, 'own labelled') in order to minimise the loss of sales at Confo shops, and to make price comparisons by consumers more difficult. Prices charged by the Commercial Division are negotiated separately with each client. The supermarkets sell the products at retail prices that are lower than the list prices in Confo's owned and franchised shops.

The Export Division sells only Confo branded products, in bulk, to overseas retailers. It has taken some time to establish relationships with new clients and develop brand awareness, but sales have started to grow.

Exhibit 3: Management accounts and operating data

Confo: Management accounts for the year ended 30 September 20Y3

	Manufacturing £'000	Retail £'000	Total £'000
Transfers to franchised shops by Manufacturing Division	8,100	–	8,100
External sales	–	24,000	24,000
Divisional transfers	18,000	(18,000)	–
Variable costs	(13,050)	(2,400)	(15,450)
Fixed costs	(8,700)	(4,000)	(12,700)
Divisional profit	4,350	(400)	3,950
Fixed franchise fees			1,200
Operating profit			5,150

Confo: Management accounts for the year ended 30 September 20Y4

	Manufacturing £'000	Retail £'000	Commercial £'000	Export £'000	Total £'000
Transfers to franchised shops by Manufacturing Division	7,500	–	–	–	7,500
External sales	–	14,400	4,320	1,760	20,480
Divisional transfers	13,000	(9,000)	(3,000)	(1,000)	–
Variable costs	(12,300)	(1,080)	(720)	(320)	(14,420)
Fixed costs	(8,200)	(3,000)	(300)	(240)	(11,740)
Divisional profit	0	1,320	300	200	1,820
Fixed franchise fees					2,500
Operating profit					4,320

Confo: Operating data for the years ended 30 September

	20Y3	20Y4
Number of boxes of sweets sold externally:		
Retail Division (owned shops) ('000s)	12,000	7,200
Franchised shops ('000s)	5,400	6,000
Commercial Division ('000s)	–	2,400
Export Division ('000s)	–	800
Total products sold externally	17,400	16,400
Number of Confo shops:		
Owned shops	150	80
Franchised shops	90	120

29 Radar Traditional Radios Ltd

The date is December 20Y4.

Radar Traditional Radios Ltd (RTR) is a family-owned company which manufactures high quality portable radios at a factory in the UK. The particular styling of the radios, which appeals to UK market tastes, means sales are made in the UK only.

Radio broadcasting

In the UK, radio stations broadcast radio programmes via two main platforms:

- Analogue, using traditional analogue frequencies (AM/FM)
- Digital, using newer digital audio broadcasting (DAB)

Digital broadcasting was publicly launched in the UK twenty years ago. The broadcasting industry is encouraging digital radio broadcasting as it offers a wider choice of radio stations than analogue, is easier to use, and is resistant to localised signal interference.

However, on the negative side, the overall audio quality on digital is poorer than analogue, and digital reception is restricted in certain areas of the UK, so a lower percentage of the population can receive digital, compared with analogue. Digital reception was available to 80% of the UK population in 20X4 and to 90% by 20Y4. Analogue reception is available to 99% of the UK population.

Radio listening

In 20Y3, 35% of radio listening hours in the UK were on digital, 60% on analogue and 5% on other platforms.

Radio programmes that are broadcast on the analogue platform can be listened to only on analogue radios. Digital radio broadcasts can however be listened to on a variety of devices. The devices used to listen to digital audio broadcasts in the UK in 20X9 and 20Y3 were as follows:

Radio listening to digital broadcasts by device

	20X9	20Y3
	%	%
Digital television	25	27
Digital radios	23	25
Internet	15	22
Smartphones	10	20
Other devices	27	6

In 20X9, there was significant optimism about the future of digital radio broadcasting. The UK government predicted that it would switch off the analogue platform in the UK by 20Y5. As a result, in 20Y1 a major UK electrical retailer announced that it would shortly stop selling analogue radios. In spite of this early optimism, however, growth in sales of digital radios has been much lower than anticipated. Digital radios are currently owned by a little less than half of UK households.

The government is now expected to require the switch-off of analogue radio frequencies in the UK by 20Y9, at the very earliest. Some industry analysts believe that digital may take many years to overtake analogue due to the modest levels of ownership of digital radios.

Radio manufacture

The manufacture of radios is a global industry with some multinational companies producing radios as part of a wide range of consumer electrical products. There are however many small national companies, like RTR, specialising in radio manufacture only for their home markets. Some companies have stopped making analogue radios. Most companies in the industry, however, currently manufacture both analogue and digital radios, though some have plans to greatly reduce, and then cease, the production of analogue radios, as analogue is being switched off in an increasing number of countries.

The price of radios to consumers in the UK varies widely. Analogue radios are significantly cheaper than digital radios, retailing from around £25. The cheaper digital radios retail at £35, and mid-market digital radios are typically £50 to £100, while top-of-the-range models are considerably more expensive.

With advances in technology, some radio manufacturers are adding additional features to digital radios including, for example, internet access. They have also added 'Bluetooth' technology, which allows the user to stream music wirelessly through a digital radio from other devices such as MP3 players and smartphones.

Company information – RTR

RTR manufactures both digital and analogue radios. Its radios contain up-to-date technology and are known for their quality, but they deliberately feature old-fashioned styling. This gives RTR a niche market, but there is continued pressure in the industry to keep the technology up-to-date to compete, not just with other radios, but also with the other devices, such as smartphones, which can receive digital broadcasts.

RTR radios are only distributed through upmarket stores in the UK, and are at the top end of the market. RTR's analogue radios sell for an average of £150 and their digital radios average £200. Over the past few years, RTR's annual sales volumes have remained constant at 100,000 radios, as follows:

RTR sales (units)	20X9	20Y3
Analogue radios	65,000	60,000
Digital radios	35,000	40,000

RTR has always had a policy of investing in research and development (R&D) to ensure its radios are innovative in function, as well as being distinctive in style. Recently it has added Bluetooth to one model in its digital range, but further investment is needed to introduce Bluetooth across the digital range and develop additional technology features.

It has become difficult for RTR to compete with larger manufacturers given rapidly advancing technology, both in radio broadcasting and in listening devices. RTR needs to decide whether to cease R&D and marketing expenditure on analogue radios, effectively phasing out their production over the next two to three years, so that all the R&D and marketing budgets can be focussed on digital radios. A board meeting was arranged to discuss these issues.

Board meeting

The R&D director was pessimistic: 'We are a small company in a big industry. We need to focus our R&D expenditure on digital products or the budget will just be spread too thin.'

The marketing director disagreed: 'We cannot abandon analogue, which is still our largest market. I agree we need to focus our resources. However, I would try to focus marketing expenditure at our target consumer groups for both analogue and digital radios, not just concentrate on one type of product. I agree the digital radio market is more challenging, so I have provided some data (**Exhibit**) to help us decide on a marketing strategy for digital radios.'

Requirements

29.1 Using Porter's Five Forces Model, explain the impact on competitiveness in the radio manufacturing industry, for the UK market, of the following **two** forces only:

- Substitutes
- Competitive rivalry amongst existing firms

(10 marks)

29.2 Explain how market segmentation can be used by RTR to identify target groups of consumers for its digital radios, and discuss how each of the components in the marketing mix (4Ps) can be used by RTR to promote its digital radio product range to these groups. **(12 marks)**

29.3 Discuss and evaluate the factors to be considered by the RTR board in determining whether, and if so when, it should decide to abandon the manufacture of analogue radios to focus resources on developing and selling only digital radios. **(9 marks)**

Total: 31 marks

Exhibit – Analysis of UK consumers for digital radios		
	UK industry average	**RTR radios**
Age of consumer	45	55
Average annual income	£23,000	£37,000
Gender	60% male	45% male

30 The Norgate Bank plc

The Norgate Bank plc (NB) is a bank whose customers are small businesses and individuals living in either the UK or France. It has no physical branches for customers to visit. Internet banking is therefore important to NB, but also its telephone call centres are key to communication and to building customer relationships.

Until last year, NB had only one telephone call centre, which was near London and served all its existing customers. Call operators included fluent French speakers to serve French customers. In December 20Y3, a major new investment was made in a new call centre in Vietnam, where some of the local population speak French. At that time, Ron Terry was appointed as the director in charge of all call centre operations.

Under the new arrangement, the UK call centre serves only UK customers. French customers are served by the call centre in Vietnam, where call operators are from the local, French-speaking population. Property costs and staff costs are much lower in Vietnam than in London. At both call centres there are two groups of call operators: one for business customers and one for individual customers.

Ron wants to conduct a post-implementation review of both call centres to ensure that physical and human resources are being used efficiently. Over the past year, Ron has used three Key Performance Indictors (KPIs) to measure call centre performance (**Exhibit**). These are:

- average time taken to answer a customer call
- average length of a customer call
- scores from customer satisfaction surveys for handling calls (where: 1 = poor; 5 = excellent)

Ron is concerned about the validity of these KPIs, and he is unsure whether they are the most appropriate means of measuring performance. He is also unsure how they might be utilised to improve the efficiency of the call centres.

Wendy West, a senior manager reporting to Ron, used to work at a call centre in a large insurance company. She believes that NB's KPIs are poor by comparison to those of her previous employer.

Requirements

30.1 Evaluate the validity of the three KPIs used for measuring the performance of NB's call centres and suggest alternative measures.   (12 marks)

30.2 Explain the benefits and problems of NB using benchmarking to evaluate performance, and to improve efficiency, in its call centres. Refer to different types of benchmark and use the data in the Exhibit where relevant.   (11 marks)

Total: 23 marks

Exhibit: Data for the year ended 30 November 20Y4

| | UK call centre (UK customers) | | Vietnam call centre (French customers) | |
	Business	Individuals	Business	Individuals
Number of calls in the year ('000s)	120	1,200	90	600
Number of call operators	20	100	12	30
Time to answer a call (minutes)	2	2	1	1.2
Length of call (minutes)	10	4	8	3
Average customer satisfaction score	3.9	4.1	3.1	3.3

31   Rocket Co

The date is March 20Y5.

Rocket Co (Rocket) is an accountancy practice with four partners. It operates from a single office in a European country that is not part of the EU and whose currency is the franc.

Information about Rocket

Rocket employs 17 professional staff, both qualified and part-qualified accountants, and five support staff. It specialises in accounting and tax advisory work in the sports and leisure sector. Rocket's clients are typically wealthy self-employed sportsmen and sportswomen. It competes with a number of big regional and national accountancy practices which service sports and leisure clients as part of a more general client portfolio.

Rocket has experienced impressive growth rates but the partners are concerned that growth appears to be slowing. An extract from Rocket's balanced scorecard for the years ended 31 December 20Y3 and 20Y4 is provided in the **Exhibit**, showing both financial and non-financial information. The partners' financial returns in 20Y4 were affected by a number of factors, including a fall in billable hours, a rent review and increased professional indemnity insurance (PII) premiums. Most significantly, Rocket had to pay higher salaries to its employees. Professional staff working on sports and leisure clients normally command a premium of around 10% on market salaries. During a recent economic downturn in Rocket's home country, Rocket had been paying its 17 professional staff just below the market rates for general accountancy staff. This was accepted by staff while they had few other employment options available, however the market is now improving and external job opportunities are growing. As a result, during 20Y4, Rocket was forced to give professional staff a substantial pay rise.

Change in strategy: creation of a multi-disciplinary practice

A new regulatory framework for the legal services market was recently introduced in Rocket's country, to increase competition and encourage efficiency. This removed the previous restrictions on lawyers forming partnerships with other professions and created a new type of professional services firm, known as a multi-disciplinary practice (MDP). An MDP is a professional firm consisting of professionally qualified lawyers and accountants working together in client-facing roles. To operate as an MDP, a licence is required from the newly-created regulatory authority which is responsible for monitoring quality and compliance.

In February 20Y5, Rocket's four partners decided to take steps to become an MDP. Clients in the sports and leisure sector often need more than one professional service to deal with matters such as contract negotiations, sponsorship deals and personal injury claims. Rocket's intention is to capitalise on this by offering legal, tax and accounting advice to its existing clients. This should also allow it to attract new clients. Typically both legal and accounting firms face high fixed costs for salaries, premises and PII. The synergies involved in becoming an MDP will allow Rocket to provide a greater volume of client services more efficiently and cost-effectively, thereby increasing both revenue and margins.

Rocket estimates it initially needs six fully-qualified lawyers, with a view to increasing this to a team of 10 once demand is established. Two possible ways of resourcing the change to an MDP are being considered:

(1)   Recruit qualified lawyers on an individual basis

(2)   Acquire a specialist team of qualified lawyers from a law firm to which Rocket has previously referred work

Announcement of the change in strategy

On 1 March 20Y5, Rocket issued the following email to its professional staff and support staff, in order to announce the firm's change of strategy and to set out the partners' expectations. There had been no prior consultation with the recipients of the email and it has caused considerable anxiety among all staff.

CONFIDENTIAL EMAIL

To: allstaff@Rocket.com
From: Rocket partners
Date: 1 March 20Y5

Re: New business structure and strategy

The partners have decided to take advantage of recent changes in legislation so, with effect from 1 June 20Y5, Rocket will become a multi-disciplinary practice (MDP) offering both legal and accounting/tax services. As you are aware, our high-profile sporting clients frequently also need legal services and this change in strategy will allow us to attract a greater share of their expenditure on professional advice, and to improve our competitive position. We are in the process of recruiting the necessary qualified lawyers.

We will be spending heavily on marketing the new services and to fund this over the next month we will be examining the potential for cost savings and efficiencies across the firm. This may have some impact on our staffing and management structure.

We estimate that 75% of a fully-qualified staff member's total workload is dependent on having completed their professional qualification. The remaining workload could be carried out by a combination of part-qualified professional staff and support staff. Therefore, we require all fully-qualified staff to identify immediately which parts of their work they can begin to pass on to other staff. This will result in financial benefits to clients as we can reduce certain fees, and it will allow our fully-qualified staff to focus on more value-added advisory work, which will enhance revenues.

From 1 June 20Y5, each client will be serviced by a multi-disciplinary account management team headed up by a partner, with at least one qualified lawyer and one fully-qualified accountant. There will be a single central support team providing administrative assistance to both legal and accounting/tax professional staff, so that clients receive a co-ordinated service. We need to improve the productivity of our support function with a view to maintaining a ratio of one member of support staff for every six professional staff (including partners).We expect all staff to be as co-operative as possible and ask you to do everything you can to make our new legal colleagues welcome. Please give them open access to your clients and all relevant client information.

Ethical issue

Alina Jay, an ICAEW Chartered Accountant with Rocket, has recently been involved in preparing a statement of personal assets and liabilities for a long-standing client of the firm, who is currently seeking loan finance. The final statement which was submitted to the client's bank was very different from the initial draft which Alina prepared and submitted to her manager at Rocket. She suspects that the Rocket manager, who is a personal friend of the client, may have agreed to a misstatement of the client's personal affairs. Alina is unsure whether she should report the client and/or the manager to her superiors, and is concerned about the impact on her job and career if she were to do so.

Requirements

31.1 Using the balanced scorecard in the Exhibit and the other information available, analyse and evaluate the performance of Rocket between 20Y3 and 20Y4.   **(18 marks)**

31.2 Analyse the impact of the following factors that may influence Rocket's ability to create a multi-disciplinary practice:

- Human resource capabilities
- Legal and regulatory issues
- Competitors and market structure   **(10 marks)**

31.3 In relation to the email announcing Rocket's proposed change in strategy, discuss the extent to which Rocket's approach meets best practice in change management. Refer to an appropriate change model such as Gemini 4Rs.   **(10 marks)**

31.4 Discuss the ethical issues associated with Alina's concerns and advise her on appropriate actions to take.

(8 marks)

Total: 46 marks

Exhibit: Extract from Balanced Scorecard for Rocket

	Year ended 31 December	
	20Y4	**20Y3**
Financial		
Note: All monetary amounts are expressed in francs (F)		
Total fee income (F'000)	7,091	6,653
Growth in fee income	+6.6%	+9.2%
Mix of fee income – Accounting Tax	47:53	45:55
Average fee charged per billable hour (F):		
Accounting services	335	300
Taxation services	415	360
Fee income per partner (F'000)	1,773	1,663
Net profit as a % of fee income	20.8%	23.1%
Clients		
Market share (sports and leisure sector)	12%	14%
% of satisfied clients (based on annual survey)	75%	85%
Innovation and learning		
Average training hours per qualified employee	14	14
Total staff turnover	23.5%	17.6%
Internal business processes		
Error rates (% of client assignments undertaken where mistakes by rocket employees are detected)	10%	8%
Utilisation rate (% of total professional staff hours spent on chargeable client work)	70.5%	66.5%
Staff ratio:		
Number of support staff: number of professional staff and partners	5:21	5:21

---

32 The Scottish Woodlands Commission

The Scottish Woodlands Commission (SWC) is a government department. It is responsible for all state-owned forests in Scotland.

SWC's mission and activities

SWC's mission is to 'manage, protect and expand the public woodlands in Scotland and to increase their value to society and the environment'. It is authorised to carry out woodland management, nature conservation and the provision of facilities for public recreation.

Woodland management requires a long-term planning process, typically involving a timescale of more than 20 years. Activities include:

- maintenance of existing trees and removal of deadwood

- felling of trees and extraction of timber

- planting of new trees

- identification and management of threats to woodland (eg, fire, pests, disease, impact of wildlife, soil erosion)

In addition to woodland management, SWC's secondary aims are:

- to protect and maintain habitats for wildlife and to manage wildlife populations

- to provide the general public with widespread access to the natural woodland environment and to promote the woodlands as a location for sports and leisure activities

SWC is governed by a board of trustees whose role is to make strategic decisions, monitor performance and liaise with stakeholders including the general public and other government departments. SWC is allocated a share of central government funds annually, but it is prohibited from borrowing money in its own right. Money is spent on replanting, making grants to private organisations and individuals engaged in woodland creation and improvement, providing education, and research. SWC is able to generate some revenue from the harvesting and sale of timber for use in house-building, paper, fencing and bio-fuels.

Holiday village

SWC has been approached by CabinCo Ltd (CabinCo), a private company, which operates a number of up-market, self-catering holiday villages in England and Wales. CabinCo has a database of around 400,000 customers. Its mission is 'to be one of the UK's leading providers of luxury short-breaks in natural surroundings'. CabinCo has been highly successful because of the high occupancy rates it achieves in its holiday villages. It wants to take advantage of the rapid growth in the short-break market (holidays of 3-5 days) and the increased demand for 'sustainable tourism' to create a new, high-quality holiday village in Campbell Forest, one of SWC's woodlands in Scotland. Customers will be able to rent a luxury self-catering log cabin and participate in a variety of activities in woodland surroundings. Due to Campbell Forest's location, on the edge of a lake surrounded by mountains, it is envisaged that there will be demand all year round and cabins will be available 365 days a year.

Structure of venture

A limited liability public/private partnership (LLP) will be set up specifically for the new venture. The LLP will have two members: CabinCo and SWC. CabinCo will provide capital in the form of £2 million cash for building the cabins and developing the site, and will provide holiday management experience.

SWC will make its capital contribution by making available Campbell Forest (current market value £2 million) for use in the venture. It will also provide expertise in woodland management and woodland activities. The LLP will be operated as a commercial venture, with the members sharing profits and losses equally. The new venture will be known as Woodsaway LLP (Woodsaway). CabinCo and SWC will each be entitled to appoint three representatives on Woodsaway's senior management committee.

Campbell Forest will continue to be owned by SWC, which will grant a long lease to Woodsaway in exchange for an annual rent of £30,000. Woodsaway will have day-to-day management responsibility for operating the holiday village and the surrounding woodland. The village will consist of 100 high-quality two bedroom log cabins, built to a unique, eco-friendly design. Construction of the village will take approximately 12 months at an expected cost of £2 million, to be funded by CabinCo's contribution to the LLP.

The government has granted preliminary approval for creation of the public/private partnership, as it believes this is the most appropriate format for the management of risk and the exploitation of benefits from the village. The financial projections for Woodsaway make it clear that cabin occupancy levels will be critical to the venture breaking even:

	%	%	%
Cabin occupancy	40	65	90
	£'000	£'000	£'000
Cabin revenue	1,752	2,847	3,942
Variable costs	(526)	(854)	(1,183)
Contribution	1,226	1,993	2,759
Fixed costs	(1,502)	(1,727)	(1,985)
Rent to SWC	(30)	(30)	(30)
Operating (loss)/profit	(306)	236	744

If the initial venture proves successful then the concept may be expanded to other SWC woodland locations and Woodsaway will be given first right of access for the development of any new holiday villages in these locations.

Governance

At a meeting of SWC's trustees, one trustee expressed concern: 'Given SWC is a public sector body and we have a responsibility as trustees to deliver public benefit, by demonstrating selflessness and objectivity among other things, won't our involvement in Woodsaway give rise to possible corporate governance issues?'

Another trustee disagreed: 'Surely corporate governance isn't relevant. As the term **corporate** suggests, it is a matter for companies and their directors only, not a public sector body like SWC'.

Requirements

You are a strategic business adviser engaged by the government. Write a report for SWC's trustees, evaluating the proposed venture using the following headings:

32.1 Strategic fit	**(9 marks)**
32.2 Financial benefits	**(10 marks)**
32.3 Risks	**(7 marks)**
32.4 Governance issues	**(8 marks)**

Total: 34 marks

33   WeDive Ltd

WeDive Ltd (WeDive) is a company which produces and sells high-performance drysuits for divers. It was set up some years ago, by a group of friends, after they experienced severe discomfort whilst scuba diving in cold waters because of leaks in their hired drysuits, which are supposed to work by keeping water out. The friends sourced a single supplier that was able to provide a special thermal fabric and designed a very tight-fitting durable suit with a unique neck seal, to offer maximum protection.

WeDive's drysuits are very expensive (up to £2,000 each) and are typically bought by professional divers (police, armed forces, oil companies, rescue organisations and salvage businesses). To achieve optimum fit the company produces a wide range of different sizes for both men and women. Each drysuit has a three year warranty and any repairs are undertaken at WeDive's production facility, located in the UK.

WeDive has grown successfully. It now has a number of major contracts with professional divers, but also distributes its drysuits to diving retailers for recreational users who want a high quality product. Total sales last year were approximately £13 million, comprising 65% professional divers and 35% recreational users. All sales were in the UK.

Drysuit production is very labour intensive. The market for recreational drysuits is dominated by several large manufacturers in China and South East Asia which benefit from economies of scale, although there are a significant number of smaller producers, like WeDive, which sell in niche markets.

WeDive's directors are keen to expand the business and are considering the following two mutually exclusive strategies:

Option 1: Expand the range of products for the UK market

WeDive would source supplies of lifestyle clothing (t-shirts, jackets and accessories) and sell them under its own brand. The products would be aimed at consumers in the UK market and distributed and sold through existing channels (diving retailers). This option would require marketing but, because of limited funds, WeDive primarily intends to use social media.

Option 2: Produce drysuits for export markets

Entering export markets would involve finding and partnering with new distributors, which WeDive hopes would promote the product on its behalf. A key aspect of WeDive's high-performance drysuit is the fit, so the product may need some redesigning or additional tailoring depending on the height and weight of the local population in each export market.

If Option 2 is pursued, a possible key market is New Zealand. If WeDive enters this market, there is a 90% chance that New Zealand market conditions will be favourable and it will generate a profit of £300,000. However, if market conditions are unfavourable, a loss of £100,000 is expected. Alternatively WeDive could delay its decision until it has undertaken market research, at a cost of £15,000, which would accurately predict the expected market conditions in New Zealand.

Requirements

33.1 So far as the information permits, evaluate the two strategic options being considered by WeDive's directors. Refer to models where appropriate. Ignore the specific information about the New Zealand market for this requirement.   **(14 marks)**

33.2 Using a decision tree, calculate whether it would be worth WeDive paying for market research on the New Zealand market. Discuss your findings.   **(6 marks)**

Total: 20 marks

34   Reyel plc

Reyel plc (Reyel) is an international company which owns and operates mid-market hotels.

On 31 March 20Y4 a new division, 'The Extended Stay Hotel Division' (the ESH Division), was set up so Reyel could enter the extended stay hotel market.

The extended stay hotel market

Hotels in this market target customers who wish to stay in a hotel for at least eight consecutive nights. Whilst customers can stay for as little as one night, the high prices charged for short stays discourage this.

The extended stay hotel market has two segments, business and private:

- Customers in the business segment include: project managers; professionals working on assignments; staff on short-term secondments; and contract workers.

- Customers in the private segment include individuals who are in the process of relocation, while looking for more permanent accommodation, or who have had to evacuate their houses due, for example, to floods or fire.

The business segment typically represents a higher proportion of total revenue than is the case for traditional hotels.

In order to meet the needs of the extended stay market, the guestrooms are larger than in traditional hotels and include living space with a kitchen as well as a bedroom. When averaged across the duration of the stay, the price per night is typically cheaper than traditional hotels, but the costs incurred are lower as the number of room change-overs (ie, when one guest leaves and another arrives) is greatly reduced, and guestrooms are cleaned weekly on average, rather than daily. Occupancy is also typically higher than for traditional hotels.

The extended stay hotel market is well developed in the US, but it does not represent a significant proportion of the European hotel market, although it is growing.

The ESH Division

The ESH Division's business model is designed to: appeal to a different type of customer than Reyel's traditional hotels; exploit cost advantages; and strengthen the wider company brand in the business market segment.

The Clarre

In order to test the business model, the ESH Division commenced trading on 1 April 20Y4 with one hotel, called The Clarre, which is located in London. It has large guestrooms, each including a living area and a kitchen, but it does not have a restaurant or bar as there are many in the local area which guests can use. The hotel offers good quality rooms, but provides a limited range of services to guests. Each guestroom is identical.

The performance of The Clarre has been closely monitored and assessed each quarter. Sales appear to have been seasonal, with the quarters ending 30 September and 31 December being the periods of highest demand. Within each quarter, there is variation in demand where occupancy in some weeks is 100% (ie, all guestrooms are full) and customers have to be turned away. There are fewer fluctuations in demand between days of the week than is the case with traditional hotels due to the longer duration of each guest's stay.

Kevin Kloster, the manager of The Clarre, has expressed concern over managing capacity and pricing:

- Managing capacity is a short-term concern involving coping with weekly and monthly fluctuations in demand. It is also a long-term concern in terms of being able to meet trends in demand over time.

- Pricing is complex with different standard prices at different times of the year. There is also a range of discounts available on the standard prices according to type of customer (business or private), length of stay and frequency of visits. Kevin also has discretion to offer a discount to achieve a booking when negotiating with customers.

The Zoy – a comparison

Performance measures monitored by the Reyel board include internal benchmarking in comparing The Clarre with a traditional hotel, called The Zoy, which is also owned by Reyel and is located nearby in the same area of London. The Zoy is a long-established traditional hotel, in a building the same size as The Clarre, but it has a restaurant and a bar which generate additional revenue. The Zoy's guestrooms are much smaller than The Clarre's, but there are more of them. Guestrooms are cleaned daily at The Zoy, but usually only weekly at The Clarre.

Quarterly financial and operating data is provided for The Clarre. Annual data is provided for The Zoy (**Exhibit**).

Concerns of The Zoy's manager

At a Reyel internal meeting, the manager of The Zoy expressed some concerns: 'Reyel should not be entering the extended stay hotel market. Our business is in traditional hotels and there will be customer confusion. Also, the cheaper prices for extended stays will damage the Reyel brand name. In the year ended 31 March 20Y5, revenues from The Zoy were 10% lower than the previous year and I think this is due to the opening of The Clarre in the same area of London, less than two kilometres away. I also believe Kevin Kloster is undercutting us on price and we just cannot compete as we need to offer a much wider range of services, which increases our costs.

'When we look at the performance of The Clarre we should look from a company-wide perspective and consider lost sales for other group hotels, not just the sales The Clarre is recording.'

An ethical problem

Most business customers in the extended stay hotel market are individuals who choose which hotel to stay in, then recharge the cost to their employers. To induce some of The Clarre's regular business customers to agree to pay a premium over the standard price for a guestroom, at their employer's expense, Kevin has been giving these individuals Reyel discount vouchers for private holidays with their families at Reyel hotels.

Requirements

34.1 Using the quantitative data in the Exhibit and the other information provided:

(a) Analyse the performance of The Clarre for each of the four quarters to 31 March 20Y5. Briefly identify additional information that would help provide a more comprehensive assessment of performance.

(b) Compare the performance of The Clarre and The Zoy for the year ended 31 March 20Y5.

(18 marks)

34.2 Explain, for the year ending 31 March 20Y6, the factors that the manager of The Clarre should consider in respect of:

- capacity management; and
- pricing.

(10 marks)

34.3 Explain how the Reyel management could estimate the loss in revenue of The Zoy for the year ended 31 March 20Y5 arising from the opening of The Clarre. (7 marks)

34.4 Discuss the ethical issues arising from the inducements given to individual business customers and advise on the actions that Reyel should take. (7 marks)

Total: 42 marks

Exhibit: Financial and operating data

Management accounts for the year ended 31 March 20Y5

	The Clarre					The Zoy
	Q1 £'000	Q2 £'000	Q3 £'000	Q4 £'000	Year ending 31 March 20Y5 £'000	Year ending 31 March 20Y5 £'000
Guestroom revenues	1,058	1,279	1,280	1,028	4,645	6,264
Other revenues	–	–	–	–	–	1,200
Operating costs	(864)	(920)	(920)	(857)	(3,561)	(6,106)
Operating profit	194	359	360	171	1,084	1,358

Operating data for the year ended 31 March 20Y5

	The Clarre					The Zoy
	Q1	Q2	Q3	Q4	Year ending 31 March 20Y5	Year ending 31 March 20Y5
Occupancy	72%	80%	78%	70%	75%	58%
Average guestroom price per night	£68.0	£74.0	£76.0	£68.0	£71.7	£100
Average length of stay (nights)	14	15	18	13	15	3

Notes

1 Both The Clarre and The Zoy are open for 90 days each quarter.

2 The Clarre has 240 guestrooms and The Zoy has 300 guestrooms.

3 Occupancy refers to the average number of nights that guestrooms are occupied as a percentage of the total available guestrooms.

4 'Other revenues' comprise restaurant and bar sales.

5 Quarterly accounting periods are as follows:

- **Q1** is the quarter ended 30 June 20Y4
- **Q2** is the quarter ended 30 September 20Y4
- **Q3** is the quarter ended 31 December 20Y4
- **Q4** is the quarter ended 31 March 20Y5

35 Home of Leather plc

The date is June 20Y5.

Home of Leather plc (HoL) is a company which manufactures good quality leather furniture. The company is located in the small town of Puddington in the South of England, where its site is comprised of a factory, distribution centre and office.

Company background

HoL was established many years ago and has been important to the Puddington economy throughout its existence. Most of the employees, who are mainly skilled workers, live in or around Puddington. Many of the suppliers, including suppliers of leather, are also from the local area. HoL is Puddington's largest employer.

Over the past 15 years, the reputation of HoL's products has grown. Its furniture is now sold throughout Europe, although 70% of sales are still in the UK market.

However, revenue growth has slowed in recent years. There has been increasing competition in the UK and European markets from overseas suppliers producing good quality leather furniture. These suppliers incur lower property and labour costs than HoL, and can therefore charge lower prices. The HoL board fears that sales could start to decline unless costs can be reduced to enable more competitive pricing.

A particular concern is that half of the UK sales come from a single customer, Grint plc (Grint), under a long-term contract. The contract is due for renewal on 31 December 20Y6 and the Grint board has already stated that the contract will be put out to tender. Grint's expectation is that prices will need to be reduced from their current average of £400 per unit to, at most, £360 per unit.

Strategic choices

The HoL board has decided that a fundamental change needs to be made in the next six months in order for HoL to continue to compete in the market. It has not yet made any announcement to the employees (including managers), but three alternative strategies have been proposed to reduce costs.

The board has set a target annual profit of £7.2 million, to be achieved irrespective of which strategy is selected.

Strategy 1 – relocate within the UK

Close the whole Puddington site and relocate all operations to a larger site in the UK about 150 kilometres away. Most, but not all, employees would be offered continuing employment at the new site, but only about 40% of existing employees are expected to agree to relocate and carry on working for HoL at the new site. The new factory would have more automated production processes than the old factory and many of the working practices of skilled employees would need to change, along with the managerial reporting structure. The employees who do not relocate would be made redundant. HoL would continue to use most, but not all, of its existing suppliers.

Strategy 2 – relocate manufacturing overseas

Close the factory in Puddington and relocate manufacturing to a larger factory in a lower cost, developing nation in South America. This would involve making 96% of existing employees redundant. The remaining 4% would continue to be employed in the existing distribution centre in Puddington, with senior managers operating from the Puddington office.

Strategy 3 – cease manufacturing and import

Close the factory in Puddington and import furniture from overseas suppliers, thereby making HoL a wholesaler. Most employees would be made redundant. Only 4% of existing employees would be retained, operating from the Puddington distribution centre and Puddington office, as in Strategy 2.

Pricing

The quality of the output under Strategy 1 will be higher than under the other two strategies. As a result, the selling price for Strategy 2 and Strategy 3 will be about 90% of the selling price for Strategy 1. However, the sales volumes will be the same under all three strategies.

Estimated data is provided for costs and revenues for each of the three strategies (**Exhibit**).

Requirements

The board of HoL has asked you, as a business advisor, to prepare a report for it as follows:

35.1 Calculate each of the following, using the information in the Exhibit, for **each** of the three proposed strategies:

    (a)   The break-even selling price

    (b)   The volume of sales which would achieve an annual profit of £7.2 million   **(9 marks)**

35.2 Evaluate **each** of the three proposed strategies. Refer to your calculations in (a) above and make any further appropriate calculations. Ignore change management issues.   **(10 marks)**

35.3 For Strategy 1 **only**, explain power-interest using Mendelow's matrix for each of the following stakeholders:

    •   Existing employees

    •   Grint   **(7 marks)**

35.4 Identify and compare the change management issues for Strategy 1 and Strategy 2.   **(8 marks)**

                    Total: 34 marks

Exhibit: Estimated data on costs and revenues

	Strategy 1	Strategy 2	Strategy 3
Expected sales volume	120,000 units	120,000 units	120,000 units
Average price per unit	£360	£324	£324
Average variable cost per unit	£200	£160	£280
Annual fixed costs	£14.4 million	£10.8 million	£1.8 million

36 Zuccini plc

The date is June 20Y5.

Zuccini plc (Zuccini) is a listed company manufacturing motorbikes, which it sells mainly in European Union (EU) countries.

The motorbike industry

Motorbike technology is constantly changing. As a result, research and development (R&D) is a key feature of product improvement and replacement. The industry is very competitive and implementing the latest technology can be important in gaining competitive advantage. However, as technology changes rapidly, any such advantage is difficult to sustain.

There were 1.2 million new motorbikes sold in the EU last year. Many of the most popular motorbikes sold in the EU are manufactured in Japan by multinational companies, which also make cars and other automotive products. There are also several smaller niche motorbike manufacturers located throughout Europe, such as Zuccini.

Company background

Zuccini is a relatively small company in the global motorbike industry. Currently it has an annual sales volume of 4,800 motorbikes. It has an R&D centre in Italy and two factories, one in Italy and one in the UK. The head office is in the UK.

The existing models

Zuccini currently manufactures two models of motorbike: the Typhoon4, a mid-market to upmarket motorbike; and the StormRaider, an upmarket motorbike.

The StormRaider is manufactured at the UK factory and was launched in 20Y3. Its launch was successful and monthly sales are continuing to increase. It is estimated to have a product life cycle of six years before it needs replacing in 20Y9.

The Typhoon4 is made at the factory in Italy. It is reaching the end of its product life cycle and sales have been gradually falling in recent months. The Zuccini board has not yet decided whether to:

(1) Replace the Typhoon4 with a completely new model, the Typhoon5; or

(2) Modify the Typhoon4 to produce a slightly updated version, the Typhoon4A, then replace the Typhoon4A with the Typhoon 5 two years later (ie, in 20Y7 if the Typhoon4 were to be modified as the Typhoon4A immediately).

New capital investment will be needed for either alternative. The Typhoon5 would be a much more significant change than the Typhoon4A, although either of these alternatives could be implemented without much delay, once a decision is made. The board has not yet decided how long to carry on manufacturing the Typhoon4, but the timing of any change is under active consideration.

A new model under development

Another model of motorbike, 'the Hurricane', is currently in its R&D phase, but technical difficulties have caused delays and some uncertainties. It could be brought to market in June 20Y6 as a basic product selling at £6,000 or, with a further two years' development, it could be brought to market in June 20Y8 as a mid-market product selling at £9,000. The life cycle would be seven years from launch for the basic version of the product, as it is less susceptible to new technology developments and would sell on the basis of price rather than features. The life cycle would be six years from launch for the mid-market version. No estimate of production costs or volumes for either of these alternatives can yet be made.

Liquidity issues

Liquidity has started to become a concern for Zuccini. There is no immediate crisis, but cash flow projections indicate that further financing will be needed by 20Y7, unless sales improve.

Requirements

36.1 Referring to appropriate models, provide reasoned advice to the Zuccini board to help it decide:

- When production of the Typhoon4 should be ended; and

- Whether to replace the Typhoon4 with the new Typhoon5, or to modify it, initially, as the Typhoon4A. **(12 marks)**

36.2 Explain the strategic, operational and financial factors which would determine whether the Hurricane should be launched:

- In June 20Y6 as a basic product; or
- In June 20Y8 as a mid-market product. **(12 marks)**

Total: 24 marks

37 Kentish Fruit Farms

Kentish Fruit Farms (KFF) is a UK organic fruit farm that is owned and run by the Fielding family. KFF grows apples and produces apple juice, both of which it sells at local markets and to retailers.

UK organic farming and food industry

Organic food must be produced using environmentally-friendly farming methods, so no genetically modified (GM) crops, growth enhancers, or artificial pesticides and fertilisers may be used. Any farmer claiming to be organic must be certified by a government-approved body, such as the UK Soil Association. Food producers must also comply with Food Standards Agency regulations regarding the production, packaging and labelling of food.

Regulatory bodies can impose sanctions for breaching regulations. They can:

- forbid the use of misleading labels and product descriptions
- issue fines for inappropriate production
- close down operations
- seek punishment of those responsible for wrongful operations

Consumers increasingly want food that is healthy and is sourced both ethically and locally. Consequently, although initially perceived as a luxury niche product, organic food is now seen as a lifestyle choice by those consumers who regard non-organic products as more harmful to health and the environment. Major supermarkets have started to stock more organic and locally grown food.

A key issue for all farmers is the weather, which significantly affects the volume (yield) and quality of a crop and hence the market price. Organic farmers are unable to use artificial fertilisers or pesticides, so have developed alternative high-tech farming methods to improve profitability and cash flow. Weather information systems help plan planting, harvesting and irrigation. Climate-controlled growing tunnels and stores provide a pest-free environment with temperature, light and humidity control. These methods increase yields, extend the possible growing season and allow crops to be stored for longer before usage or sale, with no loss of flavour or quality.

KFF operations

KFF's profitability depends on crop yields and fruit quality, and its ability to use or sell all of the apple harvest. It is also affected by the overall level of supply in the market in any given year. KFF has a weather information system and uses climate-controlled technology.

The best of KFF's apples, which conform to retailers' specifications in relation to size, shape and quality, are sold to retailers as fresh fruit. Apples that do not meet retailers' specifications are either sold at local markets or used to produce KFF own-brand organic pressed apple juice in one-litre bottles. The juice is sold at local markets and has proved very popular so it is now also being stocked by retailers.

KFF's harvest normally begins in early summer and ends in late autumn. The production of juice follows on from the harvest cycle and, because of KFF's ability to store fruit, continues after the harvest has ended. KFF has a permanent labour force for its growing, production and bottling operations and additional seasonal workers are employed for harvesting and packing the fruit.

KFF uses its own vans to transport goods to the local markets. Distribution of products to the retailers, most of which are within 80 kilometres of the farm, is outsourced.

New strategies affecting the 20Y4 results

Demand for KFF's apples and juices in year ended 31 December 20Y3 exceeded KFF's production capacity. In 20Y4, capacity increased as a result of implementing the following strategies:

Strategy 1: KFF had acquired 15 hectares of land from a neighbouring farmer in 20Y0. The land was then intensively planted with apple trees of a modern variety which were expected to produce yields 30% higher than existing varieties. The first apple crop from these new trees was harvested in 20Y4. KFF's existing trees continued to give the same yield as in 20Y3, at the same cost per hectare.

Strategy 2: In 20Y4 KFF started to buy apples from other local farmers to use in its organic juices.

KFF's board set medium-term business objectives at the start of 20Y4. These were to:

- Achieve average annual revenue growth of 15%
- Increase gross profit margin to 45%

Financial and operating data for 20Y3 and 20Y4 is available **(Exhibits 1 and 2)**. The current management information system does not separately analyse cost of sales between the fresh fruit and juice operations.

Supply chain problem

In August 20Y5, a batch of KFF's organic apple juice was tested by the Food Standards Agency and found to contain artificial pesticides. The juice was made in a large production run using fruit from one of KFF's new suppliers. 20% of this production run has already been distributed to a major retailer which has just started to sell KFF organic juice. KFF is considering whether to issue a public recall of these bottles.

KFF's marketing manager, Joe Fielding, thinks this could be disastrous for KFF's reputation locally and has suggested that they do nothing in relation to the bottles that have already been distributed, but re-label and sell the remainder as non-organic. 'The thing that most concerns me,' said Joe, 'is why we didn't identify this as a problem earlier?'

Requirements

37.1 Identify and analyse the **three** key factors from the PESTEL model which are most relevant to the UK organic fruit industry.   **(9 marks)**

37.2 Using the quantitative data in the Exhibits and the other information provided, evaluate the impact that KFF's two new strategies had on its performance in 20Y4. Identify any specific information that you require to explain more fully the effect of each strategy.   **(18 marks)**

37.3 Discuss the ethical issues for KFF arising from the supply chain problem, and advise KFF on appropriate actions.   **(8 marks)**

37.4 Explain how control procedures could be used by KFF to identify and prevent quality problems with suppliers. You should give specific examples of information that could be used to measure and monitor supplier performance.   **(8 marks)**

Total: 43 marks

Exhibit 1: Financial data for KFF			
Extract from income statement for the years ended 31 December			
	20Y3	**20Y4**	**%**
	£'000	**£'000**	**change**
Revenue			
Fresh fruit	576	889	54.3
Juice	336	525	56.3
Total revenue	912	1,414	55.0
Cost of sales	(540)	(812)	50.4
Gross profit	372	602	61.8
Other operating costs	(259)	(456)	76.1
Operating profit	113	146	29.2
Interest paid	(53)	(74)	39.6
Profit before tax	60	72	20.0

	20Y3	20Y4
Hectares of KFF trees yielding fruit	40	55
Tonnes of KFF apples sold as fresh fruit	288	468
Tonnes of KFF apples used for juice production	192	252
Total tonnes of KFF apples harvested	480	720
Tonnes of apples purchased from local farmers for juice	–	48
Number of one-litre bottles of juice produced and sold	96,000	150,000

38 Premier Paper Products plc

The date is September 20X5.

Premier Paper Products plc (PPP) prints banknotes and identity documents for a variety of central banks and governments. It operates three divisions: Banknotes, Cash Processing and Identity Systems.

Company background

PPP started over one hundred years ago with a contract to produce paper banknotes for its own country. Its reputation for high quality, elegant designs and innovative security features has made it a market leader – PPP now prints paper banknotes for over 100 countries, mainly in Europe and Asia.

To capitalise on its customer base, 60 years ago PPP started to produce banknote counting and sorting machines and banknote inspection equipment to assist banks in processing cash and detecting forgeries. It then applied its expertise in designing and printing security paper for government identity schemes. 15 years ago PPP won its first contract to print passports and driving licences, for its own government. PPP has continued to invest in the development of sophisticated security solutions. It produces passports and identity cards for 65 countries, including machine-readable e-passports with biometric data incorporated on an electronic chip.

Banknote production

A country's currency is issued by its central bank. The world's largest central banks produce all of their country's banknotes using their own state-owned printing works. However many smaller central banks outsource production to large paper and printing companies which benefit from economies of scale. As a result, PPP and its competitors print 20% of all banknotes worldwide. Since security is a major issue, banknote-printing companies must be certified and the ordering and distribution process is tightly controlled. Normally central banks outsource banknote printing to a single supplier, under a long-term contract, renewable every 10 years.

Smaller countries outsource banknote printing for economic and technical reasons. Machines required to print modern currency are expensive and are designed to produce large volumes of notes which may significantly exceed a smaller country's requirement.

Some state-owned printing works attempt to achieve critical mass by producing notes for other countries. Rapid changes in technology make it difficult for a small state-owned printing works to keep up with constantly evolving anti-counterfeiting features.

New technology means that several central banks recently decided to change from using paper banknotes to plastic (polymer) notes. Polymer notes are lighter, cleaner and have more embedded security features to protect against counterfeiting. They are also more environmentally sustainable as on average each polymer note has a life of seven years compared to three years for a paper note.

Future strategic direction: Banknote division

Although PPP remains committed to the production of paper notes, its board is unsure whether the demand for polymer notes merits investing in the new technology.

The private banknote printing sector is dominated by PPP and two other companies, one of which, Uniquel, produces polymer notes. Uniquel's share of the banknote market has increased as 25 countries have recently moved from paper to polymer notes, because costs to the central bank are reduced over the life of the banknote despite high initial costs.

Several of PPP's central bank contracts for paper notes are due to come to an end in 20X6 and some of the banks concerned are likely to adopt polymer notes. Producing and printing polymer notes would require a more highly skilled workforce and different machinery. To achieve critical mass for both existing and new machinery, PPP would need to find new customers for paper notes whilst persuading some existing customers to switch to polymer.

Extract from Banking trade journal article:

Is there a future for cash?

Society is increasingly moving away from cash to card-based and smartphone/contactless payments systems. Last year only 4.5% of the UK's money existed in the form of physical cash and the average value of a cash transaction was £9.50.

Will polymer bank notes help stop this move to a cashless society?

Polymer notes are waterproof, cleaner, more durable and more environmentally friendly than paper money and this will help them compete with plastic payment cards. Unlike credit cards and contactless payment systems, notes are not subject to identity theft.

In the UK cash is still important for person-to-person transactions and elsewhere around the world, cash prevails. In many emerging economies over 70% of all consumer transactions still take place in cash. Between 20X5 and 20X7 banknote volumes are expected to grow in some parts of Africa by up to 50%.

Requirements

38.1 Using relevant strategic models analyse the ways that PPP has expanded its business and identify the critical success factors (CSFs) which have facilitated this growth. **(10 marks)**

38.2 Prepare a risk register, setting out what you consider to be **three** significant business risks facing PPP's Banknote division.

You should present your answer in a three-column format, explaining, for each risk:

- The nature of the risk
- The possible impact of the risk and the likelihood of it occurring
- Risk management strategies **(9 marks)**

38.3 You are the manager of the PPP Banknote division. Prepare a memorandum for the board which explains the issues that should be considered in deciding whether to invest in polymer banknotes technology. **(11 marks)**

Total: 30 marks

39 Taxi Tracker

Taxi Tracker (TT) is a company which is trying to change the taxi market in a major capital city. The market currently consists of council-regulated city taxis (Citicabs) and private-hire vehicles (PHV).

Citicabs operate from taxi ranks and are also able to pick up passengers in the street. The city council controls the number of Citicab licences available and regulates fares. Critics argue that this increases waiting times and imposes high fares on customers. The council also issues licences to drivers of individual private-hire vehicles. PHVs cannot use the taxi ranks or pick up passengers in the street. They must be pre-booked but can charge whatever they like in fares. Some PHV drivers work for themselves, others register with private-hire companies which operate a centralised booking service and take a percentage of each fare charged in exchange for putting the driver in contact with passengers.

TT's business model

TT began operations in 20Y2 when it launched a 'driver for hire' application (app) for smartphones. The customer downloads the TT app for free and registers their personal details and payment card information. They can then see which PHVs are near their location, receive estimates of price and journey time, tap on the desired PHV to book, and track its arrival on their phone. TT fares are calculated according to distance and time, with the customer's phone acting as a meter. At the end of the journey the customer's registered payment card is automatically debited. TT promises to 'have a car with you within five minutes'. It seeks customer feedback on every journey and drivers are required to achieve a minimum average score of 4 out of 5.

TT does not own vehicles or employ drivers. Instead it acts as an intermediary between PHV drivers and customers. Drivers with an existing PHV licence can apply to TT, which carries out a criminal record check, and verifies licence and insurance details. Drivers who pass TT's screening process are then issued with a TT smartphone which allows them to be registered and tracked on the TT system. TT passes 80% of the fare it charges to the driver, retaining 20% as commission to cover costs and margin. TT's main operating costs are technology and marketing.

Since its launch, TT has faced intense opposition from Citicab drivers, who have argued to the city's transport regulators that TT essentially operates an unlicensed city taxi service. To the consumer, TT's service was initially cheaper than a Citicab, but more expensive than a conventional PHV. Due to the ease of booking, cashless payment, and improved customer service compared to both Citicabs and existing PHV, the number of journeys booked through TT grew rapidly.

Dynamic demand-based pricing

As a result of its initial success, in 20Y4 TT switched to a dynamic demand-based pricing model. When demand is high in relation to the number of cars available, the fare goes up in an attempt to balance supply and demand. The higher price encourages more PHV drivers to make themselves available, helping to avoid unfulfilled customer requests. For example, when it is raining, and during peak hours, the average fare typically increases by 50%. There have been some angry responses on social media suggesting this is unfair to TT's customers.

Proposed short-term fare reduction

Recently TT has been made aware of rumours that a rival firm is planning to launch its own taxi booking app in the city. TT is keen to protect its 'first to market' position. In order to generate brand loyalty from existing customers and attract new ones before the rival's launch, TT is considering cutting its fares by 25% for a limited period of four weeks. However it needs to retain the loyalty of its PHV drivers so wants to make sure it minimises the impact on them.

Requirements

39.1 Explain the concept of cost drivers and value drivers and briefly explain **three** key drivers in TT's value chain. **(8 marks)**

39.2 Discuss the benefits of TT's dynamic demand-based pricing model and comment on whether it is unfair to TT's customers. **(8 marks)**

39.3 You have been asked to evaluate for TT the impact of its proposed short-term 25% fare reduction. Assume that currently 130,000 journeys a week are booked through the TT app, at an average fare of £10 per journey.

(a) Calculate the impact on TT's profit for a four-week period if:

- demand is unaffected by the fare cut, and TT retains 20% commission

- demand increases by 15% and TT commits to maintaining PHV driver revenue at its current level

(b) Assuming that TT retains 20% commission, calculate the increase in demand that would maintain revenue for both TT and the PHV drivers at the same level as before the fare reduction.

(c) Evaluate the proposed fare reduction strategy in light of your results in both (a) and (b). **(11 marks)**

Total: 27 marks

40 Bespoke Oak Beds plc

The date is December 20X5.

Bespoke Oak Beds plc (BOB) is a listed company which manufactures high quality, hand-made wooden bed-frames.

Industry background

Sales of household furniture to consumers were £5,000 million in the UK in 20X4. Of this total, bedroom furniture sales were £1,320 million. The market is highly competitive, and is experiencing pressure on profit margins.

A key sales driver in the UK household furniture market is the number of house purchases, which in recent years have been low so sales of household furniture showed zero growth. Increases in the number of house purchases are expected over the next few years and this is a source of optimism for UK household furniture manufacturers.

The bedroom furniture sector comprises two sub-sectors: bed-frames, and other bedroom furniture (ie, wardrobes and storage units).

Bed-frame manufacturers typically sell to furniture retailers. Larger manufacturers usually also produce a range of slightly lower quality bed-frames for sale directly to other businesses, such as hotels and house-builders (the contract market).

An important trend in the market is selling full matching sets of bedroom furniture (typically a bed-frame, a wardrobe and storage units).

Company background

BOB is one of the larger upmarket UK manufacturers of bed-frames only. These are hand-made from solid oak, a hardwood. BOB only makes two types of bed-frame: the Classic and the Deco. The two products are made on the same production lines at the same factory, with production runs alternating between the two types of bed-frame according to demand. There are common raw materials and staffing for both products. The Classic is a better quality bed-frame than the Deco, being made with more raw materials and more skilled labour, thereby generating a higher sales price and higher margin. The distribution channels for both of BOB's products are mainly through upmarket furniture retailers.

Oak is sourced from Central America, as this is cheaper than using European oak. BOB has been criticised by environmental groups for contributing to destroying forests in developing nations. Also, hardwoods take far longer to grow than softwoods, so after replanting it takes more time to restore a hardwood forest that has been cut down for commercial use. The BOB board believes that sustainability issues are beginning to damage the company's reputation and it now wishes to improve the company's image.

A board meeting

The finance director, Hannah Zhou, said: "Although currently profitable, the company is in slow decline. I have produced some forecast financial data for the year ending 31 December 20X5 (**Exhibit 1**). Unless we develop a new strategy, I expect the results for the year ending 31 December 20X6 to be the same as for the year ending 31 December 20X5."

Two proposed new strategies were presented to the meeting. Only one of these can be accepted, but it is possible to reject both.

Strategy A

The marketing director, James Jones, spoke next. "There is an increasing trend for consumers to purchase full matching sets of bedroom furniture. As we only sell bed-frames, currently we are not able to offer this choice, so we are losing sales. An overseas manufacturer, Welby East Furniture (WEF), is willing to manufacture sets of oak wardrobes and storage units to match the design of our Deco bed-frames. The WEF furniture is of inferior quality to our own, but it is cheap, so I think the margins will be good. WEF furniture would be sold under the BOB brand. I have provided a briefing paper containing details about a possible arrangement with WEF (**Exhibit 2**)."

Strategy B

The commercial director, Martin Moss, said: "A major house-builder, Linton Housing plc (LH), has started selling its houses fully furnished. I am negotiating to establish BOB as the preferred contract market supplier of bed-frames to LH.

"However, prices for our current products are higher than LH will pay. A possible compromise is to sell our bed-frames to LH in the same designs as the existing Classic bed-frames, but manufactured using Canadian softwood. These would be separately branded as the 'Quebec' range. Canadian softwood is significantly cheaper than oak, and it is easier for our craftsmen to work with, so there would also be a saving in labour time. The Quebec softwood bed-frames for LH would be of lower quality than the Classic oak bed-frames for other customers. My briefing paper (**Exhibit 3**) provides further details.

"If this strategy succeeds, then we could consider extending it in future to make all our beds from Canadian softwood, instead of oak."

An ethical issue

A fault has been detected in one production run of 120 Deco oak bed-frames, all of which have now been sold by BOB. The fault will not immediately be apparent to purchasers, but the typical life of each bed-frame will be four years, rather than the normal 10 years or more. BOB products are guaranteed for three years. Disclosure of this fault to purchasers would result, not just in the cost of replacement bed-frames, but also in damage to the company's reputation. There is a reasonable possibility that, as a consequence, the factory would have to close, necessitating redundancies.

James Jones told the meeting: "We want to be ethical, but there comes a point when the massive commercial and personal consequences for all concerned outweigh what are relatively minor ethical issues regarding the shortened useful life of only 120 bed-frames."

Requirements

40.1 Using the data provided for the year ending 31 December 20X5:

    (a)   Compare the financial performance of the Classic and the Deco.
    (b)   Evaluate and explain the financial and operating performance of BOB.

    Ignore the two proposed new strategies.   **(13 marks)**

40.2 For each of the two proposed new strategies:

    (a)   Calculate the expected contribution that would be generated in the year ending 31 December 20X6; and

    (b)   Explain the benefits and risks, including any additional relevant calculations.

    Make a reasoned recommendation as to which strategy, if either, should be adopted.   **(17 marks)**

40.3 Without further calculations, explain the merits and problems of BOB changing from using oak to using Canadian softwood for all its future production.   **(8 marks)**

40.4 Discuss the ethical issues that arise for BOB from the faulty production run. Set out the actions that BOB should now take.   **(8 marks)**

    Total: 46 marks

Exhibit 1: Forecast financial data for the year ending 31 December 20X5

	Classic	Deco
Annual sales volume (number of bed-frames)	12,500	18,000
Average contribution per bed-frame	£	£
Selling price	900	720
Variable costs:		
Labour	(250)	(200)
Materials	(200)	(160)
Other	(100)	(100)
Total variable cost	(550)	(460)
Average contribution per bed-frame	350	260

Total fixed costs: £8,170,000

Exhibit 2: Strategy A: Briefing paper – prepared by marketing director

This strategy is to import from WEF sets of bedroom furniture which match the design of BOB's existing Deco bed-frame. The working assumptions are:

- Deliveries would be under annual contracts, commencing on 1 January 20X6.

- Each set purchased from WEF would comprise a wardrobe and two matching storage units.

- WEF would charge a price to BOB equivalent to £480 per set at current exchange rates.

- BOB would sell each full matching furniture set (ie, the WEF set plus a BOB Deco bed-frame) to customers for £1,300.

- Based on market research, it is estimated that BOB will sell 2,000 full matching furniture sets in the year ending 31 December 2016. The customers purchasing these 2,000 sets would have purchased 150 Deco beds from BOB in the absence of any contract with WEF.

- The contract would require BOB to purchase a minimum of 1,900 sets from WEF in the year ending 31 December 20X6.

Exhibit 3: Strategy B: Briefing paper – prepared by commercial director

This strategy is to be a contract market supplier of bed-frames for LH, a house-builder. These bed-frames would be branded 'Quebec' and would be identical in design to the current Classic bed-frames, but made of Canadian softwood, rather than oak. The working assumptions are:

- Deliveries would be under a two-year contract commencing on 1 January 20X6.

- BOB would charge LH a price of £600 per Quebec bed-frame.

- The costs of raw materials per bed-frame would be 40% lower for the Quebec range compared with the Classic range.

- The costs of labour per bed-frame would be 10% lower for the Quebec range compared with the Classic range.

- Other variable costs per Quebec bed-frame would remain at £100.

- Annual fixed costs would increase by 3% as a result of undertaking this strategy.

- Based on LH's forecast of house sales, LH would require BOB to supply 9,000 Quebec bed-frames in the year ending 31 December 20X6 and the same number in the following year.

- The contract would have no minimum or maximum quantities, and demand would be uneven and would peak when each of LH's large housing projects nears completion.

- The contract would require BOB to supply LH within one month of each order.

- Quebec bed-frames would only be available to LH. To keep its existing retail customers happy, as part of this strategy BOB would reduce the price of Classic bed-frames by 2% from 1 January 20X6, but the expected sales volume would be unaffected.

41   Drummond & Drew LLP

The date is December 20X5.

Drummond & Drew LLP (DD) is a large firm of commercial architects, based in a single office in London.

The industry

Architects plan, design and oversee the construction of buildings for clients. Architects belong to professional bodies and usually operate in professional partnerships or companies.

The scale of architectural projects varies from large commercial buildings (such as offices, shops and factories) to residential housing. Some architect firms specialise in one type of project, others operate across a spectrum of different project types. A project may involve constructing a new building or altering an existing building.

A client's project usually requires two phases of work: the planning and design phase, and the construction phase. Both phases are normally managed by the same architect firm.

The planning and design phase involves the architect ascertaining the client's requirements in detail. The architect then prepares design drawings and graphics which comply with local building and other regulations.

The construction phase requires the administration, monitoring and coordination of the construction process by the architect. This can include, for a large project: site inspections, surveys, procurement of contractors, cost appraisal, certification, valuations and project management. Most aspects of this phase require architects regularly working on site with construction company staff.

Company background

DD's structure and staffing

DD has grown gradually over many years, increasing its revenue and staff, and has built a reputation within the UK as a good quality architect firm specialising in commercial, rather than residential, projects. In recent years, however, DD's UK growth has slowed due to increasing competition from existing firms and new market entrants.

DD has 12 partners (all qualified architects) plus 93 other qualified architects, and a further 77 support staff including managers, IT specialists, chartered surveyors, semi-skilled staff and administrative staff.

The 12 partners together take all the key decisions. Jeff Drummond is the senior partner. The other qualified architects have various levels of seniority and differing specialist skills.

All DD architects are fee-earning other than the technical and regulatory team, comprising three architects, which deals with adherence to technical standards and compliance with regulations.

Additional qualified architect time is sometimes acquired on a short-term contract basis, for both complex projects and more routine work. Using short-term contract architects has helped DD manage capacity where there are variations over time in the number and size of client projects.

Individual DD architects have significant autonomy in the design process and professional decision making, but they report to the partners regarding progress compared to plan, time spent and profitability of each project.

In the design and planning phase, most architects work at the London office, with occasional visits to clients. In the construction phase, most of the architects' time is spent at the construction site, with occasional visits to the London office.

Clients and projects

DD's client portfolio includes large companies requiring the design and construction of offices, factories and other large commercial buildings.

Whilst historically most of DD's projects have been in the UK, over the past five years there has been an increasing number of overseas projects. Almost all of the growth in project numbers has been in Dubai and the other Gulf States, where there is significant commercial construction activity as the region recovers from a recent economic downturn.

The scale of projects won in the Gulf States has grown as DD's reputation has spread in the region. To date, projects in the Gulf States have been serviced by London-based DD staff, but this has proved increasingly difficult as the number and scale of projects in the region have increased. In 20X4, the equivalent of 10 architects spent all their chargeable hours on Gulf State projects. A majority of DD partners believe that many more projects could be obtained in the Gulf States if the firm had an office in the region.

A potential new project in Dubai

To be eligible to bid in January 20X6 to provide planning, design and construction services for a major building in Dubai, called the Sunrise, DD must make a commitment to establishing an office in the region from 1 January 20X7. It therefore needs now to make an urgent decision about operating an office in Dubai. If the bid is successful, design work on the Sunrise project will start in January 20X7.

DD would aim to obtain commissions for additional commercial projects in the Gulf State region during 20X6. However, to make the investment in an office in Dubai viable in the longer term, DD would also need to work on smaller projects, especially residential buildings.

The number of architects and support staff required to be located in an office in Dubai is estimated to be:

| | Number of Dubai staff | | |
Projects	20X7	20X8	20X9 and each year thereafter
Sunrise	12	18	0
Other commercial	10	14	16
Residential	5	7	10

If this international expansion does take place, there are two alternative methods: acquire an existing architect firm in Dubai; or set up a new DD office there.

Requirements

41.1 Using appropriate models, explain the nature and suitability of the existing organisational structure of DD as a professional service organisation. Ignore any new development in the Gulf States.

(10 marks)

41.2 Explain the factors that DD should consider in deciding whether or not to expand internationally by establishing an office in Dubai. Ignore the issue of whether this is by acquisition or by an office being set up by DD. **(12 marks)**

41.3 Assuming DD does decide it needs an office in Dubai, explain the factors that should be considered in determining whether it should acquire an existing architect firm in Dubai or open a new office there itself. **(8 marks)**

Total: 30 marks

42 Mississippi Muzic Ltd

Mississippi Muzic Ltd (MM) operates four London nightclubs, each with a restaurant. The four clubs are the same size but are located in different areas of London. They all aim to attract a similar clientele and are open every night of the week.

There is a small fee for life-time membership when a person first visits a MM club, but the entrance charge for each subsequent visit by a member is high, and drinks and meals are expensive. The target market is young, high-income professionals who wish to socialise, dine, drink and network with people from a similar background. The high entrance charge is viewed favourably by many club members as it keeps the environment exclusive to professional groups.

MM has attracted a loyal core of members and the clubs are, on average, 95% full on Friday and Saturday nights. The capacity of each club at any one time is 250 people. The clubs are significantly less busy for the remainder of the week as members tend to work long hours.

MM has a database of all its 7,800 current members. The membership grows each week as new members join. However the chief executive of MM, Jane Flinkstein, believes that the company is not making best use of this database for marketing. The core database includes the member's: name; contact details; gender; age; job; and interests. Each member has a membership card with a bar code to be shown at each visit to the club. Data is then recorded so the timing and frequency of each member's visits are held on the database.

MM wishes to increase revenue by marketing its clubs more effectively and has identified two possible strategies, which are not mutually exclusive.

Strategy 1 – MM would encourage existing members to visit the clubs more frequently, and dine in the restaurants more often, by using its database more effectively for relationship marketing purposes.

Strategy 2 – MM would appeal to new types of customer, other than young professionals, in order to fill its spare capacity from Sunday to Thursday.

Requirements

You are a business adviser who has been asked by Jane Flinkstein to prepare a report outlining elements of a marketing strategy for MM:

42.1 Explain how MM can use its database more effectively to market to existing customers (Strategy 1).

(8 marks)

42.2 Outline and explain the market research that MM should undertake for Strategy 2. **(8 marks)**

42.3 For Strategy 2, identify and explain:

- • a segmentation strategy; and
- • a pricing strategy. **(8 marks)**

Total: 24 marks

43 Outil plc

The date is March 20X6.

Outil plc (Outil) is a large home improvement retailer, listed on the London Stock Exchange.

It operates three divisions:

- Homestyle Division (UK only)
- Fixings Division (UK only)
- Targi Division (Eastern Europe only)

UK home improvement industry

The home improvement industry derives its income from homeowners undertaking repairs, maintenance and improvements to houses. Industry revenue has been in decline for several years. Approximately 60% of industry revenue derives from homeowners themselves (domestic customers) and the remainder from tradespeople such as builders, electricians and plumbers (trade customers). The market is influenced by the state of the economy and the volume of transactions in the housing market, with homeowners typically repairing and improving their houses either before a house sale or after a purchase.

Despite recent recovery in the UK housing market, homeowners have been slow to increase spending on home improvements. Industry experts believe this is partly due to younger homeowners lacking the necessary skills to do the work themselves, and preferring to spend their time and money on leisure activities. As a result, there is a move away from a 'Do-it-yourself' (DIY) approach to home improvements to a 'Do-it-for-me' approach, with homeowners hiring tradespeople. Retailers who service trade customers as well as domestic customers have therefore generally performed better.

Some home improvement retailers have responded by launching services to link their trade and domestic customers, and recommending local tradespeople to homeowners. Some retailers have switched to UK suppliers to reduce the need to hold inventory. Many bigger retailers are also increasing online sales or reducing the size of stores.

Company history: UK

Outil was established a number of years ago with 10 home improvement stores in the UK. It grew organically and the original chain now operates as the Homestyle Division with 252 stores.

Homestyle stores sell to both domestic and trade customers. The stores stock a vast range of home improvement products (30,000 to 50,000 different products). Approximately 30% of the store space is accessible to customers and 70% is used for storage. Stores have extended opening hours and specialist staff are available to provide advice. Homestyle stores vary considerably in size from 5,000 to 15,000 square metres. Newer large stores have demonstration areas for DIY classes plus display kitchens, bathrooms and bedrooms so that customers can plan a major home improvement project with the help of design consultants. However the availability of suitable large sites for new stores is limited by transportation and traffic problems, and by planning restrictions. New stores also require large capital investment.

The Fixings Division was created in 20X0 when Outil purchased a UK business that sold screws and fixings. The Fixings Division sells a wide range of small items (tools, nuts, bolts, piping etc) via a catalogue, website and its 395 stores. The division has grown rapidly, opening 50 new stores in 20X5. Fixings stores are specifically designed to satisfy the needs of trade customers, although they do sell to domestic customers as well. There is a simple layout with emphasis on convenience, and the majority of store space is visible to customers as it is used to display inventory. Stores carry a limited range (up to 15,000 different products) and are, typically, smaller than the Homestyle stores (up to 5,000 square metres).Their smaller size makes it easier for Outil to find sites to establish new Fixings stores, obtain planning permission and finance the necessary capital investment.

Company history: Eastern Europe

In January 20X5, Outil acquired a chain of 115 stores branded 'Targi' in Eastern Europe, which it operates as the new Targi Division. Targi only sells to trade customers. It provides equipment and materials for professional building companies and tradespeople. Stores carry a limited range of products which are sold in large quantities at low prices. This division currently operates only in Eastern Europe.

Board meeting

Outil's most recent management accounts (**Exhibit**) show a decrease in profit in 20X5. This is despite the acquisition of Targi. Outil's board has been concerned for some time about the performance of the Homestyle Division, which is a mature business.

The managing director commented at a recent board meeting:

"Given the excellent performance of our other divisions, we should refocus as a business that sells to trade customers only, so we should close the Homestyle Division. Smaller Homestyle stores could be re-branded and operated as Fixings stores, or used to establish Targi as a brand in the UK. Larger Homestyle stores are too big so would need to be closed outright. Employees, where possible, would be transferred to remaining divisions. There would be a cost in terms of lease penalties and redundancies but overall I believe that results would improve."

The director of the Homestyle Division advocated continuing the current strategy:

"20X5 was a very tough year and one of the Division's major competitors closed, but we still managed to keep sales revenue constant. Margins were affected by customers choosing lower margin products, increased delivery costs and more pricing promotions but I am confident that the market will improve eventually in line with activity in the housing market."

A different approach was proposed by the Fixings Division director:

"An alternative is to sell the Homestyle Division outright. This would generate funds for Outil to expand the Targi and Fixings brands. Our website has recently attracted lots of attention from international customers. I would like to test the market for our international expansion by initially opening four Fixings stores in Germany, on a trial basis, with a dedicated German website."

Requirements

Prepare a report for the board on the future strategic direction of Outil.

Your report should:

43.1 Use the quantitative data in the Exhibit and the other information provided to:

- evaluate the company's overall performance between 20X4 and 20X5, and
- compare the performance of the three divisions in 20X5. **(17 marks)**

43.2 Discuss the proposals for the future of the Homestyle Division. Refer to your calculations in 43.1 and the directors' comments where appropriate. Ignore the proposed German expansion for the purpose of this requirement. **(10 marks)**

43.3 Identify **two** stakeholder groups that are likely to be affected by a decision to close the Homestyle Division, and advise on the strategies that Outil could adopt to reduce any barriers to change. Refer to relevant models where appropriate. **(8 marks)**

43.4 In relation to the Fixings division, discuss:

- the merits of undertaking test marketing before a full international expansion, and
- the strategy of opening four stores in Germany, on a trial basis. **(8 marks)**

Total: 43 marks

Exhibit: Extracts from Outil plc management accounts

Financial information: Year ended 31 December (£ million)

	Home style	Fixings	UK Total	Targi	Outil Total	Outil Total
			20X5			**20X4**
Revenue	2,635	1,955	4,590	835	5,425	4,343
Gross profit	771	821	1,592	251	1,843	1,560
Traceable divisional costs	(620)	(672)	(1,292)	(178)	(1,470)	(1,167)
Divisional contribution	151	149	300	73	373	393
Apportioned central costs	(20)	(14)	(34)	(6)	(40)	(35)
Operating profit	131	135	266	67	333	358
Net assets (at carrying amount)	728	495	1,223	266	1,489	1,160

Operating information: Year ended 31 December 20X5

	Homestyle	Fixings	Targi
Number of employees	14,595	7,200	3,430
Number of stores	252	395	115
Average store size (square metres)	10,000	3,500	5,600
Average number of product lines per store	43,500	13,750	10,750

44 Dreamy Potato Products Ltd

The date is March 20X6.

Dreamy Potato Products Ltd (DPP) is a food processing company based in the west of England.

Company operations

DPP purchases potatoes from local farmers then peels, washes and processes them into two uncooked forms: whole or cut. It sells these products to food manufacturers which choose to buy from companies, like DPP, that benefit from economies of scale in procurement and processing.

DPP has grown steadily. Approximately 80% of its revenue comes from four food manufacturing clients that produce ready-meals for UK supermarkets. DPP's contracts are, typically, renegotiated every three years, although terms change frequently. This is often as a result of specific demands by supermarkets in relation, for instance, to quality or type of potato.

The food processing industry is highly regulated for health and safety. DPP's clients, prompted by the major supermarkets, also have their own strict quality control requirements. DPP's workforce consists mainly of weekly-paid workers, on the UK minimum wage. DPP is subject to restrictions on working hours, enforced by European Union regulations.

DPP's raw material costs and selling prices are driven by the market price of potatoes, which fluctuates considerably, depending on the availability and quality of the annual crop. DPP acquires its potatoes from local farms, with which it has exclusive purchase agreements. The company owns a fleet of trucks for distributing products to its clients.

Competition

The market-leader, Estima plc (Estima), has a 30% share of the UK market for processed uncooked potatoes. It is a vertically-integrated, national business which grows its own potatoes and supplies both uncooked and cooked potato products to the catering industry and food manufacturers.

A further 35% of the UK market consists of DPP and two other competitors – one in the south and one in the east of England. The rest of the market is fragmented. Many farms supply unprocessed potatoes direct to the catering industry. Some potato farmers operate their own processing plants, but these are regional businesses, often specialising in particular market niches eg, supplying processed uncooked potatoes to local schools or hospitals.

Proposals

In the year ended 31 December 20X5, DPP generated an operating profit of £352,000 on sales of £10.8 million. It is considering two opportunities for future growth:

Proposal 1: fast-food contract

DPP has been approached by a national fast-food chain that wants to buy uncooked cut potatoes. The initial contract would be for three years, at a fixed price of £210 per tonne. To implement this strategy, DPP would need to acquire a new machine to grade and cut the potatoes and rent a further 9,000 square metres of premises. Working assumptions for this contract are provided in the **Exhibit**.

Proposal 2: use of waste

Starch residue from washing the potatoes could be sold to local farmers as cattle food. DPP is also considering investing in a digester machine, which can convert potato waste into gas to power DPP's processing plant. As well as potentially improving profits, better use of waste would be positive for sustainability and help differentiate DPP from Estima.

Client request

Potters Pies (Potters), a major client, buys processed uncooked potatoes from DPP to produce pies for two supermarkets: Giant (a low-cost retailer) and Quality (a high-quality retailer). Potters' contract with Giant is due for renewal shortly and Giant has told Potters to reduce its prices if it wants to retain the business. Andrew Baxter, a director at Potters, wants DPP to drop the price that it charges Potters for potatoes for the Giant contract by 5%.

Andrew explained to DPP's sales director: "If you drop the price on the Giant contract, I am prepared to increase the price per tonne we pay DPP for potatoes for the Quality contract by the same percentage.

"I am confident that I can go to Quality and persuade them to pay more for our pies. I will convince them by pretending that we have had to pay our supplier more because they have started to supply higher quality potatoes.

"This will help ensure that we don't lose the Giant contract, which would be bad news for both Potters and DPP. If you agree, I will make sure that DPP is our preferred supplier when we renegotiate contracts later this year. If not, then I may have to move our business to Estima."

Requirements

44.1 In relation to the potato processing industry, prepare an analysis of the following elements of the Porter's Five Forces model:

- Barriers to entry
- Power of suppliers
- Power of customers

You should explain the relevance of each force for DPP. **(9 marks)**

44.2 Evaluate the fast-food contract in Proposal 1 and discuss whether it should be undertaken. Show supporting calculations. **(10 marks)**

44.3 Assess Proposal 2 for the use of waste and suggest further actions that DPP could take to enhance its sustainability. **(7 marks)**

44.4 Discuss the ethical issues for DPP and Potters that arise from Andrew Baxter's request. **(7 marks)**

Total: 33 marks

Exhibit: Working assumptions for Proposal 1: fast-food contract

1. Expected sales volume: 9,000 tonnes pa at £210 per tonne, for three years.

2. Direct labour and variable costs of processing are expected to be £65 per tonne pa.

3. In 20X5 DPP's fixed overhead absorption rate was 12% of revenue pa. Fixed operating expenses will increase by £25,000 pa as a result of this contract.

4. For the first year of the contract DPP has agreed, with its existing suppliers, a purchase price of £125 per tonne of potatoes. Industry price forecasts assume that year 3 potato prices are conditional on market prices in year 2. The predicted average purchase prices are as follows:

	Year 2				Year 3	
	Probability	Price/tonne (£)			Probability	Price/tonne (£)
Low price	0.40	125	{	Low price	0.45	115
				High price	0.55	135
High price	0.60	160	{	Low price	0.65	150
				High price	0.35	170

45 The Zed Museum

The Zed Museum (Zed) opened in Venice, Italy, a number of years ago. It hosts one of the finest collections of sculptures and modern art in the world and is a popular destination for locals and tourists.

The museum is a not-for-profit organisation, managed by trustees and largely staffed by volunteers. It charges nominal admission fees and relies on private donations. For the last three years, Zed's income has just covered the costs of operating the museum, insuring the exhibits and running educational programmes. After the recent death of Zed's wealthy founder, Emilio Zissi, the museum is experiencing a financial crisis and some of the staff and donors feel that it lacks direction. Without a significant injection of cash, the museum may have to close and, if it is found to be insolvent, the trustees may be liable for any losses.

Zed has a sizeable collection, only a small proportion of which is on display at any given time. Most of the items in the collection are not owned by Zed but were given in trust to Zed to hold, conserve and use in exhibitions or programmes for future generations. Despite their value, the items are not liquid assets and Zed is prohibited from selling them to pay for operating expenses.

The trustees have appointed a new chief executive to address Zed's financial situation and to attract a wider audience and additional revenue streams. She is keen to operate the museum on a more commercial basis and exploit its collection, as she explained at a recent meeting of the museum's trustees:

"Zed's ability to remain open rests purely on how fast we can raise sufficient additional funds – a task that I believe may be accomplished, in part, by licensing our brand and collection. I have been approached by a well-known billionaire, Kazuo Tada, who owns a Japanese island. Mr Tada is developing the island into an exclusive cultural destination. A 20-year licence to operate a Zed-branded museum on the island will attract wealthy international tourists and other world-class visitor attractions. In addition to paying the annual licensing fee for the Zed brand, Mr Tada has promised us a substantial one-off donation. The Japanese museum will be stocked by us with exhibits from our collection, in return for the annual licensing fee. Other international museums have successfully licensed their brand and collection, and I believe that we should do the same."

Some of the trustees disagree with the chief executive's proposal. They do not believe that the licence deal is appropriate for a world-class museum, which is seen as an educationally-driven entity and a steward of Italian culture. They also argue that the proposal may be contrary to the founding principles established by Emilio Zissi:

Founding principles of the Zed Museum

- Hold the collection in trust for society and safeguard the long-term public interest in the collection
- Recognise the interests of the people who made, owned, collected or donated items in the collection
- Encourage visitors to explore the collection for inspiration, learning and enjoyment
- Consult and involve the local community, users and supporters
- Review performance to innovate and improve

The chief executive is aware that some stakeholders have expressed concerns about the museum's future. She also believes that some of Zed's problems have arisen because of a failure to monitor performance adequately, and is evaluating how best to measure the museum's success. Historically, Emilio Zissi simply counted the number of visitors each year.

Requirements

45.1 Analyse the interests and influence that the following stakeholders are likely to have in their relationship with the museum:

- Trustees
- Donors
- Staff

(9 marks)

45.2 Explain the advantages and disadvantages for Zed of pursuing a licensing strategy with a third party and any specific considerations relating to the proposed Japanese museum. **(8 marks)**

45.3 Recommend an approach to performance measurement that is suitable for Zed and some specific performance measures to assist the chief executive in measuring Zed's performance. **(7 marks)**

Total: 24 marks

46 The Healthy Vegetarian plc

The date is June 20X6.

The Healthy Vegetarian plc (THV) is a listed company which operates 200 shops throughout the UK. THV shops sell ready-to-eat food, plus hot and cold drinks. All products are suitable for people who eat no meat or fish products (vegetarians). THV does not prepare food on the premises, although some snacks can be heated in the shop, on request, at the time of purchase.

Company background

Company history and development

THV has expanded organically by reinvesting operating cash flows to finance the opening of new shops. The board is not willing to borrow or raise new equity capital at this time.

Food products and operations

THV carries a range of 40 types of food and drink products. All products are purchased centrally by head office from four suppliers. Products are delivered by suppliers directly to each shop. All shops are charged the same price for each product, which is agreed by head office with suppliers.

One week in advance, the shop manager informs head office of the quantities of food and drink required for each day. Drinks can be displayed on shelves for a long time from the delivery date, but most foods can be displayed for only one or two days before being discarded, in line with hygiene regulations. Excessive delivery quantities therefore reduce the operating profit of the shop.

Each shop has one manager who decides on the number of staff to employ, but wage rates are set centrally at head office.

Head office determines capital expenditure. Depreciation on each shop's non-current assets is charged in arriving at the shop's operating profit, but no central head office costs are allocated to shops.

Markets

The target market for THV is customers who are healthy eaters. The company markets itself as selling healthy, vegetarian products, as reflected in the company's name.

Selling prices are determined by head office so, for each product, all shops charge the same price to customers.

Budgeting, performance assessment and closure review procedures

An annual budget is set for each shop at the start of each year, and the performance of each shop is assessed annually using key performance indicators (KPIs) and internal benchmarks (**Exhibit 1**). The worst performing shops are placed under 'closure review procedures' following assessment, and are then given three months to demonstrate substantial improvement, or be closed.

June board meeting

Closure review procedures

At the June 20X6 board meeting, the performance director, Tina Thomson, expressed concern about the company's closure review procedures. "There is increasing stress amongst staff about these procedures. Staff do not understand how they operate and fear the possible loss of their jobs at short notice.

"We need to develop and communicate more objective criteria for placing shops under closure review procedures. To help determine which criteria are appropriate, I have provided illustrative data for two poorly performing shops, in Leeds and Hull, which have recently been placed under closure review procedures. I have also provided relevant internal benchmarks from THV shops across the performance range (**Exhibit 2**)."

Procurement processes

The head of management information systems, Paul Potter, suggested a change in procurement processes. "Currently each shop manager has responsibility for determining the quantities of food and drinks ordered each day. I believe that we could use information technology to have automated reordering centrally. The IT system would use data on the amount and timing of historic sales for each shop to predict future sales as the basis for ordering from suppliers. Shop managers would therefore no longer be responsible for ordering.

"I have consulted one group of managers about this, who suggested an alternative approach. Their suggestion was to allow shop managers to use their discretion to purchase up to (say) 20% of their shop's products, by value, directly from local suppliers, rather than ordering through head office. These managers argued that this would better enable them to satisfy local tastes using their local knowledge. The remaining 80% of products would continue to be ordered by shop managers through head office."

Ethical concerns

In a private conversation, Andrew Aimes, a non-executive director of THV, raised a concern with the marketing director, Diana Dunn.

Andrew said: "A major element of THV's marketing is that our products are not only vegetarian, but also are healthy because they are vegetarian. However, there is high sugar content in many of our products, and it is well-established that eating too much sugar can badly affect people's health."

Diana responded: "Look, Andrew, the sugar content in grams is marked on all our products in a small, detailed table of the ingredients. If people don't want to read it, or don't understand what number of grams is high or low for sugar content, then that is their problem."

Requirements

46.1 In respect of assessing shop performance:

    (a)   Evaluate and explain the performance of the shops in Leeds and Hull (Exhibit 2). So far as the information permits, give a reasoned opinion as to whether each shop should be closed. State key additional information that you would require to make a more complete assessment of the performance of the two shops; and   **(10 marks)**

    (b)   Critically appraise the effectiveness of THV's KPIs (Exhibit 1) in identifying under-performing shops. Suggest and justify further relevant KPIs that would improve the process for implementing closure review procedures.   **(8 marks)**

46.2 Explain how THV can make better use of budgeting (Exhibit 1).   **(7 marks)**

46.3 In respect of procurement processes, explain the merits and problems of:

- permitting shop managers to purchase some of their products from local suppliers, rather than ordering only through head office; and

- using IT systems to automate ordering for all products centrally for each shop.

    Assume these two proposals are mutually exclusive.   **(11 marks)**

46.4 Explain the ethical issues for Andrew and THV arising from the matters discussed by Andrew and Diana. Set out any actions that Andrew should now take.   **(8 marks)**

Total: 44 marks

Exhibit 1: Performance assessment and budgeting

Performance assessment and closure review procedures

THV's accounting year end is 31 May. The annual performance of every shop is assessed in June each year. The performance of each shop is measured and the shops are ranked in order (from best to worst) for each of the following three KPIs:

- Revenue

- Operating profit

- Return on capital employed (ROCE) – calculated using the depreciated historic cost of the shop's non-current assets.

Staff in the best performing 50 shops are paid a bonus.

At the discretion of the board, shops which are placed bottom in the ranking for at least one KPI may be placed under closure review procedures. During these procedures, the shop manager must implement a three-month recovery plan, and the shop's monthly performance is measured against this plan. Unless the shop shows substantial improvement over the period of the recovery plan it is likely to be closed.

The closure review procedures were introduced to give an incentive to shop managers and other staff to perform well, as all the staff working in shops that are closed are normally made redundant.

The final decision to close a shop is made at the discretion of the board after considering all relevant factors.

Budgeting

Annual budgets are set for each shop, and the actual performance of each shop is compared to its budget annually. This is an additional, and separate, process to the annual closure review process.

Budgets are used for planning purposes, and also to motivate all shop managers, whether they are performing well or badly. The budgets are set by negotiation with each shop manager. However, head office does not accept shop budgets which have a lower revenue or operating profit than was actually achieved for the previous year. If a shop budget is consistently not achieved, the shop manager may be dismissed, although the shop would not be closed on this basis alone.

Exhibit 2: Performance data and related internal benchmarks

Year ended 31 May 20X6

| | Shops under closure review procedures | | | Benchmarks | |
	Leeds shop	Hull shop	Average for all shops	Average for 50 worst performing shops	Average for 50 best performing shops
Revenue	£425,000	£325,000	£480,000	£390,000	£580,000
Operating profit	£17,000	£11,000	£30,000	£20,000	£45,000
ROCE	3.1%	3.7%	9.7%	6.8%	10.0%
Number of years since opening	11 years	2 years	5 years	3 years	13 years
Floor space (square metres)	130	80	80	80	120
Non-current assets *	£550,000	£300,000	£310,000	£295,000	£450,000
Number of employees	11	7	7	7	10

* Non-current assets are property, plant and equipment valued at depreciated historic cost. At 31 May 20X6 there were no leasehold properties.

---

47 Elver Bloom Recruiting plc

The date is June 20X6.

Elver Bloom Recruiting plc (EBR) is a medium-sized employment recruitment agency. It recruits staff, on behalf of its clients, to work on permanent employment contracts in the finance industry.

The employment recruitment industry

Recruitment agencies attract, identify and select suitable candidates as employees for their clients. Staff recruited may be for permanent or temporary contracts.

Recruitment agencies may also offer other services, such as training, project management (eg, redundancy schemes and large-scale recruitment initiatives), advice (eg, on employment law) and staff appraisal. Frequently, these services are provided to existing regular clients.

Advertising available jobs in the most efficient manner, and identifying potential employees, are key processes for any recruitment agency. Increased use of the internet and social media in recent years has facilitated these processes for all companies in the industry.

Key constraints on recruitment agencies are legal issues regarding both who can be recruited and the process by which employees can be recruited.

Smaller agencies tend to specialise in: a particular industry (eg, finance, IT, hospitality, education, construction); a category of employee (eg, new graduates, seasonal workers); or a geographical region (eg, major cities or a single country). Larger recruitment agencies operate across a broad spectrum of services and sectors.

The majority of the revenue of recruitment agencies comes from charging fees to clients for achieving successful recruitment. The fee for recruiting a permanent employee is normally based on a percentage of the employee's first year salary. This can range from 10% (for large-volume, regular clients) to 30% (for a one-off assignment).

If the recruited employee does not stay in employment for more than three months, the agency pays a rebate to the employer, which is typically between 50% and 100% of the fee.

The market for recruitment agency services was weak during the recession 4 to 8 years ago. However, more recently, revenue in the industry increased by 10% in 20X4 and by 9% in 20X5. Profitability growth has been highest in the recruitment of permanent employees, with average increases in profit in the sector of 18% in 20X4 and 16% in 20X5. Many new entrants to the recruitment agency industry are being attracted by increasing profits.

EBR – company background

EBR was formed 10 years ago by Amy Cheng and Mark Prost, who had worked together in the human resources department of an investment bank. Shortly afterwards they set up an office in the financial district of London and now have 35 staff. EBR has established a base of regular clients, but it also carries out one-off assignments. The industry is competitive and new clients and assignments are gained through tenders. Each year, existing regular clients put pressure on EBR to reduce fees.

EBR specialises in permanent appointments in the finance industry (eg, banking, investment management, financial services and accounting). It seeks to attract candidates with a minimum of five years' relevant work experience. The average first-year salary of EBR's recruits is £80,000.

A further specialism is that EBR attempts to recruit candidates both in the UK and internationally, mainly for clients based in London.

Mark summarised this policy: "We use social media, the internet and industry electronic journals to recruit the best financial candidates in the world and bring them to London, which is one of the largest global financial centres. These international candidates bring language skills and knowledge of international financial markets. We recruit in three regions: Europe, North America and East Asia."

Fees – a new approach

During the recession, market conditions for EBR were difficult, as they were for all companies in the industry. Then, as the UK economy began to emerge from the recession, EBR continued to find it difficult to win new tenders, retain existing clients and increase revenue.

The EBR board therefore decided to reduce all its fees by 10% for each employee recruited from 1 April 20X5. This reduction was aimed at winning tenders and retaining clients, and thereby gaining a greater volume of business.

A board meeting in May 20X6 reviewed the success of the fee reduction policy.

Mark Prost opened: "The policy to reduce fees has been a disaster. I have produced some financial information and operating data (**Exhibit**) which shows that, while revenue has increased, operating profit has fallen. I think we should revert to our previous fee levels."

The marketing director, Nick Drapp, disagreed: "I think the policy has been a success. We have won more tenders in the year ended 31 March 20X6 than in the previous few years, and we have retained nearly all our regular clients. This gives the agency a better basis to market itself to existing and new clients and therefore to build for the future."

Amy Cheng had a different view: "I think we need to move upmarket and increase fees by 20% from their current, reduced, level. Clearly, we must offer something in return to clients, so I think we should go beyond the industry norm for offering rebates. I suggest we offer a 100% rebate to clients if our recruits leave their employment within six months of joining, and a 75% rebate if recruits leave between six months and 12 months of joining. We will then be giving a really clear signal that we have confidence in the quality and suitability of the candidates we have recruited."

Requirements

47.1 Using the PESTEL framework, explain how the following factors affect the employment recruitment agency industry:

- Economic
- Technological
- Legal

You are **not** required to discuss the other PESTEL factors. **(10 marks)**

47.2 Use the available quantitative data (Exhibit) and other information to evaluate the decision to reduce fees by 10% from 1 April 20X5. In a report to the board advise, with reasons, whether this price reduction should now be retained or reversed. Ignore Amy's proposal. **(16 marks)**

47.3 Explain the factors that should be considered in deciding whether to implement Amy's proposal. Provide a reasoned recommendation. **(9 marks)**

Total: 35 marks

Exhibit: Financial information and operating data

Financial information – years ended 31 March

	20X6 £'000	20X5 £'000
Recruitment		
Revenue: fees	12,480	11,900
Less:		
Rebates	(1,498)	(1,200)
Variable costs (eg, advertising)	(2,496)	(2,142)
Fixed costs	(3,300)	(3,300)
Operating profit from recruitment	5,186	5,258
Operating profit from other services	610	560
Total operating profit	5,796	5,818

Operating data – years ended 31 March

	20X6	20X5
Number of permanent appointments	780	700
Number of active clients	168	142

Working assumption: if the change in pricing policy on 1 April 20X5 had not taken place, the financial information and operating data for the year ended 31 March 20X6 would have been the same as that for the year ended 31 March 20X5.

---

48   TechScan Ltd

The date is June 20X6.

TechScan Ltd (TechScan) develops and manufactures complex electronic scanners, which are used by hospitals in the UK. The company has a large research and development (R&D) department.

The basic TechScan technology is common to all its products and is protected by patents. However, the patent protection ends in 20X7 and, unless new technology can be found, there will be a significant fall in profitability.

The TechScan board has identified two options:

- **Option 1** – TechScan's R&D department develops and patents new advanced scanner technology.

- **Option 2** – TechScan obtains a licence for the right to use new scanning technology which has already been successfully developed in the US by Ursa Inc, a rival company.

While the technologies under each option would be different, if TechScan's R&D is successful, the two different technologies are expected to be equally effective. It is therefore estimated that, using either technology, sales of scanners would be the same in quality, volume and price terms. The useful life of either technology would be five years, before being replaced by newer developments. Both technologies could be available to TechScan in 20X7 and 1,000 scanners could be manufactured and sold over the following five-year period, under either option.

Option 1 – R&D project

TechScan's R&D department has been working on an R&D project to develop new advanced scanner technology for six years. It has incurred substantial expenditure over that period and, while some progress has been made, there remain significant uncertainties with the project. An immediate additional investment of £45 million is required to finance the final phase of the R&D project but, even with this investment, there is only a 60% probability of its success. If the project fails, no benefit would arise. However, the licence from Ursa Inc could still then be purchased (as per Option 2).

If the R&D project succeeds, the present value of all future costs to manufacture 1,000 scanners would be £20 million (in addition to the £45 million R&D investment). All costs would be incurred in £ sterling.

Option 2 – purchase a licence

TechScan could abandon the R&D project immediately and purchase a licence from Ursa Inc. This would give TechScan the sole rights to include Ursa technology in all its scanners sold in the UK over the next five years. The present value of all future costs to develop and manufacture 1,000 scanners using Ursa technology would be £100 million, including the licence fees. All costs would be incurred in £ sterling.

Sales

The total sales volume over the five years of manufacture would be 1,000 scanners under either option. Over this period, the selling price would be subject to the same uncertainties for either option. There is a 70% probability of high prices, in which case the present value of revenues would be £160 million for either option. There is a 30% probability of low prices, in which case the present value of revenues would be £110 million for either option.

Requirements

48.1 If the board were to choose Option 2, discuss the likely impact of this decision on the R&D department and on TechScan's future R&D strategy. **(6 marks)**

48.2 (a) Calculate the expected net present values of the two options.

(b) Using the calculations in 48.2(a), and taking account of other relevant factors, advise and explain which of the two options should be selected. **(15 marks)**

Total: 21 marks

49 Guayaporto Ltd

The date is September 20X6.

Guayaporto Ltd (GPT) is a company based in Fantasia in South America. It manufactures discs (CDs and DVDs) that store digital data in audio, video or text format. It supplies these to order to Fantasian businesses in the publishing, music, education and home entertainment sectors.

Disc production process

To produce each set of discs, a template is required. GPT outsources the creation of this to a specialist supplier in Asia. For every order placed, the customer provides GPT with a confidential data file. This is sent, electronically, to the Asian supplier, which uses the data to create a glass master-disc as a template. This master-disc is transported from the supplier to GPT by secure courier.

GPT manufactures discs in-house, from polycarbonate, which it sources locally. Using the master-disc, the digital data are transferred onto each disc. A metallic reflective layer is then applied which allows the disc to be played. Once these stages are complete, colour and graphics are added to one side of each disc, according to the customer's specifications. Finally, the discs are packaged into individual plastic wallets or cases.

Quality control is very important for customer satisfaction and because high error rates and wastage result in low margins for GPT. Testing for quality consistency is undertaken at various points in the production process and any defective discs are rejected. The intellectual property contained in the confidential data files and the master-disc belongs to GPT's customer and must be kept secure at all times. The terms of GPT's standard contract with the customer requires GPT to destroy the master-disc on completion of each order.

Industry demand

CDs were introduced thirty years ago, DVDs followed 10 years later, when use of the internet was becoming popular. For 20 years, disc-based technology dominated the market for film, music and gaming. However, use of the internet for downloading data, and the rise of on-demand services for streaming film, music and games, has meant that discs are increasingly obsolete.

As businesses move away from releasing their products in disc form, retailers are devoting less shelf space to CDs and DVDs. Traditionally discs were used for storage of digital data, but they are being replaced by other devices and cloud-based storage. Computer manufacturers are increasingly producing computers and tablets without disc drives. As a result, worldwide demand for CDs and DVDs has fallen to 30% of its peak of 20 billion discs at the beginning of the 21st century.

Weakening demand has led to some manufacturers stopping disc production entirely or diversifying into other products. However, not all markets are declining at the same rate and there is still a core demand for discs for certain purposes. For example, some film producers refuse to make their films available for streaming, preferring to release them as DVDs in an attempt to maintain their revenues. 3D movies, which are increasingly popular, are often released on disc due to the large file sizes involved. DVDs, rather than downloads, are still preferred by many video-game players.

GPT's results and future direction

GPT's machines are capable of producing up to 45,000 discs per week but are not currently being used at full capacity. Most of GPT's production line is highly mechanised, but all the final packaging is carried out manually. The directors understand that manual packaging is less efficient, but they have been prepared to sacrifice some margin because they believe it is important to provide employment for the local labour force.

GPT's results have declined considerably in the last 12 months (Exhibit). GPT has not lost many customers, but typically customers are placing orders for smaller volumes. In addition, Fantasia's currency (the franc) has weakened against most other currencies. This has increased the cost to GPT of buying master-discs from the Asian supplier, despite the purchase price in Asian $ remaining constant.

Production director's suggestion

To reduce costs, the production director has suggested that GPT acquires a new machine to undertake all its packaging requirements. This would increase capacity and avoid delays currently caused by the manual packaging process. If the proposed machine purchase takes place, 60% of GPT's packaging workforce would be made redundant. The remaining 40% would be trained to operate and maintain the packaging machine.

Sales director's suggestion

The sales director has suggested that, because falling demand for its products is the problem, GPT should establish alternative revenue streams. He has made one specific suggestion already: one of GPT's regular customers, Alegre Education (Alegre), produces a range of disc-based revision guides for college students. A college has approached GPT and asked to buy some of the revision guides directly from GPT at a price that is lower than Alegre's. Since the master-disc already exists, GPT could produce own-brand versions of the Alegre revision guides, on disc, at relatively low cost.

Requirements

49.1 Explain how GPT might benefit from scenario planning to help it develop strategic responses to the uncertainty facing its industry's future. **(7 marks)**

49.2 Using the quantitative data and the other information provided, identify and explain the key causes of the decline in GPT's performance, and analyse the impact that each cause has had on its financial results. You should, where feasible, provide calculations to quantify the financial impact and set out any further information that is required to make a fuller assessment. **(18 marks)**

49.3 Discuss the issues that GPT should consider when sharing confidential data files through the supply chain and explain how these might be addressed. **(7 marks)**

49.4 Discuss the advantages and disadvantages of the proposals made by the production director and the sales director. **(12 marks)**

Total: 44 marks

Exhibit: Financial and operating data

Summary statement of profit or loss

In Fantasian currency	20X5 francs		20X4 francs	
Sales		2,205,000		2,804,400
Cost of sales:				
Master-discs	525,000		399,750	
Other production costs	630,000		841,320	
		(1,155,000)		(1,241,070)
Gross profit		1,050,000		1,563,330
Administration and distribution overheads		(835,000)		(981,400)
Operating profit		215,000		581,930

Operating data

	20X5	20X4
Total number of discs sold	1,050,000	1,476,000
Average number of discs per order	1,000	1,200
Number of orders	1,050	1,230
Purchase price per master-disc (Asian $)	$25	$25
Average exchange rate:		
Fantasian francs (f) per Asian $	f20=$1	f13=$1

MHD is a large mental health charity based in the UK. It provides services for people with mental health problems. The charity owns and operates a number of residential and day-care centres which are subject to inspection by government regulators. It also funds research into mental health conditions.

MHD is governed by a board of trustees (the board) chaired by John Adams. The board oversees the charity's activities and is accountable for the charity's performance. It ensures that MHD is run in the public interest and for the benefit of sufferers of mental health problems. The board has delegated responsibility for the day-to-day operations of the charity to a small management team, led by chief executive Vishal Garcia. The charity has over 200 employees plus many volunteers.

MHD receives some government funding, but it relies heavily on donations and sponsorship. It has experienced financial difficulties recently and its cash balances are now very low. The chief finance officer resigned from the management team three months ago and Jennifer Studley has been recruited to take over the role. Jennifer previously managed the finances for a much smaller organisation in the charity sector.

Jennifer wants to make some changes to the way MHD functions but she has encountered some resistance from the board. John and Vishal have both been involved with MHD for over 15 years. The majority of the trustees are volunteers who have been recruited by John and Vishal from among their close friends and former colleagues in the mental health sector.

Jennifer met recently with Vishal and John to discuss how to improve MHD's financial position and raised a number of agenda items:

Agenda item A: Governance and the role of trustees

Jennifer started the meeting: "I think that we should recruit some new trustees with a wider range of commercial experience. They would be able to challenge the way MHD is managed, and identify opportunities for innovation and development. This would allow the board to take a more strategic view in future."

Vishal was not convinced: "One of the big advantages of working with the current board of trustees is the fact that we all know each other and the charity well, having spent many years working together. As a result, there is little conflict in our meetings and we are usually able to reach quick, unanimous decisions. Also, some of our trustees are very wealthy and their companies have given us large donations in the past. I would not want to upset them by suggesting they have not been doing their jobs properly."

John commented: "Since MHD is a charity, I believe our role as trustees is to make sure that the management team avoids risk, wherever possible, and chooses safe strategies. This approach has served us well in the past."

Agenda item B: Sustainability and performance measurement

Jennifer suggested that MHD should consider seeking more funds to prevent any solvency issues: "There is a critical need for MHD to provide more mental health services but, as we have minimal cash, we would need to raise new funds. We will be more able to access funding, and therefore become a more sustainable organisation, if we can clearly demonstrate good performance.

"As far as I can tell the charity has done little in the past to measure its performance. If we are to attract more funding we need to be able to demonstrate to our fund-providers the impact that MHD is having in the mental health sector."

Agenda item C: Adverse publicity about MHD's ethics

Finally Jennifer said: "I feel awkward raising this, but it has come to my attention that MHD has attracted some adverse publicity recently, in a negative article about the charitable sector in a national newspaper. The journalist expressed concerns about the ethics of high salary packages paid by charitable organisations, and in particular the recent pay rises awarded by MHD to its senior management.

"The article also queried the ethics of MHD's aggressive fund-raising. As you know we are under pressure to raise more funds so we outsourced this process to a professional fund-raising organisation FundsForYou Ltd (FFY). We agreed to pay them commission based on the amount of funds raised. FFY initially sent a mailshot and an email to all the previous donors listed on our database. It then used its call centre staff to follow this up with repeated texts and phone calls."

Requirements

Agenda item A:

50.1 With reference to the views expressed at the meeting, critically appraise the governance procedures of MHD and assess their impact on the charity's ability to achieve its objectives.

(8 marks)

Agenda item B:

50.2 Explain what sustainability means for MHD and discuss the extent to which MHD is a sustainable organisation. **(6 marks)**

50.3 Explain an approach to performance measurement that MHD could use to assess the impact of its activities. You should give examples of specific performance measures relevant to MHD. **(9 marks)**

Agenda item C:

50.4 Discuss the ethical implications arising for MHD from the issues raised in the newspaper article.

(8 marks)

Total: 31 marks

51 Thistle Engineering Services Ltd

The date is September 20X6.

Thistle Engineering Services Ltd (Thistle) was formed 20 years ago by engineer Joshua Woodburn. The company is based in Scotland and provides engineering and construction services. Thistle specialises in the design, construction and installation of storage tanks and high-pressure steel pipelines for the oil and gas industry.

Management team

Joshua Woodburn (aged 60)   – Managing director and Sales director (shareholding 50%)
Tom Tabinor (aged 53)   – Operations director (shareholding 35%)
Anya Clough (aged 45)   – Finance director (shareholding 15%)

Joshua and Tom have run the business for many years. Joshua has 30 years' experience in the engineering sector and has overall responsibility for the company. Tom joined Thistle soon after it was formed, having previously worked in the oil and gas industry. Anya originally joined Thistle as financial controller many years ago. She manages its administration and finances. Thistle also employs 100 staff, the majority of whom are skilled engineers. They are all based in Scotland.

Operations

All structural steelwork is manufactured at the company's factory in Scotland, by experienced, fully-qualified welders. Pipelines and tanks are then transported to the customer's site for installation. Unlike many competitors, which rely on contract labour, all Thistle's site installation teams are directly employed by the company. Thistle also provides pipeline testing and off-site fabrication and welding services.

Thistle uses a range of Scottish suppliers for tools and other materials. It also has contracts with preferred suppliers for metals, pumps and specialist equipment. The majority of these suppliers are located in the UK.

Thistle has an established customer base in the UK and the majority of its business is on a repeat basis. 60% of sales are made to four large global companies that distribute oil and gas around the UK. Other customers include utility companies and businesses specialising in the removal of liquid waste.

Thistle has built a reputation for quality and innovation. It has developed a unique, patented 'pipe-wrapping' system which allows customers to maintain the flow of product through their pipelines whilst Thistle undertakes repairs.

The company is committed to maintaining the highest standards of health and safety. It is certified as compliant with global oil and gas regulatory standards and is acknowledged as an industry leader in environmental awareness and compliance.

International expansion

One of Thistle's major customers, Romiou Inc (Romiou), is a global company. It has asked Thistle to provide it with services for a major infrastructure project outside the UK. Exploratory drilling has identified large gas reserves at a new offshore site in the Mediterranean, and an undersea pipeline is required to transfer the gas to an onshore plant in Malta. Initial industry research has indicated that there is enormous potential for extracting natural gas in the region. Thistle believes there is a strong likelihood that Romiou will be the first of many customers seeking contracts for Mediterranean operations. As a result, Thistle is considering setting up a new base in Malta.

Setting up a Maltese base on 1 July 20X7 will require an initial investment of £425,000 and Thistle has approached its UK bank for loan finance. The bank has asked Thistle to produce a business plan in support of its loan application, specifying certain sections that are required. You work in Thistle's strategy team and have been asked to help draft information that should be included in the business plan. Anya has supplied you with the following financial information:

Three year forecast – new Maltese base

	Year 1 £'000	Year 2 £'000	Year 3 £'000	Total £'000
Sales	633	1,266	1,582	3,481
Gross profit	190	443	634	1,267
Fixed costs	(310)	(335)	(365)	(1,010)
Operating (loss)/profit	(120)	108	269	257

Thistle Ltd – summary of UK results, year ended 30 June 20X6

	£'000	Notes
Sales	6,574	
Cost of sales	(4,565)	
Gross profit	2,009	Gross margin 30.6%
Overheads	(1,593)	
Operating profit	416	Operating margin 6.3%
Interest	(49)	Interest cover = 8.5 times
Profit before tax	367	
Net assets	1,850	ROCE = 22.5%

Requirements

You are required to assist in preparing three specific sections of the business plan for a loan for the new Maltese base that would be of use to Thistle's bank.

For each of the sections set out in 51.1 to 51.3 below you should:

• prepare the section;
• explain why the section is important for the loan application; and
• identify any further information that would be useful to complete the section.

51.1 Risks of the new Maltese base, and any mitigating factors **(8 marks)**

51.2 Analysis of the three year forecast for the new Maltese base, including sensitivity **(10 marks)**

51.3 Appropriate organisational structure for international expansion **(7 marks)**

Total: 25 marks

52 Pinter Shipping Panels plc

The date is December 20X6.

Pinter Shipping Panels plc (PSP) is a listed company which manufactures steel panels for the shipbuilding industry. Shipbuilding is a global industry which is extremely competitive.

You have recently joined PSP, reporting to the chief executive, Ashley Adams. Ashley has asked you to report to him on a few important issues that have arisen recently:

"I know you are new to PSP so I have provided you with some background information (**Exhibit 1**).

"The board is concerned about performance. Although profits have improved this year the directors are not convinced that this improvement is sustainable. The finance director has provided some financial and operating data for 20X5 and 20X6 (**Exhibit 2**).

"There are also two issues for you to evaluate. Firstly, our sole supplier of steel has recently informed PSP that it will cease production on 31 December 20X6. We need to address this problem urgently, using either a sole new supplier or multiple new suppliers (**Exhibit 3**). Secondly, one of our two customers, Tinner, is challenging our pricing policy (**Exhibit 4**)."

Requirements

52.1 Using the quantitative data and other information provided in Exhibits 1 and 2, analyse the performance of PSP in 20X5 and 20X6, identifying and explaining the key drivers of profit.

(18 marks)

52.2 Explain the factors to be considered in deciding how to source supplies of steel (Exhibit 3). Provide reasoned advice regarding which supplier should be selected or whether both suppliers should be used in a multiple supplier agreement.

(13 marks)

52.3 Prepare a formal response to the email from Tinner's procurement director, Kelly Jones (Exhibit 4).

(9 marks)

Total: 40 marks

Exhibit 1: PSP – background information

Operations

PSP uses steel as a raw material to manufacture its panels. The panels are used by PSP's customers to build ships. The size and shape of the panels are standardised. The cost of manufacturing each panel is similar for all customers, although delivery costs vary according to the customer's requirements and location.

After taking account of wastage rates, one tonne of steel makes four steel panels.

Raw material – steel

Due to overcapacity in the steel industry, the global price of steel has fallen significantly from a high of £350 per tonne in 20X4 to a price of £130 per tonne in December 20X6. This has caused many steel producers to cease production.

Supply chain – upstream

For many years PSP has used a sole supplier of steel, Coastal Inc (Coastal), which is based in Brazil. Until recently Coastal supplied steel to PSP under annual fixed price contracts in which the price of steel per tonne for the next year was fixed in £ sterling on 1 January each year.

In October 20X6, Coastal Inc informed PSP it would cease production from 31 December 20X6 because it had become insolvent. Since October, the PSP board has been looking for new sources of steel and has found two possible suppliers, Lipp plc and Kerr Inc (Exhibit 3).

Supply chain – downstream

PSP has only two customers: Tinner plc (Tinner) and Falchetti Marine Construction (FMC).

Tinner

Tinner builds cargo ships at its dockyard which is five kilometres from the PSP factory in the UK. PSP is the sole supplier of steel panels to Tinner.

PSP agrees an annual contract with Tinner on 1 January each year, which fixes the price of steel panels in £ sterling for that year. PSP delivers to Tinner every two weeks, with similar quantities of panels each time. Deliveries are agreed a few months in advance. Tinner holds large inventories of steel panels in order to deal with any variations in its manufacturing requirements. PSP could deliver panels more frequently, but it has not been required to do so by Tinner.

Tinner has recently appointed a new procurement director, Kelly Jones. She wishes to negotiate the supply contract with PSP for 20X7 on revised terms and has sent an email to PSP about this (Exhibit 4).

FMC

FMC builds cargo ships at a dockyard in Italy. It uses several suppliers of steel panels. PSP supplies 35% of FMC's total requirements for steel panels.

PSP supplies FMC under quarterly contracts. These are agreed on 1 January and at three-month intervals thereafter. Each contract fixes the price of steel panels in euro for the following three months.

Exhibit 2: PSP financial and operating data – prepared by the finance director

Extracts from the financial statements for the years to 31 December:

	20X5			20X6 (Estimated)		
	Tinner £'000	FMC £'000	Total £'000	Tinner £'000	FMC £'000	Total £'000
Revenue	24,000	16,400	40,400	18,720	16,720	35,440
Cost of steel	(9,000)	(6,000)	(15,000)	(3,900)	(3,300)	(7,200)
Other variable Operating costs	(7,200)	(5,200)	(12,400)	(6,760)	(6,160)	(12,920)
Fixed operating costs			(9,000)			(9,000)
Operating profit			4,000			6,320

Operating data for the years to 31 December:

	20X5	20X6 (Estimated)
Steel used (tonnes)	50,000	48,000
Number of steel panels sold:		
Tinner	120,000	104,000
FMC	80,000	88,000
	200,000	192,000

Note: The figures for 20X6 comprise actual data for the year to November 20X6, with estimates for December 20X6.

Exhibit 3: Potential supply arrangements for steel

Only two potential new suppliers of steel for PSP have been identified for 20X7: Lipp plc (Lipp) and Kerr Inc (Kerr). PSP can select one of these companies to be its sole supplier, or it can use both companies in a multiple supplier arrangement.

Lipp

Lipp is a UK steel producer. It has been struggling financially recently, so it wants to win the contract to supply steel to PSP. It has offered an annual contract from 1 January 20X7 at a fixed price of £180 per tonne of steel under a sole supplier arrangement. If there is to be a multiple supplier arrangement it has offered a fixed price of £190 per tonne of steel under a similar annual contract. Deliveries can be made weekly.

Kerr

Kerr is a US steel producer. It is willing to supply steel to PSP from 1 January 20X7. Each delivery would be under a separate contract. Each contract's price would vary according to a pre-agreed formula based on the spot price of steel on global commodity markets on the day of ordering. Prices would be charged to PSP in US dollars. For a delivery on 1 January 20X7, the contract price is expected to be equivalent to £185 per tonne of steel.

Multiple supplier arrangement

PSP has agreed with Lipp and Kerr that, in any multiple supplier arrangement, each supplier would supply at least 40% of PSP's total annual steel requirements. The Lipp contract would be renegotiated after one year.

Exhibit 4: Extract from email to PSP from Tinner's procurement director, Kelly Jones

In the last two years, PSP has benefitted from large reductions in the global price of steel. However, because of the current fixed price contract, PSP has not shared this benefit with Tinner in the form of lower prices for its steel panels. It is not acceptable for this to continue.

I have also reviewed the level of service that PSP has been offering Tinner.

I require the following amendments to the terms in the new contract for 20X7:

- The current system of a delivery every two weeks will cease. We will require several deliveries per week. These will be of varying quantities, notified to you one day in advance of delivery.

- There will be a separate contract each week. The price for each week's deliveries will be determined separately according to an agreed formula in the contract that takes into account the spot price of steel.

If we cannot agree on these revised terms Tinner will terminate PSP's status as its sole supplier and, in future, source its steel panels from other suppliers in addition to PSP. This would result in a significant reduction in the volume of steel panels that Tinner purchases from PSP

53   Zeter Domestic Chemicals plc

The date is December 20X6.

Zeter Domestic Chemicals plc (ZDC) manufactures domestic cleaning products that are used by individual consumers.

Company background

ZDC processes raw chemicals to make domestic cleaning products, which it packages and sells to retailers.

The cleaning products are collected and distributed by lorry from ZDC's factory in the south of England. They are delivered directly to retailers which are located in the UK and France.

The acquisition of Trann Ltd

ZDC acquired Trann Ltd (Trann) on 1 October 20X4.

Prior to the acquisition, Trann had been one of three distribution companies used by ZDC.

The decision to acquire Trann was the result of a vote at a ZDC board meeting. The Chief executive, David Xuan, and the Marketing Director, Kevin Hilton, voted in favour. The Finance Director, Lisa Long, and the Chairman voted against. David Xuan had the casting vote and so the acquisition was approved.

First year post-acquisition review: October 20X5

On 1 October 20X5, ZDC's board held a meeting to review the first year of ZDC's ownership of Trann.

The board heard that, for this year, Trann's management had been allowed the autonomy to take all decisions which it believed to be appropriate for Trann. As a result, little had changed since ZDC's acquisition: Trann was still providing similar distribution services for ZDC and its other customers, and was charging similar prices as it did before the acquisition. ZDC's distribution managers also continued to use the two other distribution companies in addition to Trann.

David Xuan was unhappy: "I am wondering why we acquired Trann. In effect, it is being run as a separate entity from ZDC. Why are we still using the other two external distribution companies as well as Trann, and incurring unnecessary costs? We now have our own distribution company which we can use for all our distribution needs."

The ZDC board agreed that ZDC should use Trann for all its distribution with immediate effect. To give ZDC's distribution managers an incentive to use Trann, the Trann board was instructed to reduce its transfer prices to ZDC by 10%. Trann was also instructed to terminate its contracts with all its other customers immediately in order to create sufficient capacity to satisfy all of ZDC's transport requirements.

Second year post-acquisition review: October 20X6

In October 20X6, the ZDC board met for a further review of Trann. Financial extracts for Trann were provided to the ZDC board (**Exhibit 1**).

Lisa Long commented on these results: "It is clear that the performance of Trann was poor in the first year after acquisition and it has continued to decline in this second year. I disagreed with the decision to acquire Trann and these figures have proved me right."

Kevin Hilton disagreed: "The acquisition of Trann has been a success. I have produced key performance indicators (KPIs) (**Exhibit 2**) to show how much ZDC's distribution has improved in terms of efficiency and customer satisfaction in the year ended 30 September 20X6."

An ethical issue

David Xuan and Kevin Hilton had a conversation after the October 20X6 review.

During the conversation Kevin said: "In talking to Trann staff, I discovered that your niece has worked for Trann as a manager for several years. There is a rumour that, in supporting ZDC's acquisition of Trann, you were helping your niece. I note that she has been promoted twice within Trann since the acquisition. At the time the ZDC board voted on the acquisition, I felt that you applied pressure on me to vote with you. I hope that this was because you thought the acquisition was in the best interests of ZDC, not because of concern for your niece's career."

David responded: "At the time of the vote I said nothing about my niece's position at Trann because I did not want to influence the board, favourably or unfavourably, in the acquisition decision. ZDC's distribution function is part of your role and you are responsible for Trann. If the acquisition is not successful for ZDC, I will be asking for your resignation. The matter of my niece's employment is confidential. If you break that confidence I will dismiss you."

Requirements

53.1 Analyse the decisions made on 1 October 20X5, at the first year post-acquisition review, to:

- use Trann for all of ZDC's distribution needs, and require Trann to terminate the contracts with all its other customers; and

- reduce the transfer prices charged by Trann to ZDC by 10%.

Note: Ignore the data in Exhibit 1 and Exhibit 2. **(11 marks)**

53.2 Evaluate the views and information put forward by Lisa Long and Kevin Hilton, in October 20X6, at the second year post-acquisition review. Use the information in Exhibits 1 and 2 to provide supporting calculations. These should include, but not be restricted to, return on investment and residual income for Trann. **(11 marks)**

53.3 Explain the ethical issues for David Xuan and Kevin Hilton arising from their conversation. Set out the actions that they should each now take. **(8 marks)**

Total: 30 marks

Exhibit 1: Financial extracts for Trann – prepared by the Finance Director

Extracts from the management accounts of Trann for years ended 30 September:

	20X5	20X6
	£'000	£'000
Revenue	16,610	15,120
Operating profit/(loss)	983	(640)
Fair value of net assets	7,000	7,000

The annual cost of capital for both ZDC and Trann is 10%.

Using the fair value of its net assets, excluding Trann, ZDC has a return on investment of 18% per annum.

It is estimated that variable costs for Trann were £1.40 per kilometre in both the years ended 30 September 20X5 and 30 September 20X6.

Exhibit 2: Distribution data for Trann – prepared by the Marketing Director

KPIs – years ended 30 September	20X5	20X6
Percentage of on-time deliveries	91%	96%
Number of customer complaints related to delivery journeys	184	163
Percentage of full loads operated (ie, % of all deliveries when the lorry is full to capacity on the outward journey)	44	56
Number of delivery journeys made:		
• For ZDC	4,250	8,000
• For other customers	3,300	–
Average distance per delivery journey (kilometres)		
• For ZDC	1,100	1,050
• For other customers	1,100	–

Each delivery journey may involve deliveries to several retailers.

---

54 Hartley's Traditional Footwear Ltd

The date is December 20X6.

Hartley's Traditional Footwear Ltd (HTF) is a retailer of high quality shoes and boots (footwear) from 20 shops located throughout the UK.

Company background

HTF was established a number of years ago as a retailer of traditional leather footwear. Customers were typically from high-income groups and over 40 years old. HTF's shops are located in premium locations in shopping centres of major cities.

The HTF brand is well-known amongst high-income individuals in the UK as having high quality footwear, supported by good customer service.

A new product – Ayres boots

From January 20X5, HTF entered into a two-year contract with an Australian manufacturer of boots, The Ayres Boot Company Ltd (ABC), for the exclusive right to sell its Ayres brand boots in the UK. At that time, the Ayres brand was not well known in the UK. The contract specified that HTF could buy each pair of boots for £40 a pair from ABC until December 20X6. Sales globally were typically to consumers in the 20 to 30 years age group. Ayres boots are made mostly from synthetic fur.

For the first year, sales of Ayres boots were low. Some HTF board members started to argue that they were not suitable for HTF's customer base and had damaged the HTF brand.

In December 20X5, several celebrities were photographed wearing Ayres boots. Via social media, the boots quickly became a global fashion phenomenon. They became in huge demand as a premium product from the start of 20X6.

Global sales of Ayres boots increased rapidly and, despite retailers raising the selling price to consumers substantially, ABC could not manufacture enough boots to satisfy global demand. From January 20X6, ABC therefore limited supplies to HTF to 10,000 pairs of boots per month in the UK for the remaining term of the contract.

The following data are provided:

	20X5	20X6
Sales volumes (pairs):		
Ayres boots	8,000	120,000
Traditional footwear	40,000	36,000
Average sales prices:		
Ayres boots	£60	£200
Traditional footwear	£150	£150
Average cost:		
Ayres boots	£40	£40
Traditional footwear	£100	£100

Contract extension – December 20X6

HTF continues to sell traditional leather footwear through its shops, but HTF's reputation and brand are now closely identified with the Ayres brand.

The end of the two-year contract period with ABC is now imminent. ABC has stated that it is still willing to continue to sell its boots to HTF. However, it is considering increasing its price to HTF and ending the exclusivity agreement by making sales to other UK retailers from 1 January 20X7.

ABC's board has said that it will consider extending the existing contract with HTF, as the exclusive UK retailer, for one more year. This would be in return for a one-off payment by HTF. The extended contract would continue to run until 31 December 20X7 on the same terms of 10,000 pairs per month, at £40 per pair. To open negotiations, ABC has asked the HTF board to suggest an appropriate amount for the one-off payment.

Importing boots from Russia

As a possible alternative to buying any boots from ABC from January 20X7, HTF has found a Russian company that can supply boots of a similar design as the Ayres boots, but without a brand name. The cost to HTF would be £40 a pair. HTF estimates that these boots will sell in similar quantities to the Ayres boots if it charges customers £60 a pair.

Some HTF board members are concerned that the Russian boots may have a risk of poor quality and have suggested that sourcing from this supplier may necessitate new quality control procedures.

Requirements

54.1 In respect of HTF's branding strategy:

(a) Compare the HTF brand and the Ayres brand; and

(b) Explain the benefits and problems for the HTF brand arising from the association with the Ayres brand. **(8 marks)**

54.2 Explain why the same Ayres boots sold for £60 in 20X5 and for £200 in 20X6. Use appropriate pricing models and concepts. **(7 marks)**

54.3 Identify and explain the quantitative and qualitative factors that HTF should consider in determining the amount of the one-off payment to offer ABC for the one-year extension of the exclusive supply contract for the UK. **(7 marks)**

54.4 Explain how quality control procedures could be used to identify and mitigate problems with the supply of the Russian boots. You should give specific examples of information that could be used to measure and monitor supplier performance. **(8 marks)**

Total: 30 marks

55 Ignite plc

The date is now March 2017.

Ignite plc (Ignite) is a listed company which makes a range of products that are capable of world-wide use. These include: cigarette lighters; multi-purpose lighters; lighter fuel; and a limited range of accessories (including torches, sunglasses and pens).

You have recently joined Ignite as a corporate strategy advisor, reporting to the strategy director, Hannah Smith. Hannah has asked for your help with a report that Ignite's board has requested on the company's product portfolio.

"As you are new to the team and the business, I am hoping you will bring some innovative ideas. Our most important product has always been the Ignite cigarette lighter. Our most important market has historically been the UK, though the anti-smoking movement has caused us a number of issues here. The board has recently been discussing the sales forecasts and it is very concerned about the declining sales of Ignite cigarette lighters in the UK. I have provided some background information for you about the company's history and product range (**Exhibit 1**) and the UK cigarette industry (**Exhibit 2**). More widely, the board has asked us to evaluate Ignite's global product sales and current product portfolio, because of concern about their implications for the company's future profitability (**Exhibit 3**).

"Ignite has a strong brand image but traditionally it has struggled to attract female consumers, other than those purchasing Ignite products as gifts. One of our directors believes that this is a failure on the part of the advertising department; another director believes that the problem is the design of our product range, which appeals primarily to males in the age group 18-34.

"The board wants us to consider opportunities for growth. I believe that we should extend the current portfolio to other related products in different markets and with different customers. I have suggested some ideas (**Exhibit 4**). The board is keen to report better results for 2017. It has set targets of 15% sales growth (compared with 2016), and a 38% gross profit margin."

Requirements

Draft sections for the report on the company's product portfolio that Ignite's board has requested:

55.1 Analyse the external factors that have influenced the changing demand for Ignite's cigarette lighters in the UK between 1950 and 2016. Use the data provided in Exhibits 1 and 2 to support your analysis. **(9 marks)**

55.2 Using the data in Exhibits 1, 2 and 3 and the other information provided, evaluate Ignite's existing product portfolio:

(a) Make appropriate calculations to:

- analyse the global historic and forecast financial information for 2015-2017 (for this purpose ignore the new products in Exhibit 4)

- analyse Ignite's existing product portfolio using the Boston Consulting Group (BCG) matrix.

(b) Discuss the implications of your analysis in (a) for Ignite's future corporate strategy. Use the following headings:

- Sales growth
- Profitability
- Risk **(22 marks)**

55.3 In relation to the board's requirements for future growth:

(a) Calculate the forecast sales and gross profit margin that the new products (Exhibit 4) must achieve to meet the board's targets for 2017.

(b) Discuss the growth strategies proposed by Hannah Smith (Exhibit 4). Refer to relevant models.

(13 marks)

Total: 44 marks

Exhibit 1: Company history and product range

Ignite was established in the late 1940s as a UK manufacturer of high quality cigarette lighters. The health risks of smoking are now widely known but, at that time, smoking was marketed as a fashionable and elegant activity.

Cigarette lighters

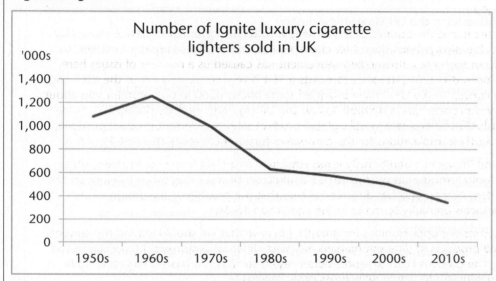

Ignite's first product was a luxury cigarette lighter with a fuel cylinder that could be refilled. The fuel could be purchased only from Ignite. As a result of their innovative design, Ignite lighters quickly became collectors' items, even being purchased by non-smokers.

In 1961, a competitor launched the first disposable cigarette lighter. Ignite reacted by introducing a lifetime guarantee for its products, promising that: "It works or we will fix it for free". This was attractive to loyal customers who valued Ignite's quality standards. However, by 1980, the use of very cheap, disposable lighters was widespread and several makers of refillable lighters went out of business.

During the 1980s, Ignite developed and patented new technology to produce lighters with a wind-resistant flame which would remain lit in all weather conditions. Ignite also expanded its marketing internationally, making use of product placement in films, television and sponsored events, to raise brand awareness.

Since 2007, as in many countries, smoking has been banned in the UK in enclosed public places. The fact that smokers are forced to go outside has increased demand for Ignite's wind-resistant lighters. However, the ban has also led to some of Ignite's customers switching to electronic cigarettes (e-cigarettes) which do not need a lighter.

To stimulate demand, every year Ignite brings out a limited-edition cigarette lighter which is widely publicised on social media. Each lighter carries unique artwork and is engraved with a date code and the initials of the worker who assembled it.

The UK market is declining so the international market is becoming increasingly important for Ignite. Today, Ignite lighters are sold in over 160 countries, and Ignite is a popular brand in Asia.

Multi-purpose lighters

In the 1990s, as UK social habits changed and outdoor entertaining became more popular, Ignite used its wind-resistant flame technology to develop multi-purpose lighters for candles, barbecues and cooking stoves. These are proving increasingly popular.

Lifestyle accessories

To capitalise on its brand name, in 2010 Ignite launched a range of lifestyle accessories for men: sunglasses, torches and pens. However whilst the technology behind the wind-resistant flame is difficult to copy, this is less true of fashion accessories. A number of cheap 'Ignite' counterfeits have been produced which has provided publicity for the Ignite brand, but reduced Ignite's sales and detracted from its quality image. The accessory range also included a range of male fragrances in cigarette lighter-shaped bottles. However, demand for Ignite fragrance has been lower than for other accessories.

Exhibit 2: Key dates influencing the UK cigarette industry

1920s–1950s	Cigarette smoking was extremely popular and increased rapidly. By 1959, in the UK, 60% of men and 40% of women smoked.
1960s	Various research papers were published about the addictive nature of cigarettes, showing a statistical link between smoking and reduced life expectancy.
1971	UK government health warnings were placed on cigarette packs for the first time.
1990s (and ongoing)	Research suggested that a 10% increase in price leads to approximately a 5% reduction in demand for cigarettes. Successive UK governments adopted a strategy of raising the price of cigarettes, through taxes, to reduce smoking.
2002	UK legislation banned cigarette advertising, promotion and sponsorship.
2004	The first electronic 'e-cigarette' was developed.
2007	UK legislation banned smoking in enclosed public places (bars, restaurants, workplaces).
2016	UK users of e-cigarettes increased from 700,000 in 2012 to 2.6 million in 2016.

Exhibit 3: Extracts of management information for Ignite's global product portfolio

Global product sales and profitability (based on 31 December year end):

	Luxury cigarette lighters £ million	Multi-purpose lighters £ million	Lighter fuel £ million	Lifestyle accessories £ million	Total £ million
Actual 2015					
Sales	127.0	34.0	32.0	20.0	213.0
Gross profit	52.1	8.2	6.1	12.0	78.4
Actual 2016					
Sales	108.0	38.0	30.0	24.0	200.0
Gross profit	43.2	9.1	5.4	14.4	72.1
Forecast 2017					
Sales	92.0	40.0	30.0	28.0	190.0
Gross profit	35.0	9.6	5.1	16.8	66.5

Global market data for the year ended 31 December 2016:

Product	Ignite's market share	Market leader's market share	Estimated market growth rate pa
Luxury cigarette lighters	26%	38%	(5%)
Multi-purpose lighters	18%	22%	14%
Lighter fuel	11%	45%	2%
Lifestyle accessories	Negligible	Note	12%

Note: No single company has more than 5% of the market

Exhibit 4: Growth strategies, suggested by Hannah Smith (strategy director)

- **New lighter**

  In response to health concerns about smoking and the success of fitness apps, Ignite has developed a new product, the Trackr. The Trackr is a cigarette lighter which includes a digital screen to monitor the number of cigarettes that have been lit that day. This enables a person to keep track of their smoking habit. This will be marketed as a device to help customers cut down on their smoking. The Trackr can be used on its own or integrated with a fitness app which monitors a range of other health-related issues (diet, exercise, alcohol etc) on a daily basis.

- **Outdoor range**

  Ignite's multi-purpose lighters are already used by many camping enthusiasts. Ignite is currently developing a range of high-quality gas barbecues to capitalise on its wind-resistant technological expertise. The negative association with smoking has been bad for Ignite's brand image. Developing more of an outdoor focus will appeal to health and fitness fans and counteract this. Once it has been established as a barbecue brand, Ignite will then develop a range of camping equipment.

- **Female market**

  To attract more customers, Ignite is also considering a new range of products for the female market: candle lighters, sunglasses, pens, fragrances. Unlike existing products, these will be designed specifically to appeal visually to women.

56 Eclo Ltd

Eclo Ltd (Eclo) sells environmentally-friendly uniforms to corporate clients. The garments are customised with the client's business logo. Eclo's target market is organisations that have created brands based on sustainability.

Company background

Eclo is a social enterprise which aims to trade in a profitable and sustainable manner. It was set up five years ago by Eve Carter, a textile engineering expert.

Eve is passionate about the environment. She wanted Eclo to avoid the traditional linear supply chain model: "take resources, make a product, use it, discard it". Instead, Eclo adopts a circular model where product materials and packaging are re-used multiple times as they are recycled into the supply chain to aim for zero waste.

Eve designs all Eclo garments with the aim that they can be repaired, re-used or re-manufactured. Customers are offered discounts off future orders as an incentive to return old products if they do not need them any longer.

Eclo has a small workforce. It operates with a very flat organisational structure, with all employees encouraged to contribute ideas and participate in decisions. It has strategic partnerships with three different Indian suppliers which currently produce all of Eclo's garments in India to standard specifications. Eclo pays an agent in India which arranges for the garments to be transported from the suppliers' factories to an Indian printing company for customisation according to the client's requirements. The agent then arranges shipping to the UK.

Sustainable production

Eclo uses environmentally sustainable processes which conform to a global certification standard. This requires Eclo to comply with high-level environmental and social criteria along its entire supply chain. A key marketing message of Eclo is that every Eclo garment can be traced back to its origins. Eclo has developed a simple eco-labelling system to evidence this.

All suppliers are required to have a fair and consistent wage policy and there are strict regulations on workers' age and working conditions. Eclo prohibits the use of poisonous chemicals and toxic additives that might damage workers' health and the environment.

Eclo's garments are made in factories that are powered by wind and solar energy. The garments incorporate wool, organic cotton and recycled polyester (RPET) fabrics. RPET is created from recycled plastic bottles which are turned into fabric so it has a much lower carbon footprint than other synthetic fabrics. The customised printing process uses environmentally-friendly dyes and low-waste, bio-degradable ink.

Supply chain management

Eclo's reliance on Indian suppliers has caused delays between client order and delivery. There have been an increasing number of client complaints about product quality and errors in printing. Eve is now considering whether to change to an entirely UK-based supply chain for garment production, and whether to establish an in-house printing operation in the UK. Eve has identified a suitable factory unit at a low rent. Eclo would need an additional equity investor to provide £100,000 for the installation of environmentally-friendly printing machines. Eve wants to acquire technology to allow clients to connect directly to Eclo's printing operation using an app so that they can upload their logos and designs and place orders without the need for Eclo's intervention.

Ethical issue: wastewater contamination

One of the Indian suppliers (AMG) makes garments for several companies, not all of which conform to the certification standard used by Eclo. Toxic wastewater from AMG's factory has been discharged, untreated, into the nearby river causing a severe impact on aquatic life and plants.

AMG has emailed Eclo to inform it about the incident, which arose during a production run for a high-fashion retailer. The contamination has not yet been made public, however AMG intends to publish an honest and open apology next week and to make appropriate compensation payments. AMG has asked Eclo to keep this information confidential until it has had a chance to publish all the facts.

Eclo's marketing manager wants to avoid any bad publicity. "Our products do not use any toxic chemical dyes so this issue cannot be anything to do with us. I think we should cancel our contract with AMG immediately. We should also make a public statement now, before the news comes out, explaining the contamination was not our responsibility. We can name the high-fashion retailer as the culprit. That way our reputation should remain intact."

Requirements

56.1 Discuss whether Eclo operates with a flexible organisational structure. Refer to relevant models.

(7 marks)

56.2 Assume that Eclo continues with its existing supply chain arrangements in India.

Discuss the control procedures that can be used to ensure suppliers are compliant with Eclo's sustainability processes and to monitor the quality of their output. **(9 marks)**

56.3 Explain the strategic and financial considerations that will determine whether Eclo should bring its supply chain to the UK and whether to invest in an in-house printing operation. **(12 marks)**

56.4 Discuss any ethical issues arising for Eclo as a result of the wastewater contamination and the proposals made by Eclo's marketing manager. Advise Eve on appropriate actions. **(8 marks)**

Total: 36 marks

57 Gighay Ltd

Gighay Ltd (Gighay) is a technology company which provides managed services to small and medium-sized enterprises (SMEs) in respect of information technology (IT). It specialises in creating flexible, cost-effective managed IT service solutions for its clients. Gighay's promise is "to enable you to make the best use of IT in your business, whatever your size, whatever your budget".

Gighay employs a team of technical experts with industry-accredited IT qualifications. It has strategic alliances with leading hardware and software providers. As a result, Gighay has access to the latest technological developments, and knowledge and experience in a range of IT specialisms. It has particular expertise in data capture and data analytics.

Gighay's managed IT services are provided by a 24-hour team which is based at its operations centre. Gighay monitors the configuration, availability and performance of client systems and applications from the same centre. It holds regular service review meetings and all clients receive a monthly reporting pack with tailored key performance indicators (KPIs).

Gighay has been approached by two potential clients, Oxna Ltd (Oxna) and Feltar Ltd (Feltar).

Oxna

Oxna is a publishing business. Many of Oxna's employees work remotely in different countries and time zones. They depend on being able to connect to Oxna's network, 24 hours a day. Oxna's business is growing rapidly and the demands on its systems are increasing. On two occasions recently, Oxna's server has crashed. This caused periods of costly downtime and required Oxna to pay for expensive emergency support. It appears that one of these incidents was the result of a targeted attack by a hacker who used malicious software to disrupt the company's systems. Oxna is therefore increasingly worried about cyber-security. It has limited in-house IT expertise and is considering whether to use Gighay's managed IT services. Oxna's operations director has asked for a document which sets out the benefits of outsourcing management of all its IT needs to Gighay and explains how Gighay will manage the service contract between itself and Oxna.

Feltar

Feltar sells speciality coffee in two forms, whole-bean and ground coffee, to individual consumers and independent cafes. It currently makes online sales via a basic website. When placing an order, customers are required to provide limited details, including their name, address, contact and payment details. Feltar's managing director has approached Gighay for advice: "One of our employees tells me that we should be making more use of social media. He also says we could use big data and data analytics to direct our marketing efforts better and to determine inventory and pricing strategies. I am not sure I even understand what big data is, let alone how we could use it to our competitive advantage. And as a small business, I am concerned about the practical implications for us of capturing and using more data about customers".

Requirements

In response to the requests by Gighay's potential clients:

57.1 Explain the benefits and problems for Oxna of outsourcing all of its IT needs to Gighay and suggest some KPIs that could be included in the service contract between the companies. **(11 marks)**

57.2 Explain how Feltar can use data analytics to achieve competitive advantage. Address the managing director's concerns about the practical implications of implementing a big data strategy. **(9 marks)**

Total: 20 marks

58 Holidays Direct plc

The date is June 20X7.

Holidays Direct plc (HD) is a UK-based, online holiday company which sells package holidays to locations outside the UK, directly to UK consumers.

The package holiday industry

Package holiday companies arrange both accommodation (ie, hotel stays) and flights, then sell these together as holiday packages. Sales are made either directly to consumers or through travel agents acting as intermediaries.

Most package holiday companies do not own aircraft or hotels. Instead, they enter into block contracts to purchase flights and hotel stays in advance from airlines and hotel operators.

In relation to flights, the package holiday company charters entire aircraft for return flights to and from a pre-agreed destination airport at a pre-agreed time. The package holiday company then sells individual seats as return flights to consumers as part of the holiday package.

The increasing use of the internet has made holiday package companies' marketing more effective, including the use of mobile devices and social media.

Company background

Company history and development

HD was established a number of years ago in the UK as an online holiday company selling holiday packages to mainland Europe, direct to UK consumers.

In 20X2, HD acquired another UK online holiday company, Helio Ltd, which sold holiday packages to worldwide destinations. Helio's European activities were quickly integrated into HD's operations, forming the European Division. Helio's operations outside Europe formed a separate Worldwide Division within HD.

In the year ended 31 May 20X6, demand was low and HD's financial performance was poor. The CEO was removed in November 20X6 and a new CEO, Oliver Orrs, was appointed in April 20X7.

The year ended 31 May 20X7 was an unexpectedly good year for HD with high demand, which exceeded forecasts.

Sales and bookings

All HD bookings are made online directly by consumers. Each booking combines return flight seats plus hotel stays (averaging one week) under a single contract for a group of two or more people. HD does not sell flight seats and hotel stays separately. Bookings can be made many months in advance, but can also be made just a few days before departure.

Flights

HD charters flights from three different airlines. Two of these airlines serve only European destination airports and one operates worldwide. Each destination airport may serve a number of different holiday sites. The fee paid by HD for each chartered flight is the same no matter how many seats are occupied on the flight.

HD agrees the number, dates and destination airports of chartered flights for the year with each airline under one large annual contract (block contract). Block contracts, which are binding, are entered into for an entire calendar year in September of the previous year. The capacity of the flights, timings and destination airports are based on HD's estimates of demand from consumers for each destination airport.

HD offers late discounts on its website to attract last-minute bookings from consumers where there are unsold seats. If HD overestimates demand for a destination airport, then some seats on some flights may remain unoccupied despite such discounts.

If HD underestimates demand for a destination airport, then it may charter some additional flights from airlines, but at a much higher price than the original block contract price.

Harriet Hubber is the manager for HD's flight chartering. She reports to the head of HD's European Division regarding European flights, and to the head of HD's Worldwide Division regarding non-European flights.

Hotels

HD purchases hotel stays from 84 different hotel operators at holiday sites throughout the world. Most of the hotel operators own hotels both in Europe and the rest of the world.

Typically, HD signs block contracts with each hotel up to three years ahead, to secure an appropriate number and type of bedroom accommodation (hotel stays). These are based on HD's estimates of demand from consumers for each holiday site.

The block contracts are binding and the full price must be paid by HD, whether or not it eventually sells the hotel stays in the block contracts to consumers.

HD offers late discounts to attract consumers if it has overestimated demand for a particular hotel. If it has underestimated demand, HD tries to purchase additional hotel stays, often at a higher cost.

Penny Price is the manager for hotels. She reports to the head of HD's European Division regarding European hotels, and to the head of HD's Worldwide Division regarding non-European hotels.

Challenges identified by the new CEO

Following his initial assessment of the company, Oliver Orrs required data to be collected and analysed to support his strategic and operational decisions. Some limited initial information has been prepared (**Exhibit**).

Oliver believes that HD's current organisational structure of two divisions, European and Worldwide, is not promoting operational efficiency. Therefore, he is considering making changes to the organisational structure.

A critical success factor for HD is matching actual consumer bookings with the block contracts made in advance to purchase flights and hotel stays. Oliver is concerned about the scale of the variances between HD's estimates and actual demand. He wants to understand the possible consequences in financial terms and wishes to mitigate this operating risk.

Ethical issue

Penny Price made the following comments, in confidence, to Harriet Hubber:

Penny said: "HD has a contract with a global car rental business to promote their car hire as an additional service to consumers. HD receives a commission on each car rental contract that our consumers book. However, I am concerned that consumers are being overcharged.

"I have a friend who operates a small car rental firm in Spain and I have told just a few consumers that it would be cheaper for them to hire through his company, rather than the car rental company that HD promotes. I have not taken any money for doing this."

Requirements

58.1 Use the quantitative data in the Exhibit and the other information provided to:

(a) Evaluate HD's operating and financial performance in the year ended 31 May 20X7, comparing it with the year ended 31 May 20X6, identifying any key further information required; and

(b) Explain the operating and financial risks which arise for HD from the potential differences in quantities between:

- The number of flights and hotel stays that have been acquired through the block contracts; and

- Demand from consumers. **(19 marks)**

58.2 Explain how monitoring the use of its website by consumers may help HD estimate future demand.
(8 marks)

58.3 Critically appraise HD's current organisational structure. Explain and justify a revised structure.
(9 marks)

58.4 Explain the ethical issues that arise for HD and Penny from the matters in Penny Price's comments. Set out the actions that should be taken by Harriet Hubber.
(8 marks)

Total: 44 marks

Exhibit: Financial and operating data for years ended 31 May

Revenue	20X6	20X7
European destinations (£'000s)	348,000	360,000
Worldwide destinations (£'000s)	148,000	184,000
Total (£'000s)	496,000	544,000
Other financial data		
Value of discounts given to consumers (£'000s)	14,880	5,440
Cost of additional flights and hotel stays purchased by HD outside block contracts (£'000s)	4,960	27,200
Number of bookings by consumers		
European destinations ('000s)	290	300
Worldwide destinations ('000s)	74	92
Total ('000s)	364	392
Operating data		
Average time of booking by consumer before departure (days)	87	76
Number of hotel stays booked by consumers ('000s)	473	470
Number of return flight seats booked by consumers ('000s)	1,092	1,176
Number of block contract hotel stays left unoccupied ('000s)	14.2	4.7
Number of block contract flight seats left unoccupied ('000s)	32.8	11.8
Website data		
Number of website visits (000s)	6,916	8,624

Definition of terms

Bookings by consumers – a booking is when a person (representing a group of two or more people) enters into a single contract for a holiday package which includes flight seats and hotel stays for everyone in the group.

Cost of additional bookings – this is the price paid by HD to make late purchases of whole flights and hotel stays in addition to block contracts.

Hotel stay – this is one bedroom, irrespective of the number of occupants. Hotel stays average one week.

Return flight seat – this is one return flight per person.

Value of discounts given to consumers – these are the discounts given to consumers in order to make late sales of unsold flight seats and hotel stays.

Website visits – a visit to the website is counted each time a consumer accesses any part of the HD website.

59   Jason Smyth Textiles Ltd

The date is June 20X7.

Jason Smyth Textiles Ltd (JST) is a manufacturer of soft furnishings including bedding, cushions and curtains.

Company background

The entire ordinary share capital of JST is owned by Jason Smyth.

A number of years ago Jason established JST and immediately acquired a factory, located in the UK, and good quality machinery at low cost from the liquidator of another company.

JST's business model has been one of cost leadership. Jason personally maintains strict operational and financial control over all the company's activities in order to minimise costs.

Price competition throughout the supply chain is intense. Whilst design and quality are important, contracts are frequently won and lost on the basis of price. JST makes sales to low-price soft furnishings retailers throughout the UK.

The main raw material used by JST is polyester, which is a cheap synthetic fabric. Polyester is imported by JST from a small number of suppliers located in developing nations. JST uses only a few suppliers to obtain larger quantity discounts and to increase the efficiency of its procurement system. It is the responsibility of suppliers to arrange delivery directly to JST's factory. The fabric purchased by JST is of basic quality, but it is fit for the purpose of manufacturing soft furnishings for JST's customers.

The labour-intensive manufacturing process involves colouring, processing and cutting the raw material polyester fabric, before making it into soft furnishings designed by JST. The colouring and design are particular features of JST products that have enabled the company to distinguish its products from those of competitors.

JST uses its own lorries for distribution to customers. It is a low-cost service which operates efficiently using an information technology (IT) system to schedule and control deliveries.

Ordering of raw materials and the scheduling of deliveries are controlled centrally by skilled employees using the company's IT systems. This permits strict inventory control. The large overall quantity of raw materials ordered by JST from each supplier enables it to impose a just-in-time inventory system.

JST managers take a strict approach to staff discipline, especially regarding customer complaints. Some training is provided for skilled staff, but little for unskilled staff.

Financing and marketing support is provided by skilled JST staff, again using the company's IT systems. This includes providing and administering credit facilities for customers. A strict 30-day credit policy is applied. Marketing is mainly through customer relationship management using captured data on each retailer customer.

Competition and pressures on costs

There has been a long-term trend for soft furnishings to be manufactured in developing nations using low cost production and locally produced fabrics. These goods are imported into the UK, and other developed countries, and sold at prices which undercut JST's prices.

The machinery that Jason originally acquired from the liquidator has given JST a cost advantage. However, it is now nearing the end of its useful life so it is becoming unreliable. As a result, an increasing number of defects have been found in batches of production. JST always replaces such items for its customers.

In the year ended 31 May 20X7, JST made an operating loss. Two factors have been identified which suggest that costs will rise in future and, as a result, financial performance is expected to worsen:

(1)   The legal minimum wage in the UK has recently increased and will further increase in the next few years. 75% of JST's staff are unskilled and paid the current legal minimum wage. Skilled staff are paid a little above the legal minimum wage. Staff turnover is high, but there is high local unemployment, so finding replacement employees is not difficult.

(2)   A fall in the value of sterling, compared with many currencies, has meant that the cost of fabric imported by JST has increased in sterling terms.

A proposed new business model

The JST board believes that the company's cost leadership position is no longer sustainable. It has proposed changing the company's strategic direction with a new business model. This involves a move upmarket by producing better quality soft furnishings in a new range of fabrics. The company will mainly use natural fabrics including cotton, wool, linen and silk. It will still use some polyester fabric, but this will be better quality than the type currently used.

The new business model will require transformational change. It will include replacing most of the old machinery and increasing automation, so new management roles and reporting structures will be needed. The model is planned to be introduced on 1 January 20X8.

Fewer unskilled staff will be needed and so many of these employees will be made redundant. Skilled staff will be retrained to upgrade and adapt their skills. There will also be recruitment of new staff with specialist skills more relevant to automated production.

Requirements

59.1 Write a report to the JST board in which you:

   (a) Draw a value chain diagram for JST's existing business model and include brief descriptions of each of JST's relevant activities in the diagram.

   (b) Explain how the elements of JST's value chain support its current low cost strategy.

   Ignore the proposed new business model. **(19 marks)**

59.2 With respect to JST's proposed new business model:

   (a) Describe its benefits and problems, and make a reasoned recommendation as to whether JST should implement the new business model; and

   (b) Explain the change management issues for JST. **(14 marks)**

Total: 33 marks

60 Portland Prawns Ltd

The date is June 20X7.

Portland Prawns Ltd (PP) processes high-quality fresh prawns and sells them to upmarket restaurants.

Company background

PP owns a processing and packaging factory in Scotland, about 750 kilometres north of London. It purchases high-quality, freshly caught prawns from a small number of suppliers located at fishing ports in Scotland.

The prawns are processed, packaged and delivered fresh to customers throughout the UK within 24 hours of being caught.

In recent years, PP's annual sales have been constant at 400,000 kilos, priced at £10 per kilo. This level of production is 80% of the factory's operating capacity.

The budgeted performance of PP for the year ending 30 June 20X8 is as follows:

	£'000	£'000
Revenue		4,000
Production costs:		
Variable	1,800	
Fixed	1,000	
		(2,800)
Variable distribution costs		(400)
Fixed administration expenses		(200)
Operating profit		600

Proposed new contract

Finlay's Finest Fish Ltd (FFF) is a chain of large, upmarket fish shops based in and around London.

FFF has offered PP a one-year contract, from 1 July 20X7, to supply FFF with frozen prawns. The following terms are not negotiable:

- Selling price per kilo will be £8.

- A minimum of 150,000 kilos will be supplied in the year, but up to 200,000 kilos in total must be supplied by PP if FFF requests this amount.

- The quality must be at least equal to that now being supplied to PP's existing customers, but prawns must be frozen rather than fresh.

- FFF will collect the frozen prawns from the PP factory, so there will be no incremental distribution costs incurred by PP.

- Large financial penalties will apply if the contract conditions are not satisfied.

- FFF has the option, but not the obligation, to renew the contract for a further year from 1 July 20X8 on the same terms. The contract may be renewed yet again on 1 July 20X9 on terms to be agreed between the two parties at the appropriate time.

- PP will be FFF's sole supplier of frozen prawns.

Variable production costs per kilo will not change in the next three years, with or without the new FFF contract. All annual fixed costs will remain the same in future if the new FFF contract is rejected, but will increase by £420,000 from 1 July 20X7 as a result of accepting the FFF contract in order to acquire and operate freezing facilities.

Market research

New market research has determined the following demand schedule from PP's existing customers (ie, excluding FFF) for the year ending 30 June 20X8:

Selling price	£10.00	£10.50	£11.00
Sales volume (kilos)	400,000	350,000	300,000

New capacity – a possible rental agreement

PP has the opportunity to sign a three-year rental agreement for an additional local factory, including machinery. The rental agreement would commence on 1 July 20X7 and would give PP annual processing capacity for an extra 150,000 kilos of prawns. The annual rental cost is £65,000.

Requirements

60.1 Determine the maximum operating profit achievable by PP for the year ending 30 June 20X8 under each of the following alternative assumptions:

(a) The FFF contract is rejected.

(b) The FFF contract is accepted and FFF demand in the year ending 30 June 20X8 is 150,000 kilos.

(c) The FFF contract is accepted and FFF demand in the year ending 30 June 20X8 is 200,000 kilos.

Advise PP's board on whether the new FFF contract should be accepted, considering all relevant factors. Ignore the rental agreement. **(15 marks)**

60.2 Explain, with supporting calculations, whether PP should sign the rental agreement. Assume that the FFF contract has been accepted. **(8 marks)**

Total: 23 marks

61 Blakes Blinds Ltd

The date is September 20X7.

Blakes Blinds Ltd (BB) manufactures and installs high-quality door and window blinds for the corporate market.

Customers

BB's customers are UK-based. They include restaurant chains, hospitals, educational establishments and owners of commercial buildings. BB undertakes one-off contracts but also has repeat business with existing customers who refurbish their premises or re-locate. BB acts as sub-contractor to several large building firms for the installation of blinds in new-build developments.

Competitive strategy

The blinds market is divided into domestic and commercial segments. It is dominated by a small number of key companies, with large marketing budgets, who compete aggressively on price. The rest of the market is fragmented. Smaller operators, like BB, often focus on one market segment or one geographical area.

Most companies that sell blinds buy low-cost, finished products from Asia and sell them to UK customers. However BB manufactures all its own products in its UK factory, based in Lemchester, which allows it to control quality. BB purchases over 60% of its components from China, mostly from one supplier, Ren Xiao Ltd (RX), with whom it has a good trading relationship.

BB offers a wide range of blinds for the control of light, heat and privacy, with a complete service from design to installation. When a customer makes an enquiry, BB carries out a site survey to advise on the best option for the customer's individual requirements. BB's blinds are then made to measure. The service is tailored to take into account customer needs in relation to delivery dates, installation times and specific budgets. Once the blinds have been manufactured, they are installed by a team of specialist fitters, who are all employed by BB.

Blinds are often subject to high usage and can therefore be damaged easily. After installation, BB offers customers the option to pay for a service contract with a three-year warranty on all components. The price of the service contract depends on the quantity and type of blinds installed. Under the service contract, BB checks all operating mechanisms on each anniversary of the initial installation. Damaged components are replaced free of charge within the three-year warranty period, but are chargeable to the customer thereafter. Service contracts help to tie customers into BB and most customers extend their contracts beyond the initial warranty period. As a result, where repairs and upgrades are necessary, BB is likely to be asked to undertake them.

In January 20X5 BB launched its innovative 'Auto-Close' system. This allows blinds to be operated by remote control or by using an app on a smartphone or tablet. The system's motorised technology can be fitted as part of an initial installation of new blinds or fitted to a customer's existing blinds, even if they were originally installed by another company. Auto- Close has proved very popular with corporate customers who need to respond quickly to changes in light and weather conditions, to maintain constant internal temperatures and to reduce energy consumption. Since BB introduced Auto-Close, several competitors have launched similar products. The only intellectual property right that BB has protected is the use of the Auto-Close brand name.

Financial performance

As a result of introducing Auto-Close, BB achieved high revenue growth in 20X6. However, the board was disappointed that, although selling prices were relatively constant, the operating profit was lower than in 20X5. Extracts from the most recent management accounts, including key performance indicators and the 20X7 budget, are provided (**Exhibit**). The board would like to understand how profitability to date has been affected by the performance of each of BB's three main revenue streams:

(1)   Blinds
(2)   Auto-Close systems
(3)   Service contracts

Possible acquisition of supplier

BB is considering the acquisition of its major Chinese supplier, RX. The board believes that eliminating the margins currently paid to RX may help improve profitability. If the acquisition goes ahead, RX's business would be operated as the component division of BB and would supply all the required components to BB's manufacturing division. In addition BB's board hopes that the acquisition will give it an opportunity to start selling blinds in Asia, by using the local knowledge and contacts of RX.

Grant application

Lemchester City Council has recently made grants available to help revive the area's manufacturing industries. Grants will be awarded to businesses which provide local employment and also have an entirely local supply chain. BB's Managing Director (MD) has told the Financial Controller to apply for a grant and to certify on the form that BB fulfils all the application criteria. The MD's justification is that all BB's blinds are manufactured locally. The Financial Controller, a qualified ICAEW Chartered Accountant, is concerned that BB does not meet the grant conditions because it buys components from China.

Requirements

61.1 Identify the factors that have contributed to BB's competitive advantage and assess the extent to which this is likely to be sustainable.
(7 marks)

61.2 Using the data in the Exhibit and the other information provided, analyse BB's financial performance to:

- explain the key reasons for the differences in performance between 20X5 and 20X6
- assess the likelihood of achieving the 20X7 budget, highlighting any areas of concern.

Identify specific further information that would assist your analysis.
(20 marks)

61.3 In relation to the proposal to acquire RX:

- Discuss the advantages and disadvantages of the acquisition.

- Assuming the acquisition takes place, briefly explain the factors that should be considered in determining transfer prices between BB's new component division and its manufacturing division.
(11 marks)

61.4 Discuss the ethical issues arising for BB and the Financial Controller as a result of the grant application, and recommend appropriate actions.
(7 marks)

Total: 45 marks

Exhibit: Extracts from BB's management accounts

Summary of financial performance (£'000)

| | Actual results | | 6 months to | Budget |
| | Year ended 31 December | | 30 June | Year ending 31 December |
	20X5	20X6	20X7	20X7
Revenue	10,530	16,460	10,370	24,165
Cost of sales	5,980	9,790	6,225	14,260
Gross profit	4,550	6,670	4,145	9,905
Fixed costs	4,133	6,260	3,694	6,970
Operating profit	417	410	451	2,935

Note: Cost of sales consists of labour and components. It includes the cost of components bought from China and invoiced in Chinese yuan renminbi (CNY). Actual costs have been translated into sterling (£) at the appropriate exchange rate:

Components bought from China	Year ended 31 December		6 months to 30 June
	20X5	20X6	20X7
Actual cost (CNY'000)	19,616	26,456	16,123
Actual cost (£'000)	2,060	3,043	1,935

Analysis of sales and gross profit by revenue stream

Year ended 31 December 20X5	Blinds £'000	Auto-Close systems £'000	Service contracts £'000
Revenue	7,660	560	2,310
Gross profit	2,756	252	1,542
20X6			
Revenue	10,299	2,869	3,292
Gross profit	3,055	1,411	2,204

Key performance indicators	Year ended 31 December	
	20X5	20X6
Gross profit margin	43.2%	40.5%
Operating profit margin	4.0%	2.5%
Revenue growth	6.7%	56.3%
Warranty costs as % of cost of sales	5.0%	8.0%
Research and development costs as % of revenue	9.8%	5.1%

62 Air Services UK Ltd

Air Services UK Ltd (ASU) is responsible for providing airspace management services to all airports and aircraft using UK airspace.

Company ownership

The company was originally a non-profit making government body. However, a number of years ago it was established as a limited company. ASU is 49% owned by the UK government and 51% privately owned. Private shareholders include several UK-based airlines and ASU staff. In the interests of national security, the government intends to retain its shareholding for the foreseeable future.

Operations

ASU's airspace management services comprise:

- **Air traffic control**

  ASU staff manage take-offs, landings and traffic in and around each UK airport. This is done from a control tower located at each airport.

- **In-flight navigation services**

  ASU is responsible for authorising access to all UK airspace and providing in-flight navigational guidance for aircraft over the UK. This is handled at ASU's two operational centres in the UK.

ASU's activities in the UK are licensed and regulated by the Civil Aviation Authority (CAA). The CAA ensures that the UK aviation industry treats consumers fairly, meets the highest safety and security standards and complies with environmental targets. The CAA, with the UK government, has committed to reducing aviation emissions.

ASU operates as a commercial company. It charges fees to the airports for managing their air traffic and to the airlines for its in-flight navigation services. Since ASU is in a monopoly situation, the CAA sets limits on the fees that ASU can charge.

Human resources

ASU operates 24 hours a day, 365 days of the year. The company employs 6,000 people comprising air traffic controllers, analysts, researchers and support staff. The majority were appointed when ASU was still a government body and have long-standing employment contracts. Up to 2,000 senior employees are expected to retire over the next 10 years (half of ASU's analysts and a third of its air traffic controllers).

Information technology

Timely and accurate management of data and information is vital for airports, airlines and air traffic control. Air traffic control systems are complex, integrating many diverse technologies, components and data. Technological developments play a key role in allowing the airline industry to meet operational efficiency and environmental targets.

Airports want to increase their capacity to handle flights, whilst maintaining safety and reducing operating costs and emissions. Airlines face high costs which are increased if there are flight delays and flight inefficiency. Effective air traffic control systems help airlines and airports to reduce costs by improving runway usage, reducing delays for inbound and outbound aircraft and designing more efficient flight routes. This also reduces the levels of emissions.

ASU has invested heavily in technology to allow better sharing of information. ASU's IT systems are connected across a wide range of organisations in different countries, with many users having real-time access. This enables controllers to manage high volumes of aircraft safely in crowded airspace, but presents increased cyber-security risks.

Through investment in research and development, ASU has developed expertise in managing unmanned aircraft systems (drones). Drones can pose a threat to air traffic management. ASU's innovative cloud-based system analyses all available real-time data to authorise a drone's flight plans. It monitors the drone in-flight and sends out electronic commands, where necessary, to redirect the drone or make it land immediately.

Suspected cyber-security incident

Recently there was a suspected hacking incident at one of ASU's operational centres. This occurred during a technical upgrade of the system responsible for airspace monitoring and aircraft control. ASU immediately shut down the system and implemented its business continuity plan. However, 300 flights were cancelled and 1,500 were delayed. After the incident, the CAA made ASU pay £7 million compensation to the airports and airlines affected.

A new global vision

Since the suspected cyber-security incident, ASU has appointed a new Chief Executive, Joan Louli. Joan previously led Germany's state-owned traffic control operation. She is keen to develop international revenue streams for ASU. Her stated vision is for ASU to become "the global leader in innovative airspace management."

Joan has set out the following three-year goals for the company:

- Achieve business growth by diversification
- Reduce the risk of accidents linked to airspace management
- Reduce emissions arising from inefficient airspace management
- Increase the efficiency of ASU's internal operations.

Joan has identified two specific international growth opportunities:

European airspace reorganisation

An agreement has been signed to reorganise Europe's airspace into nine blocks. ASU has been invited to tender to manage airspace within one or more of the blocks. Airspace management in most European countries is currently provided by state-owned operations. Joan believes that ASU's public-private ownership gives it a competitive advantage. Contracts will be awarded via a competitive tender process, based on four key criteria: safety, cost-efficiency, capacity management and environmental impact.

Drone traffic management

ASU has been asked to tender for a contract with the government of a Middle Eastern country to implement a drone traffic management service. ASU was approached after an incident involving a drone which closed the country's main airport for an hour.

Joan believes that ASU's ability to grow will depend on its information systems, its people and its ability to innovate. She wants to ensure that ASU has the right functional strategies in place to win the tenders and deliver these new contracts.

Requirements

62.1 Analyse the extent to which the three-year goals set out by Joan Louli are consistent with both her stated vision for ASU and the objectives of ASU's key stakeholders. **(10 marks)**

62.2 Explain the following two functional strategies that ASU could implement to achieve Joan Louli's stated vision:

- Human Resources (HR); and
- Research and Development (R&D). **(10 marks)**

62.3 Explain the cyber-security risks that ASU faces and how these risks can be managed. **(9 marks)**

Total: 29 marks

63 Purechoc Ltd

Purechoc Ltd (Purechoc) is a family-owned business that makes premium chocolates and chocolate bars, on a small scale for a niche market. It was established three years ago by Marine Bernard and her brother Thomas. Purechoc has four UK shops, each managed by a member of the Bernard family, who are all directors (see **Exhibit**). Purechoc's share capital is owned as follows:

Marine	35%
Thomas	35%
Jonathan (Thomas's son)	15%
Anne (Marine's daughter)	15%

Over 80% of chocolate products sold in the UK are made by three dominant confectionery producers. Some of these businesses have attracted adverse publicity recently due to the way they source their cocoa and their treatment of cocoa producers in the supply chain. This has created an opportunity for businesses like Purechoc to exploit growing niche markets.

All Purechoc products are hand-made at each shop and are available in a wide range of exotic flavours. Instead of making products from pre-processed cocoa, Purechoc starts with high-quality, fair-trade cocoa beans from a single country of origin.

Purechoc sells only to individuals and not to supermarkets or other retailers. Its products are priced at about three times the price of standard chocolate confectionery. Purechoc shops have a loyal following of local customers, although Purechoc has done no marketing. It relies instead on word-of-mouth to generate business.

A large, American confectionery manufacturer, Koreto Inc (Koreto), has recently offered to acquire the entire share capital of Purechoc. Koreto's products are very popular in the USA but relatively unknown in the UK, and Koreto wants to enter the UK confectionery market. Marine Bernard is unwell and wishes to reduce her role in the business. As a result she wants to accept Koreto's offer for her shares.

If its offer is accepted, Koreto has promised that Purechoc will keep its brand identity and that the current board can run it as a semi-autonomous subsidiary. Koreto will provide funds to allow Purechoc to expand the number of shops. However, one of the terms of the offer is that Koreto would appoint a new Chief Executive to run Purechoc.

Jonathan and Anne do not want to sell their shares. However they recognise that opening four shops in three years has created a cashflow constraint. They have put forward an alternative proposal to resolve the constraint whilst retaining control of the growth of the business. This would involve expanding the number of shops by offering exclusive franchise agreements. Each franchisee would have the right to operate a Purechoc shop, and would be provided with the recipes to make and sell Purechoc products.

Purechoc would receive an upfront franchise fee and commission based on sales revenue generated. Thomas however is concerned that franchising will destroy the unique and personal image of the Purechoc brand.

Requirements

Prepare a report for the directors that will help them to evaluate the two alternative proposals for the future of the Purechoc business: the sale of shares to Koreto Inc and the expansion by franchising.

Use the following headings:

63.1 Control
63.2 Risks
63.3 Strategic fit
63.4 Preliminary advice   **Total: 26 marks**

Exhibit: Directors and shareholders

- Marine (aged 58)

  Marine was the driving force behind setting up Purechoc. The business is currently her sole source of income and the proceeds from the sale of her shares in Purechoc will be her main source of funds in future.

- Thomas (aged 50)

  Thomas is married to a wealthy landowner and was happy to help provide initial capital for Marine to set up Purechoc. Thomas does not need income. He works in the business because of his family loyalty and his passion for Purechoc's products.

- Jonathan (aged 27)

  Jonathan joined Purechoc after completing a degree in business. He is entrepreneurial and has ambitious plans to create a larger, more successful business.

- Anne (aged 30)

  Before joining Purechoc, Anne worked for a large catering business but left because she wanted to be her own boss. She relies on the business as her main source of income.

Answer Bank

Guidance on mark plans

Introduction

This guidance has been put together by the examining team. It is possible, over time, as a result of candidates' performance in the real exams, that there may be further developments in the way in which mark plans are constructed. A document such as this can only ever provide broad guidance. The examining team set mark plans for each question on an individual basis, taking account of the overall structure of the question, the scenario, and the complexity of the analysis and argument required.

Marking documents

Business Strategy and Technology has one of the highest skills content of all the Professional Stage papers as it leads on to the Technical Integration and Case Study papers. This is reflected in the marking process where the available marks for each requirement are divided into two pools: Knowledge marks (K) and Skills marks (S), with more marks awarded for skills than knowledge.

For any particular exam paper there are three separate marking documents:

- A detailed mark plan for the paper (a full answer, containing all the likely points that candidates may make, as published for students)

- A marking grid which breaks the paper down into the K and S mark pools available for each requirement

- A separate marking guidance document issued to markers, giving an overview of the typical K and S points for each requirement, to be used in conjunction with the detailed mark plan

The marking grid and marking guidance for the December 2014 paper are included in Chapter 1 of the Study Manual.

Knowledge and skills marks

Broadly speaking, the K marks are for demonstration of appropriate and accurate knowledge and understanding from the learning materials, explicit or implied (eg, where the answer is developed using recognised models, tools and frameworks, not just common sense).

The S marks are for:

- Assimilating and using information
- Structuring problems and solutions
- Applying judgement
- Conclusions and recommendations
- Communication

For example, if the requirement was to 'analyse the competitive forces within an industry' then K marks would be available for selecting the right model and knowing the meaning of the key headings, in this case that 'competitive forces' suggests Porter's Five Forces model should be applied.

S marks would be gained for example by:

- Applying a model to the context in the question, eg, identifying relevant information from the scenario

- Analysing the information, eg, identifying causal factors that explain changes in data

- Reasoning and judgement, eg, providing reasoned advice relating to the specific terms of the scenario

The marking information set out below is used to mark the questions.

Allocation of marks

Typically it is not possible to allocate a half/one mark per point as it is in the more numerical papers. This type of approach would encourage a scatter-gun approach and reward answers making a long list of minor points, even where they fail to identify and explain the key issues.

Marks are therefore awarded in small pools which attempt to give an assessment of a candidate's performance for each sub-set of a requirement. Markers are encouraged to use discretion and to award partial marks where a point was either not explained fully or made by implications.

It is often the case that the more succinct answers are better, since it is the quality rather than the number of points which attracts marks in Business Strategy and Technology.

As a general rule, the mark plan is constructed according to the following principles:

- **Numerical elements**

    Where the requirement includes a specific calculation, the total marks available will be broken down into a series of computations for the components of the calculation. Marks will be awarded for workings and not just for the correct final figure. Additional marks will be available for stating assumptions.

- **Data interpretation/analysis**

    Specific marks for any necessary calculations/numerical analysis will be awarded as for numerical elements above. Also, however, appropriate calculations will need to be identified by the candidate and marks will be awarded for addressing the key issues.

    A greater proportion of the total marks available will be awarded for the following skills:

    – Interpretation of data (both qualitative and quantitative)
    – Considering cause and effect relationships
    – Identifying implications of the analysis
    – And for linking the data analysis to the wider strategy or issue in the scenario

    In these respects 'making the numbers talk' will be a key feature.

    Additional marks will be awarded for highlighting additional information required and/or the limitations of the analysis undertaken, even if not specifically asked for (although this may form part of the requirement).

- **Use of specific theories/models**

    Requirements will generally be open ended and candidates may be expected to identify the appropriate model to use in a particular situation. For example, a requirement to analyse the ways in which the business has grown might be answered by considering Ansoff and Lynch.

    Where a requirement calls for the application of a particular theory or model, there will be a limited number of knowledge marks for identifying the correct model and explaining its use. A greater proportion of the total marks will be awarded for the skills shown in applying the model to the scenario and discussing its limitations in the particular context.

- **Written elements**

    Each component of the requirement will be assigned a 'pool' of marks. An element of the marks in the pool will be available for demonstrating the correct knowledge but the majority will then be awarded to a candidate based on the degree of application, analysis and judgement demonstrated by the answer. Thus it is possible to identify the characteristics of various possible answers, together with their mark scoring potential:

    (a) Generic comments from the learning materials, which are not expressed in the context of the scenario. Answer includes lists of unprioritised, undeveloped and/or irrelevant points. Points listed but not explained.

    This constitutes a poor answer, scoring less than half the marks available in the pool and hence a 'fail' on the particular section of the requirement.

(b) A number of generic comments but with some attempt to apply knowledge to the scenario in the question and to link points together in the form of key issues.

An adequate attempt, scoring a little over half the marks available in the pool normally generating sufficient marks to attain a marginal pass.

(c) Succinct points, made in the context of the question with little irrelevant comment. Some insights demonstrated. Logical argument backed up by analysis of the data/scenario. Demonstrates judgement by providing clear recommendations or advice where required by the question.

A high scoring answer which would be awarded the majority of marks available in the pool (in some cases the maximum) and achieve a clear pass.

Presentation marks and workings

Generally, where specifically requested in the requirement, one knowledge mark would be awarded for presentation of a report/memo/briefing notes in an appropriate format.

Headroom

As can be seen from the sample paper and previous real exam papers, all written questions contain a degree of 'headroom' (ie, potentially there are more marks available than the maximum for the requirement), as a range of different answers are possible. For example, the requirement totals, say, 20 marks, but the mark plan contains a total of, say, 25 marks. This means that a candidate could, in fact, score 100% without producing an ideal answer.

The published answers are detailed mark **plans** and are designed to encompass many possible valid comments that a marker may see. As a result they are often more detailed than even a strong candidate would give in his or her answer.

Mark plans in the learning materials

The summary mark plans in the learning materials have been reviewed by the examining team.

However, tutors should bear in mind that the mark plans in the learning materials have not undergone the full development process as those for the real exams where mark plans are tested over a large sample of candidates' answers.

Nonetheless, the above guidance can be illustrated by looking at the past real exam papers included in the question bank.

The mark scheme provided with each solution indicates relative emphasis of the sub-areas of the question.

Note: The marks awarded in the real paper may exceed these where the candidate's answers merit this.

1 DA plc (March 2008, amended)

Marking guide

	Knowledge	Skill	Marks
1.1 Factors creating competitive advantage	2	5	6
1.2 Analysis of strategic development	4	8	10
1.3 PESTEL analysis	2	7	8
1.4 Marketing strategy	2	7	8
1.5 Strategic and cyber security risks	2	7	8
	12	34	40

1.1 Factors creating competitive advantage

Competitive advantage is anything that gives one organisation an edge over its rivals. Critical success factors (CSFs) are the areas where an organisation must excel if it is to achieve sustainable competitive advantage. DA's critical success factors concern not only the resources of the business but how these can be used to advantage in the competitive environment in which it operates.

Here a key strategic resource is the possession of a licence to operate as a CRA. Complying with the terms of this licence is fundamental to DA's ability to continue in operation. Possession of the licence acts as a barrier to entry and while it does not give DA an advantage over CC Inc, it does protect its market share from new entrants.

DA may gain competitive advantage over CC Inc by virtue of being the only UK-based CRA.

According to the resource-based view of strategy, firms develop competencies and then exploit them. Sustainable competitive advantage is obtained by the exploitation of unique resources. Thus a firm should focus only on products where it has a sustainable competitive advantage and focus on core competences which competitors do not possess or would find it difficult to copy.

A threshold competence for CRAs is compliance with the relevant UK legislation, eg, consumers have specific rights in relation to the information CRAs hold about them. Complying with this and other relevant legislation is crucial to DA's business, as it is to the business of competitors. Going beyond mere compliance, eg, by extending its free advisory and education services may give DA a competitive advantage over CC Inc.

The key factors that appear to have given rise to DA's competitive advantage would include:

(1) First to market – DA began business a number of years ago and as one of the first to market, and a primary player, it has created a strong reputation and market dominance as a result of this.

(2) Scale – with 58% of the market there are scale economies in search costs and IT costs which would give DA an advantage over its main competitor and any potential entrants.

(3) Information and knowledge systems – DA's core competences are its ability to compile and manage vast quantities of data, and extract meaning from it. This has been achieved partly by the data analytics software that it developed in-house. This has helped to give DA 'the most comprehensive credit database in the UK'. It also maintains a large database for the automotive industry.

For competitive advantage DA must have superior skills in database management and data analytics:

• Continuous access to a wide range of data sources to ensure that the consumer profile or vehicle history is complete and accurate

- The ability to integrate vast quantities of information and organise it in a user friendly form
- Maintenance of up-to-date information that can be used by large credit providers to make enhanced decisions in 'real time'

(4) Product development skills/Innovation – DA have a core competence in helping businesses reduce risk. This is best illustrated by the development of data analytics software which has enabled DA to expand the products and services it offers and the markets it serves, eg, the development of the analytical decision business. The demand for this service is evident given the fact that a large number of financial institutions have expressed an interest in using this in recent months. By making this proprietary software, DA is able to protect their competitive position and prevent copying.

(5) Relationship management skills – DA's experience in personal selling has attracted business customers in the first instance. These customers have been retained through relationship management and by developing additional products to meet their risk management needs. As a result there is significant brand loyalty.

(6) Technical resources – DA's IT systems will be important in delivering an efficient service to customers, where customers will particularly value:

- Speed of processing
- Flexibility of delivery (online, phone etc)
- Confidentiality

(7) Organisation structure – DA has divisionalised by product or brand. This should facilitate communication and decision-making, at the level of the brand and allow a fast response to a rapidly changing market.

As a listed company DA will also have good access to finance.

1.2 Analysis of strategic development

The Ansoff model is a two-by-two matrix of Products (new and existing) and Markets (new and existing).

By relating product opportunities to markets, this mix identifies four broad alternative strategies open to DA.

Market penetration

This involves selling more of existing products to existing markets. This increases the organisation's market share. DA is the largest credit reference agency in the UK market and in this field the company has only one major competitor, CC Inc. As a result each company can only increase market share at the expense of the other, unless they can each persuade businesses to carry out searches with both organisations. To some extent DA's position is protected by the fact that organisations wishing to compile credit information need a licence. As DA is clearly the market leader it could be argued that they have been very successful in achieving market penetration. This has been based on their ability to create and retain successful client relationships and their core skills of database compilation and management.

Product development

This means developing new products for existing markets. As a credit reference business, DA initially focused on financial services businesses as its potential customers. It was then able to expand by developing the technology around its existing product. Knowledge of the specific needs of this market in terms of speed of decision making, reduction of risk etc enabled DA to build and develop a wider range of products relevant to its customers, eg, the decision analysis software that DA introduced was based on the premise that businesses would value analytical rather than just factual information.

Market development

This strategy takes existing products and finds new markets for them. Having recognised a core competence in database management, DA used this strategy to offer information products to the automotive industry. This market is similar to the financial services market, in that customers value information that assists in reducing the risk associated with decisions.

Diversification

This involves moving away from core activities and developing new products for new markets. Diversification stands apart from the other strategies. It involves the greatest risk of all strategies. It requires new skills, new techniques and different ways of operating.

Having focused on the business-to-business market, DA plans to diversify into the business-to-consumer market with its new product Checksta. While the broad product area is still credit information there are overtones of diversification because it is for individual consumers. This decision recognises that many consumers want to be more in control of their credit status, to be able to monitor their credit report at any time and to protect themselves against identity fraud.

Note: Although the company perception is that Checksta represents a new market, it could be argued that this is product development rather than diversification, since DA already offers the statutory credit report to the consumer market.

Lynch Expansion method matrix

The Lynch model is another two-by-two matrix of company growth (organic growth and external development) and geographical location (home (domestic) and international). Under this model, all of DA's growth appears to have been carried out organically and products/markets have been developed domestically rather than internationally.

DA has been able to grow organically as a result of having been an initial player in the market, allowing it to develop critical mass.

Overseas expansion

It is likely that a large number of existing customers, who value the DA brand, are global businesses. In the same way that CC Inc has expanded into the UK, DA could exploit this brand loyalty and apply its information management skills to Europe or the USA. If it wishes to target overseas markets in the future, then growth by acquisition might be considered as a faster way of getting access to the necessary licences and databases.

1.3 PESTEL analysis

Political

- Only companies that are licensed CRAs can provide credit reference services and access to consumer credit files. DA and CC Inc are the two largest CRAs. Lending organisations and retailers offering trade credit have a choice of organisation with which to do a credit search, and consumers may not know which business their prospective lender will use, thus consumers are likely to want to access their file with each organisation.

- Changes in regulation may restrict DA's freedom of operations, eg, regarding pricing or ability to advertise.

- Government may choose to discourage credit, reducing the need for credit checks and hence DA's product.

Economic

- A consumer's willingness to take on credit depends on his or her confidence in their ability to repay the money. This confidence comes in part from job stability and faith in the economy. The relatively low and stable interest rates and stable employment have made consumers more willing to take on credit. While currently favourable, future changes, eg, in interest rates, may reverse this trend.

- Consumer spending is often used as an indicator of how well the economy is doing. Credit is a key factor in fuelling an economic boom. Any boom in consumer spending will mean that there is an increase in the number of credit checks lenders make through DA.

- The rejection of credit applications, especially if it is unexpected, may be an opportunity for DA as it is likely to cause individuals to want to access their credit report.

Social

- Changing attitudes to money and credit have meant it is no longer traditional to save up for things. More and more people use credit as a way of buying things they do not have the money for.

- People can apply for credit from almost anywhere: over the internet, by telephone, in a shop or supermarket, or in response to direct marketing campaigns.

- Consumers are much less loyal to one bank or finance provider and are more likely to shop around and approach several lenders to find the best deal. The above factors mean that individuals are more likely to shop around for credit and lenders have to carry out more credit checks. A desire to obtain credit on the best terms is likely to increase consumers' awareness of their credit history and increase demand for the credit scoring service provided in conjunction with Checksta.

Technological

- The credit industry has made huge technological advances. Financial products and services can now be bought online and e-commerce is now an important part of the global economy.

- The boom in e-commerce will continue to necessitate more frequent and rapid credit checks by businesses and increase the number of consumers who are likely to want real time online access to their credit history.

- DA has already upgraded its IT and knowledge management systems in response to changing technology but will need to ensure that these are kept up to date and that the necessary security systems are in place.

- The increase in identity crime represents a major opportunity for Checksta as individuals become increasingly aware of the possibilities of fraudulent access to their information and identities and will be keen to protect themselves against this.

Environmental

- Not really of major significance, though there could be a reduction in credit if society moves towards consuming less and conserving energy and resources.

- Environmental concerns, such as the desire to go 'paperless' may boost demand for an online product.

Legal

- UK legislation exists which governs how organisations can collect, use and share personal information and giving consumers specific rights in relation to the information CRAs hold about them. Continuing to comply with this and other relevant legislation is crucial to DA's business. DA needs to ensure that its plans for Checksta do not contravene this legislation or the terms of its licence.

- The consumer education programme that DA had to implement as a result of the tightening legislation has given it an opportunity to increase the awareness of its brand name among consumers and also consumer organisations.

In conclusion the environmental analysis would suggest that there is considerable scope for a product such as Checksta and that its planned introduction is well timed.

1.4 Marketing strategy

In the first instance DA should ensure that it has undertaken the appropriate market research. Market research is the systematic gathering, recording and analysing of information about problems relating to marketing of goods and services. Market research will therefore involve gathering information about the 7Ps of marketing (see below).

Target market

To the extent that it has identified customer needs and developed a product accordingly, DA would appear to have undertaken some preliminary market research and used this to identify the segments containing those potential customers that it wants to target.

In DA's case it wants to target a specific type of customer: personal rather than business, with certain behaviour preferences: users of credit and also of the Internet. As a result it will need to take account of people's ages, their gender and socioeconomic grouping in deciding on an appropriate marketing mix.

Checksta is a new UK brand. It is important to develop an image that would be appropriate for the product that is being offered. Having a profile of the most likely customer will help DA to develop a promotional campaign that positions the product in the minds of its potential customers.

Marketing mix

Next, DA needs to develop its marketing strategy using the marketing mix, which is traditionally done using the 4Ps.

Product

Checksta is based on a product that existed already – the consumer credit report. The product has been developed by allowing real time online access and augmented via support for ID fraud.

In this case, the service needs to be considered in terms of the attributes that are likely to generate demand (eg, 24-hour availability; convenience of online access; security of information; ability to predict lender's scoring).

Checksta's unique selling points (USPs) are that it allows consumers to see their credit reports online and automatically alerts them to important changes to the information held about them. This helps consumers understand what makes them creditworthy and can help them to manage their credit commitments. If there is a problem, consumers get free phone advice from credit reference specialists.

Price

The price that potential customers are willing to pay could clearly be a specific objective of any market research exercise.

DA needs to consider whether there are any regulations governing the pricing of their service. Presumably the starting point for price is the price of the statutory report = £2.

It then needs to assess the value of real time access to the customer and the value of the other services on offer.

One possibility is to price elements of the package separately eg, a basic price for online access, and then extra charges for the additional service elements such as the alert service, credit score and so on.

Some form of monthly membership scheme, with an initial free trial period would encourage new users to consider take up of the service. If they do not think the service is for them, members would then have to remember to cancel their membership, say at the end of the 30-day free trial.

DA could consider price skimming for early adopters or alternatively discounts for those who are quick to sign up, so as to build market share quickly.

Place

Checksta was developed because of the growth in e-commerce communications technology. Its 'place' or channel by which it reaches its users is the electronic medium of the internet – Checksta is an e-commerce product, available online for consumers.

Some of the support services are offered online but also via different channels – the alert service is offered via email or text (mobile phone) and the free phone help-line can presumably be accessed via landline or mobile. Thus in addition to internet users, DA is also targeting those with mobile phones.

Promotion

As a new venture, the initial impact of advertising and other promotion on price and demand should be considered.

Until recently, DA has worked mainly in the business-to-business (b2b) market. Its expertise is based on personal selling and relationship building. To succeed in the business to consumer (b2c)

market, DA will have to use a different promotional mix and needs to develop a range of different promotional strategies.

As a result of the tightening of credit legislation DA has already implemented a consumer education programme and been working with consumer groups. When DA launches its Checksta product in the UK, it should build on this existing awareness of its brand by ensuring that all free advice guides, consumer education programmes and conferences it attends also promote Checksta.

It could produce literature both online and as a paper product informing people of the dangers of identity fraud and explain how a monitoring service like Checksta could help protect them from the effects of this crime.

DA should consider using a public relations agency to help advertise the new online credit report with press releases and a television advertising campaign.

Advertising could be placed in the money/financial review sections of the press and appropriate financial/credit/consumer advice magazines.

DA could sponsor exhibitions such as the Ideal Home Show and events such as Credit Awareness Week 20X7, which its target customers may attend.

As the product is an online one and DA are targeting internet users, web-based advertising would also be appropriate. DA need to ensure there are links to its website from the various money supermarket and personal finance websites. Research should be done to ensure that DA and the Checksta brand appear when a potential customer uses a search engine.

DA could exploit links with other areas of its business, eg, advertise the Checksta service to those customers seeking finance for vehicle purchases. Direct mail those people who have previously applied for a statutory credit report and include a leaflet about Checksta with each statutory report.

Note: As DA is a service company, the marketing mix could be extended to consideration of 7 Ps.

People

This refers to anyone that is to have regular interaction with the customer. In this case a lot of the service will be provided automatically and a substantial amount of any interaction will be electronic by text or email. Customers may make personal contact if they use the free advice phone line.

DA needs to ensure that the nature of any communication gives a good impression of the company, that staff have appropriate training on the new product and the flexibility to provide a good service and that staff manning the helpline are informative and suitably concerned and reassuring.

Processes

Accuracy of information, secure access and confidentiality will be key to determining how effective the service is. DA needs to implement standard operational procedures and ensure that staff apply these consistently.

The ease of application for membership and navigation through the website will be important.

There will need to be security systems in place to verify the identity of members both online and by phone.

DA needs to ensure that the IT systems operate efficiently and that there are no significant delays in the provision of the real time information or periods when the website is down.

Physical evidence

This is the evidence that the service has been performed. It may include electronic confirmation of membership, the online report, any alerts. DA could issue a credit card sized Checksta membership card, with membership number and key contact numbers/website addresses.

Strategic risks	Risk management
DA will lose competitive advantage if it fails to utilise IT/IS as effectively as CC Inc, particularly given its renewed focus on the UK market. If the use of analytical software among DA's competitors increases and DA fails to innovate its own processes then this may result in falling behind its rivals.	DA needs to keep up to date with new technology, continuously upgrade systems and ensure continuous advancements in the products/services offered. It should undertake regular benchmarking against competitors such as CC Inc.
Since all of DA's information management and in particular the Checksta product depends on IT/IS, a breakdown in its operations threatens the business. This could arise from systems failure or natural threats such as fire, flood, electrical storms.	DA should ensure that if major failures or disasters occur, the business will not be completely unable to function. It should implement protection measures to ensure continuity of operations and to minimise the risk of systems failures, eg, back-up servers in alternative locations and regular back-ups of data.
The cost of updating and maintaining IT/IS and implementing the necessary security controls and risk management systems may reduce the operating margins that DA has enjoyed to date (currently around 25% on average). This is particularly true if, as a result of CC Inc offering a low cost web-based solution, DA has to reduce the price of its services.	The costs of the necessary systems controls and security measures need to be considered in the light of the benefits that these will bring.
Market dominance may result in DA being criticised for anti-competitive practices or investigated by the Competition and Markets Authority.	Care should be taken to ensure DA does not abuse its position and actively lay itself open to criticism.

Cyber security risks	Risk management
Loss of information as a result of corruption of the system by viruses or human error.	Particularly important is protection from viruses and the need for regular back-ups. DA needs to protect data and systems from unauthorised modification, eg, via passwords and levels of access/modification authority.
Theft of sensitive financial information or deliberate misuse of data by hackers/employees.	DA must recruit trustworthy employees, and ensure detection and reporting of security-related incidents, eg, unauthorised activity. Training is particularly important, with the aim that users are aware of information security threats and concerns and are equipped to comply with the security policy.
Penalties or intervention as a result of non compliance with regulations such as the *Data Protection Act* which could be imposed by courts if data is wrongly used or control procedures are not in place.	DA must put controls in place to ensure it monitors compliance with any relevant legal requirements such as the *Data Protection Act*.

2   e-Parts Ltd (September 2010, amended)

Marking guide

		Knowledge	Skill	Marks
2.1	Relevance of risk management/contents of BCP	3	4	6
2.2	Key IT risks and management	4	5	8
2.3	Outsourcing to implement IT strategy	3	5	7
		10	14	21

General comments:

The scenario in this question relates to an online retailer which sells parts and accessories for domestic appliances. 90% of orders are made online, and the owner has identified the dependence of the business on the inventory control system and the importance of keeping its website operational. The business has grown significantly and is now considering outsourcing all its operational systems to a specialist IT provider. The owner has also been made aware that the company needs a formal risk management policy and a business continuity plan.

Answers to this question varied in standard and although the overall performance was quite good, there were some very poor answers.

2.1   Risk management and business continuity planning

Risk management is the process of identifying and assessing the risks facing EP's business and the development, implementation and monitoring of a strategy to respond to those risks, in order to reduce threats to acceptable levels.

When running a business, risk is unavoidable and will include financial, strategic, operational and hazard risks arising from both internal and external sources. Risk management is a corporate governance issue as there is the danger that directors of companies might take decisions intended to increase profits without giving due regard to the risks. They may also continue to operate without regard to the changing risk profile of their organisation.

The point of risk management is that risks can be mitigated if management have plans to deal with problems if they occur. Risk management should be carried out by all businesses and involve all levels of staff and management. The aim is to prioritise the risks according to the ones that threaten the business most and then to take action to reduce or otherwise address the risk.

In addition to the general risks faced by all businesses, as a retailer EP faces additional IT and cyber risks because it carries large volumes of inventory and also because business is largely done online (see 10.2). Cyber risk is any risk of financial loss, disruption or damage to the reputation of an organisation from some sort of failure of its IT systems. A key issue for an online business is that technical failure has a significant and immediate impact. Problems with the ecommerce site are immediately visible and it is easy for customers to switch to a competitor if the website is unavailable. Thus cyber security is an important issue for EP. EP needs to take action to prevent/reduce losses due to excessive risk exposure that may include theft, fraud and data insecurity.

Kamal must ensure that all staff are trained and fully aware of ecommerce security issues and fraud risk.

Whether EP thrives or fails will partly be dependent on how as a business it manages risk and exploits opportunities. The aim is to reduce the probability and/or consequence of failure but retain as far as possible the benefits of success. Thus effective risk management is integral to EP's competitive advantage and will help ensure EP's survival in the longer term.

Business continuity planning is the process through which a business details how and when it will recover and restore operations interrupted by the occurrence of a massive (but rare) risk event eg, natural disaster such as a warehouse flood or fire or a major breach of security causing the website to be down for an extended period.

Where risk management is largely pre-emptive, BCP is designed to deal with the consequences of a major realised risk. The difference is also linked to the extent of the impact – for instance the difference between website disruption due to a temporary loss of internet connection and a denial of service attack that places the business's existence in jeopardy.

A BCP is concerned with crisis management and disaster recovery. It must specify the actions to be taken in order to recover from any unexpected disruptive event. Factors that should be considered by a BCP include the following:

- Securing interim management and staff
- Inventory replacement
- Restoration of data and other IT systems
- Securing interim premises
- Management of the PR issues

Methods of recovery might include the following:

- Carrying out activities manually until IT services are resumed (eg, via the call centre)

- Moving staff at an affected building to another location

- Agreeing with another business to use each other's premises in the event of a disaster

- Arranging to use IT services and accommodation provided by a specialist third-party standby site

All members of EP staff should be aware of the importance of business continuity planning, training should be given and the plan tested regularly.

Examiner's comments

Requirement 2.1 asked candidates to explain the relevance of risk management to the business as a whole and to identify the main factors that would be covered in a business continuity plan. Overall answers were of a poor standard with many candidates failing this requirement because they were uncertain about the nature and content of a business continuity plan, despite the clear hint given in the scenario about ensuring the business could continue to function in the event of a major incident. Explanations of risk management tended to be extremely generic and only the best candidates pointed out that risk management was critical given the risks faced by EP as a result of its inventory levels and the e-commerce nature of the business. Weaker candidates often mentioned Turnbull, which demonstrated a lack of understanding of its application.

2.2 **IT risks including cyber risks and how to manage them**

EP must take steps to minimise the risk of systems failure, protect the integrity of its systems, safeguard information and ensure the continuity of its operations.

Risks may be transferred, avoided, reduced or accepted.

Specific IT and cyber risks arising for EP and recommendations for risk management:

- Inaccessible website/website too slow/payment system for ecommerce website goes down. This is critical given that 90% sales are online and is likely to result in frustrated customers and lost sales as they can easily switch to another online competitor.

  Risk can be reduced by ensuring appropriate systems development and maintenance takes place and by having back-up servers. EP could also reduce the risk by providing other channels to market and ensuring that customers are directed to alternatives such as the call centre in the event of system delays or failures.

  EP could transfer the risk by outsourcing the provision of the website to a specialist provider (see 2.3).

- Identity theft/credit card fraud arising due to online payments – this would damage EP's reputation and may result in lost customers.

EP should ensure it reduces the risk by having access controls, appropriate payment verification software, firewalls and secure communication.

- Loss of critical data, particularly given there are 2m customers on the database and 100,000 different products to control. Failure of the inventory control system may cause inaccurate information to be provided regarding inventory levels or wrong products to be despatched. Failure to comply with the Data Protection Act could also result in penalties/litigation.

  EP should reduce the risk of inadequate or inaccurate information by performing regular physical inventory counts and reconciling these to computerised records.

  EP must ensure the inventory system and customer database are kept up-to date, backed up regularly and hard copies kept off site. It must have systems in place to monitor compliance with data protection regulations and ensure all data held is secure (eg, via encryption).

  Reduce the risk by ensuring all feedback is screened regularly and ensuring appropriate security features are in place to control access and content.

- IT system becomes out-of-date or is less capable than that of online competitors.

  Systems need to be upgraded regularly to ensure they are capable of providing the necessary capacity, particularly given the growth EP has experienced.

Where risks cannot be reduced or eliminated it may be possible for EP to transfer them via the following:

- Insurance (however this may be costly and it may be problematic to quantify the extent of business loss from a security incident)

- Contracting out the management of ecommerce to a third party who can host the system. The loss may still occur and impact on the business, but the service level agreement can stipulate penalties

Other more generic IT risks include the following:

- Virus attacks and/or hackers exploiting vulnerabilities in the system (steal data, damage system or corrupt information)

- Website defacement (impact on reputation/brand image)

- Denial of service

- Infrastructure failure eg, loss of internet connection

- Software/hardware systems malfunction

- Loss of key IT personnel eg, website designer/IT manager

- Risk to corporate information/intellectual property

- Human error

- Deliberate sabotage

- Fraud

- Natural threats (fire, flood, electrical storm)

More generally EP can reduce vulnerability and increase its level of confidence in its technical environment by:

- Installing firewalls, using strong authentication processes and secure communication

- Implementing policies to manage activities eg, internet and email usage

- Setting standards for firewalls, servers and procurement of PCs

- Establishing a high level of Information security and access controls, and measuring to detect unauthorised access

- Ensuring there are regular back-ups

- Undertaking appropriate systems development and maintenance

- Ensuring physical and environment security

- Complying with relevant legislation

Examiner's comments

Requirement 2.2 asked candidates to identify the key IT risks including cyber risks arising for EP as a result of its reliance on IT and to recommend how they could be managed. Answers were quite variable. Good answers concentrated on relevant IT and cyber risks for EP, including the possible failure of the website, loss of customer database information, identity theft and the possibility of damaging reviews on social networking sites. A significant number of answers discussed IT risks and the TARA model for risk management in very generic terms. The weakest candidates failed to concentrate on IT and cyber risks, mentioning any types of risk they could think of.

2.3 Considerations in outsourcing the provision of the website and inventory control system

EP is considering outsourcing all its systems relating to the website and inventory control.

Factors to consider include the following:

- EP has experienced substantial growth and its current systems may no longer be able to cope with the increasing volume of transactions. Outsourcing may reduce the chance of system breakdown and give EP access to back-up servers and systems.

- Outsourcing would provide access to specialist IT knowledge and allow Kamal to concentrate on the strategy of the company.

- As specialists, with the potential for economies of scale, an outsourcer may be able to provide better, more efficient systems for EP at a lower cost. They are also more likely to be able to keep the systems up-to-date and develop new applications which may help EP maintain its competitive advantage.

- By outsourcing, EP can transfer the risk of systems failure to the IT provider and may have recourse to compensation in the event of financial loss.

However:

- EP has a database of 2m customers. Outsourcing would require it to share confidential information with the IT provider, who may also work with competitors.

- Any problems experienced when transferring the systems over may disrupt EP's business and cause it to lose sales/customers.

- Once EP has decided to outsource it may find it difficult to switch suppliers and is unlikely to be able to revert to in-house provision as it will no longer have its own web designers/IT experts.

Other factors to consider:

- Fees charged by contractor
- Costs currently incurred in own service provision
- Potential redundancies of staff no longer required
- Time and cost involved in agreeing and monitoring service level agreement
- Attitude of influential stakeholders
- Previous incidence and consequence of system breakdown

Conclusion: if EP does decide to outsource it will need to choose a partner carefully, and assess their financial stability and track record of delivering suitable services elsewhere.

It must then agree a series of performance targets and penalties in the event of the contractor's failure to deliver.

Examiner's comments

In requirement 2.3 candidates were asked to explain the factors that should be considered by EP in deciding whether to use outsourcing as a method of implementing its IT strategy. Candidates were clearly well rehearsed for this requirement in terms of knowledge but many weaker candidates failed to obtain the available skills marks. This was due to the fact that they produced largely generic lists of pros and cons, with minimal application of EP and its IT strategy, which could have been applied to almost any outsourcing scenario. Better answers focussed specifically on the factors that would influence the choice between in-house and outsourced IT provision and the impact on risks for EP.

3 Marcham plc (September 2010, amended)

Marking guide

		Knowledge	Skill	Marks
3.1	Report format			
(a)	Info system benefits/competitive advantage	3	6	8
(b)	SFA of expansion into the banking sector	3	10	12
(c)	Organic growth v joint development	3	6	8
3.2	Ethical issues	3	6	8
		12	28	36

General comments:

This scenario relates to a major supermarket chain which is proposing to take advantage of the recent turmoil in the banking sector by launching its own banking services (rather than as a joint venture with another bank). Marcham has a 30% share of the supermarket sector and was the first supermarket to introduce a loyalty card. Along with an EPOS and inventory control system the loyalty card forms part of an integrated data analytics and knowledge management information system and is to be a key driver of competitive advantage for the expansion into banking. Candidates were provided with an extract from a national newspaper which has recently criticised Marcham for using its loyalty card to spy on customers and for abusing its suppliers.

Overall the performance on this question was quite good, although weaker candidates struggled with the requirement on ethics.

3.1 Report

To: Operations Director
From: AN Other
Date: September 20Y0
Re: Data analytics & information systems and proposed expansion into banking

(a) Benefits of a data analytics and information system for competitive advantage

- Increased revenue (from customers by analysing customer shopping data and also from sale of data to suppliers)

- Reduced costs (better inventory control)

- Increased customer service and hence improved customer retention – effectively the loyalty card acts as a barrier to exit for the customer

- Improved decision making (forecasting, scenario planning, market analysis)

- Existing database for direct marketing

- Targeted discount coupons as a form of price discrimination based on analysed customer purchase data

- EPOS system facilitates better inventory control, allowing for a Just-in-Time approach which reduces costs and wastage

Marcham's competitive advantage (CA)

In the supermarket industry, most players have EPOS systems and loyalty card schemes. In order for CA to arise, Marcham not only needs to be better at capturing data than competitors but also better at using it.

The loyalty scheme is a form of relationship marketing whereby Marcham is trying to build a long-term relationship with the customer. Marcham's CA arises because in terms of capturing the data:

- It was the first of its kind to introduce the scheme and therefore captured (and retained) an initial loyal customer base, obtaining first-mover advantage

- Its dominance within the market (30% market share and one in four adults in the UK belong to its customer loyalty scheme) means it has a more extensive database than any other competitor (data about more customers and also collected for longer). Crucially, Marcham has the data analytics software to be able to extract meaning from the data it holds.

In terms of its ability to use the data:

- It has reduced costs by increasing the frequency and accuracy of ordering, leading to lower levels of inventory and wastage

- It has more effective marketing which facilitates market segmentation and targeting, so low price goods can be promoted to certain customers and high quality ones to others

- It has better price discrimination and hence increased margins

- It can trade up sales by targeting promotions

- The percentage of customer spend can be extended by identifying products customers are likely to buy but may currently be buying elsewhere

- It has higher margins – it is cheaper to keep existing customers and to sell more to them than it is to attract new ones

- It is likely to result in a higher success rate for new product lines as it has already identified what customers want

- It shares this with suppliers, generating revenue from the sale of the database, promoting better captive relationships with the supplier and improving the matching of products with demand

Within the financial services sector none of the competitors has loyalty cards so Marcham will have first mover advantage if it uses the loyalty card within the banking sector.

(b) **Suitability, feasibility, acceptability**

Suitability (strategic logic and fit)

There is a precedent as Marcham would not be the first major retailer to get involved in financial services (Tesco, Sainsbury, M&S) although it would be the first to set up a full banking service.

Strong brand name – timing is good given some people's loss of faith in the banking sector and perceived lack of transparency surrounding banks' behaviour. The issue is whether Marcham will be seen by consumers as a credible provider of banking services, although the fact that they have been granted a licence suggests the financial services regulator, the Financial Conduct Authority (FCA) believe they are.

Both banks and supermarkets are about serving personal customers and Marcham already possesses core competence in customer service and responsiveness.

There is also a strong link between retail spending and the need for credit.

Both banks and supermarkets require a presence on the high street and Marcham can use existing infrastructure.

The loyalty card scheme offers exposure to a large number of customers and the opportunity to increase share of customers' spend.

However:

- Are financial services a core competence for retailers?

- It is a very competitive market

- Relatively, Marcham will be a very small player faced with large competition from existing banks
- Core competences in procurement and logistics would be less relevant in banking than if it expanded into other retail areas
- There are onerous compliance requirements related to data protection, identity confirmation, regulatory compliance and money laundering of which Marcham has limited experience
- Many customers now use online banking so MarchamBank's presence in stores may not be that attractive to them

Feasibility (can the strategy be implemented?)

This looks at whether Marcham have the necessary resources.

Marcham has already been granted a licence which demonstrates government support.

Branches will be located in existing stores which reduces the overhead costs associated with the operation.

Cash appears to be available although there is an opportunity cost if it is not invested in other new stores.

The loyalty card provides instant access to a database for direct marketing and profiling information which will allow Marcham to tailor products to different groups of customer.

Marcham already has systems in place to collate data about customers and process applications, so credit assessment would simply be a bolt-on.

Marcham would need to hire new staff and management with appropriate financial services knowledge – there is likely to be a big training requirement.

The pricing of financial services and processes are much more complex than individual retail transactions eg, selling a loaf of bread.

The banking sector will entail onerous compliance requirements related to data protection, identity confirmation and money laundering.

Financial services are long term in nature so Marcham will need to commit resources for a significant period. It will take time to recoup initial set-up costs and for the venture to become profitable.

Acceptability (to stakeholders)

This considers the likely benefits to stakeholders (returns) and the likelihood of failure and its associated consequences (risk).

Returns

More information is required to assess the proposed financial impact of the strategy. Here we are told that it will offer access to higher margins at a time when the retail business is under pressure, so it may result in increased profitability for shareholders. The core retail business is mature and growing slowly so this offers an opportunity for continued growth.

The government grant reduces the cost of setting up the call centre.

Customers may perceive the strategy as enhancing the service on offer which may help retain/attract new customers for the retail business.

Given the government's stated aim to increase competition they may well look favourably on the venture by Marcham.

It may provide additional career opportunities for some employees.

Risk

The biggest risk is that management have no experience/expertise in financial services products, which are complex.

From a risk point of view, adding financial services spreads the risk profile of Marcham's business. However according to Ansoff this strategy would be classed as unrelated diversification and as a result is a high risk approach to increasing profits. Given recent events, banking is no longer the safe and secure business that it was once deemed to be. Institutional shareholders will already have well diversified portfolios and it could be argued that if shareholders wanted ownership of a bank then they could just buy shares in one themselves.

Shareholders may be concerned that management will be distracted from the core business.

There is a big reputational risk for the existing business if Marcham gets it wrong and it would need to ring fence this area of the business as a separate company.

Marcham may lose customers from the retail business if it rejects applications for loans or credit cards.

Conclusion:

The fact that a number of other supermarkets have launched financial services products suggests that the strategy is viable, although further consideration needs to be given to the best method of implementing the strategy.

(c) **Organic growth versus joint venture**

Arguments against organic growth (in favour of joint venture)

Gaining competences via organic growth takes time. Marcham does not have any expertise in financial services so will need to buy it in. A partnership with an existing bank would ensure rapid access to the relevant expertise.

There are significant regulation and compliance issues in the banking sector, including barriers to entry such as the licence. Although Marcham has already been granted a licence it will lack expertise and systems to ensure compliance in areas such as money laundering legislation.

The financial services regulator, the Financial Conduct Authority (FCA), may be more favourable in the long term towards a venture that has already demonstrated financial expertise and compliance.

Most other retailers have chosen to move into financial services through partnership with banks, thus combining banking expertise with the retailer's brand strength and reputation.

Risk is shared.

Arguments in favour of organic growth (against joint venture)

Organic growth gives Marcham full control over the venture and avoids the need to share profits.

Having to buy-in operational expertise from a bank may restrict the scope for Marcham to do banking in a different way, which is a key driver for its strategy.

An alliance with a bank would not address the issue of the public's mistrust of the banking sector. Marcham's loyalty card provides access to existing customer base.

The government grant may not be available if Marcham expands with a partner.

The available choice of partner would be limited as there would be relatively few options available to choose from in terms of a bank with a reputation still intact.

It avoids placing reliance on the future reputation of the chosen partner.

Organic growth avoids any potential clash of strategy or disagreement – banking partners may be reluctant to sanction new financial services products that are critical of their own service provision or that overtly compete.

It saves the time and cost of negotiating terms of a JV agreement, profit share, exit options etc.

Conclusion:

Other supermarkets have chosen to enter financial services with banking partners for a reason and Marcham needs to consider carefully the risks involved in pursuing this strategy alone.

Tutorial note:

This answer includes more points than is necessary for the marks available but a full range of points has been provided for marking purposes.

Loyalty card:

The issue concerning the loyalty card is really one of ethical marketing and relates to the collection, use and sale of the data gathered in this way. Is Marcham behaving in a fair and transparent manner and what is the likely effect on its customers?

It is partly a question of boundaries – how much data is it reasonable to collect, what is acceptable use and is it legitimate to sell the data on?

Collection of data

The ethical argument is that collection of the data is an invasion of privacy and that it could be abused if it falls into the wrong hands.

Effectively, consumers who join the loyalty scheme trade information for product savings. Customers have a choice as to whether to shop at Marcham and whether to join the loyalty card scheme. The fact that one in four adults belong implies they do not have a problem, or perceive that the benefits are sufficient to compensate for the lack of privacy.

The Data Protection Act (DPA) strictly regulates the confidentiality, storage and use of personal information and Marcham is likely to have sophisticated security and access systems to ensure it does not fall into the wrong hands.

Marcham will also have a stated policy explaining what data is collected and how it is used/shared with preferred partners (transparency) plus an option for consumers to tick a box if they don't want their data shared.

Critics might argue that consumers know what data they have given when they apply to take out a card but lack awareness of how much data is subsequently captured and how it is used. The key ethical issue here is therefore transparency and whether informed and willing consent has been given by consumers to Marcham to utilise data in an agreed manner in return for the benefits of the scheme.

Use of data

Issues concern motives and transparency.

The debate about marketing centres on whether it is about meeting people's needs and expectations or selling people things they don't need.

It could be argued that Marcham uses the loyalty card to better identify the specific needs of different groups of customers and so wastes fewer resources because marketing is targeted. As a result it becomes more efficient at stocking shelves with products consumers want, and can therefore pass the savings on in lower prices, although some argue that this is at the expense of higher prices paid by non-loyalty card holders (lack of fairness/negative effect on some).

Marcham could use data captured to promote healthy food and provide improved education re healthy diets, hence offering a benefit to society.

Profiling could however also be used negatively to exclude undesirable customers (eg, recent case of the customer wearing pyjamas whilst shopping at Tesco) or to concentrate on a wealthier class of customers, and this would be regarded as unethical.

Sale of data

The potential issue regarding the sale to third parties (suppliers, direct mail companies, telemarketers) is that Marcham has less control over it and has also made money from it.

DPA means it is illegal for companies to sell on people's details without their consent or for uses other than those they were originally told about. Thus Marcham will give consumers an option on the loyalty card application form to tick a box if they don't want their data shared. This is standard practice engaged in by most retailers.

It is not in Marcham's interests to breach DPA as it will face consequences in terms of damaged reputation and lost customers.

Conclusion

Ultimately Marcham is no different than a whole host of other retailers also operating loyalty card schemes and consumers have the choice of whether to belong to the scheme or not. They can also shop elsewhere if they don't like it.

Treatment of suppliers

Business ethics covers the way a firm as a whole behaves and thus any victimisation of suppliers by Marcham would contravene this. Corporate responsibility would also suggest that Marcham owes a responsibility to society and its wider stakeholders and that a balance needs to be struck between making profits for the shareholders and treating suppliers fairly.

Marcham is being blamed, like a number of other supermarkets and large retailers in the press recently, for exacerbating the poverty of farmers and other weak suppliers.

The issue centres on whether Marcham is merely implementing good supply chain management or is guilty of unethical treatment due to exploitation.

Marcham's ability to dictate terms and conditions to suppliers is evidence of its bargaining power as a customer (Porter) – the bigger the company the greater its likely power to push prices down and demand better payment terms. Lower prices achieved from suppliers may benefit consumers if they are passed on. Thus terms and prices may differ between suppliers depending on their relative bargaining power in relation to Marcham.

The policy of extending payment terms is good cash flow management and could be argued to be in the interests of shareholders.

Even if it adopted standard payment terms, Marcham would be a relatively cash rich business - cash sales mean it has few receivables and JIT policies keep inventories relatively low, leading to an effective cash operating cycle.

The argument against extending payment terms is that Marcham's monopoly position in the market allows them to exploit suppliers by driving prices down, which can force smaller suppliers out of business. Marcham's terms could be compared to the industry average and to other organisations of its size to assess whether they are reasonable. Marcham might be said to be being unfair if it significantly differentiates terms between large and small suppliers, thus abusing its position of power, or if it is not adhering to Industry codes of practice.

However it is unlikely to be in Marcham's interest to drive suppliers out of business as it would then be faced with disruptions in supply or emergency supplies at premium prices. As a major player in the market and a successful plc, Marcham will not want to risk damaging its reputation. Outwardly at least Marcham it is likely to argue that that it supports local businesses and works in partnership with suppliers, adopts ethical procurement policies with transparent payment terms and conditions agreed in advance, and has grievance procedures available to unhappy suppliers.

A lack of personal ethics might lead individual managers to abuse their position or make threats to suppliers and Marcham must ensure it creates an ethical culture and has procedures in place to deal with such inappropriate behaviour.

Note that the Competition and Markets Authority has the power to act if it believes that a firm in a dominant position within an industry is abusing its monopoly power.

Finally it is worth pointing out that the newspaper article may be guilty of sensationalism and some of the criticisms may be unfounded.

Marking guide

		Knowledge	Skill	Marks
4.1	Key stakeholders	2	6	7
4.2	(a) Break-even	–	4	4
	(b) Implications	–	10	9
4.3	Business case (raise finance, sustainable value and alignment)	3	13	14
4.4	Key risks	2	7	8
		7	40	42

General comments:

This is the mini case and also the data analysis question. Bigville's rugby club is in need of a new stadium with greater capacity as a result of its recent league success (the current stadium is leased from the local council). The local football club is in a similar position. The city council have been approached by the rugby club to consider the creation of a community stadium which could be partly funded by sale of the existing stadium land to a developer for a retail site. The council has undertaken an initial feasibility study and is considering the high level business case for the venture. There is demand for a shared stadium with facilities for rugby, football and athletics, plus a range of additional commercial and community uses on non-match days. Land has been identified which would meet the necessary planning criteria. Either a basic stadium can be constructed, with a shared pitch for rugby and football and community sports facilities, or the Council can spend more on an enhanced stadium with a hotel and conference centre. Additional funding would be available in terms of grants provided certain criteria are fulfilled and a sponsorship deal could be sought with a large credit card company, Finanex, whose HQ is in the city. The stadium is likely to be run by a joint stadium management company (SMC) created by the Council and the two clubs.

Candidates were provided with a range of data concerning the build cost, capacity, forecast revenue and costs for each element of the stadium, and attendance figures for comparable rugby/football clubs.

This question was well attempted by most candidates.

4.1 Stakeholder conflict

The clubs and the Council will have different objectives, which will themselves be linked to their different stakeholders. Key stakeholders for the clubs will include the players, the fans and the governing body. Key stakeholders for the Council will be residents, local businesses, the wider community and central government.

The Council as a Not For Profit (NFP) organisation has a wider range of stakeholders and is likely to have to balance the use of limited resources to ensure it provides the best possible services and maximises benefits for the wider community. The clubs are likely to have two main aims:

- To achieve the best sporting success possible in order to retain/attract new fans
- To generate as much profit as possible in order to be able to acquire better players

In certain cases these aims may coincide with the Council's eg, if the clubs achieve sporting success, this will generate additional attendance and income which will increase the wealth of the stadium and facilitate the Council's objectives. However there is also scope for conflict between the individual clubs and between the clubs and the Council:

Construction of the stadium:

The clubs are likely to be predominantly interested in the main stadium and pitch. There may be conflict between them as to the best layout and surface of the pitch for their particular requirements. Each club will be interested in any stipulations or health and safety regulations set out by its ruling league body. Since the football club is contributing more capital, it may expect priority over decisions.

The Council will also be interested in the additional community facilities and there may be conflict between the Council and the clubs if the siting or construction of these is seen to negatively affect anything in relation to the main stadium eg, a running track around the pitch may cause the fans to feel separated from the game. Similarly the environmental sustainability of the stadium is of key importance to the Council whereas this may be a low priority for the clubs, particularly if it affects the visibility of fans or anything to do with the playing surface or training/changing facilities. The clubs may also be reluctant to pay additional capital costs for community facilities.

The two clubs may also conflict on the seating capacity if for instance there is little prospect of the rugby club ever being promoted and filling a larger stadium but there are realistic prospects of the football club achieving the new capacity. The clubs may also disagree over the size and nature of the playing surface.

Operation of the stadium:

Again the clubs are likely to have their own interests at heart. Although the clubs typically play matches on different days there may be conflict between them over scheduling of training and cup match scheduling.

Similarly if the rugby club has a big championship match on a Sunday they may not take too kindly to the football club having churned up the pitch on the previous day.

The clubs are likely to want priority over the use of the stadium on match days and for weekday training sessions (unless, like some professional clubs, they have access to separate training pitches). Weekday use may conflict with the Council's desire to make the stadium available for the community. Also the Council may want to use profits generated by the stadium to cross-subsidise the use of the community pitches for example, which may conflict with the clubs' profit motives.

Similarly the Council may want to hire out the stadium for events such as concerts. These may benefit the clubs by attracting a wider audience however the clubs may be concerned about the impact that such events might have in terms of damage to the stadium or the playing surface.

Sharing of joint costs between the Council and the clubs is also likely to be an issue.

Operational Issues for the Council will include: crowd safety and security; noise, lighting, energy, waste management, traffic and transport. In respect of these issues the clubs will be focussed on the needs of the clubs and their fans, whereas the Council will also need to take into account the needs of the wider community which may conflict with those of the fans/clubs.

Clearly the arrangements for the SMC will need to be carefully established and agreements drawn up to minimise the potential for conflict between the parties and to protect the interests of the Council.

Examiner's comments

Requirement 4.1 requested candidates to assess the potential for conflict between the three key stakeholders (Council, rugby club and football club). On the whole this was very well done. The majority of candidates recognised that the Council was a not-for-profit organisation and were able to discuss the potential for conflict between the clubs – who were likely to be focussed on commercial and league success – and the Council's need to satisfy the wider community (and possibly the stadium sponsor). Better candidates also pointed out that in addition to this conflict, there was also likely to be conflict between the two clubs over the type of pitch, match scheduling etc, and that the football club might expect to have priority given that it was contributing a larger share of the capital. In their desire to apply models, candidates must be selective – a number of weaker candidates had learnt and churned out Mendelow's matrix which tended to result in too much focus on power and interest rather than on conflict between stakeholders. Some weaker candidates also dwelt exclusively on the stakeholders' objectives and did not get round to conflicts at all.

4.2 Break-even

(a) **The break-even attendance is as follows:**

Contribution per visitor

Football £640,000/(25 × 3,200) = £8

Rugby £270,000/(15 × 3,000) = £6

Break-even

Football £644,000/£8 = 80,500 visitors p.a which with 25 matches = 3,220 per match

Rugby £214,000/£6 = 35,667 visitors p.a which with 15 matches = 2,378 per match

(b) **Discussion**

Implications of calculations

The BE attendance for the football club is marginally higher (by 20 visitors per match) than the attendance figure used in the forecast, which explains the predicted loss (20 × £8 × 25 = £4,000).

The BE figure is 12.5% higher than the current attendance enjoyed by the football club and 5.6% higher than the average for the league. Thus the projections may be quite optimistic and if the initial attendance is below this figure then the football club will make a bigger loss than predicted. (It can be seen from the appendix that there is a loss of £71,400 based on current attendance and a loss of £34,000 based on the average for the current league.) It would be useful to know what the capacity of the existing football ground is and whether, like the rugby club, it is already at full capacity.

In respect of the rugby club the BE figure is 6.4% higher than the current attendance (which would result in a loss of just under £13k) but 16.3% lower than the average for the league. As the club's existing ground appears to be at capacity there is likely to be an implied waiting list of fans wishing to attend and so the estimated attendance level of 3,000 seems reasonable and provides a margin of safety of 20.7% (3000 – 2378/3000).

Variability of attendance levels

The attendance and financial performance of any sports club is heavily dependent on its team's performance. Thus the financial success of both the football and rugby club will depend on their ability to retain their current league position or the chances of being relegated/promoted, which can be seen from Exhibit 1 to significantly affect attendance levels.

(On average, attendance levels for football clubs are 64% higher in the league above and 41% lower in the league below.)

As the break-even levels of attendance for both clubs are above the average attendance for either club in the lower league, then relegation of a club would lead to significant losses or the need to curtail costs. The financial impact of promotion/relegation is set out in the Appendix, based on the figures for a typical club in the league. These calculations make it clear that the profitability of the football club is much more at risk than the rugby club because of the high level of traceable fixed costs (discussed further below). As a result the potential results for football range from a loss of £284k if relegated to a profit of £356k if promoted, which compares to a loss of £43k and a profit of £146k for the rugby club.

In addition to variations in attendance, success in non-league tournaments during the year would lead to more matches, further increasing profits. Each additional football match would contribute an additional £25,600 on projected attendance levels, with an extra rugby match generating £18,000. Using the expected attendance levels provided, it can be seen from the appendix that 26 football matches and 12 rugby matches would be more than sufficient to break even.

To better assess the accuracy of the forecasts and the likelihood of profitability, it would be useful to know each club's position in the current league to assess the likelihood of promotion/relegation. Also the attendance levels and number of matches for the previous two or three seasons would indicate any trend – in reality the attendance is likely to vary between matches depending on the recent success of the team and who the opposition is.

Revenues and costs

The calculations of break-even attendance depend on assumptions about the average spend per visitor, contribution and traceable fixed costs. If the forecasts have been based on existing ticket prices and spending on merchandise/catering, these may increase with the new stadium, in which case the contribution per visitor might increase and the required attendance would be lower. A breakdown of the average spend per visitor between ticket price and merchandising and details of the different ticket prices, which presumably include concessions for the young and elderly, would be useful.

One of the reasons the football club is predicting a loss is because its traceable fixed costs are significantly higher than those of the rugby club leading to a greater variability of profits if relegated/promoted. This may be because of the level of wages in the market place for footballers but more information is required here.

Appendix: Financial analysis

Estimated profits at various attendance levels: £'000

	Current attendance	If relegated	League average	If promoted	Per forecast
Football					
Attendance	2,863	1,800	3,050	5,000	3,200
	£	£	£	£	£
Contribution	572.6	360	610	1,000	640
Fixed costs	644	644	644	644	644
Profit	(71.4)	(284)	(34)	356	(4)
Rugby					
Attendance	2,234	1,900	2,840	4,000	3,000
	£	£	£	£	£
Contribution	201.06	171	255.6	360	270
Fixed costs	214	214	214	214	214
Profit	(12.94)	(43)	41.6	146	56

Sensitivity to number of matches

	Fixed costs	Forecast contribution per match	BE no of Matches (fixed cost/contribution)
Football	£644,000	640,000/25 = £25,600	25.16
Rugby	£214,000	270,000/15 = £18,000	11.89

Tutorial note:

A variety of calculations were possible and other sensible approaches involving marginal increases/contribution would have attracted credit.

Examiner's comments

Requirement 4.2(a) asked candidates to calculate the break-even attendance figure per match for both rugby and football and then 4.2(b) to discuss the implications of the variability of attendance on the forecasts, providing supporting calculations.

Answers to 4.2(a) were good with a large number of attempts scoring full marks. The most common mistake was to provide the answer in the form of annual attendance rather than per match. Only a small minority seemed unfamiliar with the break-even formula or divided fixed costs by revenue instead of contribution.

Answers to 4.2(b) were slightly more disappointing ranging from a discussion with very little use of supporting data, to a set of calculations with no discussion. The key issue here is that the break-even attendance for football is in excess of that currently forecast, whereas rugby has some margin of safety, although it is not clear how the traceable fixed costs (which are considerably higher for football than they are for rugby) have been arrived at. The calculation also makes assumptions about the number of matches and is based on average spend per visitor which will almost certainly vary. Using the data provided for the 'average' club to estimate attendance, it is evident that the forecast for match profits will not be realised if either club is relegated since they will be loss making, and conversely that league promotion would considerably increase the profits available. Also the risks arising from variability in attendance are higher for football than rugby. This was capably demonstrated numerically by the better candidates. Candidates would be well advised to note that when supporting calculations are asked for, it is very hard to produce a high-scoring discussion without reference to at least some numbers.

4.3 Report

To: Bigville Council
From: A N Consultant
Date: September 20Y2
Re: Community stadium

The council has identified three criteria which it will use to assess the high level business case:

(1) Ability to raise finance
(2) Commercially sustainable venture
(3) Alignment with council's overall strategic priorities

(1) Ability to raise finance

The costs of the proposed stadium are as follows:

	£m
Stadium construction	6.75
Community facilities	3.25
Basic stadium	10.0
Additional level	1.1
Expanded stadium	11.1

Currently the following funding appears to be available:

	£m
Sale of council land	6
Club contributions	3
Finanex payment for naming rights	1
	10

Thus the Council would appear to have sufficient funding in place for the basic stadium, with a shortfall of £1.1m if the additional conference and events facilities are built. The forecasts suggest that an enhanced stadium would increase profits by £250,000 p.a. which means the additional investment would payback in less than 4.5 years (1.1m/250,000) and therefore appears on the face of it to be worthwhile.

It would be useful to know what information the build costs have been based on and whether these make any allowance for potential overruns which are often incurred on this type of project. The amount budgeted and actually spent on comparable stadiums would help assess whether the costs being put forward by the Council fall within the range of other stadiums.

If a 10% allowance was made for overruns and the Council wished to build the enhanced stadium then they would need to find around £2m extra finance. It appears that some grant funding may be available and the Council needs to ascertain the amount that is likely to be forthcoming and the relevant conditions attached (which appear to be quite closely linked to the Council's own priorities in terms of employment, participation in sports and environmental sustainability).

A significant element of the finance is to come from the sale of the land so any uncertainty over the price or timing of this would need to be considered. For example work may need to start on the new stadium before the old one is demolished and the Council will need to ensure sufficient finance is available. In addition the Council is likely to have limited resources and therefore has a duty to consider the opportunity cost of using the money for the stadium in terms of the other projects that require funding.

Overall the initial findings suggest that there is a viable funding proposition provided the Council can find a suitable buyer for the land and receive some grant income. If this is not forthcoming then the Council would need to draw on any existing reserves or use debt finance. An alternative might be to consider the costs of building a smaller stadium since at 6,000 seats the capacity exceeds the maximum attendance for either club if promoted to the league above.

(2) **Commercially sustainable venture**

Basic stadium

	Football £	Rugby £	Non-match £	Total £
Club income				
Current profit/(loss) from clubs	(4,000)	56,000		52,000
Other income				
Community pitches/sports facilities			50,000	
Stadium advertising/sponsorship			200,000	
Revenue from non-match day activities			187,000	
			437,000	
Costs				
Stadium running costs			(375,000)	
				62,000
Overall surplus				114,000

Enhanced stadium
Incremental costs/revenues

Non-match day activities (537 – 187)			350,000	
Advertising (250 – 200)			50,000	
Stadium running costs (525 – 375)			(150,000)	
Additional income generated				250,000
Total surplus (114,000 + 250,000)				364,000

The financial projections suggest that the basic stadium would generate £114,000 of annual surplus, increasing to £364,000 for the enhanced stadium (this is before the interest cost associated with any borrowing requirement, and assumes the forecasts of revenue and costs from the clubs are achieved).

This equates to a ROCE of 1.14% (114k/10m) for the basic stadium and 3.3% for the enhanced (364/11.1m). More importantly the additional tier generates a return of £250,000 on an investment of £1.1m (22.7%) and would therefore seem to be a sensible option.

The commercial viability of the venture is quite heavily dependent on the ongoing sponsorship to be received from Finanex. Without this the basic stadium would generate a loss (ignoring match revenues/costs) of £138k, with the additional commercial activities from the enhanced stadium leading to only a small profit of £62k. If the venture fails however the Council will still be in the position of owning the land on which the stadium is built.

One of the considerations for the Council will be the extent to which it shares in the profits generated by the stadium. Were the clubs to keep their own profits/losses then the predicted income for the Council would be £62,000 from the basic stadium and £312,000 from the advanced. However it appears that the suggested agreement is for the SMC to pay rent to the Council for the stadium and for the members of the SMC (of which the Council is one) to then share the profits/losses from its operation. It is not clear whether the costs of the lease are included in the forecasts provided and what the nature of the profit sharing agreement between the three parties to the SMC will be. To better assess the commercial viability from the Council's perspective it would be useful to compare the Council's share of the incremental costs and revenues of the proposed stadium with the current situation where the Council receives lease payments from the rugby club for its existing ground.

Alignment with council's overall strategic priorities

Bigville Council's recently stated strategic priorities are:

- To maintain and develop Bigville's successful economy and provide suitable employment opportunities for residents

- To ensure accessible opportunities for all to engage in culture, leisure and recreational activity

- To promote and provide support for local people to make healthy lifestyle choices

- To create, enhance and maintain cleaner, safer and more sustainable environments

Basic stadium

A shared community stadium should provide job opportunities and if the stadium is used for events on non-match days eg, concerts this may attract more visitors to the area, thus stimulating the economy. However the existing football and rugby grounds are likely to employ local people currently and amalgamation of two grounds into one may actually lead to a reduction of jobs in some cases.

Providing a new and improved stadium is consistent with the Council's aims of ensuring accessible leisure and recreational activities and promoting healthy lifestyle choices. The all-weather sports pitches and athletics track will be of benefit to Bigville's clubs, schools and colleges, thus increasing the opportunities available in the area for local people to have a healthy lifestyle. Concerts and other events on non-match days may also increase the cultural activities available.

Finally the design of the stadium appears to focus on environmental sustainability. However, it would be necessary to assess in more detail the impact on the environment of the construction activities and then the ongoing running of the stadium in terms of pollution, noise, use of resources etc.

Enhanced stadium

The extension of the stadium to provide a conference and exhibition centre is likely to significantly increase local employment opportunities, attract more visitors to Bigville, provide opportunities for its businesses and provide more economic benefit than the basic stadium.

In addition it will widen the scope of the activities available in the area. There may also be operating synergies which help the Council to minimise the costs involved in the provision of services or cross-subsidise the community activities from the profits generated by corporate hospitality etc.

Thus the plans for the community stadium do appear to be aligned in overall terms with the Council's four stated priorities and the enhanced stadium is likely to improve rather than worsen the strategic fit.

Conclusion

There does appear to be a positive high level business case for the shared stadium and the preliminary indications are that the enhanced stadium would be the most commercially viable and more likely to help achieve the Council's strategic priorities. The Council should arrange a meeting with the key stakeholders to discuss the project, their requirements and their potential involvement and then create a steering group to take the project forward and undertake a more detailed financial analysis and feasibility study.

Examiner's comments

In requirement 4.3, candidates were required to write a report to the Council assessing the high level business case for the stadium using the Council's three stated criteria from the scenario: ability to raise finance; commercial sustainability and alignment with strategic priorities. Generally candidates made a good attempt at assessing the ability to raise finance. The vast majority produced calculations showing the estimated costs of construction and the amount of finance already secured, recognising that cash was available to fund the basic stadium but that government grants would be required to build the enhanced version. The better answers pointed out the risk of over-runs and also the fact that there may be some uncertainty associated with the sale of the land to the developer. The evaluation of commercial sustainability was less well done, with the weaker candidates concentrating their discussion on the environmental aspects of the stadium (thereby overlooking the commercial element of sustainability) or merely reiterating their discussion of the variability of match profits, already addressed in 4.2(b). Using the projections in the scenario it is clear that the enhanced stadium increase profits significantly and that the additional £1.1m investment would be worthwhile. The best candidates pointed this out, some producing ROCE or payback calculations which were encouraging, and a number recognising the reliance on income from the sponsor. Only a few candidates pointed out that the Council has a dual role – as lessor of the stadium (which will guarantee a fixed rental income) and as a partner in the SMC (which will entitle them to a share of the profits (losses). Candidates felt more comfortable evaluating whether the stadium met the Councils' strategic priorities, although surprisingly few discussed whether these were better met by the enhanced rather than the basic stadium. The weakest candidates simply made passing reference to the stated priorities and failed to analyse whether and how the stadium would achieve these. Disappointingly some candidates continue to ignore the presentation mark available for formatting their answer appropriately (in this case as a report) and the marks available for further information and a preliminary conclusion (both of which were specifically asked for). Better marks were scored by those candidates who attempted to tailor their request for further information to the scenario.

4.4 Risks

The risks for the Council in relation to the construction of the stadium and its operation by SMC include the following:

Construction

Funding requirement

Risk arises because of the uncertainty regarding the level of capital requirement and the funding available, especially in terms of grants. Should there be a shortfall then the Council may need to find more capital by diverting it from other needs or by borrowing.

The Council may not find a developer willing to buy the land on which the existing stadium is built or one who is prepared to pay the asking price for it. Even if the sale can be arranged there is a risk that it takes time and that construction of the new stadium needs to be started before the finance from the sale of the land is available. Local residents may also decide that the money would be better spent on services such as health and education.

There are uncertainties regarding stakeholder commitment to the project. It is unclear how the football club for example would react to a shared stadium and to the fact that they are contributing more capital than the rugby club. In the current economic climate Finanex may face budget constraints and decide that it has higher priorities to spend its money on.

A major capital cost overrun, which is not uncommon in such projects, would leave the Council with the residual funding risk.

Location and planning

It appears that a site has been earmarked but a potential risk is that it turns out not to be suitable. Planning permission for the new venture is critical. There is a risk that issues arise during the construction period in relation to the environment eg, protestors complaining about the impact on the landscape or local residents unhappy about the noise/traffic etc.

Timing

Any delays in construction, as well as increasing costs, could result in adverse publicity for the Council if the clubs do not have a stadium to play in at the start of the season.

Construction company

The council will need to ensure that the building contractor is carefully selected in accordance with policy to avoid the risks associated with the work not being done properly.

Operation by SMC

The current plans are for an SMC jointly controlled by the Council and the clubs. The joint venture potentially reduces risks for the Council (as does the receipt of an annual lease payment) but an agreement will need to be carefully drawn up to minimise the potential for conflict between the parties and to specify profit sharing arrangements, contributions to ongoing costs etc.

Financial

As discussed in 4.2 and 4.3, the financial models are dependent on a number of assumptions and estimates. The Council should undertake more detailed sensitivity analysis/scenario planning to get comfort regarding best and worst case scenarios. Should the venture be loss-making, or Finanex decide to cease their sponsorship, the Council is likely to have to provide further ongoing support/financial assistance.

It appears that the profits of the whole venture will be shared between the three parties but this needs to be clarified. If one or other club starts to perform poorly and/or gets relegated this would cause the stadium to become financially unsustainable and would affect the SMC's ability to make the lease payments.

Alternatively the clubs may be expecting to retain match-day profits in which case the SMC may only share the profits from the rest of the stadium and conferencing. This may reduce the amount of community activities that can be undertaken as the Council is likely to need a share of the profits from the clubs to subsidise such initiatives.

Legal

There is likely to be a range of regulations affecting the Council, its role and powers and, in particular, the Council's legal position if the revenue targets are not achieved.

Changes in regulations of the rugby and football governing bodies may also affect the stadium and/or the number of matches eg, there is a risk that increased pitch specifications or health and safety requirements increase the running costs.

Other stakeholders

As commercial entities, the clubs may have more in common with each other than they do with the Council and, if the objectives conflict, the Council may find itself in a minority over certain decisions, resulting in the venture not achieving its strategic priorities.

There is a risk that the clubs fall out or that one of them becomes insolvent and that, as a result, the Council loses one of the parties to the joint venture. Any change in ownership and/or management of the clubs may significantly affect the venture. For example if the football club is acquired by a wealthy investor it may decide that it wants a stadium for its own use.

Examiner's comments

Requirement 4.4 requested candidates to consider the risks for the Council associated with the construction of the stadium and its operation by the stadium management company (SMC). This was the least well done element of question 1. Most, but not all, candidates split their discussion between construction and operation, although some candidates chose instead to structure their answers by using a model such as PESTEL and as a result sometimes lost focus on the specific requirement. A common weakness was to produce a list of risks that would be faced by all parties rather than specifically the council and to make only passing reference to the SMC. In this regard better answers were produced by those candidates who clearly appreciated the dual role of the council (referred to above) and their position as stakeholder within the SMC.

5 Beauty Soap Ltd (September 2012)

Marking guide

			Knowledge	Skill	Marks
5.1	(a)	Strategic models	3	4	7
	(b)	Appropriateness of BS's plans	2	7	8
5.2		Standardisation v adaptation	2	3	5
5.3		Merits of the two options	3	6	8
5.4		Ethical marketing	2	3	5
			12	23	33

General comments:

The scenario in question 2 concerned Beauty Soap (BS), a large UK based company which manufactures and sells personal care products throughout Europe. BS was established over one hundred years ago as a soap producer. It grew organically by investing in research and development to expand its product range, then later by the acquisition of a number of competitors and also a European dental care company. BS wants to reduce its dependence on the European market which is mature and where margins are under pressure. It is keen to expand into Latin America, as forecasts suggest there is considerable growth potential, particularly in countries like Brazil. BS is considering two options: organic expansion using a direct selling model of local workers, or the acquisition of Gomera, a local personal care business with existing product range and supply chain/distribution networks. Preliminary research has suggested that the local market needs smaller products sizes and lower prices than BS's European product model. BS has also recently announced plans to launch an education campaign, in conjunction with the governments in the countries in which it operates, promoting the regular washing of hands with BS soap to reduce infection and disease.

The question provided scope for a limited amount of data analysis as candidates were given brief information about sales revenues in the European personal care industry as a whole, together with those for BS and the market leader.

This question was also well attempted by the majority of candidates.

5.1 (a) Growth strategy

Lynch's expansion matrix is a two by two matrix of company growth (internal and external development) and geographic location (home/domestic and international).

Under this model BS's initial growth was carried out internally in its domestic market – the UK. After establishing itself initially as a household soap manufacturer BS used research and development to generate internal organic growth through new products such as shampoos and face creams. BS's growth then continued externally through acquisition. This occurred first domestically with the acquisition of the UK based dental care business and then internationally with the acquisition of other European companies making personal care products.

BS is now proposing further international expansion in respect of Brazil, but has not yet decided whether it will undertake this by internal or external development.

The Ansoff matrix is another two-by-two matrix, of products (existing and new) and markets (existing and new). Relating product opportunities to markets gives rise to four possible strategies:

Market penetration – involves selling more existing products to existing markets. In the case of BS it started as a household soap manufacturer and quickly penetrated the market due to the range of sizes and fragrances on offer.

Product development – selling new products to existing markets. BS did this initially by investing in research and development to expand its product range from soap to shampoos, face creams etc. Later BS further developed its product range in the UK by acquiring a company specialising in dental care products – an area where BS perhaps lacked expertise to develop the product itself internally.

Market development – new markets for existing products, usually requiring an investment in marketing. BS pursued this via acquisitions of personal care product manufacturers in Europe. It is likely that this route offered a faster method of entry to the market and potentially got round barriers to entry. The proposed expansion to Brazil is another example of market development.

Diversification: new products for new markets – BS does not specifically appear to have done this, however an example might be the acquisition of a perfume manufacturer based in America. Since the single-use products proposed for Brazil are already being sold to a European hotel chain this does not really constitute diversification.

(b) **Current position and appropriateness of targeting new markets**

Current market position

BS is currently operating in Europe, a market which appears to be mature. If we consider the data provided, the overall market for personal care products in Europe has shrunk by 6% between 20Y0 and 20Y1. Since prices are under pressure this could be due to a fall in average selling prices rather than sales volumes. BS's share of that market was maintained at 3.8% in both 20Y0 and 20Y1 but the 6% reduction in the size of the market has led to a 27m euro drop in BS turnover.

Relative to the market leader BS has performed slightly better, generating 30% of their revenue in 20Y0 and 32% in 20Y1.

More information is needed to ascertain the European market trend and exactly where personal care products are in the industry life cycle. At this stage of the life cycle the European market may still offer good profit and cash generating opportunities and it is likely that people will continue to buy personal care products so the market decline may take some time. However for a sustainable future and growth opportunities, BS may need to look elsewhere.

Under the BCG matrix, BS's UK and European business might be deemed a cash cow (or possibly a dog) and its desire to expand in Latin America could be seen as an attempt to create a star.

Appropriateness of targeting emerging market:

- Reduces dependence on core European market and spreads risk given threat to margins

- BS may face less rivalry initially in developing markets such as Brazil compared to mature markets and hence enjoy better margins

- The stage of the industry life cycle will be different in Brazil etc, where markets are still developing, which offers opportunities for better cash flow and profits over a longer period

- Western brands may be very attractive in this market so it could be a good opportunity to increase sales volumes

- Economic growth will boost demand and industry forecasts for personal care products are promising

- Expanding internationally outside Europe widens brand and image so BS becomes a more global company – this may also help strengthen its position in Europe

- It may help address any seasonality in terms of revenue and cash flow

- Competitors are doing this elsewhere (eg, the three multinational companies already in Brazil)

- There may be financial arguments for setting up eg, grants/incentives from local governments

However BS should be aware that there may be some downsides:

- Increased risk of operating in unknown, emerging markets. BS will need to invest time and money to understand the needs of the local market

- Political and legal risk eg, as demonstrated by the Brazilian government attitude to foreign owned companies creating value; any quotas/tariffs/restrictions on free trade; any specific regulations to comply with

- Economic and transaction risk – to date BS has only exported to Europe and been exposed to exchange rate risk in terms of the euro

- Existing competition – multinationals will be large with economies of scale; domestic competitors have the advantage of local knowledge. Will BS have any distinct competitive advantage over these players? Also as other markets are predicted to grow other companies may be considering expanding

- Will BS have sufficient resources and management skills to exploit the opportunity eg, language skills, ability to recruit local workforce?

- BS needs to consider the extent to which it needs to adapt products/marketing for other markets – these costs, when taken with the additional distribution costs and the exchange movements, may mean the margin is no better but the risk is higher

  If expansion is deemed appropriate, the method of expansion chosen may help to reduce some of the risks/downsides

Examiner's comments

Requirement 5.1 was split into two parts. Part (a) asked candidates to use relevant models to analyse the ways in which BS has chosen to expand historically and its plans for Brazil. Part (b) went on to request a discussion of the appropriateness of its strategy to move away from the European market and target other international markets. Overall this requirement was answered very well. There were a number of ways to approach an answer to 5.1(a) – as a discussion of organic growth/acquisition; products and markets; or domestic and international expansion. Those candidates who used Lynch's model and/or Ansoff's product/market development matrix to structure their answers tended to achieve higher marks. It was pleasing to see that the majority of answers were very specific to the scenario, identifying how BS had initially used R&D to expand organically through product development and then used acquisition to target other products and markets. In 5.1(b) most candidates used the data in the Exhibit to identify that whilst the European market had declined between 20Y0 and 20Y1, BS has retained its market share, which has increased in relation to the market leader. Whilst further information would be necessary to confirm the trend, this suggests that the European industry may be reaching the mature stage of its lifecycle and that other markets, at an earlier stage of development, might offer more potential for future growth. Quite a lot of candidates identified the scope to use either the BCG matrix or life cycle model here as a starting point for discussion. The better candidates realised that this was not a case of BS immediately leaving the European market, rather that to ensure future prosperity it should continue the expansion strategy discussed in 5.1(a) by finding new markets and/or products offering better potential. Some weaker candidates let themselves down by applying the BCG model very literally and concluding from the data that 'BS should shoot the dog.' Better answers were less categorical, recognising that there is some degree of uncertainty within the BCG categorisation. Sadly, some candidates wasted time here by starting to discuss the methods of expansion being proposed for Brazil, despite a specific instruction to ignore these for this requirement.

5.2 Standardisation v Adaptation

Products can be classified according to their degree of or potential for global marketing:

Local products – suitable in a single market

International products – have the potential to extend to other markets

Multinational products – adapted to the perceived unique characteristics of national markets

Global products – designed to meet the needs of global market segments

The global/local dilemma refers to the extent to which products and services can be standardised across national boundaries or need to be adapted to meet the requirements of specific national markets because of different social and cultural conditions. Adaptation may involve changes to the actual product (involving changes in production) or to the method of promotion (brand, price etc) or some combination of the two.

Whilst standardisation tends to bring benefits in terms of economies of scale it may fail to target the market needs appropriately. Conversely adaptation is likely to involve greater costs, as a minimum in terms of R&D and marketing, but may increase competitive advantage.

The multinational personal care companies have expanded into Brazil using their existing globally branded products. Gomera on the other hand is currently producing a product which is only being sold in a single market – Brazil. It appears that for the market in Brazil, BS believes it has no choice but to adapt its product for financial reasons because its standard European product is not affordable for a significant element of the domestic population. It would be interesting to see how BS products compare in size and cost to the existing products in the market place and to what extent this view is backed up by further market research. BS does however have the advantage that it already produces single-use products for the European hotel chain which should help to reduce the costs involved in adaptation.

The other choice available to BS (and other international companies) is whether to retain its manufacturing in a limited set of locations so as to exploit economies of scale and then distribute a standard product internationally, or whether to set up production facilities in South America.

Examiner's comments

Requirement 5.2 requested candidates to discuss the need for global companies to consider standardisation/adaptation of products. On the whole this requirement was poorly attempted and answers here were polarised. Some candidates clearly appreciated the nature of the problem and produced good answers discussing the trade-off between economies of scale in production and marketing on the one hand and satisfying the needs of different consumers and market places on the other. Others appeared to confuse this with Porters generic strategies and discussed cost leadership vs differentiation, and some weaker candidates missed this requirement out completely.

5.3 Method of market development

Lynch's expansion method matrix would identify the two options of acquisition vs. direct investment as external development (acquisition) vs internal development (organic growth).

Acquisition of Gomera, the local company, comes with the following advantages:

- Existing knowledge of the environment and local market providing useful initial expertise

- An instant skill base in terms of resources, employees etc is likely to mean faster growth

- It provides access to existing supply chain and distribution networks reaching into remote parts of Brazil

- A locally known established brand and reputation with an existing customer base – this may be viewed more favourably by the Brazilian government and consumers than a foreign owned brand. Once the acquisition has occurred BS can then start to introduce its other products

- Acquisition buys out a potential competitor and better enables BS to compete with the other two domestic companies

- There are likely to be synergies as BS can provide the advertising and product innovation that Gomera is lacking

- Gets round any barriers to entry in terms of resistance from the Brazilian government

- Capitalises on the market opportunity more quickly, which may be important if other European companies are also considering expansion in Brazil

Direct investment offers the following merits:

- Gomera may not be an ideal partner in terms of size or market positioning and there may be a conflict between strategies if BS is seen as a premium producer compared to Gomera. With direct investment BS is free to pursue its own strategy.

- The price BS is required to pay for Gomera may not be appropriate. Organic growth avoids paying for goodwill therefore BS can acquire a larger tangible asset base for the same cost as acquisition.

- May offer a chance for more gradual expansion and an opportunity to test the market by exporting products from Europe to be sold locally under the direct selling model before then investing in production facilities in Brazil.

- Organic growth creates a business with the same culture as BS thereby avoiding any conflict etc on integration.

- The Brazilian government may look favourably on the direct selling model proposed by BS and there may be grants or other incentives available.

- Avoids any hidden or unforeseen losses that do not come out as part of due diligence on Gomera.

On the face of it, it would appear that acquisition is probably preferable, however the final decision as to the most appropriate method of expansion will probably depend on the price that BS is likely to have to pay for Gomera and the premium on acquisition.

Examiner's comments

Requirement 5.3 asked candidates to discuss the relative merits of the two methods of expansion being considered for Brazil. This was very well done. As usual candidates were well prepared for a discussion of organic growth vs acquisition and the majority undertook this in the context of the scenario. Only the better candidates picked up on BS's proposed use of the direct selling model and questioned where BS was planning to produce the products. Those candidates who attempted to reach a preliminary conclusion as to the better method of expansion attracted higher skills marks.

5.4 Social and ethical marketing

The marketing concept suggests that a commercial organisation's goals are best fulfilled by identifying customers' needs and providing products which satisfy those needs efficiently and profitably.

The concept of social or ethical marketing extends this idea to see marketing as a social force that reflects and influences cultural values and norms. Thus marketing can extend beyond economic considerations and be used to promote the welfare of society as a whole. Here the social aim of BS's campaign is for improved education and hence better health, thus BS could argue that through marketing it is providing information and helping people make informed choices.

Marketing of BS soap to promote a healthier way of life is designed to instil awareness of the need for hygiene and then to create a behaviour change whereby people wash their hands more often – educating people re standards of hygiene could be argued to eradicate disease and enhance the benefits to society. Thus BS are using the education campaign to promote a global caring image whilst there are clearly additional commercial benefits for BS in terms of getting its brand name and soap products known. There is potentially an even wider benefit for BS in that it will increase awareness of personal hygiene as a concept which will have knock on benefits for the demand and sale of BS's other products such as shampoo.

The concept of responsible marketing suggests that companies should consider the wider social implications of their products and the needs of society at large. Thus BS's decisions to employ a team of direct sellers might be seen to help increase the wealth of local people and alleviate poverty; it will also help reach remote areas.

The BS campaign could be said to link the desire to improve education and welfare with the commercial reality of expanding the business's sales. To this end the interests of the company and the Brazilian government are aligned and soap could be seen as a product that will do social good by meeting people's functional needs.

Critics might argue that such marketing is actually just manipulative selling. The production of soap may involve chemicals which damage the environment, use of soap may pollute local water supplies, and access to clean water and street sanitation is more likely to have a significant influence on health and disease than the use of soap.

They would see BS as wasting the considerable resources needed to engage a Brazilian footballer in the campaign just to convince people to buy products they don't need, and using promotion to convince them that they will be dissatisfied or even unhealthy without them. The motivation might be seen to be to tap into a large potential market in the developing countries, when perhaps the domestic population would be better continuing to use more natural products or the traditional techniques available.

Also ethics could be considered in terms of whether BS is genuinely behind this as a concept – applying it to other countries etc – or whether it is simply a way of getting the Brazilian government to accept the company in the market.

> **Tutorial note:**
>
> Candidates could choose to apply the legality/transparency/fairness/effect model here:
>
> **Legality** – BS does not appear to be doing anything illegal
>
> **Transparency** – BS appears to be being quite open in its plans
>
> **Fairness** – there is nothing to stop other personal care companies doing the same thing (though Gomera for instance may not be able to pay the high fees of the footballer) and indeed there is nothing to stop consumers buying other soap products.
>
> **Effect** – by raising awareness and creating education BS could be said to be having a positive effect on the local community.

Examiner's comments

Finally part 5.4 asked candidates to assess the ethical implications of the proposed educational marketing campaign. This was poorly done by many candidates. There seems to be a tendency on the part of weaker candidates to approach the ethical requirements with great suspicion and to assume/conclude that what is being proposed is automatically unethical. A high number of candidates thought that the use of the Brazilian footballer was totally inappropriate and that in poorer countries it was unfair to try and influence people into buying anything at all (or indeed to wash their hands), with many focussing on the vulnerability of people in schools and hospitals. Some did apply the transparency, fairness and effect decision making approach, which tended to improve the quality of the answer by at least ensuring they were talking in ethical terms and applying a structured thought process. Only the best candidates provided an initial discussion of ethical marketing principles and concluded that linking marketing with corporate social responsibility is not necessarily unethical (manipulative selling). Some did question however whether the cost and high profile of using the footballer might undermine an otherwise reasonable attempt at CSR and ethical marketing. Answers to the ethics requirement, which is a consistent feature of the exam, continue to be variable and candidates wishing to score well are advised to adopt some form of framework for their answer and to produce a balanced argument rather than a one-sided discussion.

6 Maureen's Motors (September 2012)

Marking guide

	Knowledge	Skill	Marks
6.1 Generic strategy and market positioning	3	4	7
6.2 Service marketing mix	5	8	12
6.3 KPIs	2	4	6
	10	16	25

General comments:

Maureen's Motors is an eponymous insurance company that focuses its product on insurance for female drivers by offering benefits tailored to women that are not offered by most insurers: it provides additional cover for handbags and contents, pushchairs and car seats, and it has a network of female-friendly repairers and a helpline giving advice on all vehicle-related matters. Three famous actresses played the three Maureens in a long-running TV advertising campaign and MM then ran a competition to 'make me a Maureen' for ordinary women to star in their TV and billboard advertising campaign. Because of its brand image the current customer base for primary policy holders is 90% female. Since industry statistics show that women make significantly fewer claims than male counterparts and typically claim for lower amounts, this mix allows MM to make superior profits.

Like questions 1 and 2, this question was well attempted by most candidates.

6.1 Generic strategy and market positioning

Competitive positioning can be viewed in a number of ways but essentially means giving a product or service a place relative to its competitors in terms of factors such as quality, price, image etc. A sustainable competitive advantage can be achieved where there is the ability to outperform competitors in the long run.

Porter identified two distinct generic strategies: cost leadership and differentiation.

A cost leadership strategy attempts to achieve the position of lowest cost producer which facilitates competition on price. Differentiation strategy assumes that competitive advantage can be gained by creating attributes of the product or service which customers value and are prepared to pay a premium for. Such a strategy can be pursued broadly across an industry eg, Direct Line insurance which offers a range of cheap telephone/internet based insurance products, or by concentrating attention on one or more segments of the market (focus) eg, SAGA who provide insurance and other products for the over 50s.

MM appears to have adopted a focus-based approach within Porter's model, targeting a particular segment of the insurance industry (motor) and within that a specific market niche (female drivers).

The concept of generic strategy has been developed further by considering a possible spectrum of price/quality combinations from low price, low quality/added value (a no frills strategy) through to a high priced, high added value strategy of focussed differentiation.

MM has created differentiation through its product features and also its marketing.

The additional benefits offered by its insurance product suggest that MM has attempted to differentiate its service (through female friendly repairers, helplines, additional cover for handbags and car seats etc). It has also attempted to create a strong lifestyle brand image via use of the 3 Maureens and competitions. Whilst the product attributes may be relatively easy for other insurers to copy, the strong brand image may be harder to replicate.

Another way of looking at the issue of market positioning for MM is through Kotler's 3Cs: cost, customers, competition. This view sees the price/quality trade off in relation to competitors as the key issue. Competition for MM will come from other companies who decide to operate in the same market niche eg, Sheila's Wheels and also from the generic motor insurance products offered by the wide range of general insurance companies. Parity pricing would see MM's price and quality as equivalent to competitors – at below parity price sales may be made at the expense of profitability; above parity MM's product will be uncompetitive if identical products are available from competitors at lower prices. This is where the importance of brand comes in to reinforce perceived value, since MM customers who are loyal to the brand may feel they are getting a superior product, even if the basics of the cover are the same, and therefore may be prepared to pay more for it.

Examiner's comments

Requirement 6.1, which asked candidates to explain the strategy and positioning of MM, was very well attempted. The majority of candidates were well-prepared for a discussion of Porter's generic strategies and almost all identified MM as a differentiator, using appropriate information from the question, such as the provision of handbag cover and replacement car seats, to illustrate this. Some, but not all, recognised that instead of applying differentiation industry-wide, MM has focussed this strategy on a particular market niche resulting in a customer base that was 90% female. Whilst the weaker candidates restricted themselves to Porter, the better candidates also discussed positioning in relation to competitors and price/quality, pointing out that MM was likely to be at the higher end of the market when compared to the large motor insurers. A number also provided a discussion of Bowman's clock. Some weaker candidates spent too long on this requirement for the marks available, leaving themselves short of time for 6.2.

6.2 Marketing strategy

Target market

MM appears to have taken the results of some preliminary market research and used it to identify potential customers that it wants to target: women drivers. It has then tried to address the fact that insurance is seen by many as a 'grudge' purchase and developed a concept of a certain lifestyle to appeal to this target market. Finally it has developed its car insurance service by considering the product benefits that are most likely to appeal to a female market eg, handbag cover, female friendly repairers.

MM then needs to develop a marketing strategy to attract this target market, which can be considered using the marketing mix (the set of variables which a firm blends to produce the response it wants from its target market). In MM's case this includes the traditional 4Ps (Product, Price, Place, Promotion) and the additional 3Ps for service industries (People, Processes and Physical evidence). Attracting customers in the first instance is key to market share since industry statistics suggest that women are then less likely to switch insurer.

Product

This refers to the qualities of the product as perceived by potential customers. MM's product offering is made up of three elements:

- The basic or core product which is motor insurance

- The actual product which in MM's case is motor insurance specifically tailored for women and finally this leads to:

- The augmented product consisting of the insurance services that MM believes women particularly value and are prepared to pay for eg, female friendly repairers, additional cover for handbags, vehicle advice line etc.

Emphasising the fact that the service is particularly tailored to women will distinguish MM from the general motor insurers and is key to success.

Promotion

The MM brand is critical and promotion must be consistent with this and reinforce the image and alignment of the brand with the 3 Maureens. Advertising is likely to be the most important means of achieving this, hence the TV advertising campaign starring well known actresses has lead to coverage in women's magazines. Using the 'Make me a Maureen' competition strengthens the concept of MM being 'a reassuring brand for real women with real lives'. MM has created a strong brand image at relatively low cost but ongoing promotion will be required to maintain this, particularly if it continues to attract adverse publicity.

Brand recognition can be tested through market research.

Price

MM's pricing policy needs to be appropriate to the wider marketing strategy and consistent with its competitive positioning. The price that potential female customers are prepared to pay for additional benefits can be ascertained through market research. Given the differentiation strategy female customers may be more likely to be attracted to MM for its brand image and benefits its policy offers (perceived value pricing) rather than because it is necessarily the cheapest in price, although MM needs to consider the prices charged by competitors for similar products.

The EU directive means that MM cannot price discriminate between equivalent men and women but elements of the insurance package may be priced separately eg, children's car seat cover may not be required by all women. This would also facilitate the product being offered to male drivers who otherwise may not be prepared to pay MM's higher prices for services which they do not value eg, additional cover for handbag contents.

The pricing of insurance premiums is a largely risk-based actuarial calculation and so the cost of cover will vary depending on the nature and age of the vehicle, the age of the policy holder etc. The pricing strategy is also likely to include discounts for no claims and MM offers a loyalty bonus which will help retain customers and market share. It also offers discounts through a friend referral scheme.

MM should consider how people pay for their insurance eg, it may charge a premium for people who wish to pay by instalments rather than annually. It may also decide to offer a discount for online purchase or for new customers.

Place

Place does not appear to be a key factor in the mix as it is not mentioned in the scenario. MM's products are likely to be sold through remote distribution channels (phone and internet), rather than face to face, and primarily online. MM could consider a possible agreement with certain car manufacturers to promote MM insurance along side new car purchases.

The people involved in this process will be key for MM and so the extension of the 4Ps to the 7Ps model for the marketing of services is relevant.

People

Recruitment of the right staff and training and development will be key to offering good female friendly customer service otherwise the attrition rate will be high.

Customer service staff taking calls and handling claims and those staffing the vehicle advice line will interact with customers and be key to providing a high quality service consistent with the MM brand and its association with the 3 Maureens.

The quality of the service offered by MM will also be heavily reliant on the female friendly repairers and MM will need to have a code of practice, training and monitoring to ensure this is adhered to.

Processes

As part of customer service, efficient administrative processes underpin a high quality provision. Processes need to be female friendly but also efficient. The speed of handling claims and making payments will be critical. If true, the adverse coverage in the newspapers suggests that MM has some work to do to improve in this area.

Technology can be used to ensure efficient processes for taking calls/selling policies/handling claims.

MM also need good processes to hire staff who are perceived by customers to be female friendly and who have the appropriate knowledge if they are manning the vehicle advice line. There will also need to be processes in place to manage the network of repairers and ensure the provision of replacement car seats.

Physical evidence

This is probably of minor importance but refers to items that give substance or evidence of the delivery surrounding MM's service eg, tangibles such as the MM logo, claim forms, cover letters and policy documents. MM could also brand the replacement car seats and send out free tax disc holders or key rings to those renewing policies.

Requirement 6.2 asked candidates to discuss the marketing mix adopted by MM. Again the majority of candidates were well-prepared in respect of the knowledge for this question, with most recognising the fact that the service nature of the business meant considering the extra 3Ps (people, processes and physical evidence) in addition to the normal 4Ps of product, price, place and promotion. The aspect that was least well addressed was how to prioritise the 7Ps in relation to the facts in the question. The better answers identified the elements of the mix which were more important to MM and extracted salient information from the scenario to explain how these had been tailored to the target market. Some weaker candidates simply explained what each P represented rather than discussing how MM has chosen to use the various elements of the mix to market its insurance services. A significant minority limited their scores by discussing the 3Ps only, when it was very clear from the scenario that product, price and promotion were also relevant factors.

6.3 KPIs

MM has been criticised for concentrating on new customers rather than existing ones. If this criticism is valid then MM needs to set targets for and measure the improvement in customer service and claims handling. Possible KPIs are as follows:

Note: Candidates were expected to produce 3 KPIs in total, with at least one covering each area – more are however included here for tutorial purposes.

Customer service KPIs	Explanation
Average score from customer feedback surveys regarding claims handling/use of vehicle advice helpline/speed of response	An increase in this score over time would suggest that customers' satisfaction is increasing
Number of complaints – again split by the different elements of the service	If MM measures the % decrease in complaints received it can assess how effective the steps to improve service have been. By measuring the types of complaint MM can ascertain whether it is their staff or their associates (eg, the car repairers) that are the cause of the problem
Number of referrals by customers to friends	An increase in the number of referrals would suggest that more customers are satisfied enough to recommend MM
Claims handling KPIs	
Speed of claim settlement	A reduction in the time taken to process and settle claims would indicate greater efficiency and a higher level of service for customers
Number of claims processed per employee/ case load per employee	Measuring the workload per employee and their productivity would help assess whether MM has allocated sufficient resources to this area
% of claim paid out	Customers will be keen to ensure that they receive the maximum possible amount of their claim and that they do not lose out due to any small print on the policy

Examiner's comments

Requirement 6.3 asked candidates to explain and justify three KPIs that could be used to assess MM's claims handling and customer service. This was in the light of recent criticisms of both and the suggestion that MM cares more about attracting new customers than retaining existing ones. This part was quite poorly done by some candidates, who were clearly unsure about the distinction between KPIs and goals. For the weaker candidates, KPIs described could have been those for any business and it was not obvious that the candidate was discussing MM or specifically its need to improve claims handling and service to existing customers. Whilst customer satisfaction is relevant to all businesses and therefore customer feedback is vitally important, there was much information in the question, regarding the nature of MMs service and the recent criticisms, which could have been used to produce some high quality answers. The better candidates produced a reasoned justification of their choice of measure and demonstrated clearly how this could be used to track improvement in the relevant areas. Some candidates provided a long list of KPIs, despite the specific request for only three – these additional measures wasted time and did not attract marks.

7 Grassgrind Garden Mowers plc (December 2012)

Marking guide

			Knowledge	Skill	Marks
7.1	(a)	Analysis of performance	–	17	15
	(b)	UK market share	2	3	5
	(c)	Competitive positioning	2	6	7
	(d)	Growth strategy	3	10	12
7.2	Ethical issues		2	4	6
			9	40	45

General comments:

This is the mini case and also the data analysis question. The scenario relates to a company manufacturing lawnmowers (GGM). The company manufactures two types of upmarket, petrol-powered mower for use by UK households: tractor mowers and conventional mowers. The company is subject to a take-over bid by BB, which the GGM board is defending. A key issue is the proposed future strategy of BB, in comparison to the defensive strategy of the existing GGM board. The candidate is in the role of a business adviser for the accountants (PP) representing the existing GGM board. PP has been asked to prepare a report evaluating GGM and aspects of the bid strategies.

7.1 (a)

From: Business Adviser
To: GGM independent report to shareholders
Date: XX December 20Y2
Subject: Assessment of strategic plans

	20Y1 Conventional mowers	20Y1 Tractor mowers	20Y2 Conventional mowers	20Y2 Tractor mowers	20Y1 Total	20Y2 Total
Statement of profit or loss	£	£	£	£	£	£
Revenue	3,240,000	5,400,000	2,952,000	5,076,000	8,640,000	8,028,000
Variable cost	1,944,000	2,700,000	1,771,200	2,820,000	4,644,000	4,591,200
Contribution	1,296,000	2,700,000	1,180,800	2,256,000	3,996,000	3,436,800
Fixed cost	911,250	303,750	885,600	338,400	1,215,000	1,224,000
Profit	384,750	2,396,250	295,200	1,917,600	2,781,000	2,212,800
Profit/revenue %	11.9	44.4	10.0	37.8	32.2	27.6
% change in revenue			–8.9	–6.0		–7.1

% change in vc		−8.9	4.4		−1.1
% change in contribution		−8.9	−16.4		−14.0
% change in FC		−2.8	11.4		0.7
% change in profit		−23.3	−20.0		−20.4
% change in volume		−8.9	4.4		

20Y1

Conventional mowers

In 20Y1 conventional mowers made a contribution per unit of £160, giving a contribution margin ratio of 40%.

The profit per unit after allocating fixed costs was £47.50, giving an operating profit margin (using the method of allocation of fixed costs adopted by GGM) of only 11.9%. This reflects a high proportion of fixed operating costs in the cost structure and therefore a high degree of operating gearing.

In drawing any conclusions about the performance of each product, however, the validity of the operating profit figures depends largely on the validity of the method of fixed cost allocation. While all such allocations are arbitrary (to a greater or lesser extent) the allocation by unit of output seems to be inappropriate in determining a cause and effect relationship between fixed operating costs and production activity. This is particularly the case as the tractor mowers are significantly larger, and probably more time consuming to produce, meaning it is likely they will require more fixed costs.

Based on the information available, it is not possible to produce an accurate allocation (eg, using activity based costing) but a better measure might be sales value (as suggested by the CEO), rather than sales volume, as this gives some recognition to the relative scale of productive activity per unit.

On this basis, the following revised data would be produced:

	20Y1		20Y2		20Y1	20Y2
	Conventional mowers	Tractor mowers	Conventional mowers	Tractor mowers	Total	Total
	£	£	£	£	£	£
Contribution	1,296,000	2,700,000	1,180,800	2,256,000	3,996,000	3,436,800
FC by value	455,625	759,375	450,081	773,919	1,215,000	1,224,000
Profit	840,375	1,940,625	730,719	1,482,081	2,781,000	2,212,800
Operating profit/revenue	25.9%	35.9%	24.8%	29.2%	32.2%	27.6%

Compared to the volume based method of allocation, the operating profit of conventional mowers in 20Y1 has more than doubled from £384,750 to £840,375.

In terms of viability, contribution is the most valid measure in the short term, as the issue of allocation of fixed costs is avoided. On this basis, the conventional mower creates a healthy £1,296,000 contribution in 20Y1, making it viable. This generates a reasonable operating profit margin of 25.9%.

Tractor mowers

In 20Y1 tractor mowers made a contribution per unit of £1,000 giving a contribution margin ratio of 50%.

The profit per unit after allocating fixed costs was £887.50 giving an operating profit margin (using the method of allocation of fixed costs adopted by GGM) of 44.4%. As already noted, this reflects the rather favourable treatment of tractor mowers using the original fixed cost per unit allocation method.

Using sales value, rather than sales volume, to allocate fixed costs, this gives a rather less favourable, though still profitable, picture for tractor mowers. Operating profit margin is now somewhat lower at 35.9% than it was under the original allocation method, although it is still higher than the operating profit margin of the conventional mowers.

Other costs

The operating cost and profit figures are only part of the picture in measuring performance. After taking account of finance costs the business may not be profitable at all. More information is needed in this respect.

Overall company profit

While the allocation of fixed operating costs is arbitrary at unit level, the overall cost and profit at company level is the same irrespective of the allocation method. While such costs may not be avoidable in the short term, in the longer term it is essential that they are covered in order to sustain the business.

Nevertheless, overall operating profit of £2,781,000 has been generated on revenue of £8,640,000. This generates a healthy operating profit margin of 32.2% in 20Y1.

20Y2

Conventional mowers

There has been no change in the selling price or in variable cost per unit of conventional mowers between 20Y1 and 20Y2. The key change affecting performance has therefore been a fall in sales volume of 8.9%. As selling prices have not changed, then sales revenue has also fallen by 8.9%.

The impact of fixed operating costs on conventional tractor profitability in 20Y2 is twofold. First, total operating fixed costs have risen by 0.7%, so the pool of costs to be allocated has increased. Second, the volume of conventional mowers sold has decreased, while the number of tractor mowers sold has increased. As a result, the proportion of the fixed overhead pool allocated to conventional mowers has fallen. The net effect of this for conventional mowers (under the existing allocation method) is that while fixed operating cost per unit has increased from £112.50 to £120 (+6.7%), the total fixed operating cost allocated to conventional mowers has decreased from £911,250 to £885,600 (a fall of 2.8%).

As already noted, the method of fixed cost allocation used by the company based on volumes is questionable. The revised sales value based allocation method shows that the overall fixed costs allocated to the conventional product fell from £455,625 in 20Y1 to £450,081 in 20Y2, a reduction of 1.2%.

Using these revised fixed cost allocations the operating profit margin has fallen from 25.9% in 20Y1 to 24.8% in 20Y2. The primary causal factor explaining why this has occurred is the fall in sales volume.

Tractor mowers

In 20Y2 the key factors affecting the change in profitability of tractor mowers were: (1) a 10% reduction in selling price from £2,000 to £1,800; and (2) an increase of 4.4% in sales volume from 2,700 to 2,820. Variable costs per unit were unchanged.

The reduction in selling price may be causally linked to the increase in demand (downward sloping demand curve) but other factors may also have been relevant in that we do not know what would have happened to demand if the price had remained unchanged (see below).

Overall, in consequence of the price decrease and sales volume increase, revenues have fallen by 6% from £5.4m in 20Y1 to £5.076m in 20Y2. To the extent that the volume change was due to the price change, this would imply that demand is inelastic. As a consequence, the price reduction strategy could have significantly contributed to the fall in revenue of the tractor product in 20Y2 compared to 20Y1. The increase in fixed costs of 11.4% has also contributed to the reduction in profit of the tractor range.

Profitability of the tractor mowers has fallen as a result of the reduction in revenues. Using the sales volume basis for fixed cost allocation, operating profit has decreased by 20% from £2,396,250 to £1,917,600. Using the sales value basis for fixed cost allocation, operating profit has decreased by 23.6% from £1,940,625 to £1,482,081.

Comparison of the conventional and tractor range performance

Both conventional and tractor ranges have suffered a significant reduction in profit in 20Y2 compared to 20Y1 under both allocation bases.

In absolute terms, tractor mowers are more profitable than conventional mowers measured by both profit and contribution – although a more detailed review of overhead cost drivers may alter the data significantly.

The cause of the fall in profit for the tractor range may be largely endogenous ie, choosing internally a price reduction strategy. It may therefore be within the company's control to reverse this price increase and restore future profitability to 20Y1 levels.

Overall profit

Overall operating profit has fallen by 20.4% from £2,781,000 in 20Y1 to £2,212,800 in 20Y2 (irrespective of the cost allocation method used). While the fall is substantial, the company remains reasonably profitable with an overall operating profit margin on revenue of 27.6%. If the price reduction is reversed, then some of the fall may be recovered in 20Y3.

Examiner's comments

Requirement 7.1(a) requests candidates to analyse the performance of GGM, and each of its two products, in the financial years 20Y1 and 20Y2.

The majority of candidates answered this question in the report format that was required. The overall analysis of performance varied significantly from candidate to candidate. The higher scoring candidates used a variety of ratios such as change in revenues, profit margins and contribution. These data were used, in part, to explain the impact of the decrease in sales of conventional mowers. Also, the sales price of tractor mowers had reduced and, as a consequence, they had experienced an increase in sales volume. Some extremely good answers were produced in this respect, with candidates using price elasticity of demand to demonstrate the relationship between volume and price and thereby identify causal factors to explain the changes occurring in the data.

Only a minority of candidates developed their answers further and calculated the reallocation of fixed costs on a sales value basis. Most candidates calculated ratios for each of the two types of product separately and for the company as a whole for each year. This gave a structure for them to undertake further analysis.

The key issue which most candidates identified was the fact that tractor mowers were more profitable, but were aimed at a niche market. At the other end of the spectrum, the weaker candidates merely copied out the sales and cost figures from the question and made a vague attempt at analysing profitability. For these candidates there was normally no consideration of the relationship between price and volume, nor of the impact of changing the current method of allocation of fixed costs.

The lowest scoring candidates merely made assertions describing the changes in ratios, with little, if any, attempt at an analysis of causality. Some candidates spent too much time discussing market share in this section, rather than in 7.1(b).

(b) Market share can be determined in terms of volume of sales or by sales value. Which is selected would depend on the purpose for which the analysis is being used.

A further issue is in defining the market. The broadest useful definition is likely to be the UK mower market. As GGM does not currently produce other powered garden tools and equipment then taking this wider definition does not seem appropriate. Within the mower sector there are various sub-sectors eg, type of cutting blade; tractor and conventional; or method of power (petrol, electric, battery and hand-propelled).

The level of sub-analysis which would be appropriate could depend on a number of factors but one key issue would be whether consumers would readily substitute one good for another (eg, it carries out the same function and is in the same price range). On this basis one could argue that the tractor mower is different from conventional mowers on the grounds of price and function in its suitability only for large gardens.

Taking the market split of tractor and then conventional mowers, a **sales volume** analysis of market share is as follows:

	20Y1		Forecast 20Y2	
	Conventional mower	Tractor mower	Conventional mower	Tractor mower
GGM (units)	8,100	2,700	7,380	2,820
Market (units)	1.5m	30,000	1.5m	30,600
Market share	0.54%	9%	0.49%	9.2%

In terms of **sales value**, market share is as follows:

	20Y1		Forecast 20Y2	
	Conventional mower	Tractor mower	Conventional mower	Tractor mower
GGM Revenue (£)	3,240,000	5,400,000	2,952,000	5,076,000
UK market at retail prices (£s) (W1)	360,360,000	35,640,000	367,640,000	36,360,000
UK market at wholesale prices (£s) (W2)	288,288,000	28,512,000	294,112,000	29,088,000
Market share at wholesale prices	1.1%	18.9%	1.0%	17.5%
Total market share at wholesale prices		2.7%		2.5%

WORKINGS

(1) The UK market for mowers, by value, amounted to £396m in 20Y1 and £404m in 20Y2. Tractor mowers make up 9% of this market. However these are retail prices.

(2) Retail prices are reduced to 80% (ie, 1/1.25) to obtain wholesale prices.

Thus GGM has a very small share of the conventional mowers market at around 1%, but a reasonably significant share of the tractor mower market.

A further analysis could be of petrol-powered mowers alone but this might not add much to the usefulness of the information if petrol and electric mowers are close substitutes.

Note: The UK mower market share relates to the goods sold in the UK; as opposed to the UK mower industry, which is the goods manufactured in the UK.

Examiner's comments

Requirement 7.1(b) asks candidates to determine the current UK market share of GGM, highlighting any problems that arise in defining market share in order to produce a useful figure.

Most candidates attempted to determine market share for both products in terms of sales volume and sales value. Only a minority correctly adjusted for differences between wholesale and retail prices, and many ignored this issue altogether. Similarly, only a minority of candidates made a decent attempt at explaining the key problems in defining the market.

(c)

	20Y1		Forecast 20Y2	
	Conventional mowers	Tractor mowers	Conventional mowers	Tractor mowers
GGM Average price (per question)	£400	£2,000	£400	£1,800
Retailer price x 1.25	£500	£2,500	£500	£2,250

	20Y1		Forecast 20Y2	
	Conventional mowers	Tractor mowers	Conventional mowers	Tractor mowers
UK market				
UK market at retail prices (£s)	360,360,000	35,640,000	367,640,000	36,360,000
Market (units)	1.5m	30,000	1.5m	30,600
Average price	£240	£1,188	£245	£1,188

Conventional mower market

GGM is a minor participant in the UK conventional mower market with a market share of around 1% in both value terms and volume terms. This places it in a weak competitive position in this market.

The fall in conventional mower sales revenue in 20Y2 and the reduction in market share indicates a worsening of GGM's competitive positioning in this market. In volume terms, a decrease from 0.54% to 0.49% implies a worsening in competitiveness.

The fall in conventional mower sales revenue in 20Y2 and the reduction in value-based market share may indicate a worsening of GGM's competitive positioning in this market. Indeed, reduced conventional mower sales volume occurred despite no change in selling price by GGM and with competitors increasing selling price from an average of £240 in 20Y1 to £245 in 20Y2 (2%).

Within the conventional mower market, GGM is placed very much towards the quality end as its price of £400 becomes a retail price of £500 with a 25% mark up, which is more than double the market average of £245 in 20Y2. Its competitive position therefore needs to be considered against rival companies who also operate in the niche up-market sector of the conventional mower product market.

Tractor mower market

GGM is a significant player in the UK tractor mower market with a market share of 17.5% in value terms in 20Y2. This places it in a strong competitive position.

The fall in tractor mower sales revenue in 20Y2 and the reduction in value-based market share may indicate a worsening of GGM's competitive positioning in this market. However, in volume terms, an increase from 9% to 9.2% implies an increase in competitiveness on this basis at least.

Within the tractor mower market, GGM is placed very much towards the quality end as its price of £2,000 in 20Y1 is higher than the market average of £1,188 even allowing for differences between retail and wholesale prices. Even in 20Y2 with the price reduction to £1,800 it is still significantly higher than the market average. Its competitive position therefore needs to be considered against rival companies who also operate in the same niche up-market sector of the tractor mower product market.

The tractor mower range has increased sales volume by 4.4% in 20Y2. As already noted, part of this may be due to a price reduction. However there has also been market expansion of 2% in volume terms. So while GGM has increased sales this is partly due to market expansion and partly due to lower prices. Note that the average market price has been constant so GGM has lowered price and has captured more market share but reduced profit in the process.

Note also that as GGM has reduced price and is part of the market, then if the overall average market price has remained constant, on average competitors must have increased prices.

Overall competitive positioning:

In the UK market revenues amounted to £404m in 20Y2.

GGM's revenue is £8.028m, but when adjusted to retail prices it represents £10.035m.

GGM does not export outside the UK, so this is their total revenue. In terms of global sales therefore, GGM may overall be a small participant in the global industry and suffer competitive disadvantage in the UK market against international competitors from relative diseconomies of scale.

In requirement 7.1(c), candidates were asked to explain the competitive positioning of GGM in the UK mower market and to assess how this has changed between 20Y1 and 20Y2.

Most candidates answered this question by starting with Porter's generic strategies then making an attempt to link this with the scenario. Most did this by considering the two products separately.

A significant number of candidates said that the positioning was 'stuck in the middle' with regards to the tractor mower as they were reducing the price, but still trying to promote a quality product. Candidates also used other models such the BCG matrix and Bowman's Clock.

Very few candidates presented decent numerical analysis to this requirement. Most commented on the change in price of the tractor mower, but only stronger candidates commented on the fact that the average market price had also fallen.

(d) **GGM board's strategic plan**

The Ansoff matrix is a useful model for identifying growth opportunities. There are four routes to growth in the model's two-by-two matrix of Products (new and existing) and Markets (new and existing).

The expansion strategy proposed by the GGM Board is one of product development in the Ansoff model. This means developing and launching new products into current markets.

The strength of this proposal is that GGM has experience and understanding of buyer and consumer behaviour in this market sector. Customers for the new products (petrol-powered garden tools and equipment including hedge trimmers, strimmers, chainsaws) are likely to be the same garden centres and DIY centres that already purchase the GGM mowers. GGM may therefore have knowledge of the customers, and trust from the customers.

Economies of scope may also occur in distributing goods to common locations, which may reduce common costs.

In terms of manufacturing capability there appear to be common elements and therefore core competencies in production that can be exploited to gain competitive advantage. This is likely to include using a smaller scale version of the petrol engines used on the mowers, but also other aspects such as cutting blades for hedge trimmers and chainsaws.

In terms of the size of market, the UK garden tools and equipment market is larger than the mower market as mower sales make up only 'about 45% of the overall gardening equipment industry.'

Data analysis

	Low demand	Estimated demand	High demand
Volume (units)	20,000	25,000	30,000
Price	£150	£150	£150
	£'000	£'000	£'000
Revenue	3,000	3,750	4,500
Variable cost	(1,800)	(2,250)	(2,700)
Contribution	1,200	1,500	1,800
Fixed cost	(1,400)	(1,400)	(1,400)
Profit	(200)	100	400

Profitability

At the expected level of demand, the GGM board proposal makes a profit. However at only £100,000 this is extremely modest and will only relatively marginally add to the company's current profit for 20Y2 of £2,212,800. Even at the top end of the estimation range it will only add £400,000 a year to profit, and there may be a low probability to this level of demand occurring.

Unless there are synergies with existing production, the new strategy would not add significantly to profit and growth. Indeed, as a measure of the scale of new activity, profit in 20Y1 was £2,781,000 and so profit fell by £568,200 in 20Y2. This fall would not be made good by the new project even at the top end of the range of estimates.

Risk

A key feature of the new project is that it carries risk. In particular, while the contribution margin is high at 40%, there are also high fixed costs, making the operating gearing high. This is illustrated in the above table which shows that, in the worse case scenario, if sales volumes fall by 20% an operating loss of £200,000 will be made.

The break-even revenue is:

£1.4m/0.4 = £3.5m

Thus, the margin of safety from the 'most realistic estimate' is only £250,000 of sales. Therefore if sales fall by just 6.7% below the most realistic estimate, no profit will be made. A key issue in assessing risk therefore is how probable it is that sales will fall to this level.

While the market researchers indicate some uncertainty with respect to sales volumes this is only one variable. Other estimates are also likely to be surrounded by some uncertainty (eg, price, variable cost, fixed costs).

Conclusion

This project does not look to be sufficiently profitable to improve growth significantly and contains risks which may reduce future profits. While most competitor mower manufacturers also produce petrol-powered garden tools and equipment, and qualitatively it seems a reasonable proposition for GGM, quantitatively, based on the data provided, it does not seem a way forward for GGM. Indeed, had it been so, perhaps the company would have entered this market some time ago.

BB's strategic plan

The expansion strategy proposed by BB is also one of product development in the Ansoff model in respect of UK sales.

However, there is also an element of diversification in the Ansoff model in respect of US sales. This involves moving away from core activities and developing new products for new markets, which involves the greatest risk of all strategies. It requires new skills, new techniques and different ways of operating. This is reinforced as not only has GGM not used battery technology before, but BB has not made mowers before.

A further way of viewing the potential acquisition is from BB's perspective. It is continuing a policy of downstream vertical integration.

In terms of UK sales there are similar advantages as the GGM board proposal (albeit with a different type of new product). There are economies of scope in distribution to the same customers, and there may be some common core competencies (eg, the blades) with existing production methods and, although the battery element is new to GGM, it is core to BB.

At a marketing level however there are differences. In the BB case the new products are being separately branded so there is little reputational impact from the existing GGM brand. However BB may not be known in the UK, and consumer recognition in this market needs to be established.

The key advantage is that this proposal gives access to the US market through BB. However while BB operates in the US, it does not sell mowers in the US so the advantage of having BB to exploit its home market may be limited.

Data analysis

	High cost	Est cost	Low cost
Volume	20,000	20,000	20,000
Price	£500	£500	£500
	£'000	£'000	£'000
Revenue	10,000	10,000	10,000
Variable cost	(7,000)	(7,000)	(7,000)
Contribution	3,000	3,000	3,000
Fixed cost	(3,000)	(2,000)	(1,000)
Profit	Nil	1,000	2,000

Taking the data provided at face value, the BB proposal is far more profitable than the GGM board proposal and even at the lower end of the estimation range it does not make a loss, managing to break even. However this data has been provided by BB as part of its take-over bid hence a degree of professional scepticism needs to be applied to these estimates. Due diligence procedures will be needed to ascertain their validity.

The range of variation of fixed costs is considerable and yet only point estimates are given for all the other variables. Additional work is needed to ascertain why the variation is so high for fixed costs and no range of estimates is provided for other variables.

A further note of caution is that, unlike the GGM board's proposal, the BB plan is to produce more mowers. It may therefore be that consumers will buy the battery-powered mowers instead of buying a GGM petrol-powered mower. Due to this substitution, the sales noted above therefore may not be entirely incremental to the company.

Conclusion

Leaving aside these reservations, if the figures are valid, then the BB proposal looks to be a more substantial contribution to growth.

Tutorial note:

Candidates may instead/also use other models such as the Lynch Expansion method matrix. The Lynch model is another two-by-two matrix of company growth (organic growth and external development) and geographical location (home (domestic) and international).

Examiner's comments

In requirement 7.1(d) candidates were asked to compare the growth strategy of the GGM board with that of BB, make relevant calculations and refer to appropriate strategic models.

Again, the standard of answers here varied significantly between the stronger and weaker candidates. There was data in the question in terms of best case, worst case and estimated demand which could have been used to analyse each strategy. Only the better candidates used the information to compute the profit under the different scenarios and then went on to compute break-even and sensitivity analysis.

The majority of candidates tended to use the Ansoff model. The Lynch model was also used in the stronger answers to analyse the difference between the two strategies in terms of discussion of expanding internationally. In terms of the BB strategy, the use of the highest and lowest cost estimates was often ignored in favour of using the expected cost. For the most part, candidates concluded that the BB strategy was the most attractive because of the exposure to overseas markets.

Hardly any candidates expressed any sort of professional scepticism about the data presented by BB.

7.2 Ethics pertains to whether a particular behaviour is deemed acceptable in the context under consideration. Here the issue is that Hetty's government has different laws for health and safety than the UK, but the underlying reasons for having the safety guard remain the same.

In making a decision as to how to proceed, GGM may find it helpful to apply the Institute of Business Ethics three tests:

- Transparency
- Effect
- Fairness

Transparency – would GGM mind people (existing customers, suppliers, employees) knowing that it has manufactured potentially dangerous equipment, even if it were legal . This test is partly about whether GGM's corporate ethics are open and transparent in its actions, rather than just what they claim in ethical statements.

Effect – whom does the decision affect/hurt? GGM stand to gain a major order if they are willing to control costs (by omitting the safety guard) and lower price. In the short term GGM would be making more profit as a consequence of the order.

However GGM risk reputational damage if it came to light it had manufactured unsafe goods and there may be repercussions in terms of lost customers in future.

Other losers would be any customers of Hetty (or other users of mowers) who got hurt in the event of a safety incident.

The ethical issue here is that GGM needs to recognise that, as a business, it has an obligation to the public interest and its wider stakeholders to behave responsibly. The requirement and expectation to make profits need to be constrained by these obligations, but such issues may themselves impact on long term profit.

There may also be certain industry codes of conduct that apply, and consequences from a breach of these, irrespective of where the items are sold.

Fairness – would the decision be considered fair by those affected? The issue for GGM is that they are being asked to manufacture mowers in the knowledge that they might cause harm. Should someone be badly hurt as a result of its actions, it is unlikely that they would perceive GGM's actions as fair, particularly if GGM was seen to have gained financially by winning more business.

Honesty

A final issue is one of honesty and professional scepticism. GGM should take legal advice regarding the legality of the modification being considered in order to substantiate the assertion that any such modification would be legal in Hetty's home country.

Response

GGM may believe that, even if the deal would be in its short term commercial interests, the additional profit is not worthwhile given the breach of corporate ethics that would be involved, even if no safety incident ever transpired from the modification.

One possible course of action would be to insist on fitting the safety guard but to offer a lower price anyway and thereby take a reduced profit per unit. However, GGM may feel that it is not in its interests to do business with a client of this nature even under these conditions.

Examiner's comments

Requirement 7.2 asked candidates to explain the ethical issues arising from a request to modify its mowers for a potential export contract.

Answers to this requirement varied but were, on the whole, disappointing. Candidates tended to approach this requirement in terms of a transparency, fairness and effect framework. What candidates did not then develop, however, were the next steps or draw any sort of conclusion.

A significant number of candidates mentioned the ICAEW code of ethics, self-interest and integrity. This question did not focus on the code of ethics as the client (from whose perspective the ethical issues are being considered) may not have any ICAEW members. Rather, the question required candidates, in a commercial scenario, to assess the legality and ethics of the proposal and the corporate social responsibility of GGM as a company.

The weakest candidates failed to see the issues at the corporate level and instead presented an answer as though it was an individual's ethical issue. Only some candidates gave sensible business advice, such as providing the mowers with the safety guard but not charging for this feature in the price, in order to break into that market. Instead they just stated that the contract should be refused. Whilst the approach to ethics has improved significantly over the years, there is still an inability of candidates to apply ethical principles to business situations.

8 Care 4U Ltd (December 2012)

Marking guide

		Knowledge	Skill	Marks
8.1	SWOT analysis	3	10	12
8.2	Two strategies			
	(a) Operating profit	4	7	
	(b) Control and management	–	5	
	(c) Incentives for franchieses	–	5	
				19
		7	27	31

General comments:

The scenario in this question relates to a private company which owns a large chain of retail pharmacies. It has a good reputation but it has had problems retaining and motivating individual salaried pharmacists.

There are also issues regarding the manner in which the outlets should be controlled and managed. The board has proposed two alternative strategies to expand the chain, to attract pharmacists and increase motivation. These proposed strategies have been identified as: (1) franchising; and (2) shared ownership.

8.1 Strengths

- C4U sells essential products for both prescription items and over-the-counter (OTC) medicines so market demand is likely to be robust to changes in the economy and (for the market as a whole) price inelastic.

- C4U has a significant number of outlets providing scale economies for purchasing (enabling discounts from pharmaceutical suppliers), IT (the centralised system is likely to be mainly a fixed cost enabling additional outlets to benefit at near zero marginal cost) and other central operational services (such as central administration which is likely to have a significant fixed cost element).

- There is a history of sustaining growth through good management which has a track record of competence.

- Funding available for expansion means the company has significant liquidity which lowers financial risk and provides opportunities for growth.

- Good reputation as community pharmacies with free tests, screening and advice increases goodwill and enables a loyal customer base to be established of regular customers/patients.

- Good control through the IT system means the performance of the business is monitored and controlled at the level of each individual pharmacy.

Weaknesses

- There is a shortage of well motivated pharmacists who are good managers which means that, whilst the technical functions may be competently carried out, the same people may not have the key business skills to build revenue and control costs at the pharmacy level of the organisation which is the key interface with customers.

- There are problems retaining pharmacists. This leads to retraining costs and the continued losses of a key human resource. The temporary nature of the employment may mean pharmacists have a low level of long-term commitment to C4U.

- Generous salaries need to be paid to pharmacists which increases the cost base significantly and reduces profit.

Opportunities

- Increases in new drugs becoming available will mean that demand will increase both in terms of volume and, to the extent that new drugs are more expensive, may increase price.

- Pharmacy retailers have exited the industry thereby reducing competition from that source as there are fewer competitors remaining in the industry. There is therefore the opportunity to capture the markets of those leaving the industry.

- Capacity to charge in future for provision of advice, which is currently given free.

- Sell whole business to a large national chain.

- Expand through acquisition.

Threats

- Deregulation has made C4U susceptible to price competition for OTC drugs from supermarkets and other large companies in the industry who have scale economies and common costs with other functions in the store.

- Supermarkets are opening more in-store outlets offering increased non-price competition for all drugs. This competition comes in the form of 24-hour opening, convenience (shopping anyway for other goods), car parking out-of-town, scale of facility (and therefore range of items held in inventory giving choice).

- The prescription drugs market is susceptible to government regulation in terms of contractual conditions. Changes in such regulations are a risk to C4U.

- Government funding cuts will put pressure on prices paid to pharmacies in terms of the products that they will fund and the prices they are willing to pay for drugs and pharmacy services.

- Other goods sold by pharmacies are non-essential and are more susceptible to a sustained economic downturn and to competitive forces from a wider range of competitors outside the pharmacy sector.

- Alternative distribution channels for OTC are likely to be an increasing threat to high street pharmacy retailers (eg, on-line sales, drug stores (OTC drug only shops)).

Conclusion

Key factors are:

- Reductions in government expenditure are key as this puts pressure on pharmacies for their main source of income which makes up 80% of revenue and if recoveries from government are reduced, with constant costs, then severe pressure is put on profits. Any cuts are also likely to be sustained as governments continually look to reduce public sector expenditure.

- Competition from supermarkets which: are pervasive in most regions; are instantly recognisable by consumers; have the ability to be low cost providers and tend to be trusted as providers of services (including healthcare).

Examiner's comments

Requirement 8.1 asks candidates to prepare a SWOT analysis.

Attempts at this requirement were generally good, with candidates demonstrating a strong understanding of the SWOT model and using the information in the question to produce high scoring answers. The key strengths and weaknesses identified centred around the brand name, the established reputation and the good IT control system, together with the problems in staff retention and the lack of management experience from the pharmacists.

The opportunities and threats were not as well identified, although the majority of candidates did manage to identify that the main opportunity was the increase in new drugs, whilst the main threat was government spending cuts. Some candidates attempted to use the PESTEL model, despite the question specifically asking for a SWOT analysis.

It was quite surprising that a number of candidates failed to summarise the key issues from the SWOT analysis despite the requirement specifically requiring a conclusion.

8.2 (a) Operating profit

Profit shares for average size pharmacy (first five years)

	Total	C4U's profit under franchising	C4U's profit under shared ownership
Revenue	600,000	30,000 (ie, 5%)	
Operating costs (80%)	(480,000)		
Operating profit (20%)	120,000		
Management fee (under shared ownership option only)	(20,000)		20,000
Net profit	100,000		50,000
Up-front payment (amortised over 5 years)		5,000	–
Annual profit to C4U		35,000	70,000
Total profit for C4U (over 5 years)		175,000	350,000

Franchising

The up-front cash payment for the franchisee, averaging £25,000, is small by comparison to the shared ownership scheme which averages £40,000. However, with franchising, this payment would be recognised as revenue for C4U (amortised over five years) whereas the initial cash payment under the shared ownership scheme is a capital payment and would never be recognised in C4U's profit.

The up-front payment is small by comparison to the initial cost of opening a pharmacy so there is a small initial stake by the franchisee. This means that C4U has a high capital stake with franchising and may therefore expect a higher absolute level of profit to earn the same % return on investment.

Over the five year period the net cash investment by C4U for an average pharmacy under the franchise arrangement is £175,000 (£200,000 purchase price – £25,000 upfront fee). This is fully recovered according to the above table in terms of C4U's share of profits over the five year term (although this is not the case after tax and interest).

After five years C4U has all rights to the pharmacy business and the full profit stream. Meanwhile however there is an annual interest cost to C4U from providing the funds.

Shared ownership

C4U would receive the management fee in addition to the 50% share in profit, but the profit share is determined after the deduction of the management charge so in effect C4U is incurring half the cost of its own management charge.

As noted above, the additional capital stake is not recognised in C4U's profit.

The profit of the shared ownership scheme is overstated compared to the franchise arrangement as the revenue from intensive support is included but the incremental central costs in providing that support is not included.

The net cash investment by C4U for an average pharmacy under the shared ownership scheme is £160,000 (£200,000 opening cost – £40,000 pharmacist contribution). This is more than fully recovered according to the above table in terms of the C4U's share of profits over the five year term which amounts to £350,000. In this case profit will continue after the five years under the same arrangement unless one party decides to buy out the other.

As with the franchise arrangement, there is an interest cost to C4U in providing the initial funds to set up the pharmacy company. However to the extent that the interest is also a cost to pharmacy companies, it is an income to C4U, half of which is in effect paid by the co-owner.

Comparison

The above table shows that the profit per annum with the shared ownership scheme is double that of the franchise arrangement. At first sight this may suggest that the shared ownership route is better but:

- The start-up period may be a period of low profits as a new pharmacy business tries to become established against incumbents. If some costs are fixed this might mean low (or even zero) profitability in the short term, hence there may be little (or no) profit share for C4U at first with shared ownership. In contrast, under a franchise agreement at least some profit will be earned by C4U from a 5% share of revenue plus the amortised upfront franchise fee.

- The above table assumes that total revenue would be the same under either ownership choice. However if the incentives for the franchisee or the share ownership partner differ between the two options (see section below) then different levels of revenue may be generated from the same pharmacy and thus different levels of profit earned for C4U.

- The franchise profits are only for a period of five years after which full ownership can revert to C4U if it so choses. After the five years the profit stream to C4U would therefore be £120,000 per annum. Thus a lower short term profit will be compensated by higher long term profit with the franchise scheme compared to the shared ownership scheme.

- For both schemes, profits are likely to be overstated as there are likely to be additional central costs, interest and tax which are not reflected in operating profit.

- There may be some depreciation on the pharmacy outlet property.

(b) **Control and management**

Franchising

- Control is exercised loosely by C4U through the franchise agreement contract. This is more on a negative basis in preventing certain courses of action (eg, complying with contract terms to avoid damaging the brand) rather than on a positive basis in promoting positive actions.

- Autonomous management. Franchisees appear to be largely autonomous in being able to decide whether to accept or reject advice and support.

- Each pharmacy is separately managed so diversity of approach and management styles may develop between pharmacies.

- Some degree of auditing will be required by C4U in order to gain assurance regarding disclosed revenue figures to verify that the correct 5% franchise payment is being made. This will require direct access, or third party access, to accounting records and accounting systems.

- After five years, ultimate control reverts to C4U at which time it can choose to change or adapt the management style selected by the franchisee.

Shared ownership

- While the day to day management of pharmacies rests with the co-owner (the pharmacist), C4U manages and monitors the performances of individual pharmacies by providing 'intensive support advice, administration and IT facilities' to the company which would be 'a compulsory part of the agreement so C4U can manage the performance of its investment.'

- Thus, while the co-owner takes the day to day decisions, they have a high degree of monitoring by, and accountability to, C4U.

- If performance is poor and interest cannot be paid, ultimate control also rests with C4U, as the holder of the loan can force the company into insolvency.

(c) **Incentives**

Franchising

- The contract is only five years, so franchisees will not have an incentive to build long term reputation.

- Even if a pharmacy performs badly and makes an operating loss, C4U still receives 5% of revenue so there are strong incentives for the franchisee to perform well and increase profit.

- Franchisees have incentives to reduce costs as this will increase profit but C4U will not take any share of this as they only have a share of revenues. This may incentivise franchisees to be efficient, but may also incentivise them to reduce quality.

Shared ownership

- The co-owner earns a salary and retains a half share of profits after management charges and interest. They are therefore incentivised to increase profit.

- The initial contribution by the co-owner pharmacist (£40,000 on average) is at risk if the venture fails and thus this provides an incentive to succeed.

- If the business succeeds then the co-owner pharmacist has an opportunity to buy out the other 50% at a fair value. There is thus the chance of owning his/her own business. However the more successful the pharmacy becomes the greater the cost of the buy-out. This may give a disincentive to over-performing while the pharmacy remains in joint ownership.

Examiner's comments

Requirement 8.2 requests candidates to compare the two strategies for expansion by considering: operating profit: control and management; and incentives.

Candidates produced few calculations in answering the operating profit part of this requirement, opting to spend more time on the discussion aspects of the question in respect of control and management and incentives. Where calculations were performed, many candidates treated the upfront payment of £25,000 as a cost in the first year and did not amortise it over five years as expected. This led to a computed profit of £5,000 according to the franchising agreement in the first year. Other errors included: not recognising 5% of the revenue; under the shared ownership arrangement attributing C4U 80% of the profit, rather than 50%; and not thinking about 'profit' by recognising the full cost of the PPE as an expense. It was clear from the answers produced, that candidates were familiar with how a franchising agreement operated, but often the comments were general and not applied to the scenario. Also, there was a lack of understanding of the nature and implications of the shared ownership arrangement, with candidates failing to grasp the fact that it gave a significant amount of control and accountability to C4U.

Answers to the incentives part of the question were often relatively brief, with candidates identifying that under the franchising agreement, the pharmacists still received 5% of revenues whereas under the shared ownership, the co-owners would be entitled to a half share of profit.

Overall, the information in the question could have been better used. Many answers to this part were very brief and did not compare the two strategies in sufficient detail or with sufficient insight.

9 The Mealfest Corporation (December 2012)

Marking guide

			Marks	
		Knowledge	**Skill**	
9.1	(a) Organisational structure and performance measurement	1	6	
	(b) Pricing strategies	2	7	
				14
9.2	Benchmarking	3	8	10
		6	21	24

General comments:

The listed company in question owns a chain of mid-market restaurants controlled from Germany, but also located in France, Switzerland and the UK. The company was originally centrally controlled and had homogeneous prices for all restaurants across Europe. At the beginning of 20Y2 it restructured, forming a separate division for each country. After the restructuring the prices were homogeneous within countries, but not between countries. The Mealfest board now wishes to monitor the success of the new structure and strategy.

9.1 (a) Organisational structure

Pre-20Y2

MC is a multinational corporation. As such, its structure needs to consider not only operational size and diversity, but international variations in culture, taste, economic conditions, currencies, laws and regulations. The centralised nature of the organisational structure prior to January 20Y2 is in danger of ignoring, or minimising the significance of, these cross border variations.

Arising from this, there are a number of detailed issues with this structure and method of performance measurement (aside from the matters relating to foreign exchange rates highlighted by the finance director which are dealt with later below):

- Pre-20Y2 there was a very flat structure with each of 100 restaurants reporting performance directly to head office. This gives a wide span of control where head office staff in Berlin can have little knowledge of all local conditions and the causes behind the changes in the three performance metrics.

- The structure is also highly centralised with the key decisions relating to pricing, food sourcing and staff being taken centrally in Berlin. This may give economies of scale and discounts but narrows variety (eg, different national cultures and food type preferences).

- There are differences in laws and regulations with regard to employment and social security law. Apart from Switzerland, the other four countries are in the EU which reduces, but does not remove, employment law differences. Specifically, national regulation issues include the following: the minimum wage differs between countries; social security payments vary; rights of employees from outside the EU to work in the EU differ; employees rights on redundancy or dismissal differ.

- It is unclear whether the performance of (1) the restaurants or (2) the restaurant managers is being evaluated, or both.

- To the extent that it is the restaurant managers that are being evaluated, then they have little control over profit other than the volume of sales/customers. Menu prices, staff allocation, staff pay and sourcing of food are all fixed centrally. Restaurant managers are therefore being held responsible for matters beyond their control if they are being monitored as a profit centre.

- Centralised decisions fail to take account of local conditions. If, in a particular country, there is high unemployment, then staff may be recruited at lower pay than if labour market conditions are competitive.

Post-20Y2

The two key changes post-20Y2 are:

- a change in the degree of centralisation of decision making which is now at national level rather than corporate level (international).

- additionally measuring performance at divisional level rather than only at restaurant level.

The decentralisation of decision making to national level reduces the issues arising from cultural, economic and legal differences. However, there may still be many of the above differences in cultural taste and prosperity within countries, as well as between countries.

In terms of measuring performance at divisional level, this seems more appropriate as most of the key decisions are now being taken at this level eg, pricing (see below) and staffing, so the division is a profit centre (and also a revenue centre) and has control over most of the elements contributing to profit. The exception is food sourcing which remains at corporate level and is therefore an element of performance outside the control of divisional heads.

Other than revenue and profit, a third performance metric is return on assets. To make this a more valid element of performance evaluation, the divisional manager would need control over new investment and divestment (ie, an investment centre). This is not the case, even under the post-20Y2 regime.

Exchange rate issues

MC's primary currency appears to be the euro. Germany and France have the euro as their currency so sales in these countries are not directly affected by currency translation. Food purchases from France and local labour in these countries are also payable in euro.

In the UK and Switzerland fluctuations over the year in exchange rates mean that the euro value of sales revenue is likely to change subject to macroeconomic influences, rather than just decisions at restaurant or divisional levels. Wage costs are in the same currency as revenues and so provide some natural hedging.

Given that food costs are in euro, this makes the euro denominated profit in UK and Swiss restaurants even more volatile than their revenues.

Given that performance comparisons are in euro as a common currency, the profit of a division or a restaurant is heavily dependent on the strength of the national currency, as well as the underlying performance of the business.

In measuring the return on assets in the UK and Switzerland, consideration also needs to be given to the exchange rate at which assets are translated.

(b) **Pricing**

Pre-20Y2

Pre-20Y2 pricing exhibits three characteristics:

- The pricing decision is centralised
- Prices are uniform across all four countries
- Prices are only reset once a year

Centralisation

Centralisation means that pricing decisions fail to take account of local information which may be available to restaurant managers, but local conditions are unlikely to be known centrally on an up to date basis for all 100 locations in Europe. As a consequence, pricing decisions are unlikely to take account of local tastes and needs that customers may report back to individual managers.

Uniformity of pricing

Uniform pricing means that MC does not take account of local competitive conditions. This means that the company does not practise price discrimination by taking advantage of variations in price elasticity between either national markets or local restaurant markets.

Reset once a year

Prices are uniform within the year which means they lack inter-temporal flexibility. As an example, if there is seasonality, then prices would not reflect this. This might be particularly relevant where there is large tourist market in summer, but many fewer tourists in winter, generating different demand dynamics.

Post-20Y2

Of the three characteristics noted above, the third point remains the same (ie, set only once a year) hence the problems (eg, seasonality) are unchanged.

The first two issues (centralisation and uniformity) have changed and the underlying issues may have been moderated, but they have not been removed.

Centralisation

The degree of centralisation has been reduced from being company-wide to each national division. This is an improvement in terms of devolved decision making, but divisional managers might still not be aware of the local competitive conditions facing each restaurant manager.

Uniformity of pricing

There is still uniformity within countries, even though variations are permitted between countries. The issues here relating to a lack of price flexibility are reduced, but variations within a country in terms of competition, prosperity and taste can still be significant, leading to geographical variations in demand and price elasticity and a continued absence of exploiting price discrimination.

Exchange rate issues

Under the pre-20Y2 system of pricing, exchange rate variations have caused volatility in menu prices in the UK and Switzerland. Such exchange rate movements are likely to reflect macroeconomic conditions rather than the conditions in the restaurant market and may thus be distortionary, leading to arbitrary and suboptimal pricing.

Under the post-20Y2 system, there is discretion at national level to set prices and so the impact of exchange rates can be considered by divisional managers. A factor in this would be the relative rates of inflation in the UK and Switzerland compared to eurozone countries.

Examiner's comments

Requirement 9.1 asks candidates to compare pre and post 20Y2: (a) organisational structure and performance measurement; and (b) pricing strategies.

Answers tended to be brief and concentrated on the fact that pre 20Y2, the structure was highly centralised and flat, whereas post 20Y2, the decentralisation of decision making eliminated some of the cultural differences previously experienced. There was normally little or no reference to the impact of exchange rate fluctuations and resulting issues in terms of revenue differences between countries and the impact on performance assessment. Although candidates acknowledged that within the different structures the performance would be assessed in terms of revenue and profits, very few considered return on assets.

In terms of pricing, candidates did not really seem to know how to approach the question and this often led to brief, unstructured answers which did not focus on the differences between the pre and post 20Y2 position, but instead merely repeated from the question that there had been a move from a centrally fixed pricing system to one now fixed at national level by divisional heads. There was very little analysis of how this would affect the behaviour of managers and customers or of exchange rate risk.

9.2 Benchmarking compares the use of assets across the firm or across the industry and indicates best practice to show where assets might be better used to achieve sustainable competitive advantage (SCA).

One definition of benchmarking is 'The establishment, through data gathering, of targets and comparators, through whose use relative levels of performance (and particularly areas of underperformance) can be identified. By the adoption of identified best practices it is hoped that performance will improve.'

By comparing procedures and performance, internally and externally, MC can understand how to move towards best practice by learning how to reduce costs, improve service delivery in restaurants and thereby improve market positioning to align with market leaders in the sector.

There are four different types of benchmark that can be used: internal; competitive (industry wide); activity (best in class); and generic.

Internal (or historic) – internal benchmarking could be at the level of comparing individual restaurants or divisions with each other to determine those that are under- or over-performing. Comparisons of restaurants could be intra-country or company-wide. It may be however that certain restaurants are best at one function (eg, food quality) while other restaurants are better at a different function (eg, quality of service or ambience).

Historical comparison also looks at performance over time to ascertain trends/significant changes, etc.

Internal benchmarking is however restrictive as it could be that MC is generally under-performing and the true benchmark of best practice is to be found within external competitors who are out-performing MC.

Competitive (industry-wide) – this benchmark compares the performance of the restaurant or the division with equivalent units in other firms in the same industry or sector. This may assist MC in ascertaining ways to improve performance.

Comparing the performance of a division with a rival restaurant company in the same market sector may be possible if the rival is a company that is restricted to one country. In this case the published financial statements are likely to provide relevant data to compare key financial performance indicators. They may also provide some narrative information to evaluate non-financial performance indicators. Obtaining information about the performance and functions of rivals at the individual restaurant level is more challenging, as there is less information in the public domain. Industry publications and associations could be possible sources alongside informal contacts in the industry and personal visits to rivals.

If the whole national industry is under-performing, international comparisons may be more useful so comparisons could also be made with restaurants in other national markets (eg, the US).

Activity (best in class) – compares with best practice in whatever industry can be found eg, could compare MC table booking systems with online booking system for hotels or airline seats to ascertain whether there is scope for improved efficiency. Similarly, the levels of service could be benchmarked against other industry service practice (eg, first class airline travel; hotel reception); food preparation could be compared to cookery competitions or the best home cooking.

Generic – against a conceptually similar process eg, compare food preparation to the treatment of VIPs at visits and events. Food hygiene could be compared to a hospital operating theatre.

Examiner's comments

Requirement 9.2 asked candidates to explain how benchmarking may be used to evaluate performance of divisions and of individual restaurants.

A good knowledge was shown of the nature of internal, competitive, activity and generic benchmarking, with the majority of candidates displaying an understanding of each. However, answers' application to each type to the scenario tended to be very general with insufficient consideration of the circumstances of the scenario. Some candidates went on to use a balanced scorecard approach, identifying CSF's and KPI's. Whilst this identified some reasonable points, this approach was neither necessary nor entirely suitable for this requirement.

Marking guide

	Knowledge	Skill	Marks
10.1 Porter's Five Forces analysis	3	7	9
10.2 (a) Performance evaluation	2	11	
(b) Conclusion	–	6	16
10.3 Advantages/disadvantages	2	4	7
10.4 Critical success factors (CSFs)	3	7	9
	10	35	41

10.1 Five Forces analysis – filling stations

Threat of new entrants – low

Barriers to entry for fuel retailing are high. As well as needing sites in prime locations, there is the capital required to set up the filling station (underground storage tanks, fuel lines etc) and to comply with ongoing regulatory requirements. In addition the market is dominated by major brands (oil companies and supermarkets) and these larger players have significant cost advantages as a result of scale economies. Entry to the industry is also likely to be unattractive in the current environment given low margins and high levels of competition. As a result of these factors, the threat of new entrants is low although supermarkets may continue to open more filling stations at existing supermarket locations or new out-of-town sites.

Competitive rivalry – high

Because the industry is low margin, high volume, the level of competition is intense.

The supermarkets are keen to compete with each other on the price of fuel since if they can attract customers to the filling station they are also likely to buy other goods. The effect of competition is evidenced by the reduction in the number of filling stations and the failure of a significant number of the smaller independent filling stations.

Power of suppliers – high

Fuel supply is dominated by a few large petrol wholesalers who therefore wield significant power. This is increased by the fact that most are vertically integrated and also control some retail outlets. Suppliers are likely to exert more power in relation to the smaller independent filling stations than the supermarket-owned sites.

Power of customers – varied

Customers are fragmented so in that sense they have relatively low bargaining power in relation to the industry as a whole and the market price will largely be dictated by the petrol wholesaler and government taxes. However switching costs are low and petrol is a homogeneous commodity product so there is little brand loyalty. As a result customers are easily able to transfer business and in this respect they become more important to an individual operator within the industry as they are likely to choose the lowest price filling station in their area. Corporate buyers may have slightly more power because of the higher volume of business they represent.

Threat of substitutes – low

The threat of substitutes is limited although there is some scope for the manufacture and use of bio-fuels from vegetable oils and animal fats. The greater threat for the fuel retailing industry is that as the price of fuel increases people reduce their consumption by driving less, switching to electric cars and/or using alternative means of transport.

Conclusion

This is a highly competitive industry, which is particularly challenging for the smaller independent operators who struggle to compete with the economies of scale and brand loyalty of the supermarkets. With only three sites, Mayhews may lack sufficient throughput to sustain profitability in the fuel retailing industry in the longer term.

Examiner's comments

Requirement 10.1 requested candidates to prepare a Porter's Five Forces analysis of the UK fuel retailing industry which might help inform Mayhew's discussions regarding the viability of its filling station operations. This requirement was extremely well attempted by the majority of candidates. Whilst many were able to extract salient information from the question and use it to assess the strength of each force, only the better candidates concluded that the industry is extremely competitive, with high supplier power and that the future is relatively bleak for smaller independents such as Mayhews. A minority of candidates discussed only four of the five forces, omitting the need to consider competitive rivalry, which in the context of the scenario was one of the most important issues. A common error by weaker candidates was to discuss supermarket-owned filling stations under the heading substitutes instead of discussing substitutes for the purchase of fuel eg, the use of electric cars or public transport.

10.2 Analysis of Mayhews' performance and closure plans

Note: The data to support the following commentary can be found in the Appendix.

Mayhews' overall business performance

Between 20Y1 and 20Y2, despite the total revenue for the business remaining almost static at £4.29 million, there has been a 10.4% increase in gross profit and a 27.1% increase in net profit, resulting in an absolute increase in profit of £125,000. On the face of it therefore the business has done well in a difficult economic climate.

Although the revenue in overall terms has remained static, this masks the fact that the 11% reduction in fuel revenues has been almost exactly compensated for by an 18% increase in repairs revenue.

The movement in fuel revenue is explained by a 5.4% increase in price but a 15.5% reduction in volume. Within the industry fuel volumes are under pressure due to the economic climate and increased engine efficiency but the drop in volume of fuel sold by Mayhews may suggest that they are losing market share to competitors. This is not surprising since their average retail price is 136p/litre, over 2p/litre higher than the 20Y2 UK average and 5p per litre higher than the average supermarket price.

On average Mayhews is selling 1.47 million litres per site which is not only considerably lower than the branded petrol stations but also less than the 1.68 million litres sold by the average independent. The lack of volume will probably result in Mayhews having to pay higher prices to the wholesaler and will also result in higher overhead costs per litre, which may explain the higher prices being charged. This is also reflected in Mayhews' gross margin, which is only 11.3% whereas on average retailers keep 5% of the retail price, equating to a gross margin of 5/40 = 12.5% of the net of tax price.

The repairs revenue has grown by 18%. Given the economic climate it is unlikely that Mayhews will have put its prices up significantly and this is probably due to volume increases as a result of people needing more repairs and servicing as they hold on to their cars longer. It is also likely to reflect a move away from the dealers to local garages as customers attempt to keep their costs down.

Repairs and servicing now accounts for 44% of the total sales (compared to 37% in 20Y1). Since the gross margin on the repairs business is much higher at 52.1% than the margin on fuel (11.3%), this change in sales mix towards repairs has had a positive effect on the company's overall profit.

Operating costs have also remained relatively static at just under 16% of revenue. A breakdown of these would be helpful – since the premises are owned, in addition to the wages and salaries of the owner, filling station staff and garage mechanics, these costs are likely to consist of utilities, marketing and other administrative expenses. More information is required although on the face of it the business appears to have kept these under control.

Individual garages

If we consider the performance of the individual locations, it is clear that some garages are doing better than others. Garage C is performing best of all and contributing 40% of Mayhews' gross profit, which directly reflects its reduced reliance on fuel sales and a greater proportion of high margin servicing.

Garage B is the least successful. It is charging the highest price per litre (£1.38), selling the lowest volume of fuel (1.34m litres) and has lower margins on both fuel and repairs than the other two garages. It is also the most reliant on fuel revenues (over 62% of total revenue).

More information is required about the location of garage B but this may be in one of the less well populated rural areas or alternatively it may face strong competition in the vicinity eg, it could be close to a filling station operated by a major supermarket.

Garage A appears to be performing reasonably and accounts for 36% of Mayhews' revenue and gross profit. Comparing the net margins is not particularly useful as the operating costs of garage A include the £45,000 salary cost of Barry which, once removed, shows garage A making a net margin of 14.9%.

If Mayhews is to focus more on repairs it should try and establish what garage C is doing to achieve margins of 55% and replicate that elsewhere (eg, considering the procurement policy it has adopted for parts).

Interdependence of revenues and costs

A key issue for Mayhews is the extent to which the fuel and repairs revenue are interdependent. Should Mayhews decide to close one or more of the filling stations then they may lose some customers for repairs and servicing also.

Depending on how closely located the three garages are to each other, the Mayhews brand may be strong enough to close one garage completely but transfer its repair customers to one of the other locations.

Another consideration is the extent to which operating costs at a particular location will be reduced by closing the filling station part of the business.

Preliminary Conclusions and Recommendations

Mayhews has several choices available:

- Continue as it is

- Close some/all of the filling stations but retain all three repairs and servicing businesses

- Close one or more garages in their entirety and sell off the sites to help fund investment in the new IT system and the repairs business at the remaining garage(s)

There is intense competition in fuel retailing, and the Porter's Five Forces analysis in 10.1 suggests that this is a difficult industry for a business the size of Mayhews to make sustainable profits. Thus continuing as it is, Option (i), is unlikely to guarantee long-term future success.

Currently the filling station at each garage is making a positive contribution towards fixed operating costs. However the evidence between 20Y1 and 20Y2 indicates that it would be possible to improve profitability by increasing the proportion of the servicing and repairs business. Barry's comments about reputation indicate that there may be an opportunity to capitalise on the Mayhews brand and their reputation for honesty and reliability.

A preliminary assessment suggests that garage B is underperforming compared to the others and might be considered for closure. However more information is needed about the detailed performance of the individual garages, the likely savings in operating costs and the exit/compliance costs before deciding whether to close individual sites. An important consideration is the extent to which revenue and costs for the filling stations and repairs business are interdependent.

In the event that Mayhews decided to retain some/all filling stations, it could follow competitors and attempt to service local community needs through product diversification (forecourt shops).

In deciding on the future strategic direction of the business, another issue is succession planning, since Barry is 60. It is important to establish his personal aims and objectives for the business, including any exit plans. He may be keen to realise some of the capital tied up within the business, which the sale of one or more sites to a developer would allow him to do.

Further information required

- Details of the locations, markets and customer profiles of each garage
- Previous year's accounts for each garage
- Repairs revenue/margins split between individual and corporate customers
- Breakdown of operating costs between fuel/repairs/other to ascertain the likely savings in operating costs if one or more filling station is closed
- Exit costs associated with closure of one/more filling stations
- Break-even analysis of fuel sales
- Pricing policy for fuel sales
- Likely value of sites to developer
- Industry/sector information re gross margins/average labour costs/overheads

Appendix: Data analysis

Sales volumes and prices:

	Garage A	Garage B	Garage C	Mayhews 20Y2	Mayhews 20Y1
Litres sold (millions)	1.63	1.34	1.43	4.4	5.21
Ave price net of tax/litre	53.9pence	55.1pence	54.3pence	54.4pence	51.6pence
Ave retail price/litre (net of tax price/0.40)	£1.35	£1.38	£1.36	£1.36	£1.29

20Y2	Branded	Independent	Supermarkets	Mayhews
Litres sold per site (millions)	4.04	1.68	10.2	1.47
Ave retail price/litre	UK ave (whole market) = 133.8p		130.9p	136p
Ave price net of tax/litre	53.5p		52.4p	54.4p

Analysis by product/market:

Sales mix (%)

	Garage A	Garage B	Garage C	20Y2	20Y1
Fuel	56	62	51	56	63
Repairs	44	38	49	44	37

Gross margin (%)

	Garage A	Garage B	Garage C	20Y2	20Y1
Fuel	11.7	10.3	11.7	11.3	11.3
Repairs	51.6	48.0	55.0	52.1	52.1
Total	29.2	24.7	33.1	29.3	26.6

Breakdown of 20Y2 revenue by location (%):

	Fuel	Repairs	Total
Garage A	37	36	36
Garage B	31	24	28
Garage C	32	40	36

Breakdown of 20Y2 gross profit by location (%):

	Fuel	Repairs	Total
Garage A	38	36	36
Garage B	28	22	23
Garage C	34	42	41

Gross profit mix (%)

	Garage A	Garage B	Garage C	20Y2	20Y1
Fuel	22	26	18	21	27
Repairs	78	74	82	79	73

Operating costs and net profit

	Garage A	Garage B	Garage C	20Y2	20Y1
Operating costs as % of revenue	17.2 14.3%*	15.4	14.3	15.7	15.8
Net profit margin (%)	12.1 14.9%*	9.2	18.7	13.7	10.7
	(*) = adjusted for Barry's salary				

Mayhews: Overall change in performance 20Y1:20Y2

Decrease in fuel revenue	−10.9%
Increase in repairs revenue	+18.3%
Decrease in total revenue	Negligible
Decrease in fuel gross profit	−11.2%
Increase in repairs gross profit	+18.2%
Increase in total gross profit	+10.4%
Reduction in operating costs	−1.0%
Increase in net profit	+27.1%
Decrease in litres sold	−15.5%
Increase in average retail price/litre	+5.4%

Tutorial note:

A complete range of calculations has been provided here for marking purposes. Candidates were not expected to produce all of these given the marks and time available.

Examiner's comments

Requirement 10.2 asked candidates to evaluate the performance of Mayhew's overall business and the individual garages and to justify a preliminary conclusion as to whether the company should close one or more filling stations to focus on maintenance and repairs. There were some excellent attempts at this requirement with even the weaker candidates typically scoring over half the marks available.

Most candidates produced a range of calculations for Mayhews business as a whole and for each of its garages, typically including margins, sales mix and revenue/profit growth. Better candidates also used the data to assess Mayhews' fuel prices and volumes in relation to the competition/market. At the other end of the spectrum, some weaker candidates produced hardly any numerical analysis and simply copied out absolute figures from the question or only made a vague attempt at analysing increases/decreases.

Most candidates identified the fact that despite falling fuel volumes, Mayhews has performed well, generating a 27% increase in profit from relatively static sales revenue. The key reason for this is that the mix of sales has changed in favour of maintenance and repairs, which has a significantly higher gross margin than fuel.

In relation to the individual garages, most candidates commented that Garage C is performing best of all and that garage B is the least successful. Better answers explained that this reflects C's reduced reliance on fuel sales, whereas B – the most reliant on fuel sales – is charging the highest price per litre and selling the lowest volume of fuel. A pleasing number of candidates identified that comparing the net margins of the three garages is not particularly useful since the operating costs of garage A include the £45,000 salary cost of the owner, which needs to be removed for a more accurate assessment. Better candidates did this calculation and commented on its results.

The strongest candidates identified that more information is required about the location of the garages and that B may be in one of the less well populated rural areas or alternatively face strong local competition. The lowest scoring candidates merely made assertions describing the changes in ratios, with little, if any, attempt at an analysis of causality.

Candidates were requested to make a preliminary conclusion about the closure of one or more filling stations and most did this, recommending that the filling station at either B or C be closed. Only the better candidates went on to qualify their conclusion, pointing out that more information would be required before making a final decision. The very strongest candidates raised the issue of the possible interdependence of costs and revenues, identifying that the filling station business was making a positive contribution at all garage locations and that failure to supply fuel may lead to the loss of customers for repairs.

10.3 Benefits of new information system

There are two aspects to the investment in IT: a new engine diagnostic system which will allow Mayhews to service more modern vehicles and a new IT system which will improve parts management and have marketing benefits.

Advantages

- Mayhews will be able to handle all types of car and therefore attract greater volumes of business. It will also be able to undertake business that has previously had to be referred to the main dealer.

- A customer database coupled with data analytics functionality will increase marketing opportunities. Capturing data relating to previous garage services provided to Mayhews customers would enable the company to send out promotional offers. For example if 12 months earlier a customer had purchased a new set of a particular brand of tyre then the system could automatically generate an email offer promoting the same brand of tyre at a reduced price if purchased within a set time frame.

- There will be increased revenue opportunities eg, online booking of services and repairs, which might attract a different customer profile. When customers book a repair online the system could request some basic details of the identified fault. The data analytics software could combine the data captured from the customer with external data sources such as online databases of known vehicle manufacturer faults. This may enable Mayhews garage staff to pre-order parts in advance of the customer bringing their car into the garage.

- The database management system could be used to flag up, in advance, those customers needing an MOT or a vehicle service so that Mayhews staff can contact the customer to remind them and arrange a booking. This should improve the quality of the customer experience and enhance service levels. This may increase customer retention and lead to a greater share of their spend.

- The system should provide Barry with better management information and improve decision making – forecasting, customer profitability analysis, assessment of performance by location/product stream. The data analytics software could provide details on the make of vehicles which generate the greatest level of work and profit. Mayhews could then specialise in those reparing those vehicles.

- A new system may help reduce costs through more efficient work scheduling, parts control etc.

- The system may help with knowledge management and reduce the business' reliance on Barry.

Disadvantages

- The costs of acquiring and installing the system may be prohibitive for a small business like Mayhews.

- Existing staff may lack the skills to use the system and/or to do work on modern cars. Mayhews will need to train staff to use the new IT system and may encounter resistance. The requirement to employ individuals with experience in operating data analytics software is likely to be inappropriate given the size of the business.

- If Mayhews is currently receiving commission on referrals to main dealers it will lose this income.

- Implementation issues with the new IT system and the risk of system failures/downtime may cause delays/affect customer service levels. Data protection and cyber security issues will need to be addressed.

- As the technology is likely to change in the future, particularly in relation to engine diagnostics, the system may need replacing or upgrading regularly.

- There is a risk that competitors will do this too – is it competitive advantage or catch up?

Conclusion

As Mayhews currently does not have the facility to carry out repairs to cars with more modern engine management systems, it appears that investing in a new system will be critical to the success of the strategy to increase the focus on the servicing and repairs business.

A detailed cost benefit analysis should be carried out to ensure the new IT system is commercially viable.

Examiner's comments

Requirement 10.3 asked candidates to discuss the advantages and disadvantages of the proposed investment in information technology. The key to a good answer here was to identify that there were two aspects to the investment in IT: an engine diagnostic system that would allow Mayhews to service modern cars that they currently had to refer to the main dealers, and a new computer system which would provide a customer database and assist with parts management. Candidates who identified the two aspects tended to score well. Weaker candidates often listed the generic pros and cons of information systems, without applying this to Mayhews. Only the best candidates came to any form of conclusion – pointing out that the investment would be critical to Mayhews proposal to focus on repairs and maintenance and identifying the need for some form of cost/benefit analysis before such investment was undertaken.

10.4 CSFs for repairs and servicing

CSFs

Johnson, Scholes and Whittington define critical success factors as 'those product features that are particularly valued by a group of customers and therefore, where the organisation must excel to outperform the competition.' Mayhews has both individual and corporate clients and they may value different things eg, corporate clients may be more concerned about speed of service whereas individual customers may focus on trust and reliability.

Alternatively a wider definition of CSFs is 'a small number of key goals vital to the success of an organisation – things that must go right.' Thus CSFs can consider not just the actual product/service but other factors vital to commercial success eg, availability, competitive knowledge, cost or performance control.

Using CSFs for strategic control

The process of identifying CSFs will help Mayhews' management focus attention on what is important and the things that need controlling/improving. It will also identify areas of little value-added where for example costs could be eliminated.

Mayhews can measure achievement of the CSFs by calculating KPIs for periodic reporting (see below). These KPIs will assist in benchmarking the garages against each other and also against rivals. They can also help to guide the development of the new information system to ensure that Barry and the garage managers receive information about the factors that are critical to the performance of each location.

Possible CSFs for Mayhews repairs and servicing business

Tutorial note:

A number of CSFs have been identified below for marking purposes. Only three were required.

(1) Ability to attract and retain customers – Barry has identified that in this service-based market Mayhews has a reputation for being honest and reliable. Attracting and retaining customers will provide a stable source of income from annual MOTs and servicing and lead to word-of-mouth referrals which should generate growth. Maintaining and winning new corporate contracts will also be important.

(2) Providing top quality service levels – Mayhews wants to differentiate itself by providing dealer quality service. Customers will expect that repairs carried out are of the highest quality and comply with safety regulations and that they are undertaken as quickly as possible.

(3) Offering a competitively priced service – Mayhews has lower overheads and labour costs than the main dealers and its strategy is to capitalise on this by offering the same quality service but at affordable local garage prices. In the difficult economic climate, price may be a key factor for many customers.

(4) Ability to recruit and retain mechanics with appropriate expertise – Mayhews' ability to offer a fast and reliable service will depend on this, particularly if it starts to undertake more complicated engine diagnostics.

(5) Appropriate technology and information systems strategy to support business needs – without investing in the new engine diagnostic system, Mayhews will struggle to compete with the main dealers. The reliability of the new IT system will also affect online bookings and will enhance the customer experience by predicting service needs.

Performance measures (KPIs) linked to CSFs:

Tutorial note:

A wide range of KPIs has been identified below for marking purposes. Only one relevant KPI was required for each of the three CSFs identified.

(1) **Attraction/Retention of customers:**

Number of cars referred to main dealer (measures Mayhews' ability to carry out work)
Number of contracts for corporate servicing
Average Customer satisfaction scores on post work feedback survey
Level of repeat business for MOTs and annual servicing
Geographical area of customer base
% of enquiries converted to booking for MOT/service

(2) **Quality service levels**

Quality of work undertaken:

% of defects rectified
Warranty costs as a % of revenue
Level of complaints
% of vehicles maintained/repaired which have to be subsequently rechecked

Speed of service

Lead time between customer call and date job scheduled
Availability of parts
Hours taken per repair/service
% of jobs finished on time

(3) **Competitively priced service**

Final price as a % of original quotation
Hourly labour charge compared to main dealers' labour charges
Price of various work (MOT/routine service etc) compared to competitors
Recovery rates: hours recharged to customers/hours worked

(4) **Staffing**

Qualifications undertaken/mechanic
Number of sick/absent days
Staff turnover compared to total number of staff

(5) **Technology and information**

Number of vehicles that Mayhews is unable to diagnose/need referring to main dealer
Number of mechanics trained in the new engine diagnostic system
Number of computer system breakdowns

Examiner's comments

In requirement 10.4, candidates were asked to explain how the use of critical success factors might assist Mayhews in establishing a strategic control system. Candidates were required to justify three CSFs for the maintenance and repairs business and suggest one appropriate key performance indicator for each. This part was surprisingly quite poorly done. Many candidates restricted their marks by completely ignoring the element of the requirement relating to establishing a strategic control system and simply provided a list of CSFs and KPIs. The weakest candidates were clearly unsure about the distinction between KPIs and targets or goals. For some, the CSFs and KPIs described could have been those for any business and it was not obvious that the candidate was discussing Mayhews' repairs and maintenance business. Whilst customer satisfaction is relevant to all businesses and therefore customer feedback is vitally important, the information in the question could have been used to produce some higher quality answers. The better candidates produced a reasoned justification of their choice of each CSF and then demonstrated clearly how this could be measured. Some candidates provided a long list of KPIs, despite the specific request for only one for each CSF identified – these additional measures wasted time and did not attract marks.

Marking guide

	Knowledge	Skill	Marks
11.1 Business plan			
(a) Strengths and opportunities	1	4	
(b) Weaknesses and threats	1	4	
(c) Benefits of partnership	2	6	
			16
11.2 Additional information	2	7	8
11.3 Market segmentation	3	5	8
	9	26	32

General comments:

The scenario in this question relates to a relatively new company which uses steel shipping containers to create short-term living accommodation for events and contract clients. The directors are keen to expand globally and have begun to prepare a business plan to help attract appropriate local partners. Candidates were asked to take the role of a senior in the firm of business advisers which has been appointed to help develop the business plan.

The overall scores on this question were again very good.

11.1 Sections of Business Plan

(a) **Strengths and realistic market opportunities (section 2.2.1)**

Our key strengths:

Innovation – Cabezada are seen as a pioneer within the container accommodation industry and we have built up an extensive database, contact network and team of experienced designers and engineers.

The Cabezada product range is extremely flexible and can be adapted to meet the needs of a wide variety of customers and target markets.

There is a cheap and readily available supply of standardised containers, and with access to worldwide low-cost distribution systems we can quickly, easily and cheaply respond to customer needs.

We have a strong leadership team as a result of the skills and experience acquired in our previous roles as chief executive of a hotel group and operations director of a large construction company.

Realistic market opportunities:

We believe that there are significant opportunities for rapid expansion into global markets via our local partnership model.

Our proven success to date indicates that the container accommodation concept is likely to be successful in a range of other markets eg, student accommodation, pop-up retail stores, mobile offices.

The world's population is growing. Land shortages and cost implications mean there is likely to be an increasing need for this type of accommodation.

Similarly the global demand for sustainability and a desire to conserve resources will lead to a growing demand for container accommodation over conventional structures.

Cabezada may be able to further enhance its brand reputation and achieve recognition for corporate social responsibility by working with local governments and charities as potential partners in disaster areas/trouble zones. This and our sustainability ethos may widen market appeal and help attract future customers/investors.

(b) **Weaknesses and threats (section 2.2.2)**

There is limited scope for Cabezada to expand alone due to current size and resources, which is why we have developed a partnership model.

Some of the benefits of container accommodation are a result of the standardisation of containers, the ease of transportation and the readily available supply. These are also downsides as potentially this seems to be an easily replicated idea. Protection of IP in relation to our competitors will therefore be important. However Cabezada also benefits from experience and reputation gained as a result of first mover advantage and establishing a global network should help create barriers to entry.

We recognise that as the business expands the two of us are unlikely to have sufficient time and expertise to manage the wider business. Neither of us has a financial background and we are well aware that many businesses fail because they lack sufficient financial expertise. We currently rely on our accountants to provide this expertise but we plan to appoint a finance director in due course and as the business expands we intend to appoint other directors to the board.

Projects are heavily reliant on local infrastructure in relation to heat, light, sewerage etc. and delays may occur due to the political nature of certain projects. Cabezada's previous experience can be brought to bear here to ensure such risks are managed and to make sure that appropriate contingency plans are in place.

Legal and regulatory requirements differ between countries but this is mitigated by our use of the local partnership model.

Health and safety issues or accidents could be very damaging to our reputation. We pride ourselves on our unblemished health and safety record. We take this issue very seriously and we expect our partners to do the same.

A successful model will rely on the integrity of a wide range of local partners and we need to ensure goal congruence. Our partnership agreement will be carefully drafted to make clear the obligations on both sides to ensure the Cabezada brand is not diluted by variable standards. Our terms and conditions will also set out restrictive clauses and confidentiality agreements to protect our partners in the event that a local partner chooses to leave the business.

(c) **Benefits of partnership approach for Cabezada and its local partners (section 3)**

Global business using a local model

Working with the right local partners will allow us to capitalise on our brand image as a pioneer in container accommodation, expand rapidly and generate competitive advantage for Cabezada.

It is easier for local customers and governments to do business with local offices, from a language and timing point of view, as well as culturally.

Local teams are better able to identify opportunities in a market and define appropriate price/quality combination.

Since building standards vary from country to country and requirements also change frequently it is better for the local office to work with architects, governments and planning experts.

Support for our local partner

In addition to exclusive rights to operate under the Cabezada brand in your defined area, we will provide you with a range of benefits that result from being part of a global business, and which are unachievable by setting up business alone:

(1) A popular and tested product range suitable for many different uses in many markets and a reference list of successful projects in different countries

(2) Access to an experienced team of designers and engineers dedicated to container accommodation

(3) Marketing support including website, brochures and press articles

(4) Our supplier and customer contact network and our extensive database of technical, financial and marketing information

(5) Assistance with budgets and financial projections for projects

(6) Ongoing support from a committed partner as evidenced by the fact that we are prepared to take a 20% stake in each partner business

Examiner's comments

Requirement 11.1 asked candidates to prepare three sections of the business plan:

(a) Strengths and realistic market opportunities
(b) Weaknesses and threats
(c) Benefits of partnership for Cabezada and its local partners

This was one of the higher skills elements of the paper and answers were quite polarised. Although candidates were clearly familiar with the knowledge required, which was based on SWOT analysis and methods of business development, weaker candidates struggled to apply this in the context of a business plan to attract potential partners. Candidates who appreciated the need to focus their content on the end user of the document and wrote in an appropriate style, scored very highly. The key here was to (1) emphasise why the company's strengths put it in an ideal position to capitalise on the global opportunities (2) explain any potential weaknesses and threats and how they might be mitigated and (3) highlight how the partnership proposition would be a win-win for both parties. Surprisingly, too many candidates did not produce an answer using the numbered section headings given in the requirement, missing out on an easy format mark. Weaker candidates often provided a bullet point list for each requirement which would not have been suitable for a firm to send to a client. Weak answers were often written as if the focus was on assessing the situation from Cabezada's point of view rather than considering how the information would be received by the partner (ie, with a complete failure to consider the marketing/persuasive nature of the document). Another error was for candidates to write in 11.1(a) and 11.1(b) about the strengths and weaknesses of the partnership arrangement, rather than of Cabezada, leaving themselves with little new to say in 11.1(c).

11.2 Additional information requirements

A prospective partner will want sufficient information to be able to undertake appropriate due diligence and decide if the Cabezada business model makes sense given the current and future environment. They will use a range of criteria to assess the proposal and it is important to anticipate what these are likely to be and to cover them in the plan. The assessment criteria are likely to include the following:

- Viability of business model
- Costs
- Potential returns
- Risks (weaknesses and threats) and how these might be addressed
- Obligations of both parties
- Possible exit route

It would be useful for the plan to start with an executive summary setting out the highlights of the detail contained in the plan. In addition to the current content of the plan, a prospective partner is also likely to want the plan to include the following additional information about:

Owners of Cabezada

- Background/track record/qualifications/expertise of owners
- Any other key stakeholders besides the two directors
- Details of senior management

Financial security of the company

Recent accounts to indicate the long-term sustainability of the business and its ability to provide partners with on-going support.

Competition

Analysis of existing players in the market place, their USPs and how Cabezada differentiates itself in relation to their products/markets.

Detailed terms and conditions of joint venture

- Terms and conditions of Cabezada's stake
- Obligations of both JV parties
- Details of amount and level of support and training to be provided by Cabezada
- Restrictions on partners eg, Regional protection; minimum performance requirements
- Reporting structure for local partners
- Control mechanisms to guarantee quality and performance of other partners
- Restrictions on use of suppliers
- Exit arrangements

Detailed financial information

The required investment level – the amount partners will have to pay for the franchise fee, monthly management charge and % royalty fee on sales.

Annual projections for a typical partner, showing likely profitability and cash flow.

Cabezada's attitude to any continuing financial obligations and the arrangements for financing in the event of expansion.

Evidence of key strategic relationships

- Details of existing projects undertaken
- Supplier contracts
- Quotes/recommendations from existing satisfied customers
- Details of any existing partners/references from them

Other information

Supporting technical detail on the different types of accommodation offered, including photos, plans, diagrams etc.

Examiner's comments

Requirement 11.2 requested candidates to recommend any further information that should be included in the plan to help potential partners to adequately assess Cabezada's partnership proposition. Candidates who were familiar with the pro-forma contents of a business plan and who then applied this to the scenario tended to score well. Some weaker candidates merely provided a list of information without explaining how this might be useful to a potential partner. Better candidates provided a prioritised discussion, focussing on the fact that the current plan was completely lacking in any financial information – historic results, forecasts and details of the costs of the partnership arrangement – and that this would be vital if partners were to assess the likely returns from their investment. It is likely that partners would also want more information on the key directors with whom they were establishing a relationship.

11.3 Purpose and benefits of market segmentation

Market segmentation is the division of the market into homogeneous groups of potential customers who may be treated similarly for marketing purposes.

The purpose of segmentation is to vary the marketing mix according to the needs of each chosen segment. This is likely to increase the effectiveness of marketing.

For example by dividing the market into events and contract clients Cabezada can tailor its product. Events clients may be more concerned with the appearance of the accommodation and want a range of designs; contract clients may focus on cost and functionality.

Benefits of market segmentation include:

- Identification of new marketing opportunities because it provides Cabezada with an opportunity to spot additional sub-groups or to dominate certain segments of the market (niche).

- Competitive advantage from having a better understanding of customer's needs and attitudes to price in each segment.

- It allows Cabezada to assess returns from each segment and thus assist in performance measurement/provide information for decision making.

Segmentation options for Cabezada:

Cabezada has currently chosen to segment the market by type of buyer: one-off short term events vs contract clients requiring longer term accommodation.

It could also consider segmentation by:

- Geographical location – this may help Cabezada organise its logistical operations and adjust elements of the price/product to local needs

- Type of accommodation: hotel and leisure; key worker; housing; media; temporary disaster recovery

- Quality of accommodation: basic, luxury, environmentally friendly

Examiner's comments

In requirement 11.3, candidates were required to explain the purpose and benefits of market segmentation and discuss other approaches to segmentation that the company could adopt, besides the current split between contract and events clients.

The majority of candidates were able to define market segmentation and explain how it could be used to focus the marketing mix to specific customer needs. Again better candidates differentiated themselves by illustrating this with examples relating to Cabezada, rather than talking about segmentation in generic terms. Most candidates were able to make alternative suggestions for segmentation according to geography or quality, although a significant minority of suggestions were more appropriate for segmenting consumers than business customers. A small number of candidates discussed divisionalisation, generic strategy or product/market mix rather than segmentation; these answers were not relevant.

12 Chiba (March 2013)

Marking guide

	Knowledge	Skill	Marks
12.1 Ethical issues	2	3	5
12.2 Divestment/growth by acquisition	3	6	8
12.3 (a) Human resource management	2	3	5
(b) Change management issues	3	7	9
	10	19	27

Chiba is a Japanese company which manufactures a range of liquid foods including rice vinegar. Chiba wants to increase its market share in the UK by acquiring Malegar – a division of a large listed UK food business which makes the UK's leading brand of malt vinegar. Chiba's marketing director is however concerned that Malegar would not be for sale if it were a profitable business. Another potential integration issue is the fact that the two companies have very different cultures and attitudes to human resources management. There is also an ethical issue: the directors of Malegar are aware of a recent complaint from a major wholesaler concerning a contaminated batch of vinegar. As Malegar takes health and safety and quality control seriously, the directors believe the fault must lie with the supplier of the glass bottles and are therefore planning to keep this matter confidential from all parties, including Chiba.

The overall scores for this question were good although 12.3(a) caused problems for some.

12.1 Ethical issues

The issue here is whether it is legal and ethical for the directors to keep the contamination confidential. As well as possibly damaging Malegar's reputation, the contamination will potentially have an effect on the wholesaler(s), the supplier of the bottles, the consumers of the vinegar and the potential purchaser, Chiba.

The directors need to investigate the cause of the problem and consider whether there has been any breach of the law or other regulations that may apply to the industry eg, health and safety or food standards. It could be argued that since Malegar takes health and safety and quality control very seriously, there should have been procedures in place to avoid/detect the contamination before the product reached the wholesaler, irrespective of whoever caused the problem.

In the context of the potential acquisition by Chiba, the directors of Malegar have a duty to act in the best interests of the company and to obtain the best value for shareholders. However, since Malegar's parent, VM plc, is a UK listed company it is likely to have certain obligations regarding the disclosure of any information that could materially affect the purchase price. To this effect there may be a conflict of interest between the directors' duty to obtain the best price for their shareholders and their duty to treat Chiba fairly. The directors should therefore seek legal advice as to how much information they are required to disclose to a prospective purchaser and to what extent it is a case of 'buyer beware'. Chiba is likely to undertake due diligence to help understand the risks before taking on ownership and this will almost certainly involve an investigation into potential liabilities and warranties.

Knowingly making statements that are misleading or inaccurate is likely to be considered dishonest and unethical. The omission of information, which is a matter of transparency, is perhaps less clear cut, particularly where it might be argued that this is an acceptable treatment eg, if the directors believe that the contamination issue has arisen with the supplier and is likely to be fully compensated.

Malegar's directors need to establish the facts and ascertain the cause of the contamination and then seek legal advice before deciding on the most appropriate course of action which fulfils their ethical obligations but minimises the risk of reputational damage for the company.

Examiner's comments

Requirement 12.1 asked candidates to explain the ethical issues that arise for Malegar's directors in relation to revealing the possible contamination.

The quality of answers to this requirement varied considerably. The question required candidates to assess the ethical issues arising from the directors' intention to keep the contamination confidential and the responsibility of Malegar to its customers and the potential acquirer, Chiba. Many candidates approached this requirement in terms of a transparency, fairness and effect framework. However only the better candidates went on to develop the next steps or draw any sort of conclusion. The weaker candidates only considered the issue in relation to Chiba, ignoring the other stakeholders in the scenario (namely the wholesaler, glass supplier and end consumers). They often failed to see any grey area and simply stated that Malegar's directors must reveal the potential contamination or risk being sued by Chiba after it had acquired the business. Stronger candidates discussed the fact that the cause of the contamination was uncertain, and that the directors needed first to establish the facts and then decide whether to disclose. The best candidates also discussed whether Malegar would have any legal duty to disclose the issue to its customers or Chiba, which might be expected to undertake its own due diligence, or whether in the context of the acquisition it would be a case of 'buyer beware'.

12.2 Strategy evaluation

As Chiba's marketing director notes, the UK parent may want to sell Malegar because the market is challenging and it is struggling to maintain margins etc. Even so, Malegar may still be worth buying as Chiba may be better placed to exploit benefits due to synergy with its existing brands and the ability to target other markets based on health benefits and alternative uses (eg, cleaning).

However it could also be that the Malegar business is viable and that other reasons can be put forward for the divestment by the UK parent:

Reason for sale by UK parent

- Rationalisation of the business as a result of portfolio analysis – here we are told that VM plc wants to focus on a few key food brands (a reversal of diversification strategy). VM plc may have decided that there is a lack of strategic fit between vinegar and its other more profitable brands.

- VM may wish to generate funds for investment in other markets that will generate better growth opportunities. Malegar may be generating insufficient returns for the amount of management time/investment required.

- We are also told that the parent company has incurred significant borrowings. These may be incurring high interest costs and putting a strain on liquidity. A sale would raise funds to reduce this debt burden.

- If exit barriers are high (eg, redundancy costs, termination penalties on leases etc) then it is better for VM to sell the business as a going concern rather than just withdraw the product.

- Finally the company may be trying to sell Malegar before the contamination becomes widely known and damages its brand/reputation.

Chiba's growth by acquisition

The Ansoff model is a two-by-two matrix of 'Products' and 'Markets'. In the context of this matrix the acquisition of Malegar would involve market development and, to the extent that malt vinegar is deemed to be different from rice vinegar, product development. The Lynch expansion model is another two-by-two matrix of company growth and geographical location. Under this model, Chiba's proposed acquisition is international external development.

Arguments for growth by acquisition

- Chiba's management has identified a desire to increase its presence in the UK. Chiba has no track record in the UK market and the strong market presence of brand names such as Malegar creates barriers to entry that would make organic growth hard to achieve. Acquisition is likely to be faster than organic growth and potentially less risky.

- Acquisition of the market leader creates instant market dominance for Chiba and at the same time removes a significant player from the market.

- It will provide access to a strong brand name/reputation in the UK market and facilitate a better understanding of the UK market for a Japanese company. This reduces cultural risk and having a 'local image' may also reduce xenophobic tendencies.

- Acquisition gives Chiba instant access to the existing factory location and resources, including employees.

- The acquisition of a business in the UK may give rise to other future opportunities, eg, expansion into Europe.

The price of the acquisition will be a major factor in assessing the overall merits of sale or purchase.

Requirement 12.2 asked candidates to discuss the possible reasons why the UK owner might be divesting Malegar (in light of the comments of Chiba's marketing director) and the benefits to Chiba of growing by acquisition in the UK.

Candidates are used to being asked to discuss growth by acquisition and were well-versed in the arguments here, with the majority able to apply their knowledge to the scenario. Some were less prepared for a discussion of reasons for divestment, although most were able to expand on the two reasons given in the question regarding the parent company's desire to reduce borrowings and focus on core brands. Better answers discussed other possible reasons such as product portfolio and life-cycles, liquidity and return. Stronger candidates queried whether the contamination may have had an impact on the decision to sell. Despite the comment in the requirement, relatively few candidates linked their discussion to the marketing director's concerns that Malegar might be loss-making. The best scripts did address this however, often in some form of conclusion, explaining that the fact that Malegar might be making insufficient return for its UK parent did not necessarily mean that it would be an unprofitable acquisition for Chiba, although only the top decile pointed out that the overall benefit of the acquisition might depend on the price to be paid.

12.3 HR strategy and change management

(a) HR management by Malegar

Malegar does not seem to have adopted a strategic approach to HRM. Its approach, which is very authoritarian, treats the staff merely as another resource, rather than as a valued asset. It may have resulted in a high degree of job-related tension, poor working relationships and some manipulation of data by functional managers accountable for their performance. There are likely to be limited prospects for career development.

The disadvantages of such an approach include the following:

- There is evidence that staff motivation may be a problem as there is a high staff turnover. The loss of staff loses experience and skills for the company with the costs of retraining and learning for new staff.

- There may be dysfunctional behaviour by staff in response to short-term targets instead of focussing on longer-term value-enhancing activities eg, this may mean that short-term sales are made at the cost of long-term customer relationships.

- The hierarchical nature of the business and centralised approach to decision making may also have impeded team-working and stifled innovation.

HR management by Chiba

Chiba on the other hand appears to take a more strategic approach with emphasis on the human element. This recognises that collectively the staff are a valued asset and can contribute to competitive advantage.

Chiba is likely to do more to focus on personal and career development, gaining employees' commitment to the organisation's values and goals and creating a more participative environment.

As a result tension and manipulation are reduced and relationships are likely to be better.

The shared approach to decision making is likely to increase goal congruence, although a potential downside of Chiba's approach to HRM is that decision-making may be slower than in Malegar.

(b) Managing the change of culture

It is clear that the two businesses are very different and that acquisition by Chiba will transform the existing structure, culture and values. As a result of the acquisition, Chiba's management will need to develop a strategy for creating and maintaining the necessary culture change, although the fact that the transition will take up to 12 months may help as the changes can be made gradually.

The changes may cause resistance from those wishing to preserve the existing state of affairs and the way that the changes are put forward and implemented will be crucial to Chiba's success. However given Chiba's approach to HRM, the change may be welcomed by many Malegar employees as better than they are used to.

Barrier to change

Barriers to change may be cultural or arise as a result of things which affect individuals and cause them to see the change as a threat (personnel barriers).

Cultural resistance arises as a result of structural inertia, group inertia and power structures.

- Structural inertia – Malegar has operated with a rigid hierarchy and short term targets which will take time to change. Its recruitment and promotion processes are likely to have resulted in certain types of employee who may not fit with Chiba's collective approach and participative decision making.

- Group inertia – this may be less relevant as Malegar's existing structure is unlikely to have led to cohesive teams. However the functional managers may act as a group in resisting change implementation and if employees are in one geographical location this may be a factor in increasing group resistance.

Power structures are threatened by the redistribution of authority or changing communication lines. This will in particular affect higher management in Malegar whose roles may change significantly after the new structure is implemented, as participation and collective responsibility is encouraged. Such management may be reluctant to implement changes which will be against their own interests. For example, managers may have viewed Malegar as having been very successful in the UK, therefore resenting the need to integrate and adopt the new values of a Japanese company.

Other Malegar employees who have been discontented under the existing system may however be supportive at the outset.

Personal barriers

There are also barriers which affect individuals and result in them seeing the change as a threat.

Malegar employees may feel threatened by the changes to their habitual way of working and the lack of familiarity (fear of the unknown). Junior employees may lack the confidence or skills to take on a new challenge and may take time to get used to the participative approach with its emphasis on shared responsibility. It is important that Chiba offers support and training to assist them.

Employees may have concerns over potential income levels and job security, although given the high staff turnover this does not seem to have been a feature of employment with Malegar. Chiba could provide statistics on staff turnover to help reassure employees about employment prospects and their earning capacity.

Selective information processing may cause employees to misinterpret or ignore the arguments for change put forward by Chiba's management.

Change management

Resistance to cultural change can be managed or reduced with genuine and visible support for the change by top management and good communication/participation systems associated with the change.

Chiba's management should identify the key stakeholders and influencers among the Malegar employees and provide communication and appropriate training.

Communication should focus on the benefits of the change to employees. Management needs to communicate Chiba's vision of the future and show how the Malegar employees can contribute to this. Given the gradual nature of the transfer of contracts, a negotiation strategy may be implemented where the process of bargaining leads to a situation of compromise and agreement. The advantage of a negotiation strategy is that Chiba can note possible conflict and deal with it in an orderly fashion, which prevents such problems as industrial action. Also ex-Malegar employees are more likely to support changes made and give positive commitment if they 'own' the change or have a stake in the future of the company.

Lewin suggests that managers should recognise the current state of equilibrium with forces pushing for change on the one hand and, equally, forces resisting change aiming to maintain the present situation. As a result Chiba's management would need to adopt the following process:

- **Unfreezing** – where management convince staff of the undesirability of the present situation, creating the initial motivation to change by emphasising the benefits of Chiba's longer term, participative approach.

- **The change process itself** – which will often involve new information, new attitudes and new concepts. This would involve the communication, negotiation and training outlined above.

- **Refreezing** – which reinforces the new pattern of work or behaviour by rewards, developing the belief that the changed situation satisfies organisational and personal values. Under Chiba's management employees are likely to have more opportunities for career development, staff turnover should reduce and Chiba can also implement non-financial motivators rather than focussing on the achievement of short term targets.

Tutorial note:

This answer includes a wide variety of points for marking purposes and is far more comprehensive than would be expected for the marks available. As an alternative to Lewin, the Gemini's 4Rs framework for planned change could also be applied: Reframe, Restructure, Revitalise, Renew.

Examiner's comments

In requirement 12.3, candidates were required to (a) contrast Chiba and Malegar's differing approaches to human resource management and (b) explain the change management issues that Chiba is likely to face when integrating the Malegar employees.

Some candidates seemed less well prepared for 12.3(a), with many weaker candidates restricting their answers to a comparison of structure and decision-making, which often was in fact little more than a repetition of points made in the scenario. Better candidates contrasted Malegar's 'hard' approach to HRM which treats employees as a short-term commodity, with Chiba's 'softer', more collective approach where employees are seen as a valued asset, and discussed the impact that this is likely to have on motivation, quality of decision-making and commitment to the organisation.

As usual candidates demonstrated good knowledge of change management in 12.3(b), with most discussing barriers to change and Lewin/Schein's iceberg model (although the Gemini's 4Rs framework could also have been used). It was disappointing that more candidates did not focus on the change in the context of the very different HRM strategy and culture/values of the Japanese company – a point that 12.3(a) had been intended to highlight; weaker candidates instead discussed at length the general change management issues associated with acquisitions. The best candidates recognised that the change will transform the existing culture but is to take place over a gradual period of 12 months and, given some explanation, may be welcomed by most employees as better than their current position. Candidates who went on at length about structural inertia, group norms and job security failed to recognise that these might not be particularly relevant given Malegar's existing high staff turnover.

13 Hire Value Ltd (June 2013)

Marking guide

	Knowledge	Skill	Marks
13.1 Performance and competitive position	2	9	10
13.2 Shortfall in performance and matters requiring further attention	–	18	16
13.3 Risk register	3	7	9
13.4 Ethical issues, and implications of them	3	8	10
	8	42	45

General comments:

This is the mini case and also the data analysis question. The scenario relates to a small company (HV) operating in the self-drive, car hire industry. HV decided to expand the business just over a year ago by raising venture capital finance based on a business plan which forecast growth in sales and profits. Whilst there has been some growth, it has not matched the business plan projections and a one-year review has taken place to discover the reasons for this. The review also highlighted some transactions with directors which raised ethical issues. The question also provides information about the market leader, KK.

Data for 13.1 and 13.2

	HV plan	HV Actual	Variance	%	KK
Revenue					
Business £'000s	13,000	7,000	–6,000	–46.15	620,000
Leisure £'000s	17,000	20,000	+3,000	+17.65	580,000
TOTAL REV £'000s	30,000	27,000	–3,000	–10%	1,200,000
Profit £'000s	1,200	1,000	–200	–16.67%	56,000
Vehicles	3,000	2,800	–200	–6.67%	68,000
Days hiring ('000 days)	870	820	–50	–5.74%	21,100
Asset values					
Cars £'000s	20,250	16,800	–3,450	–17.04%	816,000
Other £'000s	10,000	10,000	0	0	664,000
Total assets £'000s	30,250	26,800	–3,450	–11.40%	1,480,000
Analysis					
% REVENUE					
Business	43.3%	25.9%			51.7%
Leisure	56.7%	74.1%			48.3%
PROFIT/REV	4%	3.7%			4.7%
REV per car pa	£10,000	£9,642.85			£17,647
REV per day hiring	£34.48	£32.93			£56.87
Days hire per car	290	293			310
Profit/assets	3.97	3.73			3.78
Profit/value of cars	5.93	5.95			6.86
Value of cars/cars	£6,750	£6,000			£12,000
Rev/value of cars	1.48	1.61			1.47

13.1 Key differences between KK and HV which make performance comparisons more difficult are: the larger size of KK; and a different business sector, with KK being upmarket compared to HV's business model. However, both companies operate in a similar product and geographical market, being in the UK.

Competitive position

In assessing market share of KK and HV they are both operating in the short term rental sector which has revenues of £5,000 million. Any assessment of competitive position appears valid in relation to this market sub-sector.

With revenue of £1,200 million this gives KK a substantial 24% share of the short term car hire sector. In contrast, HV has a market share of about 0.5%. With a total industry revenue of about £5,000 million and 100 companies, the average company has a revenue of about £50 million giving it a 1% market share – almost twice that of HV.

As a consequence, HV is very much a niche player in the industry. It appears to adopt a slightly confused business model of a mid-market position in all respects except the key asset of the quality of the vehicles, which is downmarket. Perhaps, as a consequence, it is particularly weak in the business customer sector with only 26% of revenue from business customers.

In contrast, KK generates 52% of its revenue from the business customer sector. It also competes at the upper end of the market with a wide range of large company business customers and a series of partners offering exclusive access to some airlines making it impossible, in the short term at least, for smaller car hire companies, including HV, to compete.

KK's size enables it to have economies of scale and economies of scope for cost advantages and these also provide barriers to entry into this sector of the market making it hard for smaller companies, like HV, to compete.

Performance

In absolute terms, it is clear that KK earns a greater profit than HV. However this is to be expected from a larger company and it does not follow that it has performed better on this basis.

In terms of margins, the data table shows that KK has significantly better operating profit margins at 4.7% compared to 3.7% for HV. This may be due to: better cost control; economies of scale; or premium pricing.

Similarly, revenue per car is much greater for KK at £17,647 per year compared to only £9,643 for HV (83% higher). It would be misleading to conclude however that KK has better revenue generation from its assets on this basis. The table shows that the average value of a KK car is £12,000 while the average value of a HV car is only half that at £6,000. Thus, while KK's car value is 100% greater than that of HV, the revenue per car is only 83% higher. As a consequence, the data table shows that HV's annual revenue per £1 of car value is £1.61, compared to only £1.41 for KK. This may give some support for the HV business model of sourcing two year old used cars.

A key piece of data that indicates market positioning is the price per day of hire. For HV it is only £32.93, whereas KK is able to charge an average of £56.87, although this average may reflect some very high quality vehicles.

In terms of operating efficiency, KK also appears to outperform HV. KK cars are hired out 310 days per year giving a utilisation of 85% (on a 365 day year) compared to that of 80% already noted for HV.

It is clear therefore that in financial and operating terms KK has overall outperformed HV, but nevertheless the strategy of HV may have some favourable aspects and HV may have more potential to grow if it is able to win some large business customer accounts.

Examiner's comments

Requirement 13.1 requested candidates to compare the performance and competitive position of HV with that of the market leader, KK. Attempts at this part were reasonable with most candidates producing some calculations including operating profit margin, average price per vehicle hired and average number of days hired. However, the interpretation of the data was, in many cases, limited. Candidates struggled with the comparison of a large business with a smaller business with many concluding little more than that KK had greater revenue and profit through its relatively greater size. Some of the reasons for the differences were very general, such as 'KK has economies of scale'. The comparison of competitive position was omitted altogether by a significant minority of candidates.

13.2 Revenue

The above data analysis shows that overall revenues are lower than the business plan by £3m, which is a 10% shortfall on planned sales revenues.

The analysis by sector shows that there is a shortfall of £6m in the business customer sector, but that sales revenue in the leisure sector has exceeded the business plan by £3m. The reason for the shortfall in leisure needs to be investigated further in terms of the assumptions that were expected to lead to growth (eg, number of new business customers, new lines of business, pricing policy, one or a few larger business customers expected to be won). It may be that negotiations are continuing on some accounts that are expected to be won in 20Y2/Y3 and that will come to fruition in 20Y3/Y4.

The excess over plan of leisure customer revenues should also be investigated further to continue to exploit any successes in the next period.

The impact of the revenue variances has made the company much more dependent on the leisure sector compared to the business sector (74% v 26%) than was envisaged in the business plan where the relative shares were reasonably equal (57% v 43%).

There is limited additional data on each customer sector but, looking at revenue overall, it can be seen from the above data table that the number of days hiring has fallen short of the plan by 50,000 hire days. In terms of volumes this is a 5.7% shortfall. The fact that sales revenues have fallen by 10% and volumes by only 5.7% implies that the rental charge has been lower than expected. This notion is substantiated by the revenue per vehicle hire day which was £34.48 per hire day in the business plan, but only £32.93 was actually achieved.

This result could be explained by: additional discounting, proportionately more hires of cheaper vehicles or failure to implement intended price increases. The result is, however, inconsistent with the shift in the proportion of business customers to leisure customers as business customers have 'preferential rates' and so one would expect the revenue per hire day to increase with a greater proportion of leisure customers. This matter requires further investigation and analysis by sector.

Profitability

The above data table shows that overall profit before tax is lower than the business plan by £200,000, which is a 16.7% shortfall on profit in the business plan.

The fall of 16.7% in profit based on a 10% fall in revenue may, in part, be due to operating gearing whereby fixed costs still need to be covered and therefore profit falls by a greater amount than revenue.

Profit margins are also lower than planned at 3.7%, compared to the forecast 4%. This also may be due to high operating gearing and lower sales than expected.

Return on assets

Having considered profitability in absolute terms, it is necessary to consider profitability in relation to the asset base generating that profit.

The revenue earning asset base (cars) is smaller than planned, with an actual average count of 2,800 vehicles rather than the 3,000 planned. The reasons for this need to be established. It may have been that with lower demand it was decided to reduce the number of cars held in order not to have surplus underutilised assets. It is possible however that the direction of causation is the other way around ie, that it has proved difficult to source the right type of cars at the right price and the shortfall in vehicle capacity has meant that revenues have been affected. This latter explanation seems less likely, but further investigation is needed.

The return on total assets from the data table is 3.7% compared to the level in the business plan of 4%. This has occurred as, even though the asset base is £3.45m (11.4%) lower than expected, the profit is down 16.7% on the planned level.

Further analysis of assets shows that general non-revenue earning assets are constant at £10m. As a result the entire £3.45m fall in the asset base relates to hire cars. This is a 17% reduction. As a consequence, the return on the revenue generating asset base of cars is 5.95% which is slightly higher than the planned rate of 5.93%.

Further analysis shows that the reason for the lower hire car asset base is partly volume with 2,800 cars compared to the planned level of 3,000 (6.7% lower). However the value per car is also lower than planned at £6,000 compared to the planned value of £6,750. This may be due to: a higher proportion of purchases of smaller and cheaper cars than planned; the acquisition of older cars in the period; or a greater than expected fall in the value of the entire vehicle holding due to market conditions. Further investigations would be needed to ascertain the reasons.

Efficiency and utilisation

The number of days per year that cars are out on hire reflects utilisation and is a key factor in determining profitability. The data table shows that cars were out on hire 293 days per year compared to the planned level of 290 days (ie, on a 365 day year this is 80% utilization). The most obvious reason for the higher level of utilization is that despite lower sales volumes than expected (ie, hire days are 5.7% lower) the number of cars available is 6.7% lower.

The high utilization rates are good in one respect as they reflect high usage of revenue earning assets. In another respect however the high utilization could be seen as excessive. In particular as the business is seasonal then it may be significantly higher than 80% in peak season.

On the basis of the information provided, 30% of annual sales come in each of spring or summer. If there is on average 80% utilization then in summer/spring there is 80% × 30/25 = 96%. At a peak time of the week in peak season there may be 100% utilization for at least some types of vehicle. This may mean lost sales or lack of consumer choice in vehicle selection.

The utilisation and sales loss arguments need to be balanced. Further investigations are therefore needed regarding the number of lost sales from the inability to supply suitable vehicles to customers.

The business plan and professional scepticism

The shortfall from the business plan may have been due to over-optimistic forecasts in setting the plan rather than poor performance in delivering the plan. In particular, in order to raise finance from the venture capitalists, the HV board may have been incentivised to present the forecasts expected by the venture capitalists.

Examiner's comments

Requirement 13.2 asked candidates to analyse and explain the shortfall between actual performance and the business plan forecast, then to highlight three matters for further investigation. The weakest candidates produced few or no calculations for this part, thereby providing purely qualitative answers. These types of data analysis and interpretation questions require numerical analysis of data but also explanations of underlying cause and effect relationships indicating why variances may have occurred in order to 'make the numbers speak'.

Many better candidates produced calculations which normally considered days hired, operating profit margins, return on assets and efficiency/utilisation ratios. Better answers also considered the validity of the projections in the business plan itself, questioning whether they were too optimistic in an attempt to obtain venture capital finance. The correct observation was often made that the necessary investment in new vehicles had not taken place hence somewhat diluting the firm's ability to expand the business sector.

Most candidates provided reasonable suggestions for further investigation. For example, some candidates indicated that prior year performance data would be useful in order to assess the reasons for the shortfall.

Risk	Impact and likelihood	Risk management
Legal liability from the operation of cars by customers and employees.	• High significance if there is personal injury. • Lower impact as damage will be to only one car. • With many vehicles being operated a reasonably high probability that accidents will occur.	• Insure risk. • Put in place procedures to ensure terms of insurance agreement are complied with. • Implement procedures to minimise the probability of accidents (eg, restrict hires to 'clean' licence holders).
Regulation risk which may change the terms of business or the need for compliance costs to be incurred, including tax.	• Increased environment and tax legislation to reduce pollution seems likely. • With so many vehicles owned the impact could be significant.	• Consider acquiring more environmentally friendly vehicles. • Join industry pressure group to influence government.
Strong dependence on airline industry.	• Any problems with airline industry (recession, taxation, strike) are likely to affect the car rental industry.	• Form partnerships and work together with airline industry. • Diversify with partners in other industries (eg, insurance).
Competition risk. The internet has made capture of new bookings much easier for smaller companies to compete at the lower end of the market.	Competition may significantly affect price and have a major impact on profits of small companies such as HV. This is likely to occur and at the smaller end of the market there is already significant competition with over 100 UK operators.	• Develop reputation and identity. • Holding slots at airports is one way to restrict competition.
Seasonality means a risk of redundant assets in low season and insufficient capacity in peak season.	If seasonality is pronounced then the effects at the margin may be moderately significant. Highly likely as an established demand pattern.	• Price discrimination according to season. • Rent assets to acquire vehicles to meet short-term peak rather than owning 100% of car pool. • Model seasonality so timings are predictable.
Car prices could change If cars increase in cost then this is the major capital asset and will affect profitability and liquidity.	The car industry is competitive which makes major price changes unlikely. However should it occur it may have significant impact.	• Have portfolio of different types of car of different ages. • Hold cars for longer if car prices temporarily increase.
Second hand values weaken meaning lower residuals at end of car life and greater depreciation and costs of ownership.	Second hand market is competitive but new legislation could mean older cars which are less environmentally friendly may become more costly to run and this reduces their value. Effect possibly significant.	• Lease some cars. • Monitor second hand market and new legislation affecting cars. • Hold cars for longer.

Risk	Impact and likelihood	Risk management
Operating cost increases – eg, repairs, petrol, insurance, road tax.	Very likely given past evidence. Cumulative effect likely to be significant, although customers pay for own petrol.	• Review maintenance operations. • Industry wide effect so would not materially impact upon competitive position in the industry which may enable industry wide price increase to offset cost increases.
Online communication or other computer failure would prevent all bookings for period of problem.	Likely to be short term and isolated but loss of customers to rivals and reputation risk.	IT back up facilities and contingency provisions for disaster recovery.

Note: Only **four** risks were required from candidates.

Examiner's comments

Requirement 13.3 asked candidates to prepare a risk register. There were some very general answers. For example some candidates merely cited operational or financial risk without being specific as to what these could be. That said, there were some really good answers at the other end of the spectrum which clearly identified very specific risks, their classification (eg, financial or strategic), their impact and likelihood and what could be done to mitigate them. The higher scoring answers included the risks of the airline industry and their implications, issues with the online systems, as well as increase in fuel prices, values of vehicles and the ageing and depreciation of cars. Weaker answers typically displayed some or all of the following: covering only three risks; little detail or explanation of each point: highlighting insignificant risks; or identifying unlikely circumstances which were not suggested by the scenario. Most, but far from all, candidates used the columnar format suggested in the question.

13.4 Introduction

In assessing the ethical issues and implications of the three matters raised it is important to assess both whether they are unethical, and the degree of ethical/unethical behaviour. This is particularly the case for the implications of the actions.

In the first instance, it is necessary to establish the full facts in each of the cases highlighted by Gatter LLP. At the moment they are merely accusations which need to be substantiated. An appropriate degree of professional scepticism must be applied to all concerned.

Issue 1 – private use of company vehicles by executive directors

The company is a separate legal entity from the directors and shareholders, and no-one has rights to use or take the company's assets without due authority. Potentially, the use of company assets by directors, even where there is no loss of revenue, is an illegal act in breach of their statutory duties. In addition, it appears there is a corporate governance problem in that the directors, who are the company's agents, are pursuing their own ends rather than those of the company. It may be necessary to take legal advice. Initially it will be necessary to speak to each director to gather evidence of actions. It will also be necessary to examine director employment contracts with the company to investigate whether they confer rights to use company assets under any conditions. Additionally, it should be established whether there was any direct benefit to the company in directors using the assets in this manner.

The key potential ethical issue is honesty/integrity.

In addition however there is the issue of transparency to shareholders, even if only retrospectively, of the nature and extent of any actions of this kind.

In terms of effect, it needs to be established whether there has been any direct loss to the company (eg, lost revenue) or additional cost (eg, petrol used) which needs to be made good by the directors concerned.

The fairness of the transaction is in question, in that it may be contrary to the interests of the shareholders. Even where the directors are shareholders it is contrary to the interests of the other shareholders, in particular TopFin.

If any of the directors belong to a professional body, then there may be a code of conduct and guidelines to ensure members behave in an ethical and professional manner, with disciplinary action if they do not. Any director who is a member of the ICAEW for instance would face disciplinary proceedings unless the actions were legitimately within the terms of their employment contract.

There may also be an issue in directors not declaring a taxable benefit.

Issue 2 – the lending of a company vehicle by a director to a third party

The issues are similar to issue 1 except as follows:

- With issue 1, the practice appeared to be at least well known to the other directors. It is not clear whether there was any internal transparency over this incident, other than the one director who was informed.

- It seems implausible that this type of action is part of an employment contract with the director.

- There is potential for the director receiving some benefit from the friend in return for the loan of the car. This would be a key effect and would amount to a personal gain.

- Are there any further undisclosed transactions of this type?

In order to gain transparency internally amongst the directors, as well as externally to shareholders, these facts need to be established in addition to those in issue 1.

Issue 3 – the hiring of a private company vehicle by a director to a third party for personal gain

This is potentially the most serious ethical issue as there is an increased risk of fraud against the company. The distinguishing features from the first two issues are:

- there is a probability of a direct financial gain by a director from deliberate misuse of company property, in breach of her statutory duties as a director

- there is a potential direct effect on the company from loss of revenue on this contract

- assuming the other directors were unaware of the incident, then there is an issue of internal control and transparency

The facts to be established are:

- why and how this transaction occurred

- what happened to the proceeds gained? Why were they returned to the company after such a delay?

- are there any further undisclosed transactions of this type?

Examiner's comments

In requirement 13.4, candidates were asked to explain the ethical issues and implications arising from a series of transactions by directors.

Candidates' answers to this requirement were the weakest on the paper. Whilst most candidates were familiar with ethical language in terms of transparency, fairness and effect, only a small number of candidates considered honesty/integrity, legality and steps which should be taken to deal with each issue. Moreover, few candidates indicated that the full facts would need to be established prior to forming a firm conclusion. It was apparent in this question that candidates do not adopt a logical, methodical approach, which considers any additional information needed.

Instead, many candidates merely concluded that the behaviour is illegal without questioning why or whether they have the legal knowledge or sufficient information to come to this firm conclusion. A significant number believed that Sandra Bevan's conduct amounted to money laundering. More balanced and questioning answers were required that do not assert conclusions without supporting reasoning and evidence. Few candidates questioned the powers and responsibilities of directors in the context of corporate governance or their legal duties.

14 Up 'n' Over plc (June 2013)

Marking guide

		Knowledge	Skill	Marks
14.1 (a)	Expected variable cost	1	4	
(b)	Break-even level	1	4	
				9
14.2 Report				
(a)	Original strategy	1	6	
(b)	Cost reduction programme	3	6	
(c)	Cease manufacturing	1	6	
				21
		7	26	30

General comments:

The scenario in this question relates to a manufacturer of low cost garage doors.

Although attempts had always been made to keep costs low to provide 'best value', losses had been made. As a consequence, a new chief executive was appointed a couple of years ago and pushed costs down further by reducing the quality of the raw materials and freezing all capital expenditure. Initially this had the effect of reducing costs and quality, increasing margins and turning the losses into a profit. More recently, however, there have been increasing customer complaints and falling sales, although profits remain higher than they were before the cost reduction exercise. The board is split between returning to the original strategy or retaining the new low cost strategy. The chairman has suggested a third choice, of ceasing to be a manufacturer and becoming an importer and wholesaler of garage doors from Thailand.

14.1 (a)   20Y3

Sales volume	=	£30m/£400	= 75,000 doors
Variable cost	=	£30m – £14m – £2m	= £14m
VC per door	=	£14m/75,000	= **£186.67**

(b)   Sales volume   =   £32m/£400   =   80,000 doors

20Y1

Variable cost	=	£32m – £15m + £1m	= £18m
VC per door	=	£18m/80,000	= £225
Contribution per door	=	£400 – £225	= £175
Break-even	=	£15m/£175	= **85,714.28 ie, 85,715 doors**

20Y2

Variable cost	=	£32m – £14m – £3m	= £15m
VC per door	=	£15m/80,000	= £187.50
Contribution per door	=	£400 – £187.5	= £212.50
Break-even	=	£14m/£212.50	= **65,882.35 ie, 65,883 doors**

Implications for operating risk

The high level of fixed costs of £15m and £14m in 20Y1 and 20Y2 respectively indicate high operating gearing. This is the seen more clearly when comparing fixed costs with the relative levels of variable costs of £18m and £15m in 20Y1 and 20Y2 respectively, which are only a little higher than fixed costs. The high operating gearing means that profits are volatile when changes in sales occur.

While there was a margin of safety of 14,117 units in 20Y2 (ie, 17.6%) the probability of the margin being 'used up' in 20Y3 needs to be considered in the context of increasing customer dissatisfaction and possible cancellation of large orders. The fall in expected sales in 20Y3 from £32m to £30m (6.3%) is indicative of the operating gearing consequences.

Examiner's comments

Requirement 14.1 asked candidates to compute variable costs and to calculate break-even from data provided. For the majority of candidates, the computation of variable cost and the subsequent break-even calculations did not pose any problems. There were however some mistakes in calculations, where candidates mixed up the revenue and cost figures or made calculations for the wrong years. The operating risk explanation was not dealt with very well, if at all, by many candidates.

14.2 From: Business Adviser
To: Up 'n' Over Board
Subject: Future Strategy
Date: 12 June 20Y3

(a) **Return to policy of 20Y1 and prior years**

   Benefits

   Good reputation with customers for best value. The additional costs therefore enhance reputation as a strategic base on which to build, despite recent operating losses.

   There is an existing customer base which is partially secured by some long term contracts with larger customers. This ties some major customers into UnO giving the opportunity to restore reputation before the next contract renewal if the cost reductions are reversed.

   Problems

   An operating loss of £1 million was made in 20Y1, which was the last year of the previous 'best value' policy. The break-even calculation shows that there is a negative margin of safety of 5,715 units. This means UnO would need to sell another 5,715 doors in order to break-even which would be a 7.1% increase in sales volume.

   UnO's strategic positioning is unclear. It is neither a differentiator nor a cost leader in accordance with Porter's generic strategies. It therefore runs the risk of pursuing a strategy based on a subjective concept of 'best value' and may be 'stuck in the middle'. At the very least, it needs to be aware of its positioning in terms of price-quality within the industry.

   There are 'competitive market conditions' which would make a price increase difficult as a means to increase sales revenues.

   Sustainability

   A sustainable enterprise is one that generates continuously increasing stakeholder value through the application of sustainable practices through the entire base activity (products and services, workforce, workplace, functions/processes, and management/governance).

   The continued operating losses are not sustainable in the longer term as, without profit, the wider stakeholder need cannot be met as the company will not survive. The key question of sustainability is whether the loss in 20Y1 would be typical, or whether it could be reversed by efficiency gains or improvements in sales.

(b) **Cost reduction**

Benefits

A profit is now being achieved of £3m in 20Y2 and there is an expected profit of £2m for 20Y3.

The break-even calculation shows that there is a margin of safety of 14,117 units for 20Y2. This means UnO would need to sell 14,117 fewer doors at current prices and costs before profit fell to break-even, which would be a 17.6% decrease in sales volume.

There has also been a share price increase in 20Y2. It is unclear whether this was entirely due to the cost reduction strategy or whether other factors also had an impact. However, assuming that the strategy was the major factor, this was a 114% increase in share price. While share price then fell to June 20Y3 by 29%, the share price remains above the 20Y1 level. The stock market does not therefore appear to expect UnO to return to losses.

Problems

While there was an initial favourable impact to cost reduction in achieving profit, there appears to be a lagged reputational effect as information gradually becomes available to show that the doors are becoming lower quality and less durable.

There is some evidence, from at least one customer, that they may cease to purchase doors from UnO if this continues.

There is some initial protection from large customers withdrawing arising from the long term contracts but, if they fail to be renewed, the impact may be sudden and substantial from reputational loss.

Moreover, as the large companies hold inventories, they may cease to purchase additional doors near the end of the contract and instead run down inventories.

Sustainability

The benefits of the cost reduction policy appear to be short term and unsustainable. While there is some margin of safety a major and systemic loss of reputation and customer demand from a poor quality product seems likely to push the company into losses fairly quickly.

(c) **Import from Thailand**

Benefits

- Funds generated from closure of manufacturing may enable a return of funds to shareholders or investment and diversification into other distribution activities in the new wholesaler/importer role.

- If a contractual agreement can assure quality control procedures then UnO's reputation may recover.

- Most costs will be variable so the operating gearing will decrease so there is some protection from losses if sales fall.

- The existing distribution competencies of economies of scope and customer relationships can still be exploited.

Problems

- UnO needs to ensure continuity of supply. Given a new supplier and significant geographical distance, some measure of control over failure to supply is required.

- The timing of the supply chain may be more unreliable given the geographical distance, so the lead time may be longer and more variable causing disappointed customers and lack of agility in satisfying their needs unless UnO holds inventory.

- Transport costs may be substantial but appear, even when added to purchase costs, to be less than the current operating costs.

- Exchange rate risk may cause uncertainty over price and profit.

- If the new contract fails then the manufacturing base will be lost so UnO cannot return to the old strategy.

- Are there alternative suppliers at a similar price to diversify risk and maintain security of supply?

- Is there an exclusivity clause to prevent other UK companies importing the same goods from the same supplier?

- Is the contract price fixed for any period?

Sustainability

Continuity of supply in the longer term at a competitive price is key. This may not be from the same suppliers but by changing suppliers over time there may be continuity of supply.

Aside from business sustainability, environmental sustainability may be damaged by transport over such a long distance (eg, climate change, pollution, emissions levels, waste, use of natural resources, impacts of product use, compliance with environmental legislation, air quality).

Conclusion

The cost reduction policy and the 20Y1 policy both appear to be unsustainable for different reasons.

The import policy has risks but if a suitable supplier can be found which is reliable then it may be a feasible and desirable strategy to follow.

Examiner's comments

Requirement 14.2 requested candidates to evaluate the benefits and problems of the three strategies and assess the sustainability of each. Answers to this part varied in standard quite significantly. The better answers addressed all three strategies and all three key areas of each strategy being: benefits, problems and sustainability. Some very good points were made overall, in particularly a return to the old strategy would continue to generate losses and it would leave UnO 'stuck in the middle'. Therefore, in the longer term, the strategy was unsustainable. Discussion of the cost reduction strategy identified the reputational effect and the potential loss of customers. Most candidates opted for the third strategy but recognised that there were significant risks associated with importing from Thailand such as quality control, exchange risks and management of supplier relations. Poorer candidates showed some or all of the following weaknesses: failing to demonstrate an understanding of the differing strategies; failing to comment on sustainability; not providing a conclusion; failure to refer to the numerical analysis calculated in requirement 14.1.

15 Moogle plc (June 2013)

Marking guide

	Knowledge	Skill	Marks
15.1 PESTEL analysis	4	8	11
15.2 Internal/external information	4	11	14
	8	19	25

General comments:

The scenario relates to the pet products section of a large supermarket chain. A new executive manager has been appointed to be responsible for UK pet products' profit, pricing and procurement. A key issue is the type of information the manager requires from the IT department to take decisions and control this section of the business.

15.1 Political

Taxation effects of pet food – eg, VAT may impact profitability significantly.

Social welfare policy – allowing people to keep pets in government housing, care homes and other regulated environments affects the number of possible pet owners.

Health and safety policies over pet foods may increase costs for suppliers.

Economic

The economic downturn is likely to have an impact on the number of people who own pets and the amount they are likely to spend on pet products (eg, premium foods vs cheaper alternatives) if they own an animal.

Exchange rates can affect the price of imported products.

Inflation may cause cost increases for pet food manufactures and increases in prices.

Social

Demographic changes are likely to lead to changes in pet ownership where ownership is concentrated in age groups, social classes or gender.

The total size of the population is likely to lead to changes in total pet ownership.

Trends in housing may affect the number and types of pets owned. For example, a trend towards inner city apartment dwellings is likely to mitigate against owning large dogs, compared to out of town houses with large gardens.

Use of social networking sites for pet owners can alter attitudes and demand by consumers making more informed purchase choices.

Social acceptability of owning some animals may influence market demand.

Social trends in animal accessories may also influence pet owners to purchase more (or fewer) pet products.

Technology

New technological developments may lead to new pet products (such as electronic tags) not previously available.

Information technology, including pet websites enabling purchasing on the Internet, can be a major rival to shopping in supermarkets and other pet stores. This may be particularly the case for bulk purchases of pet food which may not be easily achievable by some people (eg, who do not own a car) when visiting a store in person.

Ecological

Animals can have an impact on the environment. Restrictions on behaviour to limit this (eg, 'poop scoops') may be positive in providing an additional market for new products or negative in discouraging pet ownership.

Legal

Laws requiring minimum standards of care for animals may be the source of additional markets as owners purchase additional accessories in order to comply (eg, kennels).

New onerous laws may however discourage pet ownership and thereby reduce demand.

Health and safety laws with respect to the quality of pet food may increase costs of manufacturers which could be passed on to consumers.

Some elements of the pet market such as pet insurance are heavily regulated, in common with other types of insurance product. This may present a barrier to entry into this sector, which may impact on sales and profits.

Conclusion

The key issues in the industry appear to be:

- Economic factors, and particularly the economic downturn and customers' willingness to purchase premium foods and other luxury pet items

- Social trends determining pet ownership, which define the number and type of pets owned and therefore the scale of the pet market

Examiner's comments

Requirement 15.1 asked candidates to prepare a PESTEL analysis for the UK pet products industry. Most candidates prepared the PESTEL analysis quite well, although they did struggle for ideas in relation to the political and ecological impacts of the industry. Some weaker candidates did an analysis for Moogle, instead of the pet industry overall, others just gave a list of points from the scenario without explaining the effects on the industry. Few candidates made an attempt to prioritise the points in any way. An overwhelming majority of candidates failed to present any conclusions to their analysis. Often, political and legal issues were addressed together, with candidates identifying that the pet insurance sector was stringently regulated and that government is recently far more conscious of animal welfare and may adopt policies in the future to continue to address this. Better candidates were good at thinking about the wider industry rather than only the points mentioned in the question.

15.2 **Note:** More than three pieces of info are given to guide markers for a range of possible candidate answers

Information	Justification
Internal	
(1) UK sales from each product line compared to (a) the same period last year (b) the previous month	This is important in order to observe overall trends at an early stage but particularly to assess the success or otherwise of new product lines.
	If we change prices of our products generally it will also be necessary to view demand effects. (If prices of individual products change only in some regions, this can be monitored by store managers.)
	The comparison with last year would control for seasonality to make valid comparisons but also predict intra period variations in order to inform purchasing patterns.
	While I would not have time to scrutinise every product, I do need to look at the risk areas where major changes have occurred so I can manage by exception. Please therefore order the data by product according to the size of the variation with the highest variances first and the lowest variances at the bottom of the list.
(2) Shelf space (or floor space) for pet products in total	It is important to see whether allocations of shelf space impact on sales. If shelf space is being reduced then this could be a key factor affecting both sales and the number of items of inventory that can be procured.
	Dividing (1) UK sales by (2) shelf space would give me data to argue for efficient allocation of shelf space across the company if these data are also maintained for other product groupings.
	While I would not have time to scrutinise every store, I do need to look at the risk areas where the ratio of UK sales divided by shelf space is particularly high or low. Could you therefore extract data on a store by store basis but only report to me the top 10% and bottom 10% of stores?

Information	Justification
(3) Price changes by suppliers and notifications of price changes	In order to control costs and monitor the impact of cost changes on profit it is important that I am aware of any proposed or actual change in price by suppliers.
	This information will inform the procurement decision by triggering an investigation of the reasons for the price change, negotiations with the supplier and the possibility of ceasing to purchase from that supplier.
	This is essential in controlling costs.
	Where supplier price increases are accepted then the impact on profit needs to be monitored and the possibility of changing the prices we charge to our customers needs to be considered as a consequence.
(4) New product information	If I introduce new products (eg, pet insurance or on-line sales) this may require different types of information and closer monitoring than existing products.
	This is partly because of increased uncertainty and partly because of the different nature of products like insurance where aggregation with general sales would be unhelpful.
(5) Comparisons with our overseas stores	I would like to see key trends from our overseas stores to see if there are lessons to learn in the UK from pet product sales in the rest of the world.
	Key data may include: fastest growing product lines; successfully introduced new products; comparisons of product prices and costs (exchange rate adjusted) where there are large variations (eg, same product selling at significantly different prices).
	There may be good reasons for variations but I may need to investigate.

External

Information	Justification
(1) Market trends	I need to know changes in the UK pet market from both market research and market trends. This will include quantitative data such as the number of new products being released in the market each year, and qualitative data such as comments made by customers on social media about these new products.
	This may include our own data gathering (primary data) but also market intelligence (secondary data).
	Examples would be trends for buying the following:
	• Moist food or dried food • Premium or basic product lines • New product innovations
(2) Competitor pricing	Our prices relative to competitors are a key factor in maintaining competitive advantage and impact on the reputation of the company generally for being good value.
	For branded products these are identical and we need price comparison shopping within the month so we can adjust our prices regularly.
	However I need to know at the month end where our prices have been higher or lower than key competitors. Please report all exceptions beyond a 2% threshold.

Information	Justification
	Own brand products are not identical and therefore price comparisons are more difficult. Nevertheless I need to know price differences with our competitors beyond a 5% threshold.
(3) Innovations and product launches	I need to know in advance any plans by suppliers about new products or changes in products (eg, new recipes). We can then plan to purchase them or not at the earliest moment. We can also plan for price changes.

Examiner's comments

Requirement 15.2 asked candidates to identify three pieces of internal information and three pieces of external information that the pet products manager would need and to explain why this information was needed. Candidates struggled to identify the correct level and type of information required. Often, sales per product from each store were given as relevant information, despite the question flagging that 'the bigger picture' was needed. Candidates did not appear to focus on cost information and discussed revenue, breakdown of sales by store, breakdown of inventory by store and overall store performance. Some candidates did not offer specific information and instead just described the difference between strategic, tactical and operational information and then contrasted information with raw data. In terms of the external information, again, the level of detail requested was too great for someone wanting a strategic picture. Revenue from competitor stores, number of pet owners in the UK and a breakdown of ownership between dogs and cats, were among the types of information discussed. Again, some of these were not relevant for the scenario or suggestion being discussed, and provision of some of the information was not realistic as it would be nearly impossible to get.

16 The Contract Cleaning Corporation Ltd (December 2013)

Marking guide

		Knowledge	Skill	Marks
16.1 (a)	Appropriateness of KPIs	5	6	10
(b)	Data analysis	2	18	18
(c)	Roizer contract	2	8	9
16.2	Ethical issues	2	4	5
		11	36	42

General comments:

The scenario in this question relates to a company providing cleaning services to organisations in London. Revenue comes from medium term contracts. Last year CCC lost a major customer. In response, it opened up a new division offering maintenance services alongside the existing cleaning services. Despite this, there are concerns about performance. The company implemented a balanced scorecard system a couple of years ago but it is not well understood by the directors and there is doubt about whether all the measures are appropriate. There is an ethical issue relating to an advert published by CCC which may be misleading to customers. There is also the potential to bid on a new contract for a major company, Roizer, which is an element of a larger contract.

16.1 (a) **Balanced scorecard – general issues**

The balanced scorecard (BSC) indicators may be viewed as a vertical hierarchy, with the quality of the skills and processes measured by innovation and learning metrics, leading to improved internal business processes (quality, efficiency and timeliness) and hence customer satisfaction and loyalty; which, in turn, lead to favourable financial outcomes such as profit and ROCE. Conversely, the failure of innovation and internal processes may help explain inefficient operations, lower customer satisfaction and poor financial outcomes.

It is therefore important that CCC links the four quadrants when determining KPIs and using a balanced scorecard considering interdependencies rather than looking at each quadrant in isolation.

In addition, the types of KPIs that were suitable for CCC when it was solely a contract cleaning company may not be appropriate to its Maintenance Services Division. Moreover, even if the KPIs are suitable, the specific targets set may not be appropriate.

When considering performance it may be the target that is at fault, and therefore it might not be an appropriate benchmark by which to judge the actual outcome. It is possible that the targets set could be too ambitious, given the changes arising from the loss of a major customer in the previous year and failure to take into account difficult market conditions. Alternatively, the targets may have been deliberately ambitious, stretch targets in order to motivate employees, in which case some negative variances against target may be acceptable.

Innovation and learning perspective

The % of revenue from new clients seems appropriate, but needs to be judged against other criteria (eg, the amount spent on advertising). Similarly, there is a new maintenance division which may better be measured as a separate BSC rather than within the Cleaning Services Division's BSC. Nevertheless, it does represent a new innovation resulting in higher sales. Similarly, the extent to which new customers have been added to the existing customer base is a reasonable objective captured in this metric.

The hours of staff training measure is less appropriate as it measures an input rather than an achievement arising from the training. Merely spending more money on training does not, of itself, promote, or evidence, learning or reflect the benefits from learning. It may be better to measure learning achievements/qualifications by staff on key areas of CCC's activities (eg, health and safety; or environmental and green issues).

Internal business perspective

The internal business objective of staff numbers appears inappropriate on its own as, again, it measures an input. Some measure of staff productivity or staff efficiency might be more appropriate. An example may be the number of chargeable hours actually spent working at the client, divided by the total number of paid hours. This might measure unproductive time through travelling between clients, lateness or restricted access by clients, and therefore identify possible areas of inefficiency.

Similarly, the value of cleaning products used is likely to be a poor measure of performance and it is difficult to interpret. A high usage may mean a good quality, diligent service is being provided which will be valued by clients; or it could mean high wastage and a lack of cost control. Perhaps a better measure would relate to the application of quality controls by supervisors, for example the number of satisfactory jobs, as a % of the number of jobs where there was a need to rework or reperform cleaning tasks due to inadequate quality at first attempt.

Customer perspective

The total number of customers may be a reasonable measure as it is indicative of the number of new customers won, net of those lost during the year. A more direct way of capturing similar information would be to measure the gross figures of new customers (eg, tenders won); the proportions of customers retained and lost on contract renewal; and the proportions of customers retained and lost on break clause agreements during the year. Further data on whether customers have been lost to competitors, or where cleaning duties have been taken in-house by customers, may identify future threats.

The number of customer complaints is one way of capturing customer satisfaction, but measuring complaints is evaluating only one extreme of the satisfaction spectrum. Moreover, complaints to directors may be only the very worst cases, when it may be difficult to retain the customer if they are unhappy enough to complain at this level. A lower threshold of complaints by customers to supervisors may be a better early warning sign of customer dissatisfaction. Some more positive and comprehensive feedback on customer satisfaction may also be worth measuring (eg, a customer survey) with a numbered scaled response to each question.

Financial perspective

Revenue growth is a reasonable KPI but, as already noted, may best be measured separately for each division. Variants on measures of total revenue growth could be revenue growth per customer. ROCE does not appear to be a good measure as this company has few assets and pays out profits as dividends as far as it can with available cash. It has no debt. This means the very low capital base makes ROCE an almost meaningless figure. A measure of operating profit as a % of sales would give a better measure of revenue against the costs needed to generate that revenue.

Examiner's comments

Requirement 16.1(a) was reasonably well attempted by most candidates. Most candidates identified the use of the balanced scorecard and produced some relevant KPIs. Some candidates supported the use of ROCE, which was not appropriate in this case as CCC has few assets. Knowledge of the balanced scorecard was generally good and candidates were well prepared for this type of question. Answers were generally specific to the scenario. The best responses provided critical reviews of the original measures as well as proposing improved replacements/additions. Weaker candidates tended to suggest that the balanced scorecard and the existing measures were generally appropriate or suggested additional measures without appraising the existing measures.

(b)

	20Y3 Cleaning £	20Y3 Maintenance £	20Y3 Total £	20Y2 Total £	Jarren £	20Y2 total less Jarren £
Revenue	7,200,000	500,000	7,700,000	7,800,000	780,000	7,020,000
Employment costs	4,048,000	324,000	4,372,000	4,128,000		0
Other variable costs	2,024,000	162,000	2,186,000	2,476,800	0	0
Fixed costs	950,000	50,000	1,000,000	1,000,000	0	0
Operating profit	178,000	(36,000)	142,000	195,200	23,424	171,776
Op profit %	2.47%	(7.20)%	1.84%	2.50%	3.00%	2.44%
Revenue growth	(7.69)%		(1.28)%			2.56%
Op profit growth	(8.72)%		(27.18)%			3.73%
Customers	80	5	85	77	1	76
Staff numbers	440	30	470	430		
Wages per emp	9,200	10,800	9,302	9,600		
Rev/customer £	90,000	100,000	90,588	101,299	780,000	92,368
Rev/employee £	16,364	16,667	16,383	18,140		
Op profit/customer £	2,225	(7,200)	1,671	2,532	23,400	2,258
Op profit/emp £	404.55	(1,200)	302.13	453.49		

Overall performance – adjusting the data

In comparing the data for 20Y3 and 20Y2, two significant events have taken place, (one in each year). These are:

- the loss of the Jarren contract during 20Y2

- the commencement of the Maintenance Services Division at the beginning of the 20Y3 financial year

These two events distort underlying data trends and therefore, while recognising their impact on overall performance, need to be stripped out of the raw data provided in order to make like-for-like comparisons of the underlying elements of the business.

Revenue

Total revenue has declined by 1.28% in 20Y3 compared to 20Y2. The decline has been moderated by additional revenues from maintenance services in 20Y3 which did not exist as a division in 20Y2 and therefore made zero revenue in that year.

Stripping out revenues from maintenance services in 20Y3 enables revenues from cleaning activities only to be compared in 20Y2 an 20Y3. This shows a 7.69% decline in 20Y3 compared with 20Y2.

One of the major causal factors for the reduction in revenue has been the loss of the major customer Jarren in June 20Y2. Jarren contributed 10% of total revenue in the year ended 30 September 20Y2, that is £780,000 (even though there were only nine months of revenues from Jarren in the financial year).

Whilst the Jarren contract is a factor in assessing overall performance, it is instructive to assess the performance of the remaining cleaning activities excluding Jarren. The table above shows that in 20Y3 revenue from cleaning activities, excluding Jarren, increased by 2.56% compared to 20Y2 excluding Jarren.

One of the reasons for this increase is that the number of clients for cleaning activities, excluding Jarren, rose by 5.26% from 76 to 80. The revenue growth for this segment of the business can therefore be explained largely in terms of more customers, rather than increased revenue per customer. Indeed, revenue per customer from cleaning activities, excluding Jarren, fell from £92,368 in 20Y2 to £90,000 in 20Y3.

This reduction in revenue per customer may have been due to new contracts being smaller than the existing contracts; or there may have been downward pressure on contract prices generally, such that continuing contracts are generating less revenue on renegotiation.

The number of staff engaged in cleaning activities has increased by 2.3%. One reason for the increase may be the need to service new customers, but the table shows that annual revenue per employee has fallen considerably from £18,140 to £16,364 (9.8% fall). This may be due to the distortion from the loss of the Jarren contract, but separate employee data for this contract is required to carry out further analysis.

Operating profit

Operating profit from cleaning services (excluding Jarren) increased in 20Y3 by 3.73% compared to 20Y2 (ie, from £171,600 to £178,000). The figure for operating profit for Cleaning in 20Y3 should be treated with caution, however, as the new Maintenance Services Division has been allocated fixed costs of £50,000. Assuming these fixed costs would have been incurred whether or not the new Maintenance Services Division had been opened, then this is not comparing like with like because in 20Y2 all £1 million of fixed costs were allocated to what is now the Cleaning Services Division.

If an adjustment is made for this, then Cleaning Services Division profits drop to £128,000 (£178,000 – £50,000) giving a decrease of 25.4% from their 20Y2 level of £171,600 (excluding Jarren).

However, such a comparison is not entirely reasonable as there may be an element of fixed costs in the 12% operating profit of Jarren which has been stripped out. This would need to be added back to make a more precise comparison although the data is not currently available.

The operating profit margin is reasonably constant for 20Y3 and 20Y2 for cleaning activities, although it is clear that the Jarren contract was not only large, but had a slightly higher margin than other customers.

Similarly, operating profit per customer for cleaning services (excluding Jarren) is reasonably constant at £2,225 and £2,258 in 20Y3 and 20Y2 respectively. However, the increased number of employees means that operating profit per employee has fallen from £453.49 to £404.55 (down 10.8%), however this also includes Jarren where we do not have separate employee data.

Costs

Employee costs

Cleaning division employee costs have fallen by 1.9% (from £4,128,000 in 20Y2 to £4,048,000 in 20Y3) despite having more employees in 20Y3, and this has contributed to operating profit. The key factor here is the reduction in cost per employee from £9,600 pa to £9,200 pa. This may be the result of shorter working hours for existing employees or new employees on fewer hours. Conversely, there may have been an employee agreement given CCC's financial difficulties following the loss of the Jarren contract. For example, the lower wages and a shorter working week may have been given in return for no redundancies.

Other variable costs

In 20Y3 other variable costs were 50% of employee costs. In 20Y2 they were 60% of employment costs. This marked fall in costs has contributed to operating profit. Possible causes might be greater cost efficiency in perhaps travel and use of materials.

Fixed costs

Fixed costs have remained constant in total between 20Y3 and 20Y2 but, as already noted, the allocation of some of these costs to Maintenance Services Division has boosted Cleaning divisional operating profit in 20Y3 compared to 20Y2. Such an allocation is arbitrary and should not impact upon any assessment of performance of the division over time.

Performance of the new Maintenance Division

The new Maintenance Service Division has incurred an operating loss of £36,000 in its first year of trading in 20Y3. It could therefore be argued that it detracted from the overall performance of CCC compared with 20Y2, when the division did not exist.

However, even in narrow financial terms, this may not be the case. Ignoring the arbitrary allocation of overheads, it generated a positive contribution as follows:

Revenue	500,000
Employment costs	(324,000)
Other variable costs	(162,000)
Contribution	14,000

More generally, performance needs to be assessed strategically rather than in just narrow financial terms. It is difficult to make a profit in the first year of trading as upfront costs are incurred and there is a need to break into new markets. In this vein, the division has performed reasonably well.

Moreover, if customers demand multi-services then the maintenance division may be instrumental in retaining customers for the Cleaning Services Division, and even in winning new joint customers in future. Such interdependencies need to be considered in assessing the overall performance of the Maintenance Services Division.

Conclusion

The loss of the Jarren contract has been a major factor in damaging overall performance in 20Y3 compared with 20Y2. Nevertheless, other aspects of the business appear be performing reasonably well and have shown some improvement in revenue and profits.

It is too early to make a valid assessment of the new Maintenance Services Division but at least it has made a positive contribution in its first year of trading.

Examiner's comments

In requirement 16.1(b) the main calculations produced tended to focus on revenue and profit. However, the higher scoring answers also used the data in the question more widely and calculated, for instance, revenue per customer and profit per customer. Discussion of the quantitative analysis was varied. The poorer answers restated the ratios, but did not develop the reasons as to why revenue had declined since 20Y2 or the factors which had caused the changes.

Also, the performance of the cleaning and maintenance divisions was often not separated. The better answers presented the calculations in a clear and structured way, and then further analysed the data by removing the maintenance division performance which then resulted in an increased decline in revenue.

While most candidates discussed, or at least referred to, the impact of the loss of the major customer (Jarren), many tended to compare absolute figures without taking account of the fact that the inclusion of Jarren's contribution in the performance data distorted the figures. Very few candidates stripped out the figures relating to Jarren in order to make like-for-like comparisons.

The better candidates provided some good discussion on the positive contribution of the maintenance division and how CCC needed to expand into this area to remain competitive. Weaker candidates just pointed out that the maintenance division made an operating loss, without considering the basis for allocating fixed costs to the two divisions.

Overall, performance on this requirement was good and the data analysis answers are improved from most previous sittings.

(c) **Roizer contract**

Financial assessment

	£
Annual revenue (60,000 × £12)	720,000
Employee costs (Note 1)	(404,800)
Other variable costs (Note 2)	(202,400)
Contribution	112,800

This gives a contribution margin of 15.67%.

Notes

1 **Employee costs**

Employee costs, as a variable cost, are based on revenue. The revenue per annum of the Roizer contract is 10% of total cleaning revenues in 20Y3. As a result, the estimated employee cost is 10% of total 20Y3 employee costs (ie, 10% × £4,048,000)

2 **Other variable costs**

Other variable costs are 50% of employee costs in 20Y3.

Tutorial note:

Taking a ratio of other variable costs against revenue would give the same figure.

Benefits

- The contract makes a significant financial contribution

- If employees have been retained, despite the loss of the Jarren contract, then the Roizer contract may more fully utilise them and save potential redundancy costs

- There may be economies of scale so there could be efficiencies, such that variable costs may not increase in a linear fashion

- Coping with a major contact may lead to greater credibility in tendering for other similar contracts

- The contract may be renewed beyond the initial period

Risks

- There are two levels of the risk of termination. (1) GFP may terminate the contract with Roizer and may do so at two year intervals; and (2) Roizer may terminate the contract with CCC annually, even if the header contract with GFP is continuing.

- The contract may be short term (possibly one year) and therefore any initial set-up costs may not be covered.

- Exit costs – if the contract is terminated then there may be exit costs eg, redundancy costs for staff specifically recruited for the purpose of this contract.

- Roizer is a rival and promoting its interests may not be in the best interests of CCC. For example it may ease the entry of Roizer into the cleaning sector of the London market.

- Roizer is likely to be earning profit without doing any operational activity. CCC may therefore not be gaining the full potential value of their work.

- Roizer has a problem of recruiting staff quickly enough for this contract and so it has approached CCC. However, in accepting the sub-contract, CCC may have the same problem.

- In the above financial calculations, it is assumed that no incremental fixed costs will be incurred but, given the increase in the scale, fixed costs may be non-linear (eg, a step function) and there may therefore be some incremental fixed costs to be incurred.

Examiner's comments

In requirement 16.1(c) the financial assessment of the Roizer contract for many candidates focussed very simplistically on the increase in annual revenue of £720,000 and the gross profit margin, rather than calculating the contribution margin as directed. Weaker candidates produced no calculations at all.

The risks and benefits were often very generic in terms of the contract making a significant contribution and giving access to new markets; the fact that the contract may be terminated quickly was also frequently referred to. There was information in the question which should have been used to make the answers more detailed and of a far higher standard.

16.2 Ethics pertains to whether a particular behaviour is deemed acceptable in the context under consideration. Sam has become aware of an advert that CCC has published which may be making misleading or untrue statements.

In making any ethical evaluation it is first necessary to establish the facts. In this case, the claims made by CCC in the advert need to be assessed as to their validity.

On the face of it, some statements in the advert claim to be factual while others are less precise or are expressions of opinion.

The issue of legality and compliance with advertising regulations is crucial as any breach of such laws and regulations is unethical.

The four specific claims are:

- 'All of our staff have regular training.' This could be misleading in implying frequent training, rather than regularly every three years.

- 'We use environmentally friendly cleaning materials.' This appears to be literally true as it makes no claim as to the extent to which they are used, but may be misleading in implying that it uses only environmentally friendly cleaning materials.

- 'Customer service is our leading priority' this is a vague statement of intent.

- 'We also now offer maintenance services as a major part of our business'. Maintenance services are clearly now part of the business but at only 6.5% of sales it may be misleading to say they are a major part of the business.

In making a decision as to how to proceed, Sam may find it helpful to apply the Institute of Business Ethics three tests:

- Transparency
- Effect
- Fairness

Transparency – would CCC mind people (existing customers, suppliers, employees) knowing that it has made misleading claims?

Effect – whom does the decision to publish the advert affect/hurt? CCC stands to gain new customers at the expense of rivals if misleading claims are believed. New customers obtained on the basis of misleading claims may also be affected.

Fairness – would the claims be considered fair by those affected? The issue for CCC is that they are making claims to attract business on a basis that competitors or new customers may not consider to be fair.

Honesty

A final issue is one of honesty. The claims made may fail the honesty test on the basis of being misleading rather than untrue.

Response

An initial action would be to challenge the CCC board in relation to the claims being made in the advert, asking them to substantiate the assertions made.

If they cannot refute an allegation that the advert is misleading the CCC board could be asked by Sam to withdraw it. Legal advice should be sought in relation to the possible breach of advertising regulations that has occurred.

Examiner's comments

The answers to requirement 30.2 produced varying results. Some candidates did not apply their answers to the question appropriately and merely restated, in general terms, the main ethical values which an ICAEW Chartered Accountant should uphold. Some candidates approached this requirement from a transparency, fairness and effect viewpoint, but did not always analyse the problems caused by CCC and then recommend a course of action which could be taken.

The higher scoring answers analysed each statement, concluded on whether it accurately reflected the business practice and then considered legality, transparency, fairness, effect and resulting next steps.

---

17 The Foto Phrame Company (December 2013)

Marking guide

	Knowledge	Skill	Marks
17.1 Product life cyle	2	7	8
17.2 (a) Procurement and supply chain	4	10	13
(b) Two distribution strategies	3	12	14
	9	29	35

General comments:

The scenario in this question relates to a manufacturer of cameras which is based in Germany. The question provides a summary of developments in the industry and how changes in technology have affected product life cycles. The company in question, FPC, manufactures mid-market cameras and has global sales. The US is an important market for FPC which has grown in recent years. Distribution to the US currently takes place directly from the German factory. FPC currently has a single local supplier of lenses which is a key component. One of the main products, the MM3 camera, is due to be replaced shortly by the MM4, and FPC is taking the opportunity to review its procurement and supply chain management policies. Specifically, it is examining whether it should continue its single supplier policy or move to a policy of multiple international suppliers. It is also considering cost reduction, part of which involves reviewing the costs of tier 1 and tier 2 suppliers. It is also reviewing its distribution strategy to US customers. Two possible strategies are: to open a distribution centre in the US; or to enter into a joint venture with a Japanese camera manufacturer to develop a US distribution facility.

17.1 The product life cycle (PLC) describes the phases of development that a product goes through. The key stages of the life cycle are:

- **Introduction** – a newly invented product or service is made available for purchase and organisations attempt to develop buyer interest.

- **Growth** – a period of rapid expansion of demand or activity as the product finds a market and competitors are attracted by its potential.

- **Maturity** – a relatively stable period of time where there is little change in sales volumes year to year but competition between firms intensifies as growth slows down.

- **Decline** – a falling off in sales levels as the product becomes less competitive in the face of competition from newer products.

The way in which a product is defined is important in determining the life cycle. It could be defined in terms of the broad technology being used, such as digital cameras. Alternatively, it could be defined in terms of a particular model of camera, such as the MM4 for FPC. Typically, the wider definition of a digital camera would have a much longer life cycle which will only reach maturity when there has been a fundamental shift in industry technology.

From the perspective of FPC's new MM4 camera it is intended to introduce this in one year. It does not however follow from this the MM3 will be replaced immediately. FPC may carrying on producing the MM3 (or at least carry on selling it from existing inventories).

In this way, the PLC for successive products may overlap. As one product is declining, another is simultaneously being introduced. This may be because of continuing product loyalty by consumers for the old MM3. Alternatively, it is common to sell only the new product into key markets (eg, Europe and the US) but sell the older product at lower prices into other geographical markets such as developing nations where there is higher price elasticity. This will prevent internal competition between the two products, so long as there is no leakage between the two types of market.

If it is the intention for FPC to extend the PLC of the MM3 then this could be achieved through minor technological improvements and design modifications to the MM3.

Turning to the MM4, its PLC is likely to be uncertain as it is only about to enter its introductory phase and there are many uncertainties about the future. However factors that may affect the life cycle of the MM4 are:

- Success of R&D activities by FPC in developing replacement technology

- Success of R&D activities by FPC's rivals which may reduce MM4 sales and cause it to enter the decline phase sooner than expected

- Changes in customer tastes and preferences

- Pricing policies of FPC and its rivals

- New entrants to the industry

- Developments in competing technologies (eg, mobile phones)

- Willingness and ability of FPC to engage in product improvement for the MM4 to extend its product life

Examiner's comments

Requirement 17.1 was the best answered part of the paper. Most candidates exhibited good knowledge of the product life cycle model, often providing a diagram to explain it (although, of those who did provide a diagram, many did not label the axes correctly).

For weaker candidates, discussion of the factors affecting the length of the product life cycle tended to be generic, on the whole, with little, or no, application to the MM3 and MM4 products. Some omitted this element of the requirement altogether. The answers of the better candidates were more specific and discussed the influencing factors in terms of technology, social status, tastes and competition on the product life cycle of MM3 and MM4.

17.2 (a) **Issue 1**

There are two key issues:

(1) Whether to have one supplier or many suppliers

(2) Whether to continue solely with a current supplier or to engage with new suppliers as well

The current arrangement with Zeegle can be described as one of strategic procurement. This is the development of a partnership between a company and a supplier of strategic value. The arrangement is usually long-term, single-source in nature and addresses not only the buying of parts, products or services, but product design and supplier capacity.

This type of relationship can be beneficial for some organisations which may need to establish close links with companies in the supply chain to meet their own production needs or strategic objectives.

Some of the advantages to FPC from single sourcing with Zeegle may include the following:

- Consistent lenses (shape, size, quality, clarity) from a single supplier.

- Easier to monitor quality.

- Zeegle may be dependent on FPC as a major customer, and therefore is more responsive to FPC's needs, if a large amount of its income is being earned from FPC.

- More scale economies can be earned by Zeegle to reduce costs which can then be passed on to FPC in reduced prices.

- Communication, integration and synchronisation are easier (eg, integrated IT systems).

- Collaboration is easier and more mutually beneficial in developing new products because all the benefits come to one supplier.

- Zeegle has an existing relationship with FPC and therefore there is less risk and greater awareness.

However, there may also be some problems with Zeegle as a single source supplier, some of which have already been experienced by FPC in producing the MM3:

- If there is disruption to output for Zeegle there is disruption to supply for FPC. This may be indicated by the fact that 'there have been occasions when there have been delays in supply' which means FPC has needed to hold inventories.

- If there are variations in demand by FPC, a single supplier such as Zeegle may not be able to satisfy these in the short term (which may be another reason for FPC to hold inventory).

- Zeegle might exert upward pressure on prices if it knows FPC is tied into it for a number of years (over the product life cycle) and therefore has no alternative source of supply.

If FPC has multiple suppliers (ie, five) there are a number of benefits:

- FPC can drive down prices charged to it by encouraging competition between suppliers who know that FPC has a choice of alternative suppliers.

- Switching sources of supply is possible by dropping a supplier altogether if it is delivering a poor quality product or service.

- FPC can benefit from innovation in future product development from many companies rather than just one.

However, if FPC has multiple suppliers there may be a number of problems:

- Each supplier has a smaller income from FPC than a single source supplier and so may lack commitment.

- Multiple communications become more difficult and more expensive for FPC (eg, more difficult to integrate multiple IT systems).

- Reduced scale economies.

- Suppliers are less likely to invest in bespoke equipment and produce a bespoke product for FPC as production volumes may be insufficient.

- The lead times and uncertainty of delivery time are greater if the geographical distances are greater, such as with Japan.

- Cross-border supply chains may produce regulatory, language, cultural, exchange rate and tax problems. These are reduced because France and Germany are both in the EU, but this does not apply to Japan.

- Four of the five potential suppliers would be new and therefore this may create some initial uncertainty and front-end costs in establishing new relationships and communications systems.

Advice

The current supplier, Zeegle, has proved reliable and therefore reduces risk and gives assurance over quality. FPC may thus be best continuing with Zeegle as sole supplier but, in negotiations on price and service, the possibility of multiple suppliers could be raised in order to obtain the best possible contract terms.

Issue 2

The integrated supply chain model proposes that it is whole supply chains which compete and not just individual firms. Integration with, and information about, not only FPC's own suppliers (tier 1) but its suppliers' suppliers (tier 2) is consistent with this model.

If tier 2 suppliers can save costs, then this can be passed on to tier 1 suppliers in the form of reduced prices, which in turn can be passed on to FPC. While the integrated supply chain model is about more than cost reduction, this can be a key benefit, particularly where the components are fairly generic. Supply chain management is therefore needed to be able to obtain these benefits.

Supply chain management (SCM) is the management of all supply activities from the suppliers to a business through to delivery to customers. This may also be called demand chain management, reflecting the idea that the customers' requirements and downstream orders should drive activity or end-to-end business (e2e). In essence it refers to managing the value system.

In **Issue 2** the key theme is upstream supply chain management as it does not deal with customers.

The main themes in SCM are Responsiveness, Reliability and Relationships but the focus requested is solely on costs and the reliability aspects of SCM.

While **Issue 2** highlights reliability and cost reduction, responsiveness and building relationships can contribute to this.

While FPC, as the customer, has no legal right to investigate a supplier it can make transparency and openness conditions of FPC doing business with tier 1 suppliers. While such an investigation may appear to be an imposition on a tier 1 supplier (eg, a supplier of an electronic component) there may be mutual benefits of greater efficiency and establishing better relationships with a key customer.

The willingness of tier 1 suppliers to do this may depend on how large the supplier is and how important FPC is to it as a customer.

There is no direct contractual relationship between FPC and tier 2 suppliers. As a consequence, at first sight, there may be increased reluctance by tier 2 suppliers to grant access to FPC to investigate cost reduction and reliability of supply. However, a tier 2 supplier (eg, the manufacturer of a microchip that is used in an electronic component supplied by a tier 1 supplier to FPC) may be aware of the indirect relationship, and the fact that if FPC ceases to purchase from the tier 1 supplier then the tier 1 supplier may purchase less from the tier 2 supplier.

In terms of who would do the investigation, there may be more certainty if FPC does it itself, but FPC staff may be remote from the industry in which tier 2 suppliers operate and lack, not just the technical knowledge, but the detail of delivery schedules and processes as, unlike tier 1 suppliers, FPC is not a direct user of the output.

Advice

Managing costs down the supply chain seems entirely appropriate and in common with best practice. However, the cost-benefit trade-off from investigating tier 2 suppliers directly may not be favourable, as there is a lower proportion of FPC's costs at stake as we proceed further up the supply chain. Monitoring how tier 1 suppliers review tier 2 suppliers may therefore be the best compromise.

Examiner's comments

Requirement 17.2(a) produced some very general, and often brief, answers on the difference between a single supplier versus a multiple supplier strategy. Whilst there was some relevant discussion on how supplier management can be seen as a collaborative relationship, it was surprising that the information in the question was not always put to good use.

Quality and cost are issues in any type of supplier relationship and whilst these were mentioned, points were often not developed enough. What was expected was how the quality of the lenses could impact FPC, how lead times may be affected and what the resulting impact on customer goodwill may be if suppliers were not geographically proximate.

It was only a minority of candidates that discussed the Rs model (responsiveness, reliability and relationships) in a structured manner.

A number of candidates surprisingly considered the supplier tiers issue to be equivalent to vertical integration. Also some candidates confused the supply chain with the value chain, without attempting to link these concepts. A surprising number of candidates omitted discussion of the supplier review at all, thereby severely limiting the number of marks they could score on this requirement.

(b) Distribution is a key aspect of marketing. Distribution is also part of the supply chain. It has already been noted that supply chain management is the management of all supply activities through to delivery to customers. Distribution is therefore part of demand chain management, reflecting the idea that the customers' requirements and downstream orders should drive activity or end-to-end business (e2e).

The distribution channel comprises a number of stakeholders including: manufacturer (FPC); wholesalers; retailers; consumers. Either of the proposals shortens the channel between FPC, as manufacturer, and wholesalers/retailers. The local holding of inventory in the US also enables the distribution channel to be shortened in some cases, by cutting out the wholesaler and selling directly from FPC to retailers.

Distribution strategy 1 – acquire a US distribution centre

Benefits

- Inventory can be held 'locally' in the US to meet surges in demand more quickly and with less uncertainty for customers than by supplying directly from production output in Germany.

- As a consequence, this strategy is driven by customer need, which is central to the end-to-end business model. The US presence means that FPC is closer to the customers and could perhaps better understand their needs.

- If FPC owns the distribution facility then it has more control over this aspect of operations than with a JV.

- Presence in the US, rather than delivery directly from Germany, means we can use local employees with local knowledge.

- Reputation with customers may improve if they know they are being supplied locally (ie, the supply chain is within the US to a greater extent).

- FPC needs to respond to having 30% of its sales in the US and it appears FPC has not kept up with growth. Managing customer service for this extent of sales directly from Germany seems inappropriate, and a distribution facility seems to be a minimum response to satisfy the needs of the US market.

- A more substantial response to US sales growth would be to have a US production facility. However, having a distribution facility holding inventory is a much cheaper alternative than a second manufacturing site in the US which would increase fixed costs and would need an appropriate skills base without any history of production in the US.

Problems

- Mere location within the US still leaves a large geographical distance between the distribution facility and much of the US population. A single distribution facility may therefore only be a partial solution to the need to improve customer service. A network of multiple distribution facilities may be warranted for 30% of FPC's total sales.

- It would appear that little inventory of US-style cameras is currently held in Germany. An intermediate solution, to reduce lead time, would be to hold inventory in Germany rather than in the US.

- The fixed production facility increases fixed costs and therefore increases risk from operating gearing.

Strategy 2

Benefits

- Collaboration with the Japanese manufacturer takes advantage of common aims of both companies and sharing fixed costs from owning a distribution facility. This will give economies of scale.

- Given that both companies have common customers there are economies of scope from deliveries to the same location. Even if this were not the case, there are likely to be economies of scope from deliveries to the similar locations.

- Without a JV there may be insufficient volumes of sales for either company to sustain a feasible distribution network.

- The joint venture means that ownership of vans to make the distribution directly to customers is possible, so there is more control over all aspects of physical distribution without needing to trust third party couriers.

Problems

- There may be a conflict of interest in prioritising deliveries of each company where their needs, or the timing of needs, do not coincide.

- With a JV, one party may wish to terminate the agreement. This may require exit costs and create uncertainty over continuing viability.

- If there is common control between the two companies then issues of governance may arise if a key decision needs to be made that the two parties disagree about (eg, a decision to expand or develop).

- Governance could be contractual or through a JV entity. This would impact upon risk sharing, exit costs, control and cost sharing. This would need to be clearly agreed.

- If one party is larger than the other, and therefore gains more benefit from the JV, the issues of sharing costs, sharing benefits and sharing control arise. Unless there are transfer prices from the parent entities, the JV is not revenue generating which may create a range of problems over how the benefits and costs are shared.

Advice

The JV arrangement permits fixed costs to be shared and would facilitate operations in the US and support marketing there. The terms of the contract need to foresee the above potential problems and permit flexibility to enable alternative strategies to be pursued over time as conditions change or sales expand. Alternatively, if a JV partner decides to withdraw from the arrangement, there needs to be protection for FPC from excessive exit costs and options to facilitate alternative distribution strategies.

Examiner's comments

Answers to requirement 17.2(b) were sometimes very brief. Benefits of acquiring the US distribution centre focussed on access to US customers and use of specialist employees. Risks included exchange rates, but often little else. There was inadequate consideration of the fact that acquisition of an additional distribution centre would increase fixed costs and could therefore impact profit and operating gearing.

The joint venture appeared to be the favoured option as this 'mitigated the risk'. It would have been encouraging to have an analysis of what the 'risks' were as this was not always clear.

Service level agreements were mentioned in this part of the question and marks were awarded for this.

A number of candidates merged their answers for the two distribution strategies. Many of these answers failed to identify the key issues for each of the options.

18   FeedAfrica (December 2013)

Marking guide

	Knowledge	Skill	Marks
18.1 Market research	2	7	8
18.2 Market segmentation	2	6	7
18.3 Measuring and monitoring sustainable development	3	6	8
	7	19	23

General comments:

This is the shortest question on the paper. It relates to a NFP charity which raises funds in the UK to support projects which assist communities in Africa to feed themselves more sustainably.

Fundraising has not been successful in recent years and FeedAfrica has appointed a new chief executive to help FeedAfrica market itself more effectively to both individuals and companies. It is believed that marketing expenditure has been wasted in the past by being insufficiently targeted. In order to raise more corporate donations, FeedAfrica believes it needs to measure its performance more clearly to demonstrate how it has contributed to sustainable development.

18.1 **Market research** is the systematic gathering, recording and analysing of information about problems relating to marketing.

Market research can involve looking at all aspects of marketing, including the 7Ps. In this context of marketing for a charity, however, there is no product or service to be sold directly to the donor. Instead, the key issue is to generate donations from people in return for service to be provided to a third party.

Marketing needs to be done effectively to raise income without incurring too many costs to generate that income. It therefore needs to be targeted at the groups of people most likely to give most.

Key objectives for market research for FeedAfrica are therefore to gain information about the following:

- Who? Which groups of people are most likely to make donations?

- How? How will they prefer to make such donations (ie, in what form)?

- When? At what time and in what circumstances would they make donations?

- Why? What motivates people to make donations and therefore how can they best be persuaded, if they are uncertain whether to donate?

- Quantity? How much are the donations likely to be and can people be persuaded to increase donations?

- How often? How frequently does each group of people make charitable donations?

Desk research is the gathering and analysis of existing (or secondary) data from internal and external sources. This may include the following:

- Accessing an internal database of people who have donated in the past or are currently donating. Analysis of patterns in this behaviour can be useful in targeting the right type of promotional activities at the right people.

- Databases of charitable donors to be accessed by FeedAfrica or shared between charitable organisations

- Any publicly available research (ie, from psychology) which may help understand what motivates people to donate to charities

- Examination of published surveys/questionnaire about charitable giving (eg, by government; universities; charitable bodies)

Field research involves the collection of new (primary) data directly from respondents. This might be in the form of surveys/questionnaires, interviews and focus groups. It is usually more expensive than desk research, so it needs to be clearly focused in its objective of raising charitable contributions with a clear expectation of the benefits to be achieved.

Questionnaire surveys – existing charitable donors could be surveyed to ascertain their reasons for donating. Alternatively (or additionally), they could directly question random members of the public to ascertain: whether they give to charity; the level of recognition of the FeedAfrica name; and whether they are likely to donate to FeedAfrica in future.

In depth interviews – these are similar to a questionnaire, but more detailed responses can be obtained. This may cover general attitudes to charitable giving and a more comprehensive study of attitudes to FeedAfrica.

Examiner's comments

In requirement 18.1 it was apparent that candidates were well prepared for a 'marketing' type question and were able to identify the difference between desk and field research. The higher scoring answers identified the specific nature of the problem that there is no product or service to sell for a charity and therefore product/service characteristics were not relevant to the market research needed in this case. The type of desk and field research which would be relevant to FeedAfrica in terms of identification of donors was well articulated by the better candidates. Some weaker candidates wasted time by going beyond the boundaries of the requirement by, for instance, discussing the 4 Ps for FeedAfrica in detail.

18.2 **Market segmentation** is the practice of identifying homogeneous sub-groups within a market, to whom promotion can then be targeted in different ways.

In the situation of a charity, no product or service is being sold. Despite this, some people tend to give money, although others do not. Also some people tend to give more than others.

Given that promotional activities are not costless it is important that operations are directed towards those segments of the population who are most likely to make a significant donation. This avoids incurring marketing expenditure on sections of the population who are never likely to make donations to FeedAfrica.

It is also important that promotion is suitable for the sub-group being targeted, as what is likely to persuade one group to give is unlikely to resonate with an alternative group who may be persuaded by a different type of promotional campaign. In this way, the costs of a promotional campaign can be targeted to give the highest donation to cost ratio.

More specifically, examples of segmentation for FeedAfrica could be as follows:

Older people could be targeted with marketing materials that focus on legacies. This is partly because older people are likely to be giving more active consideration to leaving legacies and partly because the time horizon for FeedAfrica receiving such legacies is, on average, shorter than would be the case with younger people.

In terms of more general giving, then the propensity to make donations (subject to the above market research) may be greatest amongst the following:

- People with a history of making charitable donations
- Higher income groups
- Higher social classes
- People with religious conviction
- Older people
- People in a particular area of the country
- People with experience of living in Africa
- People of a particular political/social persuasion

Examples of how promotional activity could be targeted at these groups would be as follows:

- Email people on a database of making contributions to charities in the past (eg, by standing orders)

- Place television adverts for FeedAfrica during a religious television programme

- Place adverts in newspapers and magazine typically read by high income groups or higher social classes

- Advertise legacy giving where older people meet or in the journals they read

In requirement 18.2 most candidates correctly identified the nature of market segmentation and why organisations adopt a strategy of segmentation. Relevant means of segmentation were identified in terms of, for example, high income households, older people and affluent geographical areas. Better candidates took the opportunity offered by data given in the question to consider segmentation on the basis of method of donation (eg, direct debit, legacies). Some candidates did not follow the instructions in the question and addressed corporate donors as well as individual donors.

18.3 **Sustainability** is about maintaining the world's resources rather than depleting or destroying them. This will ensure they support human activity now and in the future.

Sustainable development is the process by which we achieve sustainability.

Sustainability is not limited to the environment. Interpretations of the scope of sustainable development have developed from a narrow interpretation which focuses on 'green issues' to broader interpretations which include concerns such as the following:

- Extremes of poverty and wealth
- Population growth
- Biodiversity loss
- Deteriorating air and water quality
- Climate change
- Human rights

A commonly employed and useful way of thinking about these issues is under three key headings: **social, environmental** and **economic**. Using these widely-recognised categories will help FeedAfrica demonstrate to its potential corporate donors that the charity is fully aware of all the implications of being involved with sustainable development in Africa.

FeedAfrica's charitable activities appear to be making a contribution to all three of these key aspects. In particular, rather than just donating money and/or food to meet a short-term need, they appear to be facilitating local people to have the means to grow food for themselves in the long term in a sustainable manner.

Measures of sustainable development under each of the headings may therefore include for FeedAfrica:

Economic:

- The increase in the amount of crops grown after projects supported by FeedAfrica have taken effect
- The increase in the value of crops grown as a result of projects supported by FeedAfrica
- Amount of new jobs created
- Number of farms in existence as businesses as a result of projects supported by FeedAfrica
- Number of farms moving from subsistence to profit as a result of projects supported by FeedAfrica

Social:

- Improvements to health by % of illness (eg, due to clean water, more and better food)
- Community projects commenced based on wealth generated from FeedAfrica projects
- New employment rights and other local social rights required as a condition of investment

Environmental:

- Use of natural resources eg, amount of additional clean water made available
- Use of land – amount of land brought into agricultural use as a result of water made available
- Reduced pollution of water sources – eg, size of reduction in water-bourne illnesses

All the above will need to be measured over time to demonstrate that benefits are sustained and not short-lived.

Not all the above are easy to measure and some measures may be required of the situation before any investment by FeedAfrica took place in order to make comparisons with the situation afterwards. This may be available from feasibility studies initially taken to assess the viability of the investment.

When convincing corporate donors, it may also be useful to FeedAfrica to be able to demonstrate the charity's own efficiency, economy and effectiveness. It could therefore present using key NFP indicators such as a low percentage of overheads in relation to funds spent on charitable activities in Africa.

Examiner's comments

In requirement 18.3 candidates tended to mention sustainability very briefly in their answers without elaborating on what it actually meant. It was extremely rare to see any type of discussion on economic, social and environmental sustainability, or any acknowledgement that it was specifically corporate donors that required FeedAfrica to make measurements. This is a very topical subject so it was surprising that answers were so short.

There were some relevant KPIs suggested, such as the number of new wells introduced, but others were very general and unfeasible, such as 'improvement in population health', with no real consideration of how this could be measured.

With regard to this question as a whole, the best candidates linked their discussion of the separate requirements eg, they recognised the need for market research to inform market segmentation.

19 Emelius Ltd (March 2014)

Marking guide

	Knowledge	Skill	Marks
19.1 Risk register	3	10	12
19.2 Value chain drivers	4	8	12
19.3 Emelius Northern franchise	5	12	14
19.4 Letter (benefits of digital data/performance measures)	3	8	10
	15	38	48

General comments:

This is the mini case at 48 marks and also the data analysis question. It was the best attempted on the paper.

The scenario relates to a company that offers document storage and management services. Its customers include professional services firms, banks and medical practices which need to archive large volumes of documents. The existing service is paper-based and involves various stages: collection, bar coding, storage, retrieval if required, and end of life destruction. The industry is relatively capital intensive and has high stepped fixed costs. As a result the company runs on a franchise model. Emelius has recently developed a new digital data capture service which its franchisees will have the option to offer to customers. Paper documents will be taken to a central scanning house, converted into digital form and then managed via a web-enabled platform with secure real-time access. A detailed value chain for this service was included in the scenario. One of the franchises, Emelius Northern (EN), is in discussions with a legal client (Swinburne LLP) which has approached EN regarding the physical storage of their paper archive. Swinburne has also expressed an interest in the digital service, which has not yet been introduced by the EN franchisee. Candidates were provided with operating information for the EN franchise for 20Y2 and 20Y3, and some working assumptions for volume, cost and revenue for 20Y4.

Requirements 19.1 and 19.2 relate to Emelius as a whole. Requirements 19.3 and 19.4 both relate to the EN franchise.

19.1 Key risks

Business risk is the variability of returns due to how a business operates, its markets, competitors etc.

It can be sub-divided into:

Strategic – risk relating to the company's strategic position with respect to competitors and environment

Operational – risk arising from how the business is managed and controlled on a day to day business, which also includes compliance issues

Hazard – risk arising from accidents or natural events

Financial – risk associated with how the business is financed

The key risk facing Emelius in each category is set out below:

Risk	Impact and likelihood	Risk management
Strategic – technological change renders the need for a paper-based document service obsolete	Technological developments clearly have a big impact on the nature of storage and the storage systems. Changes in technology may reduce the volume of business but are unlikely to remove the need for paper entirely, which to some extent may be regulatory.	Avoid/reduce risk by developing the digital data capture side of the service so Emelius will retain customers even if they switch archive method. Emelius may actually use this trend in their favour when nearing capacity in a warehouse.
Operational – poor standards of service by a franchisee damage the company's reputation	Emelius works with large organisations, many of which (banks, professional services) are likely to be national businesses expecting consistent standards. The existence of a number of competitors increases the likelihood that customers will go elsewhere if they are dissatisfied, which will have a large impact on Emelius.	Reduce risk by screening franchisees carefully and drawing up strict franchise agreements. Emelius already takes a strict approach to breaches of security and customer complaints which will help.
Hazard – data loss through fire at storage warehouse	Document security is of paramount importance. Loss of a client's records would be very damaging to Emelius' reputation and may result in litigation. The impact would be severe, the likelihood is unknown.	Reduce likelihood by having preventative measures such as advanced smoke detection and sprinkler systems, plus 24-hour monitoring Transfer through insurance Digital back-ups would also reduce this risk

Risk	Impact and likelihood	Risk management
Financial – failure to attract franchisees prevents further expansion	Capital investment requirements to continually open new outlets are significant. Emelius relies on franchise model to fund expansion. High operating gearing means franchise may take time to become profitable so it is not necessarily an attractive proposition. Likelihood: To date Emelius has 10 regional franchises so this does not appear to have presented a problem, although we do not know how this compares to target numbers	Reduce risk of low take-up by ensuring good profit incentives for franchisees Emphasise support offered Need to continually be on look out for prospective partners Again the data capture service may also attract different franchisees

Tutorial note:

Other relevant and important risks were awarded some credit.

Examiner's comments

Requirement 19.1 asked candidates to prepare a risk register for Emelius' paper-based document storage business, setting out one key risk in each of four categories: strategic, operational, hazard and financial. The standard of answers was generally very good, with almost all candidates following the tabular approach requested. Some candidates did not appear to be clear about the nature of the different types of risk, failing to distinguish the longer term nature of strategic risk from the more day-to-day operational risk, with the financial category being least well understood. That said, there were some really good answers at the other end of the spectrum which clearly identified very specific key risks, their impact and likelihood and what could be done to mitigate them. Weaker answers typically displayed some or all of the following: little detail or explanation of each point; highlighting insignificant risks (or more than one); or failing to discuss both impact and likelihood. A minority identified risks to the digital data capture service which were not relevant.

19.2 Value chain

The value chain is the sequence of business activities by which value is added to the products or services of an entity so that in the end it makes a profit. Value chain analysis can be used to help identify the cost and value drivers behind Emelius' digital data capture strategy and the strategically significant activities of this side of the business. Primary activities are those that create value and are directly concerned with providing the data capture service. The support activities do not create value of themselves, but they enable Emelius' primary activities to take place with maximum efficiency.

Porter's generic strategies suggest that a company should pursue a strategy of either cost leadership or differentiation. Some low cost features are present in the value chain and will help Emelius achieve profitability, although its competitive advantage is more likely to centre on the speed, security and reliability of access to digital information, once captured. As might be expected with digital data, Emelius makes heavy use of technology throughout the chain to address these critical success factors.

Key drivers:

(1) Centralisation of scanning process (inbound logistics)

Inbound logistics involves converting paper documents to digital form. A key cost driver is Emelius' use of a single centralised facility with large high-tech, high-speed scanners. The central facility can batch-process large volumes and multiple formats, reducing machine set-up costs. The use of relatively low skilled employees at the scanning house with strict targets will also help control costs although this may be counter-productive if it increases error rates, slows down the scanning process or leads to a high number of resubmissions. However Emelius's use of technology to check legibility and errors should prevent this affecting service levels.

(2) Indexing of documents (operations)

A key value driver is the way in which the documents are indexed (operations). The powerful indexing system supports a multiple search function which should make it easier for users to retrieve a range of documents without knowing the exact title (outbound logistics). It has also built in internal controls to validate the accuracy of indexing which will increase the chance of fast and accurate retrieval. The fact that the system can also generate any linked documents is likely to differentiate Emelius and be something that customers may be prepared to pay a premium for.

(3) Security of documents (service)

Another key value driver is the security associated with preserving the confidentiality of documents and access to them. Multiple levels of system security exist to prevent unauthorised access but also to ensure records are not created, altered or deleted inappropriately and Emelius is able to offer clients a clear document audit trail. The fact that Emelius keeps copies of digital documents across multiple servers reduces the risk that data will be lost and increases the reliability of the service offered to customers.

(4) Use of outsourcing/extended chain (procurement)

Linkages between activities in the chain or the wider value system of suppliers and customers also drive costs or value eg, the national courier chain has been chosen on the basis of the 24-hour secure service it offers. Centralised purchasing of all equipment and sole supplier agreement for all IT requirements are likely to lead to better prices/discounts. The maintenance of the online platform is outsourced to a specialist provider who is more likely to be an expert in this area than Emelius. Management of these wider linkages will allow Emelius to provide a better service and help to prevent Emelius' competitors from replicating its value chain.

Tutorial note:

Other relevant and important drivers were awarded some credit.

Branding (marketing and sales)

Limited marketing beyond existing branding will help keep costs down. The existing franchise manager will be responsible for attracting new customers. Since Emelius uses a franchise model, brand image is likely to be important and will be strengthened by the distinctive branding on vans, staff uniforms, website, social media.

Examiner's comments

Requirement 19.2 requested candidates to explain four key drivers in the value chain for Emelius' new digital data capture service. This was a slightly different take on the normal value chain requirement, as a detailed value chain diagram was already provided in the Exhibit. Weaker candidates had a tendency to merely re-write chunks of the diagram without explaining how the factor they had identified would help Emelius drive value or keep costs down. Better answers: discussed their answer in the context of Emelius' generic strategy using value chain terminology; identified and explained a range of both cost and value drivers; and brought out the importance of linkages in the value chain.

19.3 Data analysis

Expected profit 20Y4 (without Swinburne contract)

	Working	£
Revenue	90m × 0.036	3,240,000
Variable costs	90m × 0.0115	(1,035,000)
Contribution	90m × 0.0245	2,205,000
Fixed costs		(1,755,000)
Expected profit		450,000

WORKING

Revenue per sheet 20Y3 = 2.7m/75m = 0.036 ie, 3.6 pence

Comparison of results 20Y2–20Y4

Year	Volume (millions of sheets)	Revenue	Variable costs	Fixed costs	Profit/(Loss)
		£'000	£'000	£'000	£'000
20Y2 actual	50	1,800	675	1,500	(375)
20Y3 actual	75	2,700	937.5	1,650	112.5
20Y4 forecast	90	3,240	1,035	1,755	450

	20Y2	20Y3	20Y4
% of capacity	50%	75%	90%
Revenue/sheet	3.6p	3.6p	3.6p
Vc/sheet	1.35p	1.25p	1.15p
FC/sheet	3p	2.2p	1.95p
Increase in volume (and revenue)	–	50%	20%
Increase in FC	–	10%	6.4%
Decrease in VC/sheet	–	7.4%	8%

The EN franchise started in 20Y2 and has experienced strong growth in storage volumes (50% in 20Y3 and a further 20% expected in 20Y4), possibly due to a strong brand image and the increasing regulatory requirements requiring customers to store documents securely. Since the selling price charged per sheet has remained constant, all the revenue growth is due to this volume increase. Whilst the selling price has remained constant, the VC per sheet has fallen from 1.35 pence per sheet to 1.15 pence. This is likely to be due to economies of scale being achieved as volumes increase.

Given the high fixed costs of the business, the franchise needs to achieve high capacity in order to be profitable (the break-even volume in 20Y4 is 1,755/(0.036 − 0.0115) = 71.6 million sheets). As utilisation of capacity has increased, so has profitability but EN is now close to maximum and initially, because of the stepped fixed cost model, results are likely to deteriorate if it wants to increase the capacity beyond 100m sheets.

20Y4 forecast with Swinburne contract:

	Working	£
Revenue	102m × 0.036	3,672,000
Variable costs	102 × 0.0115	1,173,000
Fixed costs	1,755 + 750	2,505,000
Expected loss		(6,000)

This turns EN's profit into a small loss.

Assumptions:

Pricing and variable costs for Swinburne contract would be the same as for the existing business:

Revenue per sheet = 3.6p, VC per sheet = 1.15p (assumes no further economies of scale)

Swinburne contract of 12 million pages requires additional capacity and hence the step in fixed costs will be incurred.

Accept alternative calculations/justifications of impact of contract:

Store 12m additional sheets by increasing capacity

Contribution 12m × (0.0245) = £294,000
Incremental FC = £750,000
Net change in profit = £(456,000)

Store 12m sheets by turning away 2m existing business or destroying 2m documents at end of life to stay within existing capacity.

Incremental profit = incremental contribution 10m × (0.0245) = £245,000

Explanation of results and implications

Comparison of Profitability 20Y4:

Year	Volume (millions of sheets)	Revenue £'000	Variable costs £'000	Contribution £'000	Fixed costs £'000	Profit/ (Loss) £'000
Without contract	90	3,240	1,035	2,205	1,755	450
With contract	102	3,672	1,173	2,499	2,505	(6)

Assuming that Emelius Northern achieves its expected volume of 90m sheets in 20Y4, the Swinburne archive would take the storage volumes beyond the capacity of the existing facilities, necessitating a £750k increase in fixed costs. Emelius Northern has enjoyed rapid growth but 20Y4-5 represents the point at which it reaches a step in fixed costs if it is to expand further.

In this case it is perhaps unfair to treat the £750k as an incremental cost of the Swinburne contract. Assuming that demand generally for EN's services continue to grow, the opportunity for the Swinburne business is simply bringing forward the need to expand the business to 20Y4 rather than 20Y5. Even without the Swinburne contract, the expansion point may be reached in 20Y5, since the business has been growing rapidly and it would only require growth of 100/90 = 11.1% before full capacity is reached without the Swinburne contract.

Emelius Northern might be able to avoid or delay expanding the existing warehouse facility and incurring the £750k if it:

(1) Identifies documents still being stored that have reached end-of-life and writes to the relevant clients suggesting destruction

(2) Starts to offer the digital data capture service and persuades existing clients to transfer some/all of their current paper storage to digital – particularly for those clients who need to retrieve documents regularly

Certainly in relation to the Swinburne contract it appears that offering the digital capture service for 40% of the archive (4.8m documents) would delay the required expansion until 20Y5. However before making a decision to implement the digital data service, EN needs to consider the costs involved and the expectations of revenue.

Examiner's comments

Requirement 19.3 started off by asking candidates to calculate EN's expected profit for 20Y4, ignoring the Swinburne contract, and to analyse the reasons for the improvement in EN's performance since 20Y2. Attempts at the initial profit calculation were normally very good, with most candidates producing the correct figure, although some made errors with variable cost. However the quality of the subsequent analysis was much more variable. The weakest candidates ignored this part of the requirement entirely, or simply used the absolute figures from the question, with no additional calculations, which limited the quality of any discussion. Better candidates spotted that as the selling price has remained constant, the increase in revenue is entirely down to volume growth and that, given the high operating gearing, capacity utilisation is the key to EN's profitability.

Candidates were then asked to quantify the impact on 20Y4 profitability of accepting the Swinburne contract. The ability to tackle this part of the question was extremely varied. The key issue was that the new contract for storing 12 million pages would take EN over its existing capacity, necessitating a £750k step in fixed costs, which would not be covered by the additional £294k contribution. As a result the expected 20Y4 profit would become a loss. Some insightful candidates identified that it might be possible to avoid the incremental costs and accept the Swinburne contract within the current capacity, either by destroying documents at end–of–life or by turning down business from smaller clients. This approach to the calculation, if explained, was awarded full credit.

Finally candidates were asked to consider their results and the implications for EN's decision about whether to introduce digital data capture service. The point here was that if EN could digitally store the 40% of documents that Swinburne need to access regularly it might be able to accept the contract without the increase in capacity.

Better candidates discussed other relevant factors: in light of the business' current growth, other clients would probably be found in 20Y5 to help utilise the additional storage capacity created by the step and that the decision to expand should perhaps be separated from that of accepting the Swinburne contract.

19.4 Swinburne LLP
Albany Court
Leeds
L2 6FD

Emelius Northern
Unit 12,
Weyhill Industrial Park
Waverley
WY4 3XZ

19 March 20Y4

Dear Sirs,

Data storage and management

Following our recent discussions, I am writing to you to explain the benefits of outsourcing your data management to Emelius Northern and to recommend the most appropriate data management service for your current needs.

Recommended service package

I recommend that you use a combination of our data management services: paper document management for the 60% of documents that you are unlikely to need to access from the archive, and digital data capture for the remaining 40%.

Why digital?

- Storing paper records reduces your ability to retrieve business critical information quickly, and convenient access to the documents by a wide range of users is limited. Digital data capture allows for rapid distribution of critical information and reduces the inefficiencies of having to handle, copy, distribute, file, store and retrieve paper documents, which slow the execution of tasks and negatively impact the productivity of your employees. Using our web-enabled digital system, solicitors in your five offices will be able to access the same files at the same time, with minimal effort.

- Digital data prevents many of the human errors that occur with manual paper-based procedures, as well as minimising misplaced information, and allows for increased security measures in relation to identity theft and legal liabilities. We have multiple controls to prevent unauthorised access and tampering and this will be of great benefit to you given the confidential nature of your legal documents.

- The immediate availability of files and other data and our comprehensive indexing system will allow you to retrieve the main document quickly plus any linked supporting documents. This may be particularly useful to you in relation to prolonged legal cases or if information is suddenly required in a court case.

- There are many other benefits of capturing documents digitally:

  - It is more efficient and therefore will be cheaper for documents that are to be accessed regularly

  - Back-up files and records will be stored on multiple servers for disaster recovery

  - A certificate of destruction will be issued at end of life in accordance with regulatory requirements

Performance measures

The quality of our data management services can be assured and controlled through a service level agreement, with agreed performance measures. I would suggest the following three key performance indicators (KPIs):

Security of information – this is critical given the nature of your business and the data you hold about clients and cases. An appropriate KPI would be (any **one** of):

- Number of reported security breaches
- Number of unauthorised attempts at access
- Number or % of documents reported lost or unavailable

Speed of retrieval – this will assess the efficiency of the service we provide. An appropriate KPI would be (any **one** of):

- % of information retrieved within stated target time
- Average time taken to retrieve a document
- % electronic searches resulting in a document being retrieved and opened

Cost-effective service – a key benefit of our digital service is that it should help you reduce costs. An appropriate KPI would be:

- Monthly document storage and access costs

Tutorial note:

Other relevant and important KPIs, with justifications, were awarded some credit, eg:

- Number of documents not removed/destroyed after end of life
- % of documents where end-of-life certificate not issued within an agreed time limit
- % of documents not accessed after more than one year (or other appropriate time period)

We very much look forward to working with you

Yours Sincerely

Lee Gryphon
Emelius Northern

Requirement 19.4 asked for a letter setting out the benefits of digital data capture for Swinburne and three key performance indicators that EN could include in the service level agreement for the new contract. Most candidates were comfortable pointing out the benefits of digital data storage although only the better answers related these to the context of the legal firm in question. Once again not all candidates clearly understand what a KPI is, with some suggesting goals or critical success factors rather than measures that could be applied to service levels. A disappointing number of candidates did not score the mark for laying out the letter properly, either by ignoring it or by setting out their answer as a memorandum.

20 Boom plc (March 2014)

Marking guide

	Knowledge	Skill	Marks
20.1 Directors views and duties	4	10	12
20.2 Commerical and ethical issues	3	9	10
	7	19	22

General comments:

At 22 marks, this was the shortest question on the paper. It was reasonably well attempted.

This scenario concerns a large, profitable mining company, Boom plc, which is engaged in extracting shale gas by drilling through underground rock formations at various sites around the world (fracking). Boom has recently discovered a new drill site in a remote but populated area of South America (project SA). The local government is willing to grant Boom a lease to proceed with the drilling and the central government anticipates significant economic benefits in terms of jobs, GDP and tax revenue. An abundant domestic supply of natural gas could also be used to produce cleaner, cheaper electricity and fuel for the region. However there is opposition from environmental groups which claim that the local population have not been sufficiently informed as to the long-term environmental issues associated with fracking. They claim the fracking process would place large demands on already restricted water resources and exacerbate existing environmental concerns about access to drinking water in the region. Boom's mission statement is 'to maximise the investment of our shareholders whilst striving to recognise our corporate responsibility to the wider society.' The finance director (FD) believes the two elements of the mission contradict each other, whilst a non-executive director (NED) believes that, if the directors are to fulfil their legal duties, Boom must consider its impact on the wider community and the environment and the long-term consequences of any decisions.

20.1 Directors' views

Boom's mission states that the company aims 'to maximise the return on investment for our shareholders whilst striving to recognise our corporate responsibility to wider society.'

Finance director

The finance director believes this is contradictory. In the short term any measures taken by Boom to enhance the health and safety of its employees or to protect the local environment, such as spending on recycling water or controlling pollution, may increase costs and reduce profits. Reduced profits imply reduced shareholder wealth in terms of dividends foregone or lower capital growth. The finance director's view is consistent with the traditional view that it is the duty of the directors, as agents appointed by shareholders, to maximise shareholder wealth. This might suggest that social factors which sacrifice shareholder wealth should not be taken into account. This is the approach that the finance director is taking when he suggests that money spent 'keeping the environmentalists happy' may make certain projects non-viable.

However the mission statement is not necessarily contradictory – it does not say that Boom has to make sure that society is not disadvantaged in any way by its activities; rather it implies that the company will do its best to take society into account in its decision making and operations.

Non-executive director: corporate responsibility

Corporate responsibility is used to describe the duties which a business has to the wider community. It can be defined as the actions, activities and obligations of business in achieving sustainability. A sustainable business is one which is able to generate continuously increasing stakeholder value by applying sustainable practices throughout all its activities.

The last one hundred years has seen a change in society's expectations towards social responsibility and an increased focus on the extent to which a company should exceed its minimum obligations to stakeholders and society. The modification of the Companies Act has shifted the focus for directors from looking solely at shareholders' interests to taking account of other stakeholders as well when fulfilling their statutory duty to promote the success of the company. The aim is to promote an 'inclusive' approach towards the interests of stakeholders and to encourage a long term view to be taken of corporate investment.

This is more the approach that the NED is referring to when he quotes the statement from the conference that 'the directors have a legal duty to run the company for the benefits of its members as a whole.'

Boom's shareholders, as owners of the company, will be primarily interested in the long term profitability of the various mining projects undertaken. However mining is also likely to bring benefits to a wider group of stakeholders than just Boom's shareholders. For example, employees will benefit from pay, job security and employment prospects. There are benefits too for the local governments of the countries in which Boom mines, which need to be seen to satisfy the demands of their electorate. They may argue that they are doing so by attracting foreign investment, thereby creating employment, increasing the wealth of the economy and collecting additional tax revenues. Boom's activities will also financially benefit the suppliers of its materials and equipment, and mining will also benefit those customers who use the gas that Boom produces.

Nevertheless, whilst wider society might indeed benefit from drilling and mining, the local community and environment in which any of Boom's mining activities take place might be adversely affected through pollution or the use of scarce water resources.

If Boom is to be true to its mission statement, it must recognise its responsibility here and this is perhaps where the potential for conflict arises:

Corporate governance and directors' duties

Corporate governance is concerned with the direction and control of the company, and helps determine the structure of an organisation, its objectives and the relationship between the organisation's management, its board of directors and its shareholders.

Responsibilities fall on the Board collectively and there is no legal distinction between the duties of executive and non-executive directors, but they do have differing roles. The executive directors are more involved in the day-to-day running of the business, whilst the NEDs bring an independent view and help facilitate the strategic decision-making process, by providing objective challenge and criticism. Good corporate governance requires the directors to put in place a risk management strategy and the NED refers to this.

Risk management

If Boom is merely paying lip-service to corporate responsibility in its mission statement, then it is much more likely to be subject to risks resulting from the diverse range of issues relevant to external stakeholders. Therefore the possibility of corporate risk failure and potential financial volatility is increased.

Transparent and accountable governance structures should incorporate the highest standards of ethics. Sustainable business practices will help to manage and minimise Boom's exposure to a broad range of risks relating to the environment, and social and workplace issues. Minimising risk ultimately places Boom in a stronger, more sustainable market position than an unengaged competitor who is likely to be exposed to a greater number of external variables.

If Boom undertakes active and responsive engagement with a broad range of stakeholder groups, this will improve its relationships with stakeholders and give it a better understanding of the environment in which it operates. Such procedures will equip Boom to anticipate the inclinations of those who prescribe regulations and sharpen its response to third party pressures.

Conclusion

The link between social engagement and financial performance ultimately suggests that companies should be motivated to implement socially responsible strategies since this will reduce risk and aid long term profitability, maximising the value of shareholder investments.

On this basis, there would appear to be no inherent conflict in Boom's mission statement. Given that the directors' duties are owed to the members as a whole, any actions which foster long term profitability appear to be in the company's best interests and therefore both elements of Boom's mission statement are achievable simultaneously.

If Boom engages sincerely in social, environmental and other sustainability issues, it is, for example, more likely to secure future access to government controlled natural resources and therefore more likely to achieve superior profit maximisation for its shareholders.

Examiner's comments

Requirement 20.1 asked candidates to discuss the views of the two directors in relation to Boom's mission statement. They were also asked to explain the directors' duties in respect of corporate governance and corporate responsibility. Attempts at this requirement were quite polarised. Many weaker candidates chose to apply the models of Ashridge and Mendelow, but in doing so failed to address the requirement to discuss directors' duties and corporate governance. Most candidates were confident discussing the concept of corporate responsibility, wider stakeholders and sustainability. A surprising number were however unable to distinguish adequately between corporate responsibility (the activities and obligations of a business in achieving sustainability) and corporate governance (the rules governing the structure and objectives of the organisation and the relationship between management, the board and the shareholders). Better candidates discussed the fact that the roles of the FD and the NED might influence their viewpoint and highlighted the latter's responsibility to bring an independent viewpoint to strategy and standards of conduct. Risk management was mentioned in the scenario but only the better candidates discussed the duties of the Board in ensuring an appropriate risk management framework – particularly relevant in the context of fracking and the danger that decisions might be taken to increase profits without having due regard to the risks involved.

20.2 Commercial and ethical issues

Commercial issues

Boom needs to evaluate the costs and benefits of the proposed SA project to assess what level of return the company is likely to make for its shareholders.

However the decision to invest should not be made without considering non-financial aspects or those who might be disadvantaged by the project.

Financial projections can be prepared, incorporating estimates of the production volumes of gas, the price that it will be able to sell it at, the costs of leasing the land, and mining and distributing the gas.

Non-financial or indirect benefits include the number of jobs created in the local economy, the tax revenues paid to the local government, and the environmental benefits from the reduction in the use of coal and other fossil fuels.

Boom also needs to establish the likely costs to society – for example it needs to assess the likelihood of environmental damage from hazardous chemicals and take all steps possible to reduce the risk of contamination. This could increase the operating costs of the project.

Commercially however, as explained by the FD, if the costs of protecting the environment are too great the project may become non-viable which, given the potential benefits to the local community, would not necessarily be in anyone's interests. Therefore Boom would not be expected to incur costs to eliminate all environmental risks, just those that are deemed most likely and most significant, which it would seem reasonable to address.

Ethical issues

Boom needs to consider whether there are any legal or regulatory issues in relation to the project. Given the nature of Boom's business there may be voluntary industry codes of conduct which should be adhered to.

The project appears to have the support of the local government who are willing to grant the lease, and the central government who believe that there will be considerable economic benefits. Provided the government is prepared to grant Boom a lease to mine the land then there would not appear to be a legality issue. However the shale gas is presumably non-replaceable so the government/local region needs to be compensated for Boom's use of the limited resource – presumably this will be reflected in the price of the lease for the land.

Regulatory issues may also relate to health and safety and the working conditions of employees, who have the right to be safe and to be treated fairly. It is important that Boom acts with integrity to maintain its reputation for the highest standards of health and safety and does not exploit lower standards or the lack of regulation that may exist in the region.

From a sustainability point of view the project is expected to have long term environmental benefits. However Boom and the local government must balance the need to find alternative fuel sources with the need to conserve local water supplies. They need to consult the local population, farmers etc. and take their views into account. Consideration should be given to the alternative sources to using freshwater that exist (eg, salt water or non-drinking water) and the extent to which any waste water can be treated and recycled. This may result in slightly higher costs but will increase the sustainability of the project.

There is an issue of transparency. The environmental groups are claiming that the local population is not fully informed in relation to the impact of the fracking. This claim needs to be investigated and the facts established. Boom must ensure that it has been open and honest in its negotiations with the local government to obtain the lease. It also needs to consider the extent to which the environmentalists have genuine concerns which are backed up by evidence or whether these are merely overreactions or scaremongering claims. Meetings should be held with representatives of the government, the local community and the environmental groups to exchange information and to help address their concerns. One possible issue in relation to environmental damage is the fact that the long-term detrimental effects of fracking, which is a relatively new technique, are not yet known.

In relation to integrity, Boom must ensure that its dealings with the local government and others are honest and above board, that the local community is in no way misled about the development and its long term effects, and that it is not involved in any financial attempts to induce or persuade people to act in its favour.

Conclusion

Boom needs to weigh up the benefits of project SA for its shareholders and the wider stakeholders who benefit from the shale gas production, with the disadvantages to the local environment. Provided Boom has been transparent with the government and the local community and its consultations/negotiations are genuine then the company is probably likely to be deemed to act ethically.

Examiner's comments

Requirement 20.2 requested candidates to discuss the commercial and ethical issues for Boom which are involved in the decision to extract shale gas in South America.

A wide number of points could be made in relation to the commercial issues and the better candidates covered a number of these. Only a very few explained that in undertaking an assessment of the viability of the project Boom would need to consider both financial and non-financial costs and benefits, including where relevant the costs to society. A minority of candidates missed this element of the requirement out altogether and concentrated on ethical issues only.

Candidates' answers to the ethics element were quite mixed. Better candidates considered both the negative and positive sides of the problem, identifying that although fracking may bring some environmental problems locally, it will also reduce the need for fossil fuels, Boom has the support of local and central government, and there will be considerable benefits to the area, all of which are consistent with acting sustainably. Some weaker candidates failed to use any ethical language or principles such as transparency and integrity in their answers. Others applied the transparency/effect/fairness framework, but took a simplistic view, asserting that the farmers and local people would be badly affected, that Boom would not want people to find out about this and that as a result the project was probably not ethical. This approach failed to consider the need to assess the facts and evidence before assuming the environmentalists' claims are accurate. It also overlooked the wide range of benefits that fracking is expected to generate for the region. As has been stated before, the ethics issues are not always clear-cut and weaker candidates need to take note that more balanced and questioning answers are required that do not assert conclusions without supporting reasoning and evidence.

An overwhelming majority of candidates failed to present any sort of conclusion to their analysis, which is disappointing. Commercially, if the costs for Boom of protecting the environment are too great the project might become non-viable, which would cause the wider community to miss out on the possible benefits. Thus a balance needs to be found between the interests of the shareholders and the benefits to wider society on the one hand and those that will be affected by damage to the local environment on the other. Provided Boom is transparent and genuine with all parties and addresses the most significant environmental issues then it may well be acting ethically.

21 Tai Ltd and Jelk plc (March 2014)

Marking guide

	Knowledge	Skill	Marks
21.1 Product portfolio	3	8	10
21.2 Other key benefits	2	5	7
21.3 Strategic disasdvantages and management issues	3	7	9
21.4 Preliminary conclusions	–	4	4
	8	24	30

General comments:

The third question, worth 30 marks, was the least well attempted. The scenario concerns two companies considering a merger. Tai Ltd is a well-established Chinese company that manufactures travelators. It uses high quality materials and prides itself on customer service and post-installation maintenance. Jelk Ltd is a UK listed company which manufactures elevators for commercial use. It has contracts to supply and service lifts in office developments, railway stations, airports etc. It also designs, manufactures and installs stairlifts for domestic use, of which about 40% are exported, predominantly to Eurozone countries.

The products of both companies go through a similar life cycle of installation, maintenance and replacement, although the lengths of the cycles are different. Jelk's CEO believes that a merger will be of great benefit to both parties in terms of product portfolio and market coverage and that integration can be successfully managed.

Candidates were required to discuss whether the merger should proceed and were provided with the following headings to structure their answer: product portfolio benefits; other key benefits; key strategic disadvantages and management issues; and preliminary conclusions. As no particular addressee had been specified, candidates were expected to consider the merger from the point of view of both parties where relevant.

21.1 Product portfolio

The BCG and product life cycle models can help assess the balance of a product portfolio. Typically a wider portfolio of products helps spread risk and improve financial performance.

BCG matrix

The BCG matrix is a way of analysing a portfolio of products by considering their relative market share and market growth:

BCG Matrix		Relative market share	
		High	Low
% rate of market growth	High	Star	Question mark ?
	Low	Cash cow £	Dog

Considering the companies individually:

	Jelk Sales	Largest competitor	Market share: Jelk sales/ Largest Competitor	UK market growth rate	BCG analysis
Elevators	£54m	£260m	20.8%	–2%	Dog
Stairlifts	£96m	£80m	120%	8%	Cash cow
Total sales	150m				

	Tai Sales	Largest competitor	Tai sales/ Largest competitor	Chinese market growth rate	BCG analysis
Travelators	$19.6m	$342m	5.7%	15%	Problem child or ?
In £ at $1 = £0.65	£12.74m	£222m			

Jelk's stairlift product in the UK market might be considered to be a Cash cow or money earner. Jelk is well-established and the market leader in a market that is growing steadily, but slower than in the emerging markets of Asia. The presence of three large competitors should prevent new players entering the UK market. This is likely to mean Jelk has cash flows available for investment to develop new products/markets.

Jelk's elevators are however in a more challenging position, with a relatively low share and little market growth potential. The market is dominated by four global companies and due to the depressed construction sector has experienced a decline of 2%. Stairlifts are likely to generate sufficient funding to allow Jelk to maintain this position until the market regenerates, or Jelk might benefit from finding new markets.

However neither of its established products offers Jelk significant future growth potential. A major competitor has been taken over and further consolidation is likely in a mature market.

In China, Tai has just under a 6% share of an elevator market that is an emerging market, growing at 15%. This would probably put it as a question mark or problem child – a product where the market is growing but share is still limited. Tai is probably not operating at full efficiency, plus its share is likely to need defending against competitors.

Since the two companies have products in different BCG categories, the merger will result in a better balanced portfolio, with products in three quadrants of the matrix. The funds generated from sales of stairlifts can be used to help develop Tai's competitive position in the elevator market.

Product life cycle

The product life cycle concept can be used in conjunction with the BCG:

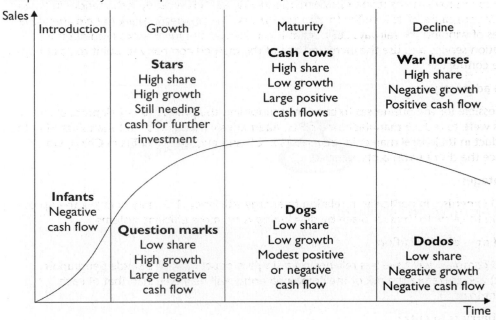

Most businesses would not want to risk having a single product or group of closely related products all at the same stage in their life cycle as they may all decline together. The life of a product can be extended and the balance of a product portfolio improved by considering markets at different stages in the life cycle and this is a key benefit of the proposed merger for Jelk Ltd. Its traditional UK market appears to have reached maturity whereas the Chinese market offers rapid growth potential for both stairlifts and elevators. From Tai's point of view Jelk's size and funding is likely to help it improve its competitive position.

Conclusion

As Jelk's CEO states, the merger will create a more comprehensive and better balanced portfolio for the new company and help sustain funds to support future needs. It will allow Jelk to access a new geographic market for stairlifts and allow Tai to benefit from the size and funding of a market leading company.

Examiner's comments

Requirement 21.1 on product portfolio benefits was well attempted by the vast majority of candidates who demonstrated good knowledge of the BCG and product life cycle models. The better candidates used the figures from the scenario to plot the different products on the BCG for the individual companies before considering the portfolio of the combined concern. Almost all candidates identified that the merger would lead to a better balanced portfolio although only the better ones linked this to the comment made by Jelk's CEO, querying whether the growth opportunities offered by China meant this would be more favourable for Jelk than Tai.

21.2 Other benefits/reasons for merger

Synergies

Both companies are independent manufacturers and leaders in their specialist markets. They both focus on product safety. Jelk pays great attentions to quality and aftersales care, and it also has a reputation for post-installation maintenance. Tai has very strong R&D. There is likely to be synergy from having strengths in different areas that are however complementary and can be used to increase competitive advantage.

Marketing advantages

As has been seen in 21.1 the combined businesses will have a more balanced product portfolio. This is likely to improve their success rates when tendering eg, Jelk recently lost a tender in Poland to a competitor because of its inability to offer travelators. The merger is likely to help strengthen Tai's chances of winning the railways contract as it can take advantage of Jelk's reputation for post-installation service and use the increased size of the merged company to point to its ability to manage the contract.

Production advantages

It may be possible for the businesses to consider centralising the production of all products in China if this were to reduce manufacturing costs. Alternatively each could start manufacturing the other's product in their local market ie, travelators in UK and elevators/stairlifts in China, which would reduce the distribution costs incurred.

R&D advantages

Tai has R&D expertise, in particular in relation to energy efficiency. This may help Jelk to improve its position in the elevator market place by developing new, more efficient systems.

Risk spreading – diversification

The merged company will have less reliance on a single product (Tai) or a single geographic market (Jelk) and therefore the risk of the combined entity will be lower than that of each individual company.

Overcome barriers to entry

The barriers to entry for either company attempting to expand geographically are high. This would probably be more difficult for Jelk to achieve in China without some sort of JV partner than it would be for Tai. Tai will however benefit from Jelk's strong brand.

Outplay rivals

Since the European (and therefore probably the US markets) are mature, most of the big companies will be looking for expansion in South America or Asia and so Jelk would be advised to get ahead of the crowd in this respect if it wants to establish its brand quickly ahead of other competitors.

Finance and management

Certainly as far as Tai is concerned, the merged entity is likely to benefit from better access to funding and Tai may benefit from the experience and skills of the Jelk team in managing global operations.

Examiner's comments

In requirement 21.2 candidates were asked to consider other key benefits of the merger. Some weaker candidates simply reiterated the product arguments they had already discussed in 21.1, missing the opportunity to consider possible synergies that might arise from the merger. Alternatively they made generic points which were not always relevant here given the geographical dispersion of the two businesses. Better candidates applied their knowledge to the scenario and were able to cite a range of points including geographical diversification, risk reduction, strategic fit, the ability to overcome barriers to entry and possible production and research advantages. Weaker candidates tended to consider benefits from Jelk's perspective only whereas stronger candidates took a more balanced view.

21.3 Strategic disadvantages and management issues

Strategic disadvantages of the merger stem from the following:

Jelk is significantly bigger than Tai so in one sense it is more likely to be a takeover than a merger.

Most of the growth opportunities seem to be in China so Jelk may stand to benefit more than Tai from the combination.

Aside from the language difference, the cultural differences between Jelk and Tai are likely to be large and bridging this gap will pose a significant challenge and business risk.

Cultural differences are likely to arise between the two firms in relation to the following:

- Values and attitudes eg, individualism vs collectivism, diversity and gender stereotypes, work ethics

- Methods of managing staff eg, unionisation, hierarchies and status systems, motivation and reward systems

- Methods of doing business eg, conventions of negotiations and tenders, need to ensure self-respect and status, hospitality

- Expectations of business conduct eg, in relation to CSR, short term vs long term time horizon of investments, government involvement

There will also be regulatory differences and the merged entity will need to ensure compliance with all legal requirements, especially in respect of employment terms and conditions.

Management issues

If the merger goes ahead, there would be significant integration challenges in relation to HR and culture. A key issue in assessing the people and cultural challenges will be understanding the level and depth of integration anticipated – from minimal integration, where Jelk and Tai continue to be run as stand-alone subsidiaries, to full integration, which since Jelk is the bigger player (£150m sales compared to Tai's £12.7m) is likely in this case to mean Tai relinquishing its identity and being subsumed into Jelk's operations. A further complication is that different parts of the organisation may be integrated at different levels, for example, minimal integration of the sales function but full integration of the supporting IT and finance function.

Understanding the similarities and differences in the way Jelk and Tai do business will enable the merged company to focus more sharply on what needs to change (in Jelk or Tai), who needs to change, and how and when these changes should take place.

A major strategic decision needs to be made in relation to how the merged firm will be managed and the shape of the new structure, and who will fill the key jobs. The eventual structure of the merged entity may not necessarily reflect the prior structure of either business.

If the merger proceeds, the change is likely to be transformational. A dedicated change management team will need to be established to manage the integration across the business units and geographies and to address a wide range of global integration challenges, including clearly defining the new organisation structure and its responsibilities, managing relevant stakeholders through clear and frequent communications, and addressing cultural differences between the two companies.

Examiner's comments

Requirement 21.3 requested candidates to discuss strategic disadvantages and management issues. Whilst Jelk's CEO has been very upbeat about the merger, it is not without its issues, not least the fact that Jelk is considerably bigger than Tai and on the face of it stands to gain more. There will also be a large language and cultural gap to breach, which will present significant integration challenges if the merger goes ahead. Better candidates discussed these and other points, distinguishing between strategic disadvantages and management issues. Weaker candidates tended to limit the scope of their answers by merging their discussion of disadvantages and management issues, and rehearsed their knowledge of change management in a generic fashion, instead of applying this to the specific issues in the scenario.

21.4 Preliminary conclusions

As Jelk's CEO states, it appears that the merger would be beneficial to both parties. The combined product portfolio will be more balanced than either of the companies individually and this is likely to increase their competitive advantage when it comes to tendering. The business risk of the combined company entity will be lower as the merger will reduce Tai's reliance on a single product and Jelk's reliance on a single market. There are likely to be some cultural issues associated with the integration, but these may be at a strategic rather than operational level, if Tai operates in China and Jelk in the UK, each distributing the other's products.

Clearly the benefits to the respective shareholders will depend on the financial structure of the transaction but, on the face of it, strategically the merger appears viable.

Examiner's comments

Requirement 21.4, the preliminary conclusion was generally well done. Those who briefly summarised the key points from each section and produced a conclusion which was consistent with their earlier discussion tended to score highly. A minority of candidates who had mismanaged their time on earlier sections or questions omitted this requirement entirely.

22 Albatross Golf Equipment plc (June 2014)

Marking guide

	Knowledge	Skill	Marks
22.1 Data analysis	2	18	18
22.2 Supply chain management and market positioning	4	11	14
22.3 Ethics	2	7	8
	8	36	40

General comments:

The scenario in this question relates to a company (AGE), which manufactures good quality golf clubs from its factory in the UK under the LazySwing brand. Sales have declined in recent years, partly due to competition from larger rival manufacturers with greater R&D expenditure. AGE has recently been acquired by a private equity firm, FF, which has appointed a new chief executive.

The chief executive undertook a strategic review, but he would like more analysis to determine the underlying causes of the decline in performance. The chief executive has also proposed to reposition the LazySwing brand from up-market to mid-market.

A further proposed strategy is to import a new range of lower-cost golf clubs from China, with two sub strategies: (1) sell these clubs through existing distribution channels with the existing LazySwing brand name; or (2) sell them through downmarket sports retailers under a new 'Eagle' brand.

An ethical issue has arisen whereby the chief executive was told in confidence by a professional golfer that the professional golfer used by AGE to promote its products is taking performance-enhancing drugs.

22.1

	AGE			Galdo		
	20Y1	**20Y2**	**20Y3**	**20Y1**	**20Y2**	**20Y3**
Number of clubs sold	250	240	234	556	519	484
% decrease		4%	2.5%		6.7%	6.7%
UK market	380,000	365,000	350,000			
% decrease		3.9%	4.1%			
Gross profit margin %	20%	18%	16%	30%	30%	30%
Operating profit margin %	6.8%	3.5%	0.2%	20.0%	19.6%	19.1%
% sales UK	80%	82%	84%	40%	40%	40%
% sales export	20%	18%	16%	60%	60%	60%
Sales revenue decrease						
UK		6.8%	5.8%		4.0%	4.2%
Export		18.2%	18.2%		4.0%	4.2%
Total revenue		9.1%	8.0%		4.0%	4.2%
Revenue per club	£88.00	£83.33	£78.63	£179.86	£184.97	£190.08
AGE/market leader						
Sales	22.0%	20.8%	20.0%			
Op profit	7.5%	3.7%	0.3%			
Market share (golf equipment market)	4.63%	4.49%	4.42%	10.53%	10.52%	10.51%
Market share (golf club market)	6.62%	6.41%	6.31%	15.04%	15.03%	15.01%

(a) **Revenues**

Total revenues of AGE have declined in 20Y2 and 20Y3 by 9.1% and 8% respectively. Part of the decline can be attributed to the shrinkage of the UK golf equipment market which is beyond the control of AGE management. However, UK market revenues only fell by 3.9% and 4.1% in 20Y2 and 20Y3 respectively. The decline in revenues for AGE has therefore been more than double the market average. More information is needed on changes in the UK golf clubs market.

To examine how this decline in AGE's revenues arose, a sub analysis of the UK market sales and export sales provides some insight. In 20Y1, AGE's UK sales were 80% of its total sales, with exports being only 20%. By 20Y3, however, these figures had changed to 84% and 16% respectively, thereby indicating an increasing relative reliance on the UK market, despite the absolute fall in sales in that market.

Indeed, there has been a decline in AGE's sales revenues in the UK of 6.8% and 5.8% in 20Y2 and 20Y3 respectively, which is still in excess of the overall decline in UK market sales for golf equipment and represents a poor performance.

The export sales performance is however far worse with a reduction in sales of 18.2% in each of the years 20Y2 and 20Y3.

In order to explore further the underlying causes for the decline, it is necessary to examine changes in sales prices and sales volumes. This detail is not analysed separately for UK and exports in the data provided, but it would be required as further information to make a more complete analysis.

Nevertheless, using the data provided, sales volumes have declined by 4% and 2.5% in 20Y2 and 20Y3 respectively. This is a smaller decrease than that in sales revenues, but the difference can be explained in lower prices.

Price can be determined by using revenue divided by volumes, thus average price changed from £88.00 in 20Y1 to £83.33 in 20Y2 (a 5.3% reduction) and then to £78.63 in 20Y3 (a further 5.6% reduction).

It is possible that there has been a change in sales mix between high value and lower value clubs to explain some of the fall in average price. More information is needed on sales volumes of different clubs within the LazySwing range.

Overall therefore, ignoring a possible change in sales mix, the decline in revenue is due to a combination of price decreases and sales volume decreases. This is indicative of weak demand as the price reductions may have been expected to have had a positive effect on sales volumes given a negatively sloped demand function.

Profit

The decline in profit over the period is even more severe than the decline in sales. The reduction of the gross profit margin from 20% in 20Y1 to 16% in 20Y3 is indicative that manufacturing costs comprise an increasing proportion of sales revenues. This is likely to be because some manufacturing costs are fixed costs and do not decline linearly with falling sales volumes, thereby forming a greater proportion of revenues.

The administrative and other fixed costs mean the operating profits are even more volatile than gross profits. As a consequence, operating profit margins have fallen from 6.8% in 20Y1 to near zero in 20Y3.

Trends

There is a clear decline over the period for which information is available, but this period is too short to establish any reliable trends. Moreover, markets can be cyclical and the poor recent performance may be reversed if there is a general upturn in the market. It would be inappropriate to ignore this possibility, but complacent to rely on it as a future strategy for growth.

Conclusion

Over the period 20Y1 to 20Y3, the performance of AGE has declined significantly, even after allowing for the overall decline in UK market sales of golf equipment. More information is needed to determine the extent to which the poor performance in export markets is attributable to a decline in those markets.

(b) **Comparison with Galdo**

The market leader provides a benchmark against which to judge performance of other companies in the industry.

In many respects it provides a better benchmark than the UK market average as it includes export markets and judges performance for a UK manufacturing base.

The relative size of a company compared to the market leader is important in making valid comparisons. In 20Y1 AGE's sales were only 22% that of Galdo and this had fallen to 20% by 20Y3. Comparisons therefore need to be relative (eg, in % terms) rather than in absolute terms.

Although Galdo is the market leader, it only has a market share of just over 10%. This implies there are many participants in the industry, or it could suggest the significance of imports to the UK market. AGE has a smaller and declining market share at 4.63% in 20Y1; falling to 4.42% in 20Y3.

Revenues

Sales revenues of Galdo have declined by 4% and 4.2% in 20Y2 and 20Y3 respectively. This is the case in both the UK market and the export market and therefore for overall revenue. This is broadly in line with the average decline in the UK market over this period of 3.9% and 4.1%. In this respect Galdo has withstood the UK market decline rather better than AGE.

The underlying causes of the sales revenue change can be better understood by examining price and sales volume changes. In sales volume terms, AGE has actually performed better than Galdo which has suffered declines of 6.7% in 20Y2 and 20Y3 compared to 4% and 2.5% for AGE. However, the changes in selling prices are causally linked to these volume changes. In 20Y1, Galdo was charging £179.86 per club compared to £88.00 charged by AGE. This is a significant difference, but by 20Y3 it had widened further, with Galdo charging £190.08 per club compared to £78.63 charged by AGE. Thus, the difference in sales volumes can be partially attributed to a shift along the demand curve caused by price changes, rather than a shift of the demand curve which would have suggested changes in underlying demand conditions.

The combined effects of price and volume are reflected in sales revenues which, as already noted, strongly favour the performance of Galdo over AGE.

In terms of export markets, Galdo is rather more dependent than AGE as 60% of sales come from export markets and, unlike AGE, this figure has remained steady throughout the period in question. Further information would be required on price, quantity and sales mix in to make more valid comparisons. Also, the specific countries to which exports are being made by the two companies would need to be known.

Market positioning

Based on price, it would appear that Galdo is in a significantly higher sector of the market than AGE and this is likely to have had an influence on performance as there is a different set of competitors.

Based on the above data, Galdo charges more than double per club than AGE and this gap has widened over the period 20Y1-20Y3 as AGE has reduced selling prices, while Galdo has increased them.

Given that Galdo's sales revenues have only fallen in line with the UK market average in this period despite the price increase, it appears that demand is more robust than for AGE, where sales revenues and volumes have fallen despite a price decrease.

These data provide some support for the chief executive's argument that the LazySwing brand can no longer compete at the high end of the market.

Profits

Whilst AGE's profits have declined severely to near zero, Galdo's operating profits have only suffered a more modest decline from £20 million to £17.6 million (12%). This is reflected in gross profit margins remaining at 30% and operating profit margins only falling from 20% in 20Y1 to 19.1% in 20Y3.

While AGE's revenues were 22% that of Galdo in 20Y1 its operating profit was only 7.5% that of Galdo indicating that Galdo is a more profitable company even after controlling for the size difference between the two companies. By 20Y3 AGE's operating profit has nearly fallen to zero and was only 0.3% that of Galdo.

Examiner's comments

The data analysis section was generally well answered, with most candidates making appropriate calculations in order to support sensible conclusions regarding relative performance. The majority of candidates examined both profit and revenue. Some also considered non-financial aspects such as R&D.

Concerning layout, whilst most candidates set out their calculations in an initial table, a minority mixed calculations within their discussion and this sometimes caused them to lose flow and structure. Some candidates looked at each year separately, while others looked only at the entire period.

Narrative explanations of relative performance over time, and in comparison to a larger competitor, Galdo, tended to be variable, depending partly on which calculations had been attempted. For example, those candidates who did not calculate revenue per club were less able to explain the overall decline in revenue for AGE.

The best answers compared and contrasted the performance of AGE and Galdo in terms of their relative positions/strategies in the industry, focusing, for example, on Galdo's ability to raise prices in a declining market and AGE's decline in revenue and sales volumes, despite a falling price per club.

The poorer answers made little attempt at identifying cause and effect relationships or key trends, for the most part simply re-stating the calculated numbers in terms of ups and downs.

22.2 Supply chain management

Supply chain management (SCM) is the management of all supply activities from the suppliers to a business through to delivery to customers. This may also be called demand chain management reflecting the idea that the customers' requirements and downstream orders should drive activity, based on the concept of end-to-end business (e2e). In essence it refers to managing the value system. SCM relates to the new products imported from China rather than the existing LazySwing products.

Key themes in SCM are Responsiveness, Reliability, Relationships. This raises important issues for AGE, but they appear to be the same for both strategies. Consideration of SCM is therefore important in determining if either strategy involving the Chinese imports is viable, but seems unlikely to be helpful in distinguishing between the two strategies.

- **Responsiveness** – the ability to supply customers quickly. This has led to the development of Just in Time (JIT) systems to keep raw materials acquisition, production and distribution as flexible as possible.

  Given the geographical distance between the UK and China then there are likely to be long lead times for orders. It is therefore essential that demand can be predicted throughout the year in order to avoid shortages and surpluses. The seasonal nature of outdoor sports could add to the difficulty of forecasting demand.

- **Reliability** – the ability to supply customers reliably. Service level agreements about the reliability of supplies should be made to enforce reliability.

- **Relationships** – the use of single sourcing and long-term contracts to better integrate the buyer and supplier. JiangGolf would appear to be a single source supplier which would assist in building relationships. However, it also builds dependency and there is a risk that if this supplier fails to deliver, for whatever reason, then AGE may be unable to supply its own customers.

A key further element is cost. It is clear that JiangGolf is cheaper than any European manufacturer of equivalent quality. This lower purchase cost needs to be balanced however with length and uncertainty over lead times.

The minimum of 100,000 golf clubs is an important constraint as it represents a high proportion of AGE's existing sales volumes. There needs to be a degree of confidence about demand volumes reaching this level before accepting this contract term. In this respect, Strategy 2 may be preferable as the lower price and the distribution through general sports equipment retailers may have a better chance of achieving higher sales volumes.

Market positioning

Market positioning relates to both the existing LazySwing products and the new products imported from China.

LazySwing products

Regarding the existing product, Lee has suggested that it may be trying to compete at too high a market position. Evidence to support this proposition is that price has been reduced but sales volumes have still fallen. While adverse market conditions are also a factor, Galdo was increasing its price over the same period, indicating it is moving upmarket.

In the absence of being able to set aside a large R&D budget, it appears likely that AGE does not have the resources to keep pace with its competitors at the high end of the market. Charging high prices without the corresponding quality is not offering customers a reasonable value proposition.

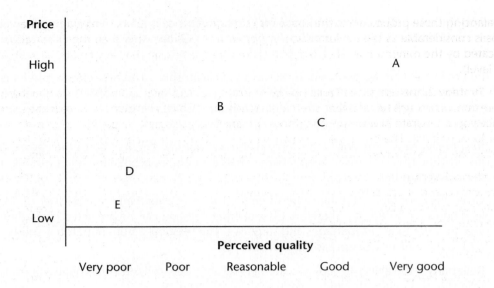

Thus in the above diagram the LazySwing brand on existing products manufactured in the UK, might be perceived to be at B. This would be dominated by product C which offers higher quality for a lower price.

In order to reposition the price would need to be reduced.

The suggestion of Lee to reduce the price to £55, from its current level of £78.63 (see table in 22.1) appears to be a move in this direction. The benefits might be increased sales volumes as LazySwing is now competing against mid-market competitors. There may also be a cost saving in R&D if there is a consumer expectation that LazySwing is not at the cutting edge of technology, but instead offers good value.

Tutorial note:

Other models such as Bowman's Clock could also have been used.

Imported goods from China

Regarding the market positioning of the imported clubs, this appears to have two possible market positions which are based on two different prices. At first sight, this might seem unusual in the context of the above diagram as the quality is the same no matter what the price and the market it is sold in. However, price can be a signal of perceived quality, as can the distribution channel used.

With Strategy 1, the imported clubs will be sold at an average price of £30 and distributed to high end specialist outlets. The price and the distribution channel might signal some degree of quality and thereby raise the market positioning as high as possible for the physical attributes of this product.

In Strategy 2 the same physical product will be sold at the lower price of £25 and distributed through channels which are further downmarket. The advantage of this is that sales volumes may increase as they are seen as better value and exposed to more potential customers.

Branding

It has already been noted that the two strategies for imported clubs involve the same physical product, but are distinguished by different prices and different distribution channels. A further distinction between the two products is their different branding.

With Strategy 1, the imported clubs use the upmarket LazySwing brand. In terms of creating a perception of quality and added value this is likely to help sales and support the higher price of £30 compared to Strategy 2. It also offers economies of scope in delivering through existing distribution channels. The downside is it might damage the perceived quality of the existing LazySwing clubs manufactured in the UK. In other words there may be confusion in the minds of consumers as to what the LazySwing brand stands for.

In balancing these propositions, the scope for damaging the sales of existing UK manufactured clubs is considerable as sales volumes are higher, at 234,000 per year, than the imported clubs as indicated by the minimum level of 100,000 (although it is recognised they could sell well beyond this level).

With Strategy 2, the use of the Eagle brand is unlikely to help sales at first as it is a new brand where consumers will be unaware of what it stands for. Over time however there is the opportunity to develop a separate brand message through marketing (eg, good value, low to mid-market, for occasional golfers). The brand will be initially perceived through the price of £25 and the distribution channel where consumers would not expect to see high quality equipment.

The main advantage with Strategy 2 might appear to be that the perceived quality of the existing LazySwing brand is protected. Even here however there is a risk in the sense that the AGE company name may itself be a brand. If consumers perceive that both Eagle and LazySwing are from the same company, there may be some reputational effect. In particular, the reputation as a manufacturer of golf clubs may be damaged once it becomes known that AGE is also an importer and wholesaler.

An additional brand risk for both strategies might be that JiangGolf sells to other UK manufacturers and wholesalers (or directly into the UK) and therefore the same golf clubs can be obtained elsewhere, under an alternative brand, perhaps at lower prices to consumers.

Conclusion

Careful consideration should be given to the business case for importing golf clubs. The clear downsides for both strategies are as follows:

- If it will not be possible to sell 100,000 units, then losses could be made from unsold inventories.

- There will be reputational damage to the LazySwing brand if there is brand confusion by customers.

Conversely, however, the existing strategy is failing and this would be an attempt to enter a different section of the market, whilst maintaining the existing products, having repositioned them.

Strategy 2 is recommended as more favourable as it has a greater probability of reaching 100,000 units with a lower price and it goes further towards protecting the existing LazySwing brand name by using a new brand. Nevertheless, significant market research is required before committing to either strategy.

Examiner's comments

Differences in candidate performance normally related to whether or not both strategies were fully evaluated in terms of both SCM, and also market positioning and branding. Poorer answers either only concentrated on one of the proposals, or mainly on either market positioning or SCM. Often, a sub-heading would be provided (eg, SCM) but then the following discussion focused mainly on market positioning, and vice versa.

Only a minority of candidates made explicit reference to the RRR framework under SCM, and some of these did not use the framework very well to inform discussion.

A majority considered adopting a mid-market position by AGE to be an example of pursuing Porter's 'stuck in the middle' strategy, with only a few referring to Bowman's clock or the price/quality trade-off matrix.

Under branding, the majority recognised the possible risk, with Strategy 1, of damage to the perceived quality of existing LazySwing products.

A majority of those who provided conclusions recommended Strategy 2 for the imported clubs.

22.3 Ethics pertains to whether a particular behaviour is deemed acceptable in the context under consideration.

In making any ethical evaluation it is first necessary to establish the facts. In this case, it needs to be established whether the disclosure about Gary is true and whether his behaviour is in fact against the law. Since the information came from a fellow professional golfer, who may be Gary's rival, it is very possible that it is false information given to damage Gary's reputation, and therefore must be carefully checked.

A key ethical principle is illegality ie, whether there is a legal duty for Lee to disclose Gary's conduct (eg, if any crime had only been committed in another country this might not be the case). If there is a legal duty there is a clear ethical imperative for Lee to obey the law.

A second ethical principle is self-interest. If there is a disclosure then AGE would lose value and Lee would also lose income. If disclosure is made on ethical grounds, then this would therefore be at a personal cost to Lee and a corporate cost to AGE.

A third ethical issue is that Lee was told 'in confidence' and therefore any public disclosure could be deemed a breach of that confidence.

A fourth ethical issue relates to honesty. Gary is being held out as a golfer with integrity, when Lee at least knows this may not be true and is therefore knowingly deceiving customers.

A key final ethical issue is the distinction between the ethics of the individual (Lee) and the corporate ethics of AGE.

In making a decision as to how to proceed, it may be helpful to apply the Institute of Business Ethics three tests:

- Transparency
- Effect
- Fairness

Transparency – at the moment Lee is the only person in AGE management who knows of the allegations. If the AGE board is to make an ethical choice then it needs to be informed of what is known, albeit that it may want to ascertain the facts. Lee has a duty to his fellow directors and to the company to disclose to them and thereby aid transparency, as there may be consequences for AGE and its stakeholders.

Effect – whom does the decision affect/hurt? Almost everyone directly concerned with the issue (Lee, AGE and Gary) stands to lose from disclosure. However, there is a wider public interest and a question of honesty to wider customers. There is also an ethical principle of 'doing the right thing' irrespective of the consequences.

Fairness – would maintaining secrecy of what could have occurred be considered fair by those affected? The issue for AGE and Lee is that they may be condoning the actions of Gary by continuing to support him and promote the brand while knowing that the image of integrity is false.

Response

An initial action would be for Lee to challenge Gary in relation to the claims being made about him and obtain any evidence.

Unless the evidence is conclusive that the claims about Gary are untrue, Lee has a duty to report the facts to the other board members, as the interests of AGE may be affected.

Lee and AGE may also take legal advice whether they have a duty to disclose the illegal act to the police and the right to disclose it to the public.

If there is evidence to support the allegation, the contract should be terminated or there should be public disclosure of what is known, so an honest position is presented to the public and to customers.

If there is not to be immediate public disclosure then the issue of transparency to other stakeholders should also be considered (existing customers, suppliers, employees).

Examiner's comments

Too many candidates failed to use appropriate ethical language or apply relevant ethical principles. Many candidates failed to identify the necessary actions that should be taken as required by the question. Many candidates also failed to recognise the key point that it is necessary to establish the facts, and not to act on rumours concerning the alleged drug-taking. Those who identified that fact-finding needed to take place and then gave options for actions, including disclosure to the authorities if illegal activities had taken place, scored well. Weaker candidates tended to describe the commercial risks to the company presented by the scenario, rather than the ethical issues.

23 Best Fresh Bakeries Ltd (June 2014)

Marking guide

	Knowledge	Skill	Marks
23.1 Risks (Best Fresh Bakeries and Stakeholders)	3	10	12
23.2 Transfer pricing	2	8	9
23.3 Governance	2	6	7
	7	24	28

General comments:

The scenario in this question relates to a family company with five shops, each baking and retailing food. The company is owned by Henry, who owns 80% of the shares, and his two sons, who own the remaining shares. The three family members comprise the board of directors.

The sons want to expand by building a central baking facility to transfer internally to the shops and to sell to third parties. Henry has different risk preferences to his sons and does not wish to incur the cost and risk of expansion. Brief biographies of the board members are provided.

A governance issue has arisen whereby the two sons are attempting to push the expansion decision through the board by outvoting their father. Henry is considering appointing two friends as non-executive directors so he effectively has the majority of board votes.

23.1 (a) Risks for BFB

The plan for expansion has significant strategic, operating and financial risks for BFB.

Strategic risks

These are the risks associated with the long term strategic objectives of the business.

The new investment in a centralised baking facility risks departing from the core marketing slogan of the business which is: 'Baked and sold on the premises on the same day.'

Whilst it will still be on the 'same day' it will not be baked on the individual shop premises and hence the change will be visible to customers. Even if there is no change in quality, this may be perceived by customers to be the case, given the overt change in the scale of baking.

More particularly, quality assurance for large scale production is more difficult than for small scale production and the brand being associated with 'high quality' may suffer from a strategy of 'high volume'.

Pricing strategy may also need to change if actual, or perceived, quality changes.

An additional strategic risk is that BFB products from the new bakery will be available to third parties who may then compete with BFB's shops, thereby reducing its sales directly to the public.

It may be that the new strategy of higher volumes will be successful and the additional sales will compensate for any lost sales from reduced quality. However, a change in strategy is a risk as this is a different market sector to the current core market.

Operating risks

The scale of the new baking facility is significant at £2 million, relative to existing operations with net assets of £3 million.

The operating gearing will be increased significantly by the new baking facility. The initial cost is £2 million, but also manufacturing is likely to have high fixed operating costs relative to variable costs. The means that profits will be volatile relative to changes in sales.

The high fixed costs are also likely to raise the break-even point. One measure of risk would be whether the break-even point is significantly above the level of internal sales, which would require significant external sales to make it viable.

Exit costs are likely to be significant if the venture fails, as there is likely to be a large financial commitment to specialist baking equipment which is likely to have a low realisable value.

Further operational risk arises from the management of a centralised baking facility and dealing with commercial customers, both of which may be outside the core competences of a management team that has experience only in managing small-scale shops with individual retail customers.

There would be a distribution risk in transporting fresh produce from the bakery to the shops. In the past this did not arise as baking was carried out on the premises. There are also health and safety risks arising from distribution.

Financial risks

The additional borrowing generates additional financial gearing which raises financial risks. This means that residual earnings after interest payments will be more volatile and there is increased risk of insolvency if repayments on the loan cannot be made.

This means that cash flows may be at risk, and therefore going concern could be questionable, if sales do not match expectations.

In dealing with commercial customers, rather than only retail customers, there is increased credit risk from bad debts.

(b) **Shareholder-director risks**

Henry

Henry's potential exposure if the business fails as a result of the new venture is the value of his shareholding of £4 million (£5m × 80%). There would also be the loss of some future income although, as he is nearing retirement, this may not be substantial.

It may also be that Henry might need to make personal guarantees for the new lending.

If the new venture fails (even if BFB survives) the value of BFB shares will fall, so Henry will be at risk from a reduced payment for his shares on retirement. Given he is risk averse, then Henry would be accepting significant risk from the new venture and it may not therefore be desirable for him.

Ralph and Nigel (common risks)

Their 10% shareholdings are at risk if the company fails (£500,000 each)

If the company fails completely, their future income as directors over many years is also at risk.

If the project succeeds, then there is a risk that the value of BFB shares will rise and the brothers may not then be able to afford to acquire Henry's shares when he retires.

There is also the risk of board conflict and loss of Henry's support. This may mean that they are removed from the board by Henry and not offered the opportunity to acquire Henry's shares on his retirement.

Ralph

Other than his shares, Ralph has few personal assets for creditors to attack, even if he has given personal guarantees.

The risky nature of the project is not inconsistent with his attitude of being willing to take 'reasonably high risks'.

For Ralph, the project may be acceptable as he will share in the upside potential and the risks are both limited by his low asset ownership and appropriate to his risk preferences.

Nigel

Nigel is risk neutral so may be less accepting of the common risks than Ralph. Also he has personal assets which would be at risk if personal guarantees have been given.

Overall it may be questionable that Nigel should accept the risks. His supportive attitude to the project may mean he has high expectations that the project will succeed and therefore accepts the associated risks. Alternatively, it could mean that he has not fully considered, or fully comprehended, all the risks.

Examiner's comments

This was generally well answered. The better answers considered strategic, financial and operating risks for BFB as a whole. However, some candidates tended to concentrate too much on financial risks at the expense of other risks. Weaker candidates did not identify different types of risks and merely listed risks randomly.

Most candidates considered the three different stakeholder perspectives, but explicit discussion of overlapping risks was only provided by a small minority.

23.2 A transfer price is the price at which one division in a group sells its products or services to another division in the same group.

The transfer prices will be important for BFB as they have a number of implications:

- They determine the profits of divisions. If the baking facility division charges a high transfer price, then most of the total profit from company sales will be attributed to it, with less to the individual shops. This will give a false measure of performance for both divisions.

- If high transfer prices are passed on to ultimate customers then sales volumes may fall and overall profits may be distorted.

- Inappropriate transfer prices can lead to dysfunctional decisions. If either division believes it can get a better deal from outside markets it may take it. For example, if the shop managers could obtain supplies of equal quality at lower cost from third parties then they may, if permitted, choose to purchase outside the company, leaving the baking facility division with reduced sales. Conversely, if transfer prices are too low, then the baking facility division management might supply to alternative channels at a higher price and leave the shops without an internal supply of produce.

The likelihood of these implications being realised depends on the way in which the transfer prices are set and imposed. There are a number of choices:

(1) Cost-based methods of setting transfer prices

This method leads to the inevitable problem of deciding which cost to use:

- **Full cost**: the variable costs plus an amount to cover the baking facility's overheads. This leaves the baking facility division in a break-even situation from internal sales if based on actual full cost. There may be some surplus/deficit arising from efficiencies or overruns if based on budgeted full cost. The baking facility division may make profit from its external sales.

- **Variable cost** (or marginal cost): this leaves the baking facility division making nil contribution and so enduring losses equal to its fixed costs from internal sales.

- **Opportunity cost**: the revenue forgone by not selling the item to the highest bidder.

In terms of cost-based transfer prices, optimal transfer pricing requires that divisions sell components at the higher of variable cost and opportunity cost.

(2) **Other methods of setting transfer prices**

The following methods of transfer pricing enable the baking facility division to record a profit.

- **Negotiated prices**: the transfer price is established by discussions between the baking facility division managers and shop managers in a bargaining process.

- **Two-part transfer prices**: the transfer price is set at variable cost to ensure corporate optimality but, in addition to this price, the baking facility division records an extra amount in its sales to arrive at a profit figure for evaluation purposes.

- **Dual pricing**: the shops record the transfer at the baking facility's standard variable cost which may aid decision making. The baking facility division reports the transfer at a higher value (eg, cost plus) to give a profit incentive. This should lead to goal congruence but may lead to poor cost control as profits are made more easily. The accounting problem makes this method unpopular.

- **Market prices**: transfer prices are set according to market prices to external customers. In this case the baking facility division charges the same price internally to BFB shops as to its external customers.

Conclusion

Transfer prices could be set by negotiation where the outcome is influenced strongly by market prices charged to third party customers by the baking facility division. This would recognise the opportunity of either division to buy from or sell into external markets on an arm's length basis.

Examiner's comments

This was reasonably well answered, on the whole. Most candidates understood the key issues involved in setting transfer prices between the divisions, and provided possible methods for setting the prices. Better answers also gave due consideration to motivation/incentives and goal congruence.

The best candidates, a very small minority, also outlined the correct principles for transfer prices – set the price at the opportunity cost of the supplying division which will be variable cost if the division has spare capacity, or variable cost plus lost contribution on external sales if at full capacity.

The vast majority of candidates failed to recommend how transfer prices should be set but instead gave a number of different options.

23.3 Governance

At its broadest, governance covers all aspects of operating and controlling the organisation including its structure and systems. Governance affects the organisational structure, determines objectives of an organisation and influences the relationship between the organisation's management, its board of directors and its shareholders.

BFB is a small private company so it has a simple structure with family-based ownership and control around three individuals. As a private company, BFB is not bound by the UK Corporate Governance Code. Nevertheless, aspects of the Code may act as guidance to best practice.

Nigel's and Ralph's voting intentions

Henry's position as the 80% shareholder gives him control over the votes in shareholder meetings.

However he does not control board meetings where he has only one of the three votes. There is therefore a conflict of control between BFB's two key decision-making bodies.

Henry has ultimate long term control both for ordinary resolutions (requiring 50% of the votes) and for special resolutions (requiring 75% of the votes) which may be needed to change a shareholder agreement. Ultimately he can therefore remove Nigel and Ralph as members of the board and take control of the board himself.

Moreover, it is clear that, from a governance perspective, best practice and company law support the view that Henry's interests, as the major shareholder, are paramount.

However, unless and until Henry decides to remove his sons as directors, the board controls the short term decisions of the company and Ralph and Nigel, acting jointly, control the board.

Nevertheless, in exercising such control the board has certain duties to act in the interests of shareholders. While not binding on BFB, the UK Corporate Governance Code embodies a shareholder-led approach to corporate governance.

In particular, the board is responsible for determining the nature and extent of the significant risks it is willing to take in achieving its strategic objectives. The board should maintain sound risk management and internal control systems. There should be emphasis on risk assessment and management, and on the long-term sustainable success of the company based on its business model.

In governance terms therefore there needs to be some agreement between the board controlled by the two brothers, and the shareholders controlled by Henry, if the company is to be managed effectively.

In conclusion, the brothers' threat to vote against Henry and exercise their short-term power over the board: is not productive in terms of effective management; is not in accordance with a board's duty to shareholders; and is not sustainable in that Henry has ultimate control over board membership.

Jon's suggestions

It is best practice that a board should include an appropriate combination of executive and non-executive directors such that no individual or small group of individuals can dominate the board's decision taking. Part of the role of the non-executives can be seen as preventing a company from being run for the personal benefit of its executive directors, rather than the shareholders.

Whilst Jon's suggestion is in accordance with this theme, by preventing Nigel and Ralph from controlling the board, it offers up the alternative of promoting control by Henry as a dominant individual.

In particular, non-executive directors should be independent from the executive directors. Jon and Gemma would merely be aligned with Henry, so the governance weakness that Jon is trying to prevent would be replaced by an alternative weakness.

Moreover, NEDs should be appointed by a formal selection process and the appointment approved by the board. It is not for Henry to appoint them on his own.

Examiner's comments

Answers were variable in quality. Many candidates either concentrated on the conflict between directors and shareholders or, specifically, the role of NEDs, but often not on both.

Only a few related the discussion back to the risk attitude profiles of the respective directors, indicating that the shift of power to Henry may be good for him, given his risk averseness, but not good for the company as a whole in that a potentially value-adding expansion may be rejected. Many candidates reflected on the ethics of Henry appointing two friends as NEDs, but few indicated that the decision on appointment is not his own personal decision but that of the shareholders as a whole.

Some candidates discussed the UK Corporate Governance Code, but did not qualify its applicability in the circumstances.

24 ElectroInfo Ltd (June 2014)

Marking guide

	Knowledge	Skill	Marks
24.1 Pricing – current and low income			
(a) Calculation of price per chargeable hour	3	2	
(b) Feasibility and benefits of charging different prices	–	8	
			12
24.2 Pricing – IT and Electrical	2	8	9
24.3 Depot heads – set prices locally	3	9	11
	8	27	32

General comments:

This scenario is about the pricing policies of a small company providing electrical and IT services to households. The company currently has 30 depots, all of which provide both services at a uniform price.

The directors are considering three alternative new policies: (1) price discriminate between households based on an approximation of incomes; (2) price each service differently; (3) allow autonomy of pricing for each depot manager locally. Market research has provided data which is available to show customer demand at a range of prices, analysed by customer type and type of service.

24.1 (a) Total demand

Price £	30	32	34	36
Variable cost £	20	20	20	20
Contribution per hr £	10	12	14	16
Demand	250,000	230,000	200,000	160,000
Total contribution	2,500,000	2,760,000	**2,800,000**	2,560,000

Thus the optimal price if charged uniformly to all customers is **£34** per session generating a total contribution of **£2.8 million**. This implies a price increase of **£2** per chargeable hour if uniform pricing is to continue.

Income
Low incomes

Price	30	32	34	36
Variable cost	20	20	20	20
Contribution per hr	10	12	14	16
Demand	85,000	70,000	45,000	20,000
Total contribution	**850,000**	840,000	630,000	320,000

Other customers

Price	30	32	34	36
Variable cost	20	20	20	20
Contribution per hr	10	12	14	16
Demand	165,000	160,000	155,000	140,000
Total contribution	1,650,000	1,920,000	2,170,000	**2,240,000**

With price discrimination based on incomes, the optimal prices per hour would be:

Low income households: £30
Other customers £36

This would generate a total contribution of:

Low income households: £0.85m
Other customers   £2.24m
Total   **£3.09m**

(b) **Discussion**

Feasibility

In order to for it to be feasible to gain advantage from price discrimination (ie, charging different prices for a similar product/service in different parts of the market) it is necessary for:

- there to be different levels of price sensitivity in each market (ie, different price elasticities)
- the markets to be segregated, so there is minimal leakage between them

To the extent that market research is reliable, it appears from the data provided that the level of price resistance (ie, price elasticity) for the two income groups is significantly different.

As the home address for IT or electrical services should be known before a price is quoted, it should be possible to estimate the value of the house from various on-line databases. However, the house value is only a rough representation for income. It is not likely to be feasible that incomes can be directly identified.

Although the market can be separated by charging different prices to different customers, if there is leakage of information between the two groups, then this may cause a loss of goodwill in the 'other customers' group, as they will have paid more per hour for the same work. This may make the operation of price discrimination more difficult, if not unfeasible. In reality, it may be hard for 'other customers' to discern the hourly rate just by knowing an overall price for a job.

Benefits

From the above table, the price discrimination policy based on incomes gives a higher overall contribution than uniform pricing for all customers, as it optimises the price in each of the two separate market segments, rather than merely the market in total.

Using the above data, the price for low income households should be reduced from the current level of £32 per hour to £30 per hour. This is advantageous to EIL, as this low income group is price sensitive (ie, there is high price elasticity) and the 6% price decrease (from £32 to £30) leads to a 21% increase in demand in terms of chargeable hours (from 70,000 to 85,000). This leads to an increased contribution of £10,000 from this group.

This increase in demand might reflect the price spectrum of sole trader competitors which is up to £28 per hour. Pricing at only £2 above this rate, EIL may appeal to many low income households wishing to obtain a good quality service and who are prepared to pay a small amount extra for this, but, for many of this potential customer group, not as much as the current price of £32 per hour.

The sensitivity of demand to price changes for 'other customers' is much lower. Using the above table, the price to 'other customers' should increase from the current level of £32 per hour to £36 per hour. This is advantageous to EIL, as this customer group is less price sensitive than low income households and, although the price increase leads to a fall in demand of 12.5% (from 160,000 to 140,000), the 12.5% price increase (from £32 to £36) more than compensates for this in terms of additional contribution from this group (contribution increases by 16.7% (£1,920,000 to £2,240,000). Overall contribution from using price discrimination increases by 10.4% (from £2.8m to £3.09m).

Even if it is not possible to separate the markets, an additional contribution can be gained compared to the current situation by increasing the overall price from £32 to £34 per hour. This will increase total contribution from £2.76m to £2.8m.

A key factor in attaining the above benefits is whether the market research is accurate. Concerns may include the following:

- The market research only explored prices up to £36 and the 'other customers' had the optimal price at this level within the range explored. However, had the research gone up to £38 and beyond, then these higher prices may have provided an even higher level of contribution

- Use of questionnaire data where customers' responses may not reflect their actual behaviour

- Past data on reaction to price changes may not reflect future behaviour to a different set of price changes

- The value of a house may not accurately reflect the available income of the householders

- There are likely to be a range of factors other than income which will impact on a customer's price resistance (eg, costs, competitors' prices, wealth, service quality)

Examiner's comments

Most candidates arrived at correct calculations and thereby could make sensible comments regarding the pros and cons of price discrimination based on income. A significant minority, however, incorrectly used revenue, rather than contribution, in their calculations. Some of these candidates said that as variable cost per unit does not change then only price/revenue needs to be used, which is not correct.

Both in this requirement, and the next requirement, a small minority attempted price elasticity of demand calculations, but failed to produce systematic calculations of contribution. Some limited credit was given for such an approach.

A majority considered discrimination based on income, in the way proposed, to be a bad idea for various reasons, especially as house values may be a poor indicator of relative income.

There was a minority who calculated average prices coming out with chargeable rates within pence of each other yet not realising they may have approached it wrongly.

Hardly any candidates made the point that prices beyond £36 could also have been explored by the market research.

24.2

Service type

IT services

Price per hour	£30	£32	£34	£36
Variable cost per hour	£20	£20	£20	£20
Contribution per hour	£10	£12	£14	£16
Demand	125,000	120,000	110,000	100,000
Total contribution	£1,250,000	£1,440,000	£1,540,000	**£1,600,000**

Electricals

Price per hour	£30	£32	£34	£36
Variable cost per hour	£20	£20	£20	£20
Contribution per hour	£10	£12	£14	£16
Demand	125,000	110,000	90,000	60,000
Total contribution	£1,250,000	**£1,320,000**	£1,260,000	£960,000

With price differentiation based on service type, the optimal prices per hour would be:

IT services	£36
Electrical	£32

This would generate a total contribution of:

IT services	£1.60m
Electrical	£1.32m
Total	**£2.92m**

Discussion

Feasibility

There would appear to be few problems of feasibility in charging different prices for the two types of service in terms of operationalising the policy. The two services are carried out by different employees and all that is required is appropriate time keeping records.

In terms of the feasibility in the market place of being able to charge different prices for the two types of service, this will depend on whether such differential pricing is acceptable to customers.

Benefits

This policy is not price discrimination as they are different types of service. The pricing policy that EIL has followed appears to be a cost based pricing policy, in that it would appear (based on the finance director's quote) that the company believes that if costs are the same, then prices should be the same.

An alternative view would be to let markets dictate optimal prices and therefore, if the two types of service are valued differently in the marketplace, they should be priced differently.

If the two services are priced according to their own markets then the above table shows that this policy gives a higher overall contribution than uniform pricing for both types of service, as it optimises the price in each of the two separate markets, rather than merely in total.

Using the above data, the price for IT services should be increased by £4 from the current level of £32 per hour to £36 per hour. The IT services market appears more resilient to higher prices than electrical services. This may be because they are more highly valued by customers or because of the pricing policies and availability of competitors. This higher price is advantageous to EIL as although it leads to a fall in demand for IT services of 16.7% (from 120,000 hours to 100,000 hours), the 12.5% price increase (from £32 to £36) more than compensates for this in terms of additional contribution from this group (contribution increases by 11.1% (£1,440,000 to £1,600,000)).

The table also shows that the current price of £32 per hour is optimal for electrical services. As a result, the contribution from electrical services would be unchanged.

Overall contribution from differential pricing of the two types of service is that contribution increases from £2.76m to £2.92m (ie, 5.8%).

As already noted, even if there was homogeneous pricing for both services, an additional contribution can be gained, compared to the current situation, by increasing the price from £32 to £34 per hour. This will increase total contribution from £2.76m to £2.8m.

Examiner's comments

Similar points regarding the use of revenue, rather than contribution, as were made in requirement 24.1 above, also apply here.

The majority concluded that considering price variation based on services, rather than incomes, was an improvement and did not suffer from many of the problems associated with the latter.

Many candidates incorrectly referred to the service approach as price discrimination, with only a small minority pointing out that it differs in principle from price discrimination.

24.3 Evaluation

The market analysis above examines only a limited range of the factors that need to be considered in pricing. Namely:

- a narrow range of specified prices
- demand according to incomes
- demand according to type of service
- variable costs

In order to achieve a more robust overall pricing strategy other factors need to be considered.

In so doing, there are two alternatives to the chief executive's suggestion of local pricing:

- The centre sets prices that apply to all depots.
- Separate prices are set for each depot based on local conditions.

Further information is required in this respect to clarify the alternative benchmark against which the local pricing policy is being judged.

In evaluating the chief executive's suggestion two key issues arise:

(1) The way in which prices are set (eg, who, when, how, why)
(2) The factors to be considered in setting prices

(1) **The way prices are set**

The above data analysis is static (ie, at a point in time). Market conditions are likely to change and therefore a method of setting prices according to changing markets over time is required, not just a decision on a revision of existing prices on a one-time basis. Consideration therefore needs to be given to how frequently they are reset and this requires a degree of agility in decision making which would be more appropriate at local depot level than for the company as a whole.

There is therefore some support for the CE's suggestion that local determination of prices by depot managers is a more responsive method of setting prices which can take account of local conditions and indeed, price based on individual transactions, rather than for groups of customers or types of service.

(2) **Factors to be considered in setting prices**

There are a range of factors that need to be considered in setting prices. The key question in this context is whether depot managers are better positioned to consider these factors than the centre.

Leakage – as the depots are 50km apart and the range for each depot is 25km then there is no leakage between markets if differential prices are set between depots (ie, there is no internal competition).

Variable costs – the average variable cost is £20 per hour across the company. However this is an average and may vary both (1) between depots and (2) within depots for different jobs. For example, there may be a variation between depots due to a need to pay higher wages for depots nearer London. Within depots, a job 25km away may be more expensive than a job 1km from the depot. These variations are almost impossible to accommodate centrally, but could be allowed for at local level with local knowledge.

Fixed costs – information is not provided on fixed costs so this is required. However, it seems likely that fixed costs will vary between depots. For example, there may be a variation between property costs, such as rentals, between depots nearer London and those further away from London. Whilst not relevant to short term pricing, the level of fixed costs would be relevant to a long term pricing strategy in order to make a reasonable return on investment.

Price discrimination – local knowledge of housing and individuals could enable a series of prices, based on a series of income levels, rather than just the two suggested by the market survey.

Competition – the industry is quite diverse between smaller sole proprietors and larger IT/electrics companies. The nature and intensity of the competition is therefore likely to vary between depots. Even if the centre is aware of this variation in local competition, it is not easy to set prices centrally for each depot as local conditions may change rapidly.

Employee level price variation – it appears there is uniform remuneration of operational employees. Notwithstanding this, the level of skill and experience is likely to vary between employees which may enable differential prices to be charged for their services based on local knowledge. Thus, for example, higher prices can be charged for more skilled or more popular employees (eg, based on customer requests).

The counter-argument

The above arguments tend to support the CE's view of a local pricing policy based on local knowledge of markets and operating conditions. However the counter view may include a few issues:

- By surrendering price control to depot managers there is a loss of control and more uncertainty at the centre.

- Depot managers may lack the experience of setting appropriate prices.

- Customers may in the long run prefer more certainty over prices and thus prefer uniform and stable prices over variable and varying prices.

Implementation

In order to be able to implement the policy of local pricing at depot level, the degree of autonomy of depot managers needs to increase significantly and this raises a series of questions relating to implementation including decision making authority, accountability, the role and competence of depot managers, and internal reporting mechanisms.

Decision making authority – giving depot managers additional autonomy in setting prices raises the question of whether this should be the only devolution of authority from the centre. For example, it may be difficult to uncouple the pricing decision from other issues surrounding pricing and which arise from a change in price, such as a change in demand. In the above table, the decision to raise the price of IT services by £4 per hour to £36 causes demand to fall from 120,000 hours pa to 100,000 hours pa. The human resource operations of this consequence therefore need to be considered alongside, and possibly in advance of, the pricing decision. To best achieve this, the local manager would also need autonomy over staffing as a consequence of having autonomy over pricing.

Accountability – in devolving decision making there is a corresponding duty of accountability on a depot manager in being responsible for those decisions and their consequences. This is likely to have consequences for internal reporting mechanisms as they report back to the centre.

Training and competence – depot managers would need the appropriate level of training in order to be competent in their wider role and to enable them to make appropriate pricing and related operating decisions.

Conclusion

Greater flexibility is needed in pricing. One conclusion would be to adopt both the policies of price discrimination based on estimated household incomes and differential pricing of IT and electrical services, but at depot level.

Further analysis of existing information from the market survey at depot level is required to be able to do this. It will require analysing responses for each of the two services according to the two income groupings.

Overall, making prices respond more flexibility to market conditions, service types and customer characteristics will present a more complex pricing structure, but there is significant scope to increase profits if this can be implemented at local level by competent managers with local knowledge and the consequences controlled at central level.

Examiner's comments

This part was the weakest part of the question for most candidates. Many referred to goal congruence issues, but often without providing examples of a lack of goal congruence.

A few candidates made the point that the geographical boundaries between depots may be unclear, thereby questioning the quality of any relative performance data.

Many candidates talked about customers going to another depot – they were failing to notice the point that this is a home service where an engineer comes to your house and you will be served by a specific depot. Those who discussed implementation issues arising from the change in structure for decision making scored well, but many ignored this element of the question.

25 Forsi Ltd (September 2014)

Marking guide

	Knowledge	Skill	Marks
25.1 Performance analysis/non-financial information	2	16	16
25.2 Exisiting structure	2	5	7
25.3 Knowledge management/implementation	3	6	8
25.4 (a) Subsidiary/forensic science division	3	6	
(b) Change management recommendations	2	5	
			14
	12	38	45

General comments:

This is the mini case at 45 marks and also the data analysis question. It was the best attempted question on the paper.

The scenario relates to a company – Forsi Ltd – which provides forensic science services to both public organisations (police, HMRC) and private clients. It was created when the UK government closed its inefficient state forensic science service and four of its leading scientists set up on their own. Forsi experienced rapid growth and quickly had to employ more scientists but over the last two years competition in the market has increased. The company has operated with an informal structure, wanting to minimise bureaucracy and focus on technical expertise. Most support tasks (payroll, accounting etc) are outsourced. Work is organised on a project basis, with an appropriate team created for each specific client request. Recently Forsi's loose structure has started to inhibit growth. There has been a lack of collaboration, with scientists preferring to work independently on each project and with delays because all discussions with clients are still handled by the four initial founders. Forsi has experienced cost overruns as there is little in-house financial control. As a result it has started to lose some contracts to competitors or has had to accept lower margins as a result of fixed price agreements. Forsi has been approached by an Australian multi-national (Aussi) which offers a range of scientific services to global private and public clients. Its forensic science division is the Australian market leader. Aussi wants to buy Forsi but does not want to destroy Forsi's research-centred culture and acknowledges its success to date has been dependent on the founders' knowledge and contacts. Aussi is not sure whether to operate Forsi as a separate subsidiary or a division but whatever the structure selected, Forsi will be required to comply with more stringent targets on price, margins and ROCE. Candidates were provided with a balanced scorecard of financial and non-financial data on Forsi and basic operating data for Aussi.

Appendix of calculations

Tutorial note:

A wide range of calculations is provided here for marking purposes. Candidates were not expected to produce all of these for the marks available

	Forsi 20Y2	Forsi 20Y3	Aussi Forensic science division 20Y3
Sales revenue £million	5.4	5.088 (2.3% of Aussi)	220.3
Direct costs £million	4.175	4.165 (2.5% of Aussi)	165.225
Gross profit £million	1.225	0.923 (1.7% of Aussi)	55.075
R&D £million	0.254	0.260 (5.9% of Aussi)	4.4
Marketing £million	0.108	0.090 (1.0% of Aussi)	9.000
Other operating expenses £million	0.268	0.270 (3.1% of Aussi)	8.645
Operating profit £million	0.595	0.303 (1.0% of Aussi)	33.03
Asset value £million	4.02	3.91 (2.1% of Aussi)	183.5
Gross margin	22.7%	18.1%	25.0%
Operating margin	11.2%	6.0%	15.0%
ROCE	14.8%	7.7%	18.0%
R&D as % of sales	4.7%	5.1%	2.0%
Marketing as % of sales	2.0%	1.8%	4.1%
Other operating expenses as % of sales	5.0%	5.3%	3.9%
Order book as % of revenue	25%	16.8%	29.5%
Order book (months)	3	2	3.5
No of employees	45	45 (2.25% of Aussi)	2,000
Revenue per employee	120,000	113,067	110,150

	Forsi 20Y2	Forsi 20Y3	Aussi Forensic science division 20Y3
Per project			
Average value of project	50,000	48,000	89,992
Direct cost per project	38,657	39,292	67,494
GP per project	11,343	8,708	22,498
No of projects	108	106 (4.3% of Aussi)	2,448
No of projects completed on time	90 (83%)	81 (76%)	2,179 (89%)
No of projects completed late	18 (17%)	25 (24%)	269 (11%)
No of projects completed in budget	78 (72%)	69 (65%)	2,252 (92%)

Forsi: Year on year change	%
Sales revenue	–5.8
Direct costs	–0.2
Gross profit	–24.7
R&D	+0.2
Marketing	–16.7
Other operating expenses	+0.7
Operating profit	–49.1
Net asset value	–2.7%
No of employees	No change
No of projects	–1.9
Order book	–36.7

Analysis of performance

Whilst still profitable, Forsi's performance has deteriorated significantly between 20Y2 and 20Y3, with a £312,000 drop in sales revenue (5.8%) and a £292,000 drop in operating profit. As a result, operating profit at £303,000 is only just over half the previous year's figure.

Sales

Sales revenue has fallen by just under 6%. The number of projects undertaken in the year was broadly similar (106 compared to 108) but the average project value has fallen from £50,000 to £48,000 which may reflect the price pressure that Forsi has been experiencing and the fact that it has had to agree lower prices to avoid losing clients. Forsi is very small in relation to Aussi's forensic science division – its revenue is only 2.3% of Aussi's. At £89,992 Aussi's revenue per project is almost twice that of Forsi's which could be a result of different pricing strategies or projects of a different size/nature.

In addition by the end of 20Y3, the value of Forsi's order book represents two months' worth of sales, compared to three months at the end of 20Y2. This suggests that order levels are falling and could either represent a lack of demand or an increased failure to win client tenders. More information is needed in this area (see below).

Forsi spent £18,000 less on marketing in 20Y3, a drop of 16.7% compared to the previous year, which could have had a negative effect on revenue, given the increasingly competitive environment. Its marketing expenditure as a % of sales is only 1.8% compared to Aussi's 4.1%. It is possible that awareness of the founders' expertise through word-of-mouth recommendations or existing contacts is diminishing and that more marketing needs to be undertaken to raise awareness of the company's services.

Given the increasing number of specialist providers, Forsi may be losing projects in particular areas of forensic science, so an analysis of revenue by field of expertise would be useful.

Revenue per employee is above that for Aussi (£110,150) although it has fallen from £120,000 to £113,067 which could reflect a lack of productivity due to delays experienced when project requirements are being re-negotiated, or an increase in the amount of scientists' time that is non-chargeable. Alternatively it could reflect the pressure on prices that has been discussed previously or the increased number of fixed price projects. Aussi's figure may be lower if it has more administrative staff – the statistic would be more meaningful if information were available to calculate it based on the number of fee earning employees.

Gross margin

The gross margin has fallen from 22.7% to 18.1%. This is below the 25% achieved by Aussi and less than the 20% target that would be required if Forsi was acquired.

Whilst revenue per project has fallen by 4%, direct costs per project have increased by 1.6%. The deterioration in gross margin could reflect a drop in recovery rates – compared to 20Y2, 7 more projects over-ran on time and/or budgeted cost. If clients are increasingly dissatisfied they may be refusing to pay for the over-runs and Forsi may be having to write off time/money spent on the project.

Expenses

With the exception of marketing (discussed above), expenditure on R&D and other operating costs has not changed significantly. As a % of revenue, Forsi spends more on R&D than Aussi, possibly because the latter has greater efficiencies/economies of scale.

ROCE

The halving of operating profit has resulted in a similar drop in ROCE, falling from 14.8% to 7.7%. This is considerably below Aussi's ROCE of 18% and the 15% target that Forsi would need to achieve if it were owned by Forsi.

Lack of management control

The fact that the number of projects over-running on time and/or budget has increased and is considerably worse than that achieved by Aussi suggests that Forsi's founders are not exerting sufficient control over costs and scheduling or that budgets are overly optimistic, perhaps in an attempt to win tenders. In some cases these over-runs may be unavoidable (eg, due to additional client demands) but in this case Forsi needs to ensure it has renegotiated passing these on to the client.

Other non-financial information that would be useful:

- Statistics on the number of tenders won vs the number actually submitted, including an analysis of which fields of forensic science these related to
- Details of the number of new clients won and existing clients lost during the year and the split of new projects/repeat business
- Breakdown of projects by private/public sector
- Amount of hours recharged to clients/hours actually spent on projects
- Breakdown of hours worked by scientists between client work and R&D
- Typical project length to establish average size of project team

Examiner's comments

In requirement 25.1, candidates were asked to analyse the performance of Forsi, contrasting it with Aussi's where appropriate and to suggest other non-financial information that may be useful.

The data analysis section was generally very well answered. Most candidates made some appropriate initial calculations based on the balance scorecard provided, in order to support sensible comments regarding Forsi's deteriorating performance. The majority of candidates examined revenue, margins and return on capital, and attempted to use the non-financial aspects, such as the increase in delays to project completion and the cost overruns, to explain the financial results. Whilst most candidates set out their calculations in an initial table, a minority mixed calculations within their discussion and this sometimes caused them to lose flow and structure or fail to address certain aspects. Some weaker candidates limited their analysis to the movement in figures across the two-year period.

Narrative explanations of relative performance in comparison to Aussi tended to be variable, depending partly on which calculations had been attempted. For example, those candidates who did not calculate ROCE were less able to discuss the shortfall between Forsi's current ROCE and gross margin and the targets that Aussi would require. The best answers compared and contrasted the performance of Aussi and Forsi, highlighting the vast difference in their size and market, and considering their relative performance in respect of the average size of the projects undertaken and their ability to complete on time and to budget.

The poorer answers made little attempt at identifying cause and effect relationships or key trends, for the most part simply re-stating the calculated numbers in terms of ups and downs. Weaker candidates also produced a generic list of additional information required, which was often financial, failing to address the specifics of the requirement which asked for non-financial information.

25.2 Existing structure:

Forsi undertakes specialised work based on expert knowledge. To some extent its structure has not really evolved from that of a simple entrepreneurial one, with the four original founders exerting total control over the running of the business.

One way of analysing Forsi's structure is with reference to Mintzberg's organisational configurations.

The key component (or building block) within Forsi appears to be the operating core, with scientists working directly on providing the technical forensic science service to clients.

Forsi's structure has developed incrementally and reflects the values and behaviour of the four original founders, who form the strategic apex of the organisation and currently control all client relationships.

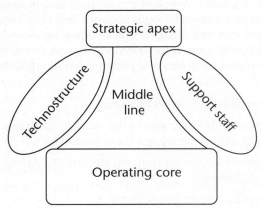

Its existing structure might be seen as Mintzberg's adhocracy or innovative configuration, suitable for a complex dynamic environment.

Key features of Forsi's structure are as follows:

- Research and innovation are key objectives and scientists (operating core) carry out their work independently.

- There is little formalisation (an absence of technostructure) and no layer of middle management (middle line). Staff are likely to be intelligent and self-motivated, with the expertise and knowledge to make the appropriate decisions whilst working in a project.

- Such a structure avoids the trappings of bureaucracy and remains flexible to encourage innovation.

- The number of support staff is limited as these functions (HR, accounting) are largely outsourced.

An alternative model might be Handy's shamrock organisation or flexible firm – with Forsi being seen as a lean organisation comprising a core of essential workers (scientists) providing specialist services to customers and supported by a contractual fringe of outside contractors, whose services are bought in as required.

Whilst the simple, flexible structure promotes innovation and allows Forsi to focus on the activities important for competitive advantage, there are some disadvantages and the informality and lack of control appear to be causing Forsi some difficulties now that it is a bigger organisation:

- The structure is lacking in coordination mechanisms

- Teams and scientists have a tendency to work in isolation rather than sharing knowledge. Such independence may result in a lack of goal congruence with personal interests being put before shared company ones

- Loose control and lack of financial awareness has led to cost overruns and impact on margins

- The founders acting as a go-between between scientists and clients has led to delays and client complaints

Recommendation:

- It may be better to have project managers responsible for liaison with the client

- Senior management could monitor projects and liaise externally to ensure Forsi is keeping abreast of industry developments, changes in competition/market. However this would necessitate an improved management information system to allow monitoring

Examiner's comments

Requirement 25.2 requested candidates to discuss the appropriateness of Forsi's existing structure, referring to relevant models. It was well attempted by the vast majority of candidates, who were clearly very well-prepared for this topic. The majority of candidates identified that the informal, largely entrepreneurial structure had initially fostered successful innovation and flexibility in a dynamic environment but was no longer suitable for the growing size of the company and was, at least in part, to blame for Forsi's deteriorating performance discussed in 25.1. Candidates were asked to refer to relevant models and those who discussed Forsi's structure with reference to Mintzberg's organisational forms and/or Handy's shamrock structure produced answers that had more depth than those who limited their discussion to functional, divisional and matrix structures.

25.3 Why knowledge management is important

Knowledge is a key strategic asset for an organisation such as Forsi which is providing a highly technical scientific service. It may have limited tangible assets other than the technical expertise of its people.

As an organisation grows it needs more formal processes to ensure that the wealth of knowledge within the business is being captured and shared. Eg, knowledge gleaned by scientists on a project for one police force may assist scientists working on a similar project for another force, thereby reducing the learning curve and cutting time or costs.

It is important that the founders recognise that a formal strategy is required and that knowledge does not just flow round the organisation of its own accord.

Forsi's knowledge management (KM) strategy needs to capture the knowledge that is critical to its competitive advantage and then disseminate and use that knowledge in the decision-making process. Eg, KM could help Forsi to identify ways to meet client needs that are better than competitors or to improve processes or develop new and innovative forensic science techniques.

Implementing a knowledge management strategy

Implementing a knowledge management strategy would involve the following steps:

(1) Identifying the knowledge that exists within Forsi

- Human capital eg, specific scientific knowledge held by a particular scientist in a particular field or discipline

- Intellectual property (the result of innovation) eg, patents over any new techniques developed

- Client data eg, lists of client contacts held by founders, details of projects undertaken by client

- Organisational infrastructure (processes and policies) eg, the negotiating skills and relationship management tools used by the founders when dealing with clients

(2) Capture/document the knowledge to create some form of knowledge base. This may include capturing knowledge from outside Forsi (eg, intelligence on competitors, renowned experts in a particular scientific field, the police's in-house labs)

(3) Disseminate the knowledge to the appropriate people so it can be harnessed to:

- improve efficiency and performance
- identify opportunities to provide a better service for customers than competitors
- innovate new forensic science techniques

(4) Determine ways in which Forsi's knowledge can be developed and tracked. KM also requires an organisation to identify any knowledge it lacks and to spend time investing in improving the knowledge of its employees (eg, technical training or update courses) or helping them to use it more effectively (organisational learning)

(5) Ensure that key strategic knowledge is kept secure and confidential within Forsi and does not leak to competitors or is not lost when staff leave eg, ensuring all scientists have confidentiality clauses in their contracts, protecting IP wherever possible

Some knowledge will be explicit eg, particular forensic science procedures or protocols. Other knowledge may be tacit (in the heads of the scientists and/or founders and therefore invisible).

It is more difficult to harness the tacit knowledge and the informal networks and communities or practices that exist within an organisation. However encouraging increased collaboration between scientists would help Forsi to transform tacit knowledge into explicit knowledge.

Forsi needs to try and break down the barriers to sharing eg, scientists may be protective of their knowledge and feel reluctant to give away their value or feel that they are losing their position of influence or professional respect if they share their expertise with everyone.

Encouraging increased collaboration between scientists and creating a culture of openness where knowledge sharing is rewarded, would help Forsi to transform tacit knowledge into explicit knowledge.

In a field such as forensic science negative knowledge is also important. A company with an effective knowledge management process will be able to build a permanent body of awareness of 'negative knowledge' which provides information to improve on – those approaches that didn't work out as hoped or anticipated, or the reasons why a particular tender was lost.

A KM strategy is likely to place significant reliance on information technology and systems and Forsi may need to invest more money in this area.

Electronic tools such as online bulletin boards, blogs, intranets and wikis may all facilitate knowledge sharing.

Examiner's comments

Requirement 25.3 asked candidates, on the assumption that the business was not taken over, to explain why knowledge management is important to Forsi and recommend steps to implement a knowledge management strategy. Answers to this requirement, which was the least well done of all the paper, were very polarised and only a small minority of candidates scored the maximum marks. The weakest candidates knew very little about knowledge management or misinterpreted the requirement and wrote about the need for a management information system. Better candidates identified that scientific knowledge was a key strategic asset for Forsi and a source of competitive advantage. They went on to discuss how IP might be protected and the steps Forsi could take to capture and disseminate the knowledge that its scientists and founders possess.

25.4 (a) **Choice of operating structure**

Irrespective of the structure chosen, ownership by Aussi is likely to provide Forsi with additional administrative support and may reduce the need for outsourcing.

Forsi will also have greater access to funding.

Better financial controls and a focus on efficiency and returns may prevent acceptance of unprofitable or unacceptable projects.

Combined organisational knowledge is likely to increase as the businesses differ in geography, culture and operating practices, so sharing experience and best practice may enhance activities for both Aussi and Forsi.

However:

The need for central sign-off of projects by Australia may delay the speed of response so Forsi could lose tenders to competition

Rejection of a project purely on financial grounds may overlook the fact that it leads to repeat business or other more profitable work

Ownership by a larger global company inevitably brings more bureaucracy which could stifle Forsi's innovation and research culture.

Specific issues relating to the two different options for structuring the management of Forsi:

Integration of Forsi within the existing division of Aussi

If Forsi is fully incorporated into Aussi as part of its forensic science operating division, then its strategy and operations will be formalised centrally.

This may help with knowledge sharing etc – Aussi is likely to have procedures in place.

Forsi may be able to increase efficiency by benchmarking its activities against the rest of the division.

Integration may also generate economies of scale. The parts of the business will be geographically separate but there may be economies in areas like procurement.

However, having too great a technostructure would seem to run counter to the needs of an innovative business and direct supervision is unlikely to be welcomed by scientists, who are used to working independently.

Decision making could become slower and inflexible and barriers between scientists and clients may increase.

Some UK clients may have a negative attitude to Australian ownership, especially those in the public sector. Conversely being part of the acknowledged market leader in Australia/Asia may give Forsi credibility at tenders and help win more business/public sector projects.

Aussi's forensic division may be more conservative in their attitude to risk which might affect the nature of projects undertaken.

Aussi's main activities are in Australia and Asia so it may not make sense to have European activities integrated in the same area when markets, regulations etc may be quite different.

It will be harder for Aussi to assess how Forsi is doing if its activities are subsumed within the existing division – Forsi will only be a very small part of the existing activities.

Separate subsidiary company

Forsi would have more freedom to operate as it has done before, retaining its research-centred culture.

Forsi's founders may continue to negotiate its own projects and have more flexibility re pricing and margins, although it will still be subject to Aussi's project screening procedures so will not be completely autonomous.

Objectives of the subsidiary may become more determined by financial considerations and the need to meet Aussi's targets.

Forsi's culture could change and this may affect the behaviour of the workforce who appear happy with the current loose informal structure.

Australian ownership may be less visible to clients if Forsi continues to operate as a separate subsidiary.

Forsi would be a very small subsidiary compared to Aussi's existing division.

Recommendation:

Forsi should be operated as a subsidiary. Aussi needs to create some overarching management principles to guide activities but not overemphasise rules, regulations and procedures, otherwise research and innovation will be stifled.

ROCE and margin targets may need to be different than for the existing division to take account of the different market place, clients etc.

(b) Change management

The acquisition will involve rapid one-off change to the culture and structure of the organisation and is likely to be viewed by Forsi's employees as transformational. It is likely to involve changes to the way activities are carried out, new management structures and new reward systems.

The change is likely to be greater if Forsi is to be incorporated within the division of Aussi than if it is to continue as a stand-alone subsidiary. The way in which Aussi manages the change will affect the future success of the business.

Integration will require a careful change management programme.

If the founders have agreed to sell then they may encourage and support the change programme, particularly if they are involved in any sort of earn-out. The founders may therefore be able to help break down any forces resisting change.

Intelligent staff such as the scientists employed by Forsi will want to feel like they are being offered the chance to participate in the change process. One danger of consultation however is that should they provide input which is ignored they might become demotivated. Thus some careful negotiation and trade-offs may be required to accommodate the wishes of all parties involved in the change.

Open communication as to the reasons for the change in structure may help Forsi's staff to accept it, although care needs to be taken that such education is not done in a patronising way. Power, coercion or manipulation are unlikely to work with the majority of the scientists and may result in the loss of key staff.

Examiner's comments

The assumption in requirement 25.4 was that Forsi's founders did agree to be taken over by Aussi. Candidates needed to discuss whether Forsi should be operated as a subsidiary or as part of Aussi's forensic science division, and to recommend how Aussi should manage the change when the takeover is announced. Again this requirement was well attempted.

Most were comfortable discussing the choice of operating structure, in the light of Aussi's desire to retain Forsi's research-centred culture. Better candidates discussed the impact the choice might have on performance monitoring, given Aussi's project screening process and requirements for target returns, and provided a preliminary recommendation as to the best option. However some weaker candidates seemed to overlook the fact that the two businesses were very dissimilar in size and geographic location. As in previous sittings, candidates were well versed in the technical knowledge for the change management requirement but an inability to apply this knowledge was again evident on the part of the weaker candidates. A key issue here was that the nature of the change, the likely barriers and the appropriate change management practice were dependent on the choice of structure, a fact that the better candidates identified.

26 ToyL Ltd (September 2014)

Marking guide

	Knowledge	Skill	Marks
26.1 Appraisal of business plan/recommendations	5	12	15
26.2 Benefits of outsourcing	2	4	6
26.3 Information requirements	2	8	9
	9	24	30

General comments:

This question was also well attempted. The scenario concerns ToyL, a provider of educational toys which will be sold to individual customers (parents, grandparents, children) and wholesale purchasers (schools and daycare centres/nurseries). ToyL is a start-up business which has developed three distinct educational toys that use interactive technology to teach young children number skills, alphabet skills and phonics. The company has been founded by Pavel and Rosemary, a team of husband (IT specialist) and wife (educational consultant). The toys are in prototype form but functionally complete. The product line is expected to grow over time as new ideas are generated. While prototypes will be designed and manufactured in-house, production will be outsourced. A website will be used as the key marketing tool. ToyL hopes to be profitable by the end of year one and expects a steep increase in sales for the next few years. ToyL is in the process of producing a business plan to attract funding and a draft version is included in the scenario.

26.1 Report on draft Business Plan

To: Rosemary and Pavel Bochev
From: AN Accountant
Date: September 20Y4

This analysis is done in two parts:

- The quality and completeness of the existing sections of the plan
- Additional sections or information that would be relevant

The current plan is lacking in critical financial detail and this is discussed further below.

Quality and completeness of existing plan

(1) Executive summary

One of the most important sections of a business plan is the executive summary. The executive summary should grab the attention of potential investors, help them understand what ToyL is about and the implications for their investment, and make them want to read the plan in more detail.

Pavel and Rosemary have correctly identified that although it is the first thing that will appear in the plan, it should be the last thing to be written.

It will need to highlight the key points from the other sections:

- Overview of the business
- Why it will be successful
- What finance is being sought
- What financial performance an investor can expect
- Any major risks and how they can be mitigated

(2) Introduction and management team

This section should introduce the business and the owners' vision for its future. Anyone investing in ToyL needs to have faith in Pavel and Rosemary's management skills and commitment to the business.

There is insufficient detail about the management team. The business is clearly going to be very dependent on the two directors and a prospective investor is likely to want more information to assess the risk that this creates:

- Ages
- Personal objectives
- Financial management experience
- CVs (include in an Appendix)
- Other personnel that the business is planning to employ to address any skills gaps – a key concern for any investor would be Rosemary and Pavel's apparent lack of financial expertise

(3) Products

This section clearly explains ToyL's products. However since the business is at a very early stage, it will be important to provide evidence about how realistic the idea is:

- USPs compared to existing products on the market
- Evidence of field testing
- Feedback on prototypes and modifications required
- Cost and time required to get product ready for market
- Details of who will manufacture the products
- Details of toy safety regulations and ToyL's compliance
- Outline of ideas for future products

(4) Marketing

The target market is clear but the language used to describe its nature and size ('we think', 'about 3.3 million', 'around 8% pa') is vague and does not inspire confidence. Evidence to show that it is a viable market is required; as it stands some of the figures seem optimistic, especially in relation to growth in the target market. The plan needs to describe the factors that drive this growth.

A more detailed marketing plan is necessary. It seems unlikely that reliance on the website will be sufficient.

More information is needed on pricing:

- What is the pricing strategy?
- How will prices compare to competitors?
- What level of price discount will be offered to/expected by wholesale clients?

Details of any market research undertaken should be included in the Appendix.

(5) Competition

This section should explain how ToyL believes it is going to compete effectively.

The information about competitors is not sufficiently detailed. It is not clear whether ToyL intends to take on the global market leaders or the regional manufacturers.

More information about the customer base and market share of main rivals would be helpful.

Evidence is required to support the superiority claimed for ToyL's products.

(6) **Strategy and operations**

The title of this section does not really match the content which is a mixture of strategy and financial information. In relation to strategy, this section could include the business' overall mission and objectives. It should also evaluate the alternative strategies open to the business in terms of market positioning. More information could be included on supply chain management and the plans to outsource production.

The figures include projected revenue but there is no information on costs or prospective margins. The expectation that the business will break-even in the first year seems quite optimistic and more evidence is required to substantiate the projected sales of £367,000 in year two and £475,000 in year three (see below).

Additional sections or information that would be relevant:

- **Financial information**

  As this is primarily a plan to attract additional finance this is a critical section and needs to be comprehensive. It should clearly identify the following:

  - What the finance needs are

    How much money is being sought from investor(s) and in what format? How has any initial capital been spent (eg, what is the breakdown of the £24,000 set-up costs) and how will any new funds be used?

  - What the financial future of the business might look like

    The plan needs to include detailed profit projections and cash flow forecasts covering a period of at least three years.

  - The business plan should have a clear statement of underlying assumptions

    An investor will be keen to assess the realism of the business plan and forecasts. It is important not to be over-optimistic.

Since the future is uncertain, it is important to include here anything that might change the forecasts or mean that things don't quite go to plan. A prospective investor will ask 'What if?' questions. Eg, What will happen to the expected profit if sales fall by 5%? What sales will need to be achieved to break even?

- **Risks and mitigation/contingency plans**

  Some business owners are reluctant to include information on the business' weaknesses or on business threats. However, a prospective investor will want to know that the owner has considered the risks facing the business and that there is a plan to manage them. Risks facing ToyL include the following:

  - Reliance on two owner directors
  - Toys aimed at young children – onerous health and safety requirements
  - Highly competitive market, lots of substitutes, easily copied
  - Products rely on technology which is rapidly changing, so they are likely to have a short life and need to be updated/amended frequently
  - Environmental/industry issues (PESTEL/Five Forces analysis)

- **Appendix of supporting documentation**

  So that the plan is concise and focussed, any detailed information should be included here, rather than in the main body of the plan.

  This section should also include any other information necessary to present a full picture of the business/its owners:

  - Statement of owners' personal wealth
  - Copies of personal tax returns
  - CVs of Pavel and Rosemary
  - Details of any market research undertaken
  - Copies of any patents/product safety certificates
  - Letters of intent or contracts with suppliers/wholesalers

Requirement 26.1 asked candidates to critically assess the content of the draft business plan and make recommendations as to how the document may be improved in order to attract the necessary investors. Although many candidates were clearly familiar with the knowledge required (the pro-forma contents of a business plan), weaker candidates struggled to apply this in the context of a plan to attract potential investment. Candidates who appreciated the need to focus their content on the end user of the document, and who wrote in an appropriate style, structuring their answer using the headings from the draft plan, scored very highly. The key here was to appreciate that the draft plan made a number of claims about the superiority of the proposed products but that the lack of substantive data/evidence in relation to the products/markets, and the absence of any real detail about the amount of finance or the expected future performance needed, would be of major concern to a prospective investor. This needed to be addressed as a priority. It is likely that an investor might also want more information on the directors with whom they were establishing a relationship, and on how Rosemary and Pavel intend to handle their lack of financial expertise. Weak answers often spent far too long appraising the existing sections of the plan, sometimes with little structure, and then identified the need for more financial information almost as an after-thought at the end. Key elements which should have been included in the business plan, such as a focused executive summary plus financial forecasts, were ignored by many candidates.

26.2 An outsourcing model is likely to be appropriate for ToyL for a number of reasons.

(1) Neither Pavel nor Rosemary has any experience of manufacturing operations/supply chain. An outsource company may provide greater expertise.

(2) Outsourcing will keep overhead costs to a minimum, making all production costs variable and reducing operating gearing.

(3) This will allow the management team to focus on marketing and new product development which makes best use of their skills.

(4) Financial risks will be reduced by not committing to the expense of a manufacturing facility. An outsourcing model will allow greater flexibility.

(5) Outsourcing will increase the scalability of the business model, which will be particularly important if ToyL succeeds in attracting a number of wholesale clients.

On the face of it outsourcing would seem sensible, however ToyL will need to consider:

- the impact on variable costs of production
- control over quality
- bargaining power as ToyL may be small relative to suppliers

Examiner's comments

In requirement 26.2, candidates were requested to explain the benefits of outsourcing as a production model for ToyL. The majority of candidates were clearly well prepared for and scored very highly on this requirement.

26.3 The information requirements will depend on the purpose for which the information is required.

Management team

Pavel and Rosemary will be managing the business on a day-to-day basis. As a result they will require information for planning, control and decision making.

Internal information

Quite a lot of the information for control purposes is likely to be operational in nature. They have identified that the implementation of strict financial controls is a critical success factor – they will need to monitor the company's performance in terms of profitability, cost control and working capital management

This means that typically they will find management accounting information more relevant than financial reporting information as they will require:

- detailed analysis of costs and revenues
- reports comparing actual performance and budget, showing variances
- detailed monthly information, analysed by product and type of customer
- development costs incurred on various products

External information

Pavel and Rosemary will need to decide which product lines to pursue and how to price them, what distribution channels to use, and how to promote the products.

To do this they will need to analyse information on the market they are operating in: competitors, market share, new products launched, educational trends etc.

They will need to collect data on the effectiveness of different marketing initiatives.

Non-financial information

Information should also focus on non-financial measures and the CSF's identified eg, customer feedback.

Equity investors

Private investors will be focussed on the quality of their investment and the returns they can expect.

The extent of the information they require may depend on the size of their stake and the nature of the role they decide to take eg, whether they are involved in some non-executive capacity.

They are likely to want information about the performance achieved by ToyL in summary or overview form. Typically this will be more like financial reporting information.

It will also relate to the longer term strategic picture, including future expected returns and value on exit. An investor will want to monitor the overall profitability, liquidity and gearing of the business.

They will also want to assess the quality of the management team (Pavel and Rosemary), their strategy and their ability to manage the risks attached to the investment.

Data about Toyl is likely to be benchmarked against other investments/sector/economy norms.

Examiner's comments

Requirement 26.3 asked candidates to explain how the information requirements of Pavel and Rosemary as managers will be different from the information requirements of the additional private investors, once the business is operational. Surprisingly this was one of the least well attempted requirements. The key here was to identify the purpose for which any information was to be used. Most candidates appreciated that whilst Rosemary and Pavel would be interested in information to manage the day-to-day operations, private investors would probably be more interested in evaluating the return on their investment. Having done so however, weaker candidates talked in generic terms and did not go on to give sufficiently detailed examples of the type of information that would be useful to each party. Only the best candidates identified that the exact requirements of the investor(s) may depend on the size and nature of their investment and therefore risk, and the extent to which they are involved in the business eg, in a non-executive capacity. Some candidates started by applying Mendelow's stakeholder matrix, but often, having identified the likely interest and power of the investor, were unsure of the implications for the information needs of managers and investors.

27 Water On Tap (September 2014)

	Knowledge	Skill	Marks
27.1 Sustainable enterprise	2	5	7
27.2 Ethics of marketing	3	6	8
27.3 Two proposals	3	9	10
	8	20	25

General comments:

The third question, worth 25 marks, was the least well attempted overall, largely as a result of requirement 27.2. The scenario relates to a social enterprise 'Ontap'. Its founder, Nala, is a keen athlete who was fed up with the amount she was spending on bottled water and the level of plastic bottle waste. The Ontap concept involves a water bottle, made from recycled aluminium foil for use by athletes, commuters and students. Once purchased from Ontap, the bottle can be taken to a range of participating cafes and shops (currently only in central London) and re-filled with tap-water for free. The Ontap website provides a list of tap locations and there is also a free mobile app showing refill sites, all of which prominently display the Ontap logo. 70% of the business' profits are donated to fund clean water projects in India and used to raise awareness of the damaging effects of bottled water on the environment. The business has been successful and is keen to expand. Two options are being considered: (1) a corporate scheme whereby companies will purchase co-branded Ontap bottles to replace the water cooler and plastic cups typically found in most offices; and (2) geographical expansion outside London. Information was also provided in the scenario about the marketing activities of the bottled water companies and supermarkets.

27.1 Sustainable enterprise

A sustainable enterprise is one that takes account of social and environmental returns as well as financial ones. As a social enterprise, on the face of it Ontap would appear to be such a business.

A key issue is the concept that a sustainable organisation is one that has a long term orientation and does not just focus on short-term results and measures when making decisions. As a social enterprise, Ontap's objectives will be wider than just financial. Its goals will be externally as well as internally focussed and will include taking account of customers'/partners' business objectives and meeting the needs of the Indian communities it is serving. Ontap will want to optimise its profits (rather than maximise them), in order to give more money away to fund water projects and raise educational awareness.

To be financially sustainable (ie, to survive in the long term), a business needs an understanding of the changing external environment so that it can respond and adapt to the opportunities and threats presented by it. So for example Nala has developed a product in response to society's changing attitudes to bottled water and environmental waste.

Sustainability is therefore an issue for any business in relation to risk mitigation, innovation and the development of new skills and capabilities to create and sustain competitive advantage over rivals. One question over Ontap's financial sustainability will be whether refillable bottles prove to be a fad and/or whether other businesses copy the idea, although in a sense this would help Ontap in its desire to persuade individuals to move away from bottled water in order to protect the environment.

In the context of environmental sustainability, an organisation should only use resources at a rate that allows them to be replenished in order to ensure they will continue to be available.

Ontap's whole concept is aiming to protect the environment by persuading individuals to move away from bottled water, thereby reducing the volume of bottles that end up in landfill. It donates profits to education campaigns and clean water projects and its own bottle is made from recycled

A socially sustainable organisation is one where decision making is linked to respect for people, communities and the environment. An increased focus on sustainability should support investment in human capital, engaging in innovation and establishing more reliable supply chains even if these do not maximise short-term financial performance. A key issue for Ontap will be ensuring that the supplier(s) of its bottles and the cafes and restaurants it partners with also act in a socially responsible manner.

Conclusion

In social and environmental terms, Ontap would appear to constitute a sustainable enterprise. The steps Nala is proposing to capitalise on the success of the business may help ensure it is also a financially sustainable one.

Examiner's comments

In requirement 27.1 candidates were asked to discuss the extent to which Ontap is a sustainable enterprise. A significant number of candidates started their discussion with the Brundtland definition of sustainability but did not necessarily explore how this related to the concept of a sustainable enterprise. Many candidates then limited their discussion by concentrating on either the environmental aspects or the financial aspects of Ontap's sustainability and it was extremely rare to see a discussion of all three aspects of sustainability: economic, social and environmental. Clearly, Ontap is striving for environmental sustainability, but the extent to which it is financially sustainable as a model may be more questionable. Disappointingly, despite having been asked to assess the extent of Ontap's sustainability, candidates often failed to reach a conclusion on this matter.

27.2 Ethics of marketing

Bottled water manufacturers

An ethical argument sometimes raised against marketing is that it wastes resources by selling people things that they don't want or using promotional techniques to persuade people that they are dissatisfied without them.

This criticism could perhaps be levied at the bottled water manufacturers, who have spent significant resources on advertising to create brand/lifestyle images (eg, Evian roller babies) in order to persuade consumers to buy water which they could otherwise choose to get free from our taps.

Some would argue that charging money for something that is freely available or certainly cheap to obtain in order to make a profit for shareholders is unethical and does not demonstrate corporate responsibility. However marketing is undertaken by most organisations so is a reality in the commercial world.

One aspect of the marketing mix is 'Product'. The bottled water product itself could also be argued to lead to environmental pollution. The financial costs to both the consumer and the environment are high:

- The cost of the actual product
- Energy required in production
- Pollution created as a result of the production process
- Transportation costs
- Packaging material that has to be discarded (75% of the 18bn bottles end up in landfill)

The way marketing is carried out may also sometimes cause ethical concerns. Information about the content and effects of products needs to be clear otherwise there is an issue of transparency, particularly if the manufacturers, either deliberately or by omission, suggest their product is something that it is not. Hence the example given in the scenario of the UK supermarkets being criticised when it became apparent that some of their own-brand bottled water was simply filtered, purified tap water.

However most businesses will abide by industry and voluntary codes of practice in how they promote their products and would argue therefore that they are behaving responsibly in marketing their products.

The bottled water companies might also argue that consumers have a free choice and, provided they are given clear information, it is up to the buyer to decide whether to buy or to choose not to buy if they think the product is unethical.

Such companies might also argue that there is an ethical good that comes from the marketing of their product in the form of creating employment and jobs. Some of the bottled water companies have also started to try and address ethical criticisms by donating funds to promote clean drinking water in the developing world or selling more ecologically responsible products, using recycled bottles eg, Volvic's Drink 1 give 10 campaign or the One Foundation.

Ontap

Marketing will be undertaken by Ontap in relation to:

- sale of water bottles
- promotion of business in order to attract cafes and restaurants as partners
- education relating to environmental impact of buying and drinking bottled water

Ontap's product is not a luxury good – it is aiming to fill a distinct need, saving customers money and protecting the environment at the same time, so it is unlikely to be subject to the same degree of criticism.

In promoting a more ecologically responsible product, aimed at persuading its target audience to voluntarily change behaviour and revert to tap water, Ontap's marketing could be argued to reduce waste and save resources. Also it is aimed at steering people to products that are helpful to them and to society.

However Ontap will face a conflict between spending resources on marketing and generating more profits to donate to good causes. By harnessing social media, the use of logos in cafés and restaurants and on bottles to build its brand image, Ontap may be able to keep its marketing spend to a minimum.

A possible criticism of Ontap might be that, like the bottled water companies, it is also trying to sell consumers a product (in this case a bottle) when they could just ask for free tap water. Also if Ontap's business model proves not to be sustainable, customers will have wasted £8 on a bottle that they may not then be able to refill for free if there are no longer participating cafes.

Overall Ontap's marketing is likely to be seen as more ethical and transparent than some other companies in the bottled water industry. Certainly, since Ontap is a not–for–profit organisation, society is likely to be less cynical about its motives compared to the for-profit bottled water companies.

Examiner's comments

Part 27.2 asked candidates to compare and contrast the ethics of the marketing activities of Ontap with its competitors in the bottled water industry. This is only the second time that ethical marketing has been specifically examined (it was last set in September 2012) and the requirement was poorly done by many candidates. Some did apply the transparency, fairness and effect decision-making approach, which tended to at least ensure they were talking in ethical terms and applying a structured thought process. Only the best candidates provided an initial discussion of ethical marketing principles and the arguments for and against marketing in the context of the activities of Ontap and the bottled water companies (providing choice/ raising awareness/ promoting responsible products vs wasting resources/persuading consumers to buy products they don't need/attempting to portray products as something they are not). Better answers pointed out that, whilst attempting to sell tap water as bottled mineral water lacked transparency, attempts to strengthen brand image through marketing is common place and legal and not necessarily unethical, providing industry advertising standards are adhered to. A small minority did question whether Ontap's own marketing activities were in reality that different, since under the umbrella of corporate social responsibility they were also hoping to make money by marketing a product that in theory people could obtain for free, and that if their business model is not financially sustainable, people will have wasted £8 on a bottle they cannot then use for its intended purpose. Answers to the ethics requirement, which is a consistent feature of the exam, continue to be variable and – as has been said before – candidates wishing to score well are advised to adopt some form of framework for their answer and to produce a balanced argument rather than a one-sided discussion.

27.3 Expansion strategies

Nala's desire to expand – general factors to consider

- Expansion will require finance which may not be available given that a significant proportion of Ontap's profits are donated

- It is likely to be harder for Nala to control a bigger business

- Ontap will need to be sure it can source sufficient supply of water bottles from ethical suppliers

- The business is likely to need to expand by taking on more staff

- There is a limited market – once a consumer has bought a bottle they don't need to replace it

- Will the Ontap concept prove to be a passing fad?

- Product concept is very easy for others to copy

- If you are an existing customer in the restaurant/café/bar you don't need a water bottle. Also Ontap cannot prevent people refilling their own bottles and containers.

- Ontap may face reaction/competition from bottled water companies

Corporate sales scheme

- This will generate significant volumes from persuading one company to buy (less time, cost and effort) although fulfilling the order may be problematic.

- Ontap needs to target businesses which want to be more environmentally responsible. Companies who are keen to improve their image may be prepared to sign up

- A partnership with a large blue chip company will enhance Ontap's reputation and co-branded bottles will raise awareness

- This idea may be popular with staff – Ontap could get existing customers to lobby their employers on Ontap's behalf

- The downside is that Ontap will be relatively small in relation to a large corporate buyer, which may insist on a substantial volume discount. Ontap's image and reputation could be badly affected if the wrong 'partner' is chosen, and Ontap's ability to source sufficient bottles may be a problem

- Perhaps Ontap could offer a corporate customer a trial scheme to start with

Geographical expansion

- It would be easiest achieved by targetting national and regional chains eg, pizza restaurants

- Getting first mover advantage and wider national coverage may create barriers to entry for the competition

- Cafes can also act as sales outlets for the bottles which would increase the potential market

- Ontap should be able to find appropriate partners as the cafes benefit from a page on the Ontap website, increased footfall, free marketing via Ontap's app. They can also attract additional customers rather than replacement ones as they will still also be selling bottled water to other consumers

- Again Ontap will need to be careful about the image/ethics of the cafes and restaurants it chooses to partner with.

- This option is likely to be harder for Nala to control than the corporate option and would result in slower growth, at least initially.

Recommendation:

The options may not both be mutually exclusive – Nala's ability to pursue them will be limited by Ontap's resources in terms of people and finance, and its ability to source bottles.

Both are probably sensible ways of expanding.

Requirement 27.3 requested candidates to discuss the problems Ontap will face in any expansion of the business and evaluate the two proposed options. Although this was the last requirement on the paper it was generally well attempted. Most candidates pointed out the expansion issues for Nala in relation to control, limited resources and available funding. Better candidates went on to then discuss the two proposals in the light of these and to reach a conclusion on which strategy might be more suitable. A number pointed out correctly that neither were mutually exclusive and that it might be feasible to pursue both options.

28 Confo plc (December 2014)

Marking guide

	Knowledge	Skill	Marks
28.1 Transfer price	3	7	9
28.2 Performance	2	15	15
28.3 Recovery plan	4	12	15
28.4 Ethics	3	5	7
	12	39	46

General comments:

This is the mini case worth 46 marks and also the main data analysis question.

The scenario is based on a manufacturer of confectionery products, Confo, which also owns and franchises retail outlets, which sell the company's products. Following a period of difficult trading, Confo implemented a three-year recovery plan which: closed a number of owned outlets, reopening some of these as franchised outlets; opened a new commercial division; and opened a new export division. There was also a change in the way the manufacturing division priced transfers to owned and franchised outlets. The change was from cost plus 20% to full cost, with franchisees also paying an increased fixed annual fee. One year into the recovery plan, the board undertook a review of progress. This review showed that the overall performance of the company had deteriorated. An additional ethical issue has arisen whereby the procurement manager of a major customer had been asking for gifts of sweets from a Confo sales manager. These requests were small in value at first, but increased in amount and frequency over time. Their eventual cessation by Confo led to the customer withdrawing its custom.

28.1 Transfer prices

A transfer price (TP) is the price at which one division in a group sells its products or services to another division in the same group.

The transfer prices will be important for Confo as they have a number of implications:

- They determine the profits of divisions. If the Manufacturing Division charges a high transfer price then most of the total profit from company sales will be attributed to it, with less to the other divisions. This will give a false measure of performance for all divisions.

- As the price to franchisees is the same as the transfer price to the owned shops, this may impact upon the willingness of third parties (favourably or unfavourably) to take up franchises and the volume of goods they purchase whilst a franchisee.

- If high transfer prices are passed on to ultimate customers then sales volumes may fall and overall profits may be distorted.

- Inappropriate transfer prices can lead to internal conflict between divisions. As shops only sell Confo's confectionery, the Retail Division cannot access outside markets to obtain lower cost products from third parties. The Manufacturing Division is therefore a monopoly supplier to owned shops and to franchisees and, from 1 October 20Y3, to the Commercial and Export Divisions.

Pre-1 October 20Y3 transfer pricing system

The transfer pricing system pre-1 October 20Y3 was on a full cost plus 20% basis.

The Manufacturing Division

From the perspective of the Manufacturing Division, the cost-plus formula guaranteed an operating profit margin of 20%. This meant that any cost inefficiencies could be passed on to the Retail Division with an additional mark-up. Perversely, this could mean that the more inefficient the Manufacturing Division was, the more profit it made.

There does not appear to be any rationale for the 20% and this figure appears to be arbitrary. More meaningful is the mark-up overall for the company.

A further concern is that, although fixed costs are not as large as variable costs, they are significant. In attempting to recover fixed costs per unit then an estimate needed to be made at the beginning of the year, not just of total fixed costs to be incurred, but also of the output volume to be achieved in order to determine budgeted fixed cost per unit and hence price. Any error would result in an under- or over-recovery of fixed costs.

A related problem is that costs (fixed and variable) need to be allocated to each type of product to set each transfer price. Given that production is likely to be interdependent between different products, costs are incurred jointly on different products and it can be difficult to identify cost drivers to separate them in order to be able to calculate each product's transfer price.

Conversely, however, there are a number of positive points that could be made for Confo's former transfer pricing system:

- The same prices were being successfully charged commercially to franchisees which may imply it was at (or below) the market rate. However, in this case, franchisees were also paying a fixed fee which needs to be considered alongside the transfer price to determine viability for the franchisees.

- The full cost may be budgeted costs rather than actual so any cost overrun would be incurred by the Manufacturing Division rather than the Retail Division (although the data shows 20% related to actual cost, it could be that the budget equalled actual).

The Retail Division

The Retail Division had no control over the transfer price it paid to the Manufacturing Division and there was no alternative supplier of confectionery it could use. The transfer prices therefore had significant implications for the validity of its status as a profit centre. Being a profit centre would imply that divisional managers had significant control over costs and revenues, but this appears not to have been the case. As a consequence, the divisional loss of £400,000 for the Retail Division had little meaning.

In favour of the transfer prices, it could be that the Confo board had set cost plus 20% as their best estimate of the wholesale market value of the confectionery. The fact that there are no identical confectionery products being sold by rival companies makes this difficult to substantiate.

Post-1 October 20Y3 transfer pricing system

The transfer pricing system post-1 October 20Y3 is on a full cost basis. This treats the Manufacturing Division as a cost centre and the other divisions (Retail, Commercial and Export) therefore recognise the full profit to be made from the sale by the company.

The Manufacturing Division

The Manufacturing Division is now a cost centre and so its performance cannot be measured on profit, but rather on its ability to control costs (eg, against budget). An example of how well it has performed in this respect is the reduction in fixed costs compared with the previous year (see below).

Given the franchisees are also acquiring the goods at the same full cost, manufacturing has few incentives to promotes sales to franchisees as there is no profit. The only advantage for the Manufacturing Division of more sales to franchisees is that fixed costs are being spread over more units of output thereby increasing its cost efficiency.

The Retail, Commercial and Export Divisions

These divisions are profit centres and have the advantage of acquiring inventories at cost price, whereas rivals would need to pay outside suppliers wholesale market rates including a mark-up for profit.

In terms of incentives, these divisions may be motivated to over-order from Manufacturing Division or under-price to consumers/customers compared to rivals as they can acquire confectionery more cheaply.

Alternative methods of transfer pricing

There may be distortions in incentives given that internal transfer prices and prices to franchisees are unlikely to be at wholesale market rates.

An alternative system of transfer pricing would be to make transfers at market rates.

This could be done by estimating the wholesale market value of each type of sweet by comparison to rivals' products (albeit there are no identical products).

A further alternative would be to let divisional directors negotiate the transfer prices by discussion in a bargaining process. This may cause conflict, but would result in an agreed set of transfer prices, rather than a centrally imposed set. It may also tend towards market prices over time. However, the problem with this is that the strongest negotiator may dominate, possibly providing a sub-optimal outcome overall.

Conclusion

Transfer prices should be set by negotiation where the outcome is influenced strongly by market prices charged to third party customers (or to franchisees) in a competitive market.

Examiner's comments

Answers were variable in quality. A significant minority failed to explain the motivational aspects of transfer pricing, particularly for the manufacturing division. For example, some considered the revised transfer pricing approach as not motivating managers in this division to control costs. Only a few candidates appreciated that any revised performance management/reward approach would incorporate success in cost control for the Manufacturing Division, as opposed to success in generating profits. Even fewer made the point that the downside could be a reduction in product quality in pursuit of lower costs.

Of those who referred to goal congruence, many did not explain this in the context of the question. The same observation applies to discussion of alternative transfer pricing approaches. With reference to transfer prices at opportunity cost, there appeared to be no appreciation of the fact that the manufacturing division only supplies internally and is a monopoly supplier to the shops. Better answers did refer to the use of market prices in this context, but normally did not consider that these may be difficult to determine, given the unique nature of the firm's products. Weaker candidates did not justify the alternative methods of transfer pricing and instead just listed various methods (such as variable cost plus, fixed cost plus, market prices, negotiated prices) without any explanation or discussion. A small minority of candidates discussed methods of pricing in general rather than of transfer pricing.

	20Y3 Owned shops	20Y4 Owned shops	20Y3 Manufacturing	20Y4 Manufacturing
Revenue per shop £	160,000	180,000		
Operating profit per shop £	−2,667	16,500		
Revenue per product £	2	2	1.50	1.25
Operating profit per product £	−0.033	0.183	0.25	0
Total cost per product £			1.25	1.25
Operating profit margin (profit/revenue %)	−1.67%	9.17%	16.67%	0%

Profit from franchisees:

	20Y3 £'000	20Y4 £'000
Profit on transfers from manufacturing (8,100 × 20/120)	1,350	0
Fees	1,200	2,500
	2,550	2,500
Profit per franchisee shop £'000	28,333	20,833

Manufacturing costs

	20Y3	20Y4
Fixed costs per unit	50p	50p
Variable costs per unit	75p	75p
Transfer price	£1.50	£1.25

Total profit for Retail and Manufacturing

	20Y3 £'000	20Y4 £'000
Manufacturing	4,350	0
Retail	(400)	1,320
Fees	1,200	2,500
Total operating profit	5,150	3,820

Overall performance of Retail and Manufacturing

In comparing the data for 20Y3 and 20Y4 for Retail and Manufacturing Divisions, four significant elements of the recovery plan have occurred. These are:

- the closure of 70 owned shops to scale down the owned network significantly

- opening 30 new franchised shops in replacement of some owned shops

- transfers from Manufacturing Division at full cost in 20Y4, rather than full cost plus 20% in 20Y3

- more than doubling, in total, of the fixed franchise fee from £1.2m to £2.5m

These decisions distort underlying data trends and therefore impact on any comparable assessment of overall performance. This makes like-for-like comparisons difficult for the underlying elements of the business.

Note: The Commercial and Export Divisions are new lines of business and are analysed separately.

Revenue – owned outlets

Total revenue for owned shops has declined by 40% from £24m in 20Y3 to £14.4m in 20Y4. Similarly, the volume of sales (number of items sold) has declined by 40% from 12 million in 20Y3 to 7.2 million in 20Y4. The average selling price has remained the same at £2, so this does not appear to be a factor in the change in revenue or volume of sales.

A key causal factor in this decline has been the scaling down of the number of owned shops by 46.7% from 150 in 20Y3, to 80 in 20Y4.

Thus, rather than reflecting poor performance, the change in revenue has been a deliberate rescaling within the recovery strategy.

Revenue per owned shop has increased from £160,000 in 20Y3 to £180,000 in 20Y4 (12.5%). This is indicative, in revenue terms at least, that the worst performing shops have been closed and the shops with higher revenue generation have remained open.

Thus, while there has been a downscaling of the number of owned shops in the network, the average sales generation performance per owned shop has improved.

Operating profit – owned outlets

Total operating profit for owned shops has improved from an operating loss of £400,000 in 20Y3 to an operating profit of £1.32 million in 20Y4.

At first sight, this appears to indicate improved performance, particularly as it has been generated by a scaled down network of owned shops.

Further analysis indicates, however, that a key causal factor in this improvement has been the reduced transfer price from the manufacturing division. Adjusting the data to show the operating profit/loss if the previous transfer pricing policy in 20Y3, of full cost plus 20%, had been maintained for 20Y4 reveals the following:

	£'000
External sales	14,400
Internal & franchisee transfers (9,000 × 1.2)	(10,800)
Variable costs	(1,080)
Fixed costs	(3,000)
Operating (Loss)	(480)

Tutorial note:

A comparable analysis could be carried out by scaling down the 20Y3 data.

Thus, rather than operating profit of the owned shops improving, had the transfer pricing policy remained at full cost plus 20%, then the operating losses would have increased from £400,000 to £480,000.

This has occurred, despite the improvement in revenue generation per shop, because the smaller network has meant that fixed costs of owned shops have decreased by only 25% (from £4m to £3m) while volumes of sales have decreased by 40% (see above) thereby increasing fixed costs per unit.

Franchised shops

The recovery strategy has been to favour franchised shops rather than owned shops. In this respect there has been some operational success in opening a further 30 franchised shops in replacement of owned shops.

Overall, the profit from franchising has decreased by 2% from £2.55m to £2.5m. This is in the context of an increase in the number franchised shops of 33.3% from 90 to 120.

As a consequence, the operating profit to Confo per franchised shop has fallen by 26.5% from £28,333 in 20Y3, to £20,833 in 20Y4. This may be indicative of poorer performance, but it could also reflect a short term policy to expand the network by offering improved conditions for the franchisee contract.

It may also reflect the fact that the newer franchisees may take some time to become established. More information would be needed on the relative performance of new and existing franchisees.

Manufacturing

The key factor affecting the 'profit' generated by the manufacturing division has been the change in transfer pricing policy from a profit centre (cost plus 20%) to a cost centre. This is a corporate level decision and is not indicative of the underlying performance of the Manufacturing Division itself.

Basing performance on its ability to control costs, it has performed well. The overall output has reduced by 5.7% from 17.4 million units to 16.4 million units. This is a reflection of reduced sales but additional information would be needed to confirm that sales were not constrained by reduced production capacity.

Variable cost per unit has remained at 75p so any reduced scale economies have not been a factor.

More significantly, the fixed cost per unit has remained constant despite the fall in sales and production output. This reflects a good performance in reducing fixed costs.

Examiner's comments

Generally, this requirement was fairly well answered, with most candidates providing up-front calculations in a reasonably well structured table. Analysis often endeavoured to explain changes and results for the two years in terms of cause and effect. Weaker candidates were poor in this regard, merely reiterating the percentage changes. Weaker candidates also provided occasional calculations within their narrative, rather than in an initial structured table.

Calculations most commonly focussed on gross and net profit margins and commented on changes year on year. Only the better candidates calculated specific ratios such as revenue per shop, operating profit per shop and cost per shop. There was some good discussion of the differences in results between the franchised outlets and owned outlets.

Better responses recognised problems in comparisons between the two years, particularly due to the change in the transfer pricing system and organisational structure changes. A very small minority adjusted the data to take out this distortion, normally by adjusting the 20Y3 data by removing the 20% mark-up on internal transfers, thus arriving at more sensible comments regarding the relative performance of the manufacturing and retail divisions. Weaker candidates omitted to comment on problems in making comparisons, or to suggest additional information that would assist analysis, despite these being required in the question.

28.3 (a) To: The Confo plc board
        From: A Student
        Date: 10 December 20Y4
        Subject: Strategy review

Both divisions are in the start-up phase of their life cycle so it is difficult to make judgements about the success of the performance or strategy at this stage. Nevertheless, there are some early indicators.

Using the Ansoff matrix these are both examples of market development whereby existing products are being sold in new markets.

Export Division

In the case of the Export Division the new markets in the Ansoff matrix are new geographical markets.

In terms of the Lynch Expansion Method it would be regarded as growth through internal development abroad (ie, exporting).

These sales are likely to all be incremental with minimal leakage between home and export markets. While this is positive in terms of generating more revenue, the strategy has a number of problems in relation to costs and risks:

(1) The costs incurred in penetrating new markets may be significant compared to the revenues earned

(2) The downstream supply chain is lengthened significantly, thereby increasing costs of getting goods to customers

(3) There may be different tastes in different countries such that products developed for the UK market tastes may be unsuitable (eg, some sweets may be unsuitable in hot climates)

(4) Additional risks apply (eg, international physical distribution and foreign exchange rate risk on settlement)

The Export Division has made a small profit of £200,000 for the year. Whilst this is unlikely to be sufficient in the long run to justify the investment, this is the start-up phase to penetrate markets.

The profit is small but, based on the above argument; it is all incremental, with little or no damage to the existing business. Indeed, as an international brand it may enhance the existing business in the UK in terms of reputation.

Commercial Division

In the case of the Commercial Division, the new markets in the Ansoff matrix are new distribution channels.

In terms of the Lynch Expansion Method it would be regarded as growth through internal domestic development.

The key strategic issue in this case is that there may be competition between Confo's existing markets and the new commercial market. If consumers become aware that the supermarkets are selling the same products as Confo's owned shops and franchisees, but at a lower price, then this strategy may reduce contribution and destroy value for Confo overall.

The Commercial Division has made a small profit of £300,000 for the year. Unlike the Export Division, we cannot be certain that this is entirely incremental. Indeed, the lost contribution on existing sales (if consumers perceive it is the same product but own-labelled) may be greater than £300,000.

(b) **Evaluation of success of the recovery plan**

In pure financial terms Confo has generated less profit in the year following the introduction of the recovery plan (£4.32m) than in the year before the plan (£5.15m). This is a reduction in operating profit of 16.1%.

However as the marking director pointed out, it would be unwise to judge performance on one year's data. This is particularly the case as it is a transitional period and only the first year of the three year recovery plan.

Positive signs included the following:

(1)   The willingness of 30 franchisees to take up new franchises
(2)   Profit in first year for Export Division
(3)   Profit in first year for Commercial Division

Negative signs include the following:

(1)   Overall reduction in volume of sales
(2)   Significant fall in operating profit per franchisee shop

Given that several simultaneous changes have been made by Confo, it is difficult to determine precisely which changes have impacted performance most in the short term. Given that the planning horizon is three years, it is appropriate to review progress after one year, but unreasonable to draw firm conclusions as to whether the changes will be successful when the three year planning horizon is reached.

Examiner's comments

The main weakness in this requirement was inadequate evaluation of the overall recovery plan, which was unsatisfactory in nature and in the level of detail in the answers of most candidates.

The majority of candidates incorporated analytical frameworks, and most who used models made use of Ansoff's matrix. A smaller number also referred to Lynch.

Only a small minority recognised potential cannibalisation of the Retail Division's sales by the Commercial Division, combined with consumer awareness that the products are identical apart from packaging. More saw the revised packaging as a protection against this.

In terms of the overall recovery plan for the company, of those who considered this, most concluded it to be favourable, on balance, as time is needed for it to come to fruition. Better candidates included calculations to support this conclusion. A few explicitly referred to the three-year time horizon.

28.4 Ethical issues

Ethics pertains to whether a particular behaviour is deemed acceptable in the context under consideration. In short, it is 'doing the right thing'.

In making any ethical evaluation it is first necessary to establish the facts. In this case, it would seem that the facts are reasonably clear in terms of what has happened, although the lack of documentary evidence to support the facts may limit the actions that can be taken.

The issue of legality and compliance with the Bribery Act needs to be considered and legal advice taken by Confo. If a crime has been committed there may be a duty to disclose in the public interest.

Both the offering, and the receiving, of an inappropriate inducement may be considered illegal and/or unethical.

In making a decision as to how to proceed, it is helpful to apply the Institute of Business Ethics three tests:

- Transparency
- Effect
- Fairness

Transparency – would CCC mind people (existing customers, suppliers, employees) knowing that these transactions have taken place. In the first instance, there appears to be a degree of internal transparency as Kirsty reported the initial Christmas gift to the commercial director. It is not known whether John reported the gift within Lenton but, given his subsequent behaviour, this seems unlikely. At this stage Kirsty may be deemed to have taken actions which are not inappropriate give the scale, context and disclosure.

Subsequent gifts made by Kirsty were not disclosed and hence the ethical test of openness does not appear to have been met. Since March 20Y4 Kirsty has made gifts of company property without notification, consultation or authority, which appears both fraudulent and unethical. The question of how she obtained the goods needs to be asked and who knew about this (as opposed to the purpose for which they were being used), if anyone.

Her refusal to make undisclosed gifts beyond £100 is appropriate, but does not compensate for her earlier actions.

Effect – whom does the decision to make the ever larger transfers of sweets affect or hurt? The initial Christmas gift may be appropriate based on its scale (small amount of £10), context (seasonal gift and industry norm) and expected frequency (annual at Christmas) in that it would be unlikely to be of sufficient size to affect John's commercial decisions about the Confo contract. However, subsequent larger gifts may have had the effect of John choosing to make purchases from Confo, rather than a rival company which might be offering preferential commercial terms to Lenton, but with no personal inducement for John. The effect in this case would be that Lenton shareholders are suffering due to John receiving inappropriate personal inducements. Conversely, Confo may be the best commercial provider and the ceasing of gifts may have made John choose an inferior provider, to the detriment of Lenton shareholders.

In this context, sweets with a relatively small financial value (even at £100) could trigger decisions on a commercial contract worth many thousands of pounds.

Fairness – would the transfers be considered fair by those affected? Confo may be obtaining an unfair commercial advantage over rivals through paying inappropriate (and possibly illegal) inducements. Similarly, John has gained a significant and unfair benefit compared to more honest colleagues who would not have engaged in such actions. Whilst the benefit is in kind, rather than cash, this is not the key issue if it amounts to an inducement. Moreover, it is possible that the confectionery could be sold by John to convert to cash.

Honesty and integrity

Further issues are those of honesty and integrity. The inducements may fail the honesty test as they are not earned, authorised or disclosed by, or on behalf of, the giver or the recipient.

Actions

An initial action for Kirsty would be now to act honestly and make transparent what has occurred to the commercial director by full disclosure of all the facts, with any supporting evidence to which she has access. The matter is likely to be of sufficient seriousness that she may offer her resignation in anticipation of possible legal action against her for misappropriating goods belonging to the company to a third party without authority.

Kirsty should co-operate in all investigations made by the company or the police.

The fact she received no direct financial benefit may mitigate, but not remove, her culpability. Indirectly, in making more sales, she may have benefited in the long run by achieving promotion or more job security.

Confo may have benefited initially from Kirsty's action and may suffer reputational damage by external disclosure, but nevertheless there is a public interest disclosure requirement if, on the basis of legal advice, a crime has been committed. The Confo board should therefore inform the Lenton board of what has occurred in order that it can make its own investigations. If the Lenton board does not make disclosure to the police then the Confo board should consider doing so, notwithstanding that documentary evidence is limited.

Examiner's comments

This requirement was well answered, on the whole, with most candidates making use of ethical principles and language to assist their balanced discussion, and recognising the potential adverse effects to be much greater than a few boxes of chocolates as it could have impacted on the cessation of the supply contract between the two companies. Legal aspects were also often referred to, including bribery, though a worrying minority dismissed the idea of there being any legal ramifications out of hand. Some considered the culpability to be only with John Drake, rather than also relating to Kirsty at Confo.

Only a minority recognised the need for a clear formulation of a company policy on the issue of gifts to business contacts. Poorer candidates failed to deal with required actions and instead just analysed the scenario in general terms using transparency, fairness and effect.

---

29 Radar Traditional Radios Ltd (December 2014)

Marking guide

	Knowledge	Skill	Marks
29.1 Porter's 5 Forces	3	8	10
29.2 Segmentation	4	9	12
29.3 Abandon	2	8	9
	9	25	31

General comments:

RTR is a family-owned company which is an upmarket manufacturer of radios with retro styling. It operates in the UK market.

RTR makes both digital and analogue radios, but it is concerned about the impact of the transfer of radio broadcasting in the UK from analogue to digital, which has been much slower than expected. As the broadcasting industry moves increasingly to digital, RTR is concerned about the increasing competition from the variety of devices that can receive digital radio broadcasting. There is also significant competition from larger global radio manufacturers which have large R&D and marketing budgets compared to RTR. Some disagreement has arisen on the RTR board as to how the R&D and marketing budgets should be targeted and focused to give maximum benefit.

29.1 Porter's Five Forces

Substitutes

A substitute product is a product or service produced by another industry which satisfies the same customer needs as the industry under consideration.

Where there are readily available substitutes accessible to consumers at reasonable cost, then this acts as additional competition and competes away industry profitability.

In the radio manufacturing industry, close substitutes exist in a range of other devices which can receive digital audio transmissions to replicate the function of radios. These include digital televisions, internet devices and smart phones.

The growth in the use of internet and mobile phones for listening to radio between 20X9 and 20Y3 (see table) indicates that they are relatively close substitutes.

Moreover, while some of the other devices are more expensive than buying a radio, they also perform other functions, so consumers are, for example, already likely to have a television and there is no incremental cost to listening to the radio. In addition, switching costs are minimal if other devices are already owned.

While the other products noted above are close substitutes, they are not perfect substitutes. For example:

- The other devices do not receive analogue broadcasts
- The sound quality (eg, from many smart phones) may not be as good as a radio
- A radio is portable unlike some other devices (eg, a television)

Nevertheless, these substitutes affect the profitability of the radio manufacturing industry through the following:

- Putting a ceiling on prices eg, it is unlikely very high prices could be charged, even for high quality radios

- Affecting volumes of demand as the market is split not only between rivals in the industry, but with manufacturers of substitute products

- Forcing expensive investments and technology improvements to keep pace with technology changes outside the industry

Defining the industry as radio manufacturing is quite narrow. Many of the larger consumer electronics manufacturers are also likely to make the substitute products noted above and hence are internally diversified. The companies most exposed to the threat of substitutes in the industry are those (like RTR) who only make radios.

Conclusion

Overall the threat from substitutes is significant and could, in the longer run, be industry destroying.

Competitive rivalry amongst existing firms

The intensity of competition amongst existing rival firms in the industry will tend to compete away the collective profitability of participants in the industry.

Competition in radio manufacture is global, even if some companies in the industry are focused, like RTR, on one national market. There are major international companies which, although not based in the UK, can distribute efficiently to the UK.

The level of competitive rivalry in radio manufacturing will depend on the following factors.

Digital radios

- Rate of market growth – the market for digital radios is changing:

  - It may be rising as fewer people buy analogue radios, which will reduce competitiveness and make the industry more profitable; or

  - It may be falling as the overall market for listening to radio is fairly constant (in listening hours) and the availability of substitutes means that the remaining demand for radios is falling, leaving the incumbent manufacturers chasing a smaller market.

- Ease of switching for buyers – buyers of digital radios can easily switch to rival products when a radio is replaced thus competition is intense in relation to every product cycle.

- Degree of uncertainty over the actions of rival firms – new digital technology could emerge on a regular basis meaning that profits could fall away for many firms in the industry. This requires high R&D budgets which reduce industry profitability.

Analogue radios

- Level of fixed costs – if there is a smaller market for analogue radios in future and as volumes fall across the industry then fixed costs per unit increase and industry profitability therefore falls

- Importance of capacity utilisation/economies of scale – a shrinking market means fewer economies of scale and more spare capacity thereby reducing industry profit

- Exit barriers – these may be high (non-current assets with a low break-up value; redundancy payments, costs of withdrawal) due to the specialised nature of the equipment which means competition remains in the industry much longer than would otherwise be the case (zombie companies)

Conclusion

Overall, the threat from competitive rivalry amongst existing firms is significant and could cause less efficient companies to exit the industry.

Examiner's comments

This requirement was generally very well answered. Most recognised the relevance of substitutes and competitive rivalry to industry competitiveness and concluded that both forces are relatively strong, hence tending towards an increasingly unattractive competitive environment. Fewer candidates emphasised the fact that analogue radio faces less of a threat from substitutes than digital.

The competitive rivalry section was less well done than substitutes, with candidates often failing to recognise that the market for radios was changing. Candidates tended to conclude that competitive rivalry was high, but often without really justifying why.

Weaker efforts tended to confuse substitutes with competitive rivalry and spent a lot of time discussing how digital radios are substitutes for analogue.

29.2 Market segmentation

Market segmentation is the division of the market into homogeneous groups of potential customers who may be treated similarly for marketing purposes.

Focus players like RTR may only be able to use market segmentation in a limited way as one segment might be their sole consumer group. Broader market players may use market segmentation to market in different ways to different groups.

RTR has a premium pricing strategy. Necessarily, there are fewer people that can afford expensive radios than can afford cheaper radios, which limits the size of the market, but also changes the characteristics of the consumer group (see pricing section below).

Market segmentation is therefore a tool of marketing strategy that can help RTR management to focus on relevant customer groups, and to use a marketing mix to arrive at a desirable marketing proposition. This enables RTR to customise its marketing mix to make it appropriate to likely customers.

The market can be segmented in a number of general different ways. For example:

- Age
- Income
- Gender

More specific segmentation might refer to the number of hours listening to the radio, or technology spending of consumers (eg, identified by purchasing technology magazines or other technology products purchased).

Different types of market segmentation can be combined in order to refine the sub group which is most likely to appeal as potential consumers of RTR radios. Thus, for instance, a particular type of radio programme might appeal to higher income groups with an age group of around 55, perhaps with more females in the audience. These can be targeted for radio advertising during these programmes.

There are a number of problems in doing this type of market segmentation:

- The groupings are crude (eg, 55% female buyers for RTR is only just above half and there is therefore little benefit above mass marketing to the population generally).

- Obtaining the information to target these groups may be difficult. It may be necessary to use databases which tend to be typical of the market segments identified, rather than use the characteristics (age, income, gender) directly. The best such database is RTR's historic customer list, as these have chosen to buy RTR radios before. Other companies' customer lists, with similar customer characteristics to RTR (where they can be legally and ethically obtained) may also be a useful means of segmentation.

The marketing mix

Following market segmentation, targeting involves selecting the most appropriate market segments.

Target marketing tailors a marketing mix for one or more segments identified by market segmentation.

Promotion

Advertising is the most obvious form of promotion, and it should be appropriate to the targeted market segment.

Radio manufacturing is related to the media industry, so advertising through this means seems one of the most obvious channels to use. This may include transmissions through other rival devices such as TV, mobiles and the internet.

The internet may take target marketing down to very small groups who have shown an interest in radios and radio broadcasting through their choice of websites.

In terms of broader radio audiences, data may be available by audience characteristics for particular programmes and placing adverts adjacent to these programmes would stand the best opportunity of reaching the RTR target customer base and gain best value for its advertising spending.

Other media might include journals and magazines used by older, high income age groups, ideally with some radio listening theme.

Price

RTR has a premium pricing strategy. Necessarily, there are fewer people that can afford expensive radios than can afford cheaper radios, which limits the size of the market, but it also changes the characteristics of the consumer group willing to pay more for radios, compared with the mass market of radio purchasing consumers.

Even within the high income group who buy RTR's radios, more customers could be created by lowering the price, but this has some disadvantages:

- Lowers the profit per unit

- Demand is likely to be inelastic in this market niche thus sales volumes may not increase significantly even if prices are substantially lower

- It sends the wrong marketing signal where this is a luxury good and the quality cannot be readily observed, thus price is a signal of quality

A key factor in assessing price is the prices being charged by the closest competitors, which should be identified in market research of competitors. In this case, however, as a signal of quality, a virtue is being made of setting prices above competitors.

Product

A product is not just the physical item with features, but the perception of the item to thecustomer and the package of benefits that it provides.

The technology features used by RTR are good quality, but the styling of the goods is important and is distinctive, being part of the brand image.

The brand name is key in representing these qualities and making the RTR radios distinct from other brands.

In the case of RTR, the company name is the brand name.

Thus, for example, the 'retro' old fashioned style may particularly appeal to the older age market segment who can remember when all radios were styled in that way.

Place

Given RTR currently only sells through retail outlets in the UK, this limits the geographical market. The distribution network should be reviewed to make sure that the shops where RTR radios are being sold are consistent in image with the high income, middle age market segmentation strategy.

However, there may also be scope for widening the perception of the attainable geographic market by marketing to similar high income, middle aged groups overseas. Further market research could reveal whether the same segmentation groups apply in other countries as they do in the UK.

In terms of distribution, a radio is small and portable so the costs of transporting them may be low and this would enhance the opportunity to open up international markets through on-line sales without damaging the relationship with UK retailers, as there is likely to be little leakage between markets.

Examiner's comments

This requirement was well answered on the whole. Most began with definitions of segmentation and applied this to the question.

A minority wasted time discussing in detail market research approaches to segmentation, but then often proceeded to ignore the data which had been provided in the question.

The best answers related each different type of segmentation to the marketing mix. Weaker efforts only discussed the latter in generic terms.

There was little discussion by most candidates of the problems of applying market segmentation.

Virtually no candidate attempted to discuss the marketing mix in the broader context of an overall marketing strategy for the firm.

29.3 Factors to consider

RTR currently makes both digital and analogue radios. Analogue still makes up most of the sales of RTR by volume at 60%, although by value it is less than this at 53% (see below) as digital radios are more expensive.

In sales value terms at retail prices:

	20Y3 £'000	
Analogue radios (60,000 × £150)	9,000	53%
Digital radios (40,000 × £200)	8,000	47%

While analogue radios are the more important product in terms of sales volumes, they are declining as they near the end of their product life cycle, due to both technology and regulation. In terms of a BCG matrix analysis of its product portfolio, RTR's analogue radios are the company's key 'cash cows' as they still generate significant cash flows which can be used to fund increased marketing and/or investment in R&D for the 'problem child' digital products. Cash flows are likely to decline soon however, as analogue radios head towards 'dog' status. In contrast, digital radios are in the growth phase of their product life cycle, but at a slow rate of only 1,000 radios per year on average.

The immediate abandonment of the major product seems implausible, and this is not being suggested. Rather, the suggestion is that RTR should no longer invest in analogue R&D and marketing and thus gradually let sales decline (perhaps over two to three years) to the point where they will then be abandoned.

If the process of decline in analogue is rapid (as two to three years may seem to be), this is very risky as the major product may be in its decline stage of the product life cycle but is still generating most of the major cash flows for RTR. Indeed, any R&D and marketing costs may be self-financing in terms of additional sales.

Despite the above, it seems clear that the UK government intends to abandon analogue broadcasting eventually, thereby ending sales of analogue radios in the UK. Whilst there may be overseas markets to sell analogue radios to (eg, developing nations) it seems clear this market will disappear over time in favour of digital radios.

In essence therefore, the key decision for RTR is not **whether** to abandon producing analogue radios, but **when**.

In making this decision the key factors are as follows.

In favour of abandoning analogue sooner and investing in digital radios

- Analogue is to cease being broadcast. In anticipation of this, consumers will cease to buy analogue radios some time before the switch-off date

- Industry support appears to be in favour of digital, so working with broadcasters in digital research may be more fruitful than analogue research

- Only 40% households own digital radios, but in total 90% of people listen to radio programmes, so there is a big potential first time buyer market

- As technology develops rapidly, consumers will wish to replace their radios more frequently with the new features

- Distribution outlets for analogue radios may shrink as retail chains stop selling them

- New features like Bluetooth are needed to keep pace with changes in technology in order to compete and R&D is needed for this

Against abandoning analogue sooner and continuing to invest in it for longer

- Digital reception is only available to 90% of the UK population. This not only restricts the market but makes it less likely in the short term that government will switch off analogue

- Uncertainty arises from the intensity of future competition in digital communications (within the industry and with substitutes)

- Analogue is still a larger market than digital by current sales volumes and current listeners

- Digital may fail to take hold in the global market and therefore fail commercially as a technology

- Analogue may continue for many years, perhaps due to the greater sound quality.

- If other companies exit the analogue market, but RTR remain in it, then it may be less competitive for RTR

Conclusion

There are significant uncertainties about the nature and timing of the relative popularity of digital and analogue. It may be appropriate to keep the real option and continue with both technologies until it is clearer about the pace of change in market preferences and the timing and certainty of the analogue switch off.

Examiner's comments

The responses to this question were mixed. The best answers were well balanced and often explicitly introduced either the product life cycle or the BCG matrix, or both. Many were implicitly aware of the relevance of these frameworks, so some credit was given.

Only a few referred to the uncertainty of the analogue switch-off date, with most assuming that this will happen in 20Y9. The weakest answers concluded that the firm should quit analogue production as soon as possible, with little consideration of the adverse cash flow impact this would have. Weaker answers also failed to make any reference to the data provided.

The higher scoring answers recognised that if other companies exited the analogue market, then RTR could benefit from this as the industry supply would be reduced to offset, to some degree, falling industry demand for analogue devices.

Additionally they tended to spend a lot of time discussing partially relevant issues such as redundancies, with little focus on the timing, product portfolio and cash flow issues.

Very few referred to the real option characteristics of the choices faced by the firm.

30 The Norgate Bank plc (December 2014)

Marking guide

	Knowledge	Skill	Marks
30.1 KPIs	2	11	12
30.2 Benchmarking	4	8	11
	6	19	23

General comments:

The Norgate Bank (NB) has both business customers and individual customers who are based in the UK and France. It has no branches but communicates with customers entirely through internet and telephone banking. Historically, NB had one telephone call centre near London, but last year it opened a new call centre in Vietnam to service all its French-speaking customers. At each centre, employees are divided into two separate groups which service business and individual customers. In the first year of operation, three key KPIs were used to measure and monitor performance being: time to answer a call; length of a call; and customer satisfaction survey results. Concern has been raised about the suitability of these measures. The company also wants to use benchmarking to evaluate performance and improve efficiency. Data on performance is provided.

30.1 KPIs

KPIs are metrics in relation to a target that will deliver the organisation's objectives in the area to which they relate.

KPIs should therefore be related to the relevant critical success factor. In the case of the call centres this means dealing with customer enquiries to satisfy customer expectations, build relationships and achieve this as efficiently as possible in terms of time and cost.

The actual KPIs achieved are given in the Exhibit but there is no target measure against which to judge these metrics in order to determine whether performance has been at an appropriate level. The idea of benchmarks to determine an appropriate target is examined below.

Dealing with the nature of the KPI's used by Ron:

Average time taken to answer a customer call

This is measure of efficiency, but also it is a measure of capacity to take calls. If the KPI achieved is not at an appropriate level of efficiency (eg, customers are ringing off before the call is answered) then this may damage relationships with customers and cause dissatisfaction leaving customer enquiries unsatisfied.

There is therefore a trade-off between efficiency, capacity and cost. If sufficient resources are dedicated to call centres then all calls could be answered immediately, but this may not meet the objective of cost efficiency as too many staff may be idle waiting when call volumes are low.

Being efficient would be trying to meet customer expectations, including unexpected peaks and troughs in call volumes, without undue idle time and therefore excessive cost.

Overall this seems to be a reasonable measure in that long waiting times are likely to be viewed unfavourably by customers. What is not clear is how to determine the target for the optimal time that customers should wait to balance service delivery with cost.

Average length of a customer call

This KPI is, to a degree, ambiguous. If the average call is long then it could be sign of quality in meeting customer needs by giving due time to resolve all the issues raised and make the customer feel in receipt of a good service.

Conversely, it could be a sign of inefficiency in being unable to deal with customer enquiries quickly and efficiently and so wastes customer time as well as NB staff time and costs.

A further alternative may be that the length of the call is dependent on the subject matter. Thus business customer calls may deal with more complex issues than calls from private individuals and may therefore take longer on average.

Overall, therefore, this seems a difficult measure to determine, not just the level of the KPI, but the direction relative to target. In this respect many of the relevant factors may be captured in the final KPI which is:

Scores from customer satisfaction surveys

Scores from customer satisfaction surveys are a good measure of whether objectives are being achieved in relation to building customer relationships and offering appropriate service.

On their own however crude measures of how satisfied customers are with a call does not of itself indicate why they are satisfied. Further qualitative detail is needed to better undertstand customer satisfaction (eg, whether it is the length of the call, ability to resolve issue quickly, friendliness). It also leaves open the question of satisfaction relative to cost.

Conclusion

The KPIs selected emphasise effective service delivery by omitting measures of the efficiency with which that service is delivered.

Additional measures of efficiency (eg, meeting peaks and troughs with the right scheduling of staff hours to meet demand at key times in the day, and for key days of the week) and capacity (idle hours to total hours ie, utilisation) would be useful.

Also there are no financial KPIs which is key to call centre financial efficiency. Cost per call could be one such measure. In this case, the costs of the Vietnam centre per call may be much lower than the London centre, even if operational efficiency is lower in Vietnam.

Examiner's comments

The quality of responses was mixed for this requirement. The best answers provided critical evaluation of each of the three KPIs after an introduction defining KPIs, their role and their relationship to critical success factors or goals. Alternatives were suggested during the course of the evaluations and, often, afterwards. Weaker candidates failed to link the KPIs with CSFs.

Relatively few candidates explicitly or implicitly discussed the trade-offs between efficiency, capacity and costs. Likewise, only a significant minority considered the issue of different types of customers and/or locations.

Additionally, a few referred to direct sample monitoring of calls as well as using the 'mystery shopper' approach to direct quality evaluation.

In order to consider critical success factors, some attempted to use the Balanced Scorecard framework, but in many instances suggested goals and measures which were largely unrelated to the performance of the call centres.

Some candidates redefined the entire requirement in terms of the Balanced Scorecard, which tended to lead to poor marks.

30.2 Benchmarking

Benchmarking is: 'The establishment, through data gathering, of targets and comparators, through whose use relative levels of performance (and particularly areas of underperformance) can be identified. By the adoption of identified best practices it is hoped that performance will improve.'

Benchmarking compares the use of assets and activities across the firm, or across the industry, and indicates where they might be used better or where they are already a source of superior performance. Once a business has identified its CSFs and core competences, it must identify performance standards which need to be achieved to outperform rivals and achieve sustainable competitive advantage. These standards are sometimes called key performance indicators (KPIs).

Benchmarks can therefore provide a means of determining target KPIs which, if achieved, will match the best standards in the industry. Such benchmarks not only set targets for existing KPIs, but may suggest different types of KPI to measure new CSFs.

In so doing, by comparing performance with other entities, NB can learn how to reduce costs and improve customer service quality. Additionally, benchmarking may help NB better understand whether it is achieving competitive advantage and superior performance in the call centre operations area of its activities.

Different types of benchmarks may provide different types of guidance:

Historic or internal benchmarking – internal benchmarking would be at the level of comparing individual units (for businesses and individuals) at each call centre (London and Vietnam) with each other to determine those that are under- or over-performing when considering the different demands and circumstances. At the moment however this is the first year of operation of Vietnam and learning may still be taking place. Conversely London may still be adjusting to losing the French customer calls. Nevertheless, internal benchmarking attempts to raise performance to the standard of the best internal unit and demonstrates to other units that this level of performance is achievable.

Historical comparison looks at performance over time to ascertain trends/significant changes, but the danger is that performance against competitors is ignored and long-standing internal inefficiencies are not highlighted. Note: For the first year of operation this is not possible in Vietnam.

In the Exhibit, it would appear that data could be used (for example) to compare the number of hours of calls handled per annum for each member of staff. In the UK call centre for individuals this is 800 hours pa ($(1,200,000 \times 4/60)/100$) but in the other three functions (UK individuals, Vietnam business and Vietnam individuals) it is 1,000 hours pa. This would at least raise some questions. The differences in satisfaction also vary between centre and between types of customer, but there is no obvious pattern.

Competitive benchmarking – compares performance with other firms in the same industry or sector. This may assist NB in ascertaining ways to improve performance – eg, comparing the performance with other banks' call centres. An alternative is to widen the definition of the industry from banks to financial services and include the experience of Ron's deputy who has worked in the related industry of insurance. The differences may be accounted for in the differences in the types of calls received by banks and insurance companies but questions may be asked to improve performance even though the comparisons are not identical.

This may involve the use of league tables, but more detailed information may be difficult to achieve as competitors may be reluctant to share data with rivals. Partnerships or industry groupings or a benchmarking centre may help overcome this lack of information.

Activity (best in class) benchmarking – compare with best practice in whatever industry can be found eg, could compare with a hotel telephone booking system, or ticket booking or emergency telephone system, whichever is 'best in class' for the function dealing with telephone calls efficiently. This has the advantage that a firm may share operations in common with non-competitor external organisations, which might be 'best in the class' for a particular function, more readily than with a rival firm in the same industry.

Generic benchmarking – this is benchmarking against a conceptually similar process eg, compare an online system of banking compared to telephone calls which can achieve the same outcome (eg, simple transactions online or by telephone). It is unlikely that this will result in comparison of detailed measures but it could identify conceptual areas for improvement.

Disadvantages

There are disadvantages to benchmarking. A full programme can overload managers with demands for information, restrict their attention to the factors that are to be benchmarked and affect their motivation by seeming to reduce their role to copying others. It can also undermine competitive advantage by revealing trade secrets. Strategically, it can divert attention away from innovation and the future by focussing it on the efficiency of current operations.

Since benchmarking is about processes rather than results, measures would have to be linked to outcomes at some stage.

Examiner's comments

Most candidates discussed three or four types of benchmarking and many also provided an introduction to the purpose of benchmarking in the performance management process of identifying critical success factors and related KPIs.

A significant minority described the approaches with little or no evaluation of advantages and problems in their application in this particular scenario. Many did mention, in general terms, the difficulties involved in obtaining competitor/comparator data. Additionally, there was a tendency to evaluate internal benchmarking only, tending to ignore the other types of benchmarking, beyond an initial description.

Good answers also related their discussion to their previous consideration of KPIs. However, a minority of weaker candidates displayed a lack of awareness of the benchmarking process and simply carried on evaluating KPIs.

31   Rocket Co (March 2015)

Marking guide

	Knowledge	Skill	Marks
31.1 Performance	2	18	18
31.2 Consideration of factors	3	9	10
31.3 Change management	4	7	10
31.4 Ethics	3	6	8
	12	40	46

General comments:

This is the mini case at 46 marks and also the data analysis question. It was the highest scoring question on the paper.

The scenario relates to a four partner accountancy practice – Rocket – which operates in a European country and specialises in accounting and tax advisory work in the sports and leisure sector. Rocket has experienced impressive growth rates but the partners are concerned that growth appears to be slowing. Candidates were presented with a balanced scorecard for Rocket for 20Y13 and 20Y14, showing financial and non-financial performance indicators.

A new regulatory framework for the legal services market has recently been introduced in Rocket's country, allowing the creation of a multi-disciplinary practice (MDP) – a professional firm consisting of professionally qualified lawyers and accountants working together in client-facing roles. Rocket has decided to begin operating as an MDP, and needs to obtain the necessary licence and recruit staff to resource the change in strategy. It will either recruit qualified lawyers on an individual basis or acquire a specialist team of qualified lawyers from a law firm to which it has previously referred work. On 1 March 20Y15, Rocket issued an email (provided in the scenario) to all staff, announcing the firm's change of strategy and the partners' expectations. There had been no prior consultation with the recipients of the email and it has caused considerable anxiety.

Rocket is also facing an ethical issue – Alina Jay, an ICAEW Chartered Accountant, suspects that her manager may have agreed to the misstatement of a client's personal affairs on a loan application because he is a personal friend of the client. Alina is unsure whether she should report the client and/or the manager to her superiors, and is concerned about the impact on her job and career if she were to do so.

31.1 Performance analysis

Appendix: Further analysis

Tutorial note:

A wide range of possible calculations have been given here for marking purposes and to illustrate the scope for additional numerical analysis.

Analysis of income

	20Y4	20Y3
Fee income F'000 (given)	7,091	6,653
Mix of fee income:		
Accounting: tax	47:53	45:55
Absolute fee income:		
Accounting F'000	3,333 (increase 11.3%)	2,994
Tax F'000	3,758 (increase 2.7%)	3,659
Average fee charged		
Accounting	F335 (increase 11.7%)	F300
Tax	F415 (increase 15.3%)	F360
Premium charged for tax (tax rate/accountancy rate)	23.9%	20%
Hours billed		
Accounting	9,949	9,980
Tax	9,055	10,164
	Total 19,004	Total 20,144
Change in total hours:	(5.7%)	
Accounting	(0.3%)	
Tax	(10.9%)	

Market information

	20Y4	20Y3
Fee income F'000 (given)	7,091	6,653
Market share (given)	12%	14%
Hence market size F'000	59,092 (increase 24.3%)	47,521

Profitability

	20Y4	20Y3
Fee income F'000 (given)	7,091	6,653
Net profit margin	20.8%	23.1%
Net profit F'000	1,475 (decrease 4.0%)	1,537
Total costs F'000	5,616 (increase 9.8%)	5,116
Fee income per partner F'000 (given)	1,773	1,663
No. of partners	4	4
Average profit per partner	368.75 (4% decrease)	384.25

Variances on non-financial indicators

	20Y4	20Y3	Variance
Market share	12%	14%	2% decrease
% Satisfied clients	75%	85%	10% decrease
Total staff turnover	23.5%	17.6%	5.9% increase
Error rates	10%	8%	2% increase
Utilisation rate	70.5%	66.5%	4% increase

Rocket uses a balanced scorecard approach to performance measurement which combines financial and non-financial information. Some of the non-financial factors in the scorecard can be used to help explain the financial performance of and the prospects for the business and give much greater insight into key operational issues within the business.

Income and market share

Fee income is up by 6.6% compared to an increase of 9.2% the previous year which suggests that growth is slowing and may explain Rocket's desire to consider new products.

However referring to the market share information (customer perspective), it is clear that Rocket has underperformed the market, losing 2% of its share at a time when the market for services (measured by revenue) has increased by 24.3%. It would be helpful to have the market share information analysed between tax and accounting to consider both lines of service separately and assess whether one is out-performing the other. The sales mix has altered with the more lucrative tax work representing only 53% of income (F3.758million), compared to 55% in 20Y3 (F3.659million), so it may be that Rocket is falling behind in this market. Since tax services command a premium rate compared to accounting, the change in sales mix will have an adverse effect on income.

The cause of the growth in fee income needs to be analysed between price and volume:

Rocket increased the fees charged for both services – accounting by 11.7% and tax by 15.3%. As a result the hours billed have fallen by 5.6% in total, from 20,144 to 19,004. This is consistent with a drop in market share. One possible reason for the increase in price would be to cover the pay rise that Rocket has had to offer staff to keep its salaries more in line with competitors.

It can be seen from the analysis that the tax services seem to have been more sensitive to the change in price, with chargeable tax hours reducing by 10.9% and thus only a 2.7% increase in overall tax revenue (compared to 11.3% for accounting). It would be useful to know to what extent the level of WIP (work done not yet billed) is comparable across the years and to try to ascertain whether the loss of chargeable hours is a timing issue or symptomatic of a loss of clients. It would also be useful to obtain competitor charge-out rates for the sports and leisure sector to see whether Rocket's fees are reasonable, although as discussed above the fact that Rocket has lost market share may be in part due to over-pricing.

Another reason for the drop in hours billed may be to do with loss of clients due to client dissatisfaction. The 20Y4 customer survey has revealed that only 75% of clients are satisfied, compared to 85% in 20Y3 – a 10% adverse variance. The cause of the dissatisfaction needs to be investigated. It may be linked to an increase in error rates from 8% to 10% of jobs (internal business) or to staffing issues – see below. Certainly if clients are being asked to pay higher fees they are likely to expect standards and quality of service to be at least maintained, so a 25% increase in the error rate is unlikely to be acceptable. It would be useful to know the reasons for the dissatisfaction and to ascertain whether one service has been affected more than the other.

Rocket has not been paying staff the appropriate market premium and this has probably led to demotivation and dissatisfaction, as evidenced by the increase in staff turnover (17.6% to 23.5% - innovation and learning). This represents one more fee-earner (5.9% x 17 fee earners) leaving and needing to be replaced. The pay rise offered may have come too late for some staff and more may choose to leave given the increasing employment opportunities in the marketplace. Continuity of staff is important as clients may resent revealing personal financial details to a variety of different people each year. Recruiting replacement staff costs the business money and there is then a learning curve period, during which perhaps errors may be made. In addition the business does not appear to be investing much in training, with qualified staff only receiving two days per year. In a specialist sector this may not be sufficient to keep abreast of developments and may be an additional cause of the error rates.

Profitability

Despite the 6.6% increase in fee income, Rocket's net profit for 20Y4 of F1.475million is 4% lower than in 20Y3.

The net profit margin has fallen from 23.1% to 20.8% as a result of the total cost increase (9.8%) exceeding that of the revenue increase. A number of factors have caused Rocket's costs to increase in 20Y4:

- Rent review

- Increased PII premiums

- Pay rise for staff (it would be useful to know how much this was and at what point in the year it was made as it does not yet appear to have stemmed the staff turnover)

One factor which will be adversely affecting profitability is the poor staff utilisation rate. Although this has improved from 66.5% to 70.5% it still means that staff are spending a considerable amount of time engaged in activities that are not billed to clients. This may be due to having to incur write-offs of time eg, on fixed fee jobs or because staff are spending time on business development, or too much time on administrative issues. Assuming staff work 7 hours a day, 5 days a week for 48 weeks, there are 1,680 hours available per fee earner. Assuming utilisation rates were between 85% and 90%, Rocket would only need 13 staff to achieve the 20Y4 billed hours. In the change management memo the partners identify the need for qualified staff to consider delegating more tasks to concentrate on higher value activities which would increase profitability.

Summary

In conclusion, although the revenue has grown and margins are still reasonable, the financial results do not show the full picture. Rocket appears to have some fundamental weaknesses in its core business that need to be addressed, if it is to continue to grow into the future. The success of the MDP proposal will be dependent on existing clients' willingness to buy additional legal services from Rocket, which they will not do if they are dissatisfied with the existing services and perceive staff to be inadequately trained.

Examiner's comments

Candidates were asked to analyse and evaluate the performance of Rocket between 20Y3 and 20Y4, using the balanced scorecard.

The data analysis requirement was reasonably attempted but certainly not as well answered as in recent sittings. The fact that a balanced scorecard of performance indicators was provided in the Exhibit seemed to discourage a surprising number of candidates from undertaking any further numerical analysis. Better candidates provided some additional up-front calculations in a reasonably well structured table to help explain some of the changes in the scorecard (fee income per service stream, billable hours, market size, profit per partner). Weaker candidates were very poor in this regard, merely reiterating the KPIs that had been given or at most providing occasional calculations of changes in figures, within their narrative.

Most candidates structured their narrative explanation using the four headings from the scorecard and made good links between the different sections, successfully drawing conclusions from the non-financial information to explain the reasons behind the financial performance.

Only the stronger candidates suggested additional information that would assist their analysis and concluded that Rocket would need to address some of its internal issues relating to client and staff dissatisfaction before becoming an MDP.

31.2 Factors affecting ability to create a multi-disciplinary practice (MDP)

Human resource capabilities

Rocket's existing partners and staff are all experienced in accountancy and taxation, not law, so it does not currently have the HR capability to implement this strategy. It would appear that it intends to use its existing support staff but will need to employ new 'fee-earners'.

It is critical to the venture's success that the legal staff have appropriate specialist expertise, otherwise there will be no incentive for existing clients to switch their legal services to Rocket. The MDP will take longer to set up if Rocket recruits piecemeal rather than acquires an existing team. However the advantage of the former is that Rocket may be more likely to integrate individuals into its own culture and may experience less resistance from staff.

From a cost point of view, Rocket may have to offer higher pay/rewards to induce staff to move, particularly if it has a reputation for poor pay and high staff turnover. The upside of recruiting an existing team however is that they may bring some clients with them.

Increasingly law firms are employing para-legal/non-lawyers to do routine work such as document processing, so Rocket will need to consider how many staff are required and what the appropriate mix is. This will depend on the expected demand for its legal services.

Legal and regulatory issues

These forces may relate to/be affected by government policies and be politically driven. They are largely outside Rocket's control.

Changes in the regulations affecting the legal services market appear to be an attempt by government to increase competition in the market. However this could change.

The new MDP will need a licence to operate and will be monitored by the new regulatory authority. It is not clear how easy it will be for Rocket to acquire the licence, the time and cost involved, what terms and conditions will apply eg, in relation to the mix of partners, governance requirements etc. and what the costs of compliance are likely to be. Rocket is presumably used to being accountable to the relevant accountancy and tax regulators so it has some experience in this area.

It will also need to consider the prospect of further regulations affecting MDPs/law/accountancy firms and also in relation to the sports sector where there are likely to be rules and regulations of different sports governing bodies, disciplinary matters etc.

Competitors and market structure

The reduction of barriers to entry is likely to increase competition and give rise to a number of alternative professional services providers.

Other accountancy firms may also decide to create MDPs.

Alternatively legal firms could develop their own accountancy and tax businesses so Rocket may lose referrals that it is currently getting from these firms.

Possible consolidation in the market place is likely to increase the size of the various players and if they are able to reduce costs, this may result in lower prices for services which will affect margins.

Rocket's advantage is that it specialises in sports and leisure, so it may face less competition in this niche than if it were targeting the whole market.

Examiner's comments

Candidates were required to analyse various factors that might influence Rocket's ability to create an MDP.

Requirement 31.2 was very well answered on the whole. The majority of candidates identified that Rocket does not currently have any legal expertise and that recruiting the necessary staff and obtaining the licence would be critical success factors for the creation of an MDP. Better candidates discussed the two different approaches to resourcing suggested in the question, in light of Rocket's current staffing issues. They also highlighted the uncertainty surrounding the MDP licence and rules given that the regulatory framework is new and designed to increase competition. Weaker candidates typically found it more difficult to discuss competition and market structure, although candidates who used their knowledge of rivalry and barriers to entry from the Porter's 5 forces model had more to say.

31.3 Change management

The change to an MDP is a major transformational change for Rocket, which is being made in response to changes in the external environment. As the internal memo points out, it may have a significant effect on the staffing and management structure of the firm.

The Gemini 4Rs framework to change involves reframing, restructuring, revitalising and renewal. To an extent, in advance of the memo, Rocket's partners have already addressed the first three of these:

- Reframing – Rocket has asked fundamental questions about what the organisation is about, decided to become an MDP and created a vision of what it will stand for: a mid-market professional services practice offering one-stop legal, tax and accounting advice for its existing wealthy sporting clients.

- Restructuring – the alignment of the physical organisation with the plan. Again the partners have addressed this by identifying the need to recruit resources, creating a central administration function and setting up appropriate account teams.

- Revitalising – this is the process of securing a good fit with the environment and explains the motivation for the change – here the partners of Rocket have quickly decided to adopt a new business model in response to the deregulation of the legal services market and are one of the early adopters in the hope of gaining competitive advantage.

This leaves the critical element – renewal - which is ensuring that people in the organisation support the change process and have the necessary skills to contribute to it.

Here the partners appear to have left the major change of culture and structure to be announced to staff in a memo. This is a coercive change approach, with little attempt at participation. As a result they have possibly underestimated the forces of resistance to change and do not appear to have attempted to harness support in favour of the new structure.

The problem with this is that change affects individuals in different ways and that the way change is introduced can influence the degree of resistance to it. Staff are likely to have lots of questions about the MDP and there will be a great deal of uncertainty surrounding the impact that the new legal staff will have on the firm's culture, structure and systems. The fact that the partners state they will 'be examining the potential for cost savings and efficiencies across the firm' is likely to cause staff to worry about earnings and job security.

Existing staff may see the change as a threat for a variety of reasons: administrative staff in particular are being told to increase efficiency and informed that there will be target staffing ratios. Qualified staff may fear that in delegating work to juniors they lose their power base or may become redundant. Junior staff may feel ill-prepared to take on the additional work that is expected of them and worry about their lack of appropriate skills and training.

Such an approach can lead to low staff morale, which may already be a problem given that Rocket is not paying the market premium for specialist staff and has experienced an increase in staff turnover.

Instead of presenting staff with a fait accompli, Rocket would have been better undertaking some consultation process in advance of the announcement, allowing discussion about individual needs and creating opportunities for staff to contribute to the changes. This would have given staff time to get used to the idea and reduced the resentment and feelings of helplessness.

Thus whilst Rocket is taking a proactive approach to changes in its environment, its chosen method of communicating the change falls short of best practice. In the aftermath of the email, Rocket would be well advised to hold meetings to address any concerns and offer staff the chance to become involved in the implementation phase of the change process.

Examiner's comments

Candidates were asked to discuss, in light of the partners' email, the extent to which Rocket's approach meets best practice in change management, referring to an appropriate change model such as Gemini 4Rs.

The main difference in the answers to this requirement related to whether candidates were familiar with the specific model suggested for use. Candidates are normally well versed in the technical knowledge for the change management requirement but the Gemini 4Rs model proved to be an exception. A significant number of candidates, clearly unable to recall the Gemini model, made comments along the lines of 'whilst Gemini 4Rs is useful, so is Lewin Schein's iceberg model' and then went on to use that as an alternative.

Candidates are advised that if the examiner recommends an approach, there is usually a good reason for doing so. Whilst credit was awarded to candidates who used an alternative model, the use of the recommended Gemini model would have created scope to make a wider variety of points. Faced with changes in the external environment, Rocket appears to have **reframed** what the practice should stand for, is **restructuring** (recruiting lawyers and creating a central admin team) and attempting to **revitalise** by being an early adopter of the MDP model. However this is a major transformational change and staff are already unhappy, yet Rocket appears to have adopted a coercive change approach with little consultation. Thus the critical element of **renewal**, ensuring people in the organisation support the change, is lacking. Better answers were produced by the very few candidates who understood the model and recognised this.

As usual, weaker candidates failed to apply their knowledge to the question, simply discussing the type of change and the likely barriers rather than evaluating Rocket's decision to announce the change via email.

31.4 Ethical issues

This situation gives rise to a number of different potential ethical issues:

- Facilitation by the manager of unethical behaviour or even possibly illegal actions by the client

- Conflict between Alina's obligations as an ICAEW professional accountant and her obligations to Rocket, her employer

- Possible issues with the tone at the top within Rocket

Every employee has a duty of loyalty to their employer and in this case Alina owes a duty to Rocket Co. As a result Alina must not just turn blind eye to suspected wrongful behaviour because saying something might put her in an uncomfortable position with colleagues or because of self-interest in relation to her job or career. Thus if there is evidence of wrongdoing then keeping quiet should not be an option. Instead she needs to consider morally and ethically what the right thing to do is in relation to her suspicions.

A longstanding personal relationship with a client may have given rise to a familiarity threat to the manager's fundamental principles of objectivity. However it is important that Alina does not automatically assume that the manager has done something wrong. She needs to try and ascertain the facts. An effective relationship with superiors needs to be open, honest and trusting – the culture of Rocket should be such that Alina feels able to go to the managers and partners she works for and discuss opinions/ask questions/even challenge. It is not clear to what extent Alina has already done this with the manager concerned in relation to the statement of wealth and what evidence she has that the client's personal wealth has been misstated. If Alina has felt unable to raise her concerns then there may be a cultural issue to be addressed here by Rocket (the manner in which the change management was handled may suggest that this is the case).

Alina also needs to consider whether there is any statutory duty here and what legislation applies. Professional accountants need to be mindful of their responsibilities to their clients and employers to keep any information they learn confidential. Certainly Alina needs to avoid spreading news of the potentially dishonest activity by discussing it with colleagues or others who do not have responsibility over the matter. However there may be anti-fraud and/or anti-money laundering legislation that might govern reporting requirements. Whistle-blower protection provisions are common in most of Europe so she also needs to consider what legislation exists in the country to protect whistle-blowers, particularly for example in relation to the disclosure of confidential information about the client concerned.

In determining the appropriate action, Alina should consider whether there is any guidance in her employment contract, staff handbook, Rocket's code of conduct, or any internal guidance on whistleblowing. She also needs to consider her professional responsibility as a qualified accountant and the IESBA code of ethics (which is likely to apply to her manager and Rocket's partners to the extent that they are qualified accountants). Alina may be able to contact the firm's HR representative for assistance and/or seek legal advice.

Discussing her concerns with superiors in Rocket may be key as a means of preventing/detecting possible fraud. It would also highlight the inadequacies in Rocket's systems and culture which have allowed this to happen. Were Alina not to take any action, this would be allowed to perpetuate.

Examiner's comments

Candidates were requested to discuss the ethical issues associated with Alina's concerns and advise her on appropriate actions to take.

This requirement was well answered, presumably because the ethical issues (the suspected provision of misleading information to the bank and the need for internal/external disclosure) were reasonably easy for most candidates to identify. The vast majority of candidates recognised that there is likely to be a legal issue here - possibly fraud or money laundering. Most candidates made good use of ICAEW ethical principles and ethical language to assist their discussion and were able to identify the potential actions open to Alina. Some weaker candidates did apply the transparency, fairness and effect decision-making approach, although this is often more relevant in relation to a business dilemma and was much less useful here.

32 The Scottish Woodlands Commission (March 2015)

Marking guide

	Knowledge	Skill	Marks
32.1 Strategic fit	3	7	9
32.2 Financial benefits	2	8	10
32.3 Risks	2	6	7
32.4 Governance issues	3	7	8
	10	28	34

General comments:

Overall this question was also well attempted, although it contained both the highest and lowest scoring sections on the paper.

The scenario concerns a government department - the Scottish Woodlands Commission (SWC) - that is governed by a board of trustees. Its mission is 'to manage, protect and expand public woodlands in Scotland and to increase their value to society and the environment'. SWC is allocated a share of government funds but is prohibited from borrowing money in its own right. It also generates revenue from the harvesting and sale of timber. Money is spent on replanting, making grants for woodland improvement, providing education, and research.

SWC has been approached by a private holiday company, CabinCo, which wants to create self-catering holiday cabins in one of SWC's forests. A limited liability public/private partnership would be set up for the new venture, Woodsaway LLP, with profits and losses shared equally. CabinCo would supply £2m investment capital for the construction of the cabins and site and provide holiday management experience. SWC would make available Campbell Forest (current market value £2 million) for use in the venture. Campbell Forest would continue to be owned by SWC, which would grant a long lease to Woodsaway in exchange for an annual rent of £30,000. Financial projections for Woodsaway are provided which make it clear that cabin occupancy levels will be critical to the venture breaking even.

One of the trustees is concerned that their involvement in Woodsaway may give rise to certain conflicts with some of the principles of public sector governance that apply to them as trustees of SWC. Another believes that there is no issue, as corporate governance only applies to companies and their directors.

Candidates were required to act as a strategic business adviser engaged by the government and to write a report for SWC's trustees, evaluating the proposed venture using given headings. For ease of reference, the four sub-headings provided have been referred to as requirements (32.1) – (32.4) in the commentary below.

32.1 Strategic fit

To: SWC's Trustees
From: Business adviser
Date: March 20Y5
Re: Woodsaway LLP

Strategic fit

SWC's mission is to 'manage, protect and expand the public woodlands in Scotland and to increase their value to society and the environment'. In order to achieve this, it is authorised to undertake woodland management, nature conservation and provide facilities for public recreation.

The Woodsaway venture is likely to increase the number of people who are able to enjoy Campbell Forest and assist SWC in fulfilling one of its subsidiary objectives, of providing the general public with widespread access to the natural woodlands environment, and to promote woodlands as a location for sports and leisure activities.

It would not appear to directly assist with woodland management or nature conservation. Indeed construction of the log cabins may have a negative impact on the habitat for local wildlife, the maintenance of which is the other of SWC's subsidiary objectives.

However if the LLP generates additional income for SWC (see financial benefits below), then it may indirectly allow it to better achieve its primary and secondary objectives by providing more financial resources. Also woodland activities undertaken by Woodsaway's customers may have educational benefits by raising awareness and, if paid for, could also generate funds for conservation.

For the venture to be a success the two members of the LLP need to have complementary and aligned objectives.

CabinCo's mission is 'to be one of the UK's leading providers of luxury short breaks in natural surroundings'. It has created a strong brand and is seeking competitive advantage from having access to Campbell forest to develop a holiday village, and first option on the development of future villages on SWC woodlands in Scotland. As a private commercial company, CabinCo's aims are likely to involve growth and profits. Its primary objectives are more likely to be financial rather than non-financial, with a probable focus on cost control and margins. However the sustainable tourism market it is targeting may be more in line with SWC's environmental aims. Also the benefit to SWC is that CabinCo brings commercial experience to the venture, which may help increase profits and hence SWC's share.

There may be possible conflicts of interest about the strategy and activities of Woodsaway, between CabinCo as a private entity and SWC as a public body, since they have very different stakeholders and different planning horizons. CabinCo as a company accountable to its shareholders is likely to have a shorter term focus than the 20 year planning horizon that woodland management entails. A balance will need to be struck between financial return and delivering a service to customers and the general public.

Also conflicts may arise between the interests of the LLP and the separate interests of the two participating members. For instance CabinCo's desire to increase the profitability of the Woodsaway venture may conflict with SWC's mission to protect the woodlands and increase their value to society.

This is further discussed under the governance heading below.

Examiner's comments

In the first section of the report, candidates had to assess the strategic fit of the proposed venture. It was well answered. Most candidates were comfortable discussing the extent to which the venture is aligned with SWC's mission and secondary aims, recognising that construction of the log cabins might be inconsistent with the achievement of some of these aims (eg, protection of the woodland and nature conservation) but might facilitate others (increasing access and education). The better candidates also highlighted the very different nature of the two organisations involved in the LLP and questioned the conflict that may arise as a result. Most, but surprisingly not all candidates, scored an easy format mark for setting out their answer in the report format required. Some candidates created a time management issue for themselves by using all three headings from the suitability, feasibility, acceptability model when in fact 'suitability' is sufficient to assess strategic fit.

32.2 Financial benefits

The public/private partnership reduces the need for investment from SWC which would have to come from central government and SWC's limited commercial funds.

CabinCo (and possibly Woodsaway) will be able to raise funds privately from banks etc as it is not under the same restrictions regarding borrowing as SWC. The access to finance could provide opportunities for SWC, which would be unlikely to be able to find the £2m building costs. In the future it would also allow extension of the concept to other sites.

The venture provides SWC as landlord with a guaranteed income stream in the form of the lease rentals of £30,000pa. Depending on the occupancy levels, SWC, as a member of the LLP, will also receive a 50% share of the profits. Provided Woodsaway does not make a loss of more than £60,000 then SWC will avoid any financial loss.

Looking at the figures in the exhibit, the financial returns to SWC are highly sensitive to occupancy, which is likely to be lower in the early years:

Occupancy rate	40%	65%	90%
	£'000	£'000	£'000
Rental	30	30	30
Share of Woodsaway (loss)/profit	(153)	118	372
Net return to SWC	(123)	148	402
Annual return on £2m land value invested	-6.15%	7.4%	20.1%

Occupancy rate	40%	65%	90%
	£'000	£'000	£'000
Cabin revenue	1,752	2,847	3,942
Contribution	1,226	1,993	2,759
Fixed costs incl rent	(1,532)	(1,757)	(2,015)
Loss/Profit	(306)	236	744

The cabins are projected to generate a gross profit of £84 per night (eg, £1,226,000/(365 × 40)). There are 36,500 available cabin nights (365 × 100 cabins). If operating costs were £1,532,000 including rent then for the Woodsaway venture to break-even it needs to sell £1,532,000/84 = 18,238 cabin nights which equates to 50% occupancy.

Were operating costs to be £1,757,000 including rent then it would need 20,917 cabin nights or 57% occupancy. In reality it appears that some operating costs are stepped (14.7% increase in operating costs for 25% increase in occupancy), so break-even occupancy is somewhere between 50% and 57%.

It would be useful to know what occupancy CabinCo currently achieves in its other holiday villages, which is said to be 'high', but if Woodsaway achieves anything over 65%, it would appear to be providing SWC with a decent return.

It is not clear who has supplied the figures and how these compare to other CabinCo ventures. More detail on the breakdown of operating costs would be useful and the assumption of 365 days availability may be over-optimistic.

As discussed above, money from Woodsaway can be used to fulfil SWC's other objectives and is a useful source of income given its reliance on government funds.

Examiner's comments

Answers to this section on financial benefits were varied and there were a considerable number of poor answers, resulting in this section having the lowest overall mark. Once again a surprising number of candidates made no reference to the numbers provided in the question, despite the fact that this was the obvious place to do so. Weaker candidates simply discussed the fact that SWC is limited in its ability to raise finance and that the venture may help with this, without considering the financial returns.

The key to evaluating the financial benefits was to identify the two separate roles of SWC in relation to the Woodsaway venture:

- As landlord in receipt of annual rental
- As a member of the LLP, sharing in 50% of the profits or losses

Better candidates recognised this and used the various projections to calculate SWC's profit share for the different occupancy levels. The best candidates used the financial projections provided to give some indication of the likely return on SWC's £2m land investment and examined the sensitivity of the venture (eg, by calculating a break-even occupancy).

32.3 Risks

A key issue for SWC is risk and who will take responsibility for managing those risks.

Compared to SWC operating a holiday village on its own, the risk of the Woodsaway venture is reduced because it is structured as an LLP and risk is shared with CabinCo, an experienced partner in the holiday sector. The public/private partnership integrates the complementary resources of the two parties. However as discussed in 32.1 above, a conflict of interest may arise between the interests of the LLP and the separate interests of the two participating members.

The Woodsaway venture brings its own additional risks:

Economic risk– financial events that would affect the management of the holiday village and/or the forest. This might include the volatility of revenue streams and profit share due to the state of the economy. Also any impact that operating the holiday site may have on revenues from the sale of timber. The construction of the cabins may require tree felling which could generate revenue initially but may then reduce the areas available for replanting, adversely impacting SWC's future revenue.

Reputational risk – the possible negative impact of the LLP and the holiday site on the image of SWC in the minds of other organisations it deals with, the general public and the government. If Woodsaway is very profitable it may not be appropriate for SWC to be seen to be associated with this, conversely the same may be true with a financially unsuccessful venture. There may also be reputational issues if Woodsaway is seen to pay high salaries/bonuses or alternatively if it treats staff poorly or causes environmental damage (see below).

Environmental risk – the creation of a holiday site exposes the woodland estate to possible additional threats in relation to damage and disease. There is a possible risk of urbanisation of forest through construction of cabins, which might destroy natural habitats, and there may be ongoing issues relating to damage due to footfall, more vehicles, creation of waste etc.

Hazard risk – similar to the environmental risk above, there is an increased risk of fire damage from the use of the forest as a holiday site.

Social risk – the holiday site may open the woodland up to more people but if CabinCo's customers are largely in England and Wales, these may not necessarily be from the community which SWC serves. Also the luxury cabins may only be affordable by a small minority and could be seen to be elitist.

SWC will need to ensure that appropriate risk management processes are put in place to address the additional risks that arise as a result of the Woodsaway venture. It needs to insist on controls in relation to woodland management, protection of habitat and leisure.

Examiner's comments

The majority of candidates were clearly well prepared to discuss the risks associated with the proposed venture and scored very highly on this section of the report. Most candidates identified a range of risks and discussed their potential impact. Better candidates also discussed their likelihood and suggested how they might be mitigated/managed if SWC is to go ahead with the proposal, pointing out that the risks are reduced by the creation of the LLP to operate the venture.

32.4 Governance issues

Applicability of corporate governance

Corporate governance generally refers to the system by which companies are directed and controlled. The aim of corporate governance is to facilitate effective, prudent management in order to deliver long term success. It is underpinned by the principles of accountability, transparency, probity (honesty) and focus on long term sustainable success.

Whilst the second SWC trustee is correct that the UK Corporate Governance Code applies to listed companies only, good governance is essential not just for companies but to any organisation, irrespective of whether it is private or public, if that organisation is to be well led and high performing.

It could be argued that good governance is even more important in the context of a public sector body, like SWC, which needs to ensure that public funds are wisely spent and that resources such as Scotland's woodlands are properly safeguarded and are used economically, efficiently, and effectively. This is the view expressed by the first trustee.

More generally therefore, governance relates to the framework of accountability to users, stakeholders and the wider community, within which organisations take decisions, and lead and control their functions, to achieve their objectives. As such it would apply to both SWC and Woodsaway. Without effective governance, the proposed public/private partnership is unlikely to be successful.

Nolan principles

Governance in the public sector has much in common with corporate governance for companies. As a publicly funded body, SWC's management board needs to act in accordance with the Nolan principles, which include the principles of integrity, accountability, openness (transparency) and honesty (probity). These are very similar to the core corporate governance principles. In addition, holders of public office are expected to comply with the additional principles of selflessness, objectivity and leadership.

Of particular relevance in the context of the Woodsaway venture are:

Selflessness: holders of public office should take decisions solely in terms of the public interest. They should not do so in order to gain financial or other materials benefits for themselves, their family, or other friends. Thus SWC needs to balance its different responsibilities and ensure that its involvement in Woodsaway does not give rise to the risk of appearing to act in a manner contrary to public interest.

Objectivity: in carrying out public business, including making public appointments, awarding contracts, or recommending individuals for rewards and benefits, holders of public office should make choices on merit. The trustees need to be seen to have considered alternative partners as well as CabinCo, which has been selected because it is the best option

Public sector organisations operate in complex legislative, political and local contexts, in which they have to make difficult decisions. Well-governed organisations balance their different responsibilities and use information to decide where to allocate effort and resources to meet competing demands.

Governance of Woodsaway

The principles of governance will apply to Woodsaway, as an LLP. A key part of good governance is risk management and this will be particularly important to SWC given the additional risks that arise as a result of the Woodsaway venture (discussed in 32.3 above).

CabinCo and SWC will each be entitled to appoint three representatives on Woodsaway's senior management committee so neither party would appear able to dictate decisions.

SWC needs to insist on controls to ensure Woodsaway LLP does not undermine SWC's objectives in relation to woodland management and the protection of habitat and nature. It will also need to agree on the methods for resolving any disputes and the exit arrangements should either party want to terminate the venture.

Conclusion

Overall the project appears likely to generate financial returns and would appear to help SWC further some of its aims. It seems to have the support of government, which has granted preliminary approval for the formation of the LLP. More work should be done on the financial projections and SWC could engage in stakeholder consultations to assess the public perception of the proposals. The LLP will need to be set up carefully to ensure that the risks and governance issues identified are properly addressed.

Examiner's comments

Answers to the governance section were very variable in quality. There were really two issues here: addressing the trustees' comments in relation to governance and considering the governance of the proposed LLP. A significant minority failed to appreciate the distinction between the UK Corporate Governance Code that applies only to listed companies and corporate governance, which is the system by which companies are directed and controlled. The better candidates recognised that the principles of good governance (accountability, transparency etc) are very similar to those enshrined in the Nolan principles and are best practice for the prudent and effective management of any organisation. Thus governance may be more, rather than less, relevant for a public sector organisation such as SWC with a wider group of stakeholders to account to and a need to act in the public interest.

Having discussed this in the light of the trustees' comments, better candidates also went on to consider governance in relation to the LLP as a critical factor in the likely success of the venture, and discussed the proposals for the structure of Woodsaway's senior management committee.

Recognising that the overall purpose of the report was to evaluate the proposed venture, most candidates provided reasoned advice at the end as to whether SWC should go ahead with the Woodsaway venture. This was pleasing to see.

33 WeDive Ltd (March 2015)

Marking guide

	Knowledge	Skill	Marks
33.1 Strategic options	3	12	14
33.2 Decision tree	2	5	6
	5	17	20

General comments:

The third question, worth only 20 marks, was also well attempted overall, with good scores on requirement 33.1 making up for poorer answers to requirement 33.2.

The scenario relates to a company which produces high-performance thermal drysuits for scuba diving. The drysuits are very expensive and are typically bought by professional divers, although WeDive also distributes its drysuits to diving retailers for recreational users who want a high quality product. The directors are keen to expand and are considering two mutually exclusive strategies:

Option 1: Expand the range of products for the UK market by sourcing lifestyle clothing and selling it under WeDive's own brand, through existing distribution channels (diving retailers). Due to limited funds, WeDive intends to use social media to market this option.

Option 2: Produce drysuits for export markets. This would involve finding and partnering with new distributors. Since a key aspect of WeDive's high-performance drysuit is the fit, the product may need some redesigning to fit the local population in each export market. Some basic financial information is provided in the form of possible outcomes, and their probabilities, for one possible market being considered - New Zealand.

33.1 Evaluation of options

Option 1: expand the range of products for the UK market

Option 1 in terms of the Ansoff matrix constitutes product development.

Advantages

- It may be less risky than targeting overseas markets as there are no language/cultural barriers.

- WeDive's brand name is already known to the UK market and seen as high-quality, so it can easily capitalise on it.

- Casual lifestyle clothing is related to the existing product range so there is some strategic fit and it may appeal to existing recreational dive customers.

- These products can probably sell through the existing distribution channels which facilitates implementation of the strategy.

- The new products may also appeal to other market segments, so this strategy could involve an element of market development too.

- The marketing of the product via social media may fit with the appeal of lifestyle clothing to a younger market.

Disadvantages

- From a generic strategy point of view, WeDive's existing product is very differentiated and it protects itself from competition by operating in a market niche. There are high levels of competition in the lifestyle clothing market already and the products are more homogeneous.

- Margins on casual clothing may be lower than on existing drysuit products and will be affected by the level of competition and the fact that there are low-cost producers outside the UK.

- There is likely to be a short product life cycle as typically these lifestyle brands come and go as far as fashion is concerned.

- 65% of sales are to professional divers and these products may be less attractive to them than the recreational divers.

- WeDive will need to source a supplier(s) as it has no experience in manufacturing.

- There is little scope for using WeDive's existing expertise.

- The new strategy will require marketing expenditure and social media may be insufficient to attract a wide customer base.

- This strategy is still UK focussed and may offer limited scope for growth.

Option 2: focus on core product but expand market overseas

Option 2 in terms of the Ansoff matrix constitutes market development.

Advantages

- Exporting drysuits builds on existing competences and is consistent with WeDive's differentiation strategy.

- WeDive already have a tried and tested product that has been well received by the market.

- It may be possible to achieve better expansion by targeting contracts with professional divers rather than recreational ones, using existing links with police, armed forces etc.

- Overseas markets may be more price sensitive/have different price elasticities which could increase their profitability.

- It may be sensible to try out one or two markets initially that are more close to the UK in terms of the size, fit and climate requirements.

Disadvantages

- WeDive's brand name may not be recognised in export markets although once established, this strategy will help to create a global brand.

- The nature of the product may not work in some countries – eg, different fabric may be required for tropical rather than cold water diving.

- The product may require amendments to the fit to suit different population sizes and characteristics.

- Risk arises due to the lack of familiarity with overseas markets although this will be reduced if WeDive find the right distribution partner.

- WeDive is likely to face competition from existing players in these markets.

- A factor to consider is where the suits will be made and whether WeDive has the production capacity to cater for the increased volumes.

Preliminary conclusions

- The existing product has a three year warranty and may not involve frequent repeat purchases so it seems sensible to consider opportunities to expand revenue.

- Either option will help reduce dependence on the existing UK market and on professional dive contracts in particular.

- Market research of either strategy offers the opportunity to reduce the risk of expansion.

- WeDive needs to consider financial projections before making a decision.

- Option 2 is probably more likely to be successful in the longer term as it makes use of existing expertise and builds on WeDive's differentiation strategy. The company could consider selling online initially as a means of export then find distributors if it becomes clear that there is demand.

Examiner's comments

The requirement to evaluate the two alternative strategies was straightforward and well done by most candidates. A significant number of candidates identified that WeDive is currently a differentiator, focussed on a niche market. Many started their discussion by positioning the proposed strategies within the Ansoff matrix as product development and market development respectively. Most candidates produced sensible answers setting out the advantages and disadvantages of the two strategies and showed good knowledge of the specific issues relating to overseas expansion. Some used the 'suitability, feasibility, acceptability' approach to good effect to generate a range of points. The better candidates went on to reach a conclusion as to which of the strategies might be more appropriate for WeDive, recognising the need to obtain more detailed financial projections before making a final decision.

33.2 Decision Tree

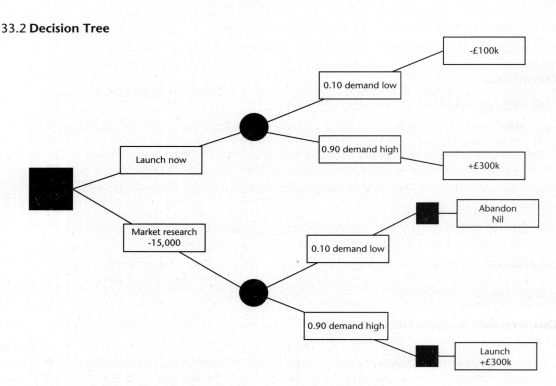

Launch now without MR: (0.9 × 300k) + (0.1 × (-100k)) = 260k

With MR: (0.9 × 300k) + (0.1 × 0) = 270k less 15k research cost = 255k

Hence financially it is better not to undertake MR but this is based on EV which is a long term average and not necessarily applicable to a one-off decision. It also ignores risk:

Without MR, actual outcomes are +300 or -100, spread of 400k in potential return

With MR, actual outcomes become +300 or zero. Therefore depending on WeDive's attitude to risk it may be worth paying £15k for the ability to minimise downside risk despite the lower expected outcome.

Examiner's comments

This was the first time that a decision tree has been examined and answers were very variable. For candidates who knew how to draw the tree, and then do the simple expected value calculations, this requirement was a source of easy marks. Many lacked the required technical knowledge however which resulted in some non-attempts. Sensible candidates who used the numbers in the scenario to produce an expected value calculation and then went on to make some relevant comments were still able to score a pass however.

34 Reyel plc (June 2015)

Marking guide

		Knowledge	Skill	Marks
34.1 (a)	Quarterly data analysis	1	11	
(b)	Comparative data analysis	1	8	18
34.2 Capacity management and pricing		4	7	10
34.3 Estimated loss		1	7	7
34.4 Ethics		3	4	7
		10	37	42

General comments:

This is the mini case worth 42 marks and also the main data analysis question.

The scenario is based on an international company, Reyel, which owns and operates mid-market hotels. A new division, 'The Extended Stay Hotel Division' (the ESH), was set up to enter the extended stay hotel market. The initial strategy, to test the market, was to establish one hotel, The Clarre, in London. Quarterly management accounts are produced to measure performance, where seasonality is an issue. The performance of The Clarre is also benchmarked against one of Reyel's traditional hotels in London, The Zoy.

Two issues that have arisen with respect to the management of The Clarre are: managing capacity and pricing.

An ethical issue has arisen whereby the manager of The Clarre has offered regular business customers discount vouchers for private holidays if they agree to a premium over the standard price for a guestroom, at their employer's expense.

34.1 (a) Quarterly data analysis: The Clarre

	The Clarre					The Zoy
	Quarter to 30 June 20Y4	Quarter to 30 September 20Y4	Quarter to 31 December 20Y4	Quarter to 31 March 20Y5	Year ending 31 March 20Y5	Year ending 31 March 20Y5
Capacity (nights)	21,600	21,600	21,600	21,600	86,400	108,000
Number of nights actually occupied	15,552	17,280	16,848	15,120	64,800	62,640
Operating profit % (based on guestroom revenue)	18.3%	28.1%	28.1%	16.6%	23.3%	*21.7%
% of annual revenue	22.8%	27.5%	27.5%	22.1%	100%	–
% of annual nights	24.0%	26.7%	26.0%	23.3%	100%	–
% of annual operating profit	17.9%	33.1%	33.2%	15.8%	100%	–

*   18.2% If based on total revenue

Revenue

The Clarre was a new start-up on 1 April 20Y4, which is the beginning of the current financial year. As such, it is likely to take some time to establish a customer base and grow, particularly as this is a new type of hotel for the Reyel group. The first year of operations is therefore probably atypical and there is likely to be growth in future years. Similarly, there is likely to be growth between quarters as the hotel becomes established during the year. Some of the underlying quarterly variation may therefore be due to early growth, rather than just seasonal variation.

Revenue in each of the two quarters ending 30 September 20Y4 and 31 December 20Y4 (Q2 and Q3) was greater than in each of the other two quarters (Q1 and Q4). In terms of revenue generated 55% of annual revenue occurred in Q2 and Q3, being equally split between these two quarters.

It terms of volumes (ie, number of guest nights) the seasonal variation is less pronounced with only 52.7% of guest nights occurring in Q2 and Q3 (being 26.7% and 26% respectively). This variation however understates the variability in seasonal demand as the lowest occupancy rates in Q1 and Q4 were incurred despite the lowest average prices of £68 per night, compared with averages of £74 and £76 per night respectively for Q2 and Q3. Had the same prices been charged throughout the year then a much more pronounced seasonal variation is likely to have occurred.

In summary, the highest demand occurred in Q2 and Q3 despite these quarters having the higher average prices. Whilst Q1 may have been disadvantaged as the start-up quarter, the same cannot be said for Q4 which had longer to establish a customer base than Q2 and Q3.

Additional information, which would be an indicator of the Q1 start-up effect, can be found by comparing revenue for Q1 with the quarter ended 30 June 20Y5, which is near completion.

Additional useful information would be:

- seasonal variation of any other extended stay hotels in the London area to use as a benchmark to strip out industry average seasonality in the geographical area (though this information may be difficult to obtain)

- variations in prices and occupancy within each quarter.

Operating profit

The quarterly operating profit margins for Q2 and Q3 (28.1% for each) show that they are much more profitable than Q1 and Q4 which had margins of only 18.3% and 16.6% respectively.

A similar picture can be seen from analysing the percentage of total operating profit for the year earned in each quarter. Almost two thirds (66.3%) of total operating profit for the year was earned in Q2 and Q3, being 33.1% and 33.2% respectively. This trend is far more pronounced than that for revenue, discussed above, which amounted to only 55% in Q2 and Q3.

There are number of causal factors which are likely to have given rise to this:

- The average price per night is higher in Q2 and Q3 so the margins are higher.

- There will be a large element of fixed operating costs in running a hotel. These will have an operating gearing effect, such that variations in revenue are magnified in operating profit as the fixed costs must still be covered when revenue falls. This means the lower demand in Q1 and Q4 gives rise to a disproportionate decrease in operating profit.

- The average length of a stay is greater in Q2 and Q3 (at 15 and 18 nights respectively, against 14 and 13 nights in Q1 and Q4), so the costs of room change-overs are reduced.

(b) **Comparison of The Clarre and The Zoy**

Difficulties in making valid comparisons should be recognised. These include:

- a different business model, although both are in the same industry
- the Clarre is a start-up whereas The Zoy is well established

Despite this, the two hotels are operating in the mid-market hotel sector, are of similar size and are in similar locations. Reasonable comparisons are therefore possible.

A key distinction is that The Zoy has two sources of revenue: room revenues and other revenues (from the restaurant and bar). The operating costs provided are not divided between these two revenue streams and this would be useful additional information in identifying the source of the performance. The interdependence of revenues and costs between these two revenue streams would however need to be recognised, even if this cost analysis information were to be available.

Guestroom revenues

Guestroom revenues generated by The Zoy are 34.9% higher than those of The Clarre. In analysing the underlying causes of why the revenue is greater there are three key factors:

- Capacity (number of room nights available)
- Occupancy
- Price

It can be seen from the above table that the number of nights occupancy (ie, volume) is similar for the two hotels, with The Clarre and The Zoy being 64,800 and 62,640 respectively for the year ended 31 March 20Y5. These figures are determined as a function of capacity and occupancy.

Despite the volume of room nights being similar, this is achieved in a different way with The Zoy having a much higher capacity (108,000 room nights compared to 86,400), but a lower occupancy (58% compared to 75%).

Given the similar volumes sold (ie, the number of room nights) the fact that The Zoy has revenue that is 34.9% higher than The Clarre is caused by an average price of £100 for The Zoy per night, compared with £71.70 per night for The Clarre (ie, 39.5% higher).

Data could meaningfully be calculated based on revenue per guest if comparing two traditional hotels or two extended stay hotels. However, given that the relative business models create very different average stays, such a comparison would be almost meaningless in comparing The Clarre with The Zoy as it would not compare like with like.

Other revenue

'Other revenue' for The Zoy is £1.2 million, which is 16.1% of the total revenue of £7.464 million for The Zoy. This is therefore reasonably substantial and makes the total revenue for The Zoy 60.7% higher than that of The Clarre. (However, the operating costs of the restaurant and bar are not separately provided so it is difficult to draw conclusions about the profitability of The Zoy restaurant.)

Operating costs

Additional information is needed analysing operating costs into the component accounts.

Overall, however, The Zoy has operating costs which are 71.5% higher than those of The Clarre. The underlying causes of this are likely to be:

- costs of the restaurant and bar
- greater levels of service (eg, daily cleaning)
- more frequent change-overs (as average stay is 3 days rather than 15 days for The Zoy)

Note however that the volume of room nights actually used is similar for both hotels.

Further information indicating the breakdown of fixed and variable costs may be useful to determine how costs relate to volumes and how operating costs are likely to change in future.

Operating profit

As already noted, The Zoy has revenue 60.7% higher than The Clarre, but operating costs 71.5% higher. Despite this, in absolute terms, The Zoy has made more profit than The Clarre in the year ended 31 March 20Y5, as revenue is greater than operating costs. Indeed, the operating profit of The Zoy is 25.3% higher than The Clarre.

Conclusion

The Zoy has outperformed The Clarre but this is not unexpected given this is the latter's first year of trading. Greater sales in future, as The Clarre generates a more established customer base, seem likely to close the gap and perhaps permit the performance of The Clarre to exceed that of The Zoy.

Examiner's comments

(a) Candidates' answers were generally reasonably good on this requirement. For most candidates, there was an improvement over previous sittings on the presentation of the data analysis by using an initial table of calculations, followed by a qualitative analysis of the results.

The majority recognised the seasonality evident in the data. Many also identified the need for a breakdown of costs into fixed and variable after recognising that there had been a more than proportional increase in operating profit relative to the increases in revenue.

The better scoring scripts analysed occupancy rates per quarter and the overall impact of occupancy on profitability. The discussion part of the question was done quite well with candidates linking seasonality, location and hotel type back to the scenario. However, only a small number identified that the data presented was from a start-up business and could be subject to major variations in the future.

Weaker candidates merely copied data from the question, often without calculating any new ratios. Where new ratios were calculated, weaker candidates tended to provide only very general ratios such as operating profit margins, without considering any indicators of performance specific to the scenario. In their narrative, weaker candidates tended to merely describe what had happened, rather than providing an analysis determining causal factors and explaining how and why a movement in the data had occurred.

(b) Calculations were mostly limited to percentage changes and basic margins. In terms of analysis, only the strong candidates highlighted the difficulties in making comparisons due to the differences in the business models of the two hotels and the fact that the Clarre was a start-up. While trying to make similar comparisons, candidates wanted to 'strip out' the restaurant but, in doing so, often deducted the revenue while not recognising some of the operating costs would be attributable to the restaurant. Conclusions were not always offered.

34.2 Capacity management and pricing

Capacity planning

Capacity planning is the process of determining the capacity needed by an organisation to satisfy changing demands for its products or services.

Effective capacity in the hotel industry is the maximum number of guests that a hotel is capable of accommodating in a given period, due to constraints such as physical resources (guestroom capacity), human resources, quality threshold issues (guestrooms in good repair and cleaned) and delays (room turnaround).

A difference between the capacity of a hotel and the demand from its guests results either in under-utilised resources (eg, available guestrooms unoccupied) or unsatisfied demand (guests turned away when the hotel is full). The goal of capacity planning is to manage this difference.

Capacity can be increased through introducing new techniques, processes or assets, or varying the number of employee hours.

Capacity management in the hotel industry can be short-term or long-term. Within each of these time frames, capacity management can also be viewed from the supply side or the demand side.

Long-term capacity management

Supply side

In the context of a hotel, the number of guestrooms sets an upper limit on physical capacity in the medium to long term. Whilst it may be possible, from the company perspective, to build new extended stay hotels, from the perspective of the manager of The Clarre, an extension of physical capacity is difficult as there are limitations of building in a city such as London. Possibilities in the longer term to raise physical capacity might be to: change common areas into more guestrooms; build additional floors; reconfigure the guestrooms to make them smaller, but more plentiful; use an overflow venue.

It would be a mistake however to consider capacity solely in terms of either (1) physical capacity or (2) only increasing capacity.

Capacity could have a number of aspects. For example, the need may be to reduce capacity in order to reduce costs, rather than increase capacity. The average utilisation of The Clarre is 75%. Maintaining the ability to service 100% occupancy, if long-term demand remains at 75% occupancy, would be an inefficient use of resources and would involve the provision of expensive and unutilised capacity.

Demand side

Demand management might involve increasing demand in order to utilise surplus capacity. This might include, in terms of long-term demand management: improving facilities to attract more people to stay at the hotel (eg, business centre, bar); improve guestroom quality; recruit more staff; reduce standard prices.

Short-term capacity management

Supply side

Flexibility in short-term capacity is needed as hotel bookings may vary unpredictably, so the need to match variations in demand with variations in capacity reduces underutilised resources or lost sales.

Labour is a key aspect of planning short-term capacity. For example, flexible contracts (eg, staff might be required to work overtime or shifts at short notice) to meet changes in demand from bookings will enable resources to be acquired quickly to match demand changes in the short term.

Short-term closure of a section of rooms, or a floor, may reduce short-term capacity (eg, from the data provided, demand is seasonal for The Clarre). This would save costs such as heating a floor.

Demand side

The use of IT and marketing models to predict variations in demand will help give management more time to manage capacity.

Demand management capacity planning may be used to reduce peak demand by switching it to the off-peak periods, such as by offering relatively lower off-peak prices. This is a form of price discrimination which is discussed below. The utilisation of the advertising budget may also be applied disproportionately to attract demand in the low season.

Pricing

Flexible prices, taking the form of price discrimination, can include charging customers different amounts to reflect their individual price elasticities. To be able to do this, there needs to be separation of markets.

Examples of effective separation of markets can include businesses which make a large number of bookings compared to individuals who may only make a single booking. The individual cannot access the business price as he/she does not normally require as many hotel stays as a business.

The objective of the pricing strategy needs to be clear. Setting prices to maximise utilisation is not necessarily a good idea if revenues can be maximised by a higher price with less than 100% utilisation.

Even revenue maximisation may not be appropriate as it may not equate to profit maximisation.

The data in the exhibit shows that demand varies between quarters, but will also vary within quarters (eg, if a major event is on in London, higher prices can be charged and yet there may still be full utilisation). These demand peaks can generate higher prices in order to reduce demand (in terms of guest nights) to the capacity level of the hotel.

Conclusion

Where there is a strict physical limit on the number of guestrooms (at least in the short term) then pricing can be one of the most effective means of capacity planning. If capacity management is aligning capacity and demand then, where capacity is upwardly inflexible, pricing is the primary means in the short term of adjusting effective demand to match available capacity.

Examiner's comments

Most candidates only considered the short term when discussing capacity management. However a range of interesting suggestions were provided. Good quality candidates tried to link capacity management and pricing policy. Few candidates distinguished supply-side and demand-side aspects of capacity management.

The treatment of pricing was variable in quality. A high proportion of candidates used the 4Cs approach to structure their answers. Many candidates recognised that varying prices could be charged due to the seasonality of the business, but many failed to recognise key issues such as price discrimination or price elasticity.

Some candidates conflated the issues of capacity management and pricing within a single narrative, which usually limited the clarity and scope of their answers.

34.3 Estimate of lost revenue

The impact of opening The Clarre on the revenues of The Zoy is the difference between the following two figures:

(1) The revenues actually generated by The Zoy

(2) The revenues that would have been generated by The Zoy had The Clarre not been opened (the counter factual).

Whilst figure (1) is known, figure (2) needs to be estimated.

The starting point is that if The Clarre had not been opened it may have been the case that The Zoy's revenues may have changed over the past year anyway, due to other factors. These other factors need to be evaluated in order to make an assessment of the figure in (2) above.

Macro and industry factors

In estimating the change in The Zoy's revenue from last year, industry trends and macroeconomic trends need to be considered, particularly in the context of the London market. Thus, if London hotels generally suffered a fall in revenues compared to last year, then this factor could be stripped out of last year's The Zoy revenue in estimating (2) above.

Internal changes

Any changes that Zoy management has made this year compared to last year need to be considered. Price changes may have had an effect on demand, as may other factors including staffing, refurbishment (or lack of it), customer service policy and advertising. These factors need to be stripped out in estimating (2) above.

Data analysis

An analysis of data might reveal more information.

For instance, if there has been a sharp fall in the number of long stays at The Zoy (of over 8 days) then this seems more likely to have been caused by the opening of The Clarre than if there had been a fall in the number of short stays, which are not the same market sector as The Clarre.

If there is a Reyel loyalty card, or company credit card, then specific evidence could be gathered on individual customers who stayed at The Zoy last year but transferred over to The Clarre this year.

Examiner's comments

The answers to this requirement were the weakest on the entire paper, and formed the highest rate of non-attempts. Many candidates failed to grasp the key issue of what would have happened to the revenue of The Zoy if The Clarre had not opened. Weaker candidates, implicitly or explicitly, assumed it would have remained at the level of the previous year.

Many candidates did not give due consideration to external factors, in addition to the internal ones, relevant to the possible impact on The Zoy arising from opening The Clarre. Few focussed on what had happened specifically to the longer stay customers of the Zoy.

34.4 Ethical issues

Ethics pertains to whether a particular behaviour is deemed acceptable in the context under consideration. In short it is 'doing the right thing'.

In making any ethical evaluation it is first necessary to establish the facts. In this case, the claims made against Kevin need to be established to assess their validity. This may include establishing the use of vouchers by The Clarre customers and tracing these back to the prices they have paid for staying at The Clarre.

The issue of legality applies; where an inducement has been given then this may come under the Bribery Act. It may also be fraud. Legal advice should be taken.

The offering of vouchers may not, of itself, be unethical and may be common practice in the industry. However, two other factors to consider are:

- the value of the vouchers and whether they are sufficiently significant to amount to a material inducement; and

- the fact that vouchers are not being offered for booking a guestroom on normal commercial terms but, rather, for individual business guests agreeing that their employers should pay in excess of the standard price set for other guests, with no clear commercial cause or benefit to the employer. There is a clear and possibly substantial benefit to the employee as an individual.

In making a decision as to how to act, it may be helpful to apply the Institute of Business Ethics three tests:

- Transparency
- Effect
- Fairness

Transparency – would the Reyel board mind people (existing customers, suppliers, employees) knowing what has happened? In particular, the issue of transparency will apply to the employers who have paid inflated amounts. This is likely to have consequences in refunding money to employers.

Effect – whom does the decision to provide inducements affect/hurt? Clearly this includes the employers who have paid more than the market rate. Other rival hotels, who were offering lower prices to employers but without additional inducements, may also have suffered.

Fairness – would the inducement be considered fair by those affected? The issue for Reyel's board is that the company may have benefited from the action of the manager, even though the board did not itself instigate the particular actions nor was even aware of them at the time.

Honesty – A final issue is one of honesty. The inducements fail the honesty test on the basis of Rexel making an improper gain. There is now the onus to make other parties (eg, employers) aware and return the excess amounts received.

Response

Where there is appropriate evidence an initial action would be to inform the employers and return any excess amounts charged. The manager's continued employment should be reviewed. The operation of the discount voucher scheme company-wide should also be reviewed.

If there is suspicion there has been a crime then disclosure to the police, based on legal advice, may be appropriate.

On the whole, this requirement was reasonably well answered. Most candidates considered the legality issue, although many then immediately dismissed it as not relevant in this case.

Many candidates adopted the transparency, effect, fairness framework. Only better students went on to identify other ethical issues outside this framework. Actions to be taken by management were often ignored. Frustratingly, this included some students who produced excellent commentary on the ethical issues, but then failed to identify any subsequent actions.

35 Home of Leather plc (June 2015)

Marking guide

	Knowledge	Skill	Marks
35.1 Break-even/volume of sales	3	6	9
35.2 Three strategies	2	10	10
35.3 Mendelow's matrix	3	4	7
35.4 Change management	3	6	8
	11	26	34

General comments:

HoL is a company which manufactures good quality leather furniture. The company is located in Puddington, where its site comprises a factory, distribution centre and office.

In order to remain competitive, HoL needs to reduce costs by making fundamental changes to its business. Three potential strategies have been identified: relocate within the UK; relocate manufacturing overseas; or cease manufacturing then import as a wholesaler. All strategies would involve redundancies to varying degrees.

The board has set a target annual profit of £7.2 million, but prices and costs vary between the three strategies. Data on costs and revenues are provided.

35.1 (a) Break-even and sales volume

To: Home of Leather plc Board
From: A Business Advisor
Date: 10 June 20Y5
Subject: Proposed reorganisation strategies

Break-even price

Strategy 1

B/E contribution = £14.4m/120,000 = £120
B/E price   = £200 + £120   = £320

Strategy 2

B/E contribution = £10.8m/120,000 = £90
B/E price   = £160 + £90   = £250

Strategy 3

B/E contribution = £1.8m/120,000 = £15
B/E price   = £280 + £15   = £295

(b) **Sales volume to achieve a profit of £7.2m**

Strategy 1

(£14.4m + £7.2m)/(360 – 200) =   135,000 units

Strategy 2

(£10.8m + £7.2m)/(324 – 160) =   109,756 units

Strategy 3

(£1.8m + £7.2m)/(324 – 280)   =   204,545 units

Examiner's comments

The performance on this requirement was generally good, although it did tend to polarise between the many candidates who managed to arrive at the correct calculations, thereby scoring full marks, and the minority who scored nominal marks. Weaker candidates often provided break-even sales volumes, rather than the volumes necessary to achieve an annual profit of £7.2 million. Others determined break-even volumes, instead of break-even prices.

Many candidates failed to achieve the mark available for presenting their answer to this question in report format.

35.2 Evaluation of proposals

	Strategy 1 £'000	Strategy 2 £'000	Strategy 3 £'000
Sales	43,200	38,880	38,880
Variable cost	(24,000)	(19,200)	(33,600)
Annual fixed costs	(14,400)	(10,800)	(1,800)
Profit	**4,800**	**8,880**	**3,480**

Strategy 1

While this strategy involves some downsizing, it is the least transformational change and therefore has fewer transition costs. Nevertheless, there would be a loss of 60% of the employees who have skills which may be difficult to replicate with a new workforce.

In terms of ongoing production, the product quality is maintained and therefore the risk of alienating existing customers in the hope of attracting new customers through a lower price-quality mix is avoided.

In terms of the data offered Strategy 1 is not as profitable as Strategy 2 (see above), but more profitable than Strategy 3.

There is however less risk with Strategy 1 than the other two strategies in a number of respects:

- There is currency matching between the currency of 70% of sales and the currency in which costs are incurred. There is therefore less risk from currency fluctuations.

- As the proposal is based on existing production there is more certainty surrounding estimates

- There is no change in market positioning

This strategy however has greater risk than the other two in having more fixed costs and therefore higher operating gearing. As an example, if the Grint contract is lost then the high fixed costs still need to be incurred and a large loss will be made.

Also, in respect of the Grint contract, the break-even price of £320 is only £40 less than the price indicated by the Grint board as a maximum, making profits only marginal on this contract.

Strategy 2

Based on the data provided, this is the most profitable contract, with an estimated annual profit of £8.88 million.

There are, however, a number of operating and financial factors which increase risk and mitigate against the higher return.

In the first instance, this strategy is likely to be the greatest transformational change and therefore have the highest initial costs from change. It is unclear whether these initial costs have been annualised into the fixed costs in the table or whether they have been treated separately.

The supply chain is lengthened significantly which may cause operational uncertainty in meeting customer delivery needs.

The break-even price at £250 is £70 lower than the break-even price for Strategy 1 at £320. However, the quality of the output is better with Strategy 1, making any given price easier to achieve. Nevertheless, if the quality differential in relation to price is correct, then Strategy 2 remains more competitive than Strategy 1 in price-quality terms.

That said, the market positioning in Strategy 2 is different from the existing market positioning and there is a risk that it may take time to adjust to a new customer base which prefers a lower price-quality mix.

Looking at the break-even data in (35.1) above there appears to be a greater margin of safety for Strategy 2 than the other two strategies. This indicates lower risk in terms of variation of price and demand.

Strategy 3

On the basis of the data presented, Strategy 3 looks to be the least favourable option as it has the lowest expected profit and the least favourable margins of safety in terms of price and volumes demanded.

The issues of price-quality mix and currency risk are the same as for Strategy 2.

The key area where outsourcing in Strategy 3 has an advantage however is that it has the lowest fixed costs and therefore the lowest operating gearing. If the Grint contract were to be lost then high fixed costs would not need to continue to be incurred. There is more financial agility with Strategy 3, even though the expected return is lower. There is therefore downside protection. Exit costs are also likely to be lower as there is only a supply contract to exit and a warehouse to sell, rather than an entire factory.

Conclusion

For the renewal of the Grint contract, it would seem that Strategy 2 and Strategy 3 offer the potential to make a more competitive bid on price than Strategy 1. However much will depend on how significant quality is to Grint in the tender process.

Examiner's comments

Generally, there was a good performance by most candidates. Not all made use of financial data in their commentary. Others made good use of the data, for example determining profits and margins of safety, but then provided limited narrative (eg, on supply chain issues). Some candidates drifted into a discussion of change management, despite being explicitly told they were not to do so. Those who used the suitability/acceptability/feasibility framework often wrote too much, yet missed key points, and were not normally helped by structuring their answers in this way. Most candidates provided a reasoned conclusion as to which strategy appeared best.

35.3 Mendelow

Strategy 1

Current employees

Power – low
Interest – high negative

The current employees have high negative interest as they are under immediate threat of losing their jobs. The power of current employees to stop or moderate any relocation decision is limited.

If the entire UK workforce is united against the move then significant costs to HoL can arise from disruption.

Given however that not all jobs are under threat, there may be limited co-operation in industrial action from the 40% of employees who are willing to relocate 150 kilometres away. This may be particularly the case if HoL pays generous removal expenses to relocate employees.

Even amongst the employees losing their jobs some may be happy with redundancy as they intend to retire or move jobs anyway.

Despite the above, it is likely that most employees have a strong negative interest in the relocation, particularly as the company is a key part of the town and perhaps families and friends are located there, who may suffer from a decline in the local economy following the closure of the factory. This may also make it harder for redundant employees to find new employment locally and therefore reinforce their negative interest.

One final qualification is employees may have a strong negative interest compared to the status quo of the factory in Puddington. If however there is an acceptance of the board's decision of the commercial need to make a change then, in relative terms, compared with the other two strategies, employees could favour Strategy 1 as there are fewer redundancies.

Grint

Power – high
Interest – moderate

Given that 35% of HoL's sales are from Grint, it has considerable power over HoL and is likely to be in a position to influence the decision to relocate production. The cost savings from transferring production are likely to be a factor in the next tender, but also the level of quality of the products that HoL can provide is dependent on which of the three strategies is selected.

Grint may however be only moderately interested in the relocation as furniture manufacture is a competitive industry, with a range of alternative suppliers being available if HoL fails to deliver the required quality at the required price. Nevertheless, HoL is presumably currently Grint's preferred supplier for good reasons, so there may be a moderate wish to continue the relationship, despite the concerns over price expressed in their communication.

Examiner's comments

This requirement was very well answered by the majority of candidates and was, on average, the best answered requirement on the paper. Relatively comprehensive rationales were usually provided to support the positioning of current employees and Grint on Mendelow's matrix.

35.4 Change management

The change management process needs to be appropriate to the nature of the change.

In this case, the change is fundamental and transformational for either Strategy 1 or Strategy 2.

The transformational and reactive nature of the change classifies it as 'Forced Change' in the sense that the company will be unable to continue to compete if it does not reduce costs by making major changes.

Whilst there are commonalities between the two strategies which may require similar change management procedures, there are also differences which suggest a different change management approach for each strategy.

In terms of managing the impact of change, then there are very different effects for employees staying with the company and those being made redundant.

While there is a major effect on those being made redundant, in the longer term they will not be employees so, while the leaving process needs to be managed, there may be limited long-term effects on motivation if the change is well-managed. For Strategy 2 the change impacts on nearly all employees.

However, in the shorter term, following announcement the employees may not know which of the two groups they will fall into, and thus all employees may be demotivated by the uncertainty in this period. This may have adverse effects on quality of work and reputation.

There is also a danger of focusing only on change with respect to employees. Other stakeholders should also be considered in change management including:

(1) Continuing customers – who need to be reassured that they will continue to be supplied quality goods and that the delivery will continue to be reliable, particularly with Strategy 2 where the supply chain is geographically extended.

(2) Suppliers – to manage the continuing relationship with Strategy 1 and the issues that may arise from the change in geographical location. With Strategy 2 there is a need to ensure reliability of supply in the closing months when UK suppliers will be aware that contracts are to be terminated.

However, change does not only involve people but also:

(1) changes in management structure due to the change in the nature of the business (eg, automation with Strategy 1) and the location of the business (with Strategy 2).

(2) change in culture. There is likely to be a change in culture particularly in Strategy 2 where employees will have a different national culture as well as management having the opportunity to work with employees to set up a new corporate culture.

Much more than Strategy 2, Strategy 1 has the change management issue of managing employees who are continuing in employment with HoL, but who may need to adapt to new practices in an automated environment and deal with a new culture.

In this context, for continuing employees, Lewin and Schein's Iceberg model has three stages in managing change:

- Unfreeze
- Move
- Refreeze

Unfreezing involves a trigger, a challenge of existing behaviour, involvement of outsiders, alterations to power structures.

Moving means making the changes, and communicating and encouraging adoption of the new situation.

Refreezing means consolidation and reinforcement of the new situation.

While these phases may be appropriate to employees moving or changing roles within the company, the changes to the factory are absolute (ie, closure) and thus there is no concept of refreezing a new situation for employees who are leaving.

The model's application is therefore limited in the context of this factory closure, as some employees are lost to the company rather than having to accept a new structure or culture.

The **coercive change** approach is where change is forced without participation. This requires the ability to push through the change without co-operation but it may be appropriate in these circumstances as there is no requirement to maintain the goodwill of most of the factory workforce post changes, as they will no longer be working for HoL.

The **Gemini 4Rs** model of reframing, restructuring, revitalising and renewal is, like the Lewin model, largely based on the needs, not just of getting rid of the old structure, but also of reformulating the new structure. In the case of factory closure and for Strategy 2, the latter part of the model is largely redundant as there is little scope for renewal for employees who are leaving.

There are likely to be barriers to change, particularly from employees, which need to be managed as part of the change management process.

(1) **Cultural barriers**

Strategy 1 is more difficult to manage as it involves maintaining elements of the existing culture/structure/ workforce despite closing the factory. In contrast, Strategy 2 is more about managing closure and a new start up than managing a continuing process.

Strategy 1 puts forward fundamental changes that will affect the culture of the organisation. Power structures within the company may be threatened by the redistribution of decision-making authority or resources, or the changing of lines of communication.

For example, this will affect management and thus management may be reluctant to implement changes which will be contrary to their own interests.

(2) Stakeholder groups

Group inertia may block change where the changes are inconsistent with the norms of teams and departments, or where they threaten their interests.

Examples might include the following:

- Strikes and other forms of resistance to change implementation by staff who are to be made redundant

- UK raw material suppliers taking legal action for contract termination if the business is now to be switched to overseas suppliers under Strategy 2

- Shareholders selling shares as a result of the changes.

(3) Individuals

There are also barriers which affect individuals and result in them seeing the change as a threat to earnings and job security.

Conclusion

The transfer overseas in Strategy 2 is operationally more difficult as it involves setting up in a new country and almost starting the manufacturing process again. However, managing employees who are to move from the old factory to the new factory in Strategy 1 also presents challenges and a greater opportunity for resistance to change from those involved in that change. Each will require elements of common change management and differences in change management.

Examiner's comments

Answers were variable in quality. Weaker candidates' answers were unstructured and often did not refer to models at all, but merely discussed common sense issues such as uncertainty, redundancy and a lack of buy-in by the employees.

For those candidates that did use change management models, such as Lewin's iceberg model, answers were mixed. Where models were used, the weaker candidates did not apply the model to the scenario, while stronger candidates tended to analyse each strategy separately and conclude how best to manage change in each case.

36 Zuccini plc (June 2015)

Marking guide

	Knowledge	Skill	Marks
36.1 Typhoon	3	10	12
36.2 Hurricane	3	10	12
	6	20	24

General comments:

Zuccini plc (Zuccini) is a niche manufacturer of motorbikes which is small in the context of the industry. It has an R&D centre in Italy and two factories, one in Italy and one in the UK. Product life cycles are a key feature of the industry and, as Zuccini is having liquidity issues, the product portfolio needs to be considered using models such as the product life cycle and the BCG matrix.

One of Zuccini's motorbikes, the Typhoon4, is nearing the end of its product life cycle and consideration is being given either: (1) to replacing the Typhoon4 with a completely new model, the Typhoon5; or (2) to modifying the Typhoon4 to produce a slightly updated version, the Typhoon4A, to extend the existing life cycle.

Another motorbike, 'the Hurricane', is currently in its R&D phase, but technical difficulties have caused delays and some uncertainties. Consideration is being given whether to: (1) launch 'the Hurricane' next year as a low-price, basic model; or (2) delay the launch and continue R&D for three years, then launch as a higher price, mid-market product.

36.1 The product life cycle

The product life cycle (PLC) describes the phases of development that a product goes through. The key stages of the life cycle are as follows:

- **Introduction** – a new product or service is made available for purchase and organisations attempt to develop buyer interest.

- **Growth** – a period of rapid expansion of demand or activity as the product finds a market and the product demonstrates its potential.

- **Maturity** – a relatively stable period of time where there is little change in sales volumes year to year but competition between firms intensifies as growth slows down.

- **Decline** – a falling off in sales levels as the product becomes less competitive in the face of competition from newer products.

The PLC can be viewed in conjunction with the BCG Matrix in determining the impact on the company's cash flow from a portfolio of products at various stages in their life cycles. The BCG Matrix portfolio analysis is useful because it provides a framework to consider and forecast potential market growth and to evaluate the competitive dimension through an evaluation of market share. (Note: As Zuccini is a niche player then, in one sense, all of its products have a small market share in relation to the largest companies in motorbike industry. Zuccini's relative market share therefore needs to be considered in comparison to the other niche players.)

The Typhoon4 appears to be in its decline phase with sales falling, and may be viewed as a 'Dog' product (or perhaps a Dodo) within the BCG Matrix with low market share, low or negative growth, and modest or negative cash flow.

The StormRaider appears to be in the growth phase with replacement not due until 20Y9. It may therefore be viewed as a 'Star' within the BCG Matrix.

The Hurricane is in its R&D phase. It will not enter its introduction phase until either 20Y6 or 20Y8 (see below). It may therefore be viewed as an infant in the BCG Matrix with negative cash flow.

Overall, the benefit of the BCG Matrix is to view Zuccini's portfolio of products as impacting cash flows and liquidity in different ways at different points in their life cycles. Thus, for example, established or growth products are financing the development of new products.

When to end Typhoon4 production

In deciding on the timing of change for the Typhoon4 it is necessary to consider it in the context of the wider company product portfolio.

Whilst Typhoon4 sales are declining, the product is not necessarily unprofitable. As it is made in a separate factory in Italy, most of the costs associated with the Typhoon4 should be readily identifiable in order to make an assessment of product profitability.

In order to determine how long the production of the Typhoon4 should be allowed to continue in its decline phase, the following factors should be considered:

- How much inventory of the Typhoon4 exists (ie, how many months' sales). If inventory is significant, then production will need to cease some time prior to sales ceasing.

- Evaluate the exit barriers to determine the optimum time to cease production (eg, at the end of a lease agreement on machinery specific to the manufacture of the Typhoon4 or at the end of the useful life of machinery for making the Typhoon4).

- Potential response of competitors to any change.

- Need for new updates (eg, a change in regulations on emissions with which the Typhoon4 does not comply, but with which the Typhoon4A and Typhoon5 do comply).

- Availability of cash to replace or modify. Even though its sales are declining, the Typhoon4 may still be cash generative. In contrast, the introduction of the Typhoon4A or the Typhoon5 would be likely initially to consume cash at a time it may be needed on R&D projects, eg, for the Hurricane (see below).

Whether to produce the Typhoon4A or the Typhoon5

At this stage, there is insufficient information to make a firm decision as to whether the Typhoon4 should be replaced or modified. There are however a number of indicative factors which can be considered.

In terms of the product life cycle (PLC) replacing the Typhoon4 with the Typhoon4A will provide an extra two years of product life, effectively pushing it back into the maturity phase, and extending its life before the replacement of the Typhoon4A is needed with the Typhoon5 in 20Y7.

Replacing the Typhoon4 with the Typhoon5 on the other hand will, in PLC terms, in effect commence a new introduction phase with a much longer extended life cycle.

One of the problems of replacing the Typhoon4 with the Typhoon4A is that it is a two-stage process, as the Typhoon4A will then need to be replaced with the Typhoon5 two years later.

This raises two key questions:

- Will the transition costs of converting from the Typhoon4 to the Typhoon5 in one step be significantly different from the transition costs of converting from the Typhoon4 to the Typhoon4A, and then later from the Typhoon4A to the Typhoon5, as a two-step process?

- If the Typhoon5 starts production two years later, will its life cycle finish two years later, or at the same time for both options, irrespective of its introduction date?

The cash needed to replace a product is much greater than the amount needed to modify one, therefore the introduction of the Typhoon5 is likely initially to consume much more cash than the modification to the Typhoon4A. This may be at a time it is needed on R&D projects, eg, for the Hurricane (see below).

Turning to marketing aspects, in trying to compete in a difficult external market it is important that Zuccini's product reputation is maintained and improved. This would indicate that the best product should be launched as soon as possible, which would be the Typhoon5. Prolonging the introduction of the Typhoon5 with the Typhoon4A may damage reputation and make future sales of all Zuccini's products more difficult.

Conclusion

Subject to more detailed information becoming available, based on the current information the Typhoon5 should be introduced as soon as possible. This will save a double change of product type and ensure that the best product is available to customers as soon as possible. The life cycles are driven by market conditions and so could well be coterminous for the Typhoon5 under either option. It may be that sales of the Typhoon4 continue to be made from inventory but, in this case, a short period of overlapping life cycles, where the old product price is discounted, is likely to be more acceptable than forcing customers into buying Typhoon4A technology which is not the best that Zuccini can offer.

Examiner's comments

Candidates appeared to be comfortable in the application of the product life cycle and the BCG matrix, identifying that the Typhoon 4 was in decline and could be classified as a dog product. The higher scoring answers also identified capital investment and the resulting liquidity position as key factors in making the decision. Disappointingly, most answers did not discuss the wider product portfolio context that in order to manage a product range, it is a sensible strategy to have a range of products all at different stages of the life cycle. Many candidates did not make sufficient distinction between types 4A and 5.

36.2 Factors

The launch of the Hurricane would introduce an extra model to the product portfolio, making it three in all. It would sit at the bottom end of the Zuccini quality range whether introduced in June 20Y6 as a basic product, or in June 20Y8 as a mid-market product.

Strategic factors

The StormRaider is an upmarket motorbike and the Typhoon4 is a mid to upmarket motorbike. The introduction of the Hurricane as a basic motorbike extends the product portfolio down the quality spectrum, which may cause brand confusion and damage reputation for the two other products in the portfolio.

There will be a significant delay of three years (until 20Y8) before the mid-market version of the Hurricane can be launched. There is significant uncertainty here as competitors are likely to launch new models during this period so the degree of competition by 20Y8 is difficult to estimate, causing additional uncertainty.

R&D plays a key role in product strategy and a number of strategic models are relevant in this context.

Porter's generic strategies: product innovation could be a source of differentiation. Process innovation may enable differentiation for the £9,000 motorbike or cost leadership for the £6,000 motorbike.

Porter's value chain: R&D is included within the support activities of technology development. It can be harnessed in the service of lower costs or improved differentiation for the £6,000 motorbike.

Ansoff matrix: R&D supports all four strategic quadrants. Strategies of market penetration and product development are relevant to Zuccini in this context.

Industry and product life cycles: the obsolescence of existing products can be accelerated by R&D by other companies and so R&D is required to provide Zuccini with replacements to compete.

Operational factors

There appear to have been uncertainties relating to technical factors in the R&D process. In this sense R&D is key to determining the nature of the product and the way it is positioned in the market. However, the very nature of R&D means that it has uncertainty of operational outcomes. The mid-market product appears to present more difficulties and therefore more delay and more uncertainty. This would favour the earlier launch of the basic product in order to reduce uncertainty.

The R&D process may have unintended externalities. In other words, R&D may discover processes and products which may be of use, not just on the Hurricane, but also on the other two models, even though this was not the original purpose of the R&D.

Financial factors

Given that the company may have liquidity issues over the next few years then this may be a key factor in deciding between the 20Y6 launch and the 20Y8 launch.

Comparing the two choices, the 20Y8 launch is cash negative in the next few years. R&D tends to be expensive and over the next three years the mid-market motorbike R&D project will be consuming cash in its R&D efforts whilst delaying the product launch and therefore the future cash inflows. Even after the 20Y8 launch, the Hurricane would be in the introductory phase of its PLC and it may take a while before it will be any more than cash neutral.

In contrast the basic model will complete the R&D outflows in 20Y6 and launch thereafter with the ability to generate cash as it comes out of its introductory phase.

More information is needed to decide which alternative will ultimately generate the greater NPV over its life cycle but if short-term liquidity is an issue this points towards the basic model.

In pure undiscounted cash terms (ie, zero discount rate) the cash flows from one unit of each product (in the absence of information on volumes) would be generated as follows:

20Y6 launch: £6,000 × 7 years = £42,000
20Y8 launch: £9,000 × 6 years = £54,000

Whilst the 20Y8 mid-market product generates more revenue, there are several financial factors which mitigate against this, in favour of the 20Y6 launch of the basic product:

- The 20Y6 launch generates cash flows earlier and so will have a higher present value on average per £1 generated

- Additional R&D costs will be incurred for the 20Y8 mid-market product

- It seems likely that for the 20Y8 launch there will be greater operational costs in producing a mid-market product rather than a basic product

Conclusion

More information is needed on costs and volumes. However, based on the information available there seem too much delay and too much uncertainty to favour the 20Y8 mid-market product. Moreover, in financial terms the 20Y6 basic product generates more cash earlier. This may support the development of other products.

Rather than damage reputation it may be considered that the 20Y6 basic product could be launched under a different brand name.

Examiner's comments

This part was attempted reasonably well, with better candidates structuring their discussion using the headings provided in the question of strategic, operational and financial factors. In this part of the answer, most candidates did think about the overall strategy of where to position the product in the market and how a delayed launch would be perceived. The majority also identified the generic strategy issue in launching the low cost model, given the firm's differentiated niche focus. Conclusions were not always offered and, if they were, they were usually not fully explained or justified.

37 Kentish Fruit Farms (September 2015)

Marking guide

	Knowledge	Skill	Marks
37.1 PESTEL factors	3	6	9
37.2 Evaluation of two strategies	2	18	18
37.3 Ethical issues	3	6	8
37.4 Control procedures	3	6	8
	11	36	43

This is the mini case at 43 marks and also the data analysis question. It was well attempted.

The scenario relates to an organic fruit farm, KFF Ltd, which grows apples that are either sold to retailers or used in producing its own brand of organic apple juice. To increase capacity, KFF has planted some additional land with a new variety of apple trees and has also started to buy in apples from other organic farmers to use to produce juice. KFF's board is keen to evaluate the success of these strategies against its medium-term business objectives for revenue and profit. A supply chain issue has however arisen as a recent batch of KFF's organic apple juice, made using fruit from one of the new suppliers, was tested by the Food Standards Agency and found to contain artificial pesticides. 20% of the production run has already been distributed to a major retailer and KFF is considering whether to issue a public recall of these bottles, and what it can do to identify such quality problems in future.

Tutorial note:

Only 3 forces need to be analysed but these need to be justified as Key. There was plenty of obvious information in the scenario to discuss Social/Technological/Ecological/Legal. There was less in the scenario to support Political/ Economic.

37.1 **The key forces are:**

Social – consumers' attitudes to organic food are changing because of concerns about health and the environment. Organic food is seen to be more socially responsible – it helps address issues around global warming and the environment and reduces concerns about the consumption of harmful pesticide and fertiliser residues. These factors will work to increase industry demand. The accountability of farmers as a result of organic certification is also likely to increase consumer confidence in what they are buying. A focus on the procurement of local goods will benefit organic farmers in their region, as will public sentiment against genetically-modified crops.

Technological – the industry relies on the use of technology to avoid using harmful fertilisers and pesticides. As a result it has developed sophisticated weather management systems and atmospherically controlled growing and storage tunnels. These factors will help increase yields and also reduce the seasonality impact and perishability problems by extending the life of the product through storage, thus benefiting cashflow. Further technical advances may help the industry reduce costs and hence prices, making the products accessible to more consumers.

Ecological (Environmental) – a key factor in the growth of the organic farming industry has been a drive for more environmentally friendly products. Organic farming is seen to be more ecologically sound – the farming methods reduce harmful waste from the manufacture and use of agrochemicals and, since it is often also more local, there is less carbon footprint associated with its distribution. However the need for environmentally friendly farming methods may mean the industry struggles to compete on price with traditional farming methods. The latter may be more pest-resistant due to the use of fertilisers or may be able to achieve greater yields through artificial growth methods. A further environmental issue is the weather which can have a significant impact on crop quality and yields and which the industry attempts to manage through technology (discussed above).

Legal (regulatory) – there is significant regulation in the food industry generally and particularly for organic produce. As well as complying with the Food Standards Agency (FSA) and EU regulations regarding production, packaging and labelling, organic farmers also need to comply with regulations specifying organic farming methods. In addition they need to be approved for and obtain certification, then comply with its terms. There are severe sanctions for breaching regulations, and as a result compliance is critical and costs are likely to be high. Any changes in standards in the future will have an impact on the industry – also different countries have different standards which can be an issue for exports.

Political (there is much less in the scenario to go on for this)

Political factors refer to the attitude and approaches of the government and other parties to the organic farming movement. Any change in government may affect future regulations. The Green Party for example supports changes in the farming industry to make food production more sustainable and protect the environment and its resources; they are also in favour of local food production. Government initiatives to promote sustainability and healthy eating are likely to increase demand for organic products and hence benefit the industry. Inevitably these are links between political factors and legal factors such as consumer protection regulations and the certification of organic farmers.

Economic (there is much less information to go on in the scenario for this)

Historically organic produce has been seen as a luxury product and is therefore less in demand when disposable incomes fall. However the move towards organic as a lifestyle choice reduces this risk for the industry, which appears to be in a growth phase. As demand increases there may be pressure to intensify farming operations which may not be consistent with organic methods. Many smaller organic farmers may find it challenging to deal with the size and bargaining power of large retail buyers, which could dictate prices and hence margins. From a financial point of view organic farmers, like traditional ones, are at risk due to seasonality of cashflows and unpredictability of weather.

Examiner's comments

This requirement was very well answered and was, on average, the best answered requirement on the paper. Most candidates used relevant information from the scenario to justify the importance of their selected PESTEL factor and explain its likely impact on the industry. A common mistake among weaker candidates was to treat PESTEL as if it were a company rather than industry model and/or to discuss relatively unimportant factors. A minority of candidates wasted time by completing a full PESTEL analysis when only three factors were required.

37.2 Data Analysis

Table 1:	20Y3	20Y4
Hectares of KFF orchards yielding fruit	40	55
Tonnes of apples harvested	480	720
Yield (tonnes produced /hectare)	12.0	13.1
Tonnes of apples sold as fresh fruit	288	468
Tonnes of own apples used for juice	192	252
Crop mix: fruit:juice	60:40	65:35
Tonnes of own apples used for juice production	192	252
Tonnes of apples bought in	–	48
Total tonnes of apples used for juice production	192	300
1 litre bottles of juice produced and sold	96,000	150,000
Bottles produced per tonne	500	500
Revenue: fresh fruit £'000	576	889
Tonnes of apples sold as fresh fruit	288	468
Fresh fruit: Revenue per tonne	2,000	1,900
Revenue: juice £'000	336	525
Total tonnes of apples used for juice production	192	300
Juice: revenue per tonne £'000	1,750	1,750
Juice: revenue per 1 litre bottle £	3.50	3.50
Sales revenue mix: fruit:juice	63:37	63:37
Cost of sales £'000	540	812
Tonnes of apples sold as fruit/juice	480	768
Cost per tonne used £	1,125	1,057
Gross profit £'000	372	602
Gross profit per tonne £	775	784

Table 2:

	20Y3	20Y4
Gross profit margin	41%	43%
Operating margin	12%	10%
Operating costs as % of sales	28%	32%
Interest cover	2.13	1.97

Table 3: analysis of yield from new trees

Incremental land	15 hectares
Incremental apple crop	240 tonnes
Yield (tonnes produced per hectare)	16 tonnes/hectare
15 hectares at standard yield of 12 tonnes	180 tonnes
Increased yield due to efficiency of new planting	60 tonnes

Table 4: analysis of changes in revenue 20Y3–20Y4

	£
Revenue generated from additional trees: Strategy 1	
Incremental fruit crop: (468 – 288) × £1,900	342,000
Incremental juice crop: (252 –192) × £1,750	105,000
	447,000
Revenue generated from fruit bought in: Strategy 2	
48 × £1,750	84,000
	531,000
Revenue lost due to reduction in market price of fresh fruit:	
288 × £(2,000 – 1,900)	(28,800)
Total incremental revenue (Note: £1,414 – £912k = £502k)	**502,200**

Commentary:

KFF's profitability is limited by its capacity to meet all the demand for its products. To generate additional capacity, KFF have implemented two new strategies that impact on 20Y4 results:

(1) The purchase of land and intense planting of new trees to increase apple production and also improve yields per hectare. The first crop from this was produced in 20Y4.

(2) The decision from 20Y4 to purchase apples from local farmers to increase juice production. This will increase sales volumes of juice but is likely to reduce the margin if it is more expensive to buy in apples than to home grow them.

It is not clear whether these strategies will have had a 12 month impact or only affected results for part of the year, and more information would be useful to assess the timing of the change.

The overall performance of the business in relation to the objectives set is as follows:

	Objective	Actual 20Y4	Comment
Annual revenue growth	15%	55%	Achieved
Gross margin	45%	43%	Not achieved

On the face of it therefore the new strategies have achieved the required revenue growth, although since this is the first year of impact, the growth achieved may not be sustainable. The gross margin target has not been met, although gross margin has increased from 41% to 43% so it is moving in the right direction.

However further analysis is required, of each strategy, of performance overall and of performance in relation to the objectives.

Strategy 1: new trees:

The purpose of acquiring the land is twofold:

- To increase supply of apples
- To improve profitability by increasing the yield per hectare

The supply of apples has increased as the new orchard has come on stream, providing an additional 15 acres which in terms of land base increases the capacity of the farm by 37.5%. Ordinarily at KFF's 20Y3 yield the new land would have produced 12 tonnes per hectare or

180 tonnes of apples in total. The new farming method was expected to increase yields by 30%. In 20Y4 the new trees actually generated an additional crop of 240 tonnes, 60 tonnes above standard output, which is an increase in yield of 33.33% and resulted in a yield of 16 tonnes per hectare.

As a result the purchase of the land and the switch to more intensive planting appears to have been successful in increasing capacity. Table 4 shows that the fruit grown on the new trees increased revenue by £447,000 in 20Y4, although as we have no detail on costs we do not know how profitable this was.

A greater proportion of the crop was sold as fresh fruit (65% compared to the previous year's 60%) which perhaps suggests better quality output, but the revenue per tonne fell which, as KFF is a price-taker, is likely to be due to market factors.

Strategy 2: purchase of other fruit:

During the year KFF acquired 48 tonnes of fruit from neighbouring farms, which it turned into juice and from which it generated £84,000 extra revenue. The additional volume of bottles did not have any impact on the price per bottle, which remained constant at £3.50 and therefore suggests strong demand. Again more information on the costs of buying in and processing the fruit would be useful. Also there is now some doubt about whether all fruit bought in met the required organic standards, and this may give rise to concerns over this strategy in the future.

Success of strategies:

No breakdown is given of the costs of either strategy. In total, they have allowed KFF to increase revenue by £531,000 in 20Y4 (58% of 20Y3 revenue). The actual revenue increase of 55% (or £502,000) is lower because the market price for fresh fruit has fallen from £2,000 to £1,900 per tonne in 20Y4.

Overall the revenue mix of fresh fruit and juice has not changed.

The increase in revenue of 55% exceeds the objective of 15%. However this type of growth would be expected in the first year of the capacity increase. The objective is for annual revenue growth of 15% but it is not clear whether that is expected to be each year or on an average basis. In 20Y5 KFF will only be able to generate more revenue by purchasing additional apples for juice or adopting more new farming methods to increase yields.

Profitability

The gross profit margin has increased overall. Purchasing fruit is likely to have reduced margin on the bottles of juice which incorporate it. The increased yield per hectare will have an upward effect on margin, although this may depend on how expensive the new farming method is. The fact that the cost of sales per tonne has fallen from £1,125 to £1,057 implies that the net effect has been positive.

In order to assess the profitability of the decisions, it would be useful to know:

- the cost per hectare of farming the new trees on the new land compared to the existing trees on the existing land

- the cost per tonne that KFF has had to pay to buy in the fruit

Although the gross margin has increased, the operating margin has fallen from 12% to 10% which is due to increased operating costs. Thus £502,000 of additional revenue has generated £230,000 of additional gross profit but only £33,000 of extra operating profit. More information is needed about the increase in operating costs.

Cash flow

Interest cover has fallen from 2.13 times to 1.97 times because of the 40% increase in interest costs. The customer mix may have changed and the additional sales may have come from retailers who have dictated longer credit terms. Thus the business' cash position has deteriorated and interest charges have increased. More information on cash flows, and on KFF's capital structure, would be useful.

Further details:

To better explain performance, the business needs to analyse costs between the old and the new trees and also separately analyse the profitability of the two product lines, juice and fresh fruit.

Management accounts for 20Y4 showing monthly statement of profit or loss and cash flow would help better assess the seasonality of the business and also the impact of the new strategies.

Examiner's comments

The data analysis requirement was well attempted by the majority of candidates. Most were well practised at providing a table of up-front calculations and a list of additional information, although this was not always tailored to the scenario. The key to a good answer was to identify appropriate financial and operational calculations which would help determine the impact of each strategy separately: both the planting of the additional trees and the purchase of apples from other farmers. The better candidates did this, providing calculations to assess the impact of the additional land capacity and the change in yield, and structuring their evaluation under two separate headings. Weaker candidates were poor in this regard, merely providing calculations of changes in financial figures, within their narrative, and evaluating the performance of the company overall, rather than the impact of each strategy against the objectives that had been set. The best candidates recognised that there was sufficient information to assess the revenue impact of the strategies but not their overall profitability.

37.3 Ethical issues

Ethics pertains to whether a particular behaviour is deemed acceptable in the context under consideration. In short, it is 'doing the right thing'.

In making any ethical evaluation it is first necessary to establish the facts. In this case, it would seem that the facts are reasonably clear in terms of a batch of KFF juice being identified as containing non-organic pesticides and the fruit having been traced to a supplier. What is uncertain is how KFF should react to this.

Given the extensive regulations affecting the organic food industry, the issue of legality needs to be considered and legal advice taken by KFF as to its responsibility. Although the fruit concerned may have come from another farm, the juice is sold under the KFF brand and KFF are likely to be held responsible for the breach by the FSA, which may apply sanctions. KFF may face losing their organic certification, which may require that everything they sell should be 100% organic.

Joe Fielding appears to be prepared to behave ethically in relation to the undistributed product, which would be relabelled and sold as non-organic, presumably at a lower price. It is the action suggested in relation to the bottles that have already been distributed which raises ethical issues.

In making a decision as to how to proceed, it is helpful to apply the Institute of Business Ethics three tests:

- Transparency
- Effect
- Fairness

Transparency – a public recall of the juice already distributed would be transparent and in the public interest. It would be consistent with the reputation KFF has built as an ethical farm. Keeping quiet about the bottles that have already been distributed and only addressing the remaining inventory is less transparent and KFF should consider whether it would mind people (existing customers, regulators, employees) knowing that it has taken this action. Lack of full disclosure may in fact not be an option as it may be imposed by the regulator as a matter of public interest.

Effect – a full recall may embarrass KFF and the retailer but would prevent harm to the end-consumers. The effect of a partial action would be to keep information from the retailer, and consumers who have already bought the juice would suffer due to KFF acting in its own and not the public interest. As a minimum this would be because consumers pay higher prices for organic juice which is in fact non-organic. More serious, although perhaps less likely, is the fact that their health may be affected by the consumption of pesticide residues.

Fairness – it is likely that competitors, the retailer and consumers would not take kindly to the fact that KFF has knowingly deceived them and mis-represented its product.

Actions

KFF should be guided by legal advice and its discussions with FSA, and should co-operate in all investigations made by the FSA. The matter may be of sufficient seriousness for FSA to apply sanctions. The best action would be for KFF to act honestly and with integrity, making a full disclosure of all the facts. Even if the FSA does not require disclosure, KFF should consider doing so, to avoid further damage to its reputation. KFF should then have discussions with the supplier concerned to establish how the use of non-organic pesticides has arisen and why it was not detected. It may have recourse against the supplier depending on the contractual terms.

Having made the suggestion that the company should be dishonest, the board should consider discussing with Joe Fielding the importance of ethical behaviour, and should review the company's overall culture to ensure that all staff are in line with the importance of maintaining ethics and also the organic status of the company's produce.

Examiner's comments

This requirement was well answered. The ethical issues relating to the possible production and sale of non-organic juice were reasonably easy for most candidates to identify. The vast majority of candidates also recognised that there was a legal/regulatory issue here given the FSA and the need for organic certification. Some candidates restricted their marks by not providing clear actions. Better answers distinguished between the actions that might be appropriate in respect of the contaminated juice that has already been distributed and the action that the company should take regarding the remaining bottles.

37.4 Control procedures and information systems

Given the nature of KFF's business, quality is a critical success factor. Quality assurance and quality control are critical to standardise the quality of fruit and juice products and also ensure that they are safe to consume.

Even if KFF was not an organic farm, the requirement to produce safe foods in a hygienic way is part of the law and there are serious penalties for contravening hygiene and food safety legislation.

In creating a new relationship with suppliers, KFF should establish a service level agreement, agreeing not just on the financial terms of supply but also on key targets/standards that need to be met and the consequence of not doing. Any expectations that KFF has in relation to ethics and sustainability and the need for suppliers to conform to KFF's policies in these areas would need to be set out.

Suppliers should be selected based on their experience and the quality of their products. Clearly verifying a supplier's organic certification and credentials would be a critical step in early due diligence, before contracts are agreed. KFF should carry out an annual inspection visit where the supplier is required to confirm that organic standards have been met. If suppliers are local then occasional drop-in visits may be feasible.

Once a supplier has been contracted then a key control procedure is to measure and monitor supplier performance. Joe is correct that early detection of problems is desirable but costs (both financial and reputational) are generally lower if KFF is able to prevent defective output rather than simply detecting it.

KFF should go through each stage of processing, from purchase of apples and other ingredients/packaging products to the bottling of the final juice, to identify where factors exist that could influence either product quality or safety and then devise procedures that control those factors.

Quality assurance focuses on procedures and standards that will ensure product problems are eliminated or minimised during the production process. In KFF's case this might include inspecting or sample testing fruit that is bought in, before using it in production, in the hope that any poor quality fruit is identified and rejected or that any traces of pesticides would be identified.

Fruit that is to be stored before use might need testing on arrival at KFF and then inspecting again after storage but before use. Any bottles, caps or other items involved in the juice production should also be inspected and tested, since these may cause quality issues.

Quality control is associated with checking a product after it has been produced and this might involve sample testing bottles of juice from every batch of production. Even if there are no pesticide issues, this may be a good idea to ensure consistency of the product over time in relation to flavour, appearance etc.

Given the importance of local reputation, the need for certification and the high level of regulation in the industry, KFF would be advised to apply quality control procedures to all its own fruit and juice production, as well as to suppliers' fruit, if it is not already doing so.

If it is unable to expand its own capacity, then for long-term sustainability of the farm, KFF needs to establish partnerships with local farmers which are transparent and add strategic value. An information system can be used to enhance this, not just from the point of view of supplier control and monitoring but also for measuring KFF's own performance, by capturing a range of data.

An information system can track performance overtime, and may be useful in identifying trends or detecting early warning signs of future problems. It also provides KFF with evidence for its own organic certification and in relation to supplier performance when discussing or renewing contracts with suppliers.

Appropriate operational measures (KPIs) to monitor supplier performance might include:

Quality assurance

Rejection rate of apples per tonne purchased – this could be compared against KFF's own achievement and also across suppliers and harvests

The reasons for reject could then also be broken down as this will help identify and address the cause of the problem eg:

- Level of pesticide/fertiliser detected on apple crop
- % of apples contaminated eg, by insects
- % of apples that were mouldy/physically damaged

These would need to be considered in relation to any agreed tolerances that have been established with the supplier but also in relation to organic standard requirements.

Quality control

- Rejection rate of bottles per batch of juice
- Level of wastage during production process
- % of bottles not meeting specifications (weight, volume, appearance, labelling etc)

Other measures useful for supplier monitoring might include the following:

- Tonnes delivered vs tonnes promised
- Number of disruptions to production caused due to late delivery/apple shortages
- Price per tonne

Examiner's comments

This was one of the worst attempted requirements on the paper but answers were quite polarised. The main difference in the standard of answers to this requirement related to whether candidates were familiar with the concept of quality assurance and control procedures. Weaker answers simply listed brief checks that KFF could undertake in relation to suppliers. Stronger candidates identified procedures and processes that could be used to prevent and detect quality issues and monitor performance. A significant number of candidates ignored the requirement to suggest some specific KPIs.

Marking guide

	Knowledge	Skill	Marks
38.1 Business development and CSFs	3	8	10
38.2 Risk register	3	6	9
38.3 Memorandum	3	10	11
	9	24	30

General comments:

Overall this question was also well attempted.

The scenario concerns Premier Paper Products plc (PPP) a company which prints banknotes and identity documents for a variety of central banks and governments. New technology means that some central banks have recently decided to change from using paper banknotes to polymer notes and PPP's board is unsure whether to invest in the new technology, which has already been adopted by one of its competitors.

38.1 CSFs for PPP

PPP's growth

Ansoff

The Ansoff model is a two-by-two matrix of Products (new and existing) and Markets (new and existing).

PPP started out as a manufacturer of banknotes (existing product) for its country's central bank (existing market). The growth of its business has then come from both geographical expansion and the development of new products.

Market development – existing products and new markets.

The expansion of the banknote production into over 100 countries across Europe and Asia is market development on a geographical basis, as is the sale of security paper to the state-owned printing works which use it to produce their own banknotes. In terms of CSFs, PPP's design skills and innovative security features are likely to have helped it build market share.

Product development – new products and existing markets.

PPP realised that its existing customer base of central banks would benefit from other products. As a result, 60 years ago, it capitalised on one of its CSFs – its existing customer relationships and contracts - by expanding its product range and moving into the related area of banknote sorting and counting machines and inspection equipment.

Further product development or Diversification – new product, new market

Growth continued with the establishment of a new product range: passports and identity cards. PPP continued to leverage its expertise in designing and printing security paper and its reputation for maintaining security and confidentiality by extending this to government identity schemes. 15 years ago PPP won its first contract to print passports and driving licences for its own government and now produces documents for 65 countries.

Although closely related to central bank clients, governments might be said to be a different market and hence this strategy might be deemed diversification.

Lynch Expansion method matrix

The Lynch model is another two-by-two matrix of method of company growth (organic growth and external development) and geographical location (home (domestic) and international). Under this model, the primary focus for PPP's growth has been through organic growth and international development. Both banknote and identity card production started with the domestic market, but because the size of this is limited, to achieve economies of scale PPP had to expand internationally, targeting a variety of global central bank and government clients.

PPP's CSFs have allowed it to grow organically rather than through acquisition. It has achieved this by continuing innovation through in-house research and development and also by leveraging its client base.

Critical success factors are the product features that are particularly valued by customers and/or the activities that an organisation must excel at to outperform the competition.

In the case of PPP, a summary of the key critical success factors discussed above that have facilitated its development are as follows:

- Innovation – expertise in evolving innovative and sophisticated security features for paper, notes and identity documents

- Reputation – for the design of high quality, elegant banknotes and for maintaining security/confidentiality

- Relationships and partnerships/contracts with central banks and governments

- Operational excellence in relation to quality, accuracy, reliability

Examiner's comments

Candidates were asked to assess the ways that PPP has expanded. A number of models could be used here and many were comfortable using Ansoff, though Lynch and Porter's generic strategies were also relevant. The better answers combined their discussion of the various expansion strategies (product development, market development etc) with an explanation of the CSFs that had facilitated each move. Candidates who merely positioned each strategy on the Ansoff matrix and then separately produced a bulleted list of CSFs tended to score less well.

38.2 Risk register

A variety of key business risks facing PPP's banknote division are set out below:

Nature of business risk	Impact and likelihood	Risk management
Strategic: technological change renders the need for banknotes obsolete	Technological developments clearly have a big impact on the industry and are changing the nature of the product and market as the demand for cash reduces and it is replaced by cards and other contactless payment methods. Changes in technology may reduce the volume of business but for the present time it seems unlikely that it will remove the need for banknotes entirely. Also the technology is likely to be adopted at different rates in different markets.	Reduce risk in short term by developing different technologies eg, polymer notes so PPP will retain central bank customers even if they switch from paper. May have to accept this as a risk in longer term PPP as a whole has reduced risk by diversifying product range eg, identity cards and passports

Nature of business risk	Impact and likelihood	Risk management
Strategic: failure to produce technologically advanced and competitive banknote products	Industry standards and security features are continually evolving. Failure to innovate would likely result in lost market share and lower margins.	Reduce risk through: continued investment in R&D and design, and employment of skilled designers. Consider JV with universities/scientists
Strategic: failure to win or renew key contracts	Contracts are often long-term so timing of renewal may be predictable. The loss of contracts is likely as this is a competitive environment and contracts are awarded by central banks which can be affected by political factors outside PPP's control. Failure to win contracts may result in PPP operating below optimal capacity, restricting growth and profitability	Reduce risk by maintaining close, trusted relationships with customers. Monitor sales pipeline and undertake production planning to ensure critical mass. Monitor activities of competitors where possible. Maintain brand and reputation for design and operational excellence. Implement/maintain a CRM system and focus on key contracts as they come due for renewal.
Operational: poor quality product or standards of service damage the company's reputation	Highly technical contracts with very detailed specifications mean this is a key risk. The very public nature of the product and the high profile central bank customer mean that if a problem does occur reputational damage is quite likely, with a serious impact including possible loss of contracts. Poor quality banknotes or errors would require re-working or perhaps contract penalty payments.	Reduce risk through quality assurance/total quality management and operational excellence programmes.
Operational: product security. A breakdown in security procedures resulting in theft of products from a site or loss of notes in transit	Likelihood: PPP's past history suggests this is reasonably unlikely Impact: PPP may be contractually liable	Reduce risk by: Security screening for all staff. Physical controls regarding site access, material stores etc would reduce the risk on site. Use of stringent controls for personnel and carriers involved in distribution. Transfer risk through Insurance.

Nature of business risk	Impact and likelihood	Risk management
Hazard: loss of a key manufacturing site or inventory at a site eg, through fire	Depending on the details of the contract, this may result in litigation. The impact would be severe, the likelihood is unknown.	Reduce likelihood by having preventative measures such as advanced smoke detection and sprinkler systems, plus 24 hour monitoring. Transfer through insurance. Contingency plan for other sites to operate as back-up.
Compliance: failure to comply with legal or regulatory requirements	Value and nature of product means there is some likelihood here and reputational impact would be high	Avoid/reduce by: Implementing code of conduct and ethics Screening and security clearance for all employees Disciplinary procedures Training in rules and procedures

Tutorial note:

Other relevant key risks were awarded credit. Only **three** were required.

Examiner's comments

The majority of candidates produced a well-structured table, identifying three risks facing PPP's banknote division, although weaker candidates did not always concentrate on the key ones. Some candidates limited their marks by not addressing all elements of the requirement comprehensively eg, focussing on the impact of the risk and its management, without considering its nature and likelihood. The strongest answers identified a range of key risks and used the TARA model to identify appropriate risk management strategies. A number of candidates wasted time and marks discussing risks facing PPP as a whole rather than the banknote division.

38.3 Memorandum

To: PPP Board
From: A Manager, Banknote division
Date: September 20X5
Re: Polymer bank notes

Factors to consider in deciding whether to invest in the technology to produce polymer banknotes include the following:

Competition

Uniquel is currently the only competitor producing polymer notes, but if these are deemed by central banks to be the way forward, then other printing companies are likely to follow suit. This will have an impact on the following:

(1) The demand for PPP's paper product
(2) The number of contracts that PPP can retain on renewal

Likely buyers and their preferences

Potential customers for polymer notes include the following:

- Central banks who already outsource production to PPP

- Central banks who outsource production to PPP's competitors (private companies or other in-house printers)

- Central banks who currently print in-house

Since a major issue for the industry is security it appears likely that more central banks will move to polymer or alternatively demand increasingly expensive security features for paper notes. A way of ensuring optimal production is to approach other in-house state printing works that do not have PPP's economies of scale and may increasingly find it too costly to keep up with security developments for a small volume of notes.

Environmental considerations

The desire on the part of governments, businesses and consumers to be more environmentally friendly and to promote sustainability may influence the move away from paper to polymer.

Timing of any adoption of new technology

PPP could wait and see to what extent central banks move to polymer as their contracts come up for renewal and make a decision once it has more information. However this will allow Uniquel and any other competitors which enter the market to steal market share. Since banknote contracts are long-term (10 years on average) and this may increase, given the seven year lifetime of the new notes, it could be locked out of the market for a long time. PPP must also consider the impact on its reputation for innovation of being seen not to adopt new technology.

Resources and competences

New machinery is required which may necessitate more factory space. In addition it will take time to recruit the appropriate workforce and source suppliers of polymer. PPP is an expert in producing security paper products – it may not currently have in-house expertise to develop, design and print polymer banknotes. Any errors or issues of quality in the early stages of the process may affect its reputation and position in the paper banknote market.

Costs

A contract for paper notes requires production of notes every three years, compared to every seven for polymer. Thus PPP will need to tender for and win new contracts every year or persuade existing customers to switch to ensure efficient utilisation of production facilities.

Other issues to consider if a decision is taken to introduce polymer are as follows:

- Whether to run the two technologies side by side or cease paper production and switch to polymer

- Whether eventually demand for banknotes will cease altogether as payments move to electronic systems in the longer term

Product portfolio

Paper notes appear to be a cash cow product for PPP currently. The question is to what extent demand will decline and to what extent PPP, as a major industry player, might influence this decline by making the move to polymer. The immediate abandonment of PPP's major product seems implausible, however over the next few years sales may decline to the point where paper notes might then be abandoned.

The adoption of polymer notes is at an early stage in the lifecycle. PPP could aim to stay in the paper notes market all the time it is making sufficient returns and as one of the biggest players it has economies of scale which will probably allow it to outlast smaller competitors. However whether in the long term there will be a dual market for both paper and polymer, or whether eventually paper notes will disappear over time in favour of polymer, needs to be considered.

The future of the banknote

The lifecycle of the banknote industry appears uncertain. Changing consumer preferences appear to have reduced demand for traditional cash payment. Thus the banknote division faces a long-term threat posed by phone, card and other digital payment mechanisms. Scenario planning may help to identify future risks and possible strategic responses. However although demand for cash is reduced, it appears likely that it will not disappear altogether and that there may be more demand for cash in some parts of the world than others, because different countries are at different stages in the lifecycle of cash and electronic payment mechanisms.

Conclusion

On balance it appears that there is a sound strategic argument for the introduction of the new technology. However forecasts need to be prepared and a detailed cost benefit analysis/investment appraisal undertaken to assess the incremental effect of introducing polymer.

Examiner's comments

Most, but surprisingly not all candidates, scored an easy format mark for setting out their answer in the memo format required. Candidates who used sub-headings to structure their answer tended to produce a wider range of points than those who merely listed a range of unconnected factors. Better candidates provided a balanced argument regarding the benefits and problems associated with investing in the polymer technology, linking their answers to the risks identified in 38.2. Most candidates provided an initial recommendation as to whether the investment was advisable and the best candidates identified the steps that should be taken to reach a decision.

39 Taxi Tracker (September 2015)

Marking guide

	Knowledge	Skill	Marks
39.1 Cost and value drivers	3	6	8
39.2 Benefits of dynamic demand-based pricing	3	6	8
39.3 Calculations and evaluation	1	11	11
	7	23	27

General comments:

The third question had the lowest average mark, which was influenced by a number of poor answers to requirement (39.3).

The scenario relates to a company, TT, which has launched a free smartphone app that allows it to act as an intermediary between private hire taxi drivers and their potential customers in a major capital city. Private hire drivers who pass TT's screening process are issued with a TT smartphone which allows them to be registered and tracked on the TT system. Customers can use the TT app to get a fare quote, book a driver and track their arrival. Fares are set using a dynamic demand-based pricing model and increase when vehicles are in short supply. TT currently retains 20% of the fare as commission. There are rumours that a rival firm is planning to launch its own taxi booking app in the city, and TT is considering cutting its fares by 25% for a limited period of four weeks but is unsure whether to alter its commission.

39.1 Cost and value drivers

An organisation's value chain is the sequence of activities by which value is added to its service. This influences the margin a customer is prepared to pay over the costs the organisation incurs in delivering the service.

Within the value chain there can be both cost and value drivers. Whilst cost drivers influence the cost of a given activity, value drivers help an organisation to differentiate itself from competitors. TT's success has been built around its smartphone app which facilitates ease of booking, cashless payment, and improved customer service compared to both Citicabs and existing PHVs. As a result it appears to be following a differentiation strategy.

Tutorial note:

Only **three** were required.

In the case of TT, the key drivers include:

Technology as a value driver of customer service – TT makes widespread use of existing technology (GPS, phone, electronic payments) to add value by making it easier for customers to book a car, track it and pay for it. Using the phone as a meter makes prices more transparent for customers and the payment system is also more secure as drivers do not handle money.

- Technology as a cost driver – the use of the smartphone app reduces the costs to TT of matching drivers and customers since this largely happens without any need for intervention by TT. It means that TT can provide a very high level of customer service at a low cost to itself, connecting customers with the nearest available driver at the touch of a button.

- Procurement (cost driver) – TT's HR model is one of independent contractors rather than employees. While this reduces cost the dynamic demand-based pricing model would also ensure that there is flexibility of supply, as drivers are incentivised to make themselves available when more cars are needed.

- After sales (value driver) – asking customers to rate journeys and drivers creates a perception that TT cares about the customer experience. The fact that drivers have to score at least 4 out of 5 to be able to continue is likely to give the customer confidence in the quality of the service.

- Customer service (value driver) – fast booking and reduced waiting times for cars, the ability to track cars and the ease of payment all create an enhanced customer service experience.

- Firm infrastructure (cost driver) – TT operates a low-cost, flexible model. It has little in the way of infrastructure costs (no requirement for investment in non-current assets such as cars) or employment costs of drivers.

Examiner's comments

This requirement was well done by most candidates, who as usual demonstrated good knowledge of Porter's value chain analysis. The better candidates linked their discussion to TT's generic strategy, identified whether each key driver selected was a cost or value driver, linked it with the relevant aspect of the value chain, and explained how it gave TT a competitive advantage.

39.2 Benefits of dynamic demand-based pricing

Dynamic demand-based pricing is an attempt by TT to find a price at which supply and demand are equal and hence could be argued to be a market-driven approach. TT increases the price in periods of peak demand, when the supply of available PHVs is lower than the number of customers. This has the effect of attracting more drivers because the journeys are more lucrative, hence increasing supply, whilst potentially reducing demand temporarily as the more price-sensitive customers decide to make alternative arrangements for their journey or wait until prices fall again. The extent to which this happens will depend on the price elasticity of demand.

Essentially this strategy is similar to one of price discrimination, used for example by railways or cinemas, where prices vary according to the time of day, or dynamic pricing used by airlines, where prices vary according to the actual level of demand compared to what is deemed a normal level.

The model allows TT to extract the maximum possible revenue by charging higher prices to people who are willing to pay more. Whilst some may argue this is unfair to customers, TT is transparent about their approach to pricing and customers have alternative forms of transport and other PHVs/Citicabs available so are making a free choice.

It could be argued that customers benefit as this approach to pricing is not just about exploiting demand but also about incentivising drivers to work at peak times in order to increase supply, thereby offering the customer a better service. Also drivers benefit as they earn more money and are therefore compensated for having to work at times that are perhaps less sociable eg, public holidays.

To some extent it is a matter of perception as to which price (the high or low fare) is seen as the norm and therefore whether TT are seen to exploit customers by increasing the price in busy periods, or considered to be offering a discount at quieter times.

Unlike Citicabs, whose prices are fixed by the regulator, TT is free to set its own prices. It would be interesting to see how the maximum prices charged by TT compare to those of Citicabs.

Examiner's comments

The discussion of the benefits of demand-based pricing was well done by the majority of candidates, with many identifying both demand and supply side factors. The requirement to consider whether this was unfair to customers was less well done and some weak candidates ignored it altogether. Better answers identified that the use of price discrimination is common in many industries. They pointed out that TT's demand-based pricing model will serve to balance supply and demand, facilitate its promise to make cars available in five minutes, and be transparent so customers can choose rivals such as Citicabs if they are cheaper.

39.3 Calculations and evaluation

(a) Evaluation of fare reduction strategy:

Current fares received	**£**
130,000 × 4 × £10	5,200,000
Split:	
Drivers 80%	4,160,000
TT 20%	1,040,000

Fares reduced by 25%, demand unaffected	**£**
130,000 × 4 × £7.50	3,900,000
Split as now:	
Drivers 80%	3,120,000
TT 20%	780,000

TT would lose £260,000 (£780,000 compared to £1,040,000) and drivers would be £1,040,000 worse off (£3,120,000 compared to £4,160,000).

Fares reduced by 25%, demand increases 15%	**£**
130,000 × 1.15 × 4 × £7.50	4,485,000
Split to maintain drivers' income:	
Drivers	4,160,000
TT	325,000

TT is £715,000 worse off (£325,000 compared to £1,040,000 previously).

Drivers are unaffected.

(b) For neither TT nor the drivers to be worse off, and there to be no change in the 20% commission structure, revenue would need to be maintained at £5,200,000 still.

Where n is the number of journeys: n x 4 x £7.5 = £5,200,000

Hence n = 173,333 (£5,200,000/£30)

This requires an increase in demand of 33.3% for the month.

(c)   Evaluation of fare reduction strategy

	TT £'000	Drivers £'000
Current strategy	1,040	4,160
25% reduction, no change in demand, 20% commission	780	3,120
25% reduction, 15% increase in demand, maintain driver income	325	4,160
25% reduction, 20% commission, 33.3% increase in demand	1,040	4,160

If fares are reduced by 25%, with no corresponding increase in demand, the total fares received are £3,900,000 and under the 20% commission, both TT and the drivers are worse off: TT would lose £260,000 and drivers £1,040,000.

This is likely to cause drivers to move away from TT and contract with other PHV operators in an attempt to maintain their income levels. A lack of availability of drivers may then affect TT's customer service levels or cause higher demand-based prices.

If fares are reduced and demand increases by 15%, the new fares received are £4,485,000.

If TT guarantees that drivers will receive the same income, then TT suffers all the impact of the fare reduction and would be £715,000 worse off than in a normal four week period.

However if the increase in demand is permanent as customers stay loyal to TT, then in future months TT's income will increase. Also TT would be able to advertise this to drivers as a reduction in its commission to 7% (£325k/£4,485k) and may actually attract more drivers as a result. This seems a sensible strategy.

For neither TT nor the drivers to be affected by the fare reduction, an increase in demand of 33.3% for the month is required, which seems an ambitious target and may depend on the elasticity of demand as well as the reactions of competitors.

Other factors to consider:

Although the fare reduction may be attractive, in peak periods when the demand-based pricing model kicks in, the reduction may not be obvious to customers and hence may not have the desired effect.

TT's price reduction may lead to a price war in the PHV market, which will end up permanently reducing every operator's prices and hence margins.

The level of demand will be stimulated if demand for TT's product is price-sensitive, but the customer's decision to use TT may be more about ease of use, service, age of customer – in which case the price reduction may not stimulate demand.

Ultimately TT may be prepared to suffer a short-term reduction in income in the hope of strengthening its loyal customer base and ensuring it retains its drivers before the entry of a new rival.

Examiner's comments

This was the worst attempted requirement on the paper. Candidates seemed to score very well or very poorly. Common mistakes in the calculations included not considering the impact for a 4 week period, confusing the percentage commission with the percentage price reduction and ignoring the constraint of maintaining the driver's income in the second calculation. Many weaker candidates ignored either the calculation element or the discussion element of the requirement completely, limiting the marks available. Better candidates used their calculations as a starting point to discuss whether the strategy was sensible, identifying that the numbers are based on certain limiting assumptions and that wider issues may be relevant.

40 Bespoke Oak Beds plc (December 2015)

Marking guide

	Knowledge	Skill	Marks
40.1 Data analysis	3	12	13
40.2 New strategies	4	15	17
40.3 Future softwood use	2	7	8
40.4 Ethics	3	6	8
	12	40	46

General comments:

This is the mini case and also the main data analysis question.

The scenario is a listed company which manufactures high quality, hand-made hardwood bed-frames.

BOB currently makes two types of oak bed-frames: the Classic and the Deco. BOB has been criticised by environmental groups for using hardwood and the BOB board believes that sustainability issues are beginning to damage the company's reputation.

Although BOB is currently profitable it is in slow decline and is trying to develop a new strategy. Two proposed new strategies are being considered: (i) purchase bedroom furniture from an overseas manufacturer, so full matching bedroom furniture sets can be sold including beds; and (ii) become the preferred contract market supplier of bed-frames to a house building company, selling a new, lower cost product line of softwood beds.

If the second strategy succeeds, then BOB could consider extending it in future to make all its beds from softwood, instead of hardwood (oak).

An ethical dilemma has arisen. A fault has been detected in one production run of Deco oak bed-frames which has already been sold. It will not become apparent to customers for some years. Disclosure of this fault would result in damage to the company's reputation and possible redundancies.

40.1

Analysis	Classic	Deco	Total
Sales revenue	11,250,000	12,960,000	24,210,000
Total variable cost	(6,875,000)	(8,280,000)	(15,155,000)
Total contribution	4,375,000	4,680,000	9,055,000
Fixed costs (equal FC per bed)	(3,348,361)	(4,821,639)	(8,170,000)
Operating profit/(loss)	1,026,639	(141,639)	885,000
Margin % (contribution/sales)	38.9%	36.1%	37.4%
% share of revenue	46.5%	53.5%	100%
% share of contribution	48.3%	5.7%	100%
% share of sales volume	41.0%	59.0%	100%
Operating margin %			3.7%
Fixed cost/Total costs % (operating gearing)			5.0%
Overall company safety margins:			
Safety margin (beds) 885,000/350 and 260	2,529	3,404	
Safety margin (%)	20.2%	18.9%	
Total costs	£10,223,361	£13,101,639	£23,325,000
Total costs per bed	£818	£728	£765
Fixed cost per bed (equal allocation per bed)	£268	£268	£268

(a) **Comparison of two products**

Caution needs to be exercised in comparing the two products, which are largely interdependent in production processes and marketing. In this sense, the performance of one product is dependent on the performance of the other product. Nevertheless, it is important to gather information about how each product is generating revenue and driving costs. The wider strategic contribution of each product would also need to be assessed to make a more complete evaluation.

It is clear from the above data analysis that neither product is significantly dominant over the other in terms of scale of production, revenue generation or costs incurred.

Whilst both products are upmarket, the selling price of the Classic is 25% above that of the Deco, placing it further upmarket in the pricing spectrum. The pricing policy, to a large extent, reflects the higher costs of materials and labour, which are also 25% greater for the Classic than the Deco.

Other variable costs are the same for both products and it is therefore this factor which creates the difference in % margin between the two products. Some care needs to be exercised in that, whilst it is a variable cost, it could be an indirect cost which has been allocated equally and arbitrarily between the two products (eg, electricity that is not metered separately for the manufacture of each product).

Fixed costs have not been allocated between the two products. It is possible that cost drivers could be identified which would show the activities which cause some of these fixed costs. At least some fixed costs could then be attributed to the two products using activity based costing. This would give a clearer indication of the individual financial performance of the two products, although it is unlikely that all fixed costs could be allocated in this way.

A very crude way to allocate fixed costs would be on a per unit basis. The assumption here is that producing each unit (a bed frame) is the best guide to what causes fixed costs. Accepting this proposition as a starting point, the average fixed cost of producing one unit of output is approximately £268 (£8,170,000)/30,500). To this figure is added the identifiable variable cost per unit.

Reviewing this data it can be seen that the Deco sells for £720 which is below the full cost calculated in this (crude) manner of £728. (See table above).

The Classic sells for £900 which is significantly above its full cost calculated in this (crude) manner of £818. (See table.)

A more important measure to evaluate comparative performance is contribution. On a per unit basis, the Classic generates a contribution of £350 per bed compared with £260 for the Deco. The Classic therefore has a 35% greater contribution per unit.

In terms of sales volumes, 18,000 Deco beds are sold in the year, compared to only 12,500 for the Classic. The Deco therefore sold 44% more beds in the year than the Classic.

Putting together the factors of margin and volume it can be seen (see table) that the lower priced, lower margin Deco is forecast to contribute over half (51.7%) of the total contribution earned by BOB in the year ending 31 December 20X5.

Examiner's comments

This requirement was generally well answered. The majority of candidates included an initial table (or an appendix) of data calculations. Weaker candidates tended to be over-descriptive and failed to provide any detailed quantitative analysis.

The quality of the calculations varied; weaker candidates restricted themselves to calculating % splits of revenue and costs. Stronger candidates provided margin calculations and overall volumes, together with respective contributions.

Fixed cost allocation was less well addressed and those who did attempt this, often allocated fixed costs equally between the two products, although sometimes recognising that any method of allocation is essentially arbitrary. Very few suggested better allocation methods, such as identifying relevant cost drivers.

In terms of the qualitative analysis, the weaker candidates, having already performed less adventurous calculations, had little to discuss and therefore simply explained the determinants in the revenues/costs per unit and in total and effectively ended up repeating information already provided in the question, with little or no added value. The stronger candidates looked beyond just the basic numbers and commented on 'other variable costs' being the same for both products (and their impact on Deco's margin in particular), and also on how the apportionment of fixed costs could significantly impact overall profits for either the Classic or the Deco.

(b) **Performance of BOB**

There are no comparison data for previous years to assess performance, but a number of issues can be highlighted.

From the perspective of the company, overall fixed costs become more meaningful as they can be viewed on a company-wide basis, rather than from the perspective of one product which requires arbitrary allocations.

In this respect, operating gearing is high, as indicated by fixed costs comprising 35% of total costs. This makes BOB subject to the risk of operating profit fluctuations as a result of changes in sales volumes.

The impact of high fixed costs and the risk of making losses are also indicated by the relatively small operating profit margin of only 3.7%, despite the relatively healthy contribution margin of 37.4%.

For the company as a whole the analysis in the table above shows the margins of safety for changes in the volume of sales of each product that would make the company, as a whole, break even.

For the Classic (assuming Deco sales remain constant) the margin of safety is 20.2% which is (£885,000//£4,375,000). An alternative calculation is a margin of safety of 2,529 units (£885,000/350). This means sales of Classic beds can fall by 20.2% (2,529/12,500) before the company reaches break-even.

For the Deco (assuming Classic sales remain constant) the margin of safety is 18.9% which is (£885,000//£4,680,000). An alternative calculation is a margin of safety of 3,404 units (£885,000/260). This means sales of Deco beds can fall by 18.9% (3,404/18,000) before the company reaches break-even.

The margin of safety can also be viewed in terms of each product's break-even point.

For the Classic (assuming fixed costs are allocated on a per unit basis) a fall of 2,932 units (£1,026,369/£350) would result in a break-even position. This is a margin of safety of 23.5% (2,932/12,500) before sales of the Classic reach break-even.

As the Deco makes a loss (assuming fixed costs are allocated on a per unit basis) there is no margin of safety.

A more likely scenario to assess risk is that both Deco and Classic bed sales volumes fall. The margin of safety would then depend on the relative proportions, but it is clear that a fall in the sales volume of 10% in both products would create a small loss of £20,500 ((1,250 × £350) + (1,800 × £260) – £885,000).

Risk is moderated to some extent by the relatively even balance between the two products, but nevertheless this is a small portfolio. If one product were to lose favour with customers then the profit from the other product would be insufficient to cover fixed costs.

Examiner's comments

Most candidates calculated overall profit, margin and market share. Only the minority calculated operating gearing and even fewer attempted break-even and margin of safety calculations, for BOB as a whole, or for the individual products.

Most did recognise the very low operating margin for BOB, although fewer explicitly commented on the significance of this.

Some attributed the low margin to strong competition in the industry rather than being more directly caused by high fixed costs. Only a minority of the better candidates said that previous years' data would be useful in this regard in order to see the trend of relative fixed cost magnitude.

40.2 (a)–(b)

(i) **Strategy A – import from WEF**

Volume WEF (beds)	**2,000**

	£
Price	1,300
WEF cost	480
Revenue	2,600,000
Costs:	
WEF	960,000
Lost revenue from 150 beds	108,000
Variable costs extra 1,850 beds	851,000
Contribution	681,000

Alternative calculation 1:

	£
Price	1,300
WEF cost	480
Revenue	2,600,000
Costs:	
WEF	960,000
Lost contribution from 150 beds	39,000
Variable costs extra 2,000 beds	920,000
Contribution	681,000

Alternative calculation 2:

Contribution of WEF:
2,000 sets at £360 (1,300 – 480 – 460) = £720,000

Lost contribution of existing 150 Deco beds
150 @ £260 = £39,000

Incremental = £681,000

Benefits

Strategy A is estimated to make a positive contribution of £681,000 in the year ending 31 December 20X6. In the short term, this would therefore appear to be favourable in generating additional profit and satisfying a trend in consumer demand for sets of bedroom furniture.

The margin on each bedroom furniture set seems reasonable. The sale price of a complete bedroom furniture set (ie, with a bed) is £1,300 and Deco beds normally sell at £720. If the remaining price of £580 is fully attributed to the WEF bedroom furniture set, then at a cost of £480 this gives a mark-up of 20.8%, which is reasonable. In total, the mark-up amounts to £200,000 (£100 × 2,000) and is one element of the contribution of £681,000. The other element of the contribution is the increased sales of Deco beds at £481,000 (1,850 × £260).

As a manufacturer of beds, BOB may not have the core competences to make other types of bedroom furniture itself. The 2,000 sets ordered from WEF may also be too small for BOB to set up a new production facility for other types of bedroom furniture. The proposal to outsource is therefore, in principle, not unreasonable.

It does however raise the question of whether the volume of 2,000 is sufficient to justify a new strategy in attempting to satisfy the consumer demand for bedroom furniture sets, particularly when these sales are expected to displace some sales that would be made in the absence of an agreement with WEF.

Risks

A major risk is loss of reputation, as the WEF furniture is inferior in quality to the BOB furniture. This may not be perceived at first by customers and consumers but, in the longer term, it may mean reduced sales, not only of bedroom furniture sets, but also of beds as the core product may lose customer confidence.

A further risk is that BOB would be tied into a one-year contract with a minimum of 1,900 bedroom furniture sets. This is close to the expected level of sales of 2,000. As a consequence, if sales of bedroom furniture sets fall below expected levels, then there may be an obligation to purchase volumes from WEF which cannot be sold in the current year. This risk could however be mitigated by taking any excess purchases into inventory for sale in 20X7, while terminating the agreement with WEF from 1 January 20X7.

A further risk includes foreign exchange risk if the contract with WEF is not in £ sterling. However, as the contracts are annual, prices can be renegotiated at the year-end if there are significant exchange rate fluctuations.

(i) **Strategy B – contract with LH**

Volume LH (beds)	9,000

	£
Price	600
Revenue	5,400,000
Variable cost – labour	2,025,000
Variable cost – raw materials	1,080,000
Other variable costs	900,000
Classic revenue loss	225,000
Increased overhead	245,100
Contribution	924,900

(ii) **Cost per bed £**

Labour	225
Materials	120
Other variable costs	100
Classic revenue loss	25
Increased overhead	27.23
Total incremental cost per bed	£497.23

Benefits

Strategy B is estimated to make a positive contribution of £924,900 in the year ending 31 December 20X6. In the short term, this would therefore appear to be beneficial and compares favourably with the £681,000 contribution generated by Strategy B.

This strategy uses the existing core competences of bed manufacturing. However, it is operating in a different sector of the market. The Classic bed is normally sold for £900 and in this contract the price is £600 which is a discount of 33.3%, albeit for a product made from an inferior softwood.

The incremental cost per bed at the estimated level of sales is £497.23. The selling price gives a mark-up on cost of £102.77 at the planned level of output. This is a reasonable mark-up on full cost of 20.7%.

Professional scepticism should however be applied to the working assumptions (eg, on price and overhead changes). If the underlying assumptions are not valid then the calculations and conclusions need to be questioned.

As a new customer, LH provides incremental revenues and profit. There is some interdependency with existing markets due to the price reduction, but this has already been taken into account in determining the above amounts.

There may be some benefit in publicity of a sustainability policy in that BOB is now using some softwoods, rather than only hardwoods. In fact, however, it is still using as much hardwood as ever and the softwood usage is incremental production.

Risks

The revenue loss and the increased overhead are fixed costs which will be incurred at any level of sales volume.

To estimate risk, a break-even value can be calculated:

Contribution per unit	=	600 − (225 + 120 + 100)	=	£155
Break-even	=	(225,000 + 245,100)/155	=	3,033 beds

There is therefore a healthy margin of safety, as sales to LH would need to fall to 33.7% of the estimated level before a loss would be incurred on the contract.

Other risks are:

- LH's policy of selling new-build houses, fully furnished may be temporary and may be withdrawn at any time as there is no minimum sales guarantee. Strategy A may therefore be longer term as it uses existing markets.

- Strategy B relies on one customer, but Strategy A is more diversified with many customers.

- The policy is for two years and therefore the commitment is longer term than Strategy A if the arrangement is not successful.

- The fact that there is no minimum quantity means that there is no effective commitment from LH who might change its mind at any time, with BOB's overheads already incurred.

- Conversely, there is no maximum, so if demand from LH is high, BOB may reach capacity and may only be able to meet contractual commitments to LH by reducing production for existing customers, thereby incurring an opportunity cost in the short term and a loss of reputation to deliver reliably in the long term.

- Even if capacity is not reached, there is a need to gear up production for a 72% increase in Classic-style beds (perhaps with incremental fixed costs) which may then not come about.

- The fact that demand from LH is uneven, and the lead time is only one month, makes the capacity problem worse.

Conclusion

The short-term financial gain is greater for Strategy B than Strategy A. However such a gain comes with greater risks. The decision would depend on how reliable the estimates are perceived to be and the extent to which additional contractual protection could be put in place (eg, a minimum and a maximum level of sales).

As it stands, the risk issue with Strategy B is significant, which on balance suggests Strategy A should be selected, despite the lower financial return.

Examiner's comments

In general, this requirement was not well answered. Only a small minority managed to calculate both contributions correctly. Most candidates calculated neither correctly. The most common error with Strategy B was to ignore the revenue loss and increased overhead, thereby arriving at a total contribution of £1,395,000. For Strategy A, most candidates omitted the lost contribution from the existing Deco sales so only calculated the contribution on the new sales, £720,000.

In general, candidates coped well with identifying the risks and benefits of each strategy, and the majority also provided a justified conclusion. Only the stronger candidates commented on break-even.

Weaker candidates produced a generalised commentary, sometimes mixing A and B up in one discussion.

40.3 Merits and problems

The shift to using entirely softwoods would be a fundamental change for BOB.

In favour of such a change would be significantly lower raw material costs (40% lower based on Strategy B) and lower labour costs (10% lower based on Strategy B).

These cost changes would however fundamentally change the nature of the product and move it downmarket significantly. It would therefore be in a lower market segment with a lower price.

Given that BOB's reputation has been built around an upmarket product and the established customer base has required good quality hardwood furniture, a sudden movement downmarket would require the establishment of a new customer and consumer base. This seems to be a substantial and unnecessary risk.

Either of the proposed two strategies would be regarded as incremental to existing production and therefore lower risk. Even if either of the two strategies themselves went wrong, the existing customer base would remain largely as it is.

One favourable aspect of the proposal to change from hardwood to Canadian softwoods for the entire production is that it could be justified as a better policy for environmental sustainability. However the production would still require wood, so the environmental damage may be reduced, but not removed.

In terms of environmental protection it could also be argued that any future environmental damage would be in a developed nation (Canada) rather than in the developing nations of Central America, as is currently the case. This may mean the social consequences of deforestation could be less severe.

Overall, a change to use only softwoods would be a major change in the entire business model with significant risks for all stakeholders. A slightly more favourable sustainability programme would seem inappropriate compensation for this major commercial risk. Other efforts to improve sustainability could be used (eg, a more intensive replanting programme; aid to local communities in areas affected; and working with agencies promoting sustainability in the affected areas).

Examiner's comments

In general, this requirement was reasonably well answered. Very few candidates failed to spot the sustainability advantages of shifting to softwood, however most focused on the fact it would reduce pressure from environmental groups and failed to consider the business sustainability aspect. Many candidates picked up on the point that softwood is more sustainable than hardwood as regrowth time was quicker.

Many candidates failed to observe the key point that this was a major change in the strategy of BOB, being a move from being a luxury product differentiator in the market, to lowering prices with a lower quality product. The majority of candidates discussed the key points regarding the potential financial impact of the change and how it could affect operations.

40.4 Ethical issues

Ethics pertains to whether a particular behaviour is deemed acceptable in the context under consideration. In short, it is 'doing the right thing'.

In making any ethical evaluation it is first necessary to establish the facts. In this case, it would seem that the facts are reasonably clear in terms of what has happened, although the extent and consequences of the faulty production run need to be clear, with reasonable certainty, before any action is taken.

The issue of legality and compliance needs to be considered and legal advice taken by BOB. If the goods are faulty, it needs to be established whether there is any breach of contract or other statutory consumer rights arising from the nature of the fault (eg, could the fault be a breach of health and safety laws?).

The fact that the warranty is three years and the fault is expected to arise only after four years implies the issue is one of commerciality and ethics, rather than legality, but this needs to be ascertained by taking legal advice.

In making a decision as to how to proceed, it is helpful to apply the Institute of Business Ethics three tests:

- Transparency
- Effect
- Fairness

Transparency – this would suggest that the issue should be disclosed (ie, made transparent). BOB needs to bear in mind how people (existing customers, suppliers, employees) would react if they found out subsequently that BOB was aware of the fault but had not disclosed it.

Effect – whom does the decision to disclose or not disclose affect or hurt? Clearly the consumers who purchased the goods would be unfavourably affected by non-disclosure, as they would not have the items replaced (as would presumably be the case if the fault were to be disclosed, notwithstanding that the expected useful life is in excess of the guarantee period). The employee stakeholder group could be adversely affected by disclosure if it resulted in redundancies. However, if there was non-disclosure, that was later made public, the employees may also be adversely affected.

Fairness – would non-disclosure be considered fair by those affected? One argument could be that the goods' useful life will still exceed the guarantee period and therefore BOB has fulfilled its obligations on sale. However, the guarantee sets a minimum and there might be a reasonable expectation that the beds would last far longer in most circumstances. As a result, knowingly not disclosing a fault may be viewed as unfair on consumers and a breach of implicit business trust. The issue of fairness would apply to the employee stakeholder group who may lose their jobs, through no fault of their own, if disclosure were to be made.

Honesty and integrity

Further issues are those of honesty and integrity, which involve not just avoiding deception (eg, lying), but also making reasonable disclosures of known facts that have consequences.

Actions

There may be commercial incentives and disincentives in making reasonable disclosure, but these are separate from ethical considerations.

The marketing director appears to be suggesting that the commercial disincentives are major and should override the need to act ethically towards consumers in this case. However, the need to act ethically and to 'do the right thing' should not be moderated by commercial consequences or by the interests of other stakeholders such as employees.

Moreover, acting ethically in dealing with the fault may establish an ethical reputation to compensate for any loss in commercial reputation from allowing the fault to occur in the first instance, if the company were able to survive and keep the factory open.

An initial action for BOB would be to use its information systems to attempt to trace the customers (furniture retailers and department stores) to which the faulty goods were sold by using the serial numbers. This is an issue where the individual products are identifiable.

If they have been sold to relatively few stores, then disclosure should be made to these stores. It may be that they are still in inventory in these stores, with no consumers affected. A key issue however is whether the faulty goods which have been sold by the retailers can be traced by the retailers to the individual consumers who purchased them (eg, did they retain records of the serial numbers?).

If they can be traced, then consumers affected can be compensated by BOB with new furniture. There seems no ethical requirement to inform any customers or consumers who were not affected (ie, who did not receive any faulty goods) as no direct consequences arise for these customers.

If the goods cannot be traced to individual consumers by retailers, then wider disclosure may be required via a general 'product recall' notice, so potentially affected consumers can come forward and identify themselves.

Examiner's comments

This requirement was reasonably well answered, on the whole.

A large majority of candidates adopted the 'transparency, effect, fairness' structure for analysing the ethical issues. However, the actual application of this structure varied in terms of success, with weaker candidates not completely sure of the correct interpretation of the principles in the context of the scenario.

Honesty and integrity were mentioned by relatively few candidates, which is surprising given that ethics questions involving these principles have been tested with regularity.

Many of those who considered the legality issue asserted conclusively that selling the faulty beds either was, or was not, illegal, without any analysis and without considering the need to take legal advice.

Actions to be taken by management were ignored by a number of candidates, or just considered briefly. Very few mentioned traceability, via the firm's information systems, of customers who had purchased the faulty beds.

Only the best answers gave due consideration to the dilemma facing BOB with regard to commercial versus ethical considerations, including its responsibility to its employees as well as to its customers.

Most candidates simply suggested a 'product recall' without thinking practically about this, eg, the feasibility of tracking down the specific customers/retailers. Alarmingly, some candidates suggested that due to the possible commercial impact of the fault becoming public knowledge, the company should not make any disclosure.

41 Drummond & Drew LLP (December 2015)

Marking guide

	Knowledge	Skill	Marks
41.1 Organisational structure	3	8	10
41.2 Expand internationally	3	10	12
41.3 Acquisition v direct investment	2	7	8
	8	25	30

General comments:

The scenario relates to a large firm of commercial architects (DD), currently based in a single office in London. DD has grown gradually over many years, but recently growth has slowed.

DD has a management structure of: partners, other qualified architects, support staff and administrative staff.

Whilst historically most of DD's projects have been in the UK, over the past five years there has been an increasing number of overseas projects, particularly in Dubai and the other Gulf States, which have been serviced from the London office.

A potential large new project in Dubai (the Sunrise) has arisen but, to be eligible to bid, DD must make a commitment to establish an office in the region. This can be achieved either by acquiring an existing architect firm in Dubai or by setting up a new DD office there.

41.1 DD is a professional service provider, based on expert knowledge. There is a need for their formal and informal structures to be appropriate to the communication and control needs of the business. The structure also needs to be appropriate to external client needs as a large amount of time is spent at construction sites.

One way of analysing DD's structure is with reference to Mintzberg's organisational configurations.

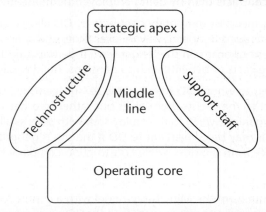

Mintzberg suggests that each component of the organisation has its own dynamic. The precise shape (configuration) of the organisation will be determined by the degree of influence each exerts.

The 12 partners who form the senior management team of the DD partnership are the strategic apex. As the owners of the business, they currently control all strategy and operations by taking all the key decisions.

The key component (or building block) within DD appears to be the operating core, with architects working directly on providing services to clients which are directly fee earning.

The managers comprise the middle line and may seek to increase control over the operating core of architects, even if they do not control the detail of their work.

Other support staff only gain influence when their expertise is vital but this may include IT where it is central to assignments (eg, graphics or management information).

The technostructure consists of the small technical and regulatory team whose reason for existence is the design of procedures and standards. The team seeks an environment that is standardised as it is highly regulated.

DD's existing structure might be seen as Mintzberg's professional bureaucracy configuration, suitable for the standardisation of skills.

Key features of DD's structure are as follows:

- The key building block is the operating core of architects who are fee earning.

- The environment is a complex static which has many elements but is not rapidly changing.

- The internal factors are professional with simple systems arising from working from one geographic location with commissions driving reporting systems.

- Skills are largely standardised professional skills but with some specialisations in complex assignments.

An alternative model might be Handy's shamrock organisation.

Handy defines the shamrock organisation as a 'core of essential executives and workers supported by outside contractors and part-time help'. This structure permits the buying-in of services as needed, with consequent reductions in overhead costs. It is also known as the flexible firm.

Handy has four elements to the shamrock:

The professional core comprises permanently employed staff who provide the core competencies and distinctive knowledge base of the organisation. For DD this would comprise the partners and architects but also some other employees (IT, administration etc)

The flexible labour force are temporary short-term contract architects who can be deployed when required by peaks in demand (eg, from variations in the number and size of commissions in progress).

The contractual fringe are external providers (specialist architects) who can undertake specialist services on complex commissions but are not required frequently and thus can be engaged more economically on short-term contracts than by being employed permanently.

The use of specialist and non-specialist temporary contracts by DD allows short-term flexibility as the number and size of commissions in operation vary over time, and specialist skills are acquired on an occasional basis as the need arises. In the longer term it permits rapid downsizing in times of recession and can save on the costs of benefits such as pensions, holiday pay and health insurance.

Customers are a fourth cluster, to whom DD may be able to 'sub-contract' some tasks. In the case of DD this is less likely to refer to the clients themselves but rather to other contractors used by clients (eg, construction companies) which may employ staff with skills similar to those of DD staff (eg, chartered surveyors). This may be convenient to DD if the site is geographically remote (eg, in parts of the UK a long distance from London) while construction company staff are on site.

Recommendation

The model of an operating core from the Mintzberg model with a contractual fringe and flexible labour force from the Handy model appears to work well for DD given its current professional bureaucracy configuration around a single head office. The ability of this structure to cope with more complex changes of multiple locations, overseas operations and a wider range of commission types would be questionable.

Examiner's comments

Candidates who used recognised frameworks or models tended to score better than candidates who referred to general types of organisational structure. Those who recognised the direct relevance of Mintzberg's structure and provided supporting contextualised discussion provided the best answers. The best candidates complemented the discussion of Mintzberg with reference to Handy's shamrock organisational structure.

Poorer answers talked vaguely about tall or flat structures or referred, in general terms, to divisionalised, matrix and functional structures. Also, weaker candidates tended to be too generic rather than applying discussion to the particular circumstances of a professional services organisation, as required by the scenario.

41.2 DD already has some revenue from international clients but as this activity expands, the capability of continuing to service clients from the UK for the construction phase of commissions becomes less plausible.

Whilst planning and design could largely be carried out from the UK, the inability to service the construction phase of the Sunrise contract is likely to mean that DD would not be used for design and planning as a single architect firm would normally be used for all phases.

The costs of setting up and maintaining a local presence in the Gulf States needs to be measured against: (1) the cost of servicing clients from the UK and (2) the ability and capacity to generate additional contribution from servicing more clients if there were to be a physical presence in the region.

The expansion being considered by DD can be evaluated using alternative strategic models.

The Ansoff model is a two-by-two matrix of Products (new and existing) and Markets (new and existing).

DD is attempting to enter a new geographical market with its existing professional service of commercial architecture. According to the Ansoff model this is market development. Having a recognised core competence in commercial architecture services, DD has used this in the UK to build its business but, due to competition, it is struggling to expand further. Overseas markets, in particular the Gulf States for DD, offer new opportunities for expansion.

It could be argued that the move into architectural services for domestic housing is a new type of service to be provided in a new market. According to the Ansoff model this is a strategy of diversification. The new service is strongly related to the existing service so it may also be termed related diversification.

Diversification involves developing new products for new markets. It involves the greatest risk of all Ansoff's strategies. In terms of providing the service it can require new skills, new techniques and different ways of operating. In terms of marketing the service it may also require adaptation to a new business-to-consumer model in addition to the existing business-to-business model.

Lynch's expansion method matrix is another two-by-two matrix matching company growth (organic growth and external development) with geographical location (home country and international).

Under this model, all of DD's traditional growth appears to have been carried out organically and services/markets have been developed largely domestically. Over the past five years there has been some international growth, mainly in the Gulf States, which has been serviced from the London office and so has been organic.

Porter's Diamond relates to developing a strategy in a global environment and the need to understand the competitive advantages DD may enjoy as result of physically locating in the Gulf States.

The factors include: firm strategy, structure and rivalry (eg, local cultural factors with respect to the architecture industry, local capital markets, rivalry from local architect firms already established in the Gulf States); factor conditions (eg, local skills available and other human resource factors; local technical knowledge and education; land for building; infrastructure); demand conditions (local demand for building projects in commercial and private building sectors); and related and support industries (eg, a well-developed local construction industry).

The more these factors in Porter's Diamond point towards favourable local conditions for architect firms, the greater the benefits from DD making a local investment and commitment to the region rather than servicing it from the London office.

Ohmae's 'five Cs' framework (The Borderless World) identified a number of reasons which might encourage a firm to act globally. This model identifies factors that may influence DD's decision of whether to establish an office in Dubai.

Ohmae's factors which may influence DD's decision include: the customer (whether the architect service requirements of Gulf States are similar to those of the UK where DD has core competences); the company (a greater volume of sales spreads existing fixed costs, although DD may incur additional fixed costs by local investment); competition (strength and response of local competition); currency volatility (currency of costs to match revenues with local investment); country (access to local resources through setting up a local office, such as HR).

Aside from these models, a key decision is needed as to whether to service client needs from London or to establish an office in Dubai (whether by setting up from scratch or by acquisition).

Key factors include the following:

A new office is likely to involve more fixed costs than servicing from London. This will increase the operating gearing of the Gulf State operations. As a result, if the Dubai office is successful then there may be advantages of lower variable costs of servicing clients (eg, reduced travel time and travel costs for architects). This may depend on whether, under existing arrangements, travel costs can be charged on to the clients without affecting competitiveness.

Under existing arrangements, 10 full time staff were used on Gulf State assignments. The data provided shows that this could increase to 27 in 20X7, then to 39 in 20X8, before falling to 26 in 20X8 and beyond as the Sunrise contract ends. This is quite a significant increase in staff and presumably there are revenues anticipated which, on the face of it, would justify investing in a physical presence in the region.

The presence in the region compared to the scale of staff at the London office would also indicate that it is substantial. If the staff are proportional to fees then this would imply a significant increase in revenue and indicates that the operation would be of a viable scale if forecasts are achieved. If however the venture fails then there may be significant exit costs of terminating the commitment (eg, redundancy, selling the office or terminating the lease).

Operating gearing risks and exit cost risks can be mitigated by keeping the real option and deferring the decision to invest in Dubai until it is known whether or not the Sunrise commission has been won assuming a commitment to future investment is acceptable under the tendering terms of the contract. This will give work for 12 staff in 20X7 along with 10 other staff on commercial work, which is only the equivalent to that already being serviced from London, so looks to be an achievable objective. Any additional staff need then only be taken on as and when new commissions are achieved.

The fall in the number of staff after the completion of the Sunrise contract could be accommodated either by sending London staff to Dubai on a two year secondment or by hiring short term contract staff, or a combination of both.

A further advantage of investing in a physical presence in Dubai would be the ability to hire local architects with local knowledge of regulations, culture and conditions.

Having an office in Dubai to house staff may also release space in the London office which may be useful if there are space constraints there.

A final factor may be foreign exchange risk. It could be viewed that the foreign investment may lead to greater foreign exchange risk but it may also be a form of natural hedging to reduce risk by incurring costs in local currencies to match against revenues earned from those countries.

Examiner's comments

Those candidates who applied a model such as Ansoff, Lynch, Porter's Diamond or Ohmae, often scored higher because their answer had structure and direction. The use of such models also widened the scope of the answers, ensuring key areas were specifically addressed. However, only a minority used such models, with the majority relying on a 'common sense' approach.

While the use of models was not specifically mentioned in the requirement, models are a core part of the syllabus and form part of the 'toolkit' for strategic analysis. Selection of appropriate models, where relevant, should therefore be considered by candidates to structure answers and to solve strategic problems in a variety of situations, and not only where directed to do so by the requirement. Candidates should not feel confined to using only one model in such circumstances.

A minority made use of Porter's Five Forces, and some credit was given for this where the analysis was appropriate.

Answers too often failed to deal with the specific issues that would be faced by DD and instead discussed very general overseas expansion issues/considerations that could apply to any company, in any industry.

The relevance of the key Sunrise development was, rather surprisingly, only referred to by a small minority.

Relatively few candidates made any reference to the data provided in the question. As a general rule, if there are numbers in the question, then there should be numbers in the answer.

41.3 According to the Lynch model, a business can expand organically (internal development) or via external development.

External development can include an acquisition or it can include working with another partner (eg, joint venture or other form of alliance). DD only appears to be considering either an acquisition or internal development.

There are a number of factors that would favour an acquisition of a local architect's practice in Dubai:

- Existing knowledge of the local environment, culture, regulations and markets providing useful initial expertise. It may be that DD has some expertise in these areas from its previous work in Dubai, but local knowledge is likely to be an additional benefit

- An instant skill base in terms of resources and employees is likely to mean faster growth.

- It provides experience of existing supply chain and networks.

- A locally known established brand and reputation with an existing customer base – this maybe viewed more favourably by local businesses and government than a foreign-owned brand.

- An acquisition buys out a potential competitor and better enables DD to compete with the other domestic companies.

- There are likely to be synergies as local staff can provide local knowledge but conversely DD can introduce innovations from its UK experience.

- Gets round any barriers to entry in terms of resistance from local architects, construction firms and government.

Direct investment by setting up a new office from scratch offers the following merits:

- It may be difficult to find a suitable partner in terms of size or market positioning in the time scale available, allowing time for negotiation and completion.

- There may be a conflict between strategies and cultures of DD and an acquired local firm which may hinder integration.

- If an acquisition is made in Dubai, the local knowledge acquired may be limited to Dubai and not stretch across all the Gulf States.

- Direct investment will allow DD to be free to pursue its own strategy.

- The price DD is required to pay for a local firm is likely to include a goodwill premium, the cost of which may outweigh the possible benefits noted above. Organic growth by setting up an office from scratch avoids paying for goodwill, therefore DD can acquire a larger tangible asset base for the same cost as an acquisition.

- Direct investment may offer a chance for more gradual expansion and an opportunity to test the market and learn. It also enables a choice of clients rather than inheriting a client list, some of which may be unsuitable for the skills base offered by DD.

- Avoids any hidden or unforeseen losses that do not come out as part of due diligence eg, litigation based on historic work by the acquired firm that has been negligently performed.

- There may be damage to, or dilution of, DD's good local reputation if a local firm is acquired with an inferior reputation or brand name.

The core competencies that have allowed DD to prosper in the UK may not be fully realised in an overseas country. The above arguments regarding the ability of DD to replicate in Dubai what it has achieved in the UK may be summarised within Kay's framework on sources of core competencies:

Architecture

Internal architecture – is the relationship with employees. These are likely to be entirely or largely new employees, where a new relationship needs to be established.

External architecture – this includes relationships with external stakeholders such as suppliers, contractors and clients.

Network architecture – collaboration between businesses and local networks needs to be established from scratch.

Reputation

It is likely that DD will need to establish a new reputation locally. This may prevent it from initially charging a price premium as in the UK.

Innovative ability

Innovation in design is likely to be able to be 'transported' from the UK to the overseas markets but it is an industry where tastes vary across countries and thus is unlikely to give the same competitive advantage.

Conclusion

Much will depend on the price of any acquisition but, given DD already has some experience and reputation in the region and an international reputation, there may be some merit in DD setting up its own office. If further local knowledge is required, an acquisition could take place later. Alternatively, some other form of strategic alliance could take place with a local firm.

Examiner's comments

Most candidates considered both direct investment and acquisition of an existing firm, and most also recognised the significance of existing knowledge and competencies.

Candidates approached this requirement in different ways. Some tried to compare the differences between organic growth and growth by acquisition, whereas others approached it by thinking about the key aspects of expansion and which method best suited DD in that respect.

Only a significant minority gave due emphasis to the importance of timing in the decision. The remainder may not have done so because they had not considered the Sunrise development in requirement 41.1. Most did nevertheless make the point that organic development will take longer than acquisition, but without much elaboration.

The candidates who scored highest related their answer to the scenario and to DD. Weaker candidates simply listed the advantages and disadvantages of each approach, without attempting to draw emphasis to which issues were more important, or to provide an overall conclusion to provide coherence to the list of points made.

42 Mississippi Muzic Ltd (December 2015)

Marking guide

	Knowledge	Skill	Marks
42.1 Database CRM	3	6	8
42.2 Market research	2	7	8
42.3 Segmentation & pricing	2	7	8
	7	20	24

General comments:

The scenario in this question was a company, MM, which operates four London nightclubs, each with a restaurant. The clubs are upmarket, the entrance charge for each visit is high, and drinks and meals are expensive. The target market is young, high-income professionals. MM has attracted a loyal core of members and the clubs are, on average, 95% full on Friday and Saturday nights.

The new CEO believes that the company is not making best use of its database of members' details for marketing.

MM now wishes to increase revenue by marketing its clubs more effectively and has identified two possible strategies:

Strategy 1 – to encourage existing members to visit the clubs more frequently, and to dine in the restaurants more often, by using its database more effectively for relationship marketing purposes.

Strategy 2 – to appeal to new types of customer, other than young professionals, in order to fill its spare capacity from Sunday to Thursday.

42.1 To: Jane Flinkstein
     From: Business Adviser
     Date: 9 December 20X5
     Subject: Marketing strategy - Mississippi Muzic Ltd

The use of the database to market to existing customers should be part of a strategy of customer relationship marketing.

This is the marketing process that seeks to attract, maintain and enhance customer relationships by focusing on the whole satisfaction experienced by the customer when dealing with the firm. Building up customer relationships requires a change of focus from the 'transaction-based approach' to a relationship approach.

The concept of a club membership and the holding of a database on members' attributes and purchase habits can facilitate retaining customers over a long period by providing them with good customer service which is appropriate to their particular needs and enables two-way communication.

The database can therefore be regarded as a Customer Relationship Management system (CRM). CRM describes the methodologies, software, and usually Internet capabilities that help an enterprise manage customer relationships.

CRM can consist of the following:

- Helping MM to identify and target their best customers, manage marketing campaigns with clear goals and objectives, and generate quality leads.

- Assisting MM to improve sales management by optimising information shared, and streamlining existing processes (for example, taking reservations of table bookings and orders using mobile devices).

- Allowing the formation of relationships with customers, with the aim of improving customer satisfaction and maximising profits; identifying the most profitable customers (eg, large groups) and providing them with the highest level of service.

- Providing employees with the information and processes necessary to know the main customer groups, understand their needs, and effectively build relationships between the company and its membership base.

The information held can be used to market the clubs' activities to individual customers in a targeted manner that will suit their individual circumstances. However, it is unlikely to be cost effective to have individual marketing for each customer's attributes. Some grouping of the data may therefore be appropriate as a form of market segmentation to enable specific marketing on a group basis.

Examples might be:

- People who have not visited for a while. These could be targeted to come back with some inducement (eg, free entry).

- Groups who visit regularly, but who have not used the restaurant (perhaps provide a restaurant voucher).

The existing information could be used to gain better communication through social media (eg, Facebook and Twitter), as a means of achieving competitive advantage. Again some inducement could be offered for initial join-up.

Social media could be particularly effective at creating a community of MM club members. When followers become part of the MM club community, it gains instant access to them. That means MM can find out what challenges they are facing and what they like and don't like about MM's offerings. MM staff can engage in ongoing dialogue that can be more valuable than any kind of paid market research.

Social media also provides MM with the opportunity to remind followers over and over again about what it has to offer, which can shorten the sales cycle dramatically.

Patterns of attendance could be established. If someone visits occasionally, but always on a Saturday when they do visit, then particular events and features on a Saturday could be marketed to that group.

In order to widen the customer base, members visiting regularly could be given incentives to bring a friend to join.

Aside from the specific attributes, more general attributes could be used to analyse and use the database, as part of a strategy of segmentation. One example would by age, whereby as members get older, then individual nights could be themed to their age group (eg, over 30s) or profession (eg, accountant only nights).

Improved data collection, storage and analysis tools may indicate previously unknown opportunities for sales. Such tools may include data-mining software which allows relationships to be discovered between previously unrelated data.

Examiner's comments

Most candidates considered both the database and marketing issues in the context of customer relationship management, a significant minority referring to the latter explicitly.

Many made use of the four 'Ps' of marketing, although only the better ones who did this used the model to focus on particular customer segments.

The majority of candidates did not use a report format for their answer despite being asked to produce a report.

42.2 Market research is the systematic gathering, recording and analysing of information relating to the marketing of goods and services.

Market research can help in identifying the potential size of specific markets and provides information about customer characteristics, needs and wants, attitude to price and quality, and competitors' products. Market research may also help in defining appropriate elements of the marketing mix (product, price, place, promotion).

There are various forms that market research can take.

Desk research

This is the gathering and analysis of existing or secondary data. This is likely to be of background significance in establishing the characteristics of the potential market identified, but is nevertheless important.

In the case of Strategy 2, much of the relevant desk research may already have been collected in relation to the initial establishment of the nightclubs. However, new relevant data might include both general economic intelligence and market intelligence.

General economic intelligence would include data about the general economy as it applies to the target markets. This might include:

- general macroeconomic data on growth, inflation, unemployment etc (as leisure is a luxury good of choice it may suffer disproportionately in a recession)

- spending habits in the UK (family expenditure survey)

- demographic trends (census): this may be of particular importance in the context of the narrow age profile that might normally attend nightclubs.

Market intelligence may include:

- industry information on the nightclub/restaurant industry (eg, prices, new trends, new music tastes, customer volume changes, advertising, trade journals, magazine articles)

- information on the demand for entertainment/leisure activities (national surveys, published local surveys, industry intelligence).

Field research

Field research involves the collection of new, primary information. It is usually more costly than desk research, but it is likely to be more relevant to the circumstances of MM.

A key advantage is that the nightclubs already exist and can thus be used as the basis for some forms of field research, as although most people are young professionals, the database would identify those members attending midweek and their attributes. The database could therefore be a key part of the field research for Strategy 2, as well as helping to develop Strategy 1.

The key answers to establish are:

- what sections of the population attend, or could be induced into attending, nightclubs on Sunday to Thursday

- how much these people would be willing to pay for entrance and for food/drink

- how frequently they would attend

- whether preferences would be concentrated for any particular night in any age group, gender, or income grouping

- whether the clubs are associated with any particular image (which may indicate the type of advertising and target market that might be appropriate)

- whether there is a demand for an alternative use midweek (eg, just as a restaurant).

Trial testing

For Strategy 2, this could involve testing the service provided by the clubs on a sample of the public. This may take the form of random sampling to extrapolate the results into the general population. This could involve free tickets for midweek nights in return for feedback on the experience. Alternatively, quota sampling may be used where the clubs are tested on a sample with predetermined characteristics (eg, age or gender), again with feedback. Some detail of the respondents will be needed if information is required on the differential response of different market segment groupings.

Experimentation

Experimentation may have some similar characteristics to trial testing, but is likely to be more controlled to isolate different factors such as slight changes in the product composition and presentation. For Strategy 2 this might involve changing the format or prices on a certain night during the week to test the appeal to target markets.

Test marketing

Test marketing involves a restricted launch of a new product in a small segment of the total market eg, a geographical region. Ideally, the test should be small, self-contained, representative and adequately promoted. The test may be based upon the results of the above types of market research.

For Strategy 2, this might involve making changes in one of the four London clubs with respect to the types of music, food or prices on particular midweek nights. It may even involve more permanent changes in the environment to develop appeal outside the core market.

Examiner's comments

Most candidates discussed desk and field research and displayed understanding of the differences between the two approaches and the uses to which each could be put. Only a small minority took this further, and considered possibilities for test marketing, trial testing and experimentation.

Stronger candidates were able to suggest specific questions that MM would be seeking to answer, whereas a weaker answer provided only generic desk/field research commentary.

42.3 Segmentation strategy

Segmentation is 'the division of the market into homogeneous groups of potential customers who may be treated similarly for market purposes'.

Strategy 2

The segmentation strategy for the existing core market is both demographic and socio-economic eg, young professionals.

It may however be appropriate to adopt a different segmentation strategy on mid-week days. The nature of the service offered could then be tailored to the new market.

Examples might include the following:

- **Students** – this is a similar demographic segmentation to the core group, but a different socio-economic segmentation, as they would be a low income group. Students may not have such long working hours and be more willing to socialise, at a lower price, during weekdays.

- **'Middle-aged' people** – a different demographic segmentation might be over 30s/40s/50s nights. More established in their careers, they might be of similar high socio-economic groups to the core market, but have different tastes in music and environment.

- **Retired** – an older age range still would be a further demographic segmentation, and might have more time flexibility, but different social and leisure needs.

- **Unemployed** – significant spare time mid-week. Could also be split demographically.

While the segments may be split on a 'day of the week' basis, there may be a danger of altering the general culture of the nightclub, making it less appealing to the core market. The physical attributes of the nightclubs (eg, décor) may also not lend themselves to different types of entertainment.

As well as splitting on a day of the week basis, segmentation could be by different types of membership. This could vary the membership fee but also facilitate subsequent targeted communication and keep the core group as a separate and distinctive membership.

Pricing

Strategy 2

The core market has a premium pricing strategy, but a nightclub can distinguish its markets on the basis of time – with each night of the week being a separate market. As such, it enables a policy of price discrimination between the different markets by charging different prices on different nights, and would thus be linked to the above segmentation strategy.

Nevertheless, this is only an advantage if there is a different price elasticity of demand in each of the markets. Given the widely different socio-economic groups being targeted, this seems very likely. Thus, while demand may be inelastic for the core market, it may be very elastic for other low income markets such as students and the unemployed. This would suggest a much lower price on these nights.

A key factor in assessing price is the price being changed by the closest competitors, which should be determined in a competitor analysis.

This should include the prices being charged for drinks and in the restaurant as well as the entrance fee. Indeed, one pricing strategy would be to have free entrance (or a minimal cost) on some nights in order to generate revenue from drink and food. This may be possible given the low marginal cost of attracting additional customers.

Examiner's comments

In general, the segmentation element of the question was dealt with much better than the pricing aspects. Poorer efforts at pricing used the four 'Cs' model with little application to the scenario, often simply 'knowledge dumping' by quoting all the pricing strategies that candidates knew. Weaker candidates also did not link their explanation of pricing strategy to their earlier discussion on segmentation.

The best responses covered market segmentation and pricing well, and explained the relationship between these, giving some emphasis to price discrimination between segments and between days of the week.

Some also made the point that it may be difficult for the club to offer a different experience on different days of the week, as it may be too focused in terms of décor and general offering on higher-end customers. Some also referred to problems of leakage between segments, thereby making price discrimination more difficult.

43 Outil plc (March 2016)

Marking guide

	Knowledge	Skill	Marks
43.1 Performance analysis	3	16	17
43.2 Discussion of proposals	2	9	10
43.3 Stakeholder analysis	3	6	8
43.4 Evaluation of test marketing and opening stores	3	6	8
	11	37	43

General comments:

This is the mini case at 43 marks, and also the main data analysis question. It was well attempted.

The scenario is about Outil plc, a large listed home improvement retailer that operates with three divisions. The Homestyle division sells DIY-related products to homeowners and tradespeople in the UK through large stores. The Fixings division sells a wide range of tools and other items, mainly to UK tradespeople, via a catalogue, website and small stores. It has grown rapidly, opening 50 new stores last year. Further development of Outil's business saw the acquisition, in 20X5, of an Eastern European trade chain, the new Targi division. This provides equipment and materials for professional building companies and tradespeople in Eastern Europe.

Outil's board has been concerned for some time about the deterioration in performance of the Homestyle division, which is a mature business (candidates were provided with extracts from the management accounts). The Homestyle director believes performance will improve in line with the housing market, especially as a competitor has gone under. However the MD believes Outil should refocus as a retail group, servicing tradespeople only. Smaller Homestyle division stores would be re-branded as Targi or Fixings outlets. The larger stores would need to be closed, but employees, where possible, would be transferred to other divisions. An alternative strategy proposed by the Fixings division director is to sell the Homestyle division to raise funds for expansion. Testing the market by opening four trial Fixings stores in Germany, with a dedicated German website, is suggested.

43.1 Report on performance

To: Outil Board
From: Business Advisor
Date: XX/XX/XX
Re: Future strategic direction

Calculations are shown in the appendix:

	Outil total 20X5	UK total 20X5	Outil total 20X4
Gross margin	34.0%	34.7%	35.9%
Contribution as % revenue	6.9%	6.5%	9.0%
Operating margin	6.1%	5.8%	8.2%
ROCE	22.4%	21.7%	30.9%

% change in

	20X4 to 20X5 Outil total	20X4 to 20X5 UK total
Revenue	+24.9%	+5.7%
Gross profit	+18.1%	+2.1%
Traceable costs	+26.0%	+10.7%
Divisional contribution	–5.1%	–23.7%
Apportioned central costs	+14.3%	–2.9%
Operating profit	–7.0%	–25.7%
Net assets	+28.4%	+5.4%

Divisional performance year to 31 December 20X5

	Homestyle	Fixing	Targi
Gross margin	29.3%	42.0%	30.1%
Divisional contributional as % revenue	5.7%	7.6%	8.7%
Operation profit margin	5.0%	6.9%	8.0%
ROCE	18.0%	27.3%	25.2%
Share of total sales	49%	36%	15%
Divisional contribution mix	41%	40%	19%
Share of net assets	49%	33%	18%
Revenue per store (£m)	10.46	4.95	7.26
Profit per store (£'000)	520	342	583
Ave store size (sq m)	10,000	3,500	5,600
Revenue per sq m	£1,046	£1,414	£1,296
Profit per sq m	£51.98	£97.65	£104.04
Employees/store	58	18	30
Sq metres covered per employee	172	194	187
Revenue per employee (£'000)	181	272	243

Commentary on overall company performance

Despite a 24.9% increase in sales revenue, Outil's total operating profit has fallen 7% and ROCE has dropped from 30.9% to 22.4%. Both gross and operating profit margins have fallen by approximately 2 percentage points.

However it is hard to properly compare the performance of the business between 20X4 and 20X5 due to substantial changes during the year, notably the acquisition of the Targi stores and the expansion of the Fixings division.

Targi needs to be excluded from the 20X5 results so that a more relevant comparison can be made of the combined results of the Homestyle and Fixings divisions. Once this is done it becomes apparent that whilst revenue has increased 5.7%, operating profit has fallen by 25.7%.

The Homestyle director says that the division's revenue is relatively unchanged year-on-year so the increase in revenue is likely to have arisen as a result of the 50 new Fixings stores. The scenario suggests the deterioration in profit is due to the Homestyle division's sales mix, increased delivery costs and promotional pricing strategies.

Segmental information for 20X4 would enable more analysis of the causes of performance.

Commentary on divisions

Comparing the divisional performance:

Almost half the company revenue comes from the Homestyle division but this only accounts for 41% of the divisional contribution. Whilst the Homestyle stores have a similar gross profit margin (29.3%) to the new Targi stores (30.1%), their operating margin is much lower (5% compared to 8%) and the ROCE considerably less (18% compared to 25.2%).

This is borne out by the fact that despite each Homestyle store being almost twice the size of the Targi ones (10,000 sqm vs 5,600), with about 45% more revenue per store (£10.46m compared to £7.26m), the average profit per store is lower at £520k compared to £583k.

This may reflect the differences in the markets (UK v Eastern Europe), customer base (consumers v tradespeople) and operating models (the Targi division carries a limited product range which it sells in large volumes at low prices).

There may also be exchange differences arising in the Targi results.

The UK based Fixings division, which sells to a mix of tradespeople and consumers, has the highest gross margin (42%) and the highest ROCE at 27.3%. It accounts for 36% of group sales and 40% of the contribution.

The Fixings stores are the smallest (3,500 sq metres and £4.95m revenue per store) but it is the most efficient revenue generator at £1,414 per sq metre, which is consistent with the information in the scenario about the majority of the store space being used to display products.

There may be differences in rental costs between the stores eg, smaller stores may be in town and therefore more expensive per sq metre than larger, out of town stores.

Given the different store sizes it is not particularly useful to compare performance measures on a per store basis, instead comparisons have been made per square metre. These show that the Homestyle division lags quite a long way behind both the Fixings and Targi divisions in terms of revenue per sq metre, profit per sq metre and revenue per employee. Since it accounts for almost half the net assets of the group, Homestyle's weak performance will have had a significant impact on the overall results.

Further information

Additional information that would be useful includes the following:

- Rental costs of the stores operated by each division

- Information regarding the age and current value of assets used by each division, including any operating leases, since this will influence ROCE

- In addition to profit-based performance measures, investors may also use measures such as EPS, PE ratio. Information regarding the investors in Outil and their target ratios would be useful.

- Wider non-financial performance measures for the divisions would also assist in comparing performance and assessing underlying causes of profitability.

Conclusion

The Homestyle division does appear to be underperforming relative to the other divisions currently. This division is the only one that relies exclusively on consumers and the performance may be a result of internal inefficiencies or a permanent decline in the DIY market. In deciding what to do with the division it is not just historic performance but also future prospects that are relevant. Therefore details of budgets/plans for the Homestyle division for 20X6 onwards would be useful.

Examiner's comments

This requirement was well answered. The majority of candidates included an initial table (or an appendix) of data calculations, covering both the company and divisional performance. The weaker candidates failed to provide sufficient quantitative analysis, often restricting their answers to a discussion with a few percentage changes thrown in. Many answers did not use a report format for their answer despite being asked to do so.

The quality of the calculations varied; stronger candidates identified that, for a like-with-like comparison with 20X4, Targi's results needed to be excluded from the overall company results for 20X5. For comparability, they also provided divisional calculations on a per square metre or per employee basis. Weaker answers considered overall movements (including Targi's 20X5 results) and/or provided calculations which ignored the differing sizes of the three divisions.

In terms of the qualitative analysis, weaker candidates who had performed more limited calculations had less to discuss and ended up repeating information already provided in the question, with little or no added value.

The stronger candidates commented on the fact that the revenue improvements in 20X5 arose as a result of the acquisition of Targi and the 50 new Fixings stores, and used the differences in the store models and the target markets to explain the varied divisional performance.

43.2 Homestyle division strategies

The managing director and the Fixings director both support focussing on the trade business and believe the group would be better off without the Homestyle division, favouring closure and sale respectively. The logic for this is to improve overall company performance, either by reducing costs or increasing return on assets by deploying resources to activities with a bigger return on capital.

On a basic level the Homestyle division is making £151 million positive contribution to group results and without it absolute profit would decrease significantly. The loss of the Homestyle division, which is contributing 49% of net assets and sales, and 41% of divisional contribution, would make Outil a much smaller company, albeit a more profitable one in terms of margins and ROCE. The fact that the company is smaller in terms of revenue, profits and net assets might affect its ability to raise finance.

The exact impact would also depend on the extent to which UK divisional sales are interdependent – if the Homestyle division is closed or sold, would customers buy from Fixings instead or would the Homestyle division customers who currently also buy from the Fixings division transfer their business elsewhere?

Other financial factors to consider are the extent to which central costs would be saved by closing or selling the division. The exit costs referred to by the managing director in terms of lease penalties and redundancies also need to be ascertained.

Sale of division vs Closure

Closure of the Homestyle division would necessitate change management, discussed in 43.3 below. However it would allow Outil to retain those Homestyle stores that are located in prime sites and creates an obvious opportunity to expand the Targi brand into the UK and to continue to open more Fixings stores. To some extent this will depend on how easy store sites are to come by and to what extent the existing Homestyle stores are located in areas where the company wants to operate.

If the change management issues and disruption arising as a result of restructuring are significant then a sale may be better and would obviously generate cash. However a key factor in the decision to sell would be whether there are any buyers and the price that they are willing to pay. This will depend on expectations of future prospects for the home improvement market. One possibility is that the managers of the division might be interested in a purchase, since according to the Homestyle division director the market is due to improve.

Retention of the division

The Homestyle director believes that the division has performed well in difficult circumstances and managed to survive when a near competitor has had to close. Whilst it is relatively not as profitable as the other divisions, it is at a different stage in the lifecycle and may be seen as a cash cow, making £151 million positive contribution.

A key consideration is whether the decline in the demand for DIY products from Homestyle consumers is a temporary or permanent situation. If the latter, then Outil may feel it is best to sell or close the division before the market declines even further. If the decline is temporary then a decision to close or sell the division may be premature.

Conclusion

Ultimately Outil needs to consider what is best for its shareholders. Outil's objective is to maximise the wealth of its shareholders, although as a listed company there may be a conflict between different groups of shareholders as to which direction the business should take.

One possible way to resolve the conflict is to consider demerging the Homestyle division so that shareholders can decide for themselves whether they wish to retain shares in it. A demerger is the opposite of a merger – the splitting up of a business into separate operating companies. Existing shareholders exchange shares in Outil plc for shares in the individual companies, but no cash is raised.

Examiner's comments

This requirement was reasonably well attempted. Most candidates used the comments from the directors to structure their answers regarding the future of the Homestyle division.

Weaker candidates tended to consider only two of the three options however and often failed to discuss the Homestyle director's proposal that the division should be kept going until the market improves. They also ignored the requirement to refer to their calculations in 43.1.

Stronger candidates used their analysis in 43.1 (as requested) to identify that the Homestyle division makes up a significant element of the group and that the group's performance might be significantly affected by any closure or sale. Many discussed the division's position in the industry lifecycle and considered the related issues of divisional interdependence and central costs.

Only a minority of candidates identified that Outil's board needs to consider what is best for its shareholders.

43.3 **Impact on two stakeholders of closure and strategies to reduce barriers to change**

The nature of the change being proposed for the Homestyle division, which involves downsizing and redundancy, is transformational and likely to be met with resistance for a variety of stakeholder groups, (for example):

- Employees
- Customers
- Investors
- Suppliers

Mendelow's matrix could be used to assess the power and interest of the various stakeholders and to identify key stakeholders who are likely to cause problems by resisting the change. For example the Homestyle employees are likely to have high levels of interest and may have some power to disrupt the change, depending on the degree of unionisation.

Tutorial note:

Discussion of two groups only was required. The obvious one, which most candidates chose to start with, was the employees.

Barriers to change	Impact	Strategies to reduce barriers
Employees		
Group inertia may block change where the changes are inconsistent with the norms of the teams/stores or where they threaten their interests	There may be strikes and other forms of resistance from the staff who are to be made redundant or transferred. Staff who are to remain may be demotivated by the loss of colleagues or the need to relocate/transfer stores.	Lewin Schein's iceberg model could be used here to assist with appropriate change management strategies. Unfreeze existing behaviour: <ul><li>Identify those stores to close and those to re-brand. Unions and staff must be consulted and the case for change made clear.</li><li>Make redundancy announcements. If staff are to be made redundant they may be motivated by reasonable redundancy terms, the provision of references and outplacement assistance, contingent on their co-operation</li></ul>
Cultural barriers: Internally the new proposal put forward will result in fundamental changes to the structure and culture of Outil. Power structures may be threatened by the re-distribution of resources and decision-making authority.	This will particularly affect the director of the Homestyle division and the store managers who may be reluctant to implement decisions that they perceive to be against their own interests.	Move to the new structure: <ul><li>Implement redundancies and provide appropriate exit support</li><li>Get retained staff on side and ready for the change.</li><li>Participation in the process may improve motivation</li></ul>
There are also barriers which affect individuals and result in them seeing the change as a threat to earnings and job security.	This will not only affect employees of the stores that are closed but also those employees who are required to work in a re-branded store for a different division which may have different working practices	Refreeze: Once the changes have been made, remaining staff will need support to adapt to the new business model.
Customers		
Customers may block change where the changes are inconsistent with the norm or where they threaten their interests	Homestyle customers who also buy from the Fixings division may choose to transfer their business to competitors	Change management will need to focus on communication of which stores will close and which will be re-branded. Key trade customers will need to be reassured that as far as the Fixings division is concerned it is business as usual. Homestyle division customers will need to be encouraged to source supplies where possible from the Fixings division. Outil will need to manage its reputation through the media by explaining how and why the decision has been taken.

Barriers to change	Impact	Strategies to reduce barriers
Investors		
Investors may block change where the changes are inconsistent with the norm or where they threaten their interests.	Shareholders may consider selling shares as a result of the changes.	Change management will need to focus on the following: • Identifying those stores which are to close and those which are to be re-branded • Announcing the change to market and other stakeholders • Managing investor relations Communication will be an essential part of the process: Shareholders will be interested in the impact on share price, profitability and dividends. Outil will need to provide reassurance regarding the state of their investment and how the strategy will benefit them. Outil will need to manage its reputation through the financial press and analysts by explaining how and why the decision has been taken.
Suppliers		
Suppliers may block change where the changes are inconsistent with the norm or where they threaten their interests.	Suppliers may take legal action for breach of contract in the event of termination.	Legal advice should be sought regarding contractual obligations with suppliers. Change management will need to focus on the following: • Communicating the change to suppliers • Managing supplier relations Communication will be an essential part of the process

Tutorial note:

In the answer above Lewin Schein's model is used to assess appropriate change management strategies, you could have also used Gemini's 4 Rs model.

Examiner's comments

This requirement was one of the best answered on the paper. The vast majority of candidates had no problem identifying two stakeholder groups that would be affected by the closure of the Homestyle division and were clearly well-versed in technical knowledge for the change management discussion. Marginal candidates tended to demonstrate one of the following weaknesses: ignoring the requirement to refer to change models, discussing the model(s) in generic terms without application to the scenario, or focussing their discussion on one stakeholder group only (usually the employees).

43.4 Expansion of Fixings division: Merits of test marketing/opening trial stores

Test marketing involves a trial run of a product or concept before proceeding to a full launch.

Test marketing the plan to expand internationally would involve a trial of all aspects of the marketing mix in a limited area. It is designed to reduce risk and gather information about the likely success prior to a full roll-out.

The marketing strategy for the Fixings division may need to be modified for international business differences in language, culture and customs. There may also need to be obvious product modifications, such as voltage changes for power tools etc. This could be minimised by using overseas suppliers rather than shipping from the UK.

Determining the appropriate pricing strategy for the international market may need to take into account increased costs – for example, shipping and export services. Fixings will need to assess competitor pricing. If the expansion is to be in Germany, Euro currency fluctuations will also need to be considered.

The test market selected should normally be small, self-contained and representative of the wider market.

Problems:

- Even the largest test market is not totally representative of the national market.

- Although the main objective of test marketing is to reduce the amount of investment put at risk, it may still involve significant costs. If a major part of the investment has already been made the reduction in risk may be minimal, for example if the Fixings division has to develop an international website or create a large central depot to service a small number of test stores.

- Test marketing may give competitors advance warning of Outil's intentions.

Conclusion:

If test marketing enables large parts of the investment costs relating to an international expansion strategy to be deferred until a reliable estimate of national sales can be made, then it is desirable.

Trial stores

Opening trial stores in Germany offers two important benefits. First, it provides Fixings division with an opportunity to test demand for its products under typical market conditions in order to obtain a measure of its sales performance. As well as enabling top management to make an accurate prediction of its potential national turnover, it may familiarise international customers with the Fixings brand.

Second, it provides an opportunity for management to identify and correct any weaknesses in the strategy or marketing plan before making the commitment to a national sales launch.

Questions to be considered are as follows:

- Where to open the stores?
- How long a test?
- What are the success criteria?

The strategy requires a specific German website to be launched which will need to be tested by a local language and culture expert.

The stores will need a wide range of inventory and if there are only a handful of them, there may not be sufficient volumes for minimum order quantities to get best prices.

If the decision to open stores is taken, this can be done organically (which is how the Homestyle division has previously grown) by opening company-owned stores, or venturing overseas via licensing deals and joint-venture partnerships.

An alternative to opening trial stores would be to test the international demand for Fixings division products via an e-commerce site in the first instance. This would allow it to see which products sell. Goods could then be dispatched from UK or direct from German/European suppliers.(Outil already operate in Eastern Europe through Targi so may already have supply and distribution networks in place.)

Conclusion:

Expanding delivery via a website is likely to be a better way of testing the waters of the German market initially. If this is successful then trial stores could be opened.

Examiner's comments

This was the lowest scoring requirement in question 1, but still reasonably well answered. In general, candidates coped well with identifying the benefits of test-marketing prior to international expansion, although only the better candidates identified this as a risk management strategy. Stronger candidates then went on to consider the merits of the specific proposal to open up four trial stores in Germany. Weaker candidates tended to mix up both elements of the requirement in one discussion, often focussing on one part to the detriment of the other.

44 Dreamy Potato Products Ltd (March 2016)

Marking guide

	Knowledge	Skill	Marks
44.1 Elements of Porter's five forces	3	6	9
44.2 Evaluation of contract (proposal 1)	2	10	10
44.3 Assessment of proposal 2	2	5	7
44.4 Discussion of ethical issues	3	5	7
	10	26	33

General comments:

This question was the best attempted overall but contained the highest and lowest scoring requirements of the paper.

The scenario relates to DPP Ltd, a food processing company based in the West of England. It buys potatoes form local farmers then peels, washes and processes them before selling them to various food manufacturers. Most of DPP's clients produce ready meals for the major supermarkets. Client contracts are typically renegotiated every three years, although terms change frequently.

DPP's raw material costs and selling prices are driven by the market price of potatoes, which fluctuates considerably, depending on the availability and quality of the annual crop. DPP acquires the majority of its potatoes from four local farms, with whom it has exclusive purchase agreements. The market-leader Estima plc is a vertically integrated business which grows its own potatoes and supplies raw and cooked potato ingredients to the catering industry and prepared food manufacturers.

DPP is considering two proposals to improve its profitability:

Proposal 1: a new contract with a famous national fast food chain to supply it with pre-prepared uncooked potatoes. To implement this strategy DPP would need to acquire a new machine to grade and cut the potatoes and rent a further 9,000 sq metres of premises. Working cost and revenue assumptions were provided.

Proposal 2: reduce costs and increase revenue through better use of waste products which would also be positive from a sustainability point of view and help differentiate DPP from Estima.

Ethical issue: Potters Pies is one of DPP's major clients and manufactures pies for two supermarkets (Giant and Quality). Potters' contract with Giant will only be renewed if it lowers the price. Andrew Baxter, a director at Potter Pies, has asked DPP to drop the price it charges Potters for potatoes for the Giant contract by 5%. In exchange Potters is prepared to increase the price it pays for potatoes for the Quality contract by the same amount. Andrew intends to recover this cost increase from Quality by pretending that the price increase is due to a change to higher quality potatoes. He has intimated to DPP that if it goes along with his wishes, he will ensure Potters retains DPP as the preferred supplier rather than moving the business to Estima.

44.1 Porter's Five forces model is used to analyse the competitive environment within an industry. An analysis of the key forces can help DPP understand the factors which will affect its profitability.

Barriers to entry:

Unless incumbents have strong and durable barriers to entry, profitable markets attract new entrants, which erodes profitability.

Barriers to entry in DPP's industry seem relatively high. They include the following:

- Economies of scale from large volume processing – evident from the fact that the ready meal manufacturers have decided to outsource and that Estima controls 30% of the market

- Investment required for capital intensive processing and specialised logistics (fresh food products)

- Existing players have three year contracts with the large ready-food manufacturers

- Heavily regulated industry with high compliance costs

- Existing firms may have access to suppliers of ingredients, possibly on favourable terms

Barriers are reduced by the following:

- Limited product differentiation and low switching costs

- Smaller entrants could avoid the need for expertise in the distribution of fresh products by outsourcing distribution

It appears that DPP is more likely to face competition from existing firms than new entrants. Local potato farmers may be too small to enter the market.

Power of suppliers:

A key issue is the availability and quality of potatoes. The price is driven by market factors so one individual supplier is unlikely to be able to drive up the price. Limited product differentiation and low switching costs also reduce supplier power. Suppliers are likely to have more power when potato harvests are poor and supplies are limited.

DPP's workforce are also a supplier but the work is probably relatively unskilled and there is likely to be a plentiful supply of workers so individually they will have low power.

DPP has exclusive contracts with four local farms which will help guarantee supply. To the extent that the farms rely on DPP for income, DPP may be in a stronger bargaining position than the suppliers. It has a weekly-paid workforce on the minimum wage and there is no indication of labour supply issues.

Power of customers

The power of customers is driven by the number of buyers in the market and the cost to the buyer of switching from one supplier to another. It is likely to be high.

If there are a few powerful ready-meal manufacturers, they will be able to dictate terms. Here the power of the buyers' buyers is also relevant. Since ready-meal manufacturers supply to large retailers their margins are likely to be low and this will influence the amount they are prepared to pay for processed potatoes. Contracts are also renewed regularly and there is little to differentiate the product.

DPP is dependent on a small number of key customers and its customers are themselves very dependent on the large retailers who have high power, as evidenced by the example of Giant and Potters Pies. This is also reflected in the fact that DPP's contracts are renegotiated every three years and contract terms tend to change frequently.

Examiner's comments

Candidates were well-prepared to discuss three of Porter's five forces and this was the highest scoring element of the paper. The best candidates discussed the model as it applies to the potato processing industry, summarised the strength of each force in the industry and then recognised the impact this would have on DPP. Weaker candidates tended to confuse the industry and company discussion.

44.2 Evaluation of fast food contract

Appendix of possible calculations

Potato prices: EV calculation

Year 1 price = £125

Year 2 price: $(0.40 \times £125) + (0.60 \times £160) = £146$

Year 3 price: $0.40 \times [(0.45 \times £115) + (0.55 \times £135)] + 0.60 \times [(0.65 \times £150) + (0.35 \times £170)] = £144.60$

Annual profits from contract

		Year 1 £	Year 2 £	Year 3 £	Total £
Revenue	9,000 × £210	1,890,000	1,890,000	1,890,000	5,670,000
Potatoes	9,000 × £125/£146/£144.60	1,125,000	1,314,000	1,301,400	3,740,400
Labour and other VC	9,000 × £65	585,000	585,000	585,000	1,755,000
Contribution	9,000 × £20/(/£1)/(£0.40)	180,000	(9,000)	3,600	174,600
Other operation cost		25,000	25,000	25,000	75,000
Profit		155,000	-34,000	-21,400	99,600

Tutorial note:

A range of different approaches could be used to determine profitability

Alternative calculation of contract profitability:

Costs	Working	£
Labour and other VC	9,000 × £65 = £585,000 pa × 3	1,755,000
Operating costs	25,000 pa × 3	75,000
		1,830,000
Potatoes	Year 1: 9,000 × £125	1,125,000
	Year 2: 9,000 × £146	1,314,000
	Year 3: 9,000 × £144.60	1,301,400
Total costs		5,570,400
Total revenue	27,000 × £210	5,670,000
Expected profit		99,600

Sensitivity to price of potatoes:

The annual revenue of £1,890,000 less labour and increased operating costs of £610,000 generates £1,280,000 per annum to cover the costs of purchasing 9,000 tonnes potatoes.

This amounts to £142.20 per tonne.

Anything paid above this price will be loss-making for DPP.

The EV is a long–term average and in fact the purchase price of potatoes will vary from £115 to £170 per tonne.

The profitability at different purchase prices can be considered:

Price	115	125	135	150	160	170
	£	£	£	£	£	£
Net revenue	1,280,000	1,280,000	1,280,000	1,280,000	1,280,000	1,280,000
Costs of Potatoes	1,035,000	1,125,000	1,215,000	1,350,000	1,440,000	1,530,000
Profit/loss	245,000	155,000	65,000	-70,000	-160,000	-250,000

Evaluation

At the proposed fixed price of £210 per tonne for the three year contract, DPP will make an additional £99,600 of operating profit overall, so on the face of it the contract is financially viable. However this is an operating margin of only 1.8% (99,600/5,670,000), which is less than the current margin (352k/10.8m = 3.3%). Also the profit is not spread evenly.

The key issue affecting profitability is the price that DPP is going to have to pay for potatoes.

On the basis of the agreed price of £125 for year 1 of the contract, there will be a profit in year 1 of £155,000. However based on the expected value calculations, the contract will make losses of £34,000 and £21,400 in the subsequent two years.

Potato prices are dependent on crops planted and harvested and market supply. It is not clear how accurate or reliable the price forecasts are. The average price used in the contract profitability calculation will not actually apply. There is a 40% chance that the actual price in year 2 is £125 and DPP will make a further £155,000 profit. However it is more likely (p=0.6) that the price will be £160, and the actual loss will be £160k.

The maximum that DPP can afford to pay for potatoes is £142.20 per tonne (see sensitivity working). Thus in year three the contract will be profitable if purchase prices are £115 or £135 and loss making at £150 or £170.

Other factors to consider:

(a) Are all the additional costs of the machine and premises space reflected in the £25,000 incremental fixed costs?

(b) If DPP turns the contract down, will it go to a competitor?

(c) If the fast food chain does not renew the contract after three years will DPP be able to use the machine and the additional warehouse space it has rented?

(d) Is there scope to add a clause to the contract for variation in prices depending on the market conditions?

(e) Can DPP pass the risk on to their suppliers by agreeing three year supply prices now?

Conclusion: further research should be undertaken before a final decision to go ahead is taken.

Examiner's comments

Answers to this requirement, which produced the lowest scores on the paper, were polarised. The weakest answers either concentrated on a numerical analysis of the proposed fast-food contract but provided no discussion, or simply produced a qualitative discussion with no supporting calculations.

The better candidates produced more balanced answers and showed good knowledge of expected values and conditional probabilities, scoring full marks on the calculations. Weaker candidates were unsure how to calculate an expected price in year 3, often averaging the numbers rather than applying the conditional probabilities. They also made errors on the fixed overheads, including the absorbed overheads as well as the incremental element.

44.3 Sustainability involves using natural resources in a way that does not lead to their decline. The Bruntland definition is: "meeting the needs of the present without compromising the ability of future generations to meet their own needs." In a wider context sustainability does not just address environmental issues but also economic and social sustainability, so would encompass long-term financial stability, working conditions and fair treatment of suppliers, among other things.

It is not really clear whether the motivation for DPP's proposed use of waste products is primarily commercial (reduced costs and increased revenues) or based on wanting to adopt a more sustainable approach to business. Certainly the conversion of potato peelings to power will reduce DPP's consumption of energy resources. The sale of starch residue is likely to generate additional revenue at relatively low cost. Whether it will be a net benefit to the environment will depend on how the residue is currently disposed of. Irrespective of environmental sustainability, the diversification of earnings streams and the ability to generate additional revenue will make DPP's business more financially sustainable.

Benefits of proposed strategy:

- In the long-run the use of waste as an energy source will reduce costs

- Sale of potato peelings for cattle food will generate additional revenue

- Accreditation for its sustainable approach may enhance DPP's reputation

- It may attract new environmentally conscious customers

- Large retailers who place emphasis on CSR may insist on suppliers adopting sustainable practices and this may help DPP win contracts.

Costs of implementing a sustainability strategy:

- Additional fixed costs associated with installing the digester

Overall the strategy would appear to be commercially viable and may help increase DPP's environmental and financial sustainability.

Other possible sustainability contributions could come from:

- Increasing the proportion of more modern, fuel efficient vehicles through a regular replacement programme

- Use of cleaner high grade diesel fuel even if this is more expensive

- Improved vehicle utilisation to reduce the number of empty load journeys which waste fuel

- Better refrigeration/chilling processes to reduce emissions

- Ensuring that health and safety is maintained at the highest standards

- Promoting diversity and equal opportunity and providing fair pay and benefits for all workers

- Working in partnership with suppliers, making sure suppliers are treated fairly and that contract terms are transparent and fair to both parties

Examiner's comments

Most candidates were well prepared for a sustainability discussion, although a surprising number still seem to believe this is limited to environmental aspects. Whilst this did gain credit, weaker students who adopted this approach restricted the marks available to them. Better answers identified the financial and environmental benefits of the proposals for waste management and considered a range of alternative proposals to improve sustainability in all three areas (economic, environmental and social).

44.4 Ethical issues

Ethics pertains to whether a particular behaviour is deemed acceptable in the context under consideration. In short, it is 'doing the right thing'.

In making any ethical evaluation it is first necessary to establish the facts. In this case, it would seem that the facts are reasonably clear: Potters is asking DPP to drop its price on one contract (Giant) but is prepared in return to pay more on another contract (Quality). A key question here is whether there is an ethical issue at all or whether this could be deemed to be a normal part of price negotiations in the ordinary course of business.

Andrew's proposal implies a lack of personal ethics on his part, both in relation to his willingness to mislead Quality and also given the implied threat in respect of DPP's contract with Potters. This may be symptomatic of a wider cultural issue within Potters. Alternatively it may be that Andrew is simply passing on the pressure that Potters has come under from Giant and reflects Andrew's desperation to retain a prestigious contract.

The issue of legality needs to be considered and legal advice taken. Andrew has not promised any direct financial incentive but has offered the inducement of a guaranteed contract renewal which might be considered a bribe.

In making a decision as to how to proceed, it is helpful to apply the Institute of Business Ethics three tests:

- Transparency
- Effect
- Fairness

Transparency – would DPP mind people (other customers, suppliers, employees) knowing that it has agreed to this transaction? In the first instance, there appears to be a degree of transparency between DPP and Potters but the same cannot be said in relation to Potters' retail customers. In particular Potters intends to deliberately mislead Quality regarding the price increase.

Effect – whom does the decision affect or hurt? To an extent the impact on Giant is positive since they win by renewing their contract with Potters at a lower price. However this is at Quality's expense. If the contract volumes are the same, DPP will be no worse off financially. However DPP might be accused of colluding with Potters to procure a contract and this may be deemed unfair to other ready-meal manufacturers who are also tendering.

Fairness – would the action be considered fair by those affected? It is likely that competitors and Quality would not take kindly to the fact that DPP has acted with Potters to knowingly deceive them and misrepresent its product as having improved in quality.

Honesty

A final issue is one of honesty. The inducements may fail the honesty test as they are not earned, authorised or disclosed by, or on behalf of, the giver or the recipient.

Actions

DPP should be guided by any legal advice.

Whilst DPP may benefit initially by agreeing to Andrew's request, it would suffer reputational damage if the transaction came to light. Having succumbed once to the implicit threats from Potters, DPP may in future come under more pressure from Potters, in return for its silence. The best action would be for DPP to act honestly and therefore not agree to Andrew's request, which is asking the company to turn a blind eye to dishonesty. DPP might also consider whether it needs to raise the issue of Andrew's behaviour with Potters' directors.

Examiner's comments

The ethics requirement was very well attempted. The vast majority of candidates now acknowledge the need for a balanced discussion which addresses any legal as well as ethical issues and uses appropriate ethical language. Weaker candidates are still tending to limit their analysis to a discussion of transparency, effect and fairness. Better candidates went beyond this to consider Andrew's thinly disguised intimidation threat and to question whether DPP would be demonstrating integrity and honesty by colluding with Andrew's proposed deception. It was encouraging to see that most candidates went on to propose some appropriate next steps to resolve the issue, which was expected for maximum marks.

45 The Zed Museum (March 2016)

Marking guide

	Knowledge	Skill	Marks
45.1 Analysis of stakeholders	3	6	9
45.2 Licensing strategy	2	7	8
45.3 Performance measurement	2	6	7
	7	19	24

General comments:

This question was reasonably well attempted.

The scenario in this question is about the not-for-profit Zed museum based in Italy. It hosts a very fine collection of sculptures and modern art and is a popular destination for locals and tourists.

After the death of its wealthy founder, Emilio Zed, the museum is experiencing a financial crisis and its future is under threat. The Zed museum has a sizeable collection, only a fraction of which is on display at any one time. However despite its valuable asset base, the assets are not liquid and cannot be sold to pay current expenses. Most of the items in the collection were given to the museum to hold, conserve, and use in exhibitions or programmes for future generations.

A new chief executive has been appointed by the trustees to address the situation and attract a wider audience and additional revenue streams. She is keen to operate the museum on a more commercial basis and exploit the museum's asset base by licensing the museum's brand and collection to a wealthy businessman, Kazuo Tada. He wants to operate a Zed museum on a Japanese island that he is developing as an exclusive cultural tourist attraction.

Some of the trustees have argued that the licensing deal is not appropriate for a world-class museum. They also argue that the proposed expansion strategy is contrary to the Museum's founding principles. The chief executive is also evaluating how best to measure the museum's success. Historically performance has simply been evaluated by measuring the number of visitors.

45.1 Stakeholders

As a NFP organisation, Zed is likely to have multiple stakeholders with a range of different interests and potentially conflicting goals. A challenge is to integrate the interests of the museum's internal stakeholders (trustees, volunteers, staff) and external stakeholders (donors, visitors, community, government donors) to allow the museum to achieve financial sustainability, make efficient use of its resources, and fulfil its educational role and public interest remit.

Stakeholders can be analysed using Mendelow's power and influence matrix:

Trustees

Trustees have significant power and influence over the day-to-day running of Zed. They may be interested in status/reputation/external recognition. They will also be concerned about the possibility of being found liable for losses if the museum is insolvent. Some trustees may have a network of contacts to assist Zed with funding/expertise or access to new collections/donations.

Trustees are key stakeholders and it is important that they are kept on board as they may attempt to block changes to the status quo, such as the proposed licensing strategy.

Donors

Donors may be interested in the proper use of their funds/artefacts. They may seek recognition or confidentiality. Overall their interest in the museum is probably medium-high. Their power may depend on the size/value of any donation and the donor's ability to raise the profile of the museum or their connections in the art world.

Given the current financial crisis, retention of existing donors or attraction of new ones is critical to the survival of the museum.

Staff

Paid staff will be interested in job satisfaction, pay and security, although volunteers may be doing the job for the love of art and the learning and experience it brings. Power and influence are based on the museum's need for their resources and the availability of labour, but it could be argued that staff are likely to have little power as individuals. However it would be easy for volunteers to withdraw their labour in disgust, since they have nothing to lose as they are not reliant on the museum for income. This could cause the museum problems, depending on the extent to which it relies on volunteer labour rather than paid staff. As a result the level of power is difficult to identify fully.

As the staff are likely to be stakeholders with high interest but possibly medium power, the key here is communication so they feel informed and involved in the museum's future.

Examiner's comments

Most candidates considered the interest and influence of the three stakeholder groups identified. Better candidates used their knowledge of Mendelow to draw this together and analyse the relative importance of each group and the impact of their relationship with the museum in light of the current scenario.

45.2 Desirability of licensing

Advantages

- The museum is in financial crisis and licence fees would offer it a quick, new source of revenue which could ensure survival.

- The assets cannot be sold and there is insufficient room to display them all so this ensures they are generating value for Zed.

- Licensing increases awareness and knowledge of the museum and raises its profile/reputation.

- Expansion risk is shared with the licensee.

- This strategy allows more people to share in/enjoy the donated items

- It increases the opportunities for learning and education due to wider reach and is consistent with Zed's constitution to "encourage visitors to explore collections for inspiration, learning and enjoyment".

Disadvantages

- Licensees may have their own agendas and the museum may suffer as a result of their self-interest.

- Zed may lose control of its collections which goes against its constitution to safeguard the long-term public interest in the collections.

- There may be conditions regarding the use of the building and the collections – restrictive legacies may prohibit them leaving the museum or specify they are for the benefit of Italian citizens only.

- The licensed museum's staff may not have suitable experience/expertise.

- Zed may be accused of allowing commercial objectives to override its constitution and licensing may not be deemed ethical for a NFP organisation.

- Licensing may create financial ties with foreign governments/nationals that restrict the museum's independence.

Specific issues relating to the Japanese museum:

- There may be disparity between the cultural priorities of Italian Zed and the Japanese billionaire.

- The sizeable donation may compromise Zed's independence.

- Will there be a demand for imported Italian culture on the Japanese island?

- There will be significant costs and logistics of transporting collections and ensuring their safety/security/conditions.

- There may be significant language and cultural differences.

Conclusion

It is not unusual for museums and art galleries to share objects and exhibitions and to put collections on loan. Some other international museums have embarked on licence strategies to strengthen their global brand.

Zed's founding principles require it to "recognise the interests of people who made, owned, collected or donated items in the collections" and to "consult and involve the local community, users and supporters" and it should engage with these people before making a final decision.

Clearly some action is required since the museum is in imminent danger of insolvency. In addition to licensing, other strategies may be available to raise revenue eg, increase admission fees, charge for special exhibitions, sell merchandise online.

Examiner's comments

The approach required here was a consideration of the benefits for Zed of a licensing strategy in general, together with the specifics of the Japanese proposal. Many candidates mixed up the two elements under one discussion of advantages and disadvantages. Whilst this approach usually scored acceptable marks, those who first considered whether licensing was a sensible option for the museum before considering some of the issues associated with the particular Japanese option tended to make a more diverse range of points. The better candidates recognised that, given the museum's financial crisis, imminent action was required.

45.3 Approach to performance measurement

Currently Zed is looking at performance from a very narrow angle: the number of people through its doors. One of its founding principles is to "review performance to innovate and improve". To fulfil this Zed needs a wider system of performance measurement and, given its NFP status, this needs to take into account both financial and non-financial aspects. An effective system of performance measurement will demonstrate to external stakeholders that the museum's founding principles and objectives are being met and show Zed's stewardship of its assets: its collections, intellectual capital, and brand.

Given the broad range of stakeholders, a balanced scorecard approach may be relevant. This highlights four perspectives: financial, customer, internal business processes, and innovation and learning. The trustees should identify critical success factors – the areas that are vital for the museum to be a long-term sustainable organisation – and these should guide the choice of KPIs and the setting of targets within each area.

Financial

It is difficult to assign monetary value to art/culture and many of the traditional financial measures of performance (eg, ROCE, profit margin) will not apply here. However given the financial crisis that Zed finds itself in, the financial perspective is vitally important. To remain viable the museum may have to manage its costs more closely. It could consider the 3Es commonly used in the public sector: Economy, Efficiency and Effectiveness. These will help assess whether the museum's resources have ben put to good use to add value to society.

Appropriate financial KPIs might include the following:

- Admission fees received
- Grant income received
- Average value of financial donations
- Average value of exhibits donated
- Sales of merchandise
- % of budget spent on marketing

- Licence fees received
- Ratio of income to operating costs
- Revenue generated from café
- Cost of restorations undertaken
- Cost of fund-raising activities

Customer

This is the only area currently being monitored. However Zed needs to know what its users feel about the museum and its exhibitions. They may be seeking education and/or entertainment.

Appropriate KPIs might include the following:

- Monthly attendance figures
- % of return visitors
- Number of first-time visitors
- Average score in visitor satisfaction ratings
- Mix of visitors – local: tourists
- % of time museum open to visitors

Internal business processes

This considers how Zed goes about delivering its services and the impact this has on its effectiveness.

Appropriate KPIs might include the following:

- % of total collection on display
- Number of new pieces acquired in the year
- % of income spent on admin rather than collections and activities
- Ratio of paid staff: volunteers
- Ratio of staff: visitors
- Number of damaged artefacts

Learning and development:

The museum should be a place of personal growth for both its staff and its visitors and it also wants to play a role in encouraging learning on the part of the visitors to the museum.

Appropriate KPIs might include the following:

- No. of articles published by museum staff in journals
- No. of institutions to which museum has lent items
- % of budget spent on staff training
- Staff turnover/absenteeism
- No. of new collections/exhibitions acquired
- No. of visits by schools/colleges

Examiner's comments

Answers to the performance measurement requirement were sometimes disappointing. Poorer efforts tended to ignore the request to recommend a suitable approach to performance measurement and simply provided a list of KPIs. Stronger candidates discussed the need to extend the current and very narrow approach to measuring performance (visitor numbers). A number of options were acceptable here in the context of a NFP experiencing financial difficulties and included balanced scorecard, the 3 Es or consideration of a range of financial and non-financial measures. The weakest candidates still appear to be confused about the difference between CSFs/goals and KPIs which are measures of the extent to which these goals have been achieved.

		Knowledge	Skill	Marks
46.1 (a)	Data analysis	2	9	10
46.1 (b)	KPIs	3	6	8
46.2	Budgeting	2	5	7
46.3	Procurement	3	9	11
46.4	Ethics	3	6	8
		13	35	44

General comments:

This is the mini case and also the main data analysis question.

The scenario is a listed company which operates a chain of shops selling ready-to-eat, vegetarian food and drinks. Healthy eating is a key feature of its marketing.

Each shop has a manager who has limited autonomy in deciding order levels and staffing levels, but most other decisions are centralised, including pricing and the supplier list.

The performance of each shop, and each shop manager, is monitored annually. All shops are ranked by three separate criteria and the lowest ranking shop is subject to closure review procedures. If performance does not then improve, the shop will be closed.

Budgets are also used to measure performance for all shops.

Two proposals have been put forward to revise procurement procedures. The first proposal is to replace the current system of shop managers placing orders by increasing centralisation of procurement. This is proposed to be achieved by determining order quantities centrally using the IT system and historic data patterns of sales for each shop. The second proposal is to partially decentralise procurement by permitting shop managers to source 20% of their shop's products directly from local suppliers, rather than ordering through head office.

An ethical dilemma has arisen as a non-executive director (Andrew) has pointed out that there is high sugar content in many THV products and that this is inconsistent with the marketing theme of healthy eating. The marketing director (Diana) has replied that the sugar content in grams is marked on all THV products and customers should read it.

46.1 (a)

	Leeds £	Hull £	Average for all shops £	Average for 50 worst performing shops £	Average for 50 best performing shops £
Per sq m					
Revenue	3,269	4,063	6,000	4,875	4,833
Op Profit	131	138	375	250	375
NCA/Sq m	4,231	3,750	3,875	3,688	3,750
Per employee					
Revenue	38,636	46,429	68,571	55,714	58,000
Op Profit	1,545	1,571	4,286	2,857	4,500
Rev/NCA	0.77	1.08	1.55	1.32	1.29
Op profit margin %	4.0%	3.4%	6.3%	5.1%	7.8%

	Leeds £	Hull £	Average for all shops £	Average for 50 worst performing shops £	Average for 50 best performing shops £
% of average for all shops					
Revenue	88.5%	67.7%	100.0%	81.3%	120.8%
Op profit	56.7%	36.7%	100.0%	66.7%	150.0%
Operating costs	408,000	314,000	450,000	370,000	535,000

Leeds shop

General issues

Based on the information available, the Leeds shop is larger in terms of floor space than the Hull shop and any of the three 'averages' given as benchmarks. This implies it could have greater potential to make more sales, so it may have an unfair advantage over smaller shops to generate revenue and profit.

Perhaps, more significantly, the cost of the property in Leeds is greater than the Hull shop and any of the three 'averages' given as benchmarks. This is true in absolute terms, but also in terms of non-current assets cost per square metre. The reason for this may be that the Leeds shop is better positioned in a prime location. This may enable it to generate more revenue. Comparisons of revenue per shop in absolute terms therefore gives unfair advantage to higher cost, bigger shops such as Leeds. Operating profit in absolute terms may also be greater for higher cost shops like Leeds, but in this case it needs to cover the additional depreciation costs.

Where the Leeds shop performs badly by comparison to all the other shops is in the ROCE KPI. Any additional profit it earns needs to be proportionate to the additional capital invested, and in this it seems to be failing.

Revenue

In terms of the total revenue generated, the Leeds shop outperforms the worst performing shops benchmark and generates 88.5% of the revenue of the average shop. Whilst not a good performance this would not place it in the very bottom of the rankings which would warrant being placed in closure review procedures.

However, when revenue is adjusted for scale using floor space, then the revenue per square metre at £3,269 is far lower than the Hull shop or the three benchmarks.

Also, revenue per employee at £38,636 is lower than the Hull shop and the three benchmarks. This may be a further reflection of scale or as a result of the inefficient use of labour resources.

Operating profit

In terms of the total operating profit earned, the Leeds shop outperforms the Hull shop, but is below the worst performing shops benchmark, despite the greater size of the Leeds shop. It generates only 56.7% of the operating profit of the average shop.

The operating margin is low at only 4%. This is little more than half the margin of the best performing shops benchmark, although it is above the margin for the Hull shop. In general it shows that despite generating significant revenue, operating costs are high.

Indeed, the operating costs of the Leeds shop are £38,000 higher than the worst performing shops benchmark despite generating only an extra £35,000 in revenue.

Operating profit per employee is the lowest of the shops in the table although similar to the Hull shop. Again this could reflect inefficient use of labour resources.

ROCE

As already noted, the ROCE of the Leeds shop is by far the lowest at 3.1%. This reflects poor utilisation of resources and a low level of return.

The ROCE uses the historic cost, but this was some years ago and the fair value may far exceed this which would make the ROCE far worse in fair value terms.

Closure decision

A distinction needs to be made between the performance of the manager and the potential performance of the shop. The causal factors therefore need to be identified to ascertain whether the poor performance is due to controllable factors (eg, poor staff management) or non-controllable factors (eg, difficult market conditions). A recovery plan can then be put in place and acted upon.

If the factors causing poor performance are non-controllable then alternative and more efficient use of the resources tied up in the Leeds shop could be gained by closing it and reinvesting the cash in alternative locations. As noted, the cash generated may far exceed the price originally paid.

Hull shop

General issues

The Hull shop is of similar size and value to the average and worst performing benchmarks, so reasonably valid comparisons can be made.

However the Hull shop was the most recently opened of the shops and therefore could still be regarded as in the start-up phase, with greater potential for future growth than other shops.

Revenue

The low level of total revenue generated appears to be the main problem. It is the lowest of the shops disclosed in the table with only 67.7% of the revenue of the average shop (ie, about a third lower) and 83.3% of the revenue of the worst performing benchmark.

In terms of revenue per square metre, the Hull shop is about the same proportion lower than the average as in absolute terms, given they are of similar size.

By the same argument, the revenue per employee for the Hull shop, compared to the average shop and the worst performing benchmark, is similarly lower as they all have the same number of staff.

Operating profit

In terms of the total operating profit earned, the Hull shop is by far the worst. This seems likely to be due to low revenue and high operating gearing, with staff and depreciation being key fixed costs.

The operating margin is the lowest at only 3.4%. This is little more than half the margin of the average shop at 6.3%. In general, it shows that low revenue and high operating gearing are having a detrimental effect on margins.

Operating profit per employee and per square metre of floor space are both higher than the Leeds shop but below that of the worst performing benchmark. Again this could reflect poor revenue generation and/or inefficient use of labour resources.

ROCE

While the ROCE of the Hull shop at 3.7% is not as low as the Leeds shop it is far below the worst performing benchmark at 6.8%, reflecting low profitability.

Closure decision

Unless there is strong evidence that the Hull shop can quickly emerge from the start-up phase and make significant improvement, consideration should be given to closure. If the Hull shop were to be sold then more efficient use of resources could be gained by reinvesting the cash in alternative locations, even if the new shop were only to earn the worst performing benchmark rate of return. There may however be closure costs and, as the shop was acquired recently, the sale price might not exceed the price paid.

(b) Closure review procedures may possibly have benefits of motivating staff at the lower end of the performance range but may also generate issues in terms of stress and uncertainty which may reduce staff morale.

Closure review procedures are unlikely to have either positive or negative motivational effects for strong performing units as it is not probable they will be affected.

Some form of criteria to decide on the viability of shops seems necessary in order to promote the efficient use of capital of the business as a whole. In this respect there are two factors:

(1)   How the criteria are applied
(2)   Which criteria are applied

How the criteria are applied

The current criteria are applied only annually. This is a long period, over which performance can deteriorate a great deal. More regular monitoring (eg, quarterly or even monthly) seems appropriate.

Conversely however once a shop is placed in closure review procedures it can be closed within three months which gives little time for it to be turned around and improved.

There also seems insufficient distinction between poor performance of the shop and the poor performance of the shop manager. Changing the shop manager may seem to be an appropriate initial response to poor performance rather than closure of the shop. Replacement of the manager only appears to occur in response to budget deficits rather than closure review procedure measures.

The measures appear to be applied in terms of relative performance compared to other shops, rather than absolute performance against a predetermined target. If all shops are performing well in absolute terms, then one shop still has to be at the bottom of the rankings and at risk of being closed. Conversely, if a large number of shops are performing badly, it is only the very worst that will be captured by closure review procedures using relative measures. Other shops, performing badly but not quite as badly, will then escape scrutiny but may warrant closure.

Moreover, relative performance measures create uncertainty in that shop managers do not know the level of performance that will place them in closure review procedures, as they do not know, in advance, how other shops are performing. Absolute criteria for closure review procedures (eg, a 5% ROCE) would at least make clear, from the beginning of the year, what is an acceptable level of performance.

Which criteria are applied

Revenue

Absolute revenue fails to allow for scale, and can therefore hide the underlying level of efficiency. A large expensive shop (such as Leeds) will easily achieve this revenue criterion, whereas a small shop may be well managed but may struggle to generate significant revenue.

Operating profit

Similarly, the absolute level of operating profit rewards scale. It also hides such factors as food wastage and theft of products amongst much larger costs.

ROCE

The ROCE as used in the closure review procedures bases the capital on the price paid for non-current assets. For older purchases, the fair value of the property may have increased a lot over historic cost. Conversely, for fixtures and equipment, they may be largely depreciated and in need of urgent replacement.

Alternative measures

Operating profit margin – this addresses the scale issue by relating operating profit to revenue generated.

Gross profit margin – this would be the difference between revenue and the cost of sales (ie, the cost of the food/drink acquired). As selling prices are uniform and the price paid for products is constant this measure would reveal inefficiencies in usage (eg, wastage and theft).

ROCE based on fair values – would give a more accurate picture of opportunity cost and the realisable value on closure. It would make comparisons between shops more valid as they would be measured on the same basis.

Non-financial measures – may include: customer satisfaction ratings; number of items sold per square metre; and number of customer complaints. A balanced scorecard could be used to identify some key non-financial measures.

Examiner's comment

Requirement 46.1(a)

The data analysis was generally very well answered by most candidates calculating relevant data and presenting their figures in a structured table. Weaker candidates did not produce an initial table of calculations, but weaved occasional random calculations into their narrative. Other weaker candidates mainly used the figures already provided in the question, with few additional new calculations.

Most candidates produced a good commentary on the data with a reasoned opinion on whether Leeds and Hull should be closed or not. The vast majority also highlighted additional information required, with most tending to do this separately, rather than integrating it into their discussion. The vast majority also provided a conclusion, although there was a lot of sitting on the fence.

Requirement 46.1(b)

Overall the critique of the KPIs was poorly done. Relatively few candidates identified the issue of scale or concept of absolute versus relative KPIs. Even fewer candidates highlighted the issue of using a ranking system for the KPIs as opposed to measurement against a target.

Candidates performed better in suggesting other KPIs with most predictably using the Balance Scorecard. However, many failed to justify the additional KPIs in the context of the given scenario. Most candidates identified the need for non-financial KPIs and a good proportion highlighted the issue of asset values and ROCE.

46.2 Budgeting

A budget is a plan expressed in financial terms.

THV appears to be currently using budgeting for three purposes:

(1) Planning – promotes forward thinking so resources can be put in place in time (eg, a cash shortfall can be financed by a planned overdraft). Potential problems are identified early, therefore giving managers time enough to consider the best way to overcome that problem.

(2) Motivating performance – having a defined target can motivate shop managers in their performance. Shop managers may be motivated by a target to achieve, but this is reinforced by the policy of penalties such as dismissal if targets are not achieved.

(3) Providing a basis for a system of control. Budgets provide a yardstick for measuring performance by comparing actual against planned performance and investigating budget variances.

Possible improvements

At the moment there may be a conflict between the ways in which THV is using budgeting.

Participation in setting targets by shop managers may lead to more commitment to achieving those targets but may also lead to a degree of biasing the budget downwards to improve budget variances. If managers fear they are going to be judged, and possibly dismissed, if they do not achieve their budget target they are likely to build in slack to make the budget more achievable. Budgets that contain slack are less useful for planning purposes as they contain bias.

An improvement would be to have less of a budget-constrained style of management and instead treat variances as an opportunity to make improvements rather than dismiss managers. With reduced consequences may come more co-operation and more accurate budgeting.

The fact that budgets below the previous year's level are not acceptable may fail to take into account changing market conditions (eg, a new competitor in a local region). If last year's performance is now unachievable, the budget may need to be revised. Only realistic budgets can form the basis for planning and control, and therefore they should be adaptable. A zero-based budget would start from first principles rather than adjust last year's figure.

Budgets enable senior managers to 'manage by exception', and thereby focus on areas where things are not going to plan (ie, the exceptions). This is done by comparing the actual performance to the budget to identify the variance. However, not all variances are under the control of shop managers. The principles of controllability and accountability apply. Shop managers can only be held responsible for budget variances arising from causes over which they have control.

The use of budgets could be extended by THV for other purposes. At the moment, there seems limited use of budgets for authorisation. Shop managers appear to have complete discretion of the number of staff hired at their shop. If they were forced to budget, then they would need to plan staff usage in advance which would make it subject to senior management scrutiny before the event. Similarly, variations from the staffing budgets would need to be justified before being authorised.

If the policy of permitting shop managers to make external purchases of food from local suppliers were to take place (see below) then this could be implemented, authorised and controlled by a budgetary mechanism at individual shop level.

The use of budgets could also be extended beyond shop level. Budgets could be applied to each of the 40 product lines to assess the profitability of each product line and trends in demand compared to expectations. Poorly performing product lines could be dropped where highlighted by adverse budget variances. Similarly, new product lines could be introduced and monitored by budgets.

Examiner's comments

There was discussion about the nature of the current budgeting system and the problems with it, but there tended to be limited detail and justification for how better use could be made of budgeting by THV. Weaker candidates struggled on this requirement providing only brief answers that lacked any real cohesion. The better responses gave due consideration to controllability by store managers in the context of performance measurement/management.

46.3 Procurement processes

Purchasing of food products from local suppliers

Currently there is a limited degree of autonomy given to shop managers. The selling prices are fixed by head office; the prices paid to suppliers and recharged to shops are fixed by head office; the location of the shop and capital expenditure are determined by head office.

The only real factors that shop managers can control therefore are:

- the amounts of food ordered each day from within the narrow range of 40 products lines purchased by head office
- staffing levels

Key advantages to permitting some purchases from local suppliers are:

- use of local knowledge to accommodate local tastes
- managers are more motivated if they have more autonomy.
- learning by head office from successful new products sold on a trial basis which can be rolled out across all 200 shops.

Disadvantages are:

- costs – head office can take advantage of economies of scale to lower the cost of purchase. Individual shops are likely to pay more.
- some central purchases would be displaced and therefore there may be the loss of quantity discounts.
- less control – risk of fraud if shop managers sell their own goods through shops and understate revenue.

- loss of homogeneity – if customers obtain different goods at different shops there may be some loss of brand identity.

Use of information technology systems for procurement

The use of automatic reordering at the level of individual shops would reduce the amount of autonomy for shop managers. In this sense, it is the opposite of the above proposal for purchasing from local suppliers. It is also probably initially incompatible with the above proposal as introducing purchases from local suppliers would make historical data patterns unreliable predictors of future sales.

Aside from the behavioural issues, there are risks of future sales patterns not following historical patterns. Local conditions, such as a new competitor, could be accommodated by a shop manager but may not be fully reflected by historic data recognition patterns over a prolonged period.

If errors are made by IT systems ordering so wastage occurs, it may not always be clear who is responsible. It would be difficult to hold shop managers responsible for wastage if they had not ordered the goods, yet wastage figures impact on profit.

Advantages would include the following:

- Releasing shop manager time to focus on customer service and staff management rather than order quantities

- Orders could be placed on a consistent basis if the shop manager was ill or on holiday

- Data management would be easier if IT systems were used rather than orders from 200 separate managers

- IT systems could be integrated with suppliers' IT systems for more efficient ordering. This could make systems more efficient as there are only four suppliers. Improved transfer of information may make the logistics and distribution systems of suppliers more efficient.

Examiner's comments

This was generally well answered with most candidates scoring well. The merits and problems of procurement and IT were well considered by most, recognising the tensions inherent in centralisation versus de-centralisation in decision making. Fewer recognised the problems associated with conflicts in brand identity due to local sourcing and/or the possibility of fraud by store managers.

46.4 Ethical issues

Ethics pertains to whether a particular behaviour is deemed acceptable in the context under consideration. In short, it is 'doing the right thing'.

In making any ethical evaluation it is first necessary to establish the facts. In this case, the claims made by Andrew need to be established to assess their validity before taking any action. This may include establishing the sugar content of a sample of products. It might also include determining the validity of Diana's counter-claim that: "...the sugar content in grams is marked on all our products...."

The issue of legality may apply if the labelling is incorrect, misleading or contrary to regulations. Legal advice should be taken.

Assuming that Diana's claim that products are labelled is correct, this leaves open the question for the board of whether the marketing theme of healthy vegetarian food is inconsistent with the facts, notwithstanding that they are labelled individually.

In making a decision as to how to act, it may be helpful to Andrew and the board to apply the Institute of Business Ethics three tests:

- Transparency
- Effect
- Fairness

Transparency – would the THV board mind people (existing customers, suppliers, employees) knowing about the sugar content in a more open way? In particular, the issue of transparency will apply to the customers who may have believed the heathy eating marketing but, if told more overtly and transparently about high sugar content, would have acted differently. The key issue is whether the prominence and clarity of the labelling amounts to adequate transparency that would lead one to believe that the customers were making an informed choice on the sugar content of their purchases.

Effect – whom does the high sugar content, without clear disclosure, affect/hurt? Clearly this could include the health of customers who would have acted differently on the basis of full information. Other rivals selling genuinely healthy food may also have suffered financially.

Fairness – would the level of disclosure of sugar content be considered fair by those affected? The issue for THV's board is the boundary between the individual customer's responsibility to read labelling about sugar and the company's responsibilities: to make labelling sufficiently clear for it to be observed, and readily understood, in the context of making a food purchase of this nature; to be fair, open and accurate in the information it provides to customers via its marketing efforts.

Honesty – A final issue is one of honesty. Is there an intention to mislead in holding out products to be healthy in marketing communications and then making the minimum possible disclosure in the expectation that customers will not understand the reality of the sugar content?

Actions

Andrew's actions should be consistent with his obligations and duties as a non-executive director. His initial action should be to inform the board. Three issues are to be highlighted: (1) whether the labelling is transparent, clear and in compliance with regulations such that there is evidence that customers are making an informed choice on the sugar content of their purchases; (2) whether the marketing message is misleading; and (3) if the labelling is within regulations, whether it is also in line with custom and practice in the industry.

Andrew needs to give the board reasonable time to respond to the issues that he has raised. If there is no adequate, timely response, and he believes the actions are illegal, then he may have a duty as a non-executive director to report to the relevant regulatory body, having taken legal advice.

He should consider resigning if this becomes necessary.

Examiner's comments

A large majority of candidates adopted the transparency, effect, and fairness structure. However, the application of this structure varied, with weaker candidates not completely sure of the correct interpretation of the principles in the context of the scenario. Many candidates failed to go beyond this TEF framework to discuss any other ethical principles. Overall the use of ethical language and principles was not as comprehensive as in previous sittings. Many candidates failed to address the legality issue or to identify suitable actions for Andrew given his role as an non-executive director. Although most candidates (but not all) identified potential actions for Andrew, there was generally a poor understanding of Andrew's role as a non-executive director in relation to this issue.

47 Elver Bloom Recruiting plc (June 2016)

Marking guide

	Knowledge	Skill	Marks
47.1 Elements of PESTEL	3	7	10
47.2 Fee reduction	4	14	16
47.3 Amy's proposal	2	8	9
	9	29	35

General comments:

The scenario relates to a medium-sized employment recruitment agency. It recruits staff globally, on behalf of its clients, to work on permanent employment contracts in London in the finance industry.

EBR has found it difficult to win new tenders, retain existing clients and increase revenue. The EBR board therefore decided to reduce all its fees by 10% from 1 April 20X5.

The board has recently been reviewing financial and operating data to determine whether the price reduction policy has been successful, but there is some disagreement on interpretation by board members.

One of the directors, Amy, has proposed an alternative policy: to move upmarket by increasing fees by 20% from their current level. The increased price is to be accompanied by offering increased rebates for unsuccessful appointments.

47.1 Key issues – notes

Economic

- Economic growth – more employees required

- More prosperity – higher salaries on which fees are based

- Labour market conditions – as the market nears full employment, it is more difficult for employers to find the right people without specialist outsourced help

- Economic cycle makes labour market and therefore recruitment particularly volatile.

- Specialist companies with dependency on one sector (eg, finance or IT) generate risk of dependency on the fortunes of that sector

Technological

- E-recruitment through social media and internet makes quick access to more potential recruits cheaper and easier

- International recruits can be accessed with social media and internet without physical presence in other countries

- Groups can be easily targeted (eg, financial services or IT potential recruits) using relevant websites and industry electronic journals

- Makes market place more competitive when cheap access makes low barriers to entry for new recruitment companies.

- Makes pricing more transparent

- Clients can more easily recruit themselves through Linkedin etc so less need for agency services

Legal

- Employment law advice is a source of income

- Employment legislation may constrain the recruitment process to avoid discrimination and promote equality. This may impose additional costs.

- Data protection may prevent e-recruitment details being accessed

- International recruitment may be constrained by immigration laws

Conclusion and synthesis

Profitability in the recruitment agency industry is dependent on cycles in the labour market which in turn are a function of the economic cycle. Agencies dependent on one sector (eg, finance or IT) will be dependent on the fortunes of that industry, which may or may not follow macro-economic conditions. Revenue generated in the recruitment agency appears to have benefited overall from the general economic recovery, thereby enhancing industry profitability.

The increased use of social media and e-recruitment seems to be lowering costs in the industry so may appear to add to profitability. However, this is not unambiguously the case if it simultaneously reduces barriers to entry and thereby increases industry competition and forces down prices.

Legal issues may similarly have an ambiguous effect on industry profitability in constraining actions of recruiters and requiring additional processes, but also offering an opportunity for advisory work.

Overall the three factors appear to have recently enhanced industry profitability but there is sufficient ambiguity of effect that not all industry participants may benefit from this.

Examiner's comments

Answers tended to use the three headings provided however the economic analysis was generally poor with few answers clearly stating the link between economic activity, the labour market and the recruitment industry. Better answers used examples for technology from social media, for employment law, and data protection. Poorer efforts tended to be somewhat generic.

47.2 To: EBR board
From: An Adviser
Date: 7 June 20X6
Subject: Report – fee level review

Year to 31 March	20X6	20X5	Change %
Fee per appointment	£16,000	£17,000	-5.9%
Rebate/revenue %	12.0%	10.1%	
Operating profit % fees	41.6%	44.2%	
Operating profit % total	46.4%	48.9%	
VC/Revenue %	20.0%	18.0%	
FC/Revenue %	26.4%	27.7%	
VC per appointment £	£3,200	£3,060	4.6%
FC per appointment £	£4,230	£4,714	–10.3%
TC per appointment £	£7,430	£7,774	–4.4%
Recruitment operating profit per appointment	£6,649	£7,511	–11.5%

% changes			
Revenue	4.9%		
Operating profit recruitment	–1.4%		
Other services	8.9%		
Operating profit total	–0.4%		

Impact of price reduction

In comparing 20X6 with 20X5, the working assumption adopted is that, in the absence of the fee change, the 20X6 financial statements would replicate those of 20X5. In other words it has been assumed that any changes in 20X6 are due entirely to the 10% fee reduction.

There has been:

- growth in revenue of 4.9%, but operating profits on fees and overall have fallen by 1.4% and 0.4% respectively. The increase in revenue as a consequence of fee reduction implies that demand is elastic. Nevertheless, the increased revenue has been outweighed by the increased costs caused by the higher level of activity, leading to a fall in operating profit.

- more appointments have been made, up 11.4%, increasing from 700 to 780. According to the working assumption, this has been generated by lower prices. This gives the opportunity for future growth and cross selling of other services (which have also increased).

- there is a danger of price being a signal for quality and the perception of positioning downmarket when trying to attract upmarket clients and recruits.

- fee per appointment has only fallen by 5.9% not 10%. This may mean a better mix of higher quality appointments or that the 10% reduction policy has not been fully implemented.

- rebates increased in absolute terms and also as a % of revenue, so there may be poorer quality appointments (although variable cost per appointment has gone up which could imply increased quality, or increased inefficiency).

- operating profit has changed only marginally in absolute and % terms. However operating profit per appointment has fallen significantly by 11.5%. This has been driven by the 10% fee reduction but also the increase of 4.6% in variable cost per appointment already noted.

- 'other services' has increased contribution – this may indicate more cross-selling.

Retain or reverse price reduction

The short term impact in 20X6 from the price reduction would indicate that the effect has been unfavourable as the operating profit has fallen. However, before deciding on the best future action, the working assumption that there were no other relevant factors affecting profit may be challenged.

Also, it may be inappropriate to judge the pricing strategy based on one year alone. The increase in the number of appointments may have a longer term beneficial effect in improving reputation and increasing cross-selling of other services.

However the longer term effects may also be detrimental to the company and the damage to the company's reputation for quality may increase over time adding to the short term adverse effect on operating profit.

Examiner's comments

Calculations were variable, with some students producing few or no calculations, whilst others made a reasonable attempt. There was generally a poor appreciation of the relationship of price/volume/variable costs, with only a minority considering the growth in other services or price elasticity and sensitivity. The discussion of the case to retain or reverse the price reduction was generally thin. Sometimes it was just added as an assertion as part of the conclusion.

47.3 Key issues

Amy's proposal is to move EBR further upmarket, not just from the current market positioning (following the 10% price reduction), but further upmarket than the traditional market position prior to the recent price reduction. This could be viewed as part of a differentiation strategy.

This would mean that EBR, under Amy's suggestion, would be charging higher prices than ever, despite the fact that it has been having difficulty in winning tenders since the end of the recession at lower prices.

Price can be taken as a signal of quality, particularly where objective evidence of underlying quality may be difficult to attain. Amy's other suggestion is therefore consistent with reinforcing the quality signal, by going beyond the industry norm in offering rebates. This gives a self-imposed penalty for poor appointments, and therefore incentives to make good quality appointments. If this is perceived by customers and potential customers, it is a consistent signal of quality with the price increase.

In terms of risk shifting, it transfers much of the risk of bad appointments from the client onto EBR. The increase in price may therefore be regarded as a risk premium being paid by clients.

From EBR's perspective there is a significant downside risk. The costs of the rebates may significantly outweigh the benefits of increased prices, particularly if the change fails to attract new customers. There is therefore a need for more information to quantify the risk to EBR. In this respect:

- Historical information about how long appointed employees have stayed with clients is needed in order to model the effects of rebates in the future.

- Market research is also needed to evaluate the likely client response to the rebate offer and to increased prices, so historical trends can be better extrapolated.

A further risk arises from competitor response. While such a policy is not common in the industry, and therefore differentiates EBR from its competitors, this is only the current position. Markets are dynamic and, if the policy is initially successful, then competitors may copy it, thereby reducing the benefits to EBR and possibly forcing down industry profits.

A final issue is that the swings in pricing policy within a short period of time, and in opposite directions, are likely to cause market confusion as to EBR's market positioning. In this respect, the previous reduction in prices may harm this proposed strategy, particularly as it is based upon the perception of quality being influenced by price, which requires stability of pricing policy.

Recommendation

The increase of prices suggested by Amy is significant and has a risk of losing existing customers and causing wide swings in pricing following the recent 10% reduction.

One proposal would be to offer all customers a choice of prices: (1) the higher price with a higher rebate; or (2) the existing (or original) pricing with existing rebates. This would enable customer preferences to determine the price-risk package, rather than the EBR board to guess what all customers may want.

Examiner's comments

Many candidates used the Suitable/Acceptable/Feasible structure but were not normally helped by this framework as they consequently tended to overlook the strategic re-positioning and quality changes. Better approaches were to discuss the price/quality relationship and the change to a differentiation strategy, followed by discussion of the price/profit/risk trade-off. A minority made direct reference to Porter's generic strategies framework, often identifying the proposal as one of focused differentiation.

48 TechScan Ltd (June 2016)

Marking guide

		Knowledge	Skill	Marks
48.1	Impact on R&D	2	4	6
48.2	Expected net present value	3	14	15
		5	18	21

General comments:

The scenario in this question is a company which develops and manufactures complex electronic scanners. The company has a large research and development (R&D) department.

The company is trying to decide whether to use its own R&D department to complete the development of a new type of scanner or to acquire the R&D rights from a rival company under licence.

If the new technology is successfully developed using internal R&D it would be much lower cost than an external licence, but there is only a 60% probability that the internal R&D would turn out to be successful.

With either internally or externally developed technology there is uncertainty in the market about the level of sales that can be achieved, with a 70% probability of high sales and a 30% probability of low sales.

48.1 Impact on R&D

Research should be intended to improve products or processes in order to gain competitive advantage. R&D should support the organisation's strategy, be properly planned and be closely co-ordinated with marketing.

There may be an impact on the R&D department arising from behavioural issues. This could arise from abandoning the current development project in favour of using licensed Ursa technology. If the best R&D staff are to be retained for developing the next generation of technology over the next five years, then motivation and staff retention will need to be prioritised. Loss of key core competences from losing key staff could be a key issue that damages the R&D capability of TechScan for many years.

R&D can have long term horizons and if Option 2 is selected, then it would seem that the next critical time is in about six years (ie, the new technology is licensed from next year and will last for five more years).

It is important that the R&D strategy should be carefully controlled; new products and technologies can be a major source of competitive advantage but can cost a great deal and have a degree of uncertainty. A screening process is necessary to ensure that resources are concentrated on projects with a high probability of success.

In this respect, R&D can be important but only if it is successful. Otherwise it is a wasted cost. If Option 2 is selected, the previous R&D project would not have produced outcomes as the board would have decided to license alternative technology from another company. Whilst it may have been successful if the final R&D phase had been financed, this would not have the opportunity to occur if there is an immediate decision in favour of Option 2. Any money spent on earlier phases is therefore wasted. A review or debriefing of what went wrong with the previous R&D project may now be appropriate in order to learn lessons about the future of the R&D department.

In the context of the board accepting Option 2, the future of R&D can be seen as part of the next product life cycle. In preparing for the obsolescence of Ursa technology, successful new technology needs to be in place for the next product life cycle in approximately six years' time. If there is early success in the new R&D, then the current product life cycle for Ursa technology may be shortened, but it is likely that contractual commitments have been made to Ursa to make licence payments over five years so these would need to be treated as a sunk cost.

Examiner's comments

This was reasonably well answered, although most concentrated either on R&D and possible closure of the department together with redundancies, or alternatively on the move to licensing. Only a minority addressed both the issue of impact on the R&D department and on the future R&D strategy. Only a minority made explicit reference to core competences in R&D and related problems, although many alluded to this indirectly.

48.2 (a) Option 1

Initial investment	R&D cost outcome	Price outcome	NPV	Probability	Expected value
(£45m)	Fail* (£100m)	High +£160m	£15m	(0.4)(0.7) = 0.28	£4.2m
(£45m)	Succeed (£20m)	Low +£110m	£45m	(0.6)(0.3) = 0.18	£8.1m
(£45m)	Fail* (£100m)	Low +£110m	(£35m)	(0.4)(0.3) = 0.12	(£4.2m)
(£45m)	Succeed (£20m)	High +£160m	£95m	(0.6)(0.7) = 0.42	£39.9m
Total				**1.0(proof)**	**£48.0m**

* If the R&D project fails, TechScan will move to Ursa Inc licensing, as future benefits exceed future costs even in a low price scenario (even though there is a loss overall, the initial £45m is a sunk cost at this stage).

Option 2

Initial investment	R&D cost outcome (£100m)	Price outcome	NPV	Probability	Expected value
0	(£100m)	High +£160m	£60m	0.7	£42.0m
0	(£100m)	Low +£110m	£10m	0.3	£3.0m
Total				**1.0**	**£45.0m**

> **Tutorial note:**
>
> A decision tree diagram can also be used to do this calculation.

Alternative approach:

Revenue in each case = (0.7 × 160 + (0.3 ×110) = 145

Costs:

Option 1: -45 + (0.6 × -20) + (0.4 × -100) = 97

Option 2: 100

Profit:

Option 1: 145 – 97 = **48**

Option 2: 145 – 100 = **45**

(b) The issues of investment in R&D or licensing deals with the concepts of risk, expected values and probabilities.

The TechScan board has to deal with decision making under uncertainty. In these circumstances there are two levels of uncertainty:

- Uncertainty of R&D success – which leads to uncertainty of costs for the R&D option but not the licensing option

- Uncertainty of market conditions – which leads to uncertainty of revenues, which is the same for both types of technology

The two types of uncertainty are independent of each other, but occur simultaneously.

The table above shows that Option 1 has a higher expected NPV than Option 2. As a result, in terms of expected values alone, Option 1 is preferable ie, undertake the final phase of the R&D project and invest £45 million.

However there are some weaknesses in using these expected values as the sole decision making criterion:

- The probabilities used when calculating expected values are likely to be estimates, particularly as R&D activity tends to have unknown uncertainties. The probabilities provided may therefore be unreliable or inaccurate.

- Expected values are long-term averages most suitable for decisions involving a high number of similar outcomes. They are less suitable for use in situations involving one-off decisions such as whether to buy the licence or engage in further R&D, where the expected value itself will never occur. They may therefore be useful as a guide to decision making rather than as a strict rule for one-off decisions.

- Expected values do not consider the attitudes to risk of the people involved in the decision making process. They assume risk neutrality which may not be appropriate for the owners of TechScan.

Looking at the data above more specifically, although Option 1 has the higher expected value (by £3m) it has a greater risk in terms of dispersion of outcomes. There is a 12% chance of making a significant loss of £4.2m, where the R&D project fails and there are low prices. For Option 2 there is no loss expected to be incurred in any circumstance.

Similarly, under Option 2 there is a 70% probability of achieving profits of £42m, which is greater than any envisaged outcome under Option 1.

Other factors

If TechScan uses Ursa technology under licence its R&D function may diminish and lose capability to engage in future R&D projects (see above)

Also, If TechScan uses Ursa technology under licence then it becomes dependent on another company which is a rival and on the terms of the licence agreement. Thus, for instance, the opportunity to export may unexpectedly arise over the next five years but TechScan would not be able to exploit this under licensing, as it only has UK rights, whereas it could export with its own R&D where it owns the intellectual property.

There is a risk that the licensing payments may vary. It is possible they are fixed in US$ terms but exchange rate fluctuation may alter their value in sterling.

It may be more difficult to legally enforce UK exclusivity under the licensing agreement than would be the case under a patent for a product that has been developed internally.

It is possible there are internal behavioural issues which could create untoward optimism for the internal R&D under Option 1. This may mean that the probability of success of the R&D project may have been exaggerated. A degree of professional scepticism should therefore be applied to these probabilities until there is supporting objective evidence.

If the R&D project is successful it may be possible to gain revenue from licensing it out to rival companies in other countries.

Conclusion

If there is reasonable confidence that the probabilities provided are reliable estimates which have been objectively determined, then there is a strong case for Option 1 and thereby retaining the core competence of R&D and control over the intellectual property rights to the technology. It also has the higher expected value.

If the R&D project fails, the licence can still be accessed from Ursa Inc at the same cost, but £45m in initial R&D will have been wasted. The wider financial strength of the company to withstand such a financial loss needs to be ascertained.

Examiner's comments

Most candidates calculated the expected NPV for Option 2 correctly. Common errors for Option 1 included selecting a zero NPV if the R&D project failed, rather than reverting to licensing. The most common incorrect answers for the ENPV of Option 1 were £80m and £30m. A small minority ignored expected values altogether in their calculations. Other errors included multiplying the NPV figures by 5 years.

In their narrative, some made use of real options terminology and concepts to enhance their analysis. Very few considered the limitations of expected values or questioned the validity of the probabilities provided. Whilst most candidates mentioned risk, far fewer spelt out the nature of the risks in using the numbers in the scenario and the limitations of expected values in this context. Consideration of other relevant factors tended to focus on keeping the option open for future R&D developments via Option 1 and thereby preserving the firm's core competences, although it was often not expressed in these terms.

Marking guide

	Knowledge	Skill	Marks
49.1 Scenario planning	2	5	7
49.2 Data analysis	2	18	18
49.3 Data sharing	2	5	7
49.4 Proposals	4	10	12
	10	38	44

General comments:

This is the mini case and also the main data analysis question. It was reasonably well attempted.

The scenario is a company, based in Fantasia, South America, which manufactures discs (CDs and DVDs) for businesses in the entertainment and education sectors. As a result of technological developments, the market for discs is declining, and GPT's financial performance has deteriorated.

GPT's customers provide it with a confidential data file from which a master-disc template is created. GPT outsources the production of the master-disc to an Asian supplier. In addition to reduced industry demand, GPT's results have also been affected by the fact that its currency has weakened relative to the Asian $.

The company is considering various strategies to improve results and address the uncertainty facing its industry. Two proposals have been put forward.

Currently GPT employs local people to carry out the disc packaging process manually. The production director has suggested acquiring a new machine which would improve quality and reduce costs but result in significant redundancies.

The sales director is keen to establish alternative revenue streams and already has one specific proposal. GPT produces a range of revision guides for Alegre, an educational publisher. A college has suggested that GPT uses Alegre's master-disc to produce its 'own-brand' version of Alegre's material which the college would then buy directly from GPT, at a lower price.

49.1 Scenario planning

Scenario planning is useful in providing a long-term view of strategy, where a few key factors may influence success. In the face of a changing industry environment, organisations can choose to do nothing, continue to make short-term forecasts or use scenario planning to consider potentially substantial shifts in the industry and its environment.

Technology has already radically changed the market for discs and this appears to be affecting GPT's results. The company is now operating below capacity.

A key question for GPT is where the disc industry will be in 5–10 years' time.

Using scenario planning GPT would attempt to consider possible future situations (favourable or unfavourable) that may occur - 'what if?'- and how these might impact on its business – 'what is the effect of?'. Consideration of these changes will help GPT determine how it can achieve a sustainable business model for the future.

The success of GPT's business depends ultimately on the demand for discs from the entertainment and education sectors. Possible scenarios to consider could be as follows:

- A reduced but ongoing demand from certain markets for discs (either geographically or based on end use)

- Complete cessation of demand for all discs as they are replaced by alternative technologies

In assessing the impact of these different scenarios GPT needs to consider the whole supply chain of which it is a part. This will include asking what will film and music producers do faced with this future, and what might competitors do?

This type of scenario planning would give general rather than precise answers because of the uncertainties involved, but might allow GPT to anticipate changes, develop contingency plans and perhaps respond earlier than some of its competitors.

Options might include the following:

- Becoming more of a niche business, servicing markets where demand remains eg, gaming
- Offering a range of complementary services eg, digital printing
- Abandoning discs and moving into a new business area/sector
- Selling the business whilst there is still some value in it

Examiner's comments

Answers to this requirement were generally disappointing.

Only a minority of candidates demonstrated a clear understanding of the nature of scenario planning. Weaker candidates failed to address the key issue of the fundamental uncertainty regarding the long-term direction of the industry. Many answers confused scenario planning with a company's normal strategic planning process and produced a PESTEL analysis. Others discussed how GPT could undertake sensitivity analysis/simulation to help evaluate the risk of the two strategies being proposed.

49.2 Data analysis

> **Tutorial note:**
>
> The requirement asked candidates to quantify the financial impact of each of the factors that have caused the decline in performance. This analysis could have been undertaken in a variety of ways. A possible approach is shown below.

Calculation are shown in the appendix:

Analysis of the differences in profit	francs
Refer to figures in (W) for 20X4 results adjusted for impact of volume change:	
Impact of reduction in sales volume on gross profit:	(451,205)
(1,563,330 actual 20X4 – 1,112,125 revised)	
Increased selling price	210,000
(2,205,000 – 1,995,000)	
Increased cost of master-disc (525,000 – 284,375)	
This may be sub analysed:	
Due to exchange rate movement:	(240,625)
1,050,000/1,000 × (500 – 325) = 183,750	
Due to smaller order size	
((1,050,000/1,200) – (1,050,000/1,000)) × 325 = 56,875	
Increase in other production costs	(31,500)
(630,000 – 598,500)	
Reduction in overheads	146,400
(835,000 – 981,400)	
Net movement in profit	(366,930)
(Check: 215,000 – 581,930)	

Other more standard performance evaluation calculations:

	20X5	20X4
Gross profit margin	47.62%	55.75%
Operating profit margin	9.75%	20.75%
Selling price per disc	f2.10	$1.90
Other production costs/disc	f0.60	$0.57
Cost/Master-disc in francs	f500	f325

% change in

	%
Sales	−21.4
Master-disc (cost of sales)	+31.3
Other production costs	−25.1
Gross profit	−32.8
Admin and distribution overheads	−14.9
Operating profit	−63.1
Volume of discs sold	−28.9
Other size	−16.7
Number of orders	−14.6
Exchange rate	−53.8
Selling price per disc	+10.5
Other production costs per disc	+5.3
Local cost of Master-disc	+53.8

Working	20X5 (based on 1,050,000 disks)	20X4 (adjusted, based on 1,050,000 discs)	Working
	francs	francs	
Sales	2,205,000	1,995,000	(1,050,000 × $1.90)
Cost of sales:			
Master-Discs	525,000	284,375	(1,050,000/1,200 × $325)
Other production costs	630,000	598,500	1,050,000 × 0.57
	1,155,000	882,875	
Gross profit	1,050,000	1,112,125	
Overheads	835,000	981,400	
Operating profit	215,000	130,725	

Commentary

During the year profit has fallen by f366,930 (63%). Gross profit margin has fallen from 55.75% to 47.62% and operating margin has fallen from 20.75% to 9.75%. The decline in profit is a result of a variety of different factors which are analysed below:

Sales

In total sales have fallen by 21.4%.

The biggest impact has been the decline in sales volume, leading to a loss in profit of f451,205. Sales volumes have fallen 28.9% by 426,000 discs which reflects the decline in industry demand and is largely due to external market factors. The number of orders placed has declined by 14.6% and customers appear to be ordering fewer discs, since the average order size has fallen by 16.7% from 1,200 discs per order to 1,000. Demand may also have been affected by customers being unhappy with delays or errors caused by manual packaging.

GPT Ltd has addressed some of the sales shortfall by increasing the price per disc from f1.90 to f2.10, leading to an overall increase in profit of f210,000. This may have been an attempt to pass on to the customer some of the increase in the cost of the master-disc or the other production costs (see below). However it is not clear whether, as a result of this price increase, customers have gone to competitors or have reduced their order volumes. Thus some of the decline in sales volume may be a result of the increase in price.

Cost of sales

A key component of cost of sales is the master-disc. The increase here has caused a profit shortfall of f240,625.

Two factors are at play:

The smaller order sizes being placed by customers has led to the need to buy more master-discs (had the order size remained at 1,200 then only 875 master-discs would have been required in 20X5 (1,050,000/1,200). This has cost an additional f56,875.

The exchange rate has depreciated significantly during the year (by 53.8%) and as a result despite the fact that the supplier has kept Asian dollar prices constant, the imported master-discs have cost an additional f183,750.

In addition other production costs have increased from f0.57 to f0.60 per disc causing an overall drop in profit of f31,500. Some of this has been recouped via the increase in selling price. This could reflect increased costs for polycarbonate, printing materials or labour rates/productivity – more information is needed to confirm this.

Overheads

These appear to have been well controlled with the effect that costs have reduced (and hence profit increased) by f146,400.

However, the machines are not working at anywhere near capacity. GPT is capable of processing 45,000 discs per week which on a 50 week year is 2,250,000 discs. Thus in 20X5 it had spare capacity of 1,200,000 discs, and is operating at 46.7% of capacity. As a result GPT will not be benefitting from economies of scale. The company needs to address this if it is to improve profitability.

Further information

Additional information that would be useful includes the following:

- A breakdown of sales and gross profit by customer and type of disc to ascertain whether some products/jobs are more profitable than others

- Competitor prices to compare with GPT

- A breakdown of overheads to assess whether there are any discretionary elements that could be cut further

- The extent to which GPT has hedged the exchange rate movements

- A forecast of market demand and exchange rates for 20X6/20X7

Conclusion

The company is in a declining market which has resulted in demand falling significantly. In addition a depreciating currency has caused the cost of importing master-discs to increase. GPT is now operating below 50% capacity and unless the company can find alternative sources of demand, its results are likely to deteriorate further.

Examiner's comments

Candidates scored reasonably well here although very few candidates fully addressed the requirement. The majority of candidates included an initial table (or an appendix) of data calculations. Most candidates were comfortable undertaking a straightforward analysis of the financial and operating data provided and discussing the causes of the decline in performance. However an extremely small minority properly answered the requirement by quantifying the financial impact of each cause separately. As a result very few candidates scored full marks on this requirement.

49.3 Data sharing

GPT Ltd is party to confidential data files which it receives from its customers and then shares in the course of its supply chain with the Asian manufacturer of the master-disc. This information may be valuable and sensitive and GPT has a contractual obligation to protect the data from unauthorised modification, disclosure or destruction.

However, once it is shared by GPT, direct control of the data files is lost. This leads to an increased risk of their confidentiality, integrity or availability being compromised.

The data files from the customer also qualify for intellectual property rights so there is some element of legal obligation for GPT to consider.

The risk of data loss or misuse occurs at various stages in GPT's process:

- The information is transferred from the customer to GPT
- GPT shares the information with the disc supplier
- The master-disc containing the information is returned to GPT
- The master is replicated and many copies of the information are made

GPT needs to ensure appropriate security measures are in place to protect the data at each stage and to prevent theft of IP, since confidential data files are only valuable if stored in an accessible form and then disclosed to others.

From customer to GPT

Make sure communication of confidential information is by secure means.

Asian supplier

Use of a single master-disc supplier reduces the risk as information is only shared with one party. GPT needs to assess the information risk in relation to the contract with the Asian supplier. It should assess the probability and impact of a potential breach and undertake assurance around controls at the supplier.

GPT should ensure there are controls in its outsourcing agreement that place specific confidentiality obligations on the recipient of the confidential data before it is disclosed. With respect to particularly valuable data files, express prior agreement to such obligations could be gained (eg, by the return of a signed confidentiality letter).

Finally it is important that the master-disc is returned via secure means and that appropriate contracts are in place with the secure courier.

At GPT

Employees

Employees automatically have duties to their employer to not knowingly misuse or wrongfully disclose confidential information. These obligations are also often expressly confirmed in their employment contracts.

GPT should only disclose confidential information to employees or third parties where reasonably necessary, and it should ensure that recipients of confidential information know that it should be treated as such, imposing express confidentiality obligations wherever possible.

Processes

GPT should ensure master-discs are kept secure whilst in use and are destroyed or returned to the customer, as agreed, after replication has finished.

It should also ensure there is no breach of intellectual property rights such as copyright eg, using information from the customer to print for other customers (see 49.4 below).

GPT needs to ensure that the replicated discs do not fall into the wrong hands (eg, theft by staff). It also needs to ensure that wasted or spoilt discs produced are disposed of securely, especially those where the disc is playable but has been rejected for errors in printing or packaging.

This was generally well answered with most candidates scoring well. The problems of sharing confidential data with the Asian supplier and the IT risks involved were well considered. Most candidates made some sensible suggestions as to how these issues might be addressed. Better answers recognised GPT's legal and contractual obligations in respect of confidentiality and clients' intellectual property, and extended their discussion to encompass these issues at all stages in the supply chain. A number of candidates referred to the 3Rs of supply chain management (responsiveness, reliability and relationships) in their answer.

49.4 Packaging strategy (production director)

Advantages:

- Automation may reduce packaging costs and increase margins.

- Improved efficiency may lead to faster processing of customer orders and increased customer satisfaction.

- A new machine may reduce error rates and wastage.

- This would increase GPT's processing capacity and may reduce bottlenecks.

- The new machine is likely to be able to cope with higher volume runs.

Disadvantages:

- GPT are not operating at full capacity (see 49.2) – it appears the number and volume of orders rather than the manual packaging process is the factor that is restricting production.

- If demand for discs is declining there may be no point in increasing capacity.

- Investment may require significant capital expenditure and GPT may not be able to access sufficient funds in future.

- Automation may convert variable costs (labour) into fixed cost (machine) and hence increase operating gearing.

- Manual packaging may have given scope to fulfil bespoke customer demands; this service will now be lost.

- Automation will result in redundancies which will incur costs.

- The change of strategy may be negatively received by the remaining workforce (change management issues).

- Redundancies will affect jobs and livelihoods – historically GPT have wanted to support the community and this goes against their previous stance on corporate responsibility.

- Adverse publicity regarding redundancies and job cuts is likely to damage GPT's reputation in the local community.

- Automation will require training and could lead to some downtime during installation and commissioning.

Alternative revenue streams (sales director)

Advantages:

- Since the market is declining, GPT needs alternative revenue streams if it is to survive.

- According to Ansoff, this can be achieved by considering new markets and/or new products.

- There may be other markets where the industry lifecycle is at a different point and has not yet reached the decline stage.

- New revenue streams will give rise to a more balanced product portfolio and diversify risk.

- The education market may represent one of the areas where demand for discs is declining more slowly.

- The Alegre proposal specifically would generate incremental contribution and utilise some spare capacity.

- GPT could explore the possibility of producing own-brand versions by licensing IP from educational businesses.

Disadvantages:

- The IP for the Alegre revision guides does not belong to GPT but to Alegre.

- In theory the Alegre master-disc should have already been destroyed according to the contract which would prevent GPT producing the guides.

- If Alegre were to find out they might stop using GPT and sue for breach of contract/use of IP.

- This specific strategy is not ethical and could also be illegal.

- It may damage GPT's brand and reputation in the marketplace.

- GPT may lack the necessary competencies/experience, particularly for a diversification strategy that involves new products and new markets.

Conclusion

Whilst the purchase of the new machine might improve efficiency and reduce costs it does not address GPT's main issue which is that of lack of demand. The sales director is correct that GPT needs to consider alternative revenue streams. Whilst it does appear that GPT needs to do this to survive, the specific suggestion does not appear to be ethical and should be rejected. Further research needs to be done to establish where demand for discs is likely to remain and GPT should then target these markets.

Examiner's comments

Answers to this requirement were mixed. Often candidates produced a good evaluation of one proposal at the expense of the other. Many candidates identified that GPT were already operating significantly below capacity and that the production director's suggestion, as well as creating reputational and change management issues, would not help to address this. However it was surprising how many candidates failed to spot the ethical and possible legal issues associated with the specific proposal to re-use Alegre's master-disc. Only the better candidates extended their discussion to consider the sales director's suggestion of other possible revenue streams.

50 MHD (September 2016)

Marking guide

	Knowledge	Skill	Marks
50.1 Governance procedures	3	6	8
50.2 Sustainability	2	4	6
50.3 Monitoring performance	3	7	9
50.4 Ethical issues	3	6	8
	11	23	31

General comments:

This question was the best attempted overall.

The scenario relates to a charity, MHD, which provides services for people with mental health problems. MHD receives some government funding, but it relies heavily on donations and sponsorship. It has experienced financial difficulties recently and its cash balances are now very low. The chief finance officer resigned from the management team three months ago. The replacement, Jennifer Studley, wants to make some changes to the way MHD functions but she has encountered some resistance from the board of trustees.

Candidates were provided with minutes of a meeting between Jennifer, the Chairman of the board of trustees and the Chief Executive, at which the following agenda items were discussed:

Agenda item A: governance and the role of trustees

The current board of trustees have spent many years working together and there is little conflict in meetings. The trustees also make sizeable donations individually. The management team avoids risk, wherever possible, by choosing safe strategies. Jennifer has proposed the recruitment of some new trustees with a wider range of commercial experience who can challenge the way MHD is managed, and identify opportunities for innovation and development.

Agenda item B: sustainability and performance measurement

MHD has minimal cash and Jennifer believes it needs to access more funding to extend its services. It has done relatively little in the past to measure performance but now needs to demonstrate to fund-providers the impact that MHD is having in the mental health sector.

Agenda item C: adverse publicity about MHD's ethics

MHD has attracted some adverse publicity recently, in a national newspaper. The article expressed concerns about the ethics of high salary packages paid by charitable organisations, and in particular the recent pay rises awarded by MHD to its senior management. It also queried the aggressive behaviour of a professional fund-raising organisation, FundsForYou Ltd (FFY), to which MHD has outsourced its fundraising.

50.1 Governance

As a charity, MHD can be considered a not-for-profit organisation (NFP). The Nolan principles set out seven standards for public sector governance which the trustees need to take into account: (selflessness, integrity, objectivity, accountability, openness, honesty and leadership.) Some of these are discussed further below.

Governance is a term used to describe the trustees' role in directing the charity in the long term, including its objectives or purposes, implementing policies and activities to achieve objectives and complying with legal requirements.

The following are the main issues that MHD need to be concerned about in respect of governance:

Stakeholders and public interest

When MHD sets objectives it must balance the interests and concerns of a wide range of stakeholders, which may conflict. This may result in a range of objectives, rather than a single over-riding one. Given that MHD is accountable to a wide range of stakeholders, the trustees need to consider to what extent they are legally obliged to involve stakeholders in the objective-setting process.

The trustees' role is one of leadership. They must act in the interests of the charity's beneficiaries, but this may not always coincide with the priorities of the board and the management team or the wishes of any corporate sponsors.

Financial solvency

Whilst MHD may not have a pure profit-making objective, it will need to ensure that it has sufficient funds to cover its costs. In addition to its stated aims of providing services and support for a range of people experiencing mental health issues, MHD's trustees will need to try and derive maximum benefit from a limited amount of resources whilst remaining solvent.

Accountability and openness

This is fundamental to the corporate governance of the charity with regard to the proper stewardship of public and donated funds.

The trustees of MHD should be as open and honest as possible about the decisions and actions that they take. They should give reasons for their decisions and restrict information only when the wider public interest clearly demands.

MHD's Board must be prepared to submit to an appropriate level of scrutiny. This will lessen any risk of being accused of acting improperly. Vishal's comment about not upsetting the trustees suggests that there may not be a culture where the trustees can be challenged.

Actions/interests of the board

Board members must take decisions in line with the objectives of the charity and in the interests of its beneficiaries. They should not do so to gain financial or other material benefits for themselves, their family or their friends. Nor should they place themselves under any financial or other obligation to outside individuals or organisations that might influence them in the performance of their duties.

Those trustees whose companies have donated funds should not be allowed to dominate or unduly influence the decision-making.

The board should ensure that they have complied with the principles set out above regarding openness, honesty and selflessness.

Composition of Board

Whilst some stability may be helpful it appears that the current trustees have all been in situ for a while and are very comfortable working with each other. Vishal's point about the meetings being easy to manage and decisions being made quickly may not necessarily be a good thing. The familiarity among the trustees may have led to a lack of pro-activity and the close relationships may make people reluctant to challenge mismanagement for fear of upsetting friends/peers. Also failure to appoint new trustees means that MHD does not have an effective succession plan. The introduction of some new trustees with a wider range of commercial experience may, as Jennifer suggests, bring fresh thinking from different sectors to assist the charity and achieve sustainability going forward.

Risk management

Charities can face a wide variety of risks which could negatively affect their beneficiaries if not dealt with properly. A risk is any event that could prevent MHD from achieving its aims or carrying out its strategies. Risks for MHD include:

*   possible damage to the charity's reputation (see 50.4)
*   receiving less funding or fewer public donations
*   changes in government policy affecting income or activities

The trustees have ultimate responsibility for managing risk but in practice this is often delegated to the management team.

John Adams is incorrect when he says that the management team needs to avoid risk at all costs. Risk management requires the trustees/management to identify any potential risks and put processes in place to assess and manage those risks. Risk avoidance is one such strategy but risks can also be transferred (eg, by insurance), reduced (eg, by widening the sources of funds) or accepted.

Conclusion

The resignation of the previous CFO may suggest that there have been some governance issues or problems between the management and trustees in the past. MHD is in a difficult situation financially and is facing possible ethical issues so implementing more robust governance procedures may help address this.

Examiner's comments

On the whole the governance requirement was well done. There were plenty of points to build on in the scenario regarding the composition of the board of trustees, risk management and MHD's financial problems. Poorer efforts tended to overlook the nature of MHD as a charitable organisation or simply reiterated the views expressed at the meeting without further analysis of the implications for MHD's achievement of objectives.

50.2 Sustainability

A sustainable enterprise is one that takes account of social and environmental returns as well as financial ones. A sustainable organisation is one that has a long-term orientation and does not just focus on short-term results and measures when making decisions.

Financial sustainability:

To survive in the long term MHD needs to be financially sustainable and financial solvency is therefore a key issue in relation to risk mitigation.

Given the low reserves, MHD will only be sustainable if it has the ability to retain existing grants/sponsors and attract new funding. The better its reputation, the more successful its activities, and the more relevant it is to a wide range of people, the greater its chances of success. The development of some income-generating services that still meet its core mission might help contribute to the development of a diverse and sustainable funding base.

Social and environmental sustainability:

As a non-profit making enterprise, MHD's objectives will be wider than just financial and its goals will be externally as well as internally focussed. This will include taking account of wider stakeholders' objectives and meeting the needs of the mental health sufferers it is serving.

A socially sustainable organisation is one where decision making is linked to respect for people, communities and the environment. The nature of MHD's activities would suggest it is socially sustainable and the research it undertakes is a forward-looking activity. However MHD has a responsibility to continue to provide services to those who are depending on it. This responsibility can only be fulfilled if it is financially sustainable.

In the context of environmental sustainability, an organisation should only use resources at a rate that allows them to be replenished in order to ensure they will continue to be available. There is little information about the extent to which MHD is environmentally sustainable.

Conclusion

With low reserves and concerns about the management of the organisation it is questionable whether MHD is currently a financially sustainable organisation. This is a problem given the needs of the beneficiaries it serves and the fact that, should the charity become insolvent, a lot of people would be left without services and many people would lose their jobs.

Jennifer is right that MHD needs to address its financial situation as soon as possible.

Examiner's comments

Candidates seemed well prepared for a requirement on this topic. The vast majority of candidates had no problem defining sustainability in a general sense. Better candidates were able to apply this to the scenario, discussing what sustainability means for MHD and identifying that unless the charity addresses its financial issues it will not be able to sustain the provision of mental health services in the future.

50.3 Monitoring performance

The board needs to implement an effective system of performance measurement as this will demonstrate to external stakeholders that MHD's mandates and objectives are being met. It may, as Jennifer says, help MHD raise more funds. However the system for measuring must not be so complicated that implementing it is prohibitively expensive.

Key performance indicators need to be established, targets set, and actual performance measured and monitored for each of those indicators, possibly in relation to other charities engaged in similar activities.

However:

(1) There is no profit motive objective so many of the traditional financial performance indicators cannot be applied.

(2) Since MHD is a large mental health charity, it may be difficult to find other, similar organisations that can be used as benchmarks for assessing MHD's performance.

Value for money is a measure often applied in the public sector. This could be used to assess whether MHD is providing an economic, efficient and effective service.

Economy – an input measure. Are the resources the cheapest possible for the quality of service desired? Eg, cost of staff in residential settings

Efficiency – Is the maximum output being achieved from the resources used? Eg, £ of funds raised per £ spent on marketing

Effectiveness – an output measure, looking at whether MHD's objectives are being met. Eg, number of new research projects undertaken

Balanced scorecard

A significant number of MHD's objectives are likely to be of a non-financial nature and as a result the balanced scorecard approach to performance measurement is likely to be particularly relevant.

The BSC approach looks at four perspectives in order to provide operational control so that the organisation's mission and objectives can be met. These perspectives are financial, customer, internal processes, and learning and growth. They are balanced in the sense that managers are required to think in terms of all four perspectives to prevent improvements being made in one area at the expense of another. MHD can identify critical success factors in each of these areas, set targets for achievement and implement KPIs to measure this. These could also take into account any government performance targets.

Financial perspective

Here the financial perspective will be in terms of economy and efficiency: allowing the available resources to be put to best use to add value to beneficiaries, providing value for money for the fund providers.

Appropriate KPIs include the following:

- Average donations
- Growth in funds raised year-on-year
- Costs of providing individual services
- Cost control of care centres (residential and day)
- Level of marketing spend

Customer perspective

A not-for-profit organisation such as MHD needs to know what its users and beneficiaries feel about its services. MHD aims to provide a range of services and fund research.

Appropriate KPIs include the following:

- Service user satisfaction statistics
- Increase in number of service users and/or areas covered by MHD
- Number of research projects funded
- Hours of mental health services provided

- Waiting list of users requiring services
- Ranking in government or local authority performance tables
- Performance in inspections carried out by regulators

Internal business process perspective

This perspective asks what processes MHD must excel at to achieve its financial and customer objectives. It aims to improve internal processes and decision making.

MHD must assess how it goes about delivering its services and what impact this has on its effectiveness.

Appropriate KPIs include the following:

- Number of service users catered for
- Percentage of revenue spent on administration
- Percentage of revenue that is spent on the publicised cause
- Number of marketing/fund-raising events held
- Number of services offered eg, counselling, workshops
- Ratio of paid staff/volunteers

Learning and growth perspective

This considers MHD's capacity to maintain and grow its position through the acquisition of new skills and the development of new services.

MHD will benefit from learning from the past (both successes and failures), to enable processes to improve over time leading to improved user satisfaction.

Jennifer is keen to attract new funding and develop services, so this is a key perspective for MHD.

Appropriate KPIs include the following:

- Number of new services implemented by MHD
- Amount of training undertaken by staff
- New funding sources identified

The introduction of a new performance measurement system may create fear and uncertainty among staff since it raises their visibility and accountability. It will be important to implement an appropriate programme of consultation, communication and training.

Examiner's comments

Although performance measurement and KPIs are a mainstream topic it is surprising how often requirements such as this one are poorly done. There were two elements to this requirement: explaining an approach to performance measurement and suggesting some specific KPIs. A reasonable proportion of candidates overlooked the former, limiting the marks available.

Most candidates identified the need for non-financial KPIs and many predictably used the Balance Scorecard. However candidates often failed to explain what each area would be measuring in the context of MHD. Weaker candidates produced a bullet list of quite generic KPIs – the better answers identified critical success factors under each balanced scorecard heading and linked their KPIs to these.

50.4 Ethical issues

A key risk for MHD as a result of the newspaper article is that the charity may suffer long-term loss of credibility with fund-providers and volunteers who trust MHD to use their money or time effectively in support of its cause.

The first step in assessing the implications would be to assess the extent to which the newspaper article is based on fact and the criticisms levied at MHD are valid.

High salary packages

Assuming the charity has indeed given substantial pay increases, the issue here is potentially one of integrity and self-interest and links to the governance discussion raised in 50.1.

It is not unethical for charities to pay their staff or to give them pay-rises. Employees of MHD, as any other organisation, are entitled to be paid a fair wage for the work that they do.

In order to attract an appropriately qualified and competent chief executive MHD needs to offer a sufficient salary that is commensurate with the complexities of the job. This may have to be at a certain level to attract relevant candidates from the private sector (or to prevent staff leaving to join the private sector).

However it may be unethical for senior staff to be given large pay-rises if this is at the expense of providing more services or reimbursing expenses to volunteers. This is particularly true if they have not earned the pay rises or are deciding on the salaries themselves. The pay rises also come at a time when the charity appears to be struggling financially.

It is important that the chief executive and management team's salaries are set independently and that they are appraised on the extent to which the charity's performance and financial position has improved.

MHD needs to ensure that:

- it is transparent about amounts paid to senior staff

- all senior staff salaries are approved by the board of trustees

- salary scales are benchmarked against other sectors

- information is provided to all stakeholders about the charity's financial position and performance

Fundraising

All charities rely on donations to provide services and the more funds MHD is able to raise, the more services it can offer.

Key ethical issues are:

(1) the cost of marketing and fund-raising activities
(2) the amount of donations spent on the end-cause.

A specific issue here is that FFY are being paid commission according to how much money they raise. This type of pricing agreement is common in the private sector and it could be argued that here it is a good thing, since it is likely to raise more money for MHD.

However this type of approach may be unethical for reasons such as these:

- The charitable element may come second to personal gain so the interests of fund-providers and service users may suffer

- FFY staff may lack involvement and interest in MHD's purpose

- FFY may use excessive pressure on potential donors to maximise their own payment

In addition, as a result of behaviour or pressure from FFY, potential donors may become disillusioned and lose faith in the charitable cause, ceasing to support MHD in future. Since it is in need of additional funding to ensure sustainability, this could present a major problem.

MHD should require any professional fund-raiser to comply with the highest legal and ethical standards eg, accurately describing the charity's work and the intended uses of the funds, not being overly aggressive or applying undue pressure to potential donors, being honest about whether the fund-raiser will benefit personally from any funds raised, and to what extent.

MHD should also be fully transparent by reporting on the percentage of income spent on raising funds and administration. It will need to ensure that donations are used to support the published purposes of the charity and are in line with the purpose for which they are solicited.

Examiner's comments

Overall the use of ethical language and principles was not as comprehensive as in previous sittings with weaker candidates simply discussing the issues raised by the newspaper in terms of their likely impact on the charity's reputation and ability to raise funds in future. A number of candidates adopted the transparency, effect, and fairness structure but only the better answers went beyond this TEF framework to discuss any other ethical principles, such as the self-interest of the management team in taking large pay-rises. A surprisingly small number demonstrated professional scepticism with regard to the factual accuracy of the claims made by the newspaper. Some marginal candidates limited their discussion to that of management pay and failed to consider the issue of the aggressive fund-raising altogether.

51 Thistle Engineering Services Ltd (September 2016)

Marking guide

	Knowledge	Skill	Marks
51.1 Risks and mitigating factors	1	7	8
51.2 Forecasts	2	10	10
51.3 Structure of venture	2	6	7
	5	23	25

General comments:

The scenario in this question is a Scottish company which specialises in the design, construction and installation of storage tanks and high-pressure steel pipelines for the oil and gas industry.

One of Thistle's major customers, Romiou Inc (Romiou), is a global company. It has asked Thistle to provide it with services for a major infrastructure project outside the UK. Exploratory drilling has identified large gas reserves at a new offshore site in the Mediterranean, and an undersea pipeline is required to transfer the gas to an onshore plant in Malta. Initial industry research has indicated that there is enormous potential for extracting natural gas in the region. Thistle believes there is a strong likelihood that Romiou will be the first of many customers seeking contracts for Mediterranean operations. As a result, Thistle is considering setting up a new base in Malta and has approached its UK bank for loan finance.

The bank has asked Thistle to produce a business plan in support of its loan application, specifying certain sections that are required. Candidates were supplied with a summary of Thistle's most recent results and a brief three year forecast for the new venture.

Overall this question was the least well answered. Many candidates failed to present the sections of the business plan in a format that would be appropriate for the bank. Easy marks were lost by candidates who did not identify any further information required or state how each section might be useful to the bank's lending decision.

Business Plan for UK Bank

Subject: Proposed Maltese Base
Prepared by: Thistle Engineering Services Ltd
Date: September 20X6

51.1 Risks and mitigants

The bank is likely to want to understand the key risks facing Thistle which will affect the profitability of the proposed venture and the ability of the business as a whole to service debt. Where possible

Thistle should provide details of mitigating factors which will reassure the bank that the risks can be monitored and managed.

The risks and potential mitigants that should be covered in this section include the following:

- **Management team**

    A key risk is the fact that the management team at Thistle is small and only experienced in UK operations. International expansion is likely to take up a significant amount of their time and attention which may result in a lack of focus on existing activities. The business is heavily dependent on Joshua's knowledge, experience and contacts, though even without the expansion this may be a problem.

    Mitigants: given Joshua's age, a succession plan is required to reassure the bank. Tom has good sector experience and has worked in the business for many years. Joshua and Tom could divide up the roles (UK/International) between them and develop a management team underneath them to take responsibility for the day-to-day operations.

- **Uncertainty of demand**

    A lack of demand beyond Romiou's current scheme would make the venture unsustainable. There is also a risk that even Romiou's proposed exploratory drilling does not prove to be as successful as expected.

    Mitigants: the bank will want to see details of industry research and results of any exploratory drilling. The fact that Romiou has suggested a contract indicates the existence of gas may now be confirmed rather than speculative.

- **Competition**

    Thistle is likely to face competition from much bigger global engineering and construction companies and may not win tenders for other contracts relating to gas extraction in the Mediterranean. It is not clear if Thistle has experience of the production and installation of under-sea pipelines, or of international tenders.

    Mitigants: initial contract with Romiou provides a good base from which to expand the business. Also a number of Thistle's existing customers are multi-national businesses so there may be scope to get contracts from them. Using the Romiou contract, Thistle will be able to establish first mover advantage in the Mediterranean area.

    The patented pipe-wrapping system is a differentiator although this is more relevant to repairs and maintenance and may not apply to the construction of new pipelines.

    Thistle is certified as compliant with global oil and gas regulatory standards and is an industry leader in environmental aspects which should act as a barrier to entry for others.

- **Supply chain**

    It is not clear whether the intention is to manufacture steelwork overseas or to continue to manufacture in the UK and ship abroad. If manufacture is to take place in the UK then the plan needs to consider capacity and ability/costs to ship overseas. Currently all suppliers are based in the UK. The expansion to production overseas is likely to require the development of new supply chain relationships.

    Mitigants: some existing suppliers may be able to provide additional capacity for overseas expansion, particularly if they already supply internationally.

- **Labour force**

    The project will require new staff and the availability of competent qualified engineers for installation will be a critical success factor.

    Mitigants: staff may need to be seconded or transferred from the UK to support those recruited locally. The use of local engineers may reduce any language and cultural barriers.

- **Exchange rate issues**

    All business is currently conducted in the UK from both a sales and supply chain point of view. International expansion will bring exchange rate risk which Anya may not have experience of.

Mitigants:

- Hedging strategies can be adopted to manage the exchange rate risk.

- Agreeing prices in the local currency may be a better strategy if costs are to be incurred locally.

- Alternatively if manufacturing is to be done in the UK, using UK suppliers, then pricing in £ may be more appropriate.

- **Health and safety risks**

  A key issue for the industry is poor H&S performance which could result in fatalities or environmental damage. Health and safety/environmental standards in the Mediterranean may be different from those in the UK.

  Mitigants: Thistle is certified as compliant with global oil and gas regulatory standards and is an industry leader in environmental aspects.

- **Financial risks**

  The new venture entails additional borrowing and will increase the financial gearing of the company.

  Mitigants: The UK business has a good track record and comfortable interest cover (8.5 times) which reduces the risk of Thistle not being able to service the debt.

Further information required:

- Evidence of any market research undertaken by Thistle
- Results of any exploratory drilling
- Details of contracts with Romiou or other potential customers
- Details of existing loan finance and repayment terms
- Further information on key staff members
- Details on existing and potential new suppliers

Examiner's comments

This was reasonably well answered. Most candidates identified a good range of risks associated with the new venture. However weaker candidates failed to set out factors that might demonstrate to the bank how these risks could be mitigated.

51.2 Forecasts

> **Tutorial note:**
>
> The requirement asked candidates to consider the sensitivity of forecasts. This could have been done in a number of ways. Some possible calculations are shown below but candidates who attempted other sensible versions of a 'what-if' calculation were given credit.

The bank will want to understand Thistle's ability to afford the debt. This may in part depend on whether the new venture is likely to provide sufficient funds to service any debt, although the loan is to the company rather than the project so if the project fails but the company is sound, the bank will probably still get paid. Thistle will want to consider whether the numbers are accurate and have been based on credible assumptions and how sensitive the forecasts are to changes in key variables and to the timing of sales.

As well as providing a commentary on the expected level of profits, forecasts should give an indication of the best and worst case scenario.

Analysis of forecasts:

Appendix:

	Year 1 £'000	Year 2 £'000	Year 3 £'000	Total £'000
Sales	633	1,266	1,582	3,481
Sales growth		100%	25%	
Gross profit	190	443	634	1,267
Gross margin	30.0%	35.0%	40.1%	36.4%
Fixed costs	310	335	365	1010
Operating (loss)/profit	(120)	108	269	257
Operating margin	(19.0)%	8.5%	17.0%	7.4%
Annualised ROCE [(257 × 1/3)/425)]				20.2%

Sensitivity:

	Year 1 £'000	Year 2 £'000	Year 3 £'000	Total £'000
Break-even sales (£'000)	1,033	957	910	2,775
Margin of safety	(63.2)%	24.4%	42.5%	20.3%
GP margin required to break-even (FC/Sales)	49.0%	26.5%	23.1%	29.0%
% change in fixed costs to achieve break-even in Y1	(38.7)%			

Commentary:

Sales

Year 1 sales are based on the contract with Romiou.

Sales are expected to double in year 2 as presumably new contracts are won and growth is expected to slow in year 3. Average annual sales are £1,160k over the period which means the overseas venture would represent 17.6% of UK sales.

Gross profit

Gross margin has been assumed at 30% which is similar to the UK margin (30.6%). This is forecast to grow in year 2 and 3 due to economies of scale. The average GP margin required to break-even over the life of the project is 29%.

Fixed costs

Fixed costs are expected to increase over the period reflecting the steps in activity level.

At the assumed margin, the break-even sales for the three year period are £2,775k – giving a margin of safety of 20%

Return on Capital employed

Over three years the expansion project is expected to make an annualised return on investment of 20.2% compared to a return on existing activities of 22.5%. At a cost of £425k, the investment is likely to have paid back after 4 years

Further information that may be required:

- Sight of the contract or letter of intent from Romiou

- List of assumptions made by Anya when creating the forecast, including assumptions re exchange rates

- A more detailed breakdown of fixed costs

- Market research and other evidence confirming the likelihood of other potential customers

Examiner's comments

Weaker candidates either produced a narrative analysis of the forecasts with few supporting numbers or alternatively focussed on calculations without appropriate discussion. Only a minority of candidates considered the sensitivity of the forecasts, despite a specific requirement to do so. This could have been done in a variety of ways and candidates who attempted some form of 'what if' analysis scored well. Whilst candidates have become well practised at data analysis in the context of performance appraisal, in BS they are expected to be able to undertake data analysis in a variety of forms. Candidates seem less comfortable with requirements that involve the analysis of management accounting type data. They need to develop the ability to analyse and challenge budgetary assumptions and to sensitise forecasts.

51.3 Structure of venture

The bank will want to ensure that the business is structured in such a way as to minimise the risks involved and to allow the performance of the new business to be monitored effectively by management. It may also want reassurance that the new venture will not adversely affect UK operations.

Various options exist for the new business.

(1)   Run as a one-off project within Thistle
(2)   Set up an overseas division of Thistle
(3)   Set up a separate company (subsidiary)

If long-term demand is expected, a further consideration which will influence structure is whether to set up a manufacturing operation overseas or manufacture all steel/pipework in the UK and distribute from there.

Since it appears that the expansion is to consist of more than just the initial project, setting up a division or subsidiary is probably a better option.

A division may have less autonomy than a subsidiary but may be more appropriate if the manufacturing is to remain in the UK. In which case issues of transfer pricing and the recharging of central costs will need to be considered.

If manufacturing is to be undertaken locally then the new business may be better as a subsidiary, fully accountable for its own results and with the freedom to make its own decisions and create its own culture. Management and employees may also be more motivated under this structure as there may be less scope for the dysfunctional decisions that sometimes occur in assessing divisional performance.

Whatever structure is chosen the business will need additional administrative support in relation to:

- financial controls
- hedging of overseas transactions

The choice may depend on the size of operations initially. To start with it may be sensible to operate the new venture as a division then expand to a subsidiary if more contracts are forthcoming. By evolving the venture in this way, Thistle retains flexibility and reduces risk.

Other considerations that might influence the choice of structure may include local tax, local regulations, the ability to raise funds in future.

Further information that may be required:

- Exact nature of the proposed base (eg, will it involve construction as well as the provision of services)

- CVs of the existing management team and other key members of staff who may be involved in the venture

- Details of likely staffing requirements in Malta

Examiner's comments

This requirement was generally well answered. Most candidates suggested some form of divisionalised structure for the new venture and discussed the need for local knowledge and input in deciding the degree to which decisions should be decentralised. Better candidates discussed the impact that the choice of structure could have on risk. In their narrative, some made use of real options terminology and concepts to enhance their analysis, recognising that the expansion may be phased over time and that initial choices could be made to provide more flexibility as the market develops.

52 Pinter Shipping Panels Ltd (December 2016)

Marking guide

	Knowledge	Skill	Marks
52.1 Data analysis	3	17	18
52.2 Sourcing steel	4	11	13
52.3 Procurement	3	8	9
	10	36	40

General comments:

This is the mini case and also the main data analysis question.

The scenario relates to a company (PPP) which manufactures steel panels for the shipbuilding industry. Despite improved profits in the current year, there are some concerns about the sustainability of the company's performance given the volatility of steel prices, which is the major raw material.

A further issue arose as the sole supplier of steel to PPP has announced it will shortly cease trading. The PPP board has the dilemma of deciding how to source future supplies of steel and has identified two possible new suppliers. It is uncertain which to select, or whether to choose both in a multiple supplier arrangement.

A final issue is that one of PPP's customers, Tinner plc, has sent an email to PPP challenging its pricing policy in failing to pass on reductions in global steel commodity prices.

52.1

	20X5			20X6			Tinner % change	FMC % change	Total % change
	Tinner	FMC	Total	Tinner	FMC	Total			
Steel cost per tonne	300	300	300	150	150	150	(50.0)	(50.0)	(50.0)
Tonnes (000s)	30	20	50	26	22	48	(13.3)	10.0	(4.0)
Panels (000s)	120	80	200	104	88	192	(13.3)	10.0	(4.0)
Price per panel	200	205		180	190		(10.0)	(7.3)	
Steel cost per panel	75	75		37.5	37.5		(50.0)	(50.0)	
Other VC per panel (£s)	60	65		65	70		8.3	7.7	

	20X5			20X6			Tinner % change	FMC % change	Total % change
	Tinner	FMC	Total	Tinner	FMC	Total			
	£'000	£'000	£'000	£'000	£'000	£'000			
Revenue	24,000	16,400	40,400	18,720	16,720	35,440	(22.0)	2.0	(12.3)
Cost of steel	9,000	6,000	15,000	3,900	3,300	7,200	(56.7)	(45.0)	(52.0)
Other VC	7,200	5,200	12,400	6,760	6,160	12,920	(6.1)	18.5	4.2
Contribution	7,800	5,200	13,000	8,060	7,260	15,320	3.3	39.6	17.8
Fixed costs			9,000			9,000			–
Operating profit			4,000			6,320			58.0

ICAEW

Revenue analysis

Total revenue has decreased by 12.3% in 20X6, compared with 20X5. The causes for the decreased revenue can be analysed in terms of price and quantity changes. Alternatively, they can be analysed in terms of the revenues generated by each customer.

The overall volume of panels sold fell from 200,000 to 192,000 between 20X5 and 20X6, which is a fall of 4%. This overall fall hides a significant difference between the sales volumes to each of the two customers. Sales volumes to Tinner fell by a significant 13.3%, while sales volumes to FMC increased by 10%.

The cause of the fall in sales volumes to Tinner is likely to be a reduction in the production requirements of Tinner as there is a single supplier agreement, so there is no competition from elsewhere. Tinner running down inventory is an alternative explanation but perhaps less plausible given the extent of the change and the regular usage and scale of annual sales.

The cause of the increase in sales volumes to FMC is more uncertain as there is a multi-supplier agreement. This means it could be because of an increase in the production requirements of FMC. Alternatively it could be that PSP's pricing has become more competitive than its other suppliers this year and so FMC is purchasing a higher proportion of its requirements for steel panels from PSP in 20X6 compared with 20X5.

Another factor causing the overall fall in revenue in 20X6 is the reduction in selling prices. Sales prices to Tinner and FMC have been reduced by 10% and 7.3% respectively. A primary cause of the fall in selling price appears to be the significant fall in the cost of steel in 20X6 (see below). Since prices have fallen across the steel panel industry it is likely that rival companies have also reduced prices, even if the full extent of the steel price reduction has not been passed on to customers. The price to FMC might also have reflected changes in the £/euro exchange rates, although there may be have been currency hedging to offset this.

Cost analysis

Steel

Steel prices paid by PSP have fallen by 50% between 20X5 and 20X6 from £300 per tonne to £150 per tonne. This is a significant percentage fall, but it is made more significant by the fact that in 20X5 steel costs of £15m made up 41.2% of the total cost of £36.4m.

The amount of steel used in 20X6 was also slightly lower at 48,000 tonnes compared with 50,000 tonnes in 20X5. Overall, this meant a fall in steel costs of £7.8m which is far greater than the increase in operating profit in 20X6 compared with 20X5 of £2.32m (see below on sensitivity of profit to steel prices).

The fall in the price of steel was therefore a key driver of the increase in profitability, although slightly moderated by the fall in selling price that seems likely to have arisen largely from the fall in steel price.

One note of caution about steel prices is that they reflect the price under an annual contract with Coastal at 1 January 20X6, rather than the average spot price during the year. As such, they may represent the benefits of the contract terms and price movements in steel prior to the commencement of 20X6 rather than favourable price movements during the year.

Other variable costs

Other variable costs per panel increased for both Tinner and FMC by 8.3% and 7.7% respectively. Both increased by the same absolute amount of £5 per panel. These are fairly significant but any increase was more than offset by the fall in steel prices.

FMC has higher other variable costs per panel than Tinner. This could be because of transport costs to Italy.

Fixed costs

Fixed costs remained constant and hence were not a contributory factor in changing absolute profit although they create high operating gearing so make profit more sensitive to changes in sales levels.

Fixed costs have not been allocated between the two customers but have been treated as a lump sum cost for the company as a whole. Analysis of the two customers can therefore only be performed at contribution level, rather than an operating profit level.

Profit and contribution analysis

The contribution from Tinner has only increased by 3.3%, despite the 50% fall in steel prices. A key factor in this respect has been the significant fall in revenue of 22% arising from a decrease in both sales volume and selling price.

In contrast, the contribution of FMC has increased very significantly by 39.6%, driven by a combination of the fall in steel prices and the increase in revenue of 2% which is turn was driven by a volume increase of 10% that outweighed the selling price decrease of 7.3%.

The operating profit showed more sensitivity to change and increased by 58% due to the high level of fixed costs and operating gearing already noted.

Sensitivity analysis

Cost of steel per tonne	=	£7.2m/48,000 tonnes
	=	£150 per tonne
Operating profit	=	£6.32m
Increase to break-even is	=	£6.32m/48,000
	=	£131.67 per tonne
Break-even price per tonne	=	£150 + £131.67
	=	**£281.67**

Implications

The superficial implication is that if steel prices rose by 87.8% from their present level of £150 then PSP would break even.

This may appear to suggest that if steel prices in 20X7 were to return to the 20X5 level of £300 per tonne then PSP would make a loss. This may appear to represent a significant risk.

However this type of sensitivity analysis is univariate in assuming all other factors will remain unchanged if steel prices increase. This seems unlikely as there appears to be a strong interdependency between the prices of panels and the price of steel (as evidenced by the fall in selling prices in 20X6 and the email from the Tinner procurement director). As a consequence, it seems likely that if steel prices did increase significantly then PSP would be able to raise its selling price – assuming it is not tied into an annual contract.

This is not to suggest that an increase in steel prices is not a significant risk to profitability for PSP, not least because of an annual contract but also because the steel price increase may not be able to be fully passed on to customers in the same way the decreases in steel prices have not been fully passed on.

Conclusion

The difference between the cost at which steel is purchased and the extent to which this influences the price at which panels can be sold is a key driver of profits. The nature of supply contracts (fixed annual or contract by contract) is important in determining the level of profit, but also the variability of profit.

Other key issues include obtaining security of supply for steel as the main raw material. In this respect, there are trade-offs between profitability and risk.

Overall, the level of profit for 20X6 seems unsustainable as PSP has been favourably affected by steel price movements and contract terms that are unlikely to be systematically repeated in future.

Examiner's comments

The data analysis was generally well answered, with most candidates calculating relevant data and presenting their figures in a structured table with appropriate columns. Weaker candidates did not produce an initial table of calculations, but weaved occasional random calculations into their narrative which tended to produce limited answers with only partial data. Other weaker candidates mainly based their discussion on the figures already provided in the question, with few additional new calculations.

Many candidates tended not to perform a sufficient number of calculations. Many calculated steel cost per panel, but fewer calculated revenue per panel. However, a number of candidates failed to analyse the data more deeply, such as splitting revenue streams between the two customers.

Most candidates produced a good commentary on the data with a reasoned discussion of the issues revealed by their data analysis. Most identified the key drivers as requested, although not all specifically mentioned 'key drivers'.

Weaker candidates failed to structure their discussion sensibly (eg, revenue/costs/profits/ conclusion). Similarly, they failed to address the two customers separately – including some of those who had done so in their calculations.

Only a minority directly addressed the issue of the sustainability of business performance. Those who did tended to reflect only on continuing steel price falls, rather than the alternative possibility of prices rising in the future.

The majority provided a conclusion, although this was often very brief, taking the form of a mere unsupported assertion which failed to make reference to their prior argument.

52.2 The key factors are:

(1) Price
(2) Terms of contract (annual, quarterly, spot)
(3) Reliability, timing and frequency of deliveries.
(4) Other risks (eg foreign currency, security of supply)

Quality could also be an issue but as a commodity product this is assumed to be largely standardised.

The issue of multi- or single-supplier arrangement needs to be considered (see separate section below).

Price

It would seem that both prospective suppliers are charging higher prices than were offered by Coastal in 20X6 (£150 per tonne). However, the prices proposed by the prospective suppliers may be higher because global steel prices are expected to be higher at 1 January 20X7 than they were at 1 January 20X6, rather than Coastal being a lower cost supplier.

Lipp is offering two prices: a lower price of £180 per tonne for the exclusivity of a single-supplier agreement and a higher price of £190 per tonne for a multi-supplier agreement. This may be due to economies of scale in production, economies of scope in making deliveries or part of the negotiating stance to provide a financial incentive for PSP to award Lipp the exclusive contract. Given Lipp's difficult financial circumstances it may be possible to negotiate lower prices than those currently being offered.

Kerr is offering a price of £185 per tonne on 1 January 20X7. This is the mid-point between the two prices offered by Lipp and does not appear to depend on whether it is a single- or multi-supplier agreement.

Terms of contract

Aside from the level of price, a key difference is that Lipp is offering a fixed price for the year while Kerr's prices will vary according to the price of steel on a contract by contract spot price basis.

Also, Lipp's price is fixed in £ sterling, while the Kerr contract is denominated in US$. Kerr's price may therefore vary if the £/$ exchange rate moves, even if the $ price of steel is stable.

Any movements in the steel price or the £/$ exchange rates could be favourable or adverse for PSP on the Kerr contract, but represent additional risk. These risks could be hedged but this may not be a perfect hedge and there would an additional cost to hedging.

Hedging could be achieved by matching the nature of the contracts to suppliers and customers. The contract with the customer Tinner is currently on an annual basis and therefore matching this with the Lipp contract, which is also on an annual basis, would mean that there is risk protection from steel price movements.

The contract with FMC is determined on a quarterly basis which is not a good match for either the Lipp or Kerr supplies, which are on an annual and spot basis respectively. Thus, if global steel prices fall and PSP is locked into an annual contract with Lipp, FMC may still demand price reductions.

Deliveries

Kerr is a US supplier so the geographical distance in the supply chain is significant.

- The lead times and uncertainty of delivery time are greater if the geographical distances are greater, such as from the US. This is made worse if Tinner is demanding supplies at more regular intervals of varying amounts.

- Cross border supply chains may produce regulatory, cultural, exchange rate and tax problems.

Risks

Lipp in particular could cease production at short notice (as Coastal did), given the competitive nature of the steel market. This gives uncertainty over security of supply for PSP, which may mitigate towards a multi-supplier arrangement.

Multi- or single-supplier arrangement

If PSP has multiple suppliers there are a number of benefits:

- PSP can drive down prices charged to it by encouraging competition between suppliers who know that it has a choice of alternative suppliers.

- There is greater flexibility in that if steel prices rise and Kerr raises its price, then PSP can purchase more from Lipp. This is particularly the case as the minimum is only 40% of total supplies so one supplier could be favoured with 60% of purchases. Conversely if steel prices fall then PSP can purchase more from Kerr which will lower prices in accordance with steel prices using the pre-agreed pricing formula.

- There is greater security of supply in case one supplier ceases to trade. Given that Lipp has difficult financial circumstances, this is particularly relevant.

However, if PSP has multiple suppliers there may be a number of problems:

- Each supplier has a smaller income from PSP than from a single source supplier agreement and so may lack commitment to the contract.

- The cost of steel is £10 per tonne higher under a multi-supplier agreement with Lipp compared to a single supplier arrangement. Using 20X6 purchases, with 40% bought from Lipp, this would cost an additional £192,000 (40% × 48,000 × £10).

- Multiple supplier communications could become more difficult and more expensive for PSP.

- Reduced scale economies and economies of scope may increase suppliers' costs and may make them more reluctant to offer reduced prices in negotiation.

- Both of the potential suppliers will be new and therefore this may create some initial uncertainty and front-end costs in establishing new relationships and communications systems.

Advice

A multi-supplier arrangement appears to offer the best option in terms of flexibility (in allocating the final 20% of supplies to either supplier) and security of supply. The two different contracts (annual and spot) are together a reasonable match for the current customer contracts.

Given that they are both new suppliers the reduction in risk and increase in flexibility appear to outweigh the relatively small short-term cost advantages from a single supplier arrangement.

Examiner's comments

This requirement was well answered by the majority of candidates. Most identified many of the key factors relevant to deciding between the two suppliers. However, the quality of answers provided tended to vary in terms of how comprehensively each factor was addressed, which allowed some candidates to score higher marks.

Some candidates concentrated on pricing and contracts but largely ignored supply chain issues. Others did the reverse. It was surprising that many candidates did not mention price as being a factor in choosing between suppliers, despite different prices being provided in the scenario. Few performed meaningful calculations for comparison.

Also surprising was the fact that a number of candidates did not address the single- versus multi-supplier issue. Others restricted their treatment to a brief mention within their conclusion. Those who did cover single- versus multi-supplier issues tended to pick up on some key points, but often missed out on some relatively straightforward marks.

Most concluded that a multi-supplier arrangement was the best way forward, usually justifying this conclusion on the basis of risk management.

52.3 To: Ms Kelly Jones, Procurement Director of Tinner plc
      From: Assistant to CEO
      Date: 6 December 20X6
      Subject: Pricing policy

Dear Ms Jones

Thank you for your recent email regarding our pricing policy and delivery scheduling.

Pricing

PSP constantly strives to price its products competitively for our customers and to provide the highest level of service. We do so in competitive markets measuring ourselves against rival companies.

As I am sure you are aware, the contract agreed between our two companies for sales in 20X6 was an annual fixed price contract. This has the advantage for both companies of giving certainty of pricing over the year and reducing the risk of significant changes in the price of panels.

A consequence for PSP of an annual fixed price agreement is that if our costs, such as the cost of steel, increase within the year we would need to bear this cost and would be unable to pass it on to Tinner in higher prices within the year. We accepted this risk as the downside from our agreed annual contract.

As it happened, in 20X6 steel prices fell and we benefited from this as the upside of our agreed contract. We believe it was clearly understood by both companies that this should happen and there was no agreement to pass on steel price reductions within the year of our annual contract.

While the price of our panels sold to Tinner was not reduced in response to steel price changes within 20X6, it was reduced by 10% from 20X5, when the price was £200 per panel to £180 in 2016.

We would not expect the prices of panels to fall by the same percentage as steel prices, as PSP has other costs which have in fact risen in 20X6 compared to 20X5. Any price based on cost would need to reflect all costs, not just steel, which is only one component of cost.

The removal of annual pricing would create uncertainty for both companies and therefore requires more discussion. If we are to move to weekly contracts for 20X7 then the formula needs to be agreed to reflect not just steel costs but other factors. We sell to our other customer in a competitive market with rival companies and these market factors need to be considered alongside other factors.

Delivery schedule

We note your comments on the requirement for weekly deliveries and penalties. As a valued customer we will do our best to accommodate your needs but 1 January 20X7 is only a few weeks away so there would need to be discussion of the logistics while we revise our operations. I am sure that you understand that this cannot be achieved instantly. In addition I am sure you will appreciate that more frequent deliveries will increase the level of delivery charges significantly.

As our production facilities are located so close to each other, we believe we can provide the best possible service in this respect.

Conclusion

Tinner is a valued customer of PSP and we wish to continue to build our relationship and provide the best possible service at competitive prices. I suggest a meeting takes place to discuss further the issues you have raised.

With kind regards

Examiner's comments

The vast majority of candidates used a generally appropriate tone, language and style for a formal communication to an external party, although the initial form of greeting in the email was often much too familiar.

Many candidates failed to provide any resistance to the client's requests or justification for the current contract and delivery schedule, and simply acquiesced to all the customer's demands. Many failed to highlight the need for costs other than steel to be covered by the price charged, and also the fact that much more frequent deliveries would result in significant extra costs. Only a minority identified the nature of risk sharing in a fixed price one-year contract and that the steel price movement was a 'two tailed risk'.

At the opposite extreme, a small minority adopted a rather aggressive tone.

Better candidates produced a conditional response, weighted by recognition of the underlying issues and stakeholder relationships, recognising the need for further negotiation.

53 Zeter Domestic Chemicals plc (December 2016)

Marking guide

	Knowledge	Skill	Marks
53.1 First-year post acquisition review	3	10	11
53.2 Second-year post acquisition review	3	10	11
53.3 Ethics	3	6	8
	9	26	30

General comments:

The scenario relates to a manufacturer of domestic cleaning products, ZDC, which has acquired one of its distribution companies, Trann. The focus is on the post-acquisition period of integration of Trann into the ZDC group and the nature of trading and operating relationships between ZDC and Trann.

In the first year after acquisition Trann continued to operate autonomously with arm's length transfer prices. In a review one year after the acquisition, the board wanted to integrate Trann more into the group by: making it the sole supplier of distribution services to ZDC; requiring Trann to terminate its contracts with other customers; and reducing transfer prices by 10%.

In a second-year review of the acquisition, the finance director produced data showing that the financial performance of Trann has worsened, but the marketing director produced KPIs to show that service levels have improved.

There is an ethical issue relating to the chief executive who had not disclosed at the time of the acquisition that his niece worked for Trann. He is attempting to intimidate the marketing director not to disclose this.

53.1 In-sourcing all distribution services

The first decision was for ZDC to in-source all distribution services by bringing them in-house using its subsidiary, Trann. This is a form of vertical integration. The rationale given by David (the CEO) was that ZDC should not use the other two external distribution companies as there would be additional costs incurred.

While the other distribution companies will charge a profit margin in addition to costs, a similar margin would be required by Trann if ZDC requires a return on its investment. Using Trann may not therefore be a lower cost to the group. (See issues below.)

A key issue is that the change-over is sudden for Trann and may create logistical problems in adjusting from supplying many customers to supplying just one customer. There is therefore a serious question of whether Trann can immediately replicate the core competences of the other two distribution companies in terms of skills and assets (eg size and type of lorries) even though the deliveries are all for ZDC which is an existing customer.

Despite these transitional issues, in the long run the greater scale of operations may permit more efficiency and better utilisation for Trann, and provide a more coherent distribution function for ZDC with better interconnectivity of information systems for transport requirements.

Terminate the contracts with all other Trann customers

In deciding to source all distribution services internally, there is an opportunity cost from cancelling the other customers of Trann in order to create the required capacity. The opportunity cost comprises the lost revenue and lost contribution from these other customers.

In order to evaluate this decision the opportunity cost needs to be compared with any reduction in costs of using Trann rather than the other two distributors previously used. (This is in addition to any lost return on the funds invested to acquire Trann.)

An additional consideration in evaluating this decision is whether Trann could have invested to create new capacity and, as a result, been able to keep its existing customers as well as providing all of ZDC's distribution requirements.

Price reduction of 10%

In the year ended 30 September 20X5, Trann seems to have been operated as an autonomous subsidiary within the ZDC group. This would mean that its financial performance could be assessed largely independently from ZDC, notwithstanding that ZDC is a major customer, as transactions are negotiated on an arm's length basis, as they were prior to the acquisition, including pricing.

Similarly, in 20X5 the transport managers of ZDC appear to have been free to use, or not to use, Trann as they had previously. As a result, in the year ended 30 September 20X5, evaluating Trann as a profit centre, or even as an investment centre, would have been broadly appropriate.

The decision to impose a transfer price at 10% below the arm's length price previously set by negotiation significantly altered the autonomy of Trann management. This reduction in autonomy was reinforced by the decision to force ZDC transport managers to acquire all distribution services from Trann and to terminate Trann's contracts with all other customers.

As a result, the financial results of Trann would, after 1 October 20X5, no longer reflect the performance of Trann as the degree of financial interdependency between ZDC and Trann would thereafter be increased. By imposing the reduced transfer price, the recorded profit of Trann would no longer act as a reasonable measure of performance or means of control.

Conclusion

The decision to make Trann the exclusive supplier of distribution services and to impose transfer prices is likely to set up dysfunctional behaviour for managers in both Trann and ZDC as it simultaneously distorts market prices, provides dysfunctional incentives, damages control mechanisms and distorts performance measures.

The decision to terminate Trann's contracts with all of its other customers may be a necessary consequence of the in-sourcing decision, and thereby impose further costs. However further consideration could have been given to increasing capacity to enable existing customers to be retained despite the exclusive in-sourcing policy.

Examiner's comments

This requirement on the first-year acquisition review produced reasonably good answers by most candidates.

The vast majority displayed an understanding of transfer pricing. A significant minority identified vertical integration but fewer candidates displayed an understanding of divisional autonomy. The answers provided for in-sourcing the distribution and contract termination for other customers were of a reasonably good standard, although some weaker candidates failed to address at least one of these issues. Marks were lost by some candidates due to the fact they attempted to cover both issues simultaneously.

Regarding the relationship with Trann, most candidates displayed an understanding of the tensions between synergy and responsiveness in corporate structures. The better candidates related the discussion of in-sourcing of all distribution back to the original decision to acquire Trann. Most considered the synergistic benefits from integration. Many considered capacity issues.

The 10% transfer price reduction was often supported by those advocating the benefits of vertical integration. However, many appropriately considered the 10% to be arbitrary. Better answers suggested that Trann was now effectively a pseudo cost centre and so conventional profitability measures for Trann were no longer valid in assessing its performance. Weaker candidates struggled to get to the crux of the transfer pricing issues and instead offered some generic commentary on transfer pricing.

A number of candidates diverted into change management and, as a result, drifted away from the requirement.

Many failed to offer a conclusion at all and often, when it was provided, it did little more than summarise what had already been stated.

53.2

	20X5	20X6
Deliveries:		
For ZDC	4,250	8,000
Other	3,300	–
Average journey km	1,100	1,050
Total km	8,305,000	8,400,000
Revenue	£16,610,000	£15,120,000
Price per km	£2.00	£1.80
Variable cost per km	£1.40	£1.40
Variable cost	£11,627,000	£11,760,000
Fixed cost	£4,000,000	£4,000,000
Operating profit	£983,000	(£640,000)

NB uses data from both exhibits

Return on investment:

20X5	£983,000 / £7m	=	14%
20X6	£(640,000) / £7m	=	(9.1%)

Residual income:

20X5	£983,000 – (£7m × 10%)	=	£283,000
20X6	£(640,000) – (£7m × 10%)	=	(£1,340,000)

Finance director

The argument of the finance director (Lisa) relates to what she perceives to be the poor performance of Trann.

In respect of the year ended 30 September 20X5 she argued "the performance of Trann was poor in the first year after acquisition".

The above table shows that Trann made an operating profit of £983,000 in the year ended 30 September 20X5, giving a return on investment of 14%. While not as high as ZDC at 18%, it is above the cost of capital threshold and therefore reasonable (without adjusting for risk). Moreover the 14% is calculated on a fair value asset basis for Trann. It needs to be ascertained that the 18% for ZDC is on a comparable basis, as if historic cost has been used for the ROI of ZDC this would artificially inflate this figure.

In the year ended 30 September 20X5, residual income for Trann is positive at £283,000, hence performance is value enhancing for the ZDC group. It may be that improvements to performance can be made but, as it stands, based on the year ended 30 September 20X5 figures, the acquisition is having a favourable impact on the group value taking account of a capital charge for the funds invested.

In respect of the year ended 30 September 20X6, Lisa argued that performance "has continued to decline in the second year."

The recorded financial information shows a decline in operating profit in the year ended 30 September 20X6 such that an operating loss of £640,000 was incurred. This clearly creates a negative ROI and residual income.

However, as already noted, the profit of Trann in the year ended 30 September 20X6 no longer provides a reasonable measure of the performance of Trann in terms of its contribution to the ZDC group, specifically because of the artificial pricing imposed by the ZDC board.

The market price of the services at £2 per kilometre was in force in the year ended 30 September 20X5 and immediately prior to the acquisition when Trann was autonomous. The 10% reduction is a cost saving to ZDC and this is reflected in the ZDC accounts as a benefit, but in Trann's accounts as a revenue reduction, leaving the group unaffected.

If the market price is reinstated to £2 to show the value to the group of the services provided by Trann by adding back the 20p per kilometre, this would amount to additional revenue and profit for the year ended 30 September 20X6 of £1.68 million (£0.20 x 8.4million km).

The revised profit figure would therefore be £1.04 million (£1.68m - £640,000). In turn, this gives the following ROI and residual income figures for Trann for 20X6:

Return on investment:

20X6   £1.04m / £7m   = 14.9%

Residual income:

20X6   £1.04m – (£7m × 10%) = £340,000

Using these revised figures and therefore making comparisons on a consistent basis: operating profit, ROI and residual income have all increased in the year ended 30 September 20X6, compared with the year ended 30 September 20X5.

The finance director's assertion that performance has continued to decline therefore lacks substance. As the ROI continues to be above the cost of capital and the residual income continues to be positive, Trann is adding value to the ZDC group, even if it is reducing the overall ROI as it is below the 18% achieved by ZDC itself.

Marketing director

Professional scepticism should be exercised over the data provided by the marketing director as he is reporting on his own area of responsibility and was key to the decision to make the acquisition. Intimidation may also have come from the CEO (see below) which may reinforce the motivation of the marketing director to present favourable data. However the argument below assumes the data to be valid in the absence of evidence to the contrary.

The key argument of the marketing director is not to refute the data presented by the finance director, but to argue that the KPIs presented show an improvement (in the year ended 30 September 20X6 compared with the year ended 30 September 20X5) in the efficiency and effectiveness (in terms of pleasing customers) of the distribution function now that it has been brought in-house entirely.

In comparing the data of the years ended 30 September 20X5 and 20X6 it is important to note that direct comparisons about efficiency may not be valid for two reasons:

- A high proportion of the deliveries made are: different journeys; to different customers; in different locations. In particular, in the year ended 30 September 20X5 only 56% of the delivery journeys were to ZDC customers, whilst in the year ended 30 September 20X6 it was 100%.

- There were more deliveries and more kilometres covered in the year ended 30 September 20X6, so comparison of absolute amounts is unlikely to be valid.

Percentage of on-time deliveries – this has increased from 91% to 96%. As noted, this could be due to different customers, but is nevertheless very high in absolute terms and can be taken to represent good performance.

Number of customer complaints related to deliveries – this has fallen significantly in the year ended 30 September 20X6 from 184 to 163. This represents complaints of 2.4% and 2.0% of total deliveries in the years ended 30 September 20X5 and 20X6 respectively. This is a low percentage but more information is needed in terms of the seriousness of the complaints. A more valid like-for-like comparison would be the number of complaints from ZDC customers who had deliveries from Trann in both the years ended 30 September 20X5 and 20X6.

Percentage of full loads operated – the increase in the percentage of full loads from 44% to 56% is an improvement in utilisation and efficiency. However, rather than resulting from effective management, the concentration of deliveries to ZDC customers is likely to produce larger single loads and higher utilisation may be an inevitable consequence of this decision to have a sole distributor.

Number of delivery journeys made – the number of journeys made is indicative of an increase in scale arising from the decision by the ZDC board to have all its distribution carried out by Trann. Thus, while the increased scale and concentration may lead to greater efficiencies, they are not of themselves evidence of greater efficiency or effectiveness by Trann management.

Average distance per delivery journey – the average distance per journey is a function of the location of customers, given the revised customer base, rather than any measure of efficiency. The short journeys may however be a challenge to improving efficiency as the turnarounds at customer premises are more frequent.

Conclusion

The arguments of the finance director are based on the data she provided. When the data is adjusted there is evidence to suggest that the financial performance of Trann is reasonable and does not unambiguously support the director's proposition that the acquisition was a mistake.

The data presented by the marketing director is less certain and it is difficult to make comparisons of efficiency between the years ended 30 September 20X5 and 20X6 given the extensive change in the nature of the distributions made in the two years. More data is needed but there is limited evidence to confirm or refute the arguments of the marketing director based on the KPIs he has provided.

Examiner's comments

Most candidates correctly calculated ROI, but a large majority failed to perform correctly the simple calculation of residual income. Many candidates did not even attempt the residual income calculation.

The weakest answers simply agreed with the finance director's comments based on the ROI data, but then also went on to agree with the marketing director as well (who had the opposite view), often referring to the KPIs in varying degrees of detail. Reference was often made to the Balanced

Scorecard in this context. Only a minority attempted to evaluate the conflict of views or reconcile the positions of the two directors.

Only the best candidates performed additional calculations to revise the second year ROI by adding back the 10% transfer price reduction, in order to make like-for-like comparisons, thereby concluding that the finance director was essentially wrong in her evaluation of financial performance. This once again highlights a weakness in many candidates when they need to critically evaluate information provided. Too many just took the numbers provided at face value.

Some candidates mistakenly said it was not surprising that, for example, the number of customer complaints had reduced given that Trann now only had one customer in ZDC.

Overall most candidates scored reasonably, but only the best candidates scored very high marks for this requirement.

53.3 Ethics pertain to whether a particular behaviour is deemed acceptable in the context under consideration. In short, it is 'doing the right thing'.

In making any ethical evaluation it is first necessary to establish the facts. In this case, a conversation about a rumour is not good evidence that what was claimed actually took place. Moreover, it is not good evidence to present to third parties in the sense that David or Kevin could deny the conversation occurred. Nevertheless, it would be appropriate as a starting point to establish the basic facts of whether David has a niece working as a senior manager for Trann and whether she has been promoted twice.

The issue of legality needs to be considered in terms of directors' duties under the Companies Act and consideration should be given to whether legal advice should be obtained.

Aside from any legal issues, there are a number of ethical issues that arise.

The first ethical threat is a potential conflict of interest between David's duty to act in the interests of the shareholders and any personal self-interest to act in favour of his niece. If self-interest were to have overridden the company's interests this would be a serious ethical breach with potential serious consequences. The issue here is David's motivation for the supporting the decision to acquire Trann and his expectations of the benefits of the acquisition for shareholders at the time the decision was made, rather than whether the outcome of the acquisition turned out to be favourable or not.

A second ethical threat is one of intimidation. David could not have voted through the acquisition on his own and may have 'pressured' or intimidated Kevin to vote with him at that time. This may have affected Kevin's motivation and willingness to make an independent decision about the acquisition for the benefit of ZDC shareholders. A second occurrence of intimidation is now taking place by David attempting to suppress Kevin's concerns and thus avoid the possibility of disclosure.

In making a decision as to how to proceed, some guidance is given by applying the Institute of Business Ethics three tests:

- Transparency
- Effect
- Fairness

Transparency – whether his niece's employment should be disclosed (ie, made transparent) by David is a key issue in this case. David needs to bear in mind how people (shareholders, directors, existing customers, suppliers, employees) would react if they found out subsequently that David may have been influenced by the interests of his niece, rather than solely by those of the ZDC shareholders. As a minimum, David should have disclosed the relationship to the other directors at the time. The idea that he "did not want to influence the board, favourably or unfavourably, in the acquisition decision" lacks credibility.

Effect – whom does the decision to disclose or not disclose affect or hurt? Clearly if the acquisition was not in the best interests of the ZDC shareholders then share value may fall as a result of the decision. It is also possible that subsequent decisions favouring Trann may have been motivated by David's personal family interests such as the decision to bring all distribution in-house with Trann.

This would also have adversely affected the other two distributors which lost ZDC as a customer. In contrast to ZDC shareholders, the Trann shareholder group could have been favourably affected by the acquisition as they willingly accepted its terms, which may not have been offered in the absence of David's conduct.

Fairness – would David's non-disclosure be considered fair by those affected? Shareholders expecting directors to act on their behalf probably would not consider it fair to suffer a loss to favour David's niece. Also, in terms of the other stakeholders, knowingly not disclosing the personal interest may be seen as unfair and a breach of business trust. For example, the other two distributors losing ZDC as a customer for non-commercial reasons may regard the decision as unfair.

Honesty and integrity

Further ethical issues are those of honesty and integrity, which involve not just non-disclosure of personal interest but also hiding the consequences of, and motivation for, the acquisition of Trann.

Actions

Transparency remains important in seeking to make clear, if only in retrospect, David's personal interests and the risk that it may have influenced his commercial decision-making.

Kevin should approach David to encourage him to make full disclosure, initially to the board. If he refuses then Kevin should disclose the circumstances initially to the chairman and then the board should be informed. This should include the potential intimidation threats by David against Kevin.

The board should decide on any appropriate further disclosure (eg to shareholders in the annual report).

However, establishing the fact of the relationship with David's niece is not direct evidence that this influenced his decision. Further independent examination of the evidence would be needed surrounding David's support of, and rationale for, the acquisition.

The niece's two promotions could also be examined to ascertain whether they were on merit and whether David had any influence. However, this would only be indirect evidence that David's decision on the acquisition was influenced.

If the facts can be established, David should consider resigning and, if not, the board should consider whether there are grounds to remove him. If there has been a legal breach there would be an impelling case for David's removal.

Examiner's comments

Generally good answers were provided by most candidates.

Ethical language and principles tended to be used by a majority. Many used the transparency, effect, fairness structure, but weaker candidates limited themselves to this framework without using the scenario to identify further ethical issues.

The majority of candidates were able to identify self-interest and intimidation threats as two key ethical issues relating to the scenario. Only better candidates noted that ethical issues arose at two different dates: the time of the acquisition and the current date of the scenario.

Many explicitly considered corporate governance, but a much smaller percentage highlighted anything specific relating to directors' legal duties.

Weaker candidates tended to provide answers that showed little cohesion but made some valid, though random, points.

An area for improvement is the actions recommended as they were, at times, too simplistic or extreme (eg to resign as a first response) or failed to show a clear understanding of the situation. Some candidates only dealt with actions for either David or Kevin, but not both, as required by the question. Better candidates provided recommended actions for both David and Kevin that were realistic and linked well with the ethical issues previously discussed.

54 Hartley's Traditional Footwear Ltd (December 2016)

Marking guide

	Knowledge	Skill	Marks
54.1 Branding strategy	2	6	8
54.2 Pricing boots	3	4	7
54.3 One-off payment	1	7	7
54.4 Quality control	2	6	8
	8	23	30

General comments:

The scenario in this question is a company (HTF) which is a retailer of high quality shoes. HTF entered into a two-year contract with an Australian manufacturer of boots, ABC, for the exclusive right to sell its Ayres brand boots in the UK.

Initially, Ayres boots were low price and little known in the UK and sales were poor. However, due to celebrity endorsements they suddenly became in huge demand as a premium product. Sales prices and sales volumes of Ayres boots both increased significantly for HTF. The contract enabled HTF to continue purchasing the boots from ABC at the original low cost making the boot sales extremely profitable for HTF. However, volumes to be supplied by ABC were now to be restricted, thereby restricting the volume of sales.

Despite the success, the relationship between the core HTF brand and the Ayres brand is an issue, with a concern about brand conflict.

The original contract giving rise to the success is shortly to reach its end date. HTF now has a choice of whether to make a one-off payment to extend the ABC contract for one year, or to use an alternative supplier of boots from Russia. These are physically similar to Ayres boots, but do not have the advantage of the Ayres brand name. There are concerns over quality control procedures for supplies of the Russian boots.

54.1 (a) HTF v Ayres brands

Brands add value to products by making them recognisable and endowing them with associations attractive to the target segment. This ability of a brand to create future value is sometimes referred to as brand equity.

As a retailer, the HTF brand is a company name, associated with good quality products. This can be contrasted with the Ayres brand, which is the name of a product, but not of the company producing it.

A further difference is that the HTF brand is owned by HTF and therefore long term, while the Ayres brand is, in effect, rented by HTF as part of the contract with ABC, and therefore temporary. In this respect, HTF is unusual in not owning a brand from which it is benefiting.

Another difference between the brands is the difference in the underlying products (HTF shoes and Ayres boots). The brand image may further distinguish the products in terms of the celebrity, young person, fashion image of Ayres, compared with the more traditional quality, over 40s image of the HTF traditional shoes. This may cause brand confusion (see below).

(b) Benefits and problems of the association with Ayres

HTF is reaping some benefits from its diversification into a product with different characteristics from its core products. Favourable effects of the Ayres brand on the HTF brand include that, after the first year, there is a distinct upmarket image to Ayres with an even higher average price than HTF shoes. This may reinforce the upmarket image of HTF and establish both products as differentiated niche items.

A further favourable effect comes from cross branding with Ayres in increasing the brand recognition of HTF by exposing it to potential new consumer sectors, albeit that they may not be one of the original target segments for HTF.

There are a number of problems that arise for the HTF brand arising from association with the Ayres brand and brand conflict:

- At first, during 20X5, Ayres boots were being sold at £60 and were low price by comparison to HTF. While making an additional positive financial contribution it seems, based on available knowledge at the time, an unusual decision in selling two very different products, with different market positioning and different target consumers. Damage to the HTF brand seems to have potentially been greatest at this time.

- In 20X6 the price of the two products is much more closely aligned, even though the products remain different. There may however be further brand confusion as, not only are the consumer groups likely to be different between the two products, they are also likely to be different between the customer buying Ayres boots at £60 a pair in 20X5 and at £200 a pair in 20X6.

- Even at £200 per pair of Ayres boots, the brands are so different there may be brand confusion by customers as to what the HTF brand stands for in terms of values, quality and image. This may damage the value of the HTF brand.

- The association with Ayres may not end at the end of the contract but it may be much reduced and may not in the longer term be directly associated with HTF, as other retailers will in future be selling the Ayres brand. As such, the significant financial benefits may be temporary but the damage to the HTF brand may be permanent.

- The HTF infrastructure (shop fittings, staff training and characteristics) have been long established to service the HTF brand image rather than the Ayres image. The appropriateness of this internal infrastructure may have been compromised in actuality, or perception, due to selling Ayres boots. For example, staff may not be able to offer as good a service selling Ayres boots to a young person as they are selling traditional shoes to an older person.

- In 20X6, Ayres boots were the dominant sales item by sales volume. The HTF brand was therefore not so much shared with the Ayres brand as potentially dominated by it. This may change the culture of the shops and relationships with long-term HTF customers, some of whom, as a consequence, may purchase shoes elsewhere in future.

Examiner's comments

This requirement was well answered by most candidates.

The majority correctly analysed positioning for the two brands into quality and market segment, as well as making comparisons between them.

Benefits and problems of Ayres' association with HTF were also well considered by most, referring to diversification benefits and potential brand damage in particular.

Poorer efforts failed explicitly to consider quality and/or segmentation when discussing positioning.

54.2 A traditional downward sloping demand curve would suggest that a lower volume of Ayres boots would be sold at a higher price.

In this case, much higher volumes have been sold in 20X6, at a much higher price, for a product which is physically the same as it was in 20X5.

Although the physical product is the same, the perceived value to consumers of the product was greater in 20X6 as it was then a fashion item with an upmarket celebrity image. As such, the demand curve has shifted to the right so significantly that, not just more can be sold at the same price, but more at a higher price.

The price for HTF is also enhanced by the supply side constraint from ABC of 10,000 pairs per month. This means that price can be increased to the point where demand is reduced to 10,000 per month whereas, if supply was potentially larger, then market forces of supply and demand could have set a potentially lower market clearing price.

In terms of product positioning, there is a relationship between price and quality. It could be argued that the price-quality relationship has shifted against consumers by the price increase from £60 to £200 (see diagram below). However, it is perceived quality that matters and the improvement in image from celebrity use could be argued to increase significantly the perceived quality.

In this case, in the diagram below, the price-quality trade-off for Ayres boots could be said to move from **B** in 20X5, to **A** in 20X6.

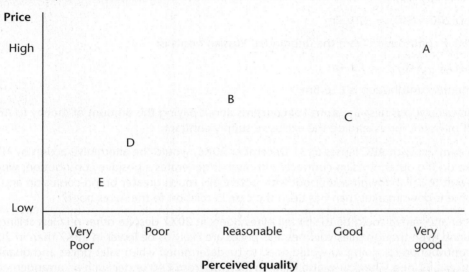

A further view could be to look at the change in terms of brand positioning. In the diagram below, it could be argued that in 20X5 Ayres was towards the top right area of the 'Economy brands' box. By increasing price substantially, but not altering the physical quality of the product, it could be that it moved upwards vertically to the 'Cowboy brands' sector.

If however quality is interpreted as perceived quality, then a more feasible and sustainable positioning is to move up into the 'Premium brands' sector.

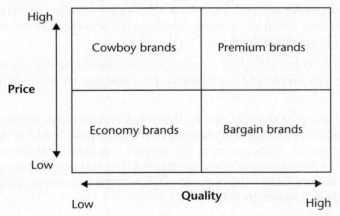

Examiner's comments

Demand and supply relationships were generally very poorly understood. Many candidates displayed a limited understanding of how demand and supply would interact to cause both the price and volume demanded to increase. Relatively few correctly identified the difference between a shift of the demand curve as opposed to a movement along the curve. Many confused a shift of the demand curve with elasticity along the curve. Better candidates noted the restricted supply of boots from ABC may also have resulted in a higher price.

Various pricing models were presented. The better answers focused on price and perceived quality relationships, relating this to willingness to pay. However, the concept of perceived value, while often cited, was often not expanded upon enough.

For many candidates, appropriate pricing models became a 'knowledge dump' with many providing discussion on as many pricing models and approaches as possible, rather than selecting those which were relevant to the scenario.

Few candidates mentioned anything to do with the brand positioning matrix.

54.3 The potential contribution to be made by extending the ABC contract is:

120,000 × (£200 − £40) = £19.2m

The alternative contribution from the unbranded Russian boots is:

120,000 × (£60 − £40)   = £2.4m

The incremental contribution is £16.8m.

These basic calculations raise a number of concerns about paying this amount of money to ABC as the one-off payment for extending the exclusive supply contract.

- If the contract with ABC lapses at 31 December 20X6, would the alternative action by HTF be to take on the other, Russian contract? Although it generates a positive contribution, would HTF want to sell a downmarket boot with potentially much greater brand confusion and movement downmarket than has been the case in relation to the Ayres boot?

- Another alternative could be to still sell Ayres boots in 20X7 despite other retailers selling them and even though sales volumes and prices are likely to be lower in 20X7 than in 20X6. The contribution for doing so would need to be determined when sales prices and quantities can be established. The cost is also likely to increase from £40 under such an arrangement. However the one-off payment would need to reflect that some contribution from the sales of Ayres boots could be made for HTF even if the exclusive contract with ABC is not extended.

- There is a suggestion that, as a fashion item, Ayres boots will have a life cycle and it may be starting to move into the downward phase of that cycle in 20X7. The above calculations assume that demand will remain at the 20X6 level, which may be optimistic.

- Even if demand remains at the 20X6 level for 20X7, the above calculations would not indicate the amount of the one-off payment to ABC for a one-year extension, as this would mean all additional contribution would be captured by ABC in the one-off payment, rather than being shared between the two companies.

- The above amounts reflect only gross margins. Any incremental fixed costs or other costs would also need to be considered in determining the final one-off payment in terms of marginal benefit.

- Aside from the amounts of financial benefit, the longer term strategic impact of extending the ABC contract need to be considered. There may have been some brand confusion over the two-year contract period. An extension of the contract may mean that damage to the HTF brand may become more embedded and permanent. The end of the contract is therefore a time to form a clear long-term strategy for the HTF business as a whole, including the image and the product lines it wishes to sell.

Examiner's comments

The qualitative aspects of this requirement were answered reasonably, but the quantitative aspects were very poor.

For many candidates, structure was again an issue, as many did not use the structure provided in the question ie, quantitative and qualitative factors.

Quantitative: this was poorly done. Only a minority made any attempt at any numerical calculations, and the vast majority of those who did simply failed to grasp the calculations needed.

Candidates rarely referred to contribution, mainly using the term profit. Some determined the contribution of £19.2 million from ABC's boots, but then failed to consider the incremental contribution relative to the alternative Russian contract.

Qualitative: this was better but still many failed to acknowledge the alternative Russian contract. The most common points identified related to fashion trends and maintaining exclusivity.

54.4 Given the nature of HTF's business, quality is a critical success factor. Quality assurance and quality control are critical to selling upmarket products.

HTF should establish a service level agreement with the Russian supplier, agreeing not just on the financial terms of supply but also on key targets/standards that need to be met and the consequences of not doing so. Any expectations that HTF has in relation to ethics and sustainability and the need for suppliers to conform to HTF's policies in these areas would also need to be set out.

Suppliers should be selected based on their reputation and the quality of their products. Clearly this would be a critical step in early due diligence, before contracts are agreed. HTF should carry out an annual inspection visit where the Russian supplier is required to confirm that quality standards have been met.

Once the Russian supplier has been contracted then a key control procedure is to measure and monitor supplier performance. Early detection of any problems is desirable but costs (both financial and reputational) are generally lower if HTF is able to prevent defective product rather than simply detecting it.

HTF should go through each stage of production processing to identify where factors exist that could influence either product quality or safety and then devise procedures that control those factors.

Quality assurance focuses on procedures and standards that will ensure product problems are eliminated or minimised during the production process. Quality control is focused on detecting defects in the output produced. In HTF's case this might include inspecting or sample testing boots that it has bought.

An information system can be used to enhance quality control, not just from the point of view of supplier control and monitoring but also for measuring HTF's own performance, by capturing a range of data (eg returned items and complaints from customers).

An information system can track performance over time, and may be useful in identifying trends or detecting early warning signs of future problems.

Measures might include the following:

- Customer complaints and returns per 100 pairs sold – this could be compared with HTF's own footwear and also Ayres boots.

- The reasons for returns could then be broken down as this will help identify and address the cause of the problem.

- These would need to be considered in relation to any agreed tolerances that have been established with the Russian supplier.

- % of boots not meeting quality criteria on initial goods receivable inspection (eg faults in manufacture or inferior materials used).

- % of boots not meeting specifications (size, volume, appearance, labelling).

- % of on-time deliveries.

Examiner's comments

Overall candidates did not perform particularly well on this requirement.

The majority of candidates displayed some knowledge of quality control but very few mentioned quality assurance. Where they did so, only a minority correctly distinguished between quality control and quality assurance.

Only a minority provided good examples of quality measures, and those who did tended to focus on customer-related measures such as customer feedback and product returns. Better candidates provided good examples of KPIs or other measures.

55 Ignite plc (March 2017)

Marking guide

	Knowledge	Skill	Marks
55.1 External factors	3	7	9
55.2 Product portfolio	3	22	22
55.3 Sales and profit margin/growth strategies	6	8	13
	12	37	44

General comments:

This is the mini case and also the main data analysis question. The average score was slightly lower for this question, due largely to requirement 55.3 (see below).

The scenario relates to a company (Ignite) which manufactures luxury cigarette lighters, and other types of product. It was set up when smoking was fashionable but has experienced declining sales as smoking has become unpopular due to changes in social attitudes, government legislation and technological developments allowing substitute products. Despite widening its product range to incorporate multi-purpose lighters for other uses and accessories, the company's sales and profitability continue to decline. Traditionally Ignite's products have appealed to a male market.

A history of developments in the UK cigarette industry and a graph of Ignite's UK sales of cigarette lighters were provided, together with key financial data for Ignite's products for 2015 and 2016, and a forecast for 2017.

The board is concerned that the forecasts suggest the existing product portfolio will not allow Ignite to meet future sales growth and profitability targets. The director of strategy has proposed various options for the future, including a lighter with a cigarette tracking app, outdoor camping equipment and products aimed at the female market.

55.1 External factors influencing demand for Ignite's cigarette lighters

To: Ignite Board
From: Business Advisor
Date: X/X/XX
Re: Product portfolio

The demand for Ignite's cigarette lighters is derived from the demand for cigarettes.

When Ignite was launched in the late 1940s, smoking was seen as fashionable and elegant. Over time demand has declined for a variety of reasons, with sales of Ignite's lighters falling from a peak of just over 1.2m lighters in the 1960s to less than 400k by 2015.

The various external factors that have caused this decline can be analysed using PESTEL and Porters Five Forces. Key factors are as follows:

Increased health consciousness (social factors)

An awareness of the addictive nature of cigarettes and health concerns has led to people cutting back on or stopping smoking. It also puts people off taking up smoking in the first instance.

Research (1960s) and health warnings (1971) have led to a decline in sales of cigarettes and hence lighters.

Taxation (political and economic factors)

From the 1990s onwards, governments have adopted a strategy of continuing to raise the price of cigarettes through taxes with a view to reducing smoking but also raising revenue to pay for the health costs associated with it. The increased cost is likely to have put consumers off buying cigarettes (a 10% price increase results in 5% reduction in demand) and also led to a drop in demand for lighters. This is particularly true during recessionary periods when there is increased pressure on disposable income.

Regulation (legal factors)

To address health concerns governments have introduced successive pieces of legislation which have had a negative impact on the image of smokers and the demand for smoking and hence lighters:

- Advertising and sponsorship restrictions (2002)
- Ban on smoking in enclosed public places (2007)

In addition to the advertising ban's indirect impact, it will have had a direct impact on Ignite's ability to advertise its own product/ brand. However the ban on smoking in public places may have helped make Ignite's windproof lighters more popular among those who continue to smoke.

Alternative products (technological factors, substitutes and competition)

Technological developments have facilitated the development of alternative products to the Ignite lighter:

- The introduction of cheap disposable lighters (1961), which were widely in use by the 1980s, can be seen to have had a significant negative impact on demand for Ignite's lighters, which almost halved between 1960 and 1980.

- e-cigarettes, first introduced in 2004, have seen almost a 300% increase in the period 2012-2016. Where consumers are switching to these for all their smoking there will be a negative effect on demand for lighters.

Summary:

The external factors considered have all had a negative impact on the UK demand for Ignite's luxury cigarette lighters, partly due to a reduction in the number of people smoking and partly due to the fact that many of those who continue to smoke are using e-cigarettes which do not require a lighter. Thus the decline exhibited on the graph is likely to continue and Ignite will need to look to international markets and/or other products to achieve sales growth.

Examiner's comments

This was well answered by the majority. Most understood that demand for lighters was derived from demand for smoking cigarettes and went on to identify several external key factors that had driven changes in demand. Many used PESTEL and/or Five Forces to structure their answers, thereby generating a better answer and ensuring a full range of points was covered. A surprising number failed to set their answers out in the form of a report.

55.2 Analysis of existing product portfolio

(a) Appropriate calculations

Appendix:

Analysis of historic and forecast financial information 2015-2017

Sales mix	2015	2016	2017
Luxury cigarette lighters	59.62%	54.00%	48.42%
Multi-purpose lighters	15.96%	19.00%	21.05%
Lighter fuel	15.02%	15.00%	15.79%
Lifestyle accessories	9.39%	12.00%	14.74%

Gross profit mix	2015	2016	2017
Luxury cigarette lighters	66.45%	59.92%	52.63%
Multi-purpose lighters	10.46%	12.62%	14.44%
Lighter fuel	7.78%	7.49%	7.67%
Lifestyle accessories	15.31%	19.97%	25.26%

£million	Luxury cigarette lighters	Multi-purpose lighters	Lighter fuel	Lifestyle accessories	Total
Gross profit margin					
2015	41%	24%	19%	60%	36.8%
2016	40%	24%	18%	60%	36.1%
2017	38%	24%	17%	60%	35.0%
Sales growth					
2015–2016	(15.0)%	11.8%	(6.3)%	20.0%	(6.1)%
2016–2017	(14.8)%	5.3%	–	16.7%	(5.0)%

Appendix: BCG analysis of existing portfolio

Product	Ignite market share	Market leader's share	Ignite's share relative to market leader	Estimated market growth rate	Analysis	Position
Luxury cigarette lighters	26%	38%	0.68	(5)%	Large share, low growth	Cash cow
Multi-purpose lighters	18%	22%	0.82	14%	Large share, high growth	Star
Lighter gas/fuel	11%	45%	0.24	2%	Small share, low growth	Dog
Lifestyle accessories	Negligible	n/a	negligible	12%	Small share, high growth	Question mark

A market growth rate of less than 10% is typically considered to be low, although this does depend on the type of market.

Positioning Ignite's products in a BCG matrix shows:

Relative market share

	High	Low
High	Star Multiple purpose lighters	Question mark Lifestyle accessories
Low	Cash cow Luxury cigarette lighters	Dog Lighter fuel

% rate of market growth

Ignite's products may actually be in a different position in different markets, for example luxury lighters may be a dog product in the UK but a star or cash cow in Asia. More information on the individual markets would facilitate a more detailed analysis.

(b) **Implications for future corporate strategy:**

Sales growth

The business has experienced a 6.1% drop in revenue between 2015 and 2016, and a further 5% fall is estimated for 2016–7. Clearly this means the Board will fail to hit the 15% growth target that it has announced to the market.

Cigarette lighters account for the majority of Ignite's sales, although for the first time in 2017 they are estimated to make up less than 50% of the overall total. This product is currently a cash cow, having reached maturity. However demand has declined as a result of the reduction in the popularity of smoking and the introduction of e-cigarettes, and it is expected to continue declining by approximately 15% per annum.

Due presumably to the popularity of outdoor activities, sales of multi-purpose lighters are increasing. However the sales growth of 11.8% is below that of the market (14%) which implies that Ignite has lost some market share and may need to increase its investment in marketing. The growth rate is expected to slow to 5.3% in the 2017 forecast.

Demand for lighter fuel is presumably derived from sales of both types of lighters, so although it has fallen by 6.3%, it would presumably have been worse without the increased sales of multi-purpose lighters.

The demand for Ignite's lifestyle accessories shows a healthy growth rate, and is the only one in excess of the Board's target. However some products eg fragrance, have been less successful than others. More information is needed to assess the sales and profitability of the individual items within this range.

Profitability

The total gross profit has fallen by 8.0% in 2016 and is estimated to fall a further 7.8% in 2017. The overall gross margin has fallen from 36.8% in 2015 to an estimated 35% in 2017, again falling short of the Board's 38% target. This reflects declining margins on both cigarette lighters and lighter fuel.

Margins on cigarette lighters are relatively high but are expected to continue falling as the market becomes increasingly mature. This is worrying since in 2016 cigarette lighters contributed 59.92% of the overall gross profit.

Overall the lifestyle accessories are the most profitable, with a consistent gross margin of 60%. Sales growth in this market means these products have contributed 19.97% of the 2016 gross profit and are expected to generate 25.26% of Ignite's profit in 2017, despite representing only 14.74% of sales. As demand for its traditional product declines, Ignite is becoming more dependent on the success of this product range.

Margins on multi-purpose lighters remain steady at 24% but are significantly below the Board's target of 38%, which may be over-optimistic.

The overall results for each product are an amalgamation of sales in different markets at different prices, and will have been translated into £. More information is needed on sales volumes, sales prices, costs and exchange rates. Information about the running costs of the business is also required to be able to evaluate Ignite's operating profit.

Risk

Currently the product portfolio is unbalanced. Ignite's business is over-reliant on cigarette lighters which make up almost 50% sales and over 50% of gross profit. This product is a cash cow but is likely to be nearing the end of its lifecycle: the market for the company's most important product is in decline and this is an industry trend which is likely to continue in the future. However there may come a point below which demand does not fall (a core of regular smokers). Identifying markets where Ignite lighters are still in demand, because a significant of the population smoke, will extend the life of the product. When these markets cease, there may remain a small income stream from sales of lighters to non-smoking collectors and to core smokers. Ignite needs to monitor the performance of its cigarette lighter range and pull out before/at the point that cashflows become negative.

Since a significant proportion of lighter fuel sales is likely to derive from sales of cigarette lighters, this interdependence increases the overall risk for the business.

To an extent Ignite have mitigated some of this risk by using the same technology for multi-purpose lighters, sales of which are increasing. This product is well-established now and although it needs promotional support, it is classified as a star and should present good prospects for the future as the market is growing.

The expansion in 2010 into lifestyle accessories has reduced the risk of the portfolio. These are expected to make up 14.74% of sales and 25.26% of gross profit in 2017. Ignite has a very small share of a growing market however and this is likely to be extremely competitive. Hence this product is classified as a problem child. Ignite has already been faced with counterfeit products which risk damaging the brand image. There is also a risk that the product sales are interdependent and that these purchases are being made because of the brand's historic image. If so, sales would be lower if Ignite withdrew its cigarette lighter product.

The products are very heavily dependent on a narrow market (males, aged 18–34) which again increases risk.

Ignite has reduced risk by targeting international sales – products are now sold in 160 countries. This helps reduce reliance on a single geographical region and also offers the opportunity to capitalise on markets where demand is at a different point in the lifecycle.

Conclusion

The Board is right to be concerned about Ignite's future profitability. Ignite appears to have under-invested in the development of new product lines. Until 2010 its entire portfolio was based on lighter-related products. Developing a wider range of products is vital if the business is to have a sustainable future. The existing portfolio is also focussed on a relatively small core market of 18-34 year old males. Widening the market of customers will also help increase sales – this should be possible for the multi-purpose lighter and accessories.

Examiner's comments

The data analysis was generally well answered although some candidates clearly mis-managed their time on this requirement as a whole.

Most candidates calculated relevant data for 2015-2017 and presented their figures in a structured table with appropriate columns. The vast majority of candidates also made a good attempt at analysing the product portfolio using the BCG matrix, although on the whole their conclusions regarding each product could have been better presented, for example using a table or diagram.

Weaker candidates did not produce an initial table of calculations, but weaved occasional random calculations into their narrative which tended to produce limited answers with only partial data. Another common error was not to calculate relative market share or for weaker candidates to assume that a relative market share of anything less than 1 counted as 'small' in the BCG analysis.

Many candidates produced a good commentary on the data with a reasoned discussion of the issues revealed by their data and product portfolio analysis, specifically identifying that Ignite's main product is in the decline phase of its product lifecycle. Weaker candidates, as usual, reiterated the figures they had calculated, without adding value.

The requirement had been constructed in two parts, asking for calculations first and then narrative using a given set of headings. A significant number of candidates provided an evaluation of the 2015-2017 figures using their own headings and then repeated something very similar, using the specific headings given in the question. This meant that they mismanaged their time considerably.

Few candidates identified further information that might be useful and only a minority provided a brief summary of whether the Board was right to be concerned about the balance of the existing portfolio and its implications for future success.

55.3 (a) **Calculation:**

£m	Target 2017	Forecast – existing products 2017	Performance required of new products (balance) 2017
Sales	230	190	40
	(200 × 1.15)		
Gross profit	87.4	66.5	20.9
	(230 × .38)		
GP margin	38%	35%	52.25%

(b) **Growth strategies**

Trackr:

Using the Ansoff matrix, this would be classified as market penetration or product development, depending on whether it is seen as a new product or a revamp of an existing one. Whilst there may be some demand for this product, it is still focussed on the declining market of cigarette smokers. The reputed 'health benefits' are likely to be small and Ignite may be accused of being unethical and damage its reputation if it makes too much of this angle for its marketing. This product is likely to have a short life-cycle. It may also be costly to produce because of the technology involved and there is no evidence that Ignite has expertise in this area. It may be better to launch this product as a joint venture with one of the businesses that specialise in fitness apps.

Outdoor range:

These products are more likely to be within Ignite's range of expertise. If these are targeted at the existing customers then this strategy would be considered one of product development.

However barbecues may also attract a new and wider market. This strategy is likely to be the least risky option and could probably be implemented fastest. However the current 'outdoor' multi-purpose lighters only achieve a margin of 24% so this range may not be sufficiently high margin for the Board.

Female market:

To the extent that Ignite already sells multi-purpose lighters to women, the sale of candle lighters might be seen as one of market penetration. Were Ignite to sell its existing sunglasses, pens and fragrance to the female market, this strategy could be seen as market development (a new target market for existing products). However if these products are to be radically different then the strategy could be seen as one of diversification (new products and new market).

The evidence to date suggests that Ignite's products have had limited appeal to the female market.

Although historically the brand image was one of elegance and glamour the existing brand appears to have developed more of a 'rugged outdoor' image, and comes with the negative connotations of smoking. It is sensible to attempt to widen the market beyond 18-34 year old males but it may be necessary to do this under a different brand. Alternatively Ignite may need to identify a range of celebrities to help promote the product and change its image.

Board's targets:

If the Board's sales growth target is to be achieved, new product sales would need to be £40m (see (a)) – the same level as those forecast for the multi-purpose lighters in 2017. This may be ambitious if the products have not yet been launched. The margin of 52.25% from new product sales also looks to be unachievable, unless Ignite is successful in introducing higher margin accessories for the female market.

Conclusion

In order to generate a financially sustainable business, Ignite should focus on changing the brand image from a lighter brand to a lifestyle and outdoor brand, and widening the appeal to reduce reliance on a young male market. In addition to considering new product streams, the Board should identify other geographical markets for market development of the existing products. The targets set by the Board for 2017 look over-ambitious.

Examiner's comments

Whilst candidates were generally comfortable with the discursive element of the requirement, answers to the calculation element regarding sales and gross profit margin were polarised, with many candidates scoring full marks but also a disappointing number scoring zero. Candidates are expected to have a degree of numerical agility and the calculation of target sales and profit figures is a basic skill that should have offered easy marks.

The requirement to analyse the three proposals for new products was well answered by the majority. Most used the Ansoff matrix to position each strategy. Better candidates went on to discuss whether the strategy was likely to be successful in delivering the additional sales and profit required by the board.

Many candidates who had mismanaged their time on requirement 55.2 gave a truncated answer to this part of the question.

56 Eclo Ltd (March 2017)

Marking guide

	Knowledge	Skill	Marks
56.1 Organisational structure	2	5	7
56.2 Control procedures	2	8	9
56.3 Strategic and financial considerations	3	10	12
56.4 Ethical issues	2	7	8
	9	30	36

General comments:

The scenario relates to a manufacturer of environmentally friendly corporate clothing. Eclo is a small company, set up by entrepreneur Eve Carter, with a relatively flat organisational structure. Eclo's products are produced and printed in India, where Eclo has strategic partnerships with a few key suppliers. Sustainability is key to the ethos of the company.

Due to some issues with quality, Eclo's is now considering bringing its supply chain back to the UK and possibly setting up an in-house printing facility, although this would require an additional equity investor.

There is an ethical issue relating to the contamination of a river by one of Eclo's suppliers, although this apparently occurred whilst the supplier was producing goods for another business. The supplier has informed Eclo that it intends to make a public announcement. However Eclo's marketing manager has suggested that Eclo makes its own announcement before the supplier has a chance to do so, denying any involvement and naming the other business involved.

56.1 Structure

Eclo currently appears to have a simple structure. It is a small business which is relatively young and the organisation is very flat: Eve the entrepreneur sits at the top with a wide span of control and the rest of the employees are encouraged to participate in decisions. As the organisation grows, this structure may become less flexible if all decisions have to go through Eve.

According to Mintzberg's theory of organisational forms, Eclo seems to fit with the adhocracy/innovative configuration. Eve the entrepreneur sits at the strategic apex with the operating core as the key building block, likely to be coordinated by mutual adjustment.

There is little formalisation (absence of technostructure) and no layer of middle management (middle line). This means the organisation is flexible and quick to adapt/innovate but it may limit the scope for expansion.

An alternative model is that of the flexible firm or, according to Handy, the shamrock organisation – a core of essential workers supported by a contractual fringe of external providers (the strategic partnerships with suppliers and the agent in India). This sees Eclo as an organic organisation which can respond to changing circumstances and evolve incrementally. For example if the new printing app is introduced, Eclo will subcontract some of the printing tasks to its customers (as the fourth part of the shamrock).

Modern businesses are developing along the lines of the boundary-less/borderless structure.

There is some evidence of this at Eclo:

- Collaborative approach with suppliers
- Outsource non-value added activities
- Outsource some operations to specialists
- Offshore some elements of process to different countries

Overall Eclo appears to have a reasonably flexible structure. The relatively informal, fluid approach reflects the values and behaviour of Eve at the top of the organisation (social entrepreneur). Should Eclo take on a new investor, this may change the structure as they may want a different approach. As the business grows it may need some more formal mechanism for control over finances, and more people responsible for customer relationships.

Examiner's comments

The requirement on structure produced good answers from most candidates, with many referring to models such as Handy's shamrock and Mintzberg. Some candidates also identified the elements of Eclo's structure that reflect the newer types of flexible organisation. The weakest answers tended to discuss Eclo's flat, entrepreneurial structure but not go beyond this.

56.2 Control procedures

The ethos of Eclo is that of a social enterprise. Its own ethos is one of sustainability and it targets organisations that have created brands based on sustainability. In a wider context sustainability does not just address environmental issues but also economic and social sustainability, so would encompass long-term financial stability, working conditions and fair treatment of suppliers, among other things.

Ensuring that all elements of the supply chain reflect Eclo's brand ethos is critical as there is a big reputational risk if they do not. Eclo can achieve this by working in partnership with suppliers, making sure suppliers are treated fairly and that contract terms are transparent and fair to both parties. For long-term sustainability Eclo needs to pay suppliers enough so their businesses are economically sustainable (although suppliers may have other customers/economic relationships and therefore may not be entirely reliant on Eclo).

To ensure suppliers are compliant with Eclo's sustainability approach:

- Eclo should undertake appropriate due diligence on suppliers - quality assurance and quality control are critical to ensure sustainability compliance so Eclo should seek assurances that suppliers are also firms with an ethically sound CSR policy.

- There may be reputational and other penalties if Eclo advertises products as organic/sustainable when they are not. Also a key marketing message is that every Eclo product can be traced back to its origins. Eclo must ensure that suppliers are able to produce this information for its simple eco-labelling system and that it is verifiable.

- In developing its relationship with suppliers, Eclo should instigate a service level agreement, agreeing not just on the financial terms of supply but also on key targets/standards that need to be met and the consequences of not doing so. Any expectations that Eclo has in relation to ethics and sustainability and the need for suppliers to conform to Eclo's policies in these areas would need to be set out. Aside from product quality, other aspects that Eclo should consider are processes to ensure that health and safety is maintained at the highest standards and that suppliers promote diversity and equal opportunity, providing fair pay and benefits for all workers.

- Suppliers should be selected based on their experience and the quality of their products. Clearly verifying a supplier's certification and credentials would be a critical step in early due diligence, before contracts are agreed. Eclo should arrange for an annual inspection visit where the supplier is required to confirm that all Eclo's standards have been met. This could be undertaken by a third party agent.

- Once a supplier has been contracted then a key control procedure is to measure and monitor supplier performance for prevention and early detection of problems.

Monitoring the quality of output:

This is critical as there have been an increasing number of client complaints about product quality and errors in printing. Eclo has also experienced delays between client order and delivery.

- Eclo should go through each stage of the production process, to identify where factors exist that could influence product quality and then devise procedures that control those factors. Quality assurance focuses on procedures and standards that will ensure product problems are eliminated or minimised during the production process. In Eclo's case this might include inspecting or sample testing fabrics and dyes before using them in production, so that any traces of toxic materials would be identified.

- Quality control is associated with checking a product after it has been produced and this might involve sample testing garments from every supplier. Even if there are no toxic/ non-organic issues, checking is still a good idea to ensure consistency of the quality of the product over time.

- An information system can be used to track performance over time, and may be useful in identifying trends or detecting early warning signs of future problems. It also provides Eclo with evidence for its own eco-friendly certification and in relation to supplier performance when discussing or renewing contracts with suppliers. Eclo could monitor areas such as quality of service (e.g the percentage of deliveries received on time) and the level of customer complaints/returns.

After a couple of recent sittings where the topics of sustainability and control procedures were not always well done, it was nice to see that the vast majority of candidates were well-prepared for this requirement. The candidates whose answers covered both quality assurance (linked to sustainability) and quality control (linked to output) tended to score higher marks.

56.3 Bringing some/all operations back to the UK

There are two issues:

(a) whether to use UK suppliers instead of Indian suppliers; and
(b) whether to bring printing in-house

Strategic considerations:

(a) In relation to Indian vs UK suppliers

Key considerations in supply chain management are responsiveness, reliability and relationships. As far as relationships are concerned, Eclo currently has partnerships with three Indian garment suppliers and an Indian printing company. This may be consistent with the ethos of a sustainable enterprise and a circular economy – providing jobs and returning income to the economies where the raw materials are sourced. Eve should consider to what extent this has been part of Eclo's marketing strategy as there may be reputational damage if contracts with Indian suppliers are terminated.

However there have been issues with the Indian suppliers in relation to quality (reliability) and lead times (responsiveness) which are affecting customer service. The issue of delays may be reduced if suppliers are in the UK rather than India as the speed of supply should increase. However raw materials may need to be imported into the UK, in which case the delay may simply be transferred to an earlier point in the supply chain.

Political and cultural risks relating to overseas operations will be reduced if the supply chain is brought back to the UK. However relationships would need to be established with a range of new UK suppliers and Eclo's bargaining power may be limited if it is small relative to potential suppliers. The issue of quality control will remain, although the lack of language barriers and the proximity of supplier locations may make it easier to undertake test visits and ensure adherence to standards if UK suppliers are used.

(b) In relation to a decision to bring printing activities in-house:

Eclo has limited direct experience of printing and an outsourced company will have greater expertise. An outsourcing model also allows Eve to focus on what she is best at (design) and makes best use of her skills.

An outsourcing model for printing allows greater flexibility (expansion/contraction) and shares risk. For a small business like Eclo it increases the scaleability of the business model – which is particularly important if there is rapid growth. Eclo's structure (see 56.1) is one of a flexible business/network and bringing activities in-house will move away from this.

However the downside of continuing to outsource printing is the possible issue of lack of control over standards and quality. There is an option to establish a printing facility in a nearby factory unit. If the printing errors in India have been ongoing and are indicative of poor supplier performance then this may be a sensible opportunity. Eclo will be able to control quality and ensure processes are sustainable.

Since Eclo's strategy is based on customisation of the garment, to the extent that this takes place at the printing stage it may be sensible to bring it in-house as a core added value activity, rather than use a supplier which also works for competitors.

The facility to allow clients to create their own designs via an app may help Eclo increase sales (although it is possible that this could still be done using an external printing supplier).

Financial considerations:

(a) In relation to Indian vs UK suppliers

More information is needed about the relative costs of UK/Indian suppliers. The garments may be more expensive to manufacture in the UK. However the increased cost of manufacture may be offset by reductions in transport and distribution costs and the profit margins paid to the third party agent and suppliers.

The decision to use UK-based suppliers only would remove exchange rate risk for Eclo and transfer it to each UK supplier which is importing the materials (although this may be reflected in the cost of the garment to Eclo).

(b) In relation to a decision to bring printing activities in-house:

The current arrangement keeps printing costs variable and reduces operating gearing. An in-house printing facility will convert variable costs to fixed costs and potentially raise the break-even point.

Currently financial risk is reduced by not committing to the expense of a printing facility. However Investment in a printing facility requires relatively small investment (£100,000) and if a suitable equity investor can be found, this may be a good first step.

Eve needs to consider whether an investor can be found who would support the ethos of the business.

Conclusion

Eclo is a small company. A sensible transition approach may be to evaluate the Indian suppliers, then to identify a suitable UK-based garment supplier and use them in conjunction with the better performing Indian suppliers. A cost benefit analysis should be done of the in-house printing facility. If a suitable equity investor can be found, a UK- based garment supplier may facilitate the strategy of allowing customers to create and print their own designs, as it will increase the speed to market.

Examiner's comments

Overall most candidates scored reasonably, but only the best candidates scored very high marks for this requirement. The question asked for the strategic and financial considerations relating to two different issues – (a) bringing the supply chain back to the UK and (b) bringing printing in-house. Typically weaker candidates let themselves down by not considering all four elements or by producing imbalanced answers. Few candidates scored full marks on this requirement. This was often due to discussing supply chain management using a common sense approach which, whilst scoring reasonably well, did not demonstrate some key areas of technical knowledge such as the relative risk of international vs domestic operations and the impact on financial and operating gearing.

56.4 Ethical issues

Ethics pertains to whether a particular behaviour is deemed acceptable in the context under consideration. In short, it is 'doing the right thing'.

There are two ethical issues to consider here:

(a) The contamination of the river by wastewater from the supplier
(b) The marketing manager's suggestion regarding the way this should be dealt with

In making any ethical evaluation it is first necessary to establish the facts concerning the original incident.

It appears reasonably certain that one of Eclo's Indian suppliers, AMG, has discharged damaging wastewater into the river, which may be illegal. The uncertainty surrounds whether Eclo has any responsibility for this – the supplier appears to be saying that it does not.

A key question here is whether there is an ethical obligation on Eclo to be aware of all activities at the supplier or just those involving its own production processes and products.

Even though Eclo may not have had any involvement, its reputation may be damaged by association with AMG when the incident comes to light. However AMG appears to be intending to deal with the problem in an open and transparent way and to make good its fault. Assuming the contamination is an accident, it is not necessarily indicative of deliberately unethical behaviour on the part of the supplier.

There are two elements to the marketing manager's proposal.

Depending on the terms of the supplier contract, Eclo may be within its rights to cancel all orders with AMG, although this may be seen as unfair/unethical if it results in job losses for local workers without any notice.

The proposal to release confidential information to the market, which AMG has supplied in good faith, implies a lack of personal ethics on the marketing manager's part, since this is a breach of confidentiality. Also the issue of legality needs to be considered and legal advice taken. Eclo does not know for certain that the high-fashion retailer is responsible and could face legal action if it states this publically.

In making a decision as to how to proceed, the Institute of Business Ethics three tests:

- Transparency
- Effect
- Fairness

could also be applied.

Transparency – AMG's intention to make an announcement suggests it is dealing with the incident in a transparent manner. If this is the case, there may be no need for Eclo to pre-empt AMG's statement.

Effect – an earlier announcement by Eclo and any termination of the supply contract would have a detrimental effect on AMG's business and its employees. This is not in keeping with the concept of sustainability.

Fairness – the marketing manager's suggestion to allocate blame away from Eclo may be unfair to the high-fashion retailer, particularly given that Eclo may not yet have all the facts and AMG has provided this information in confidence.

Actions

Eclo should be guided by any legal advice.

The most reasonable action would appear to be to draft a statement that can be released at the same time as or soon after AMG publicises its apology.

Rather than terminating the supply contract, which would compound the supplier's problems, if Eclo has a long-standing relationship with AMG then it might take steps to help the company identify the problems in its processes and implement control procedures to prevent this happening again.

The marketing manager's suggestion to make an advance statement is unethical and this should not happen. Eve should discuss the inappropriateness of this suggestion with the manager, and consider whether there is a good fit between the manager's values and those of Eclo as a social enterprise.

Examiner's comments

This requirement was very well attempted by most candidates. The majority of candidates were able to identify that there were really two key ethical issues in the scenario – the first being the contamination of the river by the supplier and the second relating to the proposed announcement by the marketing manager.

Many candidates recognised that ethically the supplier is proposing to do the right thing by making an open and honest apology and offering compensation. The less clear issue is whether there is a public interest argument for Eclo making an announcement before the supplier has a chance to do so, and what the marketing manager's motives are for suggesting that Eclo breaches confidentiality by naming and shaming the other business involved.

Ethical language and principles tended to be used by a majority. Many used the transparency, effect, fairness structure, but weaker candidates limited themselves to this framework without using the scenario to identify further ethical issues, such as confidentiality. Weaker candidates tended to provide answers that showed little cohesion but made some valid, though random, points.

It is encouraging that more candidates seem to have developed the ability to provide recommended actions that are realistic and linked well with the ethical issues previously discussed.

57 Gighay Ltd (March 2017)

Marking guide

	Knowledge	Skill	Marks
57.1 Outsouricng and KPIs	3	9	11
57.2 Data analytics and competitive advantage, and big data strategy	2	8	9
	5	17	20

General comments:

The scenario in this question is a company (Gighay) which provides IT services. Information was provided about two potential clients.

The first client Oxna, a publishing business, has limited in-house IT expertise and, in view of recent cyber-security issues, is considering whether to outsource management of all its IT needs to Gighay. The second client, Feltar, sells speciality coffee and the managing director wants to understand more about how the company could capture and use data for competitive advantage.

57.1 Benefits and problems for Oxna of outsourcing IT

Benefits:

- Outsourcing services to Gighay provides Oxna with greater flexibility which is especially important if Oxna is growing rapidly and its IT requirements are changing.

- This is likely to result in reduced service and support costs as Gighay is likely to have better purchasing power and will benefit from economies of scale. It also allows Oxna to budget more predictably.

- Oxna will benefit from better quality of service, fewer IT failures and less downtime. This is important given the recent server crashes.

- Oxna does not have a core competence in IT. It will get access to accredited technical expertise and a wide range of skills without having to train its own staff. There is also a reduced risk of an in-house IT specialist leaving the company and taking their knowledge with them.

- Gighay provides round-the-clock access to a 24-hour support desk that can resolve problems for staff remotely and rapidly, whatever the time of day or their location. This is critical given that Oxna's remote employees need to connect 24 hours a day. It should also help reduce the need for costly emergency support.

- Oxna has experienced a recent cyber-security issue. Gighay will have access to the latest applications and hardware and will be better placed to ensure security of systems and data and prevent such attacks in future. An outsourcing agreement helps to transfer the risk and responsibility for dealing with problems to Gighay.

- Oxna gains access to consultancy advice on other IT issues

Problems:

- Oxna will have to trust Gighay with potentially confidential information about its business.

- If IT services are out-sourced it will be very difficult to bring them back in-house at a later date.

- Oxna may become very dependent on Gighay and find it difficult to switch IT supplier in the event that Gighay increases its prices in future or Oxna becomes unhappy with the service.

- Outsourcing does not necessarily prevent a cyber-security attack occurring although it may reduce the financial consequences.

- Gighay's particular expertise is in data capture and data analytics which are not services that Oxna requires.

- Oxna will need to draw up a service agreement to carefully monitor the quality of the service provided.

Managing the contract: KPIs

A balance of measures will be important to cover all aspects of the support service. It could include some of the following:

- Cost per help request

- Number of help requests dealt with in the period (to give an indication of workload)

- Speed of response to initial query - how long does it take for Gighay to answer the phone or respond to emails?

- First contact resolution rate

- How often do Gighay provide a solution or outcome to a request for support at the first instance or on the same day the issue was raised?

- Average time taken to resolve issue (how soon are technicians put to work and problems resolved?)

- Number of unplanned IT security or downtime incidents

- Average amount of server downtime per week/month

- Number of cyber-security incidents detected and prevented

- Average score in customer satisfaction feedback surveys (voluntary short questionnaires could be sent to Oxna staff after each support case is closed).

Examiner's comments

This requirement was very well answered by most candidates, who were clearly well versed in the arguments for and against outsourcing. It was pleasing to see that most tailored their discussion and their KPIs to the scenario in the question. Weaker candidates tended to ignore the cyber-security issue, and make generic points. Some continue to confuse KPIs with goals or targets.

57.2 Big Data

Big Data encompasses information from multiple internal and external sources. It might include information from Feltar's systems, transactions with its customers, social media, mobile devices etc.

Companies can analyse this data and use it to adapt their products to better meet customers' needs and find new sources of revenue.

Big Data is often defined by considering the V's: volume, velocity, variety, value:

Volume – refers to the scale or amount of data which is now available for organisations to access, store and use. Widespread use of the internet, smart phones and social media has increased the volumes of data available to businesses. This data can be used to give insights to customers'

requirements by identifying trends and buying patterns. Currently Feltar are only collecting a very limited amount of data from customers.

Velocity – refers to the speed at which 'real time' data is gathered and used by modern organisations. At the moment Feltar simply records the final sale at the end of a customer transaction. Many online retailers compile records of each click and interaction a customer makes while visiting a website and use this to recommend additional purchases to a customer when they visit the company's website.

Variety – big data comes from a variety of sources and in different forms, structured and unstructured. For example Feltar could gather unstructured content from social media eg Twitter, Youtube, and use it in conjunction with more structured database information gathered from Feltar's customers via the website.

Value – refers to the uncertainty that surrounds the accuracy of a lot of the data. The reliability of the data will influence the value of the predictions/outcomes of the data analysis.

Using data for competitive advantage

Marketing and sales:

Feltar could build brand loyalty by establishing a customer loyalty scheme – this would allow it to collect data and analyse and profile customers and their needs/buying habits.

Data analytics software could be used to analyse the type of coffee individual customers buy, the frequency of purchases and the amounts typically spent.

In addition to collecting database information, Feltar could use Twitter/social media data to get better insights into what customers plan to buy, rather than just reacting to historical purchases.

Recording customers' preferences will help Feltar tailor its marketing e.g by delivering targeted advertising and discounts directly to customers' mobile devices. It could also help increase sales volumes by promoting related/similar products to those purchased before they check-out on the website or recommending items purchased by customers with similar tastes.

Inventory and pricing:

Collecting data about customers will not only help tailor the shopping experience to each individual but will also help Feltar to predict inventory requirements and potentially negotiate favourable rates with suppliers of the most popular coffee lines.

Trends identified in online sales in real time could be used to help improve inventory and pricing decisions. If a particular line of coffee is not selling very well, then an automatic price offer could be triggered.

Alternatively Feltar could send discounts to customers whose buying behaviour shows that they have not returned to the site for a while.

Competitors' prices can be monitored and analysed so that Feltar can respond quickly with its own deals.

Customer service:

Many retailers offer customers the opportunity to leave feedback on the experience of shopping with the company. Some customers also give public feedback via social media.

If Feltar were to capture and analyse such feedback it could deal proactively with potential issues and respond quickly to customer complaints.

Practical implications

IT strategy

Feltar currently operates a basic website and captures limited data. This suggests that it has made limited investment in IT. The management team may need to take a more strategic attitude towards the use of technology.

Cost

A big data strategy is likely to need significant up-front investment in IT systems, which will require funding. Capturing and processing more data about customers will also have an ongoing cost.

Skills

As Feltar is a small business it may not have people with the skills to identify the appropriate data to capture, nor to extract meaningful insight from the data that is captured and processed. An alternative to employing its own experts is to outsource this to Gighay, since it has expertise in this area.

Time

Establishing the necessary databases and acquiring suitable analytical software is likely to take a significant amount of time.

Impact on customers

Consideration will need to be given to any potential disruption that the implementation of a big data strategy may cause, particularly if enhanced data capture requires changes to the website.

Data protection and security

Collecting and holding personal data about customers has legal and security implications. Feltar's management team will need to ensure that appropriate controls are put in place to prevent customer information falling into the wrong hands and to ensure compliance with the Data Protection Act. Again Gighay may be able to assist with this.

Examiner's comments

Most candidates were able to make some general points about how retail businesses can capture and use customer data. Better candidates picked up on the three areas highlighted in the scenario - marketing, inventory and pricing – and illustrated specifically how this might be done in the context of a coffee business. It was noticeable that those candidates who had studied the new topics in the learning materials were able to talk about big data and data analytics, rather than just the analysis of data traditionally captured in a company's customer database. Surprisingly few pointed out that Gighay, with particular expertise in data capture and data analytics, would be well placed to help Feltar overcome any practical difficulties. Candidates who discussed the 4Vs of big data and applied it to the relatively small coffee business tended to score highly.

58 Holidays Direct plc (June 2017)

Marking guide

	Knowledge	Skill	Marks
58.1 (a) Data analysis	2	11	
(b) Risks	2	7	19
58.2 Website	2	6	8
58.3 Structure	2	8	9
58.4 Ethics	3	5	8
	11	37	44

General comments:

This question was the mini case and also the main data analysis question.

The scenario in this question is a UK-based, online holiday company (HD) which sells package holidays (flights and accommodation) directly to UK consumers. All HD bookings are made online directly by consumers. Each booking combines return flight seats plus hotel stays.

HD has two divisions: a European Division and a Worldwide Division. HD charters flights from three different airlines under block contracts in September of the year prior to travel.

HD purchases hotel stays from 84 different hotel operators at holiday sites throughout the world using block contracts with each hotel, made up to three years in advance of the actual stay.

Following a year of poor performance, a new CEO was recently appointed by HD. He is considering making changes to the organisational structure. He is also concerned about the risks involved in a mismatch between advance block bookings made by HD and actual outcomes in terms of demand from consumers.

An ethical issue has arisen where HD's hotels manager, Penny Price, has been informing some customers that a friend's car hire firm is cheaper than the company that HD officially recommends.

58.1 (a)

	20X6	20X7	% change
European (£'000s)	348,000	360,000	3.4%
Worldwide (£'000s)	148,000	184,000	24.3%
Total (£'000s)	496,000	544,000	9.7%
Bookings by consumers			
European (000s)	290	300	3.4%
Worldwide (000s)	74	92	24.3%
Total (000s)	364	392	7.7%
Average time of booking before departure (days)	87	76	(12.6)%
Hotel rooms booked (000s)	473	470	(0.6)%
Flight seats booked (000s)	1,092	1,176	7.7%
Hotel rooms vacant (000s)	14.2	4.7	(66.9)%
Flight seats empty (000s)	32.8	11.8	(64.0)%
Number of people per hotel room	2.31	2.5	
Value of discounts given to consumers (£'000s)	14,880	5,440	(63.4)%
Cost of additional bookings by HD (£'000s)	4,960	27,200	448.4%
Website visits (000s)	6,916	8,624	24.7%
Revenue per booking:			
European (£s)	1,200	1,200	–
Worldwide (£s)	2,000	2,000	–
Total (£s)	1,363	1,388	1.8%
Revenue per person (ie, flight seat) (£s)	454	463	2.0%
Discounts as a % of revenue	3%	1%	
Additional HD bookings as a % of revenue	1%	5%	
% vacant hotel rooms	3%	1%	
% empty seats	3%	1%	
Website visits per booking	19	22	15.8%

Financial performance

Overall revenue has increased by 9.7% in 20X7 compared with 20X6. In total, both the number of flight seats booked and the number of bookings have increased by 7.7%. However, these overall figures hide different trends in the European and Worldwide Divisions.

The European Division has experienced revenue growth of only 3.4% in the year. There has been an equivalent change in the number of bookings of 3.4% between 20X7 and 20X6. An initial conclusion might therefore be that the increase in revenue for the European Division has been the result of an increase in volumes rather than prices.

The Worldwide Division has experienced significant revenue growth of 24.3% in the year. Again, there has been an equivalent change in the number of bookings of 24.3% between 20X7 and 20X6. An initial conclusion might again be that the increase in revenue for the Worldwide Division has been the result of an increase in volumes rather than prices.

The initial conclusions of revenue changes resulting from volume changes rather than price can be challenged based on changes in underlying trends in consumer behaviour. Specifically, the number of hotel rooms booked has fallen by 0.6% despite the increase in the number of flight seats booked of 7.7%. This is due to the number of people per hotel room increasing from an average of 2.31 to an average of 2.5.

Operating performance

The increase in the number of people per hotel room may be part of a trend for more people squeezing into a hotel room to save on the price of the holiday. An alternative explanation is that the hotel rooms being sold are larger (eg, family rooms).

Overall, it seems likely that the revenue generated from operations relating to flights has increased more than that from accommodation operations, as there are more individuals flying. Also, the greater growth in the Worldwide Division may suggest that a larger part of the price of these holidays comprises the flight, compared with shorter haul European holidays.

Some trends can also be explained by the fact that a greater proportion of revenues in the mix are being generated by the operations of the Worldwide Division compared with the European Division. For example, there has been an overall increase of 1.8% in revenue per booking, despite the revenue per booking being stable for each individual division.

Additional information

- The information provided relates mainly to revenues and sales. Information on costs would be needed to determine margins and profit for each line of business and to make a more complete analysis of performance.

- A breakdown of discounts and additional flights between destinations would help to assess where the forecasting errors are occurring (eg, in one division in particular).

- Information on competitor performance from industry intelligence would help to assess HD's relative performance compared with competitors in a changing market.

- Monthly data would help to assess short-term patterns and trends in demand within the year, rather than just between years.

- Granular data on each hotel (eg, bookings, margins, occupancy) would help to determine differing trends in demand for individual hotels within destinations to assess performance at the level of individual hotels.

(b) **Operating risks**

Demand from consumers appears to be volatile.

Two issues arise from variations in demand:

- The extent to which demand is predictable (eg, through forecasts and market research)

- The extent to which demand is controllable (eg, through discounts, advertising, new or improved hotels and better destinations)

For HD predicting demand involves:

- predicting industry demand for the UK tour operators sector (eg, macroeconomic growth; competition from self-packaging; competition from consumer trend to holiday within the UK)

- predicting market share (pricing, marketing and quality of flights/hotels/service)

The key operating risks of **underestimating** demand:

- Lost goodwill and lost repeat bookings from customers who cannot book through lack of availability

- The feasibility of late additional bookings of flights and hotels by HD is limited, and are likely to be residual bookings that other tour operators do not want (eg, less favourable destinations/hotels)

- Late bookings by HD on top of block bookings require a double coincidence of availability of flights and hotels for the same location

- If an airline or a hotel cancel a booking (eg, mechanical failure of an aircraft or flood at a hotel) then there is no operational flexibility to cope with the excess demand

- If a destination suffers an incident (eg, terrorist attack or natural disaster) there is limited operational flexibility to offer alternative accommodation or flights

The key operating risk of **overestimating** demand:

- Late discounts may need to be offered which may damage goodwill of customers who have paid full price.

- Discounts may become expected, therefore incentivising consumers to delay bookings until they are available. This could make discounts the norm for an increasing proportion of consumers, thereby reducing profit and increasing uncertainty in forecasting demand.

The issues of under- and overestimating demand relate to each destination rather than overall. However, there is a little more flexibility for flights as each airport can serve multiple destinations for hotels.

As a result, there may be overestimated demand at one location and underestimated demand at another with limited operational ability (eg, due to flights) or consumer desire to transfer between the two locations.

Turning to specific data analysis in respect of the above:

Flight seat utilisation

The total of seats which were unoccupied in 20X7 was 11,800. This was a significant decrease of 64.1% from 32,800 unused seats in 20X6.

One of the factors causing the higher utilisation rate may have been that demand increased in 20X7 compared with 20X6 and this increase was not expected. It may have been that, following low demand in 20X6, HD expected demand to remain at a lower level for 20X7 rather than attempting to predict demand afresh.

This data may suggest that variations in demand have not been well predicted by HD and predictions for next year may have been too much influenced by demand in the current year.

Even when demand is high in 20X7 there are still 1% of flight seats vacant. This may suggest operating inefficiency, poor prediction of demand for some locations or random events at some locations (natural disasters).

In 20X6, when demand was lower, 3% of flight seats were vacant. The causal factor here however is not that demand was low per se, but that demand was not predicted to be low and so it was unexpected, resulting in overcapacity.

Vacant hotel rooms

The total of vacant hotel rooms in 20X7 was 4,700. This was again a significant decrease of 66.9% from 14,200 vacant rooms in 20X6.

The factors causing the higher utilisation rate in 20X7 are likely to have been the same as for flights.

Even when demand is high in 20X7 there are still 1% of hotel rooms vacant. In 20X6, when demand was lower, 3% of hotel rooms were vacant.

Whilst these data may suggest that there was operational inefficiency in misestimating demand, it does suggest, at least, that the hotel block bookings and flight block bookings were aligned at each destination.

Other operating risks

Other operating risks which may cause a difference between block contracts and demand:

- Random events (natural disasters and terrorist attacks)

- Flights – disruption of schedules (grounding of aircraft for technical problems, strikes, weather events)

Financial risks

Financial risks of overestimating demand

A key financial risk of overestimating demand relates to the cost of unsold flight seats and hotel rooms which still need to be paid for by HD even though there is no revenue from bookings.

Another of the key financial risks in overestimating demand is that discounts need to be offered in order to sell holidays (ie, flight seats and hotel rooms).

In this respect, the above data represent the residual effect in being unable to sell holidays to some destinations even after discounts.

Again, these effects are particular to each location. It is likely some destinations are overbooked and some underbooked.

The discounts have decreased by 63.4% from £14.88m to £5.44m. This is further evidence that the increase in demand in 20X7 compared with 20X6 was not fully anticipated. However, the overall increase in demand may not have been present across all destinations, as some discounts were still required in 20X7, which amounted to 1% of total revenue, despite this being lower than the 3% of total revenue in 20X6.

Financial risks of underestimating demand

The key financial risk of underestimating demand relates to lost revenues from unsatisfied demand and this will impact on profit.

One of the financial risks in underestimating demand is that additional late bookings of flights and hotel rooms may need to be made by HD. These are likely to be at higher cost than block bookings and are subject to availability of the flight and hotel at the same destination.

It may be that this results in lower profit or that the increased cost can be passed on to consumers in higher prices. Notwithstanding this, better operational efficiency in forecasting would have enabled better planning of flights, hotel rooms and prices.

Other financial risks

Other financial risks which may arise from a difference between block contracts and demand:

- Foreign exchange – if the £ falls (eg, between the time of the block contract booking and the time of consumer bookings), then oil prices (and therefore fuel costs) in $ will rise in sterling terms. Also, the cost of Worldwide accommodation will rise in sterling terms if the £ falls in relation to a range of currencies. These changes in sterling costs may need to be passed on by HD in price increases to consumers, which will impact demand and profit.

- Counterparty credit risk from failure of hotel chains and airlines holding deposits may cause a short-term reduction in supply and financial loss.

Examiner's comments

Requirement 58.1(a) was generally well answered. Most candidates provided a well-structured table for data analysis, focusing on changes between the two years, financial data and non-financial data.

The qualitative discussion was also good in many cases, providing reasons for the data trends and suggesting causal relationships. However, the non-financial data was generally less well analysed than the financial data.

Many candidates initially considered the firm's demand forecasting ability to be good, as evidenced by the decline in the value of discounts given to customers, but then often changed their minds when they came to consider the increase in the cost of additional bookings.

The weaker minority did not produce a data table and instead tended to weave some numbers into their narrative. They tended to lose marks by failing to present the data systematically, thereby failing to identify data patterns which would have revealed important issues facing the firm.

Of the better candidates, a few made the point, in the additional information section, that a complete evaluation of the firm's overall performance cannot be made as information provided was mainly restricted to revenues, with no overall cost or profit data given.

Many produced rather lengthy lists of additional insignificant information requirements, which were often very generic in nature and not directly relevant to the question.

In respect of 58.1 (b) most candidates performed well on this requirement. The majority devoted most of the discussion to the central issue of over/under estimation of demand. However, most candidates made insufficient use of the basic data provided in the question to illustrate their arguments.

Some candidates did not separate out the risks into operating and financial, thereby providing an unstructured, and frequently generalised, risk answer.

58.2 Website visits

Monitoring of the number of website visits in each period may be a lead indicator of the level of interest in the holidays and therefore the number of eventual bookings.

This may help predict future demand and therefore improve on the operational inefficiencies noted above.

The total number of visits in 20X7 increased by 24.7% compared with 20X6. This meant there were over 22 visits per booking in 20X7, compared with 19 per booking in 20X6.

This could have been an early indication of increased demand in 20X7 compared with 20X6 but it would have been necessary to monitor the visits each day/week/month rather than annually. An alternative explanation is that more visits occurring is consistent with more people accessing the internet from more types of devices.

Better data relating to visits would be obtained if the particular pages visited could be identified on the website, so changes in consumer tastes for each destination or type of holiday could be better monitored to estimate future demand in each segment of the business. This data indicating future demand could be used to support a segmentation strategy.

Bookings

Monitoring the numbers of, and trends in, actual bookings is key data in predicting eventual demand.

The fact that there has been a trend for later bookings in 20X7 (76 days before departure) compared with 20X6 (87 days) may be indicative of a change in customers' behaviour relating to the later timing of making a booking. In this case, extrapolating trends by comparing bookings this year with the number of bookings at the equivalent time last year, may be less valid, or at least may need to be adjusted.

The bookings system provides key information for Harriet and Penny in adjusting the block bookings of hotels and flights for each destination and for each week of the year. This may impact not just on block bookings but on the timing and extent of discounts and additional bookings.

Further details on demographics and social attributes of consumers may help tailor marketing of particular locations (eg, for retired people who may be flexible with travel arrangements) and timings (eg, families who are not flexible on timing and may be sensitive to price changes).

Data Analytics

HD can use data analytics software to organise and analyse the website data collected to discover trends and patterns that might not otherwise be apparent.

The website data collected can also be combined using data analytics software with other internally (eg, previous bookings) and externally (eg, from social media) available data about customers to build up a more detailed profile.

This can help HD gain a deeper understanding of customer requirements. This information can then help predict future demand, for example by using models to forecast sales trends and the likely impact on costs.

Examiner's comments

This was reasonably well answered by most candidates. Most recognised the relevance of the website information for overall demand prediction. Fewer discussed issues around segmentation and/or seasonality and how this information can be used to estimate future variations in demand in different geographical areas or segments of the business.

A minority discussed, in some detail, the technicalities of 'Big Data' – displaying knowledge in this area – but then some became distracted by this theme, missing the key issues of demand/segmentation prediction.

The validity of the data for prediction of demand was raised by a minority.

58.3 The current organisational structure seems to be a divisionalised structure which is the legacy of a previous acquisition.

In essence, the two operating divisions are based upon different geographical markets according to the location of the consumers' holidays.

It also has elements of a matrix structure as it includes Penny and Harriet reporting to both divisional heads, as flights and accommodation bookings cut across both geographical divisions. This may cause conflicts of interest, confused reporting lines and clouded areas of performance measurement.

The first key issue is whether the booking and marketing aspects of the business need to be split between Europe and Worldwide Divisions. Both use the same booking system and there appears to be little difference in the nature of the holidays to justify separation. The main difference is just distance of travel.

Joining marketing and booking into one division may generate economies of scale in sharing marketing and advertising. If the divisions are being monitored for performance separately it may also avoid competition between divisions.

The accommodation function is currently split across two divisions, despite the hotel chains having global presence across both geographical regions. This may be preventing composite contracts for the company as a whole, or at least some flexibility between bookings within and beyond Europe.

The booking of flights does appear to be in line with the current system of Europe and Worldwide with two airlines serving Europe and one elsewhere. However, this may be a consequence of having two divisions, rather than being coincident with them. If the divisions were to be merged, then there may be the facility to have all airlines serve both European and global markets with consequent economies of scale.

Revised structure

A revised structure could be for three main separate operating divisions (sales, hotel bookings and flight bookings) reporting into a single head of operations who would have overall control. Other support divisions (eg, HR, administration etc) may also be needed but could be monitored separately from operating divisions.

A key issue for business efficiency and risk is integrating sales, flights and accommodation for each location. This requires shared information and shared decision making which could take place between functions under the umbrella of a single divisional head.

The consequence of the need for coordination is interdependency so performance measurement is difficult under the old two divisions. However, it can be measured with one operating division and one operating head who can take overall responsibility for all aspects of operating performance.

Examiner's comments

Most candidates identified the current structure as divisional. Some also considered it to be partly matrix as well, or they considered it to be, in part, functional. A significant minority referred to Mintzberg and/or Handy, but often inappropriately. Most candidates were able to identify some advantages and disadvantages of the current structure.

Most candidates also provided reasonable suggestions for an alternative structure, after outlining the drawbacks of the existing structure. Many suggested a functional structure. Fewer provided a strong justification for their suggested structure in the specific context of the firm's operations.

58.4 There are two potential ethical issues:

(1) Penny disclosing information to customers about car hire charges.

(2) HD using its position of access to information, and trying to persuade consumers to pay more than necessary for car hire, in order for HD to take a commission.

In making any ethical evaluation it is first necessary to establish the facts. In this case, the claims made by Penny need to be established to assess their validity before taking any action. This may include establishing not just what Penny has disclosed but the extent of her actions (which she may have understated). In particular, it needs to be established whether over-charging of customers for car rental is actually taking place. It also needs to be established that Penny has not taken any money as she asserted.

A key issue is that she has disclosed general market information **to** customers, not **about** customers.

The issue of legality may apply if the charging information or personal details have been accessed in order to provide information to selected customers. Legal advice is needed to ascertain whether this is contrary to criminal law in the UK or other countries where HD operates, or breaches regulations or contractual agreements signed by HD.

For HD, illegality may relate to mis-selling if pressure was applied to customers, but again legal advice is required.

Irrespective of legality, in making an ethical decision as to how to act, it may be helpful to Penny and to HD apply the Institute of Business Ethics three tests:

- Transparency
- Effect
- Fairness

Penny

Transparency – would Penny mind people (divisional heads, the HD board, existing customers, suppliers, other employees) knowing about what she has done? In particular, the issue of providing transparency in disclosing car hire rates to customers could be viewed as the opposite side of a breach of confidentiality of HD's pricing.

Effect – whom does Penny's disclosure affect or hurt? Clearly this could include the benefits of reduced car hire fees to some customers who acted differently on the basis of full information. On the other hand, her employer could lose legitimate commission income. Car hire companies in Spain dealing with HD would lose income but Penny's friend could gain.

Fairness – would it be considered fair by those affected? The issues are whether mere disclosure of information is unfair and whether the circumstances under which it was made (by an employee) are fair. Also, disclosure was only made to holiday-makers going to Spain. Other holiday-makers may feel it is unfair that they did not gain the same information. In addition, the disclosure was not just general information that car hire through HD was expensive but a specific recommendation to use a firm related to Penny.

HD

Transparency – would HD mind people (existing customers, suppliers, employees) knowing what it was doing? In particular, the issue of deliberately pushing customers towards high car hire rates to make commissions for HD could be viewed as inappropriate exploitation of their position and therefore mis- selling. Conversely, it could be argued that earning commission for recommendations of firms with which it has contractual relationships is a legitimate business activity given that the consumers were free to look elsewhere if they chose to do so.

Effect – whom does the disclosure affect or hurt? Clearly this could include the harm to customers, who would have acted differently on the basis of full information, of being persuaded to pay higher car hire fees.

Fairness – would it be considered fair by those affected? The issue could be whether HD's superior information position was exploited or that information was readily available (eg, on websites) to customers to enable them to make an informed choice, but they were willing to pay an additional amount for ease and reassurance.

Actions

Penny's actions should be consistent with her obligations and duties as a senior HD employee.

Although Penny made no direct personal gain (if her claims are true), it may have facilitated a relationship with her Spanish friend to her benefit and may therefore still have involved self-interest.

Harriet's initial action should be to inform the HD board. It seems unlikely there is illegality but unauthorised direct contact with HD customers for a purpose contrary to the interests of HD whilst an employee of HD may be a breach of Penny's duties as an employee.

Harriet may also question the board on whether the arrangement amounts to mis-selling.

Examiner's comments

The answers to this requirement were variable in quality. Most candidates did not apply professional scepticism to establish the facts. For example, many candidates uncritically accepted that the firm is over-charging customers for car rental, and that Penny has not taken any money as she asserted. Discussion also often tended to focus on Penny to the exclusion of HD although, with some candidates, it was the other way around.

Many candidates used the Transparency, Effect, Fairness (TEF) structure and language, although surprisingly not everyone. However, many candidates limited their discussion to these three TEF principles rather than going on also to explore other ethical principles and issues raised by the scenario. They thereby produced a restricted and narrow answer which was constrained by the TEF framework rather than enhanced by it.

Some candidates provided a reasonable discussion of the ethical issues/principles but then provided a weak discussion of the actions. Most candidates set out suggested actions for Harriet as required, but others then went on to stray beyond what was asked in the requirement by also setting out actions for HD and Penny.

Marking guide

	Knowledge	Skill	Marks
59.1 (a) Value chain diagram	4	8	
(b) Value chain – low cost strategy	2	7	19
59.2 (a) New business model	2	7	
(b) Change management	2	5	14
	10	27	33

General comments:

The scenario in this question is a UK-based manufacturer of soft furnishings (JST).

JST's business model has been one of cost leadership, using low cost labour, overheads and imported materials.

The cost leadership model is becoming difficult to sustain due to increases in the legal minimum wage and a fall in the value of sterling, making imported materials more expensive.

A new business model has therefore been proposed. This involves a move upmarket by producing better quality soft furnishings in a new range of higher priced fabrics. The new business model will require transformational change.

59.1 (a)

	IL	O	OL	M/S	S
FI	Profit-orientated culture. Tight financial and operating control.				
TD	IT ordering systems, inventory control, payables management		Delivery IT systems	IT systems and data capture to facilitate relationship marketing	IT receivables/ payables management systems IT based marketing support
HRD	Some training for skilled staff	Some training for skilled staff Limited training for unskilled staff	Delivery IT systems training	Discipline relating to customer issues	
Procurement	Bulk buying, managing supplier relationships, payables management	Low cost factory historically used			Financing and administration of payables systems
Primary activity	Optimal delivery systems, JIT, sourcing low cost synthetic materials	Low cost factory, low cost unskilled labour Labour intensive Colouring and design	Direct delivery to customers in bulk	Relationship marketing	Make good defaults Receivables administration and management Credit facilities

(b) The value chain can be used to examine where value can be created using the resources of the business to generate strategic options.

The primary activities are those that create value and are directly concerned with providing the output of soft furnishings. The support activities do not create value of themselves but enable the primary activities to take place with maximum efficiency and effectiveness.

Value drivers for JST include the colouring and design activities that have enabled JST to distinguish its products from those of competitors and create competitive advantage.

Overall, JST is pursuing a cost leadership strategy in accordance with Porter's generic activities and should thus focus upon low cost resources to produce a low-cost product. This requires identification of cost drivers within the value chain.

Examples are the low labour and materials costs on the supply side and efficient operating activities throughout the value chain up to the truncated delivery chain to customers, which provides only a basic service.

However, to maintain the position of cost leadership it is not just internal costs that need to be controlled, but costs throughout the supply chain. This includes costs from suppliers of raw materials and other inputs.

In particular, costs relating to support activities that do not support appropriately the primary activities in adding value for customers, or that create excess costs in so doing, should be reduced or removed.

Examples of low cost features, built in throughout JST's value chain, include:

- low cost production machines (acquired from a liquidator)

- low cost labour at the minimum wage for unskilled staff

- low cost raw materials (polyester) which are imported from developing countries

- low distribution costs through own lorry fleet and improved efficiency using IT

- costs of inbound logistics shifted to suppliers so inward transport and inventory holding costs are minimised (JIT)

- only a small number of suppliers, so payables management and procurement systems costs are reduced.

The abilities to add value by reducing costs to a minimum need to be linked and applied consistently for all costs in the value chain to be able to sell at a low price and therefore be competitive in the market for basic soft furnishings.

Whilst this model has been successful historically, two key costs are increasing: wages, due to the increase in the minimum wage; and raw materials, due to the decrease in the value of the £. These changing cost drivers in the value chain make it more difficult for JST to add value and remain competitive on a sustainable basis.

Examiner's comments

Requirement 59.1(a) was well answered by most candidates. Most correctly identified the primary and secondary activities of the value chain and provided descriptions of the relevant activities. The descriptions were sometimes within the value chain diagram boxes and sometimes cross-referenced to a more detailed narrative outside the value chain diagram. Either approach was acceptable.

Some candidates answered 59.1(a) and (b) jointly, normally resulting in an unstructured approach to answering these requirements.

Weaker candidates did not know the basics of the activities within the value chain or the structure of the diagram. Examples would be: mixing rows and columns inappropriately; treating support activities as primary and vice versa; or just simply omitting some activities completely.

In respect of requirement 59.1(b), a significant minority failed to identify the cost leadership strategy pursued by the firm as central to their answer. Only a small minority referred to cost/value drivers. However, most candidates were able to use examples from the scenario to illustrate the nature of the low-cost strategy.

Linkages between primary and support activities were only explicitly considered and evaluated by the best candidates. Many candidates tended to provide a rather generic/descriptive discussion of each activity in isolation.

Better candidates were able to link the strategy to the value chain activities and discuss the relevance of value drivers and cost drivers.

59.2 (a) The new strategy consists of two elements:

- Abandoning the current model of low cost production and its associated markets

- Entering a new position in a related market with revised production techniques and improved procurement quality

Benefits

- The current market is one of cost leadership according to Porter's generic strategies. It appears to be an unsustainable strategy due to low margins and increasing costs. The new strategy offers higher prices with the potential for increased margins. The new strategy would be a move to be a differentiator in Porter's generic strategies by creating tangible and intangible product features that consumers are willing to pay for and therefore to create margin.

- The new strategy is to launch a new product in the existing market (Ansoff's product development), so there is likely to be some overlap of market knowledge and networking contacts. However, it could be argued that the new strategy is in a different sector of the same market.

- The JST brand name for soft furnishings is still relevant to the industry under the new business model.

- If competition in the new sector of the market is more about quality, design and service, and less about cost and price, then there is an opportunity to compete on more favourable terms with imported goods by taking advantage of proximity to customers.

- Whilst rival companies in developing nations may benefit from lower wage costs and lower production costs compared with JST they may suffer from the fall in the value of the £. Rivals' products will have become more expensive in £ terms and the revenue generated for these rival in £s is less attractive when converted back into their own currencies.

- Whilst the new natural products are largely a departure from existing production and markets, the continued use of polyester (albeit of better quality) may give JST a continued foothold in existing markets and production techniques as a transition to the new business model.

Problems

- The new strategy may involve new skills (eg, in processing natural fabrics) which may not be primarily within the existing core competences of JST, notwithstanding some overlap.

- The move upmarket may mean that new relationships need to be established with an entire range of new customers. The existing customer relationships may be largely lost as the new quality products may be outside the price range for their customers' range of products.

- Whilst the JST brand name may continue to have some relevance, it may send the wrong signal in suggesting a low-cost product when the firm is trying to promote the opposite, upmarket image.

- One of the reasons that a low-cost operation has been sustainable is that the factory and machinery were acquired at low cost from the liquidator. Now that this initial machinery is failing, the question of replacement arises – presumably at much greater cost. This has a number of risks:

  - The increased costs of machinery will increase overall costs and this may mean that the new business model may not be competitive even at higher prices.

  - The increase in machinery costs are fixed costs which raise operating gearing further and increases operating risk.

  - Any new investment would be a sunk cost and may not be recoverable if JST's new strategy becomes unviable.

Conclusion

The new strategy is extremely risky and a better response to the demise of existing markets may be to exit the industry. Much will depend on market research and the ability to establish a new range of customers in sufficient quantity to make the new business model viable.

(b) The type of change will strongly influence the way in which change is managed. Change in this case seems transformational (a major significant change) and is planned to take place on 1 January 20X8 as a rapid one-off change on the introduction of the new machinery. This involves the introduction of new production systems and affects all employees significantly, but unskilled employees are most at risk.

The changes also affect other stakeholders such as suppliers and customers, although customers are well protected in competitive markets where they can purchase elsewhere.

The way in which the changes are introduced will be very important in them being implemented successfully. There will be cultural and individual barriers to change. Resistance and barriers to change need to be acknowledged and may be lessened by involving the employees in planning and implementation. There are two main groups of employees which will need to be managed differently and present different barriers to change:

- Those skilled employees who are required to retrain and have changed roles
- Those unskilled employees who may be required to leave the company

Barriers to change

Change management to reduce barriers to change involves managing people's expectations and attitudes since many changes may be resisted by employees. The key staff affected here will be the skilled employees to be retrained and those unskilled employees whom JST wishes to retain. The change is unlikely to be successful unless key employees can be persuaded of the need for change and the benefits of change to them.

The current business model is generating losses for JST and these are expected to worsen, so convincing employees of the need for change is facilitated as the current business model is unsustainable. However, this does not mean employees will approve of the specific new business model being proposed.

Various barriers to change are possible.

(1) **Cultural barriers**

Power structures within JST may be threatened. This will, in particular, affect management and others in authority who may be protective of their current roles and decision-making authority and be reluctant to implement changes which will be against their own interests.

Structural inertia: the existing systems of planning and decision making may act as a barrier to change to a new approach.

Group inertia may block change where the changes are inconsistent with the norms of team working and departments, or where they threaten their interests. JST's unskilled workers may therefore bond together to resist change (eg, strike action) as they are most affected, particularly as they may not obtain other jobs as local unemployment is high.

(2) **Personnel barriers**

There are also barriers which affect individuals and result in them seeing the change as a threat. Here habit and fear of the unknown may mean some individual JST managers are unwilling or reluctant to take on additional responsibility involved in new roles.

Approach to change

A mixture of the adaptive and coercive approach is likely to be appropriate. Adaptive change alone may be too slow, and JST's management may need to emphasise that it is vital that changes are made soon if the company is to survive.

Jason may need to actively demonstrate a willingness to delegate and adopt a more hands-off approach to management of the change. Otherwise managers may perceive that their involvement is simply a token and that the substance of decision making is outside their control. JST managers will need educating that the existing manufacturing systems are insufficient to allow successful improvements to meet competitive conditions. Jason will need to provide managers with training and support to increase their ability to make decisions within the new business model.

Models

Lewin/Schein's 3-step iceberg model of change would prescribe the following approach:

- Unfreezing standard operating procedures (identifying the restraining forces and overcoming them);

- Move to new patterns of behaviour (eg, carrying out the change to higher quality production); and

- Refreezing to ensure lasting effects (eg, reinforcing working with the new automated systems and natural fabrics).

While these phases may be appropriate to employees retaining roles within JST, they will not apply to those who are to be made redundant, as they will not have to accept a new structure or culture.

The **Gemini 4Rs** framework could also be used here:

Reframe – create the will and desire to change (the current JST business model is unsustainable due to rising costs of labour and imported materials).

Restructure – redesign the structure and culture to facilitate the new approach of higher quality materials and outputs. This may involve setting up new teams and processes as part of a learning culture.

Revitalise – creating a culture of teamwork between the new incoming employees and the existing employees who are being retained.

Renewal – ensure the change is supported on an ongoing basis and that individuals involved have the necessary skills eg, training in the new manufacturing systems.

The **coercive change approach** is where change is forced without participation. This requires the ability to push through the change without co-operation.

Examiner's comments

Requirement 59.2(a) was well answered by the majority of candidates. Most recognised the proposal as a change in generic strategy, moving towards differentiation and away from cost leadership. Most candidates also recommended that the new business model should not be adopted, even though the current strategy is not sustainable.

Those who clearly structured their answer by separately identifying benefits and problems tended to score well. Weaker candidates did not separate out the benefits and problems and therefore tended to produce generic and unstructured answers. Weaker candidates also tended to produce rather thin answers. For example, for key benefits their discussion got little beyond obtaining higher prices.

Requirement 59.2(b) was well answered by most candidates. A majority incorporated a relevant model for change management, mostly Lewin, and a variety of barriers to change. However, weaker answers tended to provide very generic discussion of models and barriers to change.

60 Portland Prawns Ltd (June 2017)

Marking guide

	Knowledge	Skill	Marks
60.1 FFF Contract	2	15	15
60.2 Rental	1	7	8
	3	22	23

General comments:

The scenario in this question is a company (PP) which processes and packages fresh prawns.

PP has been offered a large, one-year contract to supply frozen prawns which must satisfy minimum and maximum sales volume contractual requirements. The factory has a capacity constraint which means that all existing customers and the demand from the new contract cannot both be supplied in full.

There are large penalties if the required quantities in the contract are not provided. Sales volumes to existing customers could be reduced to meet capacity constraints by increasing prices.

PP has the opportunity to sign a three-year rental agreement for an additional local factory to expand capacity.

60.1 (a) The FFF contract is rejected.

Price £	10.00	10.50	11.00
VC £	4.50	4.50	4.50
Selling cost £	1.00	1.00	1.00
Contribution pu £	4.50	5.00	5.50
Sales volume kg	400,000	350,000	300,000
Total contribution £	1,800,000	1,750,000	1,650,000
FC £	1,200,000	1,200,000	1,200,000
Profit £	600,000	550,000	450,000

Thus **£600,000** remains the highest attainable profit which is achieved at a price of £10 per kilo if the contract is rejected.

(b) The FFF contract is accepted and demand is **150,000 kilos**.

	Existing customers per (a)	FFF	Total
Price £	10.50	8.00	
VC £	4.50	4.50	
Selling cost £	1.00	–	
Contribution pu £	5.00	3.50	
Sales volume kg	350,000	150,000	500,000 (capacity)
Total contribution £	1,750,000	525,000	
FC £	1,200,000	420,000	
Profit £	550,000	105,000	**£655,000**

Alternative presentation of calculations

Total contribution from FFF = £[8 – 4.5) × 150,000] – £420,000 = £105,000

Maximum contribution from existing customers:

Capacity = 400,000 kg/0.8 = 500,000 kg

Maximum available supply for existing customers = (500,000 – 150,000)kg = 350,000 kg

Highest price to sell 350,000 kg = £10.50

Profit from existing customers = £550,000 (see schedule above)

Total profit = **£655,000** (£105,000 + 550,000)

(c) The FFF contract is accepted and demand is **200,000 kilos**.

	Existing customers per (a)	FFF	Total
Price £	11.00	8.00	
VC £	4.50	4.50	
Selling cost £	1.00	–	
Contribution pu £	5.50	3.50	
Sales volume kg	300,000	200,000	500,000 (capacity)
Total contribution £	1,650,000	700,000	
FC £	1,200,000	420,000	
Profit £	450,000	280,000	**£730,000**

Alternative presentation of calculations

Total contribution from FFF = £[8 – 4.5) × 200,000] – £420,000 = £280,000

Maximum contribution from existing customers:

Maximum available supply for existing customers = (500,000 – 200,000)kg = 300,000 kg

Highest price to sell 300,000 kg = £11

Profit from existing customers = £450,000 (see schedule above)

Total profit = **£730,000** (£280,000 + 450,000)

Discussion

If the FFF contract is rejected, the market research indicates that the optimal price for PP is the current price of £10 per kilo (see schedule above).

In the short term, the FFF contract would generate additional profit irrespective of whether demand is as low as 150,000 kg or as high as 200,000 kg.

If FFF demand is low (150,000 kg) however the additional profit is small at only £55,000 and this can be achieved only by reducing the volumes sold to existing customers by 50,000kg (ie, to 350,000kg) due to the annual operating capacity constraint of 500,000kg. The reduced target level of sales to existing customers does however enable the price to these customers to be increased to £10.50 in order to maximise operating profit.

If FFF demand is high (200,000 kg) the additional profit is £130,000. This is achieved by reducing the volumes sold to existing customers by 100,000kg (ie, to 300,000kg) due to the annual operating capacity constraint of 500,000kg. The reduced target level of sales to existing customers does however enable the price to these customers to be increased to £11.00 in order to maximise operating profit.

Clearly if demand is between these limits then the additional profit would be between £55,000 and £130,000.

These results however depend on a number of assumptions:

- Penalties are avoided.

- The quality of processing can be maintained with additional output and with the new freezing process.

- A supply of quality additional prawns can be obtained to satisfy both FFF and existing customers.

- If demand is seasonal (and fresh prawns cannot be effectively stored) then processing may already be at full capacity at certain times of the year and thus the opportunity cost of lost sales from existing customers may be greater than indicated.

- Demand from FFF is known at the beginning of the year, so the price to other customers can be set accordingly at that time to accommodate residual capacity (ie, at the beginning of the year it might not be known whether demand from FFF is 150,000 kg or as high as 200,000 kg, so PP does not, at that time, know whether to set a price to other customers of £10.50 or £11).

If the FFF contract is terminated after one year or after two years, there is a longer-term issue that the existing customers, who have been discouraged by price increases, do not return.

The contract with FFF may improve PP's reputation and lead to further sales in future or alternatively to a hardening of selling prices.

With the new FFF contract, production would be at capacity, so there is a risk that any stoppage of processing (strike, breakdown etc) will result in lost sales and profit. Penalty clauses may apply if there is such a failure.

Each current customer is small and thus there is little individual customer power. FFF however is a significant customer and may be able to dictate future terms.

There is no certainty of contract renewal in future thus lost customers may be a permanent opportunity cost. Similarly, the marketing survey may be incorrect and existing customers may be more resistant to price increases than the survey indicates.

There are significant additional fixed costs associated with the new contract and this increases operating gearing.

Examiner's comments

This requirement was not well answered by most candidates, but a number of the better candidates scored full marks. The marks therefore tended to polarise.

The calculations were not complex but they required an understanding and application of the basic business issues of demand and pricing where there is a capacity constraint.

Many candidates initially used a structured approach and obtained £600k if the contract is rejected. However, some jumped to this answer without demonstrating it as optimal by exploring the alternative price/volume relationships provided in the question (ie, they ignored the market research data provided). Some candidates incorrectly calculated the theoretical 'maximum profit' as if 500kg were sold. Other added the sales volumes (400k + 350k + 300k) and multiplied by the price, completely missing the point of the price/demand market research information.

Other calculation errors were: failing to alter the variable distribution costs for selling lower volumes; deducting the £65,000 rental cost which only applies to the final requirement (as explicitly stated in the requirement).

Even some of those candidates who arrived at the correct calculations did not then provide much comment or qualitative analysis.

Weaker candidates failed to grasp the fundamentals of how to deal optimally with the capacity constraint while accepting the new contract.

Where candidates made incorrect calculations, credit was given for their discussion under the 'own answer' principle. There were also marks for discussion of non-data issues relating to the terms of the contract, although candidates' answers were often too narrow and did not address these issues.

60.2 The FFF contract is accepted and demand is 150,000 kilos with rented factory

	Existing customers per (a)	FFF	Total
Price £	10.00	8.00	
VC £	4.50	4.50	
Selling cost £	1.00	–	
Contribution pu £	4.50	3.50	
Sales volume kg	400,000	150,000	550,000
Total contribution £	1,800,000	525,000	
FC £	1,200,000	420,000	
Profit £	600,000	105,000	**705,000**
Factory rental cost £			(65,000)
Revised total £			**640,000**

The FFF contract is accepted and demand is **200,000 kilos with rented factory**

	Existing customers per (a)	FFF	Total
Price £	10.00	8.00	
VC £	4.50	4.50	
Selling cost £	1.00	–	
Contribution pu £	4.50	3.50	
Sales volume kg	400,000	200,000	600,000
Total contribution £	1,800,000	700,000	
FC £	1,200,000	420,000	
Profit £	600,000	280,000	**880,000**
Factory rental cost £			(65,000)
Revised total £			**815,000**

With the rental contract, the total capacity of both factories would be 650,000 kilos (500,000 + 150,000).

This would be sufficient to satisfy both the optimal demand from current customers (400,000 kg) and the highest demand from FFF (200,000 kg). It would also leave 50,000 kg spare capacity to accommodate any sales growth.

At the maximum demand from FFF, this would generate a total contribution of £880,000 (£600,000 + £280,000), an increase of **£150,000** compared with not having the extra capacity (£880,000 – £730,000).

At the lower demand from FFF, this would generate a total contribution of £705,000 (£600,000 + £105,000), an increase of **£50,000** compared with not having the extra capacity (£705,000 – £655,000).

As a result, if demand from FFF is at the lower end of the range in the year ending 30 June 20X8 then the additional contribution generated by having the new factory (£50,000) would not be sufficient to cover the additional rental cost in that year of £65,000.

In contrast, if demand from FFF is at the higher end of the range in the year ending 30 June 20X8 then the additional contribution generated by having the new factory (£150,000) would be more than sufficient to cover the additional rental cost in that year of £65,000.

An assessment would need to be made of how probable it is that demand from FFF would be towards the higher end of the contractual range.

More significantly, there are major risks arising from the fact that this is a three-year rental agreement and there is no guarantee that the FFF contract will be renewed for either 20X8 or 20X9. This would leave PP with unnecessary spare capacity serving its existing customers and an obligation to pay rentals of £65,000 pa for possibly two more years.

It may however be possible to sub-let the factory to a third party if the FFF contract does not run for more than one year, although this may not be for £65,000 pa or for the full period.

There is some upside potential if the FFF operations lead to obtaining similar customers requiring frozen prawns and thereby utilise the spare capacity.

Overall the advice is that the risks of signing the rental contract are too great at 1 July 20X7 as this would add to the existing risks from the FFF contract. Deferring the decision to keep the real option of waiting to see how the FFF succeeds may be the best decision. It can then be determined whether spare capacity is needed, either at the new factory currently being offered, or at an alternative location.

Examiner's comments

Marks on this requirement again tended to polarise with some better candidates scoring full marks while many candidates failed to grasp some fairly basic principles on contribution and decision making in a situation of constrained capacity.

As with the first requirement, the calculations were basic, but they required an understanding and application of the fundamental business issues of the costs and benefits of obtaining additional capacity by entering into a rental agreement for an additional factory.

These basic calculations were then 'pegs' on which to hang a brief discussion of the quantitative benefits, alongside the more general qualitative business issues relating to uncertainty of demand over the period of the rental contract.

61 Blakes Blinds Ltd (September 2017)

Marking guide

	Knowledge	Skill	Marks
61.1 Factors creating competitive advantage/ sustainability	2	5	7
61.2 Analysis of financial performance/areas of concern	1	22	20
61.3 Advantages/disadvantages of acquisition/transfer pricing	4	8	11
61.4 Ethical issues	3	5	7
	10	40	45

General comments

This is the mini case and also the main data analysis question. Candidates generally performed well on this question.

The scenario relates to a company (BB) which manufactures and installs high-quality door and window blinds for the corporate market. Most of BB's competitors buy low-cost, finished products from Asia and sell them to UK customers. However BB manufactures all its own products in its UK factory. It provides a complete service from design to installation and an optional after sales service with a three-year warranty.

BB has recently launched an innovative 'Auto-close' system which has led to increased revenue though this Is now being copied by competitors. However the Board is concerned that, despite the increased revenues, operating profit has fallen. It is considering the acquisition of its Chinese supplier of components, RX.

The question contains an ethical issue relating to a grant application. The MD has asked the Financial Controller to apply for a council grant which is available to businesses that have an entirely local supply chain. The MD and has told the Financial Controller, an ICAEW chartered accountant, to certify that BB meets all the grant conditions, despite it buying components from China.

61.1 Competitive advantage

In accordance with Porter's generic strategies, BB operates a differentiation strategy manufacturing and installing high quality blinds and shutters. This means that clients are prepared to pay a premium to the extent that they perceive BB's product is different or has added value. BB's strategy is focussed on the niche market of corporate clients in the UK.

The following are value drivers which give BB a competitive advantage in terms of its differentiation strategy:

- Unlike most blind and shutter companies, which buy in ready-made products, BB undertakes all its manufacturing in-house. This allows it to control the quality which is important to the underlying strategy.

- It also provides a one-stop service from site visit through to servicing. BB is able to tailor products to individual requirements and take into account delivery dates, installation times, and specific budgets.

- The offer of a service contract also helps tie customers into BB and generate future repeat business.

- Through Research and Development BB has developed its innovative 'Auto-close' system which appears to be highly valued by corporate clients. This competitive advantage is protected in a sense as a result of the brand being trademarked.

Sustainability:

Porter's five forces looks at how easy it is to sustain profitability within an industry given the nature of the competitive forces. There are a number of businesses in the blinds and shutters market making it a competitive market and it appears that barriers to entry are relatively low. Switching costs for clients are also likely to be low so retention of clients and customer loyalty is key to sustaining market share, since there is little to stop other businesses operating a similar strategy to BB. The 'Auto-close' system offers a distinct competitive advantage, however it depends heavily on technology, which is constantly evolving and it appears that other competitors have already brought out similar products.

As a result it is likely that BB has first mover advantage here only rather than a long-term sustainable advantage. This is especially true if competitor's products can be retro-fitted to BBs blinds.

Examiner's comments

This was very well answered by the vast majority of candidates who were very comfortable discussing competitive advantage. However surprisingly few chose to use a specific model to structure their answers and ensure a full range of points were covered.

In terms of Porter's generic strategies, many answers either referred to differentiation or focus, but not focused differentiation which is the strategy being adopted by BB. Some better candidates used Porter's value chain to analyse sources of competitive advantage linked to the chosen generic strategy.

Very few used Porter's five forces to analyse the sustainability of competitive advantage, although this was implicit in many of the better answers. Some candidates missed this element of the requirement out altogether. A significant minority focused on the broader Bruntland definition of sustainability which was not really relevant here, although since most did consider economic sustainability as part of this discussion, they were awarded some marks.

Evaluation of performance 20X5–20X6

The Board is right to be concerned. Despite an increase in revenue of £5.9 million (56.3%) between 20X5 and 20X6 ,operating profit has fallen by £7,000 from £417,000 to £410,000. There are two reasons for this reduction in profitability:

- The gross profit margin has fallen from 43.2% to 40.5%; and
- The fixed costs have increased by 51% between 20X5 and 20X6.

As a result the operating margin is only 2.5% for 20X6, compared to 4% the previous year.

To further explain the reasons for the decline it is important to analyse the individual revenue streams. The fall in gross margin has been driven by the reduction in the profitability of the core business – blinds and shutters. Here the margin has fallen from 36% in 20X5 to 29.7% in 20X6. Over 60% of BB's components are sourced from China. One reason for the loss of profits is the increase in cost of sales caused by exchange rate movements. Between 20X5 and 20X6 it appears that CNY has appreciated from £0.105 to £0.115. This resulted in purchases costing an extra £265,000 in 20X6 (CNY26,456 × (0.115 – 0.105)). More information is needed about the extent to which BB undertakes hedging of its foreign exchange risk and whether this was down purely to exchange rate movements or included foreign currency losses.

The sales growth is largely attributable to the development of the new 'Auto-close' system which launched at the beginning of 20X5. This accounted for 5% of sales in 20X5 but had grown to 17% in 20X6.

Without the development of the auto-close system the decline in gross profit in 20X6 would have been greater. The fact that this is trademarked, sought after technology explains why this product is relatively more profitable, with a GP margin of 49.2% in 20X6 (45.0% 20X5). This is to be expected as early adopters of the technology will be prepared to pay a premium, however as competitors bring out similar automated systems price competition is likely to increase and profitability will fall as BB loses market share. Thus the long term margins may not remain at this level. Also BB is likely to have spent large sums on research and development to generate the system, which effectively need to be recovered. Thus if costing were to be done on a life-cycle basis, taking into account all the costs of design and development, the product would appear less profitable.

The service business accounts for a relatively consistent proportion of sales, 20% in 20X6 (22% 20X5) and is BB's most lucrative area, generating a margin of 67% in both years. It would be useful to know what % of clients take up service contracts be whether there is scope to develop this area further. Again to properly assess the profitability, the warranty costs associated with the free-of-charge repairs should be taken into account. These seem to have increased given that they represented 8% of cost of sales in 20X6, compared to 5% in 20X5, which may indicate some quality problems.

A key issue for BB is that the product lines are interdependent, since service demand is a derived demand from the sales of the underlying product. Also the existence of the service contracts then provides BB with the opportunity to undertake upgrades or install replacement products.

To the extent that the auto-close system can be retro-fitted to any blinds/shutters there is an element of sales that is independent. However it is again likely that the many clients using this system have already purchased BB blinds and shutters and that some clients are attracted to buy BB blinds and shutters because of the system. An analysis of auto-close sales by existing and new customers would be helpful.

In conclusion, it is really the overall price for any contract that matters, rather than the price for each of the three elements. Therefore in evaluating performance it is not really possible to evaluate the performance of each element separately in any meaningful way. More information is also required about the sales volumes for each revenue stream.

Ability to achieve 20X7 budget

Sales

The 20X7 budget is ambitious. It assumes another year of very high revenue growth (46.8%), presumably on the back of further sales of the Auto-close systems. This may not be achievable if competitors have brought out similar products. Indeed the growth achieved in the first six months of 20X7 is only 26% (assuming no seasonality). More information is required to understand the seasonality of BB's sales including a breakdown of budgeted revenue by revenue stream. However on the face of it the 20X7 sales budget may be over-ambitious unless there are significant contracts planned for the second half of the year.

Gross profit

The budget assumes a margin of 41%. This may be due to an assumption that the auto-close systems, which are highly profitable (20X6 margin 49.2%) will represent a greater mix of sales in 20X7. However the actual overall margin in the first six months is only 40% so again this does not seem to have happened. Since over 60% of components are bought from China, the margin on shutters and blinds is also affected by the exchange rate movement. The cost of sales note suggests that the CNY has continued to strengthen during the first six months of 20X7 (average rate for purchases of CNY = £0.12) and this will have further reduced the margins on blinds and shutters.

If the first six months of the year are replicated, then compared to the budget, by the end of 20X7 there will be a 14.2% sales shortfall and a 16.3% shortfall in gross profit.

Again the detail of the budget by revenue stream is required.

Fixed costs

Fixed costs have grown by 18% in the first six months of 20X7, assuming no seasonality, whereas the budgeted increase for the year is only 11.3%. This, coupled with the GP margin has resulted in a margin of safety of 10.9% compared to a budget of 29.7%.

In 20X6, warranty costs rose from 5% of cost of sales (COS) to 8% and this trend may explain some of the higher actual costs in 20X7. In 20X6 there was a cutback of R&D expenditure in relation to sales. BB may have had to increase this if competitors have started to bring out new products. Indeed, if it has not done so, this would give further cause for concern in relation to its ability to achieve the sales growth.

The fixed costs figure may also have been affected by timing issues and may not represent the true costs for a six-month period if accounting adjustments such as accruals have not been made in the six-month management accounts.

A detailed breakdown of fixed costs by cost category is required.

Conclusion

Ultimately in the first six months of 20X7, BB has achieved more operating profit than it did in the whole of 20X6 (£451,000 compared to £4,210,000), however it has only actually achieved 15.4% of its budgeted operating profit. Admittedly, we are only comparing six months of actual figures to the budgets for the full year, but nonetheless unless significant contracts are planned for the second half of 20X7 it would appear that the 20X7 budget is unrealistic and over-ambitious.

Appendix of additional calculations

	Blinds and shutters	Auto-close	Service contracts
20X5			
GP margin	36%	45%	67%
Sales mix	73%	5%	22%
GP mix	61%	5%	34%
20X6			
GP margin	30%	49%	67%
Sales mix	63%	17%	20%
GP mix	46%	21%	33%

	20X5	20X6	20X7
Exchange rate for purchases CNY =	£0.105	£0.115	£0.12

Components cost	Increase 20X5–X6
CNY	35%
£	48%

	20X5	20X6
Fixed costs as % of total cost	40.9%	39.0%

	Actual 6 months to 30 June 20X7 (£'000)	Estimated Scaled to 12 months (£'000)	Budget Year ended 31 December 20X7 (£'000)	Variances Estimated 12 months vs budget (£'000)
Revenue	10,370	20,740	24,165	(3,425)
Cost of sales	6,225	12,450	14,260	1,810
Gross profit	4,145	8,290	9,905	(1,615)
Fixed costs	3,694	7,388	6,970	(418)
Operating profit	451	902	2,935	(2033)

	% changes		
	20X6 vs 20X5	20X7 budget vs 20X6 actual	20X7 12mth estimated vs 20X6 actual
Revenue	56%	47%	26%
Cost of sales	64%	46%	27%
Gross profit	47%	49%	24%
Fixed costs	51%	11%	18%
Operating profit	-2%	616%	120%

	Actual 6 months to 30 June 20X7	Budget Year ended 31 December 20X7
GP margin	40.0%	41.0%
OP margin	4.3%	12.1%
Margin of safety	10.9%	29.7%
Sales growth compared to 20X6	26%	46.8%
Increase in overheads compared to 20X6	18.0%	11.3%

Examiner's comments

The data analysis requirement was generally well answered, although comparing performance was better done than evaluating whether the budget would be achieved. Several performance indicators were already provided in the scenario. Many candidates identified and calculated additional relevant data (such as exchange rate movements and analysis by product) and presented their figures in a structured table with appropriate columns. Weaker candidates often reproduced all the data already given in the question, which simply wasted time without scoring marks. Some weaker candidates only considered percentage changes in data or did not produce an initial table of calculations, but weaved occasional random calculations into their narrative which tended to produce limited answers with only partial data.

Many candidates produced a good commentary on the actual data with a reasoned discussion of the performance of the various product streams. Weaker candidates, as usual, reiterated the figures they had calculated, without adding value. Evaluation of the company's ability to achieve the budget was less insightful, although most concluded that the budget is optimistic and, given current performance, unlikely to be achieved. Only a very small minority referenced the Board's concerns or discussed the issue of interdependencies between product lines. Most candidates identified further information that might be useful although in some cases this was very generic.

61.3 Acquisition of supplier

The acquisition of RX, BB's major Chinese supplier is a strategy of vertical integration, with BB moving backwards in the supply chain.

Advantages of Vertical integration

- This removes the margin that is currently being paid to RX and means BB are only covering the cost of producing the components, so may improve profitability or allow BB to reduce prices.

- This may give BB greater control over quality, which is important given the bespoke nature of its products. BB already has a close relationship with RX but the increased warranty costs may suggest there have been some problems recently.

- BB may be able to take advantage of the fact that they will control the supply chain to ensure more reliable delivery dates and shorter lead times which would enhance customer service. However there will always be some lead time given the location in China.

- If components are a source of competitive advantage then this allows BB to prevent competitors using the same ones and enhances their differentiation strategy.

- The acquisition of RX may provide BB with a foothold in the Chinese market and could use this to develop sales of the main products in Asia which would represent market development.

Disadvantages

- This does not remove currency risk which appears to have been a significant contributor to the decline in profit.

- In addition to the exchange risk on transactions, acquisition of the Chinese supplier will create exchange risk on asset values as well.

- BB's operating gearing will be increased significantly by the acquisition which will convert variable costs into fixed operating costs. The high fixed costs may raise the break-even point and means that profits will be more volatile relative to changes in sales. Any additional borrowing generates additional financial gearing which raises financial risks.

- This strategy may not improve performance – it depends on how RX supplier is performing and what % of its sales are external.

- Exit costs are likely to be significant if the venture fails, as there is likely to be a large financial commitment.

- Flexibility of operations is reduced eg the ability to shop around if other suppliers bring out better or more technologically developed components.

- Further operational risk arises from the management of the Chinese business which may be outside the core competences of the current BB management team that has UK experience only.

- It will involve some costs of integration (although BB may continue to run it as two separate businesses).

Transfer pricing

The transfer price is the price at which RX (the component division) will sells its components to BB's manufacturing division.

The following factors should be considered:

- Whether the divisions are to be treated as cost or profit centres. If they are to be profit centres then the transfer price will determine the profits of divisions. If the component division charges a high transfer price, then most of the total profit from company sales will be attributed to it, with less to the manufacturing division. This will give a false measure of performance for both divisions.

- If high transfer prices are then treated as costs by the manufacturing division and passed on to BB's ultimate customers, sales volumes may fall and overall profits may be distorted.

- Inappropriate transfer prices can lead to dysfunctional decisions or internal conflict between divisions. If either division believes it can get a better deal from an outside market it may take it. For example, if the manufacturing division could obtain supplies of equal quality at lower cost from third parties eg alternative Chinese suppliers, then it may, if permitted, choose to purchase outside the company. This could leave the component division with reduced sales. Conversely, if transfer prices are too low, then management of the component division might prefer to sell its supply through alternative channels at a higher price and leave the manufacturing division without components.

- There are various methods of setting transfer prices:

  Basing the transfer price on standard cost rather than using RX's actual costs should incentivise the component division to control costs. An issue to consider is whether to base the price on variable costs or to include an element of fixed costs, which brings with it the need for apportionment. If the component division is to be a profit centre then some form of cost plus price may be appropriate.

  The capacity of the component division should also be considered – if it will lose out on external sales by transferring components to BB's manufacturing division then this opportunity cost should be reflected in the transfer price.

Preliminary conclusion

A lot will depend on the price of the acquisition – BB already have a close relationship and a strong partnership with RX so acquisition may not help. It reduces flexibility and does not remove the exchange rate risk. If the only motive is in relation to the supply chain then it may not be sensible. However the Asian market is large and profitable so if there is an opportunity to sell BB's products through RX then the acquisition may be worth considering.

If the acquisition goes ahead, transfer prices could be set by negotiation and need to recognise the opportunity for either division to buy from or sell into external markets on an arm's length basis.

Examiner's comments

This requirement was reasonably well answered, on the whole, although a sizeable number of candidates talked in terms of acquisition generally rather than explicitly mentioning BB's backwards vertical integration of its main supplier. Most were well rehearsed in the advantages and disadvantages of this form of strategy, and the international considerations, although only a minority considered increase in operating gearing among the disadvantages.

The requirement on the implications for transfer pricing was generally poorly done. Few candidates discussed the concept of cost and profit centres and the need to identify how the division would be assessed. Suggestions for different approaches to setting the transfer price were on the whole very wooden, although better candidates did justice to behavioural considerations and taxation issues.

61.4 Ethics

Ethics pertains to whether a particular behaviour is deemed acceptable in the context under consideration. In short, it is "doing the right thing".

The issue here seems to be one of possible fraud and is potentially a legal issue as well as a moral one. In making any ethical evaluation it is first necessary to establish the facts. In this case, it would seem that the facts are reasonably clear. BB's Financial Controller (FC) has been told by the Managing Director (MD) to apply for a grant from Lemchester City Council, stating that BB fulfils all the application criteria.

The council's criteria for the grant are that the company provides local employment and has an entirely local supply chain. BB would appear to fulfil the criteria in relation to providing local employment and if it is awarded the grant, may be able to use this to increase capacity and benefit the local area. However more information is needed to ascertain the Council's definition of local supply chain and also to understand whether the Council's criteria are open to interpretation, since whilst BB manufactures its products in the UK, it sources over 60% of its components from China.

What is not clear is the extent to which the MD is deliberately trying to mislead the council by telling the Financial Controller to make a materially inaccurate/false statement or whether the MD has misinterpreted the criteria and equated local manufacturing with local supply chain.

If the MD is trying to get the grant under false pretenses then this conduct is dishonest, lacks transparency and implies a lack of personal ethics. The application may even be considered fraudulent and potentially illegal.

As the Financial Controller is a qualified ICAEW Accountant, he/she is bound by the ethical code for professional accountants. Going along with such behaviour would conflict with the fundamental principle of integrity and objectivity and if the Financial Controller signs the application they may also be guilty of a criminal act.

The MD may also be using their position to pressurise the Financial Controller who is likely to be concerned about the implications of going against the MD's wishes and perceive some form of intimidation threat.

Actions

Before making the application, the Financial Controller needs to consider the grant documentation and obtain more information in relation to the Council's criteria for awarding the grant, in particular their definition of local supply chain.

If the Financial Controller believes the Managing Director intends to act dishonestly then the FC should tell the MD that the application should not be submitted as it stands and that they are unable to sign it. If however BB provides full information to the council about its manufacturing activities, including its supply chain, then it may reasonably leave it up to the Council to decide whether to award the grant.

If the MD continues to insist that the application is submitted then the FC will be left in a difficult situation since if they go against the MD they may find their position untenable or end up facing dismissal. The FC may need to consider BB's whistleblowing policies, seek legal advice, and contact the ICAEW ethics helpline about their position.

Examiner's comment

The ethics requirement was very well attempted by most candidates. The majority of candidates were able to identify the key ethical issues in the scenario – the MD's desire to be less than transparent in applying for the grant and the threats presented to the Financial Controller's fundamental principles. Ethical language and principles tended to be used by a majority and many referred to the ICAEW Code of Ethics. However weaker candidates limited themselves to the transparency, effect, fairness structure which restricted their ability to score marks. Many candidates pointed out that the application for the grant may be fraudulent as well as dishonest. Better candidates identified that this may depend on the council's definition of "entirely local supply chain", discussed how the possible acquisition of RX may impact on this and suggested that BB have an open conversation with the council about whether it could apply.

It is encouraging that more candidates seem to have developed the ability to provide recommended actions that are realistic and linked well with the ethical issues previously discussed.

Marking guide

	Knowledge	Skill	Marks
62.1 Consistency of three-year goals	2	9	10
62.2 Functional strategies (HR and RD)	2	9	10
62.3 Cyber-security risks/risk management	3	7	9
	7	25	29

General comments:

Candidates generally performed well on this question.

The scenario relates to a company, ASU, that provides airspace management services to all airports and aircraft using UK airspace. It is 49% owned by the UK government and 51% by private shareholders that include UK airlines and the company's employees. ASU is licensed and regulated by the Civil Aviation Authority (CAA).

ASU has two strands to its operations:

- Controlling take-offs, landings and air traffic at each UK airport; and

- Authorising access to all UK airspace and providing in-flight navigation services for aircraft over the UK to airlines.

Recently there was a suspected hacking incident at one of ASU's operational centres, causing flight delays and cancellations and resulting in a £7 million fine for ASU.

As a result it has recently appointed a new Chief Executive, Joan Louli, who has set out her vision and goals for the company. She has also identified two international growth opportunities but believes ASU will need to ensure it has the right functional strategies in place to be considered for these tenders.

62.1 Vision and goals

Joan's vision is for ASU to be "the global leader in innovative airspace management."

To achieve this she has set the following goals:

- Achieve business growth by diversification
- Reduce the risks of accidents linked to airspace management
- Reduce emissions related to airspace management
- Increase the efficiency of ASU's internal operations

Consistency of Goals and Vision

Business growth through diversification is likely to raise awareness of ASU's brand and increase its customer base, thereby helping it to become a global leader.

Three of the four goals are focussed on safety, cost efficiency and environmental management. If ASU succeeds in these areas it is more likely to achieve its goal of growth as it will be a supplier of choice. ASU currently has an excellent track record but any accidents or incidents linked to poor air traffic management would be very damaging for ASU's reputation and brand image and hinder the achievement of Joan's vision.

Currently ASU is in a monopoly position in the UK so growth can only come internationally. If ASU can demonstrate a good track record in safety, cost efficiency and environment it will be in a position to win international contracts. This will lead to increased market share and facilitate its vision to be global market leader. So there is some consistency between the vision and the goals.

However innovation is also key to the vision and to ASU's competitive advantage and yet no specific goals have been set in this area (although some innovation may be implicit in the other goals.) So given the vision of "innovative airspace management" Joan should consider setting an additional goal in this area.

Consistency of Goals and Stakeholder objectives

ASU's key stakeholders include private shareholders, the government (as shareholder), CAA (representing public interest), airlines, airports, passengers and staff. Since there are multiple stakeholders, some of their objectives may conflict.

- Reducing the risks of accidents associated with airspace management

  This goal is likely to appeal to CAA, government, airlines, airports and passengers. A first class safety record is also likely to help ASU win contracts – for example this is one of the criteria for the European airspace tender and is likely to be relevant to the drone contract.

- Reduce emissions related to airspace management

  Again this is likely to appeal to CAA, government, airlines and airports. It will also help reduce negative interest from environmental groups. Whilst some private shareholder's may not want to pursue sustainability at the expense of profits, environmental impact is one of the criteria for the European airspace tender and therefore reducing emissions may enhance future profits

- Increase the efficiency of ASU's internal operations

  This is most likely to appeal to shareholders (private and government) as the efficiency of operations will directly affect ASU's profitability. However more efficient air traffic control is also in the interests of the users of ASU's services – the airport and airlines and the CAA as regulator. It may also make life easier for staff although some may perceive this goal as threatening their jobs.

- Achieve business growth by diversification

  Again this goal is likely to be more of interest to private shareholders as growth should provide an opportunity for added value in terms of shareholder wealth. Indirectly it may also appeal to staff since growth will facilitate job security and career development prospects. However it may be less appealing to the UK government who may prefer ASU to concentrate on activities closer to home.

Conclusion:

Whilst some of ASU's stakeholders may be more or less interested in certain goals, three of the four goals are likely to be consistent with the objectives of most of the stakeholders. The one concern is over the government's attitude to diversification and as a key stakeholder Joan would be advised to consult with them as soon as possible to ascertain whether this goal has their support.

In general terms the goals do not seem to be in conflict with each other and could therefore be said to be aligned. Indeed if ASU succeeds in reducing accident risk, reducing emissions and increasing efficiency, then growth is likely to follow and in a sense the goals could be seen as forming a hierarchy which will help Joan achieve ASU's vision.

Examiner's comment

This requirement was very well answered by the majority of candidates, who considered Joan's vision for ASU to become "the global leader in innovative airspace management" in relation to both the four stated goals and the likely objectives of key stakeholders.

Many good answers identified that ASU has multiple stakeholders whose objectives are likely to conflict. However weaker candidates tended to focus on only one element of the requirement or restricted their consideration of stakeholders to ASU's owners. The best candidates reflected critically on the goals and identified that, given Joan's vision, an explicit goal was missing in relation to 'innovation'.

62.2 Functional strategies

A successful company is often one that is outward looking, and has accepted the reality of constant change. As well as delivering business as usual to the highest standards, ASU needs to look to the future towards new markets, innovative processes, and improved efficiency.

Functional strategies that are critical to ASU's vision include:

- Human resources
- Research and development

These areas are both interlinked with technology:

Human resources

Human resources considers ASU's requirements in terms of people and how these needs may be met:

- As part of succession planning ASU needs to recruit and retain the best talent – innovative organisations tend to attract and retain higher quality staff, who want the opportunity to contribute to the development of a forward-looking organisation.

- Staff retention does not seem to be the issue – ASU has staff with long employment records but a significant number will retire in the next few years and as part of succession planning ASU needs to start hiring appropriate numbers of staff with the right skills.

- Different skillsets may be required for international markets which may increase staff diversity. ASU operates in a dynamic environment and needs staff to be flexible and adaptable to change. It is likely that the drone contract would need to be operated from the Middle East. Consideration needs to be given to whether to employ local staff or second staff from the UK. Language skills may also be required.

- ASU is likely to need people with scientific and engineering backgrounds, as well as wider business skills such as finance, administration. In order to expand the business it may also need staff with sales skills.

- Continued success depends on getting the best from its employees. ASU needs to foster a culture of innovation (see below). Cross-disciplinary teams may allow employees to be more involved in the development of new processes, to move around and generate fresh ideas. Training and development will also be key.

- ASU has already invested significantly in technology to allow better use of information by staff and business partners and to ensure its IT systems are connected with others across a wide range of organisations and countries. This should help facilitate international expansion.

- ASU needs to ensure it has an appropriate knowledge management system. This needs to capture all the knowledge that is valuable and deliver it to the people in such a way that it can be acted on quickly, to the competitive advantage of the business. This is particularly true in relation to the knowledge held by the staff who are due to retire.

Research and development

Research and development is aimed at the innovation/improvement of both products and processes. This is a key source of competitive advantage and ASU needs to ensure that it continues to invest in this area, particularly given Joan's vision.

ASU can help foster a culture of innovation by:

- creating a culture that promotes and rewards creativity and inventiveness and supports individual and team abilities;

- implementing a management style and structure designed for innovation: praising new ideas, encouraging staff to explore possibilities;

- being aware of and making use of common information/resources available to the airline industry and monitoring the development and processes used by other air traffic control organisations; and

- using multiple sources of innovation – R&D, employees, customers, partners, outsourcing and joint ventures, working with the government and other public sector initiatives.

A key area of research will be finding new technological developments. ASU has already developed expertise in the management of unmanned aircraft systems and drones, which has created the opportunity for the new contract in the Middle East.

Continued investment in technology is therefore key, particularly given how fast technology changes. However technology is also a key area of risk that needs to be managed (see 62.3). As it is partly privately funded, ASU may be better placed than the government owned bodies it is competing against to attract finance for ongoing investment in research and development.

Examiner's comment

Answers to this requirement were polarised. There were some excellent attempts but some candidates omitted part 62.2 entirely. This is surprising given the fact that functional strategies are covered in detail in the learning materials and candidates should at least have been able to write from a common sense point of view, based on their own experiences and using the information in the scenario. Human resource strategy was generally answered well but for RD many candidates only gave consideration to process innovations rather than product innovations. The better candidates discussed how these strategies could be implemented to help ASU achieve the goals and vision discussed in 62.1.

62.3 Cyber security

> **Tutorial note:**
>
> This answer includes a wide range of points for marking/learning purposes and is longer than candidates were expected to produce in the time available.

Cyber risk is any risk of financial loss, disruption or damage to the reputation of an organisation from some sort of failure of its IT systems. Cyber security refers to the prevention of systems failure and the protection of networks and data from unauthorised modification, disclosure or destruction.

ASU's business is extensively reliant on computer systems. ASU's cyber security needs to be directed towards protecting its IT systems from risks which will threaten its ability to ensure the safe and uninterrupted operation of the airspace system.

The risks to ASU's IT systems and data predominantly feature some degree of human involvement:

- Human threats: hackers may be able to get into ASU's internal network, either to steal data (personnel or financial) or to damage the IT system. Political terrorism is a major risk in the era of cyber-terrorism and there have been a number of real-life examples of co-ordinated attacks on the computer systems of different airlines/airports. For ASU in extreme situations this could involve hackers taking control of aircrafts or drones.

- Denial of Service (DoS) attack: is an attempt by attackers to prevent legitimate users of a service from using that service. Such an attack could be intended to cause communication difficulties eg between the plane and the air traffic controller or to prevent systems responsible for scheduling aircraft and flight plans from operating properly.

- Viruses and other corruptions: could spread through the network to all of ASU's computers eg malware in staff email accounts or embedded Trojans which may prevent radar systems or communication channels from operating effectively .

- Deliberate sabotage: for example, malicious damage by employees or other users with access to the system could disrupt ASU's operations

- Accidents: on a more minor level, staff are a physical threat to IT installations, and there is a risk of accidents including spilling a cup of coffee over a desk, or tripping and falling, thereby doing some damage to an item of IT equipment.

ASU has developed its IT infrastructure to allow widespread use by a variety of parties which delivers more efficiency and competitive advantage but in doing so increases the risk that it is vulnerable to attack – particularly through the weakest links in the systems chain. Its use of cloud-based systems, for example in relation to drones, may also increase cyber security risks.

Risk management

Effective risk management is integral to ASU's competitive advantage and is fundamental to survival in the longer term. Global airspace is extremely crowded and a systems failure could in the worst case scenario result in a plane crash and fatalities. If a system is not operating properly ASU may need to ground all planes as a precaution since it cannot run the risk of this happening. Whilst this minimises the risk of an accident, it causes disruption for airports, airlines and passengers, potentially leading to financial loss for ASU. A key issue for ASU is that any technical failure has a significant and immediate impact and is likely to be high profile, as evidenced by the recent incident leading to flight cancellations and delays and a £7 million fine. Reputation is a key aspect and ASU may need to undertake PR to manage the negative publicity associated with the recent flight delay incident that has arisen.

ASU needs to ensure that there is a clear responsibility and accountability for cyber security and that it has individuals with the specialist skills and expertise to help the organisation protect itself against cyber-attacks. It also needs to take into account the fact that facilities and systems are accessed by third parties. ASU's board need to regularly consider their risk tolerance and risk appetite in relation to cyber security and reflect this in risk management strategies.

ASU needs to spend time identifying the various potential causes of a system breach, take steps to reduce the likelihood of this occurring and plan different strategies so that it is ready to react in the event that a breach occurs. Risks may be transferred, avoided, reduced or accepted. ASU must take steps to minimise the risk of systems failure, protect the integrity of its systems, safeguard information and ensure the continuity of its operations. However accepting that there is still the possibility of a breach, ASU should consider putting appropriate insurances in place to mitigate the effects of any cyber-attacks that do occur. It also needs a business continuity plan in place to reduce the need to shut down the systems or at least minimise the time that this has to be down for (see below).

The international security standard, ISO17799 recommends various measures for combating IT risks and ensuring security, which ASU could consider:

- Personnel security: this covers issues such as recruitment of trustworthy employees, and also reporting of security-related incidents. Training is particularly important, with the aim that users are aware of information security threats and concerns and are equipped to comply with the organisation's security policy.

- Physical and environmental security: measures should be taken to prevent unauthorised access, damage and interference to ASU's premises, assets, information and information facilities and prevention of theft.

- Systems access control: this includes protection of information, information systems, networked services, detection of unauthorised activities and security when using the systems. ASU needs to ensure that all the different users of its systems have appropriate controls in place.

- Systems development and maintenance: this includes security measures and steps to protect data in operational and application systems and also ensuring that IT projects and support are conducted securely.

Business continuity plan (BCP)

- A BCP is concerned with crisis management and disaster recovery. It must specify the actions ASU will take to recover and restore operations interrupted by the occurrence of a massive risk event eg a major breach of security resulting in a major systems failure or air disaster.

- ASU already has such a plan but it should be reviewed in the light of the recent incident to assess how successful it is and whether additional steps can be taken.

- All members of ASU staff should be aware of the importance of business continuity planning, training should be given and the plan tested regularly.

- Factors that should be considered by a BCP include:

    - Restoration of data and other IT systems
    - Securing interim premises
    - Securing interim management and staff
    - Management of the PR issues – this is a key issue for ASU

- Methods of recovery might include:

    - Carrying out activities manually until IT services are resumed (eg, via the call centre)

    - Moving staff at an affected building to another location

    - Agreeing with another business to use each other's premises in the event of a disaster

    - Arranging to use IT services and accommodation provided by a specialist third-party standby site.

Examiner's comments

Overall most candidates were well prepared for the discussion of cyber risk and scored highly. Relevant cyber risks were generally well identified although the suggestions for managing the significant risks were weaker. Some candidates introduced the TARA framework but did not then make use of it to aid discussion of risk management strategies. Given the critically important nature of air traffic management it was surprising that only a minority of candidates made reference to the need for a business continuity plan. More candidates referred to a back-up plan, but often only in relation to IT systems back-up.

63 Purechoc Ltd (September 2017)

Marking guide

	Knowledge	Skill	Marks
63.1 Control section of report	3	5	8
63.2 Risks section of report	2	6	7
63.3 Strategic fit section of report	2	6	7
63.4 Preliminary advice section of report	1	3	4
	8	20	26

General comments:

Candidates performed very well on this question, which had the highest overall average score.

The scenario concerns a family company, Purechoc, that sells premium chocolates and chocolate bars in its four shops. Each shop is managed by a different family member. The chocolates are hand-made in each shop using high quality fair trade cocoa beans from a single country of origin. The business conducts no marketing, instead relying on word of mouth. This has been largely successful, with each shop having a loyal following.

The original founder is unwell and the company is considering two possible strategic options:

(1) A take-over by a large American confectionery manufacturer, Koreto Inc, which has promised that the business can continue to run semi-autonomously, but wants to appoint its own Chief Executive. This option is preferred by the original founder.

(2) Expansion by franchising. This option is liked by the two younger family members.

To: Purechoc Board
From: Business Advisor
Date: X/X/XX
Re: Future strategy

Two possible options are being considered:

- Sale of shares to Koreto Inc
- Franchising

63.1 Control

Sale of shares

If all the directors sell their shares to Koreto then they will lose control in the form of ownership. Purechoc becomes dependent on Koreto which is a much bigger business. Although Koreto have promised that Purechoc can be run semi-autonomously, they own the business and may interfere in its running, as evidenced by their desire to appoint a new CEO.

The Bernard family will have reduced influence on the board of directors and this may lead to their wishes being overridden when it comes to important operating decisions. It may be very difficult to work with new American owners who are used to a much bigger business.

Despite the loss of ownership, Purechoc may have more influence over day-to-day running of the shops than under a franchise arrangement.

Franchise

Purechoc will maintain some general contractual control over franchisees but will lose some operational control.

If franchising is to be taken up by many small operators, then Purechoc is not dominated by its business partner(s). However it may be more difficult to influence or change the strategic direction of the business in the future if franchisees have a degree of autonomy in the running of their shop, as they may each have different objectives.

In a niche market, brand image is critical, so Purechoc will need to monitor quality control and consistency of products. Franchisees must be chosen carefully and contracts need to be drawn up to ensure Purechoc's reputation is protected.

Purechoc will need to provide training in chocolate production. Franchisees may also expect central support with procurement and marketing. Purechoc may need to take on additional manpower to provide training and support and manage the franchisees.

Examiner's comments

This was very well answered, although as usual some candidates lost easy marks by not presenting their answer in report format. Most candidates recognised that there was a difference between control in the context of ownership and control in relation to day-to-day operations. A small minority assumed that not all shareholders would be selling their shares. Although this may be a possibility, none referred to the need to seek agreement from the American company given that they are, initially at least, interested in 100% ownership. As usual, most candidates were good at discussing franchising although some weaker ones appeared to think that this option would involve relinquishing complete control of operations to the franchisees – better candidates pointed out that control could be maintained by choosing franchisees carefully and implementing a carefully worded franchise agreement.

63.2 Risks

Sale of shares

The sale of shares to Koreto means the directors no longer own the company and therefore lose their voting rights as shareholders. This transfers the risk of ownership from the Bernard family and may help reduce the risk to the business that is presented by Marine's ill-health and the current lack of cashflow.

However there is a risk that resources input by Koreto may not compensate for the loss of control by the Bernard family. Whilst Marine is keen to retire, the other members of the family are not and Koreto may decide to replace the current team.

Koreto may not fulfil their initial promises in respect of brand retention, autonomy of operations or finance. Requirements for dividends/management fees or exit route by Koreto may limit future availability of funds for Purechoc's expansion.

Koreto has no experience of the UK and there may not be able to transfer its core competences to operate successfully in a different market. Also Koreto's ownership may bring adverse publicity or damage Purechoc's brand (see 63.3 below).

Franchise

Purechoc faces reduced financial risk by having franchisees' own capital for expansion.

Compared to organic growth, there are fewer risks from franchisee losses as the cost of failure is shared with the franchisee. This reduces the maximum potential loss from the failure of a shop but also provides an increased incentive for the franchisee to succeed.

However:

Franchisees will gain access to Purechoc's intellectual property (in the form of the recipes) and successful franchisees may break away to set up in competition.

Poor quality franchisees may harm Purechoc's brand name which risks damaging the existing business and shops. There is a need to monitor the franchisees and the existing management may be overburdened as the number of franchises grows.

There is a risk that franchisees may not want to take up the opportunity – there needs to be some incentive to purchase a franchise and Purechoc may be relatively unknown outside its immediate geographical market, especially given its lack of marketing.

Examiner's comments

Again this was a high scoring requirement. Most candidates were able to make sensible points about how each of the strategic options increased downside risks for Purechoc. However only the better candidates identified that the strategies may also help the business reduce or share some risks. The strongest answers also considered upside risk from the point of view of the existing owners, recognising that, in the case of Koreto, the risks of ownership would be removed from the family entirely.

63.3 Strategic fit

Sale of shares

Koreto offers opportunities for expansion in two respects:

- Access to increased financial capital and other resources
- Possible access to Koreto's market in the USA

Purechoc is a small-scale business, operating an ethical procurement policy. It has a premium pricing policy based on its differentiation strategy. Koreto is more likely to adopt a low cost, high volume business model. It is not clear what Koreto's procurement policy is – some of the other dominant confectionery producers have already attracted adverse publicity for their sourcing of cocoa and their treatment of suppliers. Thus Purechoc's business may not fit with the existing strategy and brand image of a large confectionery manufacturer like Koreto.

However this may not be a problem if Purechoc is to be retained as a separate brand. Koreto will be able to provide access to more resources, established distribution channels and a marketing budget to raise awareness of the brand. It also provides strong potential for overseas expansion.

Franchise

Franchisees are likely to be individuals so unlike Koreto will not be able to provide financial or operational support for any large scale expansion. Under a franchise, Purechoc grants the franchisee the right to use its brand, its know-how and its products. There is also likely to be a requirement for Purechoc to provide some degree of central control and support. In return, the franchisee will provide a lump sum upfront and contribute a share of earnings.

In the context of the chocolate shops, a franchise is likely to be on a geographical basis in order to segregate the markets for the individual franchisees. The expansion of the business through individual shops may be more in keeping with the niche market and the brand ethos. Since each franchise will be unique to its area, this may help to maintain its image as a family company.

Purechoc can screen applicants carefully to identify like-minded franchisees and use the franchise agreement to ensure that franchisees adhere to the appropriate quality.

Examiner's comments

Generally the requirement to discuss strategic fit was well attempted, with many referring to the need to protect Purechoc's niche strategy and values, the latter often considered with regard to the firm's ethical procurement policy.

The best responses compared Purechoc and Koreto in terms of their respective generic strategies, assumed (reasonably) to be high volume cost leadership in the case of Koreto. The possible implications of this for Koreto's future business conduct were also well explored. Some candidates chose to adopt a suitability, feasibility, acceptability approach to this requirement which often proved disappointing and also caused them to run out of time.

63.4 Preliminary Advice

Before deciding on which option to pursue, the objectives of the different shareholders and their eventual plans for exit need to be considered.

Both options address the issue of limited resources and share the risk of expansion but also require the family to accept reduced control and share the future profits of the business.

If significant new capital is provided by Koreto, then growth could be rapid in terms of the number of outlets. Purechoc's business will be able to benefit from access to Koreto's expertise in the confectionery market and Koreto may be able to provide support for procurement, marketing, training etc, which is the inverse of the franchise situation.

Franchising offers a slower growth route, with Purechoc providing the expertise, but retaining control of the direction of the business. More consideration needs to be given to the terms of a franchise agreement and whether there would be any interested franchisees.

If Marine wants an exit in the short term then the Koreto offer may be attractive, depending on the price Koreto are prepared to pay. If she needs to raise cash then it may be better to sell now than a few years down the line when there is increased competition and a more mature market. As he is less reliant on the income, Thomas's decision may be more influenced by quality of life than money. However if he were to decide to sell too then Koreto would have sufficient shares for a majority holding, although it is not clear whether partial ownership would be acceptable to Koreto – they will need to be consulted on this. Jonathan and Anne seem more likely to want to retain control of their own destiny. They may not take kindly to reporting to a new Chief Executive appointed by Koreto. If this option is not attractive then an alternative may be for them to offer to buy out Marine and then to implement the franchising model.

Examiner's comments

The requirement to give preliminary advice was well answered by most, although omitted by a considerable number. Weaker efforts tended to concentrate on either sale or franchise, with little or no consideration of alternatives as a means of comparison. A significant minority suggested that, if the franchise option is chosen, the other shareholders can offer to buy out the founder.

REVIEW FORM – BUSINESS STRATEGY AND TECHNOLOGY: Question Bank

Your ratings, comments and suggestions would be appreciated on the following areas of this Question Bank

	Very useful	Useful	Not useful
Number of questions in each section	☐	☐	☐
Standard of answers	☐	☐	☐
Amount of guidance on exam technique	☐	☐	☐
Quality of marking guides	☐	☐	☐

	Excellent	Good	Adequate	Poor
Overall opinion of this Question Bank	☐	☐	☐	☐

Please return completed form to:

The Learning Team
Learning and Professional Department
ICAEW
Metropolitan House
321 Avebury Boulevard
Milton Keynes
MK9 2FZ
E learning@icaew.com

For space to add further comments please see overleaf.

REVIEW FORM (continued)

TELL US WHAT YOU THINK

Please note any further comments and suggestions/errors below.